Lecture Notes in Computer Science   12642

Marinos Ioannides · Eleanor Fink ·
Lorenzo Cantoni · Erik Champion (Eds.)

Digital Heritage

Progress in Cultural Heritage: Documentation, Preservation, and Protection

8th International Conference, EuroMed 2020
Virtual Event, November 2–5, 2020
Revised Selected Papers

 Springer

Editors
Marinos Ioannides (iD)
Cyprus University of Technology
Limassol, Cyprus

Lorenzo Cantoni (iD)
USI – Università della Svizzera italiana
Lugano, Switzerland

Eleanor Fink
Arlington, VA, USA

Erik Champion (iD)
Curtin University
Perth, WA, Australia

ISSN 0302-9743   ISSN 1611-3349 (electronic)
Lecture Notes in Computer Science
ISBN 978-3-030-73042-0   ISBN 978-3-030-73043-7   (eBook)
https://doi.org/10.1007/978-3-030-73043-7

LNCS Sublibrary: SL3 – Information Systems and Applications, incl. Internet/Web, and HCI

Cover Illustration: Wall painting of the 6th century A.D. which are considered of the few remaining early Christian mosaics in the world, from the Church Panagia Kanakaria Lithrangomis (Παναγία Κανακαριά Λυθράγκωμης) after it has been forcefully removed, following the 1974 Turkish invasion and occupation. With permission of the Ministry of Transport, Communications and Works, Department of antiquities, Lefkosia, Cyprus.

This Springer imprint is published by the registered company Springer Nature Switzerland AG
The registered company address is: Gewerbestrasse 11, 6330 Cham, Switzerland

Preface

EuroMed is a traditional biennial scientific event, and this year due to the COVID-19 pandemic EuroMed 2020 was held online.

Several organizations and current EU projects (H2020 ERA Chair MNEMOSYNE, EU Study on Standards, Methodologies and Guidelines for 3D Digitisation of Cultural Heritage, H2020 Marie Skłodowska Curie ITN CHANGE, Interreg Greece – Cyprus DigiArc, ERASMUS+ EU-OBP, Creative Europe OPHERA, H2020 IMPACTOUR, Europeana Common Culture, Europeana Archaeology, Virtual Multimodal Museum Plus, Research Infrastructure CLARIN CY ERIC and DARIAH-CY) and the UNESCO Chair on Digital Cultural Heritage decided to join EuroMed 2020 and continue cooperation in order to create an optimal environment for the discussion and explanation of new technologies, exchange of modern innovative ideas, and in general to allow for the transfer of knowledge between a large number of professionals and academics during one common event and time period.

The main goal of the event was to illustrate the programs underway, whether organized by public bodies (e.g., UNESCO, European Union, national states, etc.) or by private foundations (e.g., Getty Foundation, World Heritage Foundation, etc.) in order to promote a common approach to the tasks of recording, documenting, protecting, and managing world cultural heritage. The 8th European-Mediterranean Conference (EuroMed 2020) was a forum for sharing views and experiences, discussing proposals for the optimal attitude as well as the best practices and the ideal technical tools to preserve, document, manage, present/visualize, and disseminate the rich and diverse cultural heritage of mankind.

This conference was held during the last part of the EU Framework Programme, Horizon 2020, which is the largest in the world in terms of financial support on research, innovation, technological development, and demonstration activities. The awareness of the value and importance of heritage assets has been reflected in the financing of projects since the first Framework Programme for Research and Technological Development (FP1, 1984–1987) and continues into the current Horizon 2020, which follows FP7 (2007–2013). In the past 37 years, a large community of researchers, experts, and specialists have had the chance to learn and develop the transferable knowledge and skills needed to inform stakeholders, scholars, and students. Europe has become a leader in heritage documentation, preservation, and protection science, with COST Actions adding value to projects financed within the FP and EUREKA program, transferring knowledge to practice, and supporting the development of SMEs.

The EuroMed 2020 agenda focused on enhancing and strengthening international and regional cooperation and promoting awareness and tools for future innovative research, development, and applications to protect, preserve, and document European and world cultural heritage. Our ambition was to host an exceptional conference by mobilizing also policy-makers from different EU countries, institutions (European

Commission, European Parliament, Council of Europe, UNESCO, International Committee for Monuments and Sites ICOMOS, the International Committee for Documentation of Cultural Heritage CIPA, the International Society for Photogrammetry and Remote Sensing ISPRS, the International Centre for the study of the Preservation and Restoration of Cultural Property ICCROM, and the International Committee for Museums ICOM), professionals, as well as participants from all over the world and from different scientific areas of cultural heritage.

Protecting, preserving, and presenting our cultural heritage are actions that are frequently interpreted as change management and/or changes in the behavior of society. Joint European and international research yields a scientific background and support for such a change. We are living in a period characterized by rapid and remarkable changes in the environment, in society, and in technology. Natural changes, war conflicts, and man-made interventions and changes, including climate change, as well as technological and societal changes, form an ever-moving and colorful stage and pose a challenge for society. Close cooperation between professionals, policy-makers, and authorities internationally is necessary for research, development, and technology in the field of cultural heritage.

Scientific projects in the area of cultural heritage have received national, European Union, or UNESCO funding for more than 30 years. Through financial support and cooperation, major results have been achieved and published in peer-reviewed journals and conference proceedings with the support of professionals from many countries. The European Conferences on Cultural Heritage research and development and in particular the biennial EuroMed conference have become regular milestones on the never-ending journey of discovery in the search for new knowledge of our common history and its protection and preservation for the generations to come. EuroMed also provides a unique opportunity to present and review results as well as to draw new inspiration.

To reach this ambitious goal, the topics covered include experiences in the use of innovative technologies and methods as well as how to take the best advantage to integrate the results obtained so as to build up new tools and/or experiences as well as to improve methodologies for documenting, managing, preserving, and communicating cultural heritage.

We present here 67 papers, selected from 326 submissions, which focus on interdisciplinary and multidisciplinary research concerning cutting-edge cultural heritage informatics, physics, chemistry, and engineering and the use of technology for the representation, documentation, archiving, protection, preservation, and communication of cultural heritage knowledge.

Our keynote speakers, Harry Verwayen - Executive Director Europeana Foundation, Dr. Christoph Fröhlich and Christoph Held from Zoller & Fröhlich GmbH, Prof. Petros Patias from Aristotle University of Thessaloniki, Prof. Roko Žarnić and Prof. Vlatka Rajčić from Bene Construere, Alastair Rawlinson from Historic Environment Scotland, Prof. Andreas Georgopoulos and Prof. Charalabos Ioannidis from National Technical University of Athens, Prof. Raffaella Brumana from University of Polimi, Dr. Herbert Maschner from Global Digital Heritage, Prof. Sander Münster from Time Machine Organisation, Ronald Haynes from Cambridge University, Edward Silverton from Mnemoscene, Prof. Doug Boyer from Duke University/MorphoSource, Carla Schroer,

Director of Cultural Heritage Imaging, Dr. Rebecca Dikow, Research Data Scientist from the Smithsonian Institution Data Science Lab, Martin Schaich, Chief Executive Officer, ArcTron 3D GmbH, Dr. Isto Huvila, Professor in Information Studies at Uppsala University, Patricia Harpring, Managing Editor from Getty Vocabulary Program, Maximilian Nowottnick, Data Scientist from Supper & Supper GmbH, and Prof. Diofantos Hadjimitsis, Cyprus University of Technology and EXCELSIOR H2020 Teaming Project & Eratosthenes Centre of Excellence are not only experts in their fields, but also visionaries for the future of cultural heritage protection and preservation. They promote the e-documentation and protection of the past in such a way that it is preserved for the generations to come.

We extend our thanks to all the authors, speakers, and those persons whose labor, financial support, and encouragement made the EuroMed 2020 online event possible. The international Program Committee, whose members represent a cross-section of archaeology, physics, chemistry, civil engineering, computer science, graphics and design, library, archive and information science, architecture, surveying, history, and museology, worked tenaciously and finished their work on time. We would also like to express our gratitude to all the organizations supporting this event and our co-organizers, the European Commission, the director general of Europeana Mr. Harry Verwayen, the Getty Conservation Institute and World Monuments Fund, the Cyprus University of Technology, the Ministry of Energy, Commerce, Industry and Tourism especially the permanent secretary and digital champion Dr. Stelios Himonas, the Ministry of Education and Culture, and particularly, the director of Cultural Services Mr. Pavlos Paraskevas, the director of the Cyprus Library Mr. Demetris Nicolaou, the Department of Antiquities in Cyprus, all the members of the Cypriot National Committee for E-documentation and E-preservation in Cultural Heritage, and finally our corporate sponsors, CableNet Ltd and the Cyprus Tourism Organization.

We express our thanks and appreciation to the board of the ICOMOS Cyprus Section for their enthusiasm, commitment, and support for the success of this event. Most of all we would like to thank the organizations UNESCO, European Commission, Europa Nostra, and ICOMOS that entrusted us with the task of organizing and undertaking this unique event and wish all participants an interesting and fruitful experience.

February 2021

Marinos Ioannides
Eleanor Fink
Lorenzo Cantoni
Erik Champion

Acknowledgments and Disclaimer

The EuroMed 2020 Conference was partly supported by the Republic of Cyprus, by the Cyprus University of Technology, by the Cyprus Tourism Organization, ICOMOS Cyprus and the aforementioned EU projects.

However, the content of this publication reflects the authors' views only, and the European Commission, the Republic of Cyprus, ICOMOS, ICOMOS-Cyprus, Getty, Cyprus University of Technology, and the EU projects H2020 ERA Chair MNEMOSYNE, EU Study on Standards, Methodologies and Guidelines for 3D Digitisation of Cultural Heritage, H2020 Marie Skłodowska Curie ITN CHANGE, Interreg Greece – Cyprus DigiArc, ERASMUS+ EU-OBP, Creative Europe OPHERA, H2020 IMPACTOUR, Europeana Common Culture, Europeana Archaeology, H2020 Virtual Multimodal Museum Plus, Research Infrastructure CLARIN CY ERIC and DARIAH-CY, and the UNESCO Chair on Digital Cultural Heritage at Cyprus University of Technology are not liable for any use that may be made of the information contained herein.

Organization

Conference Chairs

Marinos Ioannides
Eleanor Fink
Lorenzo Cantoni
Erik Champion

Local Organizing Committee

Andreas Makromallis
Douglas Pritchard
Eleanna Avouri
Eliana Iliofotou
Francesco Ripanti
George Tryfonos
Giulia Osti
Harriet Cliffen

Ilias Nobilakis
Maria Katiri
Marina Toumpouri
Nenad Jončić
Skriapas Konstantinos
Theodoros Gkanetsos
Thomas Rigauts
Vasilis Athanasiou

International Scientific Committee

Anastasiou, Magdalini, Greece
Anastasovitis, Leyteris, Greece
Anichini, Francesca, Italy
Arakadaki, Maria, Greece
Banzi, Fabrizio, Italy
Barazzetti, Luigi, Italy
Bebis, George, USA
Bertini, Marco, Italy
Bimpas, Matthaios, Greece
Boochs, Frank, Germany
Bouzakis, Kostantinos, Greece
Brambilla, Laura, Switzerland
Bueno, Gumersindo, Spain
Cantini, Lorenzo, Italy
Caridakis, George, Greece
Cheng, Ying-Mei, Taiwan
Chmelik, Jiří, Czech Republic
Chondros, Thomas, Greece
Condoleo, Paola, Italy

Conzalez, Jorbi, Spain
Costa, Stefano, Italy
Cushing, Amber, Ireland
De Felice, Giuliano, Italy
Della Torre, Stefano, Italy
Diakoumakos, Iason, Greece
Doulamis, Nikolaos, Greece
Gattiglia, Gabriele, Italy
George, Sony, Norway
Georgiadis, Charalambos, Greece
Georgoula, Olga, Greece
Giannoulis, George, Spain
Issini, Giovanni, Italy
Granić, Andrina, Croatia
Grimoldi, Alberto, Italy
Guiseppe Landi, Angelo, Italy
Hadjidaki Marten, Elpida, Greece
Handžić, Meliha,
    Bosnia and Herzegovina

Iliopoulos, Ioannis, Greece
Jo, Sang-sun, South Korea
Kaimaris, Dimitrios, Greece
Kakavas, George, Greece
Karanikolas, Nikos, Greece
Kerle, Norman, Netherlands
Kosmopoulos, Dimitrios, Greece
Koukouvou, Angeliki, Greece
Kuo, Chiao-Ling, Taiwan
Laužikas, Rimvydas, Lithuania
Lefaki, Styliani, Greece
Liarokapis, Fotis, Czech Republic
Livanos, George, Greece
Lougiakis, Christos, Greece
Maietti, Federica, Italy
Makantasis, Kostantinos, Cyprus
Merchán, María, Spain
Merchán, Pilar, Spain
Migliori, Luisa, Italy
Mitrakos, Dimitrios, Greece
Nikolaidis, Efthymios, Greece
Oreni, Daniela, Italy
Palombini, Augusto, Italy
Pereira, Pedro, Portugal

Poulopoulos, Vasilis, Greece
Previtali, Mattia, Italy
Protopapadakis, Eftychios, Greece
Roumeliotis, Manos, Greece
Stamnas, Tasos, Greece
Stathaki, Tania, UK
Tassopoulou, Maria, Greece
Tavares, Alice, Portugal
Thomas, Suzie, Finland
Tian-Yuan Shih, Peter, Taiwan
Tokmakidis, Kostantinos, Greece
Tsafarakis, Stelios, Greece
Tsiafaki, Despoina, Greece
Tsioukas, Vasilios, Greece
Tsita, Christina, Greece
Tucci, Grazia, Italy
Vassilakis, Costas, Greece
Von Mannen, Sebastian, Germany
Voulodimos, Athanasios, Greece
Yen, Alex Ya-Ning, Taiwan
Yngve Hardeberg, Jon, Norway
Zervakis, Michalis, Greece
Zuppiroli, Marco, Italy

Contents

**Project Papers: Remote Sensing for Archaeology
and Cultural Heritage Management and Monitoring**

Project Papers: Modelling and Knowledge Management

Project Papers: Interactive Environments and Applications

**Project Paper: Visualisation Techniques (Desktop, Virtual
and Augmented Reality)**

Project Papers: Storytelling and Authoring Tools

Project Papers: Tools for Education

Short Papers: DATA Acquisition and Processing

**Short Papers: Digital Data Acquisition Technologies in CH / 2D
and 3D Data Capture Methodologies and Data Processing**

Short Paper: 2D and 3D GIS in Cultural Heritage

**Short Papers: Remote Sensing for Archaeology
and Cultural Heritage Management and Monitoring**

Short Paper: On-Site and Remotely Sensed Data Collection

Short Papers: Modelling and Knowledge Management

Short Papers: Interactive Environments and Applications

Short Papers: Reproduction Techniques and Rapid Prototyping in CH

Short Papers: Preservation and Use and Re-use

Short Papers: e-Libraries and e-Archives in Cultural Heritage

**Short Papers: Virtual Museum Applications
(e-Museums and e-Exhibitions**

Project Papers: DATA Acquisition and Processings

Project Papers: Digital Data Acquisition Technologies in CH / 2D and 3D Data Capture Methodologies and Data Processing

Recognizing the Design Patterns of Complex Vaults: Drawing, Survey and Modeling. Experiments on Palazzo Mazzonis' Atrium in Turin

R. Spallone[1]([✉]) [iD], M. C. López González[2] [iD], M. Vitali[1] [iD], G. Bertola[1], F. Natta[1], and F. Ronco[1]

[1] Department of Architecture and Design, Politecnico di Torino, Turin, Italy
{roberta.spallone,marco.vitali,giulia.bertola,fabrizio.natta,
francesca.ronco}@polito.it
[2] Department of Graphic Expression in Architecture, School of Building Engineering,
Universitat Politècnica de València, València, Spain
mlopezg@ega.upv.es

Abstract. This paper shows the results of research advances on complex vaulted systems produced by the integration of laser scanner survey techniques and three-dimensional modeling for the geometric interpretation of built architecture to recognizing the geometric matrices of the design conception. The integration between TLS techniques and digital modeling methods led to the definition of new workflows, aimed at optimizing the use of data and at refining the quality of the geometrical interpretation. The process incorporates the traditional activities of freehand drawing of eydotipes, aimed at a deep understanding of the peculiar characteristics of the artifact. In particular, from these procedures new opportunities for the research arise to better understand the relationships between survey data, geometric matrices and compositional rules.

The case study presented here, the atrium of Palazzo Mazzonis in Turin was chosen among a small number of atria that present characteristics of originality and uniqueness in a panorama of realizations strongly characterized by compliance with well-established compositional schemes.

Keywords: Complex vaults · Drawing · Survey · Modeling · Palazzo Mazzonis

1 Introduction

The research presented in this paper is one of the results of the international collaboration for the project "Nuevas tecnologías para el análisis y conservación del patrimonio arquitectónico", funded by the Ministry of Science, Innovation and the University of Spain. This allowed Concepción López to join the research group coordinated by Roberta Spallone and Marco Vitali at the Politecnico di Torino. From 2012, the Politecnico's group has been conducting investigations about bricks-made complex vaulted systems in several Baroque buildings of Piedmont, aiming to identify the geometric matrices of the vaults

M. Ioannides et al. (Eds.): EuroMed 2020, LNCS 12642, pp. 3–14, 2021.
https://doi.org/10.1007/978-3-030-73043-7_1

shapes and to re-construct them through three-dimensional models, in light of constant comparison with coeval treatises and manuals, and archival sources (when existent).

The present successful collaboration provided the necessary cues to test the value of the digital reconstruction method on data derived from a metric survey campaign carried out using terrestrial laser scanning (TLS). The integration between TLS techniques and digital modeling methods led to the definition of new workflows, aimed at optimizing the use of data and at refining the quality of the geometrical interpretation. In particular, from these procedures, new opportunities for the research arise to better understand the relationships between survey data, geometric matrices, and compositional rules.

The case study presented here, the atrium of Palazzo Mazzonis in Turin was chosen among a small number of atria that present characteristics of originality and uniqueness in a panorama of realizations strongly characterized by compliance with well-established compositional schemes.

2   Interpretative Models of Complex Vaults

The intrados surface of the vaulted atria analyzed from 2012 was represented by digital models that give back the idea of the designer, net of asymmetries, irregularities of the plan, and construction accidents. The interpretation work, applied to a relatively large number of vaulted atria, has structured the methodology of geometric decomposition and digital re-construction, successfully applied to the homogeneous classes of vaults [1, 2].

The workflow involves, in the first step, the subdivision of the vaulted surface into elements organized according to a structural and geometrical hierarchy that responds to rules of symmetry (axial longitudinal and transversal) and provides for the identification of the main surface, secondary surfaces (generically oriented along the axes) and angular surfaces. It should be noted that the most delicate phase of this work consists in the recognition of the geometrical matrices of the main surface, of which only portions remain in the built architecture. In particular, the longitudinal and transversal sections of the vaults always intersect only portions of the main surface, making the geometrical interpretation of generatrices and directrices more complex, and requiring additional sections at the imposts. The geometrical recognition of secondary and angular surfaces, rarely referable to geometrical primitives, and more often assimilated to surfaces generated by sections, is simpler.

Then the logic of the geometric composition of the main surface with the secondary and angular surfaces is defined. Digital re-construction can be addressed through two alternative composition rules: a first method, which we can call "by intersections", involves the geometric intersection of the main surface with secondary shapes (cylinders, cones, portions of torus, spheres, ellipsoids or ovaloids); a second method, which we can call "by cuts and fills", consists in cutting portions of the main surface through surfaces with a vertical generatrix (mainly pairs of planes) and filling the space left free with surfaces generated by sections that rest seamlessly on the edges of the cut of the main surface.

The digital models resulting from this work of geometric interpretation and re-construction have been described through an exploded axonometric that represents the recognized primitive surfaces, the logic of composition, and the sequence of geometric operations necessary for their combination.

The vaulted system of the atrium of Palazzo Mazzonis shows unique features in comparison with well-established patterns recognized in the historical city center. The historical information about the palace is so scarce that it is supposed to be the result of an enlargement of the pre-existing 17th-century building, which belonged to the Marquises Solaro della Chiusa. A survey of the building dated 1845 (Fig. 1), was used as the basis for planning the campaign of survey and drafting the eidotypes.

The passing atrium is divided into two main areas by two pairs of columns. Although the surface of the vaulted system is fragmented by the presence of the lintels and arches setting on the columns, this first portion of the atrium produces a unitary perception of space, suggesting a continuity of surface between the three fields in sequence. The caesura between the portion overlooking the street and that on the the courtyard is underlined by the presence of the architraved pillars, associated with columns, which define three spans symmetrical with respect to the longitudinal axis.

3 Interpretative On-Site Drawings and Geometric Reconstruction

The geometric interpretation and re-construction of the real building need to be based on knowledge phases that start with on-site drawings. Direct contact with the architecture is in fact a very important step in the process, which makes it possible to optimize the subsequent phases of the work. Indeed, this gives the opportunity to investigate modularity and proportioning of spaces, axiality, symmetries, recurrence, geometry of the surfaces that make up the vaulted system, through the drawing intended as a tool for investigation and knowledge. Moreover, the graphic transposition of the spatial characteristics of architecture requires to understand its peculiarities: the graphic activity, in fact, becomes an instrument of verification and control of this understanding and allows, as in the present study, to analyze and solve through the geometric construction problems of intersection and composition of surfaces. The evaluation of these aspects cannot disregard direct observation – it is in fact much more difficult and risky to rely on photographic or video, or even iconographic materials – which makes it possible to constantly change the point of observation, to support evaluations in the execution of some simple measurement operations as well as to make critical selections of information that would not be as easy and safe by other means.

In Palazzo Mazzonis the geometric interpretation method has been supported by the study and the use (on-site) of the archive drawings that were used as a proportioned basis for trying to find proportional criteria or a basis for 2D or 3D geometric graphic interpretative sketches and drawings (Fig. 1).

The analysis of the plan-proportioned drawing suggests the presence of a longitudinal axis that connects the entrance (and the first portion of the atrium, of almost square plan) to the courtyard (and the second portion of the atrium, of rectangular module corresponding to half of the first square), and two transversal axes of symmetry of the two vaulted systems, totally independent, as underlined by the double pillars and the double arches that constitute the main caesura of the space.

The subdivision into sub-modules emphasizes the position in plan of the free supports (pilasters and columns) which are arranged to emphasize an expansion of the unitary

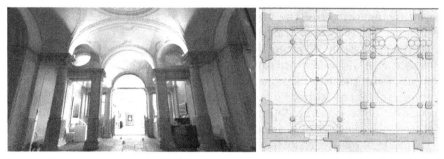

Fig. 1. Atrium of Palazzo Mazzonis in Turin; excerpt of the survey drawing dated 1st July 1845 with superimposition of graphical analysis. Source: Archivio Storico del Comune di Torino, Tipi e dis., cart. 63, fasc. 9, dis. 1, tav III. Photo: F. Natta. Graphic processing: F. Ronco.

space of the first portion of the atrium and a compression and fragmentation of the modules facing the courtyard. The two pseudo-circular decorative elements that characterize the intrados surface of the two main vaults clearly respond to this modular grid. The geometrical analysis of the intrados surface of the two vaulted systems starts from the proportional representation, in a three-dimensional scheme, of the characteristic sections of the vaults: starting from the three sections conducted along the axes of symmetry, the directrices of the surfaces involved in the composition are qualitatively defined and to these are added the longitudinal and transversal sections in correspondence of the pillars (to define the geometrical course of the arches that subdivide the vaulted fields) and the section of the surfaces in correspondence of the perimeter walls.

The construction of this three-dimensional scheme makes it possible to evaluate, surface by surface, which are the additional sections to be studied for each vault (to be produced in the following phase, the digital re-construction, starting from the point cloud) and to predict the results of the geometrical modelling operations based on the recognized logic of composition. In the specific case of Palazzo Mazzonis the two vaulted systems that characterize the atrium have different features. The portion of the atrium towards the courtyard is covered by the vaults set on the three bays (the central sail vault and the two lateral groin vaults), separated by arches. The portion facing the street presents a decidedly more complex configuration, in which the three portions defined by the two transversal arches are resolved in the central field by intersection of a barrel vault arranged longitudinally and two transversal barrel vaults, in the adjacent fields by intersection of pseudo-conical vaults with veloidic angular surfaces. The joining arch between these latter surfaces would seem to suggest a break defined by vertical planes arranged along the axis of the supports, as suggested by the archive drawing. On-site observation also reveals a different arches layout: the projection in plan is curvilinear and the surface that constitutes it has different heights in the two edge curves. The subsequent phases of data extraction from the point cloud therefore constitute a salient step in the definition of the reconstructive geometric model.

4   Eidotypes Aimed to Survey Project

Starting from the geometric reconstruction made on site, we continued to the realization of eidotypes: series of life drawings containing useful information for an in-depth knowledge of the building. They allowed to know and investigate in advance some visible and knowable aspects of the different areas analyzed and defined through the subsequent phases of measurement.

The eidotype, besides being an important guideline during the measurement operations, was also a useful memory support during the following phase of graphic restitution of the survey, in particular during the orientation and point cloud overlapping phase.

The processes and modes of production of the sign are the structural components of the drawing and are therefore closely linked to its purpose and role [3]. For this reason, two types of eidotypes have been realized. The first, made on the A5 format notebook (Fig. 2 right), contain a synthetic and schematic representation of the plan of the atrium of Palazzo Mazzonis. This plan was used to design the laser capture sequences, establishing the positioning of the laser scanner, in one or more stations concerning the object to be detected. The choice of the scanning points must guarantee the best and greatest visibility of the area to be detected and reduce shadow phenomena due to the presence of objects. In the case of the atrium, 18 gripping points were required to ensure geometric homogeneity of the metric survey. The second type of eidotypes was instead made on A3 cardboard (Fig. 2 left) and the drawings were made on an always approximate but larger scale, to include more information useful for understanding the building such as details, mouldings, architectural orders, projections of the vaulted ceilings and height differences, paying particular attention to the proportional aspects. This operation has attempted to render a work such as architecture in a two-dimensional key to obtain as much information as possible about the shape of the architecture being studied. Particular attention has been paid to geometric features, not trying to reproduce reality "as seen" but introducing geometric laws to better understand it. The geometrical and constructive characteristics and the shape and volume of the rooms have been investigated through the use of the double orthographic projection method, trying to keep on the same sheet the plan, and the section, together with back elevation. As conventionally, we chose to set the horizontal cutting plan just above the windowsill of the ground floor. The order of execution of the eidotypes suggests the order of the scans. It starts from the entrance hall, which can be easily connected through the door to the external facade of the building, and then the other rooms are drawn, following a path that corresponds to that of a person entering the building. For architectural drawings of this type it was necessary to resort to certain graphic conventions, avoiding giving into particular pictorial effects.

Their correspondence to the truth must manifest itself only through a technical sign in which the shape and structure of the various elements must prevail over the figurative appearance. The drawings, executed by hand without the use of "auxiliary tools" such as rulers and squares, were made using only pencils of three different hardness: one for the elements cut from the section planes and the other for the visible lines and the third for the decorative elements.

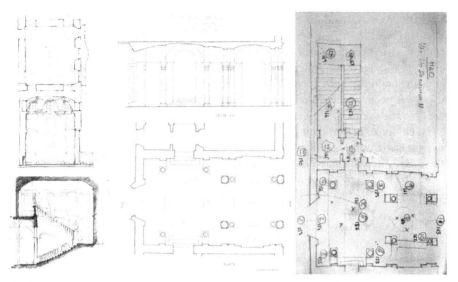

Fig. 2. Eydotipes of: the staircase and main hall, the atrium, the atrium's plan with scanning stations. Eydotipes: G. Bertola, M. C. López González.

5   Survey Methodologies: Choice of Tools and Strategies Applied to the Vaulted Systems

This complex framework of vaults above described encloses a beautiful example of compositional design only understandable through the expertise of the geometry and sensitivity by the author. The symmetry in the direction of the access axis produces a sense of depth accentuated by the lateral columns, which approach the center in the second vault. The parallelism of the diaphragmatic arches divides the space through sequential scopes, offering dynamism emphasized by the typological change between the first and second bay. The two solutions used in each of them make these vaults a complex geometric problem. Its study requires a premeditated methodology that contributes to the elaboration of digital models easily analyzed in their geometric, metric, and typological form.

As in any investigation related to the architectural heritage, it is necessary first to carry out an analysis of the written and graphic documentary references to subsequently undertake the virtual reconstruction of the vaulted system. The ideal tools to tackle the data collection of curvilinear surfaces are those that provide clouds of defining points of mentioned surfaces. The most advisable tool is the terrestrial laser scanner (TSL). This system has an added value because it is a container of qualitative-topological information since, in addition to geometric information, it provides other values such as color or reflectance [4]. However, before using it, it is necessary to consider a series of issues concerning the lighting, the distance up to which the accuracy values of the device can be assumed, and the visibility limitations that require multiple scanning stations. The curvilinear shape of the vaulted surfaces and the bas-relief decoration gives rise to shapes and textures of high reflectivity. Therefore, it is necessary to carry out the scans at a short distance, short duration, and great overlap, since if large sweeps were performed, we would obtain imprecise results. In order to make the complex vaults visible and to explore and manipulate the images obtained from the point cloud, various programs generally linked to the brand of the laser device used can be used.

There are also other generic programs of free access. These programs perfectly manage point clouds and their calculation algorithms, obtaining pinpoint accuracy in the records of the different scans, and facilitating the cleaning of noise. Some allow obtaining orthophotos scaled in JPG or TIF format that can be treated later with Photoshop software improving the results. They are especially advantageous for visualizing the contours of the intrados of the vaults and calculating the radius of curvature in the direction of the main axes (Fig. 3).

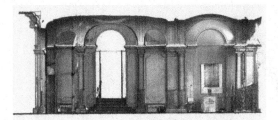 

Fig. 3. Orthophotos of the longitudinal and transversal sections. Processing: M. C. López.

Its use is very appropriate in the study of the geometric configuration relating it to the exposed in the treatment, to follow the guidelines of the old architects [5]. In some cases, these programs also allow the creation and optimization of the triangulated mesh known as TIN (Triangulated Irregular Network), which is very convenient in the study of curvilinear surfaces and in the analysis of spatial arrangement through 3D modeling. This mesh of triangles can be imported for visualization, measurement, or analysis purposes to 3D modeling programs and can even be viewed from web browsers.

The resulting cloud can be imported into CAD software proceeding to its vectorization through different formats. In this way a rigorous two-dimensional graphic representation of the real state of the vaults is obtained, that is, of its geometry, not of the geometric ideal. The vault is represented with its deformations, damages, and seats due to the construction process or the passage of time.

If we were left with only the two-dimensional representation, we would be wasting the potential of this massive data capture system [6]. Therefore, it is necessary to develop strategies that allow obtaining methodologies aimed at improving the expression and understanding of the vaults by extracting a semantic content from the management of the point cloud. The work methodology used in Palazzo Mazzonis has been based on obtaining graphic representations through the use of the terrestrial laser scanner because it is the ideal tool for taking data from vaulted systems. The Focus 130 × 3D model of the Faro brand has been used for its maneuverability, precision (2 mm for 25 m), autonomy (4 h of battery), and an integrated camera that allows it to assign to each point its natural color.

To ensure the overlap of points and the absence of blind points it was necessary to scan from 18 positions parking lots with an approximate duration of 8 min each and an average distance between scans of 3 m. The scanner location and that of the referential spheres were previously programmed.

6   From Scanning to 3D Modelling

The registration of point clouds has been carried out with the Lighthouse Scene 19 software. It offers an intuitive interface, has pinpoint accuracy in the records of the different scans, allows obtaining orthophotos scaled in.jpg format, and enables the creation and optimization of the triangulated mesh.

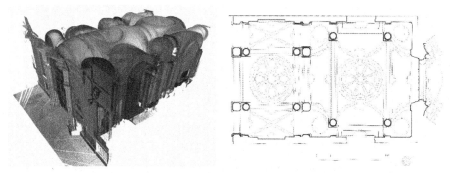

Fig. 4. Union of point clouds and surveyed plan drawing in scale 1:50. Scanning: M. C. López. Processing: F. Natta. Drawing: M. Vitali.

The import of the final cloud to AutoCAD 2020 has been done through the.e57 format from where it has been possible to make the two-dimensional drawings that specify the real geometry of the vaulted system (Fig. 4). Then, the main sections indicated in the previous paragraph have been carried out. From these sections, the distinctive sections of each vaulted surface have been extracted: if they correspond to the symmetry of the composition, they have been superimposed.

For example, taking into account the vaulted system on the portion of the atrium facing the street, a series of elements can be interpreted starting from pairs of sections, as in the case of arches on columns symmetrical to the central field, while others can be described by the overlapping of four sections symmetrical to the two axes, longitudinal and transversal, as in the case of the four pairs of sections necessary for the correct geometrization of the perimeter arches of the angular veloidic surfaces. A separate approach has been dedicated to the geometric reconstruction of intersection curves between surfaces, which cannot be derived from flat sections of the point cloud.

In fact, the vaulted system facing the street presents surfaces that seem to follow a combinatorial logic of intersection, as in the case of the barrel vaults that cover the central span. In this case a first possibility of data extraction from the point cloud could be made through the construction of a 3D polyline with object snap on the points of the cloud:

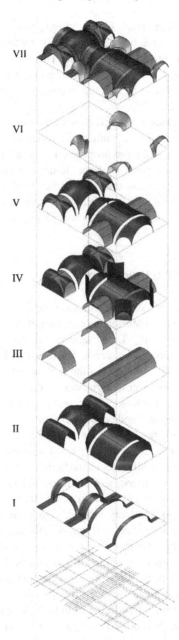

Fig. 5. De-composition of the atrium's vaulted system. The interpretative geometric model in exploded axonometric view highlights the primitive reference surfaces, the logic, and the hierarchy of composition Modelling: F. Ronco.

this procedure, however, does not allow the geometrization operations necessary for the construction of the interpretative model and has therefore been abandoned. Alternatively, to guarantee, also for these elements, a correct simplification in geometrical terms of reality, the intersection curves have been obtained starting from the plan and elevation projections of the curve, appropriately geometrized. The "geometrical" projections have been extruded perpendicularly to the projection planes: from the intersection of the two surfaces it has been possible to extract the intersection curve in its interpreted and geometrically simplified version.

A similar reasoning was made for the creation of the connection arcs of the pseudo-conical vaults with the veloidic angular vaults. As already mentioned, these arcs do not consist of cylindrical surfaces and have no projection in a linear plan: the procedure previously described was also applied to these elements highlighting, as noted in the on-site geometric interpretation, how the edge curves of the arches do not have the same height. Once all the distinctive sections of each surface have been defined, the interpretative model has been created using modeling tools of Rhinoceros software (Fig. 5).

7   Towards a Scalable Methodology

In recent decades, the rise of metric survey methods using Terrestrial Laser Scanning (and low-cost ones using Structure from Motion photogrammetry) has progressively replaced instrumental survey techniques using Total Stations and stereoscopic photogrammetry, and direct survey using traditional instruments. These last techniques were based on an approach consolidated since the beginning of the practice of metric survey: the critical selection of points, intersections, edges, alignments, which characterize every architecture as a *unicum*. This practice involved a deep architectural culture by the surveyors, based on knowledge of architectural and construction history, which allowed the correct recognizing of architectural elements, building structures, orders, materials, ornamentations, and constructive techniques. Moreover, it was needed a rigorous attention to the formal, structural, and stylistic peculiarities of the building subject of the analysis, to the historical period in which it was realized, also about coeval buildings and to the context in which it rises, to the constructive materials used, and to transformations and calamitous events happened over time. Documentary materials, archival, bibliographic and iconographic sources contribute in a fundamental way to this knowledge. The objective of representing the artefact, as the outcome of the process of knowledge and measurement, through two-dimensional drawings in reduction scales strictly dependent on the aims of the survey (documentation, project, restoration, transformation), addressed the same methodologies, techniques and choices concerning the survey instruments.

All these experiences and practices drawn from the past, can and must be integrated with today's metric survey techniques, and in particular with the TLS techniques, as in the case study analyzed, which is intended to be used as a paradigm for setting a scalable work process on other similar cases. Indeed, the automatic acquisition of a big amount of points irregularly distributed, that is the point clouds, creates a big database, useful *a posteriori* for multiple interpretations and thematic analyses, for drawing plans, elevations and sections, and, currently, for 3D modelling with different techniques (geometric, parametric, BIM). Nevertheless, it is necessary paying attention to the reduction scales provided in the survey project of laser scanning settings.

3D models, temporally parallel to the rise of laser scanner survey, represent a relatively new product, compared to traditional representations by orthographic projections. These digital 3D models are the result of a synthesis operation performed by the scholar who, pursuing a specific communication objective, selects the information of what is nothing other than a geometric figure representing an architecture [7].

Therefore, consistently with the objectives of the research, the cognitive and heuristic potential of hand-drawing and digital modeling have been used at different times within the workflow that has profitably integrated the database offered by the laser scanner acquisition. The selection of the data for 2D drawings representing the building in today state derived from the horizontal and vertical sections of the point cloud the metric and geometric information which, integrated with the features identified in the preliminary eidotypes, allow to draw up metric reliable and architecturally significant plans and sections. The selection of data for 3D reconstructive models of the design idea presents greater complexity. Indeed, it is a matter of identifying a series of significant sections of the point cloud, suitable to verify the preliminary geometric hypotheses deriving from the consultation of the original design documents (rarely preserved) and from the observations and hypotheses formulated *in situ* about generative shapes, proportions and geometries of the vaulted systems investigated.

The workflow set up in this way for the analysis of complex vaulted systems highlights today's relevance of the definition of the architectural survey as an open system of knowledge as stated in the "Chart of Architectural Survey" [8].

8 Conclusion

This paper shows the results of research advances on complex vaulted systems produced by the integration of laser scanner survey techniques and three-dimensional modeling for the geometric interpretation of built architecture to recognize the geometric matrices of the design conception. The interpretation process is enriched, concerning the tools used, with new steps for the definition of the geometries supporting the built shape and identifies new procedures, still in a study and refinement phase, for the control of the outcome curves of operations of geometric intersection of surfaces. The verification of the results of the work, carried out in this case study through the control of characteristic sections and intersection curves, requires further investigation in order to find the correspondence between the point cloud and the interpretative model through the overlapping of them, and the evaluation of the precise deviations, currently being elaborated. With regard to the process of geometric interpretation, on the other hand, there are new issues related to the process of conception and realization: some portions of the complex vaulted systems highlight the relationship between geometry and architectural ideation (in general, surfaces in which it is easier to recognize pure geometric surfaces, or described in treatises or manuals), while others (surfaces that derive from the need to relate even very different curves, as in the case of angular vaults) open reflections on the relationship between architectural design and building techniques, especially the construction and positioning of the ribs and the masonry equipment.

Acknowledgements. The atrium of Palazzo Mazzonis is the main entrance to the Museo d'Arte Orientale (MAO) in Turin. The research was carried out within the framework of an agreement between the Museo d'Arte Orientale and the Politecnico di Torino, aimed to surveying, drawing and digital modeling in order to communicate the architectural features of Palazzo Mazzonis. We would like to thank Dr. Marco Guglielminotti Trivel, Director of the Museum, and Mrs. Patrizia Bosio, from Technical and Security Office, for having favored the current research.

This paper is the result of the research on complex vaulted systems carried out by the research group. The authors wrote together paragraphs 1 and 8, M. C. López González wrote paragraph 5, R. Spallone paragraph 7, M. Vitali paragraph 2, G. Bertola, paragraph 4, F. Natta paragraph 6, F. Ronco paragraph 3.

References

1. Spallone, R., Vitali, M.: Star-shaped and Planterian Vaults in the Baroque Atria of Turin, Aracne, Ariccia (2017)
2. Vitali, M.: Geometric abstraction and three-dimensional modeling for the definition of a spatial grammar of the 'a fascioni' vaults. In: Atti del 40° Convegno Internazionale dei Docenti delle Discipline della Rappresentazione, pp. 861–870, Gangemi, Roma (2018)
3. De Rubertis, R.: Il disegno dell'architettura. La Nuova Italia Scientifica, Roma (1994)
4. Puche Fontanilles, J., Macias Solé, J.M., Toldrá Domingo, J.M., Solá-Morales, P.: Beyond metrics. Point clouds as semantic graphic expression. EGA Revista de expresión gráfica arquitectónica 31 (22), 228–237 (2017)
5. Sánchez, R.M., González, C.L.: La escalera del Real Colegio Seminario de Corpus Christi de Valencia (1599–1601) hipótesis de traza. Informes de la construcción **70**(550), 1–12 (2018)
6. Fantini, F.: Modelos con nivel de detalle variable realizados mediante un levantamiento digital aplicados a la arqueología. EGA Revista de expresión gráfica arquitectónica **19**, 306–317 (2013)
7. Bertocci, S., Bini, M.: Manuale di rilievo architettonico e urbano. Città Studi Edizioni, Torino (2012)
8. Almagro, A., et al.: Verso la "Carta del Rilievo Architettonico". In: Cundari, C., Carnevali, L. (eds.). Il Rilievo dei Beni Architettonici per la Conservazione, Edizioni Kappa, Roma, pp. 33–57, (2000).

Autonomous Aerial Systems in Service of Cultural Heritage Protection from Climate Change Effects

Artur Krukowski[1](✉) and Emmanouela Vogiatzaki[2](✉)

[1] RFSAT Limited, Dublin, Ireland
Artur.Krukowski@rfsat.com
[2] RFSAT Limited, Dublin, Ireland
emmanouela@rfsat.com

Abstract. The article reports on both past and ongoing work in such research projects as SCAN4RECO or ARCH, both funded by the European Commission under the Horizon 2020 program. The former one concerns multi-modal and multi-spectral scanning of Cultural Heritage (CH) assets for their digitization and conservation via spatio-temporal reconstruction and 3D printing, while the latter one aims to support better preservation of cultural heritage areas from hazards and risks, both natural and human-borne ones. Both projects have adopted co-creation methodologies to help pilot hosts (preservation institutions and cities) to save their cultural heritage from the effects of progressing climate change effects. This included developing disaster risk management frameworks for assessing and improving the resilience of historic areas to climate change and natural hazards. Tools and methodologies have been designed for local authorities and practitioners, urban population, as well as national and international expert communities, aiding authorities in knowledge-aware decision making. In this article we focus on presenting novel approaches to performing 3D modelling of object geometry using 3D photogrammetric methods using autonomous and automatic control systems for achieving very high model accuracies using consumer types of devices, attractive both to professions and hobbyists alike. We also present practically adopted approaches for remote monitoring of weather and climate effects in local and global scales as well as means of assessing possible negative effects that such natural climatic effects might pose on the level and speed of degradation of Cultural Heritage.

Keywords: 3D modelling · UAS · Cultural heritage · Preservation

1 Introduction

The cultural heritage and the way we preserve and valorize it is a major factor in defining Europe's place in the world and its attractiveness as a place to live, work, and visit; a powerful instrument that provides a sense of belonging amongst and between European citizens. The need to preserve, provide advanced access to and understanding of cultural heritage is clearly of utmost importance, especially when considering its wealth

© Springer Nature Switzerland AG 2021
M. Ioannides et al. (Eds.): EuroMed 2020, LNCS 12642, pp. 15–25, 2021.
https://doi.org/10.1007/978-3-030-73043-7_2

throughout Europe. The European cultural heritage is enormous, with a vast and rich variety of cultural items, ranging from buildings to museum artefacts. These items consist of materials of diverse types, the condition of which deteriorates with time, mainly due to environmental conditions and human actions. The effective documentation of the cultural items, so that information about them is easily accessible to researchers and the public. The preservation of objects against the effects of time to be passed unaltered to next generations, are also matters of uttermost importance and have attracted significant focus.

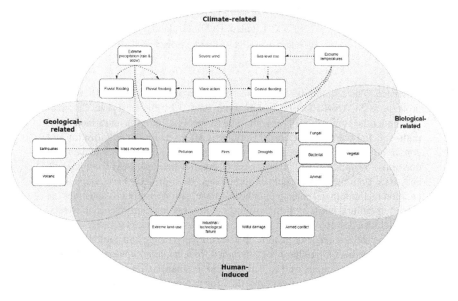

Fig. 1. Taxonomy of hazards to cultural heritage

Factors responsible for the deterioration of the state of cultural items, in case of indoor environments, include but are not limited to, humidity, temperature, exposure to light, as well as the effects of human activities, such as the transportation of the items. These factors are eliminated by keeping the cultural items in specifically designed facilities, such as museums and galleries, where environmental conditions are con-trolled by following specifications established after extensive research. However, there is a lack of research concerning the effect of the environment and the means to eliminate it, in cases of uncontrolled indoor environments. Such cases include objects and artworks hosted in historical buildings and monuments of public access, where people activities are not restricted, as in museums. The increased human activity, in combination with the uncontrolled environmental conditions of such facilities affects the objects of interest in a significantly higher degree, than the controlled environment of a museum.

In this respect, several monitoring and simulation technologies can be effectively used in order to assist in the documentation of cultural objects, as well as the evaluation of the effects of the environment on them and the development of procedures to handle those effects, in order to achieve preventive conservation. Optical, infrared, ultrasounds, x-ray and other elaborate sensors can be used to scan an object and create a rich 3D representation of it. The 3D representation is the most complete way to represent the whole structure of an object. Apart from the shape and appearance of the object, other information, resulting from various sensors, can be integrated in the 3D model, such as the materials of the object and stratigraphy information. Automatic missing part reconstruction techniques can also be adopted, to fill missing parts of the object and make the whole shape of the object available.

The rich 3D representation of a cultural object is also valuable for conservators. The 3D model constitutes an accurate virtual representation of the object and contains information about its materials and its internal condition. It thus allows the conservators to view areas of the object, which are susceptible to damage from external factors, without needing a direct access to the physical item, reducing thus, the amount of intrusion. In addition to the information of the 3D models of the objects in a facility, temperature, light and humidity sensors can constantly monitor the environmental conditions around a cultural item, for the conservation personnel to be aware of fluctuations of these conditions, which may result in the deterioration of the object. By combining environmental monitoring with continuous observation of state of an object, by updating its 3D representation, the conservator can gain an overview of how the state of the item is affected by environmental conditions over time. Such measurements can assist in preventing damage to the items and in designing strategies for better preservation.

The ARCH project [1] developed a novel, portable, integrated and modular solution for customized and thus cost-effective, automatic digitization and analysis of cultural heritage objects (CHOs). One of the main goals of the project is to create highly accurate digital surrogates of CHOs, providing also detailed insight over their surface and the volumetric structure, material composition and structure of underlying materials, enabling rendering either via visualization techniques or via multi-material 3D printing. The ARCH project analyzed object with various scanning technologies with aim to understand the heterogeneous nature and complex structures of material used, to identify the broad and varied classes of materials and to understand their degradation mechanisms over time, deriving context-dependent ageing models per material. Single material models are going to be spatiotemporally simulated, based on environmental phenomena modeling, so as to collectively render imminent degradation effects on the multi-material objects, enabling prediction and recreation of their future appearance, as well as automatic restoration, reaching even back to their original shape. ARCH project facilitates conservation by indicating spots/segments of cultural objects that are in eminent conservation need and require special attention, while suggestions are provided by a Decision Support System (DSS) about conservation methods to be followed.

2 System Architecture

The original SCAN4RECO offered a cost-efficient, portable, integrated system, based on multi-modal and multi-discipline, modular, scalable and open-architecture (presented in Fig. 1) extendable platform that will be able to provide multispectral scanning of a variety of cultural asset (e.g. wall-paintings, painting, metallic objects of various sized, carved marble, statues, etc.) non-destructively. It efficiently processes the multi-sensorial input in such a hierarchical way, to produce VR models of improved quality and information according to the demands of the end-user or the use-case/application itself, utilizing each time a diverse set of sensors. This way the complexity and the quality of the multi-layered and multi-dimensional VR model of the cultural object of interest will vary per demand (Fig. 2).

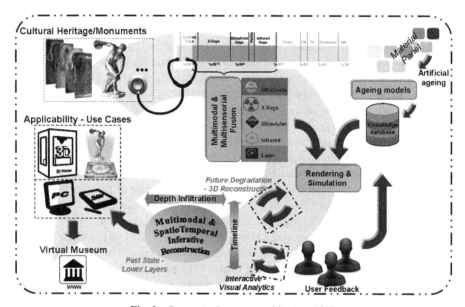

Fig. 2. Conceptual system architecture [21]

An important part of the project focuses on the study and modeling of materials commonly found in a variety of common cultural objects. This way, inter-disciplinary knowledge (e.g. physics, chemistry, history, etc.) is combined with computer science (e.g. spatiotemporal simulation, 3D rendering, DSS suggestions, visualization, etc.). The ultimate goal will be not only the material identification, stratigraphy revealing and automatic, accurate digital 3D representation and reconstruction of the object in its original state, but also the automatic inference of both previous states (i.e. restoration) and forthcoming state/shape of the object in certain times in the future, leading thus, to a 4D representation in Virtual Reality (VR) where three dimensions represent spatial information (including depth information of possible stratigraphy under the visible surface) and an extra dimension corresponds to temporal changes through simulation.

3   3d Modelling of Cultural Objects

One of the main components of the Scan4Reco system is the 3D scanning of the object geometry. It serves as a pre-requisite for being able to visualize together multiple results from a variety of surface and penetrating scanning of small parts of the object. Those include e.g. multispectral visualization from infrared to ultraviolet, depth scanning like

X-ray or Raman, to micro surface variations (roughness) using microprofilometry. Furthermore, object geometry serves also as a reference for simulated prediction of future degradations of the object over prolonged periods of time. Such changes involve both physical erosion of the surface as well as chemical changes that affect the steadiness of the object surface and give raise to speeding up of the object deterioration. Since such changes occur very slowly, having a very accurate and high-resolution 3D object representation is even more important. Over recent years, 3D scanning has become part of a coherent and non-contact approach to the documentation of cultural heritage and its long-term preservation. High-resolution 3D recordings of sites, monuments and artefacts allow us to monitor, study, disseminate and understand our shared cultural history – it is essential that the vast archives of 3D and color data are securely archived. An integral component of this work is to record surfaces and forms at the highest possible resolutions and archive them in raw formats, so the data can continue to be re-processed as technology advances. In some cases, the data will need to be re-materialized as a physical object - where a great deal of misunderstanding exists.

Digital models are used to be associated with virtual environments, but now the ability to rematerialize data as physical 3D objects is demanding new explorations into the types of information the data contains. The levels of damage and destruction of heritage sites caused by mass tourism, wars, iconoclastic acts, the ravages of time, commercial imperatives, imperfect restoration and natural disasters has led to a re-evaluation of the importance of high-resolution facsimiles. Exact representations are being made possible through advances in 3D recording, composite photography, an assortment of multi-spectral imaging techniques, image processing and output technologies. Many different 3D scanning methods exist, each with their own advantages and limitations. The challenge is to identify the right system for the right application. No one system can do every-thing. The diverse methods of capturing 3D data evidences this. Time of flight, triangulation, photogrammetry and a host of different approaches are redefining the relationship between image and form. The 3D data can be on a vast scale, recording the topography of a landscape from great distances or it can be close range and accurate enough to document the surface of a carving; marks that are not easily visible to the human eye can be visualized for reconstruction study or condition monitoring. While some systems can obtain color data as well as 3D information, currently no 3D scanner is able to record color to the standard required to produce an exact replica. All 3D recording is based on metrology; the science of making measurements. Outlined below are the main techniques and scanners that are commonly used and the reasons they are used in the way they are. The project needs are twofold, from one side a correct representation of object shape (geometry), from the other one dealing correctly with difficult materials to capture their correct color and appearance. The focus of this chapter is capturing the global shape, whereby some of the presented commercial technologies show potential for correct representation of object appearance as well.

Photogrammetry or stereoscopic scanning is the technology of making depth measurements from raster photographs. It can be used for quick recording of vulnerable and inaccessible sites. Photogrammetry is also ideal way to obtain 3D information in situations where it is not possible to use 3D scanners (inaccessible locations, conflict zones), or when high-speed recording is required (scanning people, living organisms, liquids in movement). It is ideal for the recording of translucent surfaces like alabaster and marble. Due to the composite nature of the image capture, color and form can be extracted from the data. Until recently achieving highest resolution recording of surface for facsimile production and featureless, reflective and dark surfaces was not feasible. However, recent software developments (e.g. by Pix4D Mapper, Autodesk ReMake and many other ones) it became possible through improvements to photogrammetry technology to become soon the dominant method for recording at risk cultural heritage in 3D and color. A special version of the photogrammetry is structured light scanning, whereby pre-defined shapes (commonly horizontal and vertical lines) are projected onto the object surface. By analyzing the change in line shapes from images captured by the camera, the shape of an object can be determined.

4 Automated 3D Modelling System

The photogrammetric 3D modelling provides not only the precise representation of the object geometry, but offers also a reference for positioning partial scans from other modalities. It also captures the object condition at a time that can be then aged artificially through digital simulation. The 3D modelling is done from several 50MPixel raster images taken with high-overlap (more than 70%) on a regular grid, thus providing high number of matching features among many images. The precise positioning and orientation of the camera in three dimensions (repeatable to single centimeters) is achieved by using a computer controlled mechanical arm. Images are then processed either locally (rough model only, due to a limited computational power of the rack PC) and/or using remote processing server where it can take advantage of the high processing power boosted by CUDA cores of multiple Nvidia GTX 1080TI graphics cards.

5 Simulating Ageing Effects

The H2020-ARCH project offers technology transfer from dealing with tangible objects to larger spaces whether they are buildings, statues, city areas, archeological sites [20] etc. As a result, technologies need to be extended from lab-type as in SCAN4RECO to portable, in many cases deployable on autonomous systems, such as aerial [19] ones able to capture objects well above the ground level and thus offer new way of analyzing their condition and assess risks of degradations, both due to natural erosion caused by natural environments, but also speeded up effects from Climate Change, natural events and/or human-borne incidents. Thus, it aims to strengthen the resilience of historic areas to climate change-related and other hazards by supporting decision makers in addressing the specific needs of those areas when formulating sustainable protection and reconstruction strategies. From technological perspective it offers means of determining current condition of tangible and intangible cultural objects, as well as large historic areas, gathered within an information management system for georeferenced properties of historic areas, structures, buildings, and artefacts, e.g. build material and existing protection measures. It includes an information management system for hazard data, captured via existing climate services and novel monitoring techniques leading to provision of simulation

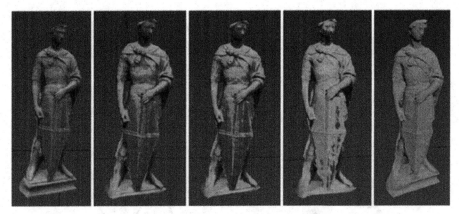

Fig. 3. Simulated ageing of a bronze statue of Saint Giorgio at 5-year intervals

models for what-if analysis of the effects of hazards and potential measures, ageing and hazard simulation.

As such it extends 3D modelling and ageing simulations from SCAN4RECO [21], shown on an example of Saint Giorgio statue in Fig. 3, adding means of monitoring climatic and weather changes that might have direct effect of degradations to cultural heritage objects.

6 Autonomous Scanning and Monitoring

Since 3D scanning and monitoring of large areas stretches beyond current capabilities of UAVs, new methods of operating large number of devices simultaneously over areas of interest, as suggested in Fig. 4, are proposed whereby initially flight control is linked to the pilot console (current legal requirement), though applied R&D is directed to fully relay autonomous mission control onto a dedicated embedded computer deployed on autonomous UAS.

7 Example Experiments

Several technology validations on different types of objects have been performed. The test showing the power of the technology was to 3D scan of a Saint Michael icon from Mount Athos monastery in Halkidiki (Greece). Here the highest resolution commercial camera Canon 5DS-R was used, which incorporates a 50Mpixel CCD sensor. A 20-years old icon has already shown signs of ageing with physical surface deteriorations and discolorations, thus being a suitable subject for high resolution analysis in both 2D and 3D. High resolution images allowed to achieve feature discrimination at accuracy reaching 57 μm (Fig. 4). A high-performance PC with i7–3.8 GHz processor and dual Nvidia GTX1080 graphics cards allowed to perform the processing in less than 8 h. A zoom into the selected features of the icon shows the precision of representation of both flat and recessed parts of the object to accuracy reaching 50 μm.

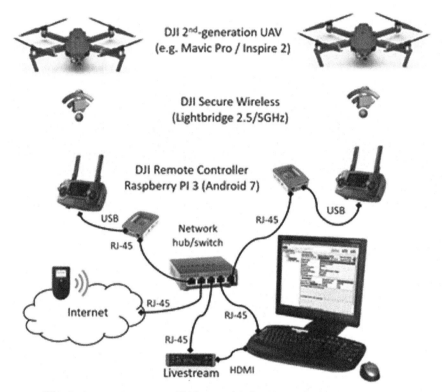

Fig. 4. Autonomous swarm UAS operation for 3D monitoring of large areas

These experiments show the capabilities for this technology to produce 3D models with accuracies reaching the precision usually required by CH restoration facilities. In our experiments, we have used commercial photogrammetric software, such as Autodesk ReMake [8] (formerly known as Autodesk Memento) and ReCap, Pix4D Mapper Pro [7], AirTek Studio [10] and Agisoft Photoscan [9]. The performance and processing time varied significantly among those applications. After several attempts, we concluded that Autodesk ReMake and Pix4D Mapper were most suited to scanning the types of objects used in the SCAN4RECO projects (painting and icons, as well as metallic 3D objects up to the size of a life size statues) and conditions under which images were taken (indoor and outdoor with natural light). ReMake is an end-to-end solution for converting reality captured with photos or scans into high-definition 3D meshes. These meshes that can be cleaned up, fixed, edited, scaled, measured, re-topologized, decimated, aligned, compared and optimized for downstream workflows entirely in ReMake. It handles reverse engineering as support for design and engineering, for asset creation for AR/VR, film, game, art, for archiving and preserving heritage, digital publishing interactive for Web and mobile experiences. ReMake plays well with Autodesk® ReCap 360, helping clean up, fix, edit, optimize and prepare the generated meshes from laser scans or photos for downstream use. ReMake simplifies complex processes since it was designed for users who require top-quality digital models of real-life objects but have little or no 3D

Fig. 5. 3D model (right) of Saint Michael icon (left) with 50MP camera

modelling expertise. The early experiments with Autodesk ReMake in the SCAN4RECO project have shown several advantages, such as smoother edges and cleaner model mesh as compared to Pix4D Mapper, although precision is significantly lower and models lack high object count, yet.

8   Extending from Objects to Cultural Areas

Such a system will enable high level of autonomy in decision making in varying environmental conditions, monitored by e.g. a CIPCast-DSS system by ENEA that collects data from diverse sensors ranging from ground to aerial ones (Fig. 5), important during disasters or in cases where instant surveillance of large areas is required (Fig. 6).

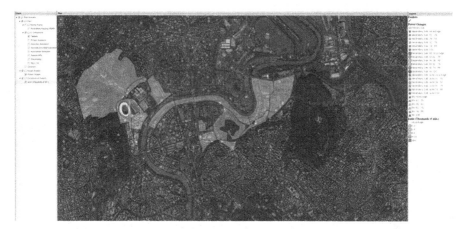

Fig. 6. CIPCast decision support system from ENEA used in ARCH project [22]

9   Conclusions and Further Work

In this article we summarized the main concepts behind use of new 3D scanning/modelling and simulated ageing of cultural heritage objects as proposed in the SCAN4RECO project, taking advantage of novel autonomous systems for monitoring large objects as well as large cultural areas of e.g. cities, excavations and/or disaster areas, as first proposed in the FP7-AF3 [18] project and currently extended in the H2020-ARCH [17] project. The vast amount of research performed in all three mentioned projects could only be signaled in this publication and therefore interested readers are suggested to explore online resources of publications, prototypes, demos and presentations available on the WEB portal of each of the mentioned projects.

Acknowledgments. The research leading to these results has been partially funded by the European Union Horizon'2020 Research Framework under Grant Agreement N° 665091: SCAN4RECO, No. 820999: ARCH and No. N° 607276: AF3.

References

1. H2020-SCAN4RECO project: https://cordis.europa.eu/project/id/665091
2. Smith, T.F., Waterman, M.S.: Identification of common molecular subsequences. J. Mol. Biol. **147**, 195–197 (1981)
3. May, P., Ehrlich, H.-C., Steinke, T.: ZIB structure prediction pipeline: composing a complex biological workflow through web services. In: Nagel, W.E., Walter, W.V., Lehner, W. (eds.) Euro-Par 2006. LNCS, vol. 4128, pp. 1148–1158. Springer, Heidelberg (2006). https://doi.org/10.1007/11823285_121
4. Foster, I., Kesselman, C.: The Grid: Blueprint for a New Computing Infrastructure. Morgan Kaufmann, San Francisco (1999)
5. Czajkowski, K., Fitzgerald, S., Foster, I., Kesselman, C.: Grid information services for distributed resource sharing. In: 10th IEEE International Symposium on High Performance Distributed Computing, pp. 181–184. IEEE Press, New York (2001)

6. Foster, I., Kesselman, C., Nick, J., Tuecke, S.: The physiology of the grid: an open grid services architecture for distributed systems integration. Technical report, Global Grid Forum (2002)
7. Krukowski, A., Vogiatzaki, E.: UAV-based photogrammetric 3D modelling and surveillance of forest wildfires. In: Workshop on UAV & SAR: using drones in rescue operations, ISA, Rome (Italy), 29th March 2017
8. Pix4D Mapper Pro: https://pix4d.com/product/pix4dmapper-pro
9. Autodesk ReMake: https://remake.autodesk.com
10. Agisoft Photoscan: https://www.agisoft.com
11. ArTec 3D Studio: https://www.artec3d.com/3d-software/artec-studio
12. Pix4D Capture: https://pix4d.com/product/pix4dcapture
13. NVidia GeForce cards: https://www.nvidia.com/en-us/geforce/products
14. CUDA (15th of March 2017): https://www.nvidia.com/object/cuda_home_new.html
15. Steward, J., Lichti, D., Chow, J., Ferber, R., Osis, S.: Performance assessment and calibration of the Kinect 2.0 time-of-flight range camera for use in motion capture applications, FIG Working week 2015, Wisdom of the Ages to the Challenges of the Modern World, Sofia, Bulgaria, 17–21 May 2015
16. Structure.io sensor: https://structure.io
17. H2020-ARCH project: https://cordis.europa.eu/project/id/820999
18. FP7-AF3 project: https://cordis.europa.eu/project/id/607276
19. Krukowski, A., Vogiatzaki, E.: Autonomous aerial systems in service of cultural heritage protection from climate change effects. In: International Conference on Heritage Tourism, Cultural Heritage and Preservation (ICHTCHP'2021), Amsterdam, The Netherlands, 21–22 January 2021. (https://panel.waset.org/conference/2021/01/amsterdam/ICHTCHP)
20. COST Action CA15201: https://www.cost.eu/actions/CA15201 and https://www.arkwork.eu
21. Krukowski, A., Vogiatzaki, E.: High resolution 3D modelling of cultural heritage. In: 12th International Conference on Non-Destructive Investigations and Microanalysis for the Diagnostics and Conservation of Cultural and Environmental Heritage (ART 2017), Politecnico di Torino, 22–24 November 2017, Torino, Italy (2017)
22. http://sue.enea.it/product/citta-sicure-e-sostenibili/sistema-di-supporto-alle-decisioni-cip cast/

3D Thermal Mapping of Architectural Heritage

Up-To-Date Workflows for the Production of Three-Dimensional Thermographic Models for Built Heritage NDT

Efstathios Adamopoulos[1]([✉]) [iD], Giacomo Patrucco[2] [iD], Monica Volinia[2],
Mario Girotto[2], Fulvio Rinaudo[2] [iD], Fabio Giulio Tonolo[2] [iD], and Antonia Spanò[2,3] [iD]

[1] Department of Computer Science, University of Turin, Corso Svizzera 185, 10149 Turin, Italy
efstathios.adamopoulos@unito.it
[2] Department of Architecture and Design, Polytechnic University of Turin,
Viale Pier Andrea Mattioli 39, 10125 Turin, Italy
{giacomo.patrucco,monica.volinia,mario.girotto,fulvio.rinaudo,
fabio.giuliotonolo,antonia.spano}@polito.it
[3] The Future Urban Legacy Lab, PoliTo FULL, Toolbox coworking.
Via Agostino da Montefeltro 2, 10125 Turin, Italy

Abstract. The combination of thermographic and geometric recording has always been an issue for architectural heritage diagnostic investigations. Multidisciplinary projects often require integrating multi-sensor information—including metric and temperature data—to extract valid conclusions regarding the state-of-preservation of historical buildings. Towards this direction, recent technological advancements in thermographic cameras and three-dimensional (3D) documentation instrumentation and software have contributed significantly, assisting the rapid creation of detailed 3D thermal-textured results, which can be exploited for non-destructive diagnostical surveys. This paper aims to briefly review and evaluate the current workflows for thermographic architectural 3D modeling, which implement state-of-the-art sensing procedures and processing techniques, while also presenting some applications on case studies of significant heritage value to help discuss current problems and identify topics for relevant future research.

Keywords: 3D thermography · Thermal imaging · Data integration · Non-destructive testing · Architectural heritage · Heritage conservation

1 Introduction

Infrared thermography (IRT) is a consolidated remote sensing technique for the non-destructive assessment of architectural heritage surfaces. Over the last years, the sensors used for the documentation and assessment of thermal phenomena have evolved and diversified. Therefore, IRT has been extensively applied regarding cultural heritage for the evaluation of the state-of-preservation of traditional and historical materials and structures [1], the behavior of replacement materials [2], the effectiveness of the cleaning of architectural surfaces, the efficacy of consolidation interventions, the compatibility of

© Springer Nature Switzerland AG 2021
M. Ioannides et al. (Eds.): EuroMed 2020, LNCS 12642, pp. 26–37, 2021.
https://doi.org/10.1007/978-3-030-73043-7_3

masonry restoration interventions by repair mortars [3, 4], the extent of plaster detachment and integration [5], the moisture content [6], as well as for the uncovering of hidden features and subsurface construction [7, 8].

Thermographic investigations of architectural heritage are often conducted independently from the acquisition of the structure's geometry and examine thermal phenomena on a local scale by acquiring two-dimensional (2D) thermograms. This is mainly a result of thermal-infrared (TIR) sensors' technical characteristics, such as their low resolution. However, the significance of geometry in the field of heritage diagnostics is high, which has led to various approaches towards the combination of 3D metric surveying and temperature mapping. These integrated geomatics approaches aim to produce either 3D models or 2D derivative orthoimages combined with TIR information, enabling accurate measurements of discontinuity locations and further diagnostical data fusion. The presented work tracks the developments in 3D temperature mapping for architectural heritage investigations by briefly reviewing techniques for 3D shape and TIR data acquisition, and integration, in the relevant literature. Some practical examples from the authors' recent work are also presented in the following to evaluate the current state-of-the-art in applicable non-destructive testing (NDT) techniques.

2 Methods and Applications

Measuring a historical building's or single building component's 3D geometry is the first integral part of accurate thermographic modeling—and accurate documentation in general—which can be performed with different sensors and concerning different purposes [9, 10]. Contemporary methods for 3D metric surveying widely used for architectural heritage applications include, but are not limited to, terrestrial and UAS-based light detection and ranging (LiDAR; active sensing) and digital photogrammetry (passive sensing). The produced metric results can be integrated into various forms and datatypes with the TIR images. Nevertheless, the latest methodological developments enable the direct extraction of 3D metric information from thermal imagery itself, employing photogrammetric-based thermographic data acquisition and multi-image processing workflows.

2.1 LiDAR and Infrared Thermography

LiDAR approaches use active range sensors to record the 3D position of every point inside the sensor's field-of-view (FOV) along with the intensity of backscattered radiation. They can produce dense or sampled point clouds of an object in considerably less time than passive methods, making them extremely valuable for high-resolution surveys of existing buildings and architectural elements. In thermographic surveys, LiDAR has often been considered as an optimal complement, given its capacity to swiftly provide point clouds that can be textured with the TIR images directly or after 3D model production. In order to perform the thermal texturing, the geometric relation between the thermographic images and the 3D geometry of the object has to be known. The position and orientation of the TIR images can be estimated with different methodologies.

When the TIR camera and the LiDAR sensor are not affixed, and their relative position and orientation are not measured during the acquisition phase, the 3D relation between each thermal image and the produced point cloud has to be estimated individually. The foundation for this estimation's solution is based on correspondence features recognition between the point cloud or the derivative documentation products—which contain metric spatial information—and the TIR images. The relative position and orientation-matrix of each TIR image can be estimated using the manual identification of corresponding (homologous) points [6, 11–14]. Figure 1 showcases the result of TIR image-texturing for a partial model of the East façade of *Castello del Valentino* in Turin (Italy), aiming to identify deterioration patterns, such as detachments, dampness, and biological colonization.

Fig. 1. The thermographic 3D model is generated with the registration of products: the thermal images and the 3D mesh produced with terrestrial LiDAR.

More advanced thermal texturing approaches of the geometric products address the automated matching of 2D features on the TIR images with the corresponding 3D features on the object's model. Hoegner and Stilla [15] described two workflows for matching infrared photos with 3D building models and 3D point clouds. The first included registering a building model with a sequence of terrestrial thermal images, using geometrical constraints generated from the model's geometry to refine thermal images' orientation. The second workflow used an Iterative Closest Point (ICP) strategy to register an RGB imagery-produced 3D point cloud and a TIR image-based 3D point cloud, to assign thermal values to the dense RGB point cloud. Lagüela et al. [16] and González-Aguilera et al. [17] extracted features from point clouds and LiDAR-produced range images respectively, to facilitate their registration.

Approaches for the simultaneous acquisition of thermal and 3D geometrical data from terrestrial LiDAR—in the form of point clouds—have also been developed for rapid 3D thermographic mapping. The utilization of commercial multi-sensor solutions or custom-made instrumentation requires the orientation of the different integrated sensors used for the acquisition. Borrmann et al. [18] built and calibrated an automatic moving setup for the simultaneous acquisition of 3D laser scan data, thermal, and RGB images combining an Optris PI 160 TIR camera, a Riegl VZ-400 laser scanner, and a Logitech QuickCam Pro 9000 webcam, mounted on a modified VolksBot RT 3 platform. They tested the robotic system to perform thermal recording at the Bremen City Hall (Germany)—a historical building of Brick Gothic and Weser Renaissance architecture. Merchán et al. [19] developed a hybrid thermal scanning system employing a Riegl VZ-400 laser scanner, a Nikon D90 color camera, and a FLIR AX5 TIR camera. The hybrid instrument was calibrated with targets incorporating both visible and thermal reflectance discriminants, distributed over a wide area of the scene. It was also used for the Baritel de San Carlos's interior thermal mapping in Almadenejos and the Nuestra Señora de la Candelaria church in Fuente del Maestre (Spain).

2.2 Single-Thermographic Image Rectification

In principle, thermographic sensors, such as those used for building inspections, can be handled as standard photogrammetric cameras [20]. As in optical photography, the thermal images are subject to distortion effects. Quite often in architectural photogrammetry, the optical axis of the camera is not vertical to the architectural surface, resulting in distortions of the object on the image. Thus, a photogrammetric single-image digital processing procedure is required [21] to allow the correct data interpretation by generating rectified thermal images, which can be used directly or for texturing point clouds and reconstructed 3D models. Image rectification is one of the simplest and most economic photogrammetric methods and can take two forms.

1. with known camera parameters and availability of a 3D model of the object
   When the internal orientation of the TIR camera is known, the geometry of the acquisition is restored, and the position and external orientation parameters of the camera are needed so that the point positions can be estimated as the intersection of rays from the camera to the surface with the surface known for its geometry. To estimate the camera's external orientation parameters, at least three points with known coordinates on the object are needed. If the digital surface model of the object is available, then the thermal values can be projected on it to create an orthographic view of the object's plane, a so-called orthophoto or orthoimage. An alternative rectification method can be the use of scale bars—instead of points with known coordinates—appropriate for the thermographic approach.
2. without knowledge of camera parameters and almost planar objects
   For the application of the rectification process, in this case, a projective transformation is needed between the plane of the thermal image and the object's surface (projective plane). Estimating the transform parameters requires at least four points with known coordinates on the object plane [22].

2.3 Multi-image 3D Reconstruction and Infrared Thermography

Multi-image 3D reconstruction approaches constitute a cost-effective alternative to traditional close-range photogrammetry, which can effectively involve both nadiral and oblique imagery to generate accurate and high-resolution metric products. Nowadays, thanks to the improvements in the fields of photogrammetric computer vision technologies and image-matching algorithms, these solutions are characterized by a high level of automatization. As a result, these techniques have become widely applied in architectural heritage recording. However, despite the fact that user-friendly and almost automatic solutions exist, it should be underlined that the role of the operator is still fundamental to ensure that the metric and thematic accuracy of the final products meet the user requirements [23]. Using robust automated Structure-from-Motion (SfM) and Multiple-View-Stereo (MVS) algorithmic implementations, dense 3D point clouds and models can be generated from properly overlapping images.

Terrestrial Applications

Recently, few approaches have been reported using multiple-view image-based reconstruction techniques to digitize both 3D shape and thermal texture using only TIR images for building related-applications (Fig. 2) [24, 25].

Fig. 2. The thermographic 3D point cloud is generated after the application of photogrammetric principles to thermographic images.

Laguela et al. [26] highlighted that certain specifications have to be met for the successful generation of 3D point clouds directly from thermographic imagery, such as the acquisition of orthogonal and oblique images, which will be used for the accurate implementation of the photogrammetric principles, maintaining a robust geometry for the reconstruction, and exploitation of only the orthogonal images for texturing the 3D results—to avoid the inclination and convergence effect.

Due to the inherently different characteristics between TIR and RGB images, research on thermographic modeling for architectural heritage has mainly concentrated on workflows reconstructing 3D shape from RGB images and applying the texture from registered TIR images, and hybrid workflows which apply the photogrammetric principles on both RGB and TIR images and use only the latter for texturing. Previtalli et al. [27] developed an approach to compute photogrammetrically the orientation of both thermal and RGB images together in a combined bundle adjustment (using the collinearity equation) in order to improve co-registration accuracies and map the infrared images on models of building façades. Lin et al. [28] proposed a thermal mapping workflow based on registration between the thermal point cloud and RGB point cloud performed using fast global registration and image resection of TIR images.

Aiming to tackle the problems caused by TIR images' low spatial resolution, we developed a cost-effective thermal mapping method employing optical and IRT terrestrial datasets from a TIR camera and a high-resolution digital RGB camera. The RGB and TIR sensors of the thermographic camera were calibrated to model the image distortions. Then, undistorted TIR images were registered with a projective transformation to match the system of the undistorted RGB images—captured with the optical sensor of the thermographic camera—using the same transformation parameters for each strip of images. The imagery dataset from the high-resolution RGB camera was used to improve and densify the photogrammetric reconstruction produced with RGB images derived from the thermographic camera. After 3D point cloud and final model generation, the oriented RGB images were replaced by the corresponding transformed TIR images to apply the thermal texture (Fig. 3). Since the thermographic images were not used for generating the geometric model, a higher number of points was reconstructed, resulting in an accurate higher resolution model. Simultaneously, the spatial resolution of the thermal information was higher due to the large number of used TIR images that were acquired from a close range [29].

Fig. 3. Model textured with thermal images, generated with the workflow described in 2.3.

UAS-Based Applications

As is well-known, nowadays, UAS (Unmanned Aircraft Systems)-based photogrammetry presents an effective and relatively low-cost solution for cultural heritage metric documentation, allowing a rigorous and accurate geometric reconstruction of the built and landscape environment [30]. The developments of new COTS (Commercial Off-the-Shelf) UAS platforms and the improvements in photogrammetric SfM-based algorithms lead to increased and effective use of UAS for mapping purposes in different application domains. Nowadays, specialists in many fields of expertise (including researchers operating in the framework of heritage valorization) are successfully using UAS photogrammetry to carry out their research.

The introduction of COTS drones equipped with high-performing thermal sensors allows researchers in the field of cultural heritage to acquire and analyze thermal data from an aerial perspective—integrating and complementing traditional close-range approaches (with a higher level of detail with respect to manned aerial or satellite platforms). As evidence of the growing interest in this research topic, several commercial and open-source SfM-based software are implementing new algorithms to process thermal data in order to successfully perform 3D reconstruction, including specific templates for UAS acquired thermograms [31, 32].

The possibility to process UAS TIR images using SfM-based algorithms allows thermal information and 3D geometry data of the object to be integrated for monitoring, inspection, or diagnostic purposes.

Considering the intrinsic vulnerability of the assets belonging to built heritage, the opportunity represented by using a remote diagnostic tool such as IRT data for photogrammetric applications is particularly interesting for the disciplines connected to documentation and restoration. The low spatial resolution of the thermal images can impose a severe obstacle to the proper reconstruction of the surveyed structures' geometry. Moreover, the radiometric characteristics of TIR images make the direct use of SfM challenging [31]: for this reason, some critical issues are generally encountered during the tie-points extraction phase [33], especially if the acquisition has been performed without following rigorous photogrammetric overlapping criteria.

In the case of UAS based acquisitions, as underlined in the previous section, a multi-sensor strategy can represent a valid solution to avoid topological errors during the 3D reconstruction phase—which could cause some projection miscalculations during orthoimagery production—and to achieve better results in terms of the geometric and spatial resolution of the final model [34, 35]. Following this strategy, and by integrating thermal and optical images, it is possible to exploit the higher geometric and spatial resolution of the traditional true-color images to generate a more detailed, accurate, and topologically correct 3D mesh, which can be used as a geometric reference surface both for the texturization process of the achieved 3D model with IRT data and the generation of thermal orthoimagery. This approach requires the registration of both thermal and optical images in the same reference system, which is based on the identification of the Ground Control Points (GCPs) also in thermal images, a challenging task due to the intrinsic characteristics of this kind of data. This problem can be solved using the image geo-tag [33], which is often embedded in the acquired images (if the system used is equipped with a GNSS receiver). However, this solution's positional accuracy is generally low (few meters) unless RTK-enabled platforms are adopted [36].

A practical solution consists of using specific artificial targets made of materials characterized by a low emissivity, in contrast to the traditional photogrammetric targets (usually made of paper or plastic, which are characterized by an emissivity value up to 0.99). This solution has been used in Hill et al. 2020 [37], where aluminum targets have been used to detect them easily and unambiguously in TIR images.

Lastly, a third workflow—which has been used in Patrucco el al. 2020 [34] in the context of an experience on an abandoned alpine hamlet subject (in the framework of

10.5 °C   39.40 °C

Fig. 4. (a) Level of detail differences between the mesh obtained from thermal dataset only (on the left) and optical dataset (on the right). (b) 3D mesh obtained from optical dataset texturized with co-registered thermal images.

research on the regeneration of small alpine settlements)—assesses the possibility to use natural points as control points, when clearly detectable on both optical and thermal images.

As is possible to observe in Fig. 4, following a traditional SfM-based workflow and using the aforementioned approaches, it is feasible to generate high resolution and high detailed 3D models with a thermal texture or generate thermal orthoimagery.

3   Discussion and Conclusions

The fusion of geomatics and thermographic techniques has a great added value for the implementation of thermographic surveys for historical architecture. This review presented several methods focused on this application domain, including techniques for simultaneous or independent acquisition of geometric and thermal information, as well as state-of-the-art workflows employing SfM/MVS-based approaches. The results showcase the potential for combined non-destructive evaluation of the state-of-preservation of built heritage.

The registration of single thermograms to LiDAR or photogrammetry-produced point clouds and 3D models is a simple-to-implement method to investigate local phenomena. The generation of extensive thermal orthophoto-maps with this method may prove time-consuming if corresponding features have to be separately computed for each image. Additionally, feature correspondences may not be visible between IRT data and optical imagery, making the registration unfeasible without placing any artificial targets detectable in both the visible and infrared spectra. However, the implementation of automated feature matching techniques can make the methodology more efficient. A significant drawback for product registration is that the relative planarity of the architectural façade or element is required so that occlusions and other geometrical irregularities will not affect the thermal texturing.

Single TIR-image rectification has proven to be a cost-effective method to create spatially correct 2D thermal products. It maximizes the potential for radiometric and spatial measurements, which can be obtained by a single thermal photo after appropriate corrections have been performed. However, it requires calibration of the thermal sensor and, as with product registration, can be used to study only localized phenomena with sufficient spatial resolution.

The application of multi-image 3D reconstruction principles to exploit the geometrical data directly captured with TIR images is a cost-effective approach for rapid 3D diagnostics, but the thermograms' low-resolution significantly restricts the resolution of spatial results. However, hybrid methods involving both RGB and TIR images can produce extensive and even full-building 3D models in high resolution. This either involves RGB and TIR images' simultaneous orientation in the same photogrammetric dataset to acquire accurate orientation information or image registration for accurate thermal texturing of high-resolution reconstructed 3D products from RGB images for terrestrial and aerial applications both. The ability of contemporary 3D temperature mapping approaches to produce high-resolution results reveals an excellent potential for holistic multidisciplinary and multi-sensor approaches towards protecting cultural heritage.

Acknowledgments. This project has partially received funding from the European Union's Framework Program for Research and Innovation Horizon 2020 (2014–2020) under the Marie-Skłodowska Curie Grant (Agreement 754511) and from the Compagnia di San Paolo.

References

1. Grinzato, E., Bison, P.G., Marinetti, S.: Monitoring of ancient buildings by the thermal method. J. Cult. Herit. **3**, 21–29 (2002). https://doi.org/10.1016/S1296-2074(02)01159-7
2. Lerma, C., Mas, Á., Gil, E., Vercher, J., Torner, M.E.: Quantitative analysis procedure for building materials in historic buildings by applying infrared thermography. Russ J Nondestruct Test. **54**, 601–609 (2018). https://doi.org/10.1134/S1061830918080065
3. Avdelidis, N.P., Moropoulou, A.: Applications of infrared thermography for the investigation of historic structures. J. Cult. Herit. **5**, 119–127 (2004). https://doi.org/10.1016/j.culher.2003.07.002
4. Moropoulou, A., Labropoulos, K.C., Delegou, E.T., Karoglou, M., Bakolas, A.: Non-destructive techniques as a tool for the protection of built cultural heritage. Constr. Build. Mater. **48**, 1222–1239 (2013). https://doi.org/10.1016/j.conbuildmat.2013.03.044
5. Volinia, M.: Integration of qualitative and quantitative infrared surveys to study the plaster conditions of Valentino Castle. Presented at the AeroSense 2000, Orlando, FL March 30 (2000). https://doi.org/10.1117/12.381566.
6. Lerma, J.L., Cabrelles, M., Portalés, C.: Multitemporal thermal analysis to detect moisture on a building façade. Constr. Build. Mater. **25**, 2190–2197 (2011). https://doi.org/10.1016/j.conbuildmat.2010.10.007
7. Brooke, C.: Thermal imaging for the archaeological investigation of historic buildings. Remote Sens. **10**, 1401 (2018). https://doi.org/10.3390/rs10091401
8. Glavaš, H., Hadzima-Nyarko, M., Buljan, I.H., Barić, T.: Locating hidden elements in walls of cultural heritage buildings by using infrared thermography. Buildings **9**, 32 (2019). https://doi.org/10.3390/buildings9020032
9. Georgopoulos, A.: Data acquisition for the geometric documentation of cultural heritage. In: Ioannides, M., Magnenat-Thalmann, N., Papagiannakis, G. (eds.) Mixed Reality and Gamification for Cultural Heritage, pp. 29–73. Springer International Publishing, Cham (2017). https://doi.org/10.1007/978-3-319-49607-8_2.
10. Chiabrando, F., Sammartano, G., Spanò, A., Spreafico, A.: Hybrid 3D models: when geomatics innovations meet extensive built heritage complexes. IJGI **8**, 124 (2019). https://doi.org/10.3390/ijgi8030124
11. Costanzo, A., Minasi, M., Casula, G., Musacchio, M., Buongiorno, M.: Combined use of terrestrial laser scanning and IR thermography applied to a historical building. Sensors **15**, 194–213 (2014). https://doi.org/10.3390/s150100194
12. Mileto, C., Vegas, F., Lerma, J.L.: Multidisciplinary studies, crossreading and transversal use of thermography: the castle of Monzón (Huesca) as a case study. In: Editorial Universitat Politècnica de València (ed.) Modern Age Fortifications of the Mediterranean Coast – Defensive architecture of the Mediterranean (FORTMED2015). UPV Press, Valencia (2015). https://doi.org/10.4995/FORTMED2015.2015.1786.
13. Spanò, A., Volinia, M., Girotto, M.: Spatial data and temperature: relationship to deepen integrated methods for advanced architectural diagnosis and metric documentation. In: Marabelli, M., Parisi, C., Buzzanca, G., Paradisi, A., (eds.) 8th International Conference on Non Destructive Investigations and Microanalysis for the Diagnostics and Conservation of the Cultural and Environmental Heritage, pp. 405–412. Italian Society for Non-Destructive Testing Monitoring Diagnostics AIPnD, Brescia (2005)
14. Zalama, E., Gómez-García-Bermejo, J., Llamas, J., Medina, R.: An effective texture mapping approach for 3D models obtained from laser scanner data to building documentation: an effective texture mapping approach. Comput.-Aided Civil Infrastruct. Eng. **26**, 381–392 (2011). https://doi.org/10.1111/j.1467-8667.2010.00699.x

15. Hoegner, L., Stilla, U.: Mobile thermal mapping for matching of infrared images with 3D building models and 3D point clouds. Quant. InfraRed Thermography J. 1–19 (2018). https://doi.org/10.1080/17686733.2018.1455129.
16. Lagüela, S., Díaz-Vilariño, L., Martínez, J., Armesto, J.: Automatic thermographic and RGB texture of as-built BIM for energy rehabilitation purposes. Autom. Constr. **31**, 230–240 (2013). https://doi.org/10.1016/j.autcon.2012.12.013
17. González-Aguilera, D., Rodriguez-Gonzalvez, P., Armesto, J., Lagüela, S.: Novel approach to 3D thermography and energy efficiency evaluation. Energy Buildings **54**, 436–443 (2012). https://doi.org/10.1016/j.enbuild.2012.07.023
18. Borrmann, D., Elseberg, J., Nüchter, A.: Thermal 3D mapping of building façades. In: Lee, S., Cho, H., Yoon, K.-J., and Lee, J. (eds.) Intelligent Autonomous Systems 12, pp. 173–182. Springer Berlin Heidelberg, Heidelberg (2013). https://doi.org/10.1007/978-3-642-33926-4_16.
19. Merchán, P., Merchán, M.J., Salamanca, S., Adán, A.: Application of multisensory technology for resolution of problems in the field of research and preservation of cultural heritage. In: Ioannides, M., Martins, J., Žarnić, R., Lim, V. (eds.) Advances in Digital Cultural Heritage. LNCS, vol. 10754, pp. 32–47. Springer, Cham (2018). https://doi.org/10.1007/978-3-319-75789-6_3
20. Luhmann, T., Piechel, J., Roelfs, T.: Geometric calibration of thermographic cameras. In: Kuenzer, C., Dech, S. (eds.) Thermal Infrared Remote Sensing, pp. 27–42. Springer Netherlands, Dordrecht (2013). https://doi.org/10.1007/978-94-007-6639-6_2.
21. Franzen, C., Siedler, G., Franzen, C., Vetter, S.: Orthogonal IRT imaging. In: 2013 Digital Heritage International Congress (DigitalHeritage), pp. 633–636. IEEE, Marseille, France (2013). https://doi.org/10.1109/DigitalHeritage.2013.6743805.
22. Hemmleb, M., Wiedemann, A.: Digital rectification and generation of orthoimages in architectural photogrammetry. Int. Arch. Photogramm. Remote Sens. Spatial Inf. Sci. XXXII-5C1B-1997, 261–267 (1997)
23. Santagati, C., Inzerillo, L., Di Paola, F.: Image-based modeling techniques for architectural heritage 3D digitalization: Limits and potentialities. Int. Arch. Photogramm. Remote Sens. Spatial Inf. Sci. **XL-5/W2**, 555–560 (2013). https://doi.org/10.5194/isprsarchives-XL-5-W2-555-2013.
24. González-Aguilera, D., Lagüela, S., Rodríguez-Gonzálvez, P., Hernández-López, D.: Image-based thermographic modeling for assessing energy efficiency of buildings façades. Energy Buildings **65**, 29–36 (2013). https://doi.org/10.1016/j.enbuild.2013.05.040
25. Dlesk, A., Vach, K., Holubec, P.: Usage of photogrammetric processing of thermal images for civil engineers. Int. Arch. Photogramm. Remote Sens. Spatial Inf. Sci. **XLII–5**, 99–103 (2018). https://doi.org/10.5194/isprs-archives-XLII-5-99-2018.
26. Lagüela, S., Díaz-Vilariño, L., Roca, D., Filgueira, A.: In: Riveiro, B., Solla, M. (eds.) Non-Destructive Techniques for the Evaluation of Structures and Infrastructure, pp. 233–252. CRC Press (2016). https://doi.org/10.1201/b19024.
27. Previtali, M., Barazzetti, L., Redaelli, V., Scaioni, M., Rosina, E.: Rigorous procedure for mapping thermal infrared images on three-dimensional models of building façades. J. Appl. Remote Sens. **7**, 073503 (2013). https://doi.org/10.1117/1.JRS.7.073503
28. Lin, D., Jarzabek-Rychard, M., Tong, X., Maas, H.-G.: Fusion of thermal imagery with point clouds for building façade thermal attribute mapping. ISPRS J. Photogramm. Remote. Sens. **151**, 162–175 (2019). https://doi.org/10.1016/j.isprsjprs.2019.03.010
29. Adamopoulos, E., Volinia, M., Girotto, M., Rinaudo, F.: Three-dimensional thermal mapping from IRT images for rapid architectural heritage NDT. Buildings **10**, 187 (2020). https://doi.org/10.3390/buildings10100187

30. Fernández-Hernandez, J., González-Aguilera, D., Rodríguez-Gonzálvez, P., Mancera Taboada, J.: Image-based modelling from unmanned aerial vehicle (UAV) photogramme-try: an effective, low-cost tool for archaeological applications. Archaeometry **57**(1), 128–145 (2015). https://doi.org/10.1111/arcm.12078
31. Javadnejad, F., Gillins, D.T., Parrish, C.E., Slocum, R.K.: A photogrammetric approach to fusing natural colour and thermal infrared UAS imagery in 3D point cloud generation. Int. J. Remote Sens. **41**(1), 211–237 (2019). https://doi.org/10.1080/01431161.2019.1641241
32. Gonzalez-Aguilera, D., et al.: GRAPHOS – Open-source software for photogrammetric applications. Photogram. Rec. **33**(161), 11–29 (2018). https://doi.org/10.1111/phor.12231
33. Jarząbek-Rychard, M., Lin, D., Maas, H.G.: Supervised detection of façade openings in 3D point clouds with thermal attributes. Remote Sens. **12**(3), 543 (2020). https://doi.org/10.3390/rs12030543
34. Patrucco, G., Cortese, G., Tonolo, F.G., Spanò, A.: Thermal and optical data fusion supporting built heritage analyses. Int. Arch. Photogramm. Remote Sens. Spatial Inf. Sci. **XLIII-B3**, 619–626 (2020). https://doi.org/10.5194/isprs-archives-XLIII-B3-2020-619-2020
35. Wakeford, Z.E., Chmielewska, M., Hole, M.J., Howell, J.A.: Combining thermal imaging with photogrammetry of an active volcano using UAV: an example from Stromboli Italy. Photogram. Rec. **34**(168), 445–466 (2019). https://doi.org/10.1111/phor.12301
36. Sammartano, G., Chiabrando, F., Spanò, A.: Oblique images and direct photogrammetry with a fixed wing platform: first test and results in Hierapolis of Phrygia (TK). Int. Arch. Photogramm. Remote Sens. Spatial Inf. Sci. **XLIII-B2**, 75–82 (2020). https://doi.org/10.5194/isprs-archives-XLIII-B2-2020-75-2020
37. Hill, A.C., Laugier, E.J., Casana, J.: Archaeological remote sensing using multi-temporal, drone-acquired thermal and near infrared (NIR) imagery: a case study at the enfield shaker village new hampshire. Remote Sens. **12**(4), 690 (2020). https://doi.org/10.3390/rs12040690

Crowd-Based Tools for Indirect Condition Assessment and Conservation of Cultural Heritage

Adriana Marra[1](✉) and Giovanni Fabbrocino[1,2]

[1] ITC-CNR, Institute for Construction Technologies, Italian National Research Council,
L'Aquila Branch, 67100 L'Aquila, Italy
{marra,fabbrocino}@itc.cnr.it
[2] Structural and Geotechnical Dynamics Lab StreGa, DiBT Department, University of Molise,
86100 Campobasso, Italy

Abstract. The enhancement of digital technologies, the diffusion of the crowd-sensing paradigm envisage useful applications to cultural heritage and depict novel approaches to the condition assessment and forms of conservation and preventive conservation. A large amount of inhomogeneous data is available to the community and, therefore, effective and reliable tools able to facilitate their processing and management are needed to design proper safeguarding and valorization measures. The present paper discusses a methodology that integrates traditional approaches for the knowledge and condition assessment of cultural heritage with those based on well-known web applications available at a large scale on different devices. In other terms, it investigated the feasibility and the reliability of the crowd-sourcing paradigm applied to the acquisition of data related to the current condition of architectural and valuable assets. The methodology is applied to two relevant but different examples of the International cultural heritage, for which a flexible and scalable database has been populated. Processing of data provides encouraging results both in the area of the indirect survey and preventive conservation.

Keywords: Preventive conservation · Indirect survey · Monitoring

1 Introduction

In recent years, the field of cultural heritage has been strongly renewed by the use of digital technologies, which have changed the way of approaching the processes of knowledge, valorization and fruition of historical heritage due to the digitization of several types of information and the development of complex three-dimensional models [1, 2]. The digitization of information has promoted also new ways for dissemination of results that become available online to a wide community, not always expert. At the same time, this enabled the analysis of cultural heritage through innovative approaches that integrate the traditional ones with those based on the use of novel technologies [3, 4]. The implementation of complex three-dimensional models resulting from the processing of point clouds or images acquired in situ during the survey phases or through

M. Ioannides et al. (Eds.): EuroMed 2020, LNCS 12642, pp. 38–50, 2021.
https://doi.org/10.1007/978-3-030-73043-7_4

specific platforms (crowdsensing platforms) is becoming widespread. Common practice has also become the development of informative systems to disseminate and share of critical information and to guide the design of suitable measures for the prevention and conservation of cultural heritage [5, 6]. These systems effectively support the planning phases of interventions but also bring several advantages in the management of cultural heritage, supporting the managing body decisions about timely with rational and efficient actions deriving from a shared and common knowledge [7].

Based on this awareness and on the approaches traditionally used in cultural heritage, the paper introduces a novel SUrvey and CoNDition AssessmEnt catalogue (SUNDAE catalogue), which is populated by data coming from web mapping and social media platforms, so that their processing and analysis exploit the resources offered by novel technologies and crowdsensing tools to assess the conservation state of cultural heritage and to implement complex informative systems useful for the valorization and the development of proactive conservation plans based on a holistic vision of the artefact.

The indirect condition assessment and survey are applied to two significant and different examples of cultural heritage at International level: the Monastery of Haghpat, North Armenia, and the Church of Santa Maria della Strada, South Italy. Results in terms of the evolution in history and the materials used, as well as the damage observed and the state of preservation, are illustrated and discussed.

2 Crowdsensing Tools for the Preservation of Cultural Heritage

The process of knowledge and preservation of cultural heritage takes several advantages from technological innovation and from different information available on the web. Such tools may play a relevant role in the preliminary phases of the asset's knowledge, as well as those of on-site survey and diagnostics, facilitating the detailed design of survey and testing that must be carried out to achieve extensive knowledge of asset and to plan the useful intervention to safeguard it. The acquisition of information derived from the web and of images accessible online, such as those made available by users on blogs, social networks, open access web mapping tools, if properly collected and analyzed can provide useful information about typological and construction characteristic of artefacts, as well as on the damage observed and conservation state. In this way, the research can be directed to other fields of analyses in order to find further information to complete the knowledge framework already identified. Indeed, the correlation of data acquired through crowdsensing tools with those derived from traditional approaches, such as bibliographic and iconographic research and in situ surveys, allows to understand the fragility of cultural heritage and, as consequence, to accelerate the planning process of conservation interventions, which will be driven from a holistic vision of the artefact.

Therefore, digital technologies and crowdsensing tools involve the whole community in the conservation process, so the same community becomes the main player in the conservation and preservation of the widespread cultural heritage. Such a concept is inherent in crowdsensing systems. These identify those processes aimed at obtaining services, ideas and contents, or at solving problems, taking the advantage of the community support that provides its aid both sharing information through smartphones or other portable devices and interacting directly with data already available on the web or other specific platforms [8, 9].

In the context of cultural heritage, crowdsensing promotes new forms of knowledge and, consequently, new forms of dissemination and communication [10]. Several users already support the selection and the updating of digital contents in libraries, archives or museums, reducing the costs related to these processes [11, 12]. At the same time, the images acquired on specific platforms, websites and open access web mapping tools can be used to create digital models useful to disseminate knowledge and history as well as to understand and assess, also through deep-learning algorithms, the state of conservation and maintenance of cultural heritage [13–16].

It is therefore clear that crowdsensing tools are the basic component of a complex informative system that combines three dimensional or virtual models to databases including bibliographic data, images collected online or on-site, information on historical evolution, materials, construction techniques and conservation state. Such an informative system would make more efficient the process of preservation and management of heritage, significantly reducing the time required to define the strategies to be implemented for the safeguard and enhancement of the site. These would be able to act on the basis of a unique vision of the asset by using the common knowledge shared through this informative system [7].

Starting from these assumptions, the SUrvey and CoNDition AssessmEnt catalogue (Fig. 1) has been implemented.

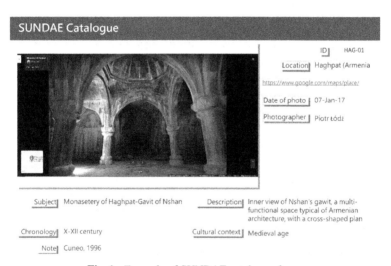

Fig. 1. Example of SUNDAE catalogue form.

The SUNDAE catalogue allows the collection of images acquired through crowdsensing systems and provides a critical assessment of the conservation state of an artefact under analysis. The chronological ordering and the analysis of acquired images enables the assessment and quantification of degradation and/or damage phenomena and to evaluate their evolution over time. In order to implement the form at the core of the SUNDAE catalogue, the F form provided for inventory and cataloguing of photos by the Central Institute for Catalogue and Documentation (the Italian ICCD) has been taken as reference [17]. In particular, 11 fields have been selected in order to record all data useful for the identification of the object to be catalogued according to the information of inventory level identified by F form. Moreover, the crowd-based information can be further processed to define a three-dimensional scaled view of assets. The development of these activities represents the starting point for the implementation of the informative system previously mentioned.

3 Implementation and Results

The development of SUNDAE catalogue allows to implement a novel approach to the survey and assessment of the current state of cultural heritage starting from crowd image-based tools. The approach requires the research of main bibliographic sources and the collection of information from crowdsourcing systems to understand the current condition of cultural heritage and the development of a three-dimensional model that allows to critically assess the actions to be implemented for the conservation, management and valorization of cultural heritage. The results achieved depend on the information collected, highlighting the limits proper of crowdsensing approaches. The quality and quantity of data are indeed related to the relevance, therefore knowledge, in the local, national and international culture of the asset under investigation. Consequently, more or less detailed information can be found, but still suitable for the preliminary phases of the knowledge process. In the following, two different case studies are presented to emphasize the advantages and limits of the SUNDAE catalogue. They refer to listed heritage; however, the adopted approach appears to be appropriate for any existing structure, including the minor ones, and other valuable assets of cultural heritage.

3.1 The Monastery of Haghpat

The monastic complex of Haghpat (Fig. 2) is included since 1996 in the World Heritage List as "the highest flowering of Armenian architecture between the 10th and 13th centuries" [18]. The monastery is located on a plateau in the north of Lori Region in Armenia, near the city of Alaverdi, and is characterized by the presence of several buildings, built at different time over the centuries, which gave to the complex an asymmetrical but volumetrically balanced and harmonious view perfectly integrated with the landscape [19]. The foundation dates back to the second half of the 10th century, by the queen Khosrovanush, and was extended within a polygonal surrounding wall and around the Church of St. Nshan during the 12th–13th centuries, according to the principle of successive aggregation and without a planning scheme (Fig. 2).

During the centuries the monastic complex has suffered several restoration and conservation works, many carried out during the 17th century, with the aim of repairing the damages caused by invasions, earthquakes and degradation phenomena. Between 1939–1940, and then in 1960 and 1980, further restoration works were carried out by the Committee for the Preservation of Monuments of the Armenian SSR [18].

Fig. 2. Monastery of Haghpat: general view and plan. (Photo by: Heretiq - https://en.wikipedia. org/wiki/File:Haghpat-Nshan.jpg; plan by: https://www.armenica.org/cgi-bin/armenica.cgi?698 337748279208=2=ba=4====baz0000 = = =).

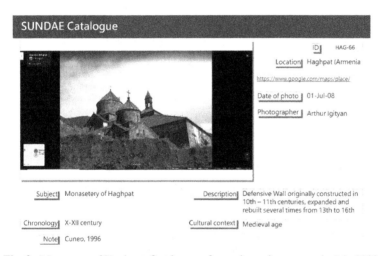

Fig. 3. Monastery of Haghpat: first image of crowdsourcing system in July 2008.

In the first phase of research, about 120 photos representing the several buildings of the complex were collected from Google Maps. In a second phase, the SUNDAE catalogue has been integrated with other images retrieved from social networks (Instagram and 500px). The 183 collected images were taken by 130 different users and cover a time span of about 10 years, from July 2008 to September 2020 (Fig. 3 and Fig. 4).

The comparative analysis of collected photos allows to understand the evolution of degradation phenomena and the safeguard actions implementation to mitigate them. Considering the photos taken in the last 5 years, it is possible to detect a widespread

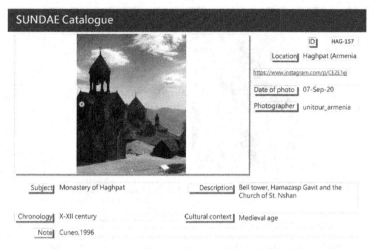

Fig. 4. Monastery of Haghpat: last image of crowdsourcing system in September 2020.

Fig. 5. Degradation phenomena detected in May 2015.

presence of infesting vegetation both on the roofs and on the masonry surfaces, where run-off phenomena, biological patina and efflorescence can be also found (Fig. 5). In the photos taken in the last year, the limited presence of the phenomena mentioned above suggests that recent maintenance interventions have been carried out by the authorities having in charge of the protection (Fig. 6).

An additional experiment has been carried out in order to understand if an indirect survey of the architectural asset can be carried out; to this end, a set of 45 images of the Church of Virgin have been processed by the Agisoft Metashape software. The result of the image processing and of the three-dimensional reconstruction of the church is

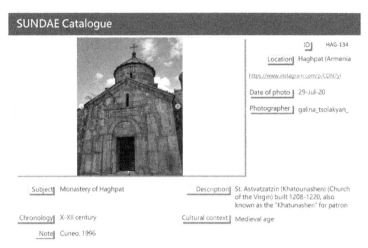

SUNDAE Catalogue

ID	HAG-134
Location	Haghpat (Armenia
	https://www.instagram.com/p/CDN7yf
Date of photo	29-Jul-20
Photographer	galina_tsolakyan_

Subject	Monastery of Haghpat	Description	St. Astvatzatzin (Khatounashen) (Church of the Virgin) built 1208-1220, also known as the "Khatunashen" for patron
Chronology	X-XII century	Cultural context	Medieval age
Note	Cuneo, 1996		

Fig. 6. Monastery of Haghpat: state on conservation in July 2020.

reported in Fig. 7; it is worth noting that the dense point cloud (3.148.834 points) is not fully optimized, but is able to provide a good 3D model (629.766 faces), which can be adopted as the base of the design of further and detailed knowledge and assessment procedures.

Fig. 7. Church of the Virgin: orthomosaic.

3.2 The Church of Santa Maria Della Strada in Matrice (South Italy)

The Benedictine monastery of Santa Maria della Strada (Fig. 8), an extraordinary example of Romanesque architecture, is located on a hill close to the minor municipality of

Matrice, near Campobasso in Molise Region (south Italy). The dating of the foundation is still uncertain but it was consecrated in 1148 [20]. In 1889, it was declared National Monument because it is one of the most significant churches in Molise.

After the 2002 earthquake several structural interventions were carried out to repair damages caused by the event and to recover the stone surfaces, with a high historical and artistic value, seriously deteriorated [21].

Fig. 8. Location of Molise region and of the Church of Santa Maria della Strada.

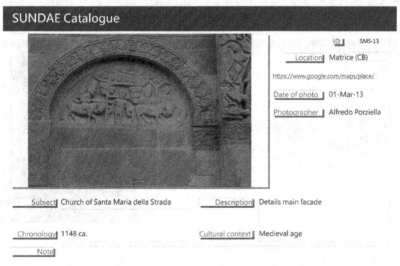

Fig. 9. Church of Santa Maria della Strada: image of crowdsourcing system of a detail of the main facade.

The SUNDAE catalogue has been populated by searching relevant data from Google Maps, Facebook and Flickr; about 147 photos taken by 40 different users have been loaded and checked. The collected images cover a time span of about 10 years, from August 2008 to August 2020 (Fig. 9–Fig. 10).

Particular attention was paid to the bell tower of the Santa Maria della Strada monastery, which stands on the right side of the facade and is detached from the church creating an isolated building of the architectural complex. The comparison of photos depicting the bell tower from 2013 to 2020 shows the evolution of several degradation phenomena but also the interventions carried out in past and recent times.

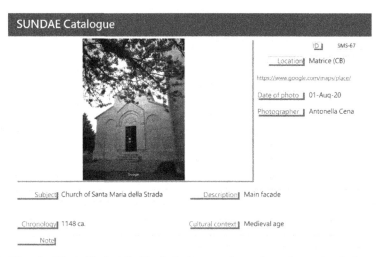

Fig. 10. Church of Santa Maria della Strada: last image of crowdsourcing system in August 2020.

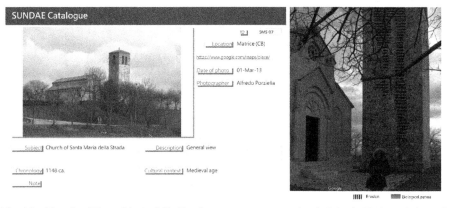

Fig. 11. Church of Santa Maria della Strada: state on conservation in March 2013 (on left) and degradation form (on right).

The photos taken in 2013 show the masonry surfaces of the bell tower covered by the widespread presence of a biological patina and localized phenomena of infesting vegetation and erosion on stone surfaces (Fig. 11). Starting from 2017 the biological patina that affected the structure is completely absent. Instead, run-off phenomena are visible in the upper part of the tower, as well as localized phenomena of erosion of stone surfaces and infesting vegetation (Fig. 12). This circumstance suggests that the periodic preservation interventions have been executed on the asset.

In the upper part of the bell tower, in particular in the area of the belfry, it is possible to find interventions carried out in the past to repair the structure. Indeed, it is visible a change in the masonry texture that suggests the rebuilding of the bell tower after one of the seismic events that affected the region over the centuries (in particular can be recalled the 1465 event that strongly damaged the architectural complex).

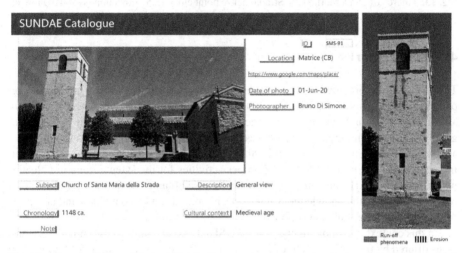

Fig. 12. Church of Santa Maria della Strada: state on conservation in June 2020 (on left) and identification of degradation form (on right).

Finally, the test related to the construction of the 3D model has been carried out; 31 images representative of the complex have been processed in Agisoft Matashape software. Results achieved for the Italian asset are similar to the ones of the Church of the Virgin of the Monastery of Haghpat. The lower number and quality of the base images influence on the results, but they are still good compared with the computational effort and the activities related to its construction.

The photos have a good resolution (about 300 dpi) but some of them have optical distortions that cannot be corrected through their manipulation. The software has provided a partial and not fully optimized model of the complex (Fig. 13).

However, the results obtained for the Monastery of Haghpat and the Church of Santa Maria della Strada confirm that real applicative opportunities exist and that the collection of images from crowdsourcing systems may play a role in the creation of three-dimensional models of cultural heritage for its preservation and valorization.

Fig. 13. Church of Santa Maria della Strada: dense point cloud (3.574.698 points) and 3D model (426.055 faces).

4 Final Remarks

The possibilities provided by new technologies and the diffusion of crowdsensing paradigm have enabled the development of novel solutions for the current condition assessment of cultural heritage. The huge amount of data that can be retrieved, indeed, greatly facilitates the preliminary phases of survey and knowledge, encouraging also a large-scale assessment of cultural heritage. The advantages deriving from the use of innovative systems in the planning of proper activities for the safeguarding are clearer when data collected online are integrated with those obtained with the traditional approach. In this way, the knowledge frameworks identified can be completed and complex informative systems can be developed.

In this context, the implementation of the SUNDAE catalogue highlights the advantages offered by the development of a big database that can be used both for knowledge and for the development of digital models to be used in conservation. The data collected online on the two examples presented confirm the ability of the catalog to track the evolution of degradation phenomena. At the same time, the modeling results put to the attention the need to select and elaborate appropriately the images before their processing. Indeed, although of good quality, several images have optical distortions and problems related to lighting variation (bright sunshine, clouds, shadows, dusk light and other issues) that cannot be neglected and underestimated to achieve optimal results. However, the three-dimensional models obtained highlight the opportunities related to simple and crowd-based tools in preventive conservation.

The encouraging results provided by the crowd-based data set suggest the areas of further investigation and point out the potentialities of an automated implementation of repetitive actions in view of the development of a complex informative system for the safeguard and valorization of cultural heritage.

References

1. Pieraccini, M., Guidi, G., Atzeni, C.: 3D digitizing of cultural heritage. J. Cult. Herit. **2**(1), 63–70 (2001). https://doi.org/10.1016/S1296-2074(01)01108-6

2. Tscheu, F., Buhalis, D.: Augmented reality at cultural heritage sites. In: Inversini, A., Schegg, R. (eds.) Information and Communication Technologies in Tourism 2016, pp. 607–619. Springer, Cham (2016). https://doi.org/10.1007/978-3-319-28231-2_44

3. ICOMOS: ICOMOS Charter – Principles for the Analysis, Conservation and Structural Restoration of Architectural Heritage (2003). https://www.icomos.org/en/resources/charters-and-texts. Accessed 15 July 2020

4. Trizio, I., et al.: Versatil Tools: Digital survey and virtual reality for documentation, analysis and fruition of cultural heritage in seismic areas. Int. Arch. Photogrammetry Remote Sens. Spatial Inf. Sci. **XLII-2/W17**, 377–384 (2019). https://doi.org/10.5194/isprs-archives-XLII-2-W17-377-2019.

5. Meyer, É., Grussenmeyer, P., Perrin, J.-P., Durand, A., Drap, P.: A web information system for the management and the dissemination of Cultural Heritage data. J. Cult. Herit. **8**(4), 396–411 (2007). https://doi.org/10.1016/j.culher.2007.07.003

6. Biagini, C., Capone, P., Donato, V., Facchini, N.: Towards the BIM implementation for historical building restoration sites. Autom. Constr. **71**(1), 74–86 (2016). https://doi.org/10.1016/j.autcon.2016.03.003

7. Marra, A., Sabino, A., Bartolomucci, C., Trizio, I., Mannella, A., Fabbrocino, G.: On a rational and interdisciplinary framework for the safety and conservation of historical centres in Abruzzo region. Int. J. Architectural Heritage, 1637478 (2019). https://doi.org/10.1080/15583058.2019.1637478.

8. Doan, A., Ramakrishnan, R., Halevy, A.Y.: Crowdsourcing systems on the World-Wide Web. Commun. ACM **54**(4), 86–96 (2011). https://doi.org/10.1145/1924421.1924442

9. Faggiani, A., Gregori, E., Lenzini, L., Luconi, V., Vecchio, A.: Smartphone-based crowdsourcing for network monitoring: opportunities, challenges, and a case study. IEEE Commun. Mag. **52**(1), 106–113 (2014). https://doi.org/10.1109/MCOM.2014.6710071

10. Delnevo, G., Melis, A., Mirri, S., Monti, L., Prandini, M.: Discovering the city: crowdsourcing and personalized urban paths across cultural heritage. In: Guidi, B., Ricci, L., Calafate, C., Gaggi, O., Marquez-Barja, J. (eds.) GOODTECHS 2017. LNICSSITE, vol. 233, pp. 132–141. Springer, Cham (2018). https://doi.org/10.1007/978-3-319-76111-4_14

11. Oomen, J., Aroyo, L.: Crowdsourcing in the cultural heritage domain: opportunities and challenges. In: Proceedings of the 5th International Conference on Communities and Technologies, pp. 138–149. AMC, New York (2011). https://doi.org/10.1145/2103354.2103373.

12. Bonacchi, C., Bevan, A., Keinan-Schoonbaert, A., Pett, D., Wexler, J.: Participation in heritage crowdsourcing. Museum Manage. Curatorship **34**(2), 166–182 (2019). https://doi.org/10.1080/09647775.2018.1559080

13. Stathopoulou, E.K., Georgopoulos, A., Panagiotopoulos, G., Kaliampakos, D.: Crowdsourcing lost cultural heritage. ISPRS Ann. Photogrammetry Remote Sens. Spatial Inf. Sci. **II-5/W3**, 295–300 (2015). https://doi.org/10.5194/isprsannals-II-5-W3-295-2015.

14. Ch'ng, E., Cai, S., Zhang, T.E., Leow, F.T.: Crowdsourcing 3D cultural heritage: best practice for mass photogrammetry. J. Cult. Heritage Manage. Sustain. Dev. **9**(1), 24–42 (2019). https://doi.org/10.1108/JCHMSD-03-2018-0018.

15. Wang, N., Zaho, X., Wang, L., Zou, Z.: Novel system for rapid investigation and damage detection in cultural heritage conservation based on deep learning. J. Infrastruct. Syst. **25**(3), 1–16 (2019). https://doi.org/10.1061/(ASCE)IS.1943-555X.0000499.

16. Dhonju, H.K., Xiao, W., Mills, J.P., Sarhosis, V.: Share our cultural heritage (SOCH): Worldwide 3D heritage reconstruction and visualization via web and mobile GIS. ISPRS – Int. J. Geo-Inf. **7**(9), 360, (2018). https://doi.org/10.3390/ijgi7090360.

17. Berardi, E.: Normativa F – Fotografia (v. 4.00). Strutturazione dei dati e norme di compilazione (2015). http://www.iccd.beniculturali.it/getFile.php?id=5403. Accessed 23 Mar 2021

18. ICOMOS: Inscription on the World Heritage List: the Monastery of Haghpat (Armenia) (1996), https://whc.unesco.org/en/decisions/2975. Accessed 11 Apr 2020

19. Cuneo, P.: The Armenian architecture of the 10th to 13th centuries renaissance: regional schools and the case of Haghbat. In: Piccolotto, M., Shaninian, S. (eds.) Armenien: Tagebuch einer Reise in das Land des Ararat, pp. 185–198. Institut für Hochschulverlag, Zurich (1996)

20. Gandolfo, F.: Una abbazia molisana e il suo programma decorativo: Santa Maria della Strada presso Matrice. In: Quintavalle, A.C. (ed.) Le vie del Medioevo: Atti del Convegno internazionale di Studi, Parma, 28 settembre – 1° ottobre 1998, pp. 208–222. Electa, Milano (2000)

21. ICR: The main façade of the Santa Maria della Strada church in Matrice (2020). http://icr.beniculturali.it/pagina.cfm?usz=5&uid=73&rid=36. Accessed 26 Mar 2021

Conservation Process of Porta Tiburtina, Rome: A Tool to Map, Protect, and Requalify the Gate

Jui Ambani$^{(\boxtimes)}$ ⓘ, Maria Paz Abad Gonzalez$^{(\boxtimes)}$ ⓘ, and Rossana Mancini$^{(\boxtimes)}$ ⓘ

Sapienza University of Rome, Piazzale Aldo Moro 5, 00185 Roma RM, Italy
arjui.ambani@gmail.com, pazabadg@gmail.com,
rossana.mancini@uniroma1.it

Abstract. Porta Tiburtina is a historic gate within the Aurelian walls in Rome. It is connected to an ancient Augustan arch that carried three aqueducts. This arch served as an opening to an ancient street, Via Tiburtina, that connected Rome, and Tivoli. This paper describes the methodology used to understand this vast subject of the practice of Heritage Conservation in the context of the regular practice of architecture that has either been largely misunderstood or, at worse, regarded as architecture with an outdated twist. It focuses on a three-stage study process starting from the current state, followed by an elaborate historical data collection that leads to the declaration of the need for an intervention. Phase I talks about the awareness of the current context, both urban and structural, with architectural features that are key to acknowledging the threats and dangers to the monument. The next phase focuses on historical data collection and arrangement that helps understand the value lost on the monument and documents every change and transformation it has been through to make a more informed decision. The final stage is a proposed project plan that tends to be respectful, minimal, and in-context. It demonstrates the value of a methodology organized on an individually tested analysis to explore and confirm different aspects of the historic development of the monument. The main question it tries to answer is, how does an architect decide whether to conserve, preserve, restore, while retaining its material authenticity, and the memory and identity of the monument?

Keywords: Conservation · Historical data collection · Built heritage · Process · Identity · Minimal intervention · Porta Tiburtina · Aurelian Walls

1 Introduction to Porta Tiburtina

The research described here is part of the work undertaken for a master's degree in architecture conservation which explored the process of conservation of a monument in the city of Rome. Porta Tiburtina is a gate within the Aurelian walls that were built through 272AD (Under Emperor Aurelian) to 279AD during the reign of Probus. It encapsulates a preexisting monumental arch composed of travertine stone erected during the time of Augustus in 5BC constructed to permit the flow of water within the three aqueducts (Iulia, Tepula, and Marcia) superimposed over the arch [1–3]. The gate derives its name from the ancient path that passes via the arch, Via Tiburtina that connects

© Springer Nature Switzerland AG 2021
M. Ioannides et al. (Eds.): EuroMed 2020, LNCS 12642, pp. 51–63, 2021.
https://doi.org/10.1007/978-3-030-73043-7_5

Rome and Tivoli. Through the times, the gate changed many names based on either its ornamental or aesthetical features (Porta Taurina) or construction of an important church in the vicinity, basilica San Lorenzo (Porta San Lorenzo).

Rome is an ancient city, based on tangible and intangible cultural and built heritage. This includes the historic city center, the Aurelian walls, as well as the remains of the more ancient Servian walls. City gates currently constitute the extent of world heritage in Rome and yet, some unattended and under-maintained parts, monuments, and gates are constituted within these limits, Porta Tiburtina being one of them (Fig. 1).

Fig. 1. Map showing the extent of world heritage city and the location of Porta Tiburtina (Source: WHC, UNESCO. IT/VA91 bis, 2015)

The map above shows the limits of the Historic Centre in the list of world heritage cities, while showing the monuments added in 1990, follows the line of the Aurelian wall. The property area of the Historic Centre of Rome (in Italy) was stated as 1446,2 ha. The property area of the Properties of the Holy See (in the Holy See) was stated as 38,9 ha. There is no buffer zone [4].

How do we start the process of understanding and protecting cultural heritage in such a complex context? The project is developed to understand in conflicts, its causes (structural or proximal), and repercussions on heritage. It is to divide them in typologies to understand vulnerability to instigate resilience. What can be linked to memories to be bought back and what needs to evolve into a new memory to create its own unique identity? While the project is a gate, in a city wall, it constitutes an original documentation of the past that can be preserved via architecture and conservation (Fig. 2).

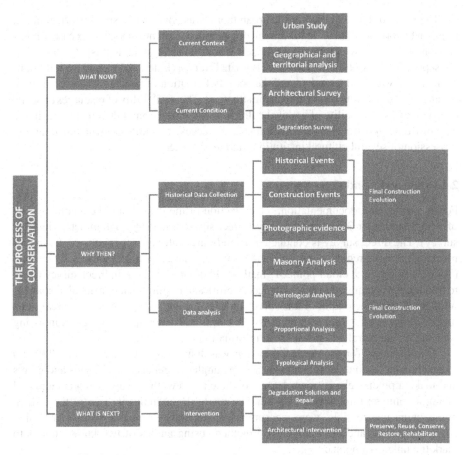

Fig. 2. Diagram of the process of conservation. (Source: Authors)

2 How to Architect? Beginning of a Process

2.1 Current Context - Geographical Analysis

The approach was developed to collect data that would help study the geographical and territorial context of the monument. Starting from a photographic collection of the site, and a recognition of other important landmarks in the area gives a wider perspective of area development and fabric growth. Urban and regional planning bodies and archives of cities are the usable sources to map the transformation of fabric, as for Rome, the PRG 2008 [5] is the most current development plan that underlines land use, zoning, and facilities around the chosen building.

The study of the evolution of the urban fabric was conducted using historical maps, found in historical archives, hand-drawn, or generated over the years. In this case, a comparison of the PRG with maps by Ludovico Muratori (1732), Giambattista Nolli (1748), Giuseppe Vasi (Late 1700's), Giovanni Battista Piranesi (Late 1700's), and Rodolfo Lanciani (1901) was used to understand the period of creation of streets, structures around, expansion of city limits connecting to the site [6, 7]. The availability of resources depends on every city's availability of archival collection and protection of documents. As in the case of Rome, most of this information is easily accessible online, documented, and in possession of several cultural institutions and universities.

2.2   State and Condition - Survey

For the survey and documentation, the collection of the data should be a combination of a total station or 3D scanner survey (direct survey), and photogrammetry (indirect survey). The direct survey is conducted to study the material consistency of the monument and to make reconstructions of the historical phases by a geometrical 2D method (Total Station) and a cloud point 3D method (Photogrammetry). Indirect survey (Photogrammetry) is required in case of inaccessibility and requirement of a detailed analysis of its geometry. The output of this survey enables the architect to measure in real time, precise dimensions of higher or inaccessible points and generate a 3D model comprising accurate architectural and geometrical information.

The 2D survey for geometrical drawings was done using total station Leica TPS700 to generate co-ordinates and points measuring angles to get accurate heights and points and make a precise elevation skeleton. As the city grew, the levels of roads increased giving a complex three levels of ground points to the monument. Two of these three points being inaccessible, were measured independently through a distometer (Using angle correction) and the triangulation method (using angles of two known points to mark the unknown point).

While with this method, the external lines were drawn precisely, the architectural survey demanded a more detailed output to study its features. This was comprehended using an indirect survey method, photogrammetry, a method that can be used with simple instruments such as camera, phone or a professional DSLR (Digital Single-Lens Reflex camera). For more accurate results, the use of a 3D laser scanner is possible, but at a higher expense. This process enables one to capture overlapping clear images to generate million-point clouds using the collineation process. Agisoft Metashape generates this cloud into a dense cloud and then processes the 3D based on location, geometry, and coordinates of these points to create a photographic clone of the monument with its features, degradation, and scaled measurements. This gives you two types of drawings for the next phase: geometrical drawings; technical, simple drawings of the general shape of the monument; and architectural drawings, detailed drawings of the current condition of the monument, and the elements within the site [8] (Figs. 3 and 4).

This process enabled us to identify discrepancies in construction, changes, and transformations of levels over time with the gate to the archeological area, identification of

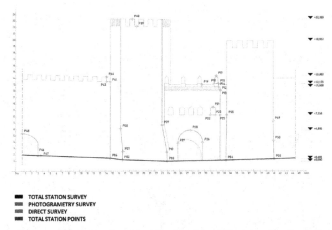

TOTAL STATION SURVEY
PHOTOGRAMETRY SURVEY
DIRECT SURVEY
TOTAL STATION POINTS

Fig. 3. Geometrical survey of the East Façade, showing different methods of the survey using color-coding. (Source: Authors)

Fig. 4. Architectural survey of the East Façade because of a holistic survey. (Source: Authors)

degradation and structural failures, and lack of symmetry and proportions in some areas. It is important to quote that this survey is a representation of the reality of the monument, so if some parts are inaccessible, or not seen, should not be drawn, and represented. After the creation of the complete drawings is time to start the first phase of analysis (Fig. 5).

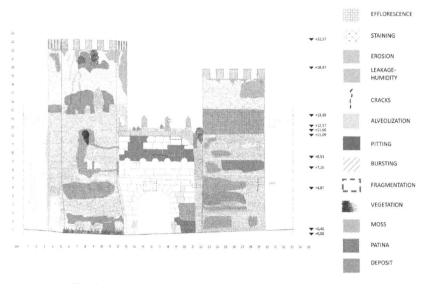

EFFLORESCENCE

STAINING

EROSION

LEAKAGE-
HUMIDITY

CRACKS

ALVEOLIZATION

PITTING

BURSTING

FRAGMENTATION

VEGETATION

MOSS

PATINA

DEPOSIT

Fig. 5. Degradation mapping east façade. (Source: Authors)

The photographic catalog achieved from documentation will be the guide to proceed with the degradation analysis. It is necessary to map and identify every type of failure and disintegration on the monument to detail zones and areas that need intervention and fully understand the being of the monument. An important document guide for understanding damage is the *Illustrated Glossary on Stone Deterioration* published by ICOMOS, where each of these phenomena is explained in detail with images, descriptions, and causes to help identify them on one's project [9]. This analysis is usually based on visual observation, unless a heavy failure is observed, and non-destructive testing are involved for a deeper and accurate analysis.

3   Where Does It All Come from? Summary of Historical Data Collection Process

3.1   Historic Survey

To make historical and cultural decisions:
Once we have the current state of a building, we can proceed to the analysis phase which includes extensive historic data collection. This answers to, what are the main events connected to the monument? How did the construction process start? What are the stages of transformation and layering? At what point did the monument lose its identity? These are some of the questions we need to solve to generate a cohesive timeline.

The historical sources can be divided into two groups: primary sources, the direct witnesses of an event; and secondary sources, which is the work based on the primary sources. On the other hand, another way of classifying the sources is:

- Verbal sources: these sources can be written or oral, and are all the chronicles, biographies, annals, epigraphs, coins, etc.
- Non-verbal sources: this category includes all the monuments, landscapes, iconography, and everyday items.

The best way to research history in Rome is to explore the archives, libraries, and databases. For the Antique monuments, there are different Databases. One of them is called Census.de [10], which documents the main events from each renaissance monument with multiple written references. For the Aurelian Walls, in general, and on Porta Tiburtina, in particular, important information can be taken from archaeological and architectural studies on the monument [11–15] (Fig. 6).

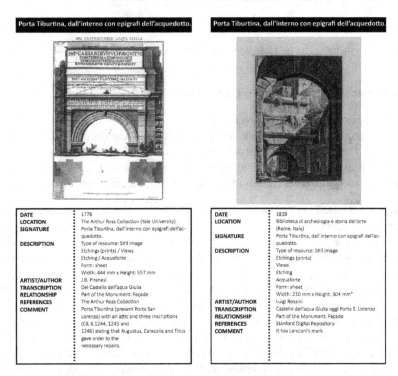

Fig. 6. Examples of document data sheets. (Source: Authors)

One of the important tools used to organize the information is by generating datasheets [16]. This format organizes images, photographs, and drawings, according to their date of creation. Through this method, we compare the physical changes, or the existing ornaments interpreted by the artist in the period of creation, we can also understand the social interaction of the community with the monument in that period. Datasheets can be divided based on evidence, documents, events, and iconography. Each of these sheets evaluates and reference the events to reach a final timeline that helps understand the monument (Fig. 7).

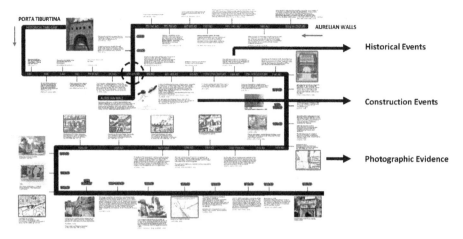

Fig. 7. Final timeline. (Source: Authors)

3.2 Reconstruct Its Beginning to Understand What Leads to Today

To make structural and technical decisions:

For this project, before we made a structural or technical decision, we divided the analysis into four main parts. The following type of analysis evaluates different structural components into materials, studying its age and process of degradation as well as determines a proportional precision of the monument concerning the current units.

Masonry Analysis. For this analysis, we identified all the types of masonry presented in the monument and we created individual tables, where, with the appropriate bibliography, we recognized the main characteristics of them. This process leads to further analysis of mortar and stone for dating and shows the layering on a monument; supports the process of differencing the original materials and the repairs performed through the years. This process helped us understand the different periods of construction according to the materials and construction techniques. Masonry analysis is mainly important in ancient monuments with layers of intervention and transformation, constructed in bricks or stones. This analysis was carried out using a tabular format that serves as a data sheet documenting information on the typology, stratigraphy, origin, and period of that masonry. Porta Tiburtina identified with 7 types of masonry, added along with its transformation and repair. This ranged from original remains from 272AD to the most recent intervention in the early 1900s. This process further clears the need for material testing for original masonry to study its degradation and identify solutions to major decay based on their material specification, mortar granulometry. In the future, this way of documentation can help in sample testing and dating. To identify the dating of certain masonry, some important sources are brick stamps and emblems. By the early 2nd century CE, brick stamps included the name of the consuls for the year of production, thereby making it easier for archaeologists to date a specific construction [17]. This analysis was carried out with reference-based on archival sources, iconography, and historic evidence found before, as well as further analysis of typologically similar monuments (Fig. 8).

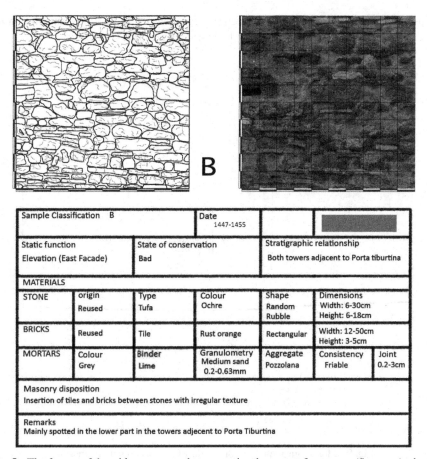

Fig. 8. The format of the table was created to recognize the types of masonry. (Source: Authors)

Proportional Analysis. This analysis describes the relationship between the structural and ornamental elements in the monument, also to see if there is symmetry in their geometric shape. It deals with the placement of openings with the ratio to build walls and structural elements. This analysis helps piece back broken elements that might have been squandered and understand the ratio and proportions of construction.

Metrological Analysis. An important analysis while studying an ancient monument, metrological analysis proves to be one of the most important steps to reconstruct the history of a monument. Due to its original time of construction, the units used to measure and build, are different and varied to the ones we use today. Italy observed a wave of many units such as the Roman foot (29.48 cm), used by the Romans, the Lombard foot (28.75 cm), used before the Italian conquest, up to 1861, the Carolingian foot (34 cm) found from the 8th to 9th century, Byzantine foot, etc. [18, 19] This analysis is conducted by a trial and error process where each of these measurements suspected to be used in the period of construction, is perceived as a proportional circle of the current unit (m) and superimposed over the geometrical drawing for an accurate conclusion. This process helps understand the process of construction, discrepancies to find the best solution in case of reconstruction to be factually and historically accurate (Fig. 9).

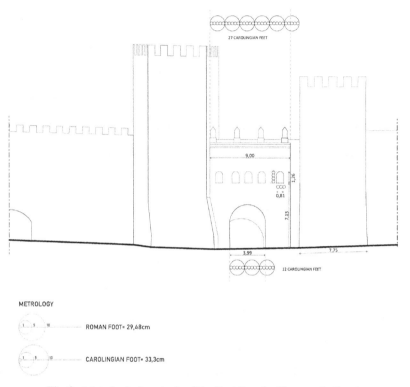

Fig. 9. Metrological analysis of the East Façade. (Source: Authors)

Typological Analysis. It is the study of similar structures and with uses meant to serve a similar purpose. This study works like a case study to compare aesthetical, structural, and architectural elements. In terms of conservation, this process also helped understand gates built in Roman times within city walls across Europe [20]. A few of these comparisons include Le Mans walls, France, Segusium (Susa), Torino, etc. Gates for comparison were chosen based on their physical characteristics such as the shape of the gate, presence of courtyard (controporte), presence of defense chambers, and merlons. The study produced results based on dimensional quality, material difference, and current condition/use. This helped conclude the analysis phase by filling gaps of missing information within the monument. Porta Tiburtina was best compared to other gates built in the Aurelian walls, Porta Flaminia, Porta Salaria (demolished in 1921), Porta Asinaria, Porta Ostiense, all built during the 3rd century (Fig. 10).

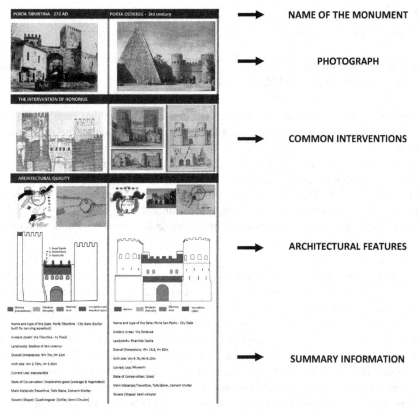

Fig. 10. Example of a typological analysis. (Source: Authors)

4 What Do We Do Now? How Do We Reach an Intervention?

4.1 The Idea of Opening the Monument to the People

Ancient monuments ought to have a minimal intervention. By this stage, an architect has enough data analysis, sources, and evidence to make a well-informed decision of the type of intervention required by the monument. The main intervention is repairs and cleaning processes based on degradation mapping achieved through the initial survey. A basic intervention was developed to re-open Porta Tiburtina to the public, to use the gate as a passage. The concept is based primarily on the idea of highlighting the archaeological area by creating a platform, going over the archaeological site, and crossing the gate. Decisions made for chemicals and mechanical processes for cleaning and repairs were based on material analysis and the most suitable and least harmful materials viable for the same. Degradation solutions were planned in stages of pre-consolidation, protecting the monument, basic cleaning, and then coating or structural repairs.

Goal. Accessibility

• To reconnect the traces of the ancient road, Via Tiburtina

- To make use to the gate as a transition as well as a cultural point
- To leave the current heritage and archeological site undisturbed.

Principles. Based on international heritage charters for good practice of conservation such as the Venice charter and NARA charter [21–23].

- Minimal construction: The intervention is devised in a way that requires minimal construction leading to low disruption to the site and maintaining the respect of its existence.
- Reversibility: The intervention material is easily reversible as well as can be dismantled without causing damage.
- Minimal intrusion: This intervention will not intrude with the current function but enhance its use and capability to a respectable cultural point of view.
- Contextual conservation: The choice of intervention fits the context of the monument and neighborhood.

Conservation is a movement-activated by the realization that the natural and cultural resources of this planet are limited and are being eroded at an alarming rate. Architecture is an irreplaceable cultural resource. For heritage, Reuse is not an alternative, is a tool that we use to prevent new damages due to the abandonment or disintegration. The architectural conservation aims to prolong the life of buildings and the built environment of historic cities so that future generations can enjoy them profitably [24]. This follows the premise that the future of the past is as, if not more, important than the past itself. As Giovanni Carbonara states, "The project is, in fact, the creative synthesis of the various needs, where what is done to remove barriers takes becomes a normal providence destined to ensure, to all, the best use of the heritage" [25].

References

1. Ashby, T.: The Aqueducts of Ancient Rome. The Clarendon Press, Oxford (1935)
2. Volpe, R.: Mura e Acquedotti: coincidenze e persistenze. In: Edizioni Roma. TRE-Press, pp. 103–113, Rome, Italy (2017)
3. Hodgkin, T.: The Walls, Gates, and Aqueducts of Rome. John Murray, London (1899)
4. World Heritage Convention, UNESCO. https://whc.unesco.org/en/list/91/documents/.
5. Roma Capitale Urbanistica, Piano Regolatore Generale 2008 (2008). https://www.urbanistica.comune.roma.it/prg.html
6. Muratori, S., et al.: Studi per un'operante storia di Roma, C.N.R., Roma (1963)
7. Zampilli, M.: Roma. Fasi formative tessuti e tipi edilizi della città storica. https://www.google.com/search?q=Michele+Zampilli%2C+%E2%80%9CRoma%2C+Fasi+Formative+Tessuti+e+Tipi+Edilizi+della+Citta%2C%E2%80%9D&oq=Michele+Zampilli%2C+%E2%80%9CRoma%2C+Fasi+Formative+Tessuti+e+Tipi+Edilizi+della+Citta%2C%E2%80%9D&aqs=chrome..69i57.484j0j8&sourceid=chrome&ie=UTF-8
8. Canciani, M., Conigliaro, E., Del Grasso, M., Papalini, P.,Saccone, M. 3D Survey and Augmented Reality for Cultural Heritage. The Case Study of Aurelian Wall at Sastra Praetoria in Rome. International Society of Photogrammetry and Remote Sensing (2016). https://www.int-arch-photogramm-remote-sens-spatial-inf-sci.net/XLI-B5/931/2016/

9. ICOMOS.: Illustrated glossary on stone deterioration patterns. In: Monuments and Sites XV. Ateliers 30 Impression, Champigny/Marne, France (2008)
10. Census of Antique Works of Art and Architecture Known in the Renaissance, developed by Humboldt-Universität zu Berlin Institut für Kunst- und Bildgeschichte / Census. https://www.census.de/
11. Richmond, I.A.: The City Walls of Imperial Rome. An account of its Architectural Development from Aurelian to Narses. The Clarendon Press, Oxford (1930)
12. Cozza, L.: Osservazioni sulle mura aureliane a Roma. Analecta Romana Instituti Danici **16**, 25–138 (1987)
13. Cozza, L.: Mura di Roma dalla Porta Nomentana alla Tiburina. Analecta Romana Instituti Danici **25**, 7–113 (1998)
14. Mancini, R.: Le mura aureliane di Roma. Atlante di un palinsesto murario. Edizioni Quasar, Rome (2001)
15. Dey, H.W.: The Aurelian Wall and the Refashioning of Imperial Rome AD 271–855. Cambridge University Press, Cambridge (2011)
16. Lanciani, R.: Stralcio della zona di Porta Tiburtina 1893–94. FORMA URBIS ROMAE, Rome (1893)
17. Pfeiffer, G.J., Van Buren, A., Armstrong, H.: Stamps on Bricks and Tiles from the Aurelian Wall at Rome. Supplementary Papers of the American School of Classical Studies in Rome, pp. 1–86 (1905)
18. Martini, A.: Manuale di metrologia, ossia misure, pesi e monete in uso attualmente e anticamente presso tutti i popoli. Loesher, Torino (1883)
19. Salvatori, M.: Manuale di Metrologia per architetti studiosi di storia dell'architettura ed archeologi. Liguori, Napoli (2006)
20. Intagliata, E., Barker, S.J., Courault, C. (eds.): City Walls in Late Antiquity: An Empire-wide Perspective. Oxbow Books, Oxford (2020)
21. Jokilehto, J.: Preservation theory unfolding. Future Anterior J. Hist. Preserv. Hist. Theory Criticism **3**(1), 1–9 (2006)
22. The Nara Document on Authenticity (1994). https://www.international.icomos.org/charters/nara-e.pdf
23. The 2nd International Congress of Architects and Technicians of Historic Monuments, Venice, 1964. ICOMOS INTERNATIONAL (1964). https://www.international.icomos.org/charters/venice_e.pdf
24. Malmberg, S., Bjur, H.: Movement and Urban Development at Two city Gates in Rome: The Porta Esquilina and Porta Tiburtina. En Laurence, R., Newsome, D., Rome, Ostia, Pompeii: Movement and Space, pp. 361–385. Oxford University Press, Oxford (2011)
25. Carbonara, G. Restauro Architettonico: principi e metodo. In: Mancosu Editore. Rome, Italy (2013)

Evaluation of Soil Loss by Water in Archaeological Landscapes by Using the (R)USLE Model and GIS. The Case Study of Paphos District, Cyprus

Nikoletta Papageorgiou[1,2](✉) and Diofantos G. Hadjimitsis[1,2](✉)

[1] Department of Civil Engineering and Geomatics, Faculty of Engineering and Technology, Cyprus University of Technology, Saripolou 2-8, 3036 Limassol, Cyprus
Nt.papageorgiou@edu.cut.ac.cy, d.hadjimitsis@cut.ac.cy
[2] Eratosthenes Centre of Excellence, Saripolou 2–8, 3036 Limassol, Cyprus

Abstract. Soil erosion is one of the most significant environmental issues, as it seriously threatens archaeological sites and monuments. In recent years, several models have been used in the in the relevant scientific literature in order to estimate soil erosion rates. The models range from empirical to physical or process-based and differ significantly in complexity, accuracy, inputs and outputs. Among these, the Revised Universal Soil Loss Equation (RUSLE) has become the most commonly used in different environmental conditions and on varying scales.

The present study calculates average annual soil erosion in terms of spatial and temporal patterns based on the Revised Universal Soil Loss Equation (RUSLE) model, combined with Geographic Information Systems (GIS) in the area of Paphos District. This study also implemented satellite remote sensing images and available data sources such as meteorological data, a digital elevation model (DEM), land use and soils maps for soil erosion analysis. The whole methodology is based on the estimation of soil loss per unit area and takes into account specific parameters such as rainfall factor, steepness and slope length factor, cover management, practice factor as well as soil erosion factor. The results indicate that the mean annual soil erosion was estimated from 0 to 235.532 t/ha.

Keywords: Soil erosion · RUSLE · Archaeological sites · Remote sensing

1 Introduction

Soil erosion is a natural phenomenon of soil loss which includes the detachment, transport and deposition of soil particles mainly caused by water runoff and wind [1]. Currently, soil erosion is defined as one of the most severe and widespread forms of destruction and degradation of archaeological sites, rural and urban landscapes and monuments amplify the natural deterioration and reduce the ability of the soil to preserve Cultural Heritage. The process can be accelerated and intensified by climate change and some human activities (e.g. intensive agricultural and pastoral activities, inefficient or inadequate irrigation

© Springer Nature Switzerland AG 2021
M. Ioannides et al. (Eds.): EuroMed 2020, LNCS 12642, pp. 64–77, 2021.
https://doi.org/10.1007/978-3-030-73043-7_6

systems), which are affecting structure stability and producing significant negative consequences on the preservation of the archaeological artefacts. Although, the effects of soil erosion have been recorded in the literature, few researchers have carried out studies on the monitoring and assessment of soil erosion on archaeological sites [2]. To obtain an overview of all existing studies, Scopus engine (https://www.scopus.com/) was used, searching for published articles within the period 1998 to 2020. A bibliometric analysis based on the collected literature data was carried out to demonstrate the spatiotemporal patterns of modelling approaches for evaluation soil loss on archaeological sites, over the last years. All the collected publication data were consolidated by year to indicate the increase year - on- year (Fig. 1).

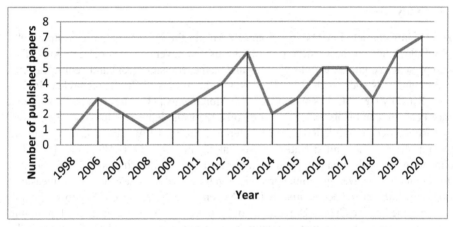

Fig. 1. Literature count of articles from 1998 to 2020, introducing soil erosion and Cultural Heritage, extracted from the Scopus database (last access 12 September 2020)

A significant number of models have been developed over the past decades in order to assess the soil erosion at various temporal and spatial scales which are categorized into empirical models, conceptual models and physically based models [3]. Among these, the universal soil loss equation (USLE) and its revised version—the revised universal soil loss equation (RUSLE) developed by [4] have been widely used in order to estimate the soil erosion risk because of its high compatibility with Geographic Information Systems (GIS). This model can predict erosion rates within the spatial limits of a watershed basin and to illustrate the spatial heterogeneity of soil erosion. The RUSLE retains the basic principle of the USLE model and introduced improvements in soil erodibility, a method for measuring cover and management factors, improvements in how topographical impact is integrated into the model, and upgraded soil conservation practices values [5]. The RUSLE model consists of several sub-factors that explain the key elements of soil erosion processes, including rainfall erosivity, soil erodibility, topographic factors, and cover and practices management [6, 7]. The detailed analysis of the RUSLE factors is presented by [8] and [9]. In addition, several innovative Earth observation (EO) approaches (e.g. satellite remote sensing, field spectroscopy, and aerial photos) have been investigated for their potential and impact on monitoring soil properties and the corresponding soil erosion phenomena [10]. Remote sensing offers a unique opportunity to map, monitor, quantify, and analyze, in detail, the processes that contribute to soil loss as a result of water erosion.

The overall objective of the study is to present a methodology to assess and quantify soil erosion risk by using the Revised Universal Soil Loss Equation (RUSLE) model, in combination with GIS and Remote Sensing techniques in the area of Paphos District. The area has been previously examined in [11], that was taken as the main literature reference for the tests and comparison on the results.

2   Materials and Methods

2.1   Study Area

The Paphos district (Lat: 34.76°, Long: 32.41°, in the World Geodetic System 1984 (WGS-84)), lies on the western part of Cyprus and covers an area of 1393 km^2. This area presents a complex geomorphology and has several significant archaeological sites and monuments such as the Nea Paphos and the Tombs of the Kings archaeological sites, listed by UNESCO as World Heritage Monuments [11]. The soils on Paphos area vary between cambisols, calcisols, vertisoils, regosols, leptosols, luvisols, gambisols, gypsisols based on the WRB (World Reference Base) of FAO (Food and Agriculture Organization of the United Nations) soil classification system (FAO, 1989) [12]. The climate in the study area is typical Mediterranean with mild winters and long, hot and dry summers. The average annual precipitation for the wider area of Paphos is measured at around 430 mm and occurs mainly from November to March, according to the rainfall data provided by the Cyprus Department of Meteorology. The average annual minimum and average yearly maximum temperature remain between 12 °C and 25 °C, respectively. Figure 2 shows the Digital Elevation Model (DEM) of the study area.

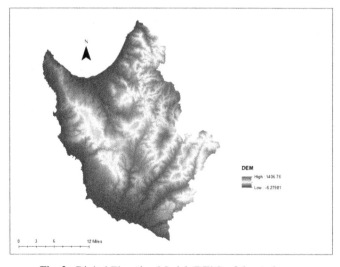

Fig. 2. Digital Elevation Model (DEM) of the study area

2.2 Data

In this research different geospatial datasets were collected, processed and analyzed in a raster format according to the five factors of the RUSLE model for calculating the soil loss (Table 1). The datasets included rainfall, remote sensing images, soil, and land use/cover data. Landsat TM remote sensing images captured on 2002, 2010, 2014 and 2015 were downloaded from the United States Geological Survey's (USGS) Earth Explorer website (https://earthexplorer.usgs.gov), with a spatial resolution of 30m. Also, a digital elevation model (DEM) with a spatial resolution of 30 m was obtained from Advanced Spaceborne Thermal Emission and Reflection Radiometer (ASTER) Global Digital Elevation Model (GDEM) website. The Soil data was derived from the "European Soil Database (ESDB) v2.0" provided by the European Soil Data Centre (ESDAC) of Joint Research Centre (JRC). A time-series of annual rainfall data covering a period from 1999 to 2019 acquired from NASA GPM (Global Precipitation Measurement).

Table 1. The datasets used for the RUSLE model

RUSLE factor	Datasets	Data source
R	Annual rainfall data from 1999 to 2019	Website for NASA Precipitation Measurement Missions
K	Soil type data	Food and Agriculture Organization of the United Nations (https://www.fao.org/home/en/) Digital Soil Map of the World (2008) (1:5,000,000 scale)
LS	ASTER global digital elevation model (GDEM) version 2 (resolution 30 m × 30 m)	United States Geological Survey (USGS) website (https://earthexplorer.usgs.gov)
C	Landsat 7 TM dated 2002, 2010, 2014 and 2015 of 30 m × 30 m spatial resolution Land use/land cover (LULC) map	United States Geological Survey (USGS) website (https://earthexplorer.usgs.gov)
P	Landsat 7 TM dated 2002, 2010, 2014 and 2015 of 30 m × 30 m spatial resolution	United States Geological Survey (USGS) website (https://earthexplorer.usgs.gov)

3 Methodology

3.1 RUSLE Model

This study is concentrated on the integration and application of the Revised Universal Soil Loss Equation (RUSLE) model and Remote Sensing and GIS techniques in order both to estimate long–term average annual soil loss and to map erosion hazard. The Universal soil loss equation (USLE) and its revised version (Revised Universal Soil

Loss Equation (RUSLE)) is an empirical soil erosion model and calculates the mean annual soil loss rates by sheet and rill erosion [13]. The RUSLE model is based on the following equation [4]:

$$A = R \times K \times LS \times C \times P \tag{1}$$

where A is the average annual erosion rate (t ha^{-1}), R is the rainfall erosivity (MJ cm ha^{-1} h^{-1}), K is the soil erodibility (t ha h MJ^{-1} ha^{-1} cm^{-1}), L is the slope length (dimensionless), S is the slope steepness (dimensionless), C is the vegetation cover and management factor (dimensionless) and P is the support practice factor (dimensionless).

All the above independent RUSLE factors were produced and multiplied using the ArcGIS 10.3 software raster calculator to estimate the annual soil loss of the cultural heritage sites in the Paphos area. All geographical data were projected into the Cyprus Geodetic Reference System (datum: CGRS93). Earth Resources Data Analysis System (ERDAS) Imagine 9.3 was implemented to process (e.g. geometric, radiometric, and atmospheric pre-processing corrections) the Landsat 7 TM satellite Images derived from United States Geological Survey (USGS) website (https://earthexplorer.usgs.gov). The methodology that was implemented in the study is represented in Fig. 3 as a flowchart.

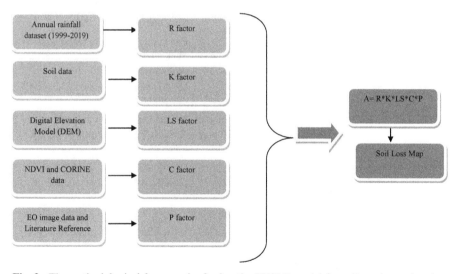

Fig. 3. The methodological framework of using the RUSLE model for soil erosion estimation

3.1.1 Rainfall-Runoff Erosivity Factor (R)

The Rainfall Erosivity Factor (R) represents the potential erosivity of soil erosion caused by precipitation, and it depends on the intensity, duration, amount of rainfall and energy and size of rain drops (Xue et al. 2018). According to [13] the R factor is described as the average annual value of the product storm kinetic energy (E) of a storm and its maximum intensity during 30 min (I_{30}):

$$R = \sum_{n=1}^{N}(EI_{30})n/\gamma \qquad (2)$$

Nevertheless, in Cyprus these data are not available for this estimation. Thus, in this study, the R-factor calculation is based on the mean annual rainfall data of 20 years (1999–2019) and was carried out using the following simple linear Eq. 3 as suggested by [14]:

$$R = 38.5 + 0.35P, \qquad (3)$$

where, R = Rainfall Erosivity Factor, P = Mean Annual Rainfall in mm.

Then, the ordinary kriging method was applied in order to interpolate the average annual rainfall data for each grid cell.

3.1.2 Soil Erodibility (K-Factor)

The soil erodibility (K-factor) is an empirical measure and it can be expressed as the impact of soil physical and chemical characteristics on soil erosion [15]. The main soil properties affecting K factor are soil texture, organic matter, structure, and permeability of the soil profile. In the present research, erodibility (K) factor values were obtained from the Food and Agriculture Organization of the United Nations (FAO) soil data and computed by applying the following Eq. (4) provided by [16]:

$$K = Fcsand * Fsi - cl * Forgc * Fhisand * 0.1317, \qquad (4)$$

Where,

$$Fcsand = [0.2 + 0.3\exp\left(-0.0256\,SAN\left(1 - \frac{SIL}{100}\right)\right)] \qquad (5)$$

$$Fsi\text{-}cl = \left[\frac{SIL}{CLA + SIL}\right]0.3, \qquad (6)$$

$$Forgc = \left[1.0 - \frac{0.25C}{C + \exp(3.72 - 2.95C)}\right], \qquad (7)$$

$$Fhisand = \left[1.0 - \frac{0.70SN1}{SN1 + \exp(-5.51 + 22.9SN1)}\right] \qquad (8)$$

where, *SAN, SIL* and *CLA* are % sand, silt and clay, respectively; *C* is the organic carbon content and *SN1* is sand content subtracted from 1 and divided by 100.

Fcsand = it gives a low soil erodibility factor for soil with coarse sand and a high value for soil with little sand content.

Fsi-cl = it gives a low soil erodibility factor with high clay to silt ration.

Forgc = it is the factor that reduces soil erodibility for soil with high organic content.

Fhisand = it is the factor that reduces soil erodibility for soil with extremely high sand content.

3.1.3 Topographic Factor (LS)

The topographic factor was determined from two sub-factors: a slope-length factor (L) and a slope gradient factor (S). The LS factor expresses the ratio of soil erosion for the given conditions to the soil erosion from an experimental plot of slope length of 22.13 m and slope steepness 9%. The L factor represents "the distance from the point of origin of overland flow to the point where either the slope gradient decreases enough that deposition begins or the runoff water enters a well-defined channel". The soil loss rises as the slope length increases. The S factor defined by [13] as "soil loss increases much more rapidly than runoff as slopes steepen".

In the current study, the LS factor was calculated from a Digital Elevation Model (DEM) with 30 by 30-m resolution of the study site. This factor was determined from the flow accumulation and slope steepness in the ArcGIS environment. After that, the LS factor is calculated as empirical Eq. (9) developed by [17, 18]:

$$LS = (\lambda/22.13)^m * (65.4 \sin^2\beta) + 4.56 \sin^2\beta + 0.0654) \tag{9}$$

Where λ is the horizontal projection of slope length [m], t is the constant dependent on the value of the slope and P is the slope angle [deg].

3.1.4 Cover Management Factor (C)

The Cover management factor (C) is described as "the ratio of soil loss from the land under specified conditions to the corresponding loss from clean-tilled, continuous fallow" [9]. This factor calculates the effects of vegetation cover on the soil erosion, ranging between 0 and 1 where higher values show no cover effects, whereas lower values indicate a strong cover effect. For determination of C factor, LANDSAT TM satellite image at 30m resolution produced by United States Geological Survey (USGS) website was used. The NDVI is defined by Rouse [19] as the ratio between the difference and the sum, respectively, between the Near Infra-Red spectral reflectance (NIR) and the Red one (R):

$$NDVI = (NIR - R)/(NIR + R) \tag{10}$$

In this study, Normalized Difference Vegetation Index (*NDVI*), was applied to calculate *C* factor values according to the following equation proposed by [21]:

$$C = \exp\left[-a\left(\frac{NDVI}{\beta - NDVI}\right)\right] \tag{11}$$

Where, α and β are constants with value 2 and 1, respectively.

In addition, CORINE Land Use / Land Cover map done in 2000 of the study area were used to access the C factor (Fig. 4). In ArcGIS the features with the same land-use classes were combined, and for each land-use type, C values were assigned according to the literature [22]. Table 2 presents the C values used for the study.

Table 2. C values were assigned based to land cover map

Land use class	Land cover code	C factor
Continuous urban fabric	111	0.10
Discontinuous urban fabric	112	0.10
Industrial or commercial units	121	0.10
Road and rail networks and associated land	122	0.10
Airports	124	0.10
Mineral extraction sites	131	0.15
Dump sites	132	0.20
Construction sites	133	0.20
Sport and leisure facilities	142	0.20
Non-irrigated arable land	211	0.10
Permanently irrigated land	212	0.23
Vineyards	221	0.35
Fruit trees and berry plantations	222	0.10
Olives	223	0.25
Pastures	231	0.12
Annual crops associated with permanent crops	241	0.23
Complex cultivation	242	0.16
Agriculture with natural vegetation	243	0.13
Broad-leaved forest	311	0.15
Coniferous forest	312	0.01
Natural Grasslands	321	0.06
Sclerophyllous vegetation	323	0.06
Transitional woodland & Shrub	324	0.03
Beaches, dunes, sands	331	0.50
Bare rocks	332	0.05
Sparsely vegetated areas	333	0.37
Water bodies	512	0.30
Sea and ocean	523	0.50

3.1.5 Conservation Support Practice (P)

The P factor indicates "the ratio of soil loss with a specific support practice to the corresponding loss" [4, 13]. The value of P factor varies between 0 and 1 (i.e., 0 shows good conservation practice and 1 indicates poor conservation practice). In this study, P was set equal to 1 because there is no erosion-control works in the basin for preventing soil erosion.

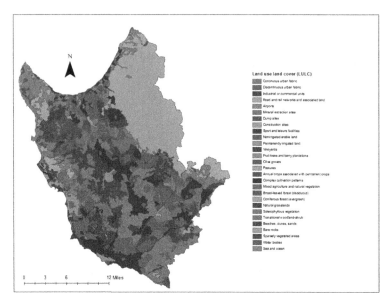

Fig. 4. CORINE Land Use / Land Cover map (European Environment Agency-EEA)

4   Results and Discussion

The erosivity factor (R) estimated by Eq. (3) ranges from 38.962 to 162.501 MJ mm ha^{-1} h^{-1} year^{-1} with the highest value occurred in the northeast part of the region and the lowest in the southwest region (Fig. 5). High rainfall values indicate higher erosivity in the northern and western areas of the Paphos district. The southwestern part is less vulnerable to erosion due to low values of rainfall.

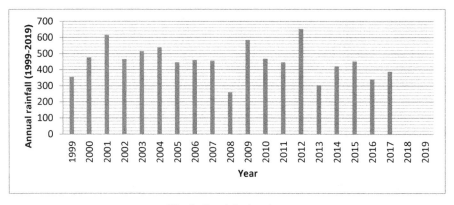

Fig. 5. Precipitation data

The soil erodibility (K) factor values were derived according to different eight soil types (cambisols, calcisols, vertisoils, regosols, leptosols, luvisols, gambisols, gypsisols)

(Table 3). The predicted K values varied from 1.18 to 9.7 T ha MJ^{-1} mm^{-1} with the highest value occurred in the north and south part and the lowest in the western part of the area (Fig. 6). The areas located in the southern and northern parts of the area were more susceptible to erosion because of their higher values of K factor, while the western parts had the lowest K values.

Table 3. Soil type at the case study area (FAO, 2008)

Soil type	K Factor
Regosols	6.470331
Leptosols	3.233758
Vertisols	2.852761
Cambisols	3.107987
Luvisols	1.342144
Gambisols	1.186563
Calcisols	1.317713
Gypsisols	1.860069

The map of LS factor demonstrates the impact of slope and length on soil erosion (Fig. 7) The topographic factor ranges from 0 in the lower part of the study area to 39.8264 in the steepest slope upper part of the area. Most of the area contains low and moderate slope or low to moderate values of the LS factor, thus indicate that the area is prone to low to moderate soil loss.

The C factor was implemented using the NDVI analysis from the Landsat satellite images and the computation in Eq. 11. The C factor varied from 0.367884 to 0.90086 (Fig. 8). The higher C factor values represent more susceptibility to soil erosion. The C factor values can range between near zero for a very well-protected soil due to existence non-irrigated arable land and areas of natural vegetation.

The Support Practice Factor (P) value varied from 0.55 to 1 where higher value shows there is no any support practice (Fig. 9). Hence, most areas of the archaeological site of Paphos are covered by vegetation, meaning the soil is protected from soil erosion. The areas with relatively high and low P values were similar to those for the C values.

To obtain the annual mean of soil loss in the study area due to soil erosion, all five factors (R, K, LS, C, P) have been multiplied within a GIS environment. According to the results the spatial distribution of soil erosion represented that the areas with high soil erosion were mainly scattered in the north-central part of the area where steep slopes occur. The total soil erosion of the archaeological site estimated from 0 to 235.532 t ha^{-1} yr^{-1}. Figure 10 shows the spatial distribution of soil erosion in the area of Paphos District.

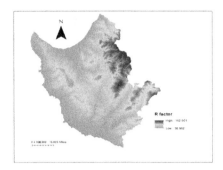

Fig. 6. R factor

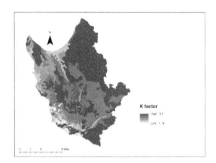

Fig. 7. K factor

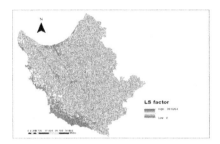

Fig. 8. LS factor

Fig. 9. C factor

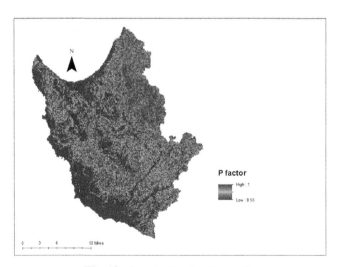

Fig. 10. Support Practice Factor (P)

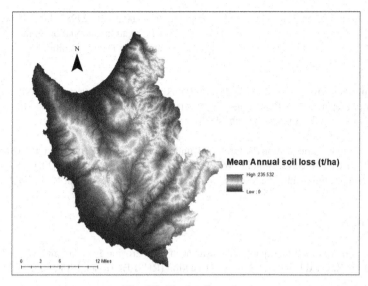

Fig. 11. Total soil erosion

5   Conclusions

The present study, describes processing chain for each of the five factors of the RUSLE equation and it proposes a chain for combination of all the factors for quantifying and map the spatial distribution of potential soil erosion areas in the Paphos district. Soil erosion risk in the current study was calculated by using the geospatial data downloaded from various sources based on the five factors that effects the soil erosion by water include rainfall erosivity, soil erodibility, topography, cover and support practices. Results showed that the study area generally suffered from a moderate erosion intensity with the annual average soil loss is from 0 to 235.532 t ha^{-1} yr^{-1}. The rate of soil erosion differs due to the topography and land use-land cover.

In this project, however, the validation of the results is complicated due to the lack of additional data. Therefore, further studies are required for the accurate assessment of erosion modeling. Despite of this, the above methodology and results could help the planners and policymakers to take preventative measures according to the obtained values of soil erosion. Consequently, the use of satellite images (e.g. SAR images) and other data related for example with soil and rainfall would lead in more precise estimation from the RUSLE model.

6   Conflicts of Interest

The authors declare no conflict of interest.

Acknowledgments. The authors acknowledge the funding and support of the RESEARCH (REmote SEnsing techniques for ARCHaeology) project H2020-MSCA-RISE-2018 of the European Commission. This project has received funding from the European Union's Horizon 2020 research and innovation programme under the grand agreement No 823987 (https://www.re-se-arch.eu/). This paper is also under the Research and Innovation Foundation grant agreement EXCELLENCE/0918/0052 (Copernicus Earth Observation Big Data for Cultural Heritage).

Author Contributions. Conceptualization, NP.; methodology, NP.; investigation, NP.; writing—original draft preparation, N.P.; writing—review and editing, NP.; project administration, GH. All authors have read and agreed to the published version of the manuscript.

Funding. This communication is submitted under the RESEARCH project H2020-MSCA-RISE-2018 that has received funding from the European Union's Horizon 2020 research and innovation programme under the Marie Skłodowska-Curie grant agreement No 823987.

References

1. Maqsoom, A., et al.: Geospatial Assessment of Soil Erosion Intensity and Sediment Yield Using the Revised Universal Soil Loss Equation (RUSLE) Model. ISPRS Int. J. Geo-Inf. **9**, 356 (2020)
2. Agapiou, A., Lysandrou, V., Hadjimitsis, D.G.: A European-scale investigation of soil erosion threat to subsurface archaeological remains. Remote Sens. **12**, 675 (2020).
3. Merritt, W.S., Letcher, R.A., Jakeman, A.J.: A review of erosion and sediment transport models. Environ. Model. Softw. **18**, 761–799 (2003)
4. Renard, K.G., Foster, G.R., Weesies, G.A., Mccool, D., Yoder, D.C., Predicting soil erosion by water: a guide to conservation planning with the Revised Universal Soil Loss Equation (RUSLE). In Agriculture Handbook; U. Department of Agriculture (USDA): Washington, DC, USA (1997)
5. Igwe, P.U., Onuigbo, A.A., Chinedu, O.C., Ezeaku, I.I., Muoneke, M.M.: Soil erosion: a review of models and applications. Int. J. Adv. Eng. Res. Sci. **4**(12), 138–150 (2017)
6. Hu, S., et al.: Estimation of soil erosion in the Chaohu lake basin through modified soil erodibility combined with gravel content in the RUSLE model. Water **11**, 1806 (2019)
7. Baiamonte, G., Minacapilli, M., Novara, A., Gristina, L.: Time scale effects and interactions of rainfall erosivity and cover management factors on vineyard soil loss erosion in the semi-arid area of southern sicily. Water **11**, 978 (2019)
8. Kinnell, P.I.A.: A review of the science and logic associated with approach used in the universal soil loss equation family of models. Soil Syst. **3**, 62 (2019)
9. Alewell, C., Borelli, P., Meusburger, K., and Panagos, P., Using the USLE: Chances, challenges and limitations of soil erosion modelling. Int. Soil Water Conservation Res. (2019)
10. Alexakis, D.D., Tapoglou, E., Vozinaki, A.-E.K., Tsanis, I.K.: Integrated use of satellite remote sensing, artificial neural networks, field spectroscopy, and gis in estimating crucial soil parameters in terms of soil erosion. Remote Sens. **11**, 1106 (2019)
11. Alexakis, D., Agapiou, A., Themistocleous, K., Lysandrou, V., Sarris, A., Hadjimitsis, D.G.: Natural and human risk assessment of the archaeological sites of Paphos area (Cyprus) with the use of Remote Sensing and GIS", Bulletin of the Geological Society of Greece, vol. XLVII 2013, Proceedings of the 13th International Congress, Chania, September 2013
12. FAO/IIASA/ISRIC/ISS-CAS/JRC., Harmonized World Soil Database (Version 1.0). FAO, Rome, Italy and IIASA, Laxenburg, Austria (2008)
13. Wischmeier, W.H., Smith, D.D.: Predicting rainfall erosion losses – a guide for conservation planning. p. 537 (1978)

14. Morgan, R.P.C.: Soil Erosion and Conservation. Third edition. Blackwell Publishing, Malden, U.S.A. (2005)
15. Koirala, P., Thakuri, S., Joshi, S., Chauhan, R.: Estimation of soil erosion in nepal using a RUSLE modeling and geospatial tool. Geosciences **9**, 147 (2019)
16. Sharpley, A. N., Williams, J. R., EPIC - Erosion/Productivity Impact Calculator: 1. Model Documentation. U. Department of Agriculture Technical Bulletin, v. 1768, p. 235 pp. (1990)
17. Moore, I.D., Burch, G.J.: Modelling erosion and deposition topographic effects. Trans. ASABE **29**, 1624–1630 (1986)
18. Moore, I.D., Burch, G.J.: Physical basis of the length slope factor in the universal soil loss equation. Soil Sci. Soc. Am. J. **50**, 1294–1298 (1986)
19. Rouse, J.W., Haas, R.H., Chelfl, J.A., Deerin, D.: Monitorin vegetation systems in the Great Plains wig ERTS. In: Proceedings nircf~arth Resources Technology Satellite-1 Symp. Goddard Space Fli ht Center, NASA SP-351, Science and Technical Information okce, NASA, Washington, D., pp. 309–317 (1974)
20. der Knijff, J.M., Jones, R.J.A., Montanarella, L.: Soil Erosion Risk Assessment in Europe (2000). https://www.preventionweb.net/files/1581_ereurnew2.pdf. Accessed 21 Nov 2018
21. Panagos, P., Borrelli, P., Meusburger, K., Alewell, C., Lugato, E., Montanarella, L.: Estimating the soil erosion cover-management factor at the European scale. Land Use Policy **48**, 38–50 (2015)

Documentation and 3D Digital Modelling: The Case of a Byzantine Christian Temple and an Ottoman Muslim Mosque in Ioannina City, Greece

Athina Chroni[1](✉) and Andreas Georgopoulos[2]

[1] Hellenic Ministry of Culture and Sports-General Directorate of Antiquities and Cultural Heritage, Postdoctoral Researcher-National Technical University of Athens, 20, Paramithias Street, 10435 Athens, Greece
athina.chroni@gmail.com

[2] Laboratory of Photogrammetry, National Technical University of Athens, 9, Iroon Polytechniou Street, 15780 Athens, Greece
drag@central.ntua.gr

Abstract. The specific paper forms part of the Postdoctoral Research Project (Implemented by Athina Chroni, Dr. Archaeologist, supervised by Professor Andreas Georgopoulos, Laboratory of Photogrammetry-National Technical University of Athens.) focusing on Ioannina city's Ottoman period (1430–1913) and its multicultural profile as depicted in buildings, public or private, religious or secular, conventional or more elaborate, each having its own historical and architectural interest.

Unfortunately, most of the landmark buildings have been destroyed due to natural disasters, religious hatred and the unbridled, often uncontrolled modern constructions. However, the existence and form of several of those edifices survived thanks to fragmentary information of various kinds, while their location in the urban web and their dimensions can be clarified, in several cases, by their comparative studies with buildings recorded at the same representations whose location and dimensions are known or buildings preserved until today.

Under this perspective, a variety of data like historiographic, bibliographic, archaeological, cartographic, topographic, remote sensing imagery, optical displays, travelers' descriptions, other literary sources, local legends, inhabitants' interviews have been collected, analyzed, cross-examined and digitally processed, thus leading to the development of a Geographic Information System, the 3D landmarks digital models, a web data base and QR tags at the specific sites, where the landmark buildings used to stand, thus connecting the intangible (digital) with the tangible (physical space) and achieving interaction of the project with the local community. Moreover, cultural walks within the city's urban web, related to the project's axis are also proposed.

Keywords: Cultural heritage · Tangible · Intangible · Documentation · Digitization · Photogrammetry · 3-D modelling · G.I.S. · Open sources · Ioannina

© Springer Nature Switzerland AG 2021
M. Ioannides et al. (Eds.): EuroMed 2020, LNCS 12642, pp. 78–89, 2021.
https://doi.org/10.1007/978-3-030-73043-7_7

1 Introduction

In 1611, a failed Christian uprising[1] would lead to the abolition of the privileges the Ioannites[2] had secured with the *Decree by Sinan Pasha* in 1430, when surrendering to the Ottomans. After that year, 35 Christian churches and monasteries were destroyed, of which 18 were located inside the Castle of Ioannina. Any attempt to identify the sites of the Castle's extinct temples, other than the *Cathedral of Taxiarchis Archangel Michael* and the adjacent *Church of Pantocrator*, in the *Inner Acropolis* (*Its Kale*) of the Castle, would be in vain, as no relevant tradition has been passed over from generation to generation [9].

From 1430 to 1913, 17 mosques were built inside and outside the Castle, two metzites inside the Castle [1, 6, 15] and three *tekes*, each one at each entrance of the city [6]. "Christian churches and monasteries existed in most of the metzitia standing" [1]. In the years 1920s–1950s, 14 of the 19 mosques in the city of Ioannina have been destroyed [10].

The Jewish synagogue inside the Castle had already been built since the 9th century [1, 9], while in 1540 a second synagogue had been founded outside the Castle [13]. The last one has been destroyed in the years 1960s.

2 Selection of Landmarks: Reasoning

The 3D digital approach for specific landmarks of the city, has been one of the scientific fields of the afore-mentioned Postdoctoral Research Project. The landmarks, coming from all the three cultures of the city, Christian, Jewish and Muslim, often stratigraphically and chronologically succeeding one another, create an interesting **cultural palimpsest** reflecting the fluidity of human reality.

In the framework of the specific paper, the following landmarks have been selected to be presented:

- *Taxiarchis Archangel Michael* Christian church, the first Cathedral of the Byzantine period, dated in the 13th century, a landmark completely destroyed in 1795, as estimated.
- *Fethiye* Muslim mosque, having three construction phases as following:
- 1st phase: 17th c. to 1770.
- 2nd phase: 1770 to 1795.
- 3rd phase: 1795 until today, i.e., the building still standing.

Both afore-mentioned landmarks are situated at the *Inner Acropolis* (*Its Kale*) of the southeastern corner of the Castle of Ioannina.

In both cases it is observed:

- Uninterrupted identical use of the same site as a religious one, until the end of the Ottoman period of Ioannina.
- Successive construction of religious buildings of different religions.

---

[1] Organised by Dionisius, Metropolitan of Larissa-Trikki. [12].

[2] *Ioannites* are called the inhabitants of Ioannina city.

3 Methodology

Concerning the specific afore-mentioned landmarks, only the building of Fethiye mosque, dated after 1795, is preserved in its entirety, except for the porch. The Fethiye building preceding the year 1795, has been absorbed by the latter. The Byzantine Cathedral has been completely destroyed.

Taking into account that the typological development of the plan view of the surviving mosques of Ioannina, as well as of those whose composition has been detected with certainty, always follows the same type, it is almost certain that the pre-1795 Fethiye might have the same form as the existing one, probably having differences only in size.

Detecting the form of the Byzantine Cathedral has been the great challenge of the specific part of this research, given the absence of extensive archaeological findings to substantiate and figure out the type of the Christian Cathedral, as well as its exact location at the southeastern acropolis of the Castle, in relation to Fethiye mosque's successive construction phases.

Consequently, the research has been based on the following documentation data:

- Historical data on the city of Ioannina.
- Bibliographic reports-testimonies- fragmentary archaeological findings.
- Typological data on Byzantine Christian churches' and monasteries' as well as on Muslim mosques' architecture.

4 Taxiarchis Archangel Michael Christian Cathedral and Fethiye Muslim Mosque: Location and Dating

The intensive, cross-examined study of the related bibliographic references, archaeological findings and testimonies lead to the safe conclusion that:

- The existence, at the southeastern citadel of the Castle, of a temple dedicated to Taxiarchis Archangel Michael, a Christian church which was at the same time the Cathedral of the Late Byzantine period of Ioannina, cannot be disputed.
- Nor can be disputed the fact that an earlier Fethiye mosque building, with two successive construction phases should have existed before 1795.

4.1 Location

The location of the Cathedral of Taxiarchis Archangel Michael can be assumed in combination with the study of the location of the pre-1795 Fethiye mosque, in its two successive construction phases,[3] as well as with the consideration of the location of the after-1795 Fethiye Mosque, existing nowadays.

---

[3] 1st phase: 17th c.-1770. 2nd phase: 1770–1795.

It is likely that the existing Fethiye mosque is spatially identified, with small differences, with the pre-1795 existing mosque,[4] after the implementation of Ali Pasha's building program, in the framework of which the mosque had, probably, been resized.[5]

However, it is not clear whether Fethiye mosque is completely spatially identified with the pre-existing Christian church of Taxiarchis Archangel Michael, the city's first Cathedral. Most likely, the mosque was originally built very close to it, since until 1770 the walls of the Christian church were visible, the frescoes as well. Exactly in that year the Christian temple was completely destroyed, on the occasion of the reconstruction of Fethiye mosque, until then adjacent to the church: it is when the area of the temple was integrated in the Muslim mosque.[6]

In this light, it results that the Cathedral of Taxiarchis Archangel Michael, concerning its location, is probably not entirely identical with the location of the existing, nowadays, Fethiye Mosque: it should have been located approximately where the Fethiye Mosque is today or, rather, a little further, to the center of the plateau of the southeastern citadel [8]. We should also always take into consideration that the pre-1795 mosque, as finally formed after the interventions of 1770, might be not entirely identical with the after-1795 mosque, regarding the size and the location.

4.2 Dating

Taking into consideration the historical data it becomes clear that the date of construction (or reconstruction) of the Cathedral of Taxiarchis Archangel Michael should be determined at the time of the re-inhabitation of the city of Ioannina, i.e., shortly after 1204 [8, 16].

---

[4] The mosque having taken its final form after 1770.

[5] If we accept the dimensions referred by Celebi,for Fethiye mosque then it turns out that the current building of Fethiye, as it was formed after the construction works of Ali Pasha, is larger than the pre-1795 Fethiye, and not limited according to Vranoussis [16]. This is a conclusion quite strong, since it would not be reasonable for Ali Pasha to reduce the size of the top-mosque of Ioannina, his city-headquarters, but rather to render the specific mosque bigger.

[6] The mosque having three construction phases:

- 17th century to 1770: The mosque is adjacent to the church. The church is still existing, although as ruins.
- 1770 to 1795: The mosque is adjacent to the church. The church is destroyed in 1770. The mosque undergoes major renovation and "absorbs" the ruined church.
- 1795 until today: Reconstruction of the mosque with radical alterations concerning the location and the size of the building.

5   Taxiarchis Archangel Michael Christian Cathedral: Form and Characteristics

5.1 Form

Taking into account the data on Byzantine temple typology concerning the Middle[7] and Late[8] Byzantine period, we consider highly probable that the Christian temple of Taxiarchis Archangel Michael, must have followed the type of the *basilica*, rather *three-aisled* and, perhaps, *vaulted*, given that the *dome basilica* has already appeared since the Early Byzantine period: as a result, we find multiple examples of temples following the type of the *vaulted basilica with a dome* in the Middle Byzantine period.

It is worth mentioning that, according to Xyggopoulos [17] most of the Cathedrals of the 11th and 12th c., and even later, follow the *basilica* type, probably in order to keep the tradition and pay respect. Additionally, this type of building is very spacious and suitable for gathering a large number of people [16].

Moreover, in 1670 the Ottoman traveler Evliya Celebi, referring to Fethiye mosque, describes it as an "ancient mosque with a saddle-type roof" [7, 15]. Perhaps Fethiye mosque had already incorporated a large part of the, rather adjacent, temple of Taxiarchis Archangel Michael: we could, therefore, conclude that the "saddle-type roof" belongs to the Christian Cathedral of Taxiarchis, which, therefore, would have been rather *vaulted* and, perhaps, *domed*.

Considering the afore-mentioned, the Christian church of *Hagia Sophia in Ohrid*,[9] (Fig. 1) dated in the end of the 9th c. until the middle of the 11th c.[10] [5], which was also founded as a Cathedral [11] and belongs to the type of the "*vaulted basilica with a dome*", [11][11], has been considered to be the right choice as a model for the probabilistic

---

[7] 867–1204 AD.

[8] 1204–1453 AD.

[9] The years after 901–907, the Diocese of Ioannina will continue to belong to the Metropolitan of Nafpaktos, except for a short period of time that it came under the Archdiocese of Ohrid, immediately after its establishment. [8]: the connection between Ioannina and Ohrid is already confirmed by a *sigil* of the Emperor Vasileios B´, dating in the year 1020, related to the Archdiocese of Ohrid, according to which is determined the extent of the ecclesiastical power of the Archdiocese of Ohrid, after the overthrow of the Bulgarian state. For the years before 1319, the Bishops of Ioannina are not mentioned by name, except for Zacharias (879) who is considered as controversial. Concerning Ioannina, for the year 1020, a Bishop under the Archbishop of Bulgaria, named Ioannis is mentioned, while for the year 1232 an anonymous Bishop under the Metropolitan of Nafpaktos is mentioned. [19].

[10] According to Gioles it is considered more probable today the founding of the church during the reign of Tsar Samuel at the end of the 10th century and its completion around the middle of the 11th century by Archbishop Leon (1037–1056), who also implemented the frescoes. [5].

[11] According to Moutsopoulos, [11] the basilica of Hagia Sophia [in Ohrid] existed during the reign of Tsar Samuel (976–1014). It was probably founded during the reign of Boris, at the end of the 9th century. After the defeat of Samuel's successors in 1018, Vasileios, the Byzantine Emperor, thrashed the Patriarchate of Ohrid and established an Archdiocese. During the time of Archbishop Leon, the basilica had been repaired. In the years of Komnenos, i.e. in the 12th and 13th century, alterations on the facades of the basilica had taken place. At that time, little domes on each side of the chancel were added, as well as to the western part of the temple [11].

3D digital approach of the form of the Cathedral of Taxiarchis Archangel Michael, at the southeastern citadel, since:

- Chronologically, it precedes, the construction of the Christian Cathedral in Ioannina, dated during the reign of Michael A' Komnenos Doukas, for which it constituted, probably, a model.
- It belongs to the type of the *vaulted basilica with a dome*, the type which we assume that the Christian Cathedral, constructed during the reign of Michael A' Komninos Doukas, also followed.
- The specific landmark had been also built on a pre-existing *basilica*, perhaps Early Christian [5, 11].

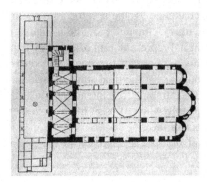

Fig. 1. Hagia Sophia in Ohrid, North Macedonia. Late 10th century. Plan view. (Source: Gioles, 1987, p. 60)

5.2 Characteristics

Orientation
In the Byzantine temple, the position of the sun in the middle of the morning-time on the day of the temple's celebration is chosen as the building's orientation axis. This axis is, of course, largely identical with the point f sunrise, i.e., the east [14].
Length, Width and Height of the Building

- If we take into account the dimensions given by Evliyia Celebi for Fethiye mosque of 1670 "sixty feet wide and one hundred [feet] long" [7, 15].
- If we assume that until then the Byzantine temple still exists, even in ruins, next to Fethiye, then we must also assume that Fethiye, if not larger than the Byzantine temple, in order to symbolize the imposition of the Muslim on the Christian, would certainly be of a similar scale, both in plan view and in vertical section.
- It is also very possible, as already mentioned, that the mosque had already incorporated a large part of the pre-existing Cathedral.

Consequently, we will make the assumption that the Christian church would be similar in size to Fethiye mosque building that existed until 1795, as far as it concerns the plan view, i.e., approximately 5.40 m wide and 9.00 m. long,[12] and the height as well, i.e., approximately 9,5 m. for the building and 23.5 m. For the bell tower.[13] In addition, in order to approach the probable form of the Christian temple, we must take into account the proportions of other parallels of this period as derived by Moutsopoulos [11] Filov [4] and Boskovic-Tomovski [2].

6   3D Digital Model Development

6.1   Reasoning

Developing the 3D digital model for the Byzantine Cathedral of Taxiarchis Archangel Michael has been a great challenge for the specific phase of the Postdoctoral Research Project due to the **fragmentary character** of the available data. This is exactly the reason for which the 3D digital representation of the Christian temple has been chosen to be abstractive, in order not to impose the researcher's point of view but just imply the form of the building by applying, at the final stage of work, the architectural typology data of Middle and Late Byzantine period, intending, thus, to activate the imagination of the recipients, i.e., the people who will visit the website or will make use of the QR tags set in the physical space of the city.

Concluding, a minimalistic optical approach of the past has been the axis of the research.

6.2   Methodology

Basic condition for the 3D digital model development has been its integration in a 2D map of the city of Ioannina, by georeferencing it. Under this perspective, the plan view of Hagia Sofia in Ohrid[14] should be inserted in a Geographical Information System, to be georeferenced and, additionally to acquire an attribute table furnishing the visitor of the G.I.S. with all the necessary information. At a successive stage of work the georeferenced plan view would form the basic image for the 3D digital model development.
Data

Remote Sensing Imagery
A physical color ortho-image of the city of Ioannina has been considered to be the optimal choice for the georeferencing of the 3D digital model's plan view, combining

---

[12] If we take into account Evliya Celebi's report in 1670 for Fethiye and Aslan Pasha mosques dimensions and compare the specific sizes to the ones as derived from architectural plans of modern times, always having in mind that the existing Fethiye mosque comes from its last construction phase, i.e., after 1795.

[13] We could accept that the bell tower, as an architectural element with symbolic dimensions in the Christian churches, corresponds to the architectural element of the minaret in the Muslim mosques.

[14] Plan view-model for Taxiarchis Archangel Michael Cathedral.

the characteristics of the image, i.e., the optical realistic representation of the city, with those of a map, i.e., the georeferencing and metrics info.

The ortho-image has been provided by *Hellenic Cadastre*[15] (Fig. 2) [18] for exclusive use in the framework of the specific Postdoctoral Research Project implementation. It consists of 132 sub-ortho-images, type LS025, dating in 2015, at a resolution of 25cm, georeferenced at *EPSG:2100-GGRS87/Greek Grid-Projected* georeference system.

Byzantine Cathedral Plan View
The plan view of the Byzantine temple of Hagia Sofia in Ohrid [5] has been the starting point for the 3D digital model development (Figs. 1 and 3).

Software
The "open access to culture" concept has been the axis of the Postdoctoral Research Project. Under this reasoning only free software has been chosen:

- The G.I.S. development has been implemented by making use of the *QGIS* free software [20].
- The 3D digital model development has been implemented by making use of the *SketchUp Make 2017* free software [21].

Fig. 2. G.I.S. screenshot. The Castle of Ioannina city. The *Hellenic Cadastre* ortho-image is the basic imagery for georeferencing the Byzantine Cathedral plan view. At the right bottom corner of the castle is the southeastern citadel of the Castle where *Taxiarchis Archangel Michael* Cathedral and *Fethiye* Muslim mosque are located. (Imagery source: The *Hellenic Cadastre.* Copyright © Hellenic Cadastre) Digital processing by Athina Chroni.

3D Digital Model Development
At a primal stage of the 3D developing, the G.I.S. imagery digital product, resulted from merging the ortho-image and the architectural plan view-prototype for the Byzantine Cathedral, has been inserted in *SketchUp* software.

---

[15] The imagery has been provided by the *Hellenic Cadastre* for exclusive use in the framework of the specific Postdoctoral Research Project.

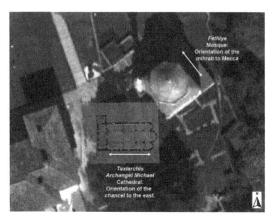

Fig. 3. G.I.S. screenshot. Top view. Detail of Fig. 2. The *Hellenic Cadastre* ortho-image is the basic imagery for georeferencing the Byzantine temple plan view. The red rectangle represents the digitized polygon, which was created for georeferencing the plan view of Hagia Sofia in Ohrid, used as a prototype for Taxiarchis Archangel Michael Cathedral, which should have had its *chancel* oriented to the east, while Fethiye mosque has its *mihrab* oriented to Mecca. (Imagery source: The *Hellenic Cadastre.* Copyright © Hellenic Cadastre) Digital processing by Athina Chroni.

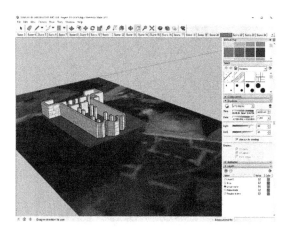

Fig. 4. *SketchUp* software screenshot. Masonry texture on the walls of the Cathedral. Oblique view of the Byzantine Cathedral's 3D digital model as developed by making use of the G.I.S. imagery digital product. The 3D digital model has been georeferenced. (Imagery source: The *Hellenic Cadastre.* Copyright © Hellenic Cadastre) Digital processing by Athina Chroni.

Taking into account the fact that stone is, over time, the basic building material of the wider area, whether for public or private buildings, secular or religious,[16] the rendering of the texture of the masonry was chosen to represent the structure of the temple's wall (Fig. 4).

---

[16] As evidenced by corresponding buildings or buildings' relics of the Ottoman period. It should be accepted as highly possible that the same data might apply for the 13th century as well, i.e., estimated period of construction of the Byzantine Cathedral.

An additional component for the representation of the specific temple under research, has been the issue of shadows and lighting: the choice focused on the early morning hours, during which the sun rises and the first part of the church building to illuminate is the chancel, which, in turn, and vice versa, indicates the point of sunrise. As a result, 08:00 UTC for Ioannina has been chosen,[17] more specifically, the position of the sun at this time for the 8th November, the name day of Taxiarchis Archangel Michael, Protector of the Cathedral.

Fig. 5. *SketchUp* software screenshot. Oblique view of the Byzantine Cathedral's 3D digital model as developed by making use of the G.I.S. imagery digital product. The 3D digital model has been georeferenced. (Imagery source: The *Hellenic Cadastre*. Copyright © Hellenic Cadastre) Digital processing by Athina Chroni.

The abstractive rendering of the Byzantine Cathedral's digital 3D model and its virtual integration at the plateau of *Its Kale* (*Inner Acropolis*) of the southeastern citadel of the city of Ioannina, at the probable site where Taxiarchis Archangel Michael was located in the past,[18] contributes effectively to the study of the buildings complex of the specific site, constituting, at the same time, a motive for further research in the future (Fig. 5).

At a final stage of the 3D digital model development, a virtual walk-through-the-3D-digital-model has become possible by producing an mp.4 digital file under the perspective of offering a more vivid experience to the visitor of the web site which has been developed as a portal to the specific research study.

7   Conclusion

The current physiognomy of Ioannina, as well as the collective memory of its inhabitants has been shaped in a fruitful and creative way thanks to the multiculturalism that has characterized this place over time.

If all the destroyed religious buildings of the Byzantine period of Ioannina were preserved, the physiognomy of the city as a Byzantine center would become clear, an element which is not perceived due to the Ottoman phase that followed, which, to a large extent is still projected as the main characteristic of the city, mainly due to the

---

[17] Ioannina, Greece: EET (UTC + 2).

[18] Completely destroyed in 1795.

survival of most of the destroyed nowadays, Ottoman period buildings in photographs, paintings, extensive bibliographic descriptions and architectural drawings. The Castle in particular, as a Byzantine castle city, is however an indisputable reality that influenced the next phase of the city.

For this very reason, the components of the city's physiognomy should regain the weight of their cultural contribution.

Moreover, for the fulfillment of an additional objective of the specific research project, that is, community participation and interaction [3], a participatory interactive web-based platform,[19] a virtual museum[20] as well as digital signage at the specific sites, where the landmark buildings used to stand, and, also, cultural walks within the city's urban web, related to the project's axis, are being developed, under the perspective of "inviting" the citizens to take an active role in cultural heritage issues.

References

1. Aravantinos, P.: Chronography of Epirus. Volume II. Vlastos S.K. Publications, Athens (1856). Reprint: Koultoura Publications, Athens (2004)
2. Boskovic, Dj., Tomovski, K.: L'architecture Medievale d'Ohrid. Dans: Recueil de Travaux, Musée National d'Ohrid, Edition Spéciale, Ohrid (1961)
3. Chroni, A.: Cultural Heritage Digitization & Copyright Issues. Proceedings of the 7th International Euro-Mediterranean Conference-EuroMed 2018 on Digital Heritage: Documentation, Preservation, and Protection, Editors M. Ioannides et al., Springer Nature, ISSN 0302–9743, ISSN 1611–3349 (electronic), Lecture Notes in Computer Science ISBN 978–3–030–01761–3, ISBN 978–3–030–01762–0 (eBook), https://doi.org/https://doi.org/10.1007/978-3-030-01762-0, Library of Congress Control Number: 2018956722, Switzerland, (2018). Chapter 34, pp. 396–407
4. Filov, B.: Geschichte der Altbulgarischen Kunst. Berlin, (1932).
5. Gioles, N.: Byzantine Church Architectural Typology. Kardamitsa Publications, Athens (1987)
6. Kanetakis, G.: The Castle: Contribution to the Urban History of Ioannina. Published by the Technical Chamber of Greece, Athens (1994)
7. Kokolakis, M.: Evliya Celebi in Ioannina. Skoufas Magazine, Issue HD-1991/1, Ioannina (1991)
8. Kordosis, M.: The Byzantine Ioannina. Athens (2003)
9. Koulidas, K.: Ioannina that left. Ioannina (2010)
10. Koulidas, K.: The Muslim vakif of the city of Ioannina. Publications of the Society on Epirotic Studies, Ioannina (2004)
11. Moutsopoulos, N.: The basilica of Agios Achilleios in Mikri Prespa. Bulletin of the Christian Archaeological Society, No. 4 (1964–1965), Period IV-In memory of George A. Sotiriou (1881–1965), pp. 163–203, Athens (1966)
12. Papadopoulos St.: Liberation struggles of the Greeks during the Turkish occupation. Issue A´ (1453–1669), University Lectures, University of Ioannina Publications, Thessaloniki (1982)
13. Papazois, A.: Land uses-typical types of houses-morphology of buildings in the Jewish quarter of Ioannina-historical data-example of application. Bachelor's thesis, Technological Educational Institute of Piraeus, Piraeus (2008)

---

[19] *IASIS* web-based platform: https://athinachroni.wixsite.com/my-site-1

[20] *IOANNINA, 1430–1913* web-based virtual museum: https://www.artsteps.com/view/5feca5aaf e659e68d58a48c8

14. Potamianos, I.: The light in the Byzantine Church. University Studio Press, Thessaloniki (2000)
15. Smyris, G.: The mosques of Ioannina and the urban planning of the Ottoman city. Epirotic Chronicles, vol. 34, Ioannina (2000)
16. Vranoussis, L.: On historical and topography of the Medieval Castle of Ioannina. Publications of the Society on Epirotic Studies, Ioannina (1968)
17. Xyggopoulos, A.: The monuments of the Serbs. The Society for Macedonian Studies and the Foundation for the Studies of Aemos Peninsula, No. 18, Athens (1957)
18. Hellenic Cadastre. www.ktimatologio.gr Accessed 08 Sep 2020
19. Holy Metropolis of Ioannina. https://www.imioanninon.gr/main/?page_id=164. Ιερά Μητρόπολις Ιωαννίνων. https://www.imioanninon.gr/main/?page_id=164. Accessed 08 Sep 2020
20. QGIS. https://www.qgis.org/en/site/. Accessed 08 Sep 2020
21. SketchUp Make 2017. https://download.cnet.com/SketchUp-Make-2017/3000-6677_4-102 57337.html. Accessed 08 Sep 2020

Terrestrial Laser Scanning and AutoCAD for Measuring Deformations of Cultural Heritage Structures. Case Study of *El Atik*'s Minaret in Sétif-Algeria

Rania Mechiche$^{(\boxtimes)}$ ⓘ and Hamza Zeghlache

Mediterranean Architecture Laboratory, Department of Architecture,
Ferhat Abbas Sétif 1 University, El Bez, 19000 Sétif, Algeria

Abstract. Today, digital technologies represent an important tool for emergency preparedness of any heritage at risk. The use of devices such as 3D modeling makes it possible to have an endangered heritage recognized. This paper deals with the terrestrial laser scanning survey (TLS) using AutoCAD and point clouds for calculating deformations of cultural heritage structures. In doing so, this study focuses on one of historic key buildings – that look very vulnerable –, in Sétif's city in Algeria: the minaret of *El Atik*'s mosque. A major novelty is the use of cross section method based directly on high accuracy model generated from the point clouds. This method is used to determine the tilted direction and tilted distance along the tower of the minaret of *El Atik*'s mosque regarding to the main axis of its base.

Keywords: Emergency preparedness · Heritage at risk · Terrestrial laser scanning survey · AutoCAD · Point clouds · Cross-section · Deformations

1   Introduction

Since the beginning of mankind, Man has created built structures that remain today as the results of an ancient occupation of a place and spaces. Many of these remains help us to understand the history of past cultures and civilizations. Today these remains are considered as the Built Cultural Heritage of humanity, expressing social, economic, political, territorial and environmental values.

Unfortunately, this Cultural Built Heritage is constantly exposed to natural threat factors (i.e. swarms, floods, landslides, volcanic eruptions and earthquakes) and human activities (i.e. pollution, inappropriate use, war, acts of vandalism and other conflicts). Indeed, the archives recount the troubled history of some of the most emblematic sites of Cultural Built Heritage; most of them are located in countries stroked by war, a complex context in which it is extremely difficult to ensure the safeguarding and protection of heritage properties. In this field, Algeria is faced with the task of safeguarding its heritage, including French colonial heritage where many buildings have disappeared or have been

© Springer Nature Switzerland AG 2021
M. Ioannides et al. (Eds.): EuroMed 2020, LNCS 12642, pp. 90–99, 2021.
https://doi.org/10.1007/978-3-030-73043-7_8

demolished, taking with them a part of the collective memory. The minaret of *El Atik* mosque is a relevant example.

El Atik was the first mosque built in 1838 by the French military engineers in Sétif, a northern city in Algeria. The mosque is located a few meters from the mythical fountain of *Ain El Fouara*, in the Frantz Fanon street. The mosque is considered as a place of worship, culture and religious teaching (See Fig. 1). It was listed in the Additional Inventory of Protected Cultural Properties following the Order N° 4538 of 04/11/2015 signed by the *Wali* of Sétif. However, the minaret of *El Atik* mosque is confronted with the risks of climate change, its deformation is slowly increasing with passage of time. Indeed, visible cracks are recognized on its walls, which affected its accessibility currently closed.

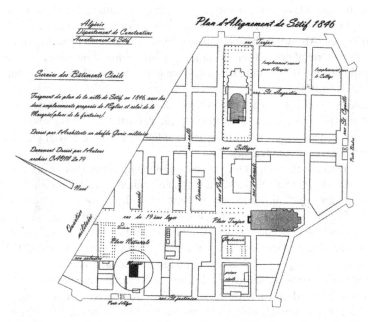

Fig. 1. Sétif Alignment Plan established by the French Military Engineers in 1846 Source: CAOM 2N79, *in* Mahdadi Noureddine and Tachrift Abdelmalek, The Influence of the *El Atik Masjed* on the Architecture of the Plans of the Sétif *Masjeds*, Algeria. (2017).

As previously mentioned, in recent years, there has been a growing interest in the conservation and protection of this Built Cultural Heritage. However, the measures implemented for its protection remain ineffective. This paper discusses the effective use of New Technologies in monitoring the conditions of Built Cultural Heritage in order to better understand changes and manage them. The paper considers New Technologies as an alternative approach to the restrictive techniques of traditional archiving currently used in conservation and urban planning practices.

2   Preparedness of Cultural Built Heritage at Risk with Digital Dataset

'Understanding the physical fabric of a site is an important first step in finding the right conservation strategy, and documentation is the first step in understanding' (Clark 2017). This sentence highlights the primary role of documentation and the interdependence between knowledge and conservation strategy (Grazia and Valentina 2012). Indeed, the preventive surveying and documentation of the Built Cultural Heritage is a first step of its conservation and restoration. In modern times, the only possible way to Preparedness of Built Cultural Heritage at risk and to hand over its documentation to future generations is through Digital Dataset.

As a matter of fact, the former way of operating the Built Cultural Heritage survey has been replaced by a Digital Process of Modeling (Varady and Martin 1997), using new technologies. All of which give us – as architects – several opportunities such as: The Automatic Orientation, High Accuracy 3D Modeling, Remote Access and Web Representation of the Built Cultural Heritage and also the possibility of Monitoring its deformations over time.

This research consists of gathering reliable digital data on a specific monument, the minaret of *El Atik*'s mosque. It aims to study the deformations of the minaret using a measurement technique that is intended to be reliable, accurate and at the same time inexpensive and easy to implement.

In the literature of the subject matter, the commonly used methods are LIDAR technique surveying (Light Detection and Ranging, also called Laser Scan). It is a technique of Lasergrammetry that allows the digitization of Built Cultural Heritage (Valentina et al. 2015). The main advantages of this technology are a fully remote and non-contact measurement and the collection of dense, detailed and three-dimensional points clouds representing the object of interest (Manuel et al. 2020; P; Gawronek et al. 2019). Also, the undeniable advantage of TLS is that although individually recorded points are not very accurate (position accuracy from $\pm$ 2 mm to $\pm$ 50 mm depending on the measuring device) the model fitted into a dense point cloud is a more precise representation of the structure and can be extremely effective in recording changes in a shape of the measured structure (Zan et al. 2019; Thomas et al. 2016).

3   Literature Review and Method

In practice determining the deformation of a structure based on terrestrial laser scanning data is performed by comparing multimillion-point scans acquired at different times (Roderik and Norbert 2005; Tsakiri et al. 2015). Several main methods of analyzing changes in cultural heritage structures based on point clouds, has already been done. We would like to mention some of the most commonly used methods: The comparison between GRID models generated based on point clouds acquired before and after deformation (Michal et al. 2012); Thomas et al. 2004), the analysis and detection of changes in elements of a building's façade and its interiors with the use of octree structures and algorithms which compare scans cloud-to-cloud (Stuart et al. 2003), The use of three-dimensional, surface models that are created by fitting simple geometric models into point clouds representing individual parts of the structure. The deformation is measured by comparing the resultant figures (Roderik 2015; Mario et al. 2016; Zhou et al. 2014).

Most of these methods are, however, usually carried out on objects of relatively large sizes, such as heaps of materials, embankments, or earth masses (Maurizio and Margherita 2013). Scans for determining displacements of architectural objects are much less frequently used, especially when changes in the position of structure points are of the order of single millimeters, and the structure is under preservation by a conservator (Luis Javier et al. 2018). In response to this need, the authors proposed a methodology for solving the problem. The Skelton of the research was the CAD geometric analysis of TLS data. This analysis was based mainly on the cross-section method, the aim of which is to study the tilt situation of the minaret. The scope is the enhancement of emergency preparedness networks, plans and expertise for French Colonial Built Heritage in Sétif (Algeria).

3.1 Workflow

With regard to the above-mentioned objectives, the research work was carried out in two stages: The first concerns hardware data acquisition, the second concerns software data processing.

- Hardware Data-Acquisition:

Based on TLS survey, 39 scans (See Table 1) were carried out in the light of a prior-digitization plan, which determines the position of different laser-scanner stations and trajectories, so that all the material properties of the minaret – collected in the form of point clouds – could be aligned. (See Fig. 2) All obtained scans created an extensive database of point clouds, which was used to train an accurate 3D model of the object.

- Software Data-Processing:

This step concerns the assemblage of different Scan Worlds obtained, which has been done according to the quadrilateral contour of the minaret's exterior walls as a correspondence between two cloud/meshes. As seen in Fig. 3, a rigid pairwise alignment was applied using iterative closest points, so that each two cloud/meshes'fit converges to minimum errors (>1 mm).

The pairwise alignment of all the scans allows us to generate a high accuracy 3D model which was then, streamlined for a reduced size and refined by an automatic meshing process to reduce noise and fil the holes in the minaret (Fig. 3). The obtained model was used to carry out the tilt situation of the minaret (Fig. 4).

Fig. 2. Prior-Digitization Plan designing ten different Laser-Scanner Stations and Trajectories at the exterior of the mosque. Source (Authors).

Table 1. Data volume and processing time of the project. Source (Authors).

Data type	Size	Device name	Scan position	Processing time
LIDAR. terrestrial	9928 Mb	Leica Scan Station P16	39	1 month

The first stage of the deformations analysis included the extraction of different cross-sections at set altitude and constant intervals (0.5 m) along the base of the main tower of the minaret. Eight slices were obtained each with a distinguishable color. Using

Constraint	Scanworld	Scanworld	Function Value (sq m)	RMS (m)	Avg (m)	Min (m)	Max (m)	Overlap Points	Status
Cloud/Mesh 1	Station-007: SW-007 (Leveled)	Station-013: SW-013 (Leveled)	0.00001097	0.008	0.003	0.000	0.092	190566	Aligned

Fig. 3. Pairwise alignment of two Scan-Word: SW 007/SW 013 (Plan and Elevation view).

Fig. 4. High accuracy 3D model of the tower minaret of *El Atik* mosque.

cad software, the authors Simulate the sliced point cloud into a standard geometric quadrilateral, the center's coordinate of each slice can be acquired accurately (See Fig. 5).

The horizontal projection of the center of the different slices allows to study the variation trend of geometric center of each slice regarding to the main axis of the central core of the minaret. Figure 6 shows the horizontal projection of the geometric center. Points 1 to 8 represent eight geometric centers. The distance marked in the figure represent the projection distance of the geometric centers on the horizontal plane.

The results show the increasing shifting of every slice's center, from the bottom to the top of the base of the main tower's minaret, which requires that the minaret's tower is displaced compared to its main axis.

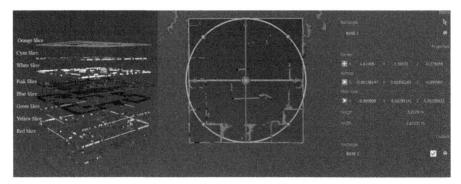

Fig. 5. Simulation of slices into a standard geometric quadrilateral and assimilation of center's coordinate.

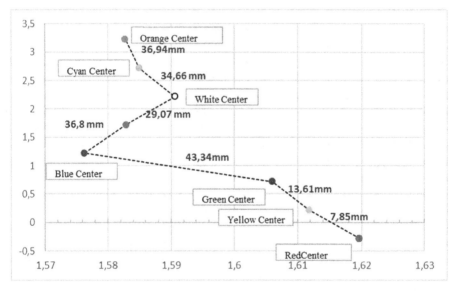

Fig. 6. Variation trend of the geometric centers.

To know how much and toward which direction the minaret is displaced, the second stage of the research work includes the same approach of the first stage for the whole main tower of the minaret. The extraction of different cross-sections, at this stage, at a fixed interval of 4 m. Four slices were obtained each with a distinguish color. Using CAD software, the authors simulate the sliced point cloud into a standard geometric circle. The quadrilaterals. The Center's coordinate and radius of each slice can be acquired accurately (See Fig. 5). The analysis data was mainly based – at this stage – around the tilted direction and tilted distance in regard to the main axis obtained from the base of the minaret illustrated in the Red Slice (See Fig. 7).

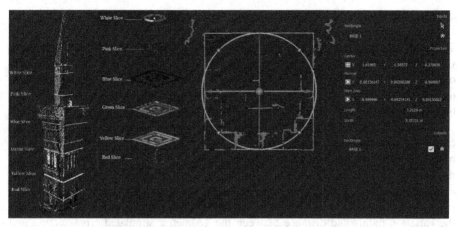

Fig. 7. Simulation of slices into a standard quadrilateral/circle and assimilation of center's coordinate and radius. (Color figure online)

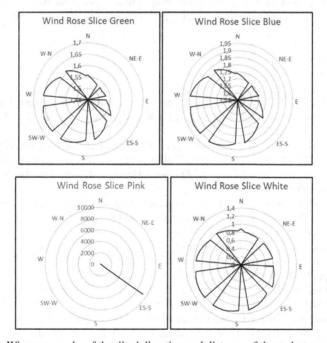

Fig. 8. Win-rose graphs of the tilted direction and distance of the main tower of the

El Atik mosque minaret.

Figure 8 is a wind-rose graphs of successive cross-sections extracted along the main tower of *El Atik*'s minaret. The result shows that the displacement of the minaret is more important on the South and Southwest side which means that the minaret has been subjected to shear stress.

4   Conclusion

The main motivation of this research was to show the effective use of geometric analysis of TLS data in calculating deformations of cultural heritage structures. The results obtained by the authors confirmed that it is possible to determine the deformation of historic structures with millimeter accuracy using CAD software and cross section method based on a data set from TLS.

In the first stage of the study, the variation trend of the geometric centers at the base of the minaret was identified. The projection distance of the geometric centers on the horizontal plane shows an increasing shifting between different slices which requires a displacement of the minaret's base from its main axis. The second stage of the study consisted on the tilt direction and distance of the main tower of the minaret. Besides measurements results were supplemented by the determination of the differences in the variation radius and distance between the geometric simulated cross-section and the main axis of the minaret's base. A structural deformation with value of 10% to 20% was identified in south and southwest side. These findings allow us to identify the type of stress (in this case, it is about shearing stress), and to measure changes on the current condition of cultural heritage which can be helpful to bring effective engineering solution.

References

Arianna, P., Elena, B., Claudio, G.: Enzo, B: Laser scanning and digital imaging for the investigation of an ancient building: Palazzo d'Accursio study case (Bologna, Italy). J. Cult. Herit. **V13**(2), 215–220 (2012)

Clark, K: Informing conservation, in recording, documentation, and information management for the conservation of Heritage places, p. 3. Chabbi, A., Eppich, R. Associated Editors (2017)

Eleonora, G.: Fabio, R: Classification of 3D Digital Heritage. Remote Sens **11**(7), 847 (2019). https://doi.org/10.3390/rs11070847

Gogcic, Z., Zhou, C., Weiser, A.: The perfect match 3D point clouds matching with smoothed densities. In: IEEE Conference on computer Vision and Patters Recongnition, 201, pp. 5545–5554. https://doi.org/10.1109/CVPR.2019.00569.

Grazia, T., Valentina, B.: New Technologies for Cultural Heritage Documentation and Conservation: The Role of Geomatics. In: Iconarch - 1 Architecture and Technology International Congress. pp. 15–17 November 2012 Konya. Published in 2014

Ladislav, D., Jana, M.: Digitization of the Cultural Heritage of Slovakia Combining of Lidar Data and Photogrammetry. SDH, 1(2), 590–606 (2017)

Lee, R.: Building maintenance management, Italian U. Hoepli, Milan (1993)

Luis Javier, S.A., Susana, D.P., Luís F, R., Andrés, A., Francisco, M, F.: Heritage site preservation with combined radiometric and geometric analysis of TLS data. Automation in Construction, vol. **85**, 24–39 (2018). https://doi.org/10.1016/j.autcon.2017.09.023

Manuel, C., Belén, R., Borja, C., Ana, S.R.: A case study of measurements of deformations due to different loads in pieces less than 1 m from lidar data. Measurement **151**, 107196 (2020). https://doi.org/10.1016/j.measurement.2019.107196

Mario, A., Luigi, F., Federico, P., Marco, S., Paolo, V.: Structural monitoring of a large dam by terrestrial laser scanning. Int. Arch. Photogram. Remote Sens. SpatialInform. Sci. **36**(5) (2006) 6. https://www.researchgate.net/publication/228653597_Structural_monitoring_of_a_large_dam_by_terrestrial_laser_scanning. Accessed 05 Sept 2020

Maurizio, B., Margherita, F.: Monitoring of large landslides by terrestrial laser scanning techniques: field data collection and processing. Eur. J. Remote Sens. **46**(1), 126–151 (2013). https://doi.org/10.5721/EuJRS20134608

Tsakiri, M., Vasileios-Athanasios, A: Change detection in terrestrial laser scannerdata via point-cloud correspondence. IJEIR **4**(3), 476–486 (2015). https://www.researchgate.net/public ation/282001967_Change_Detection_in_Terrestrial_Laser_Scanner_Data_Via_Point_Cloud_ Correspondence. Accessed 20 Sept 2020

Michal, K., Rafal, Z., Anna, F., Michalina, W., Paulina, B.D.: Noninvasive methods of determining historical objects deformation using TLS, Struct. Anal. Hist. Constr. **3**, 2582–2588 (2012). https://www.researchgate.net/publication/266201887_Noninvasive_methods_of_dete rmining_historical_objects_deformation_using_TLS. Accessed 0 Sept 2020

Minaroviech, J.: Digitization of the Cultural Heritage of Slovakia. Combining of Lidar Data and Photogrammetry. Stud. Digital Heritage **1**(2), 590–606 (2017)

Noureddine, M., Abdelmalek, T.: The Influence of the *El Atik*masjed on the architecture of the plans of the sétifmasjeds, Algeria. J. Architecture Plann. **31**(1), 103–118, Riyadh (2019/1440H)2017.

Pelagia, G., Maria, M., Bartosz, M., Tadeusz, G.: Measurements of the vertical displacements of a railway bridge using TLS technology in the context of the upgrade of the polish railway transport. Sensors **19**, 4275 (2019). https://doi.org/10.3390/s19194275

Roderik C, L., Norbert, P.: A statistical deformation analysis of two epochs of terrestrial laser data of a lock. In: Proceedings of the 7th Conference on Optical, pp. 61–70 (2005). https://www.researchgate.net/publication/228847312_A_statistical_deformation_anal ysis_of_two_epochs_of_terrestrial_laser_data_of_a_lockAccessed 20 Sept 2020

Stuart, G., Derek, L., Mike, S., Jochen, F.: Structural Deformation Measurement Using Terrestrial Laser Scanners. In: Proceedings, 11th FIG Symposium on Deformation Measurements, Santorini, Greece (2003).

Thomas, S., et *al.*:Deformation measurement using terrestrial laser scanning at the hydropower station of Gabcikovo. In: NGEO 2004 and FIG Regional Central and Eastern European Conference on Engineering Surveying Bratislava, p. 10. Slovakia (November 11–13, 2004).

Thomas, W., Niemeier, W., Daniel, W., Christoph, H., Frank, N., Heiner, K.: Arealdeformation analysis from TLS point clouds – the challenge. Allgemeine VermessungsNachrichten (AVN) **123**, 340–351 (2016). https://www.researchgate.net/publication/311795322_Areal_Def ormation_Analysis_from_TLS_Point_Clouds_-_The_Challenge. Accessed 20 Sept 2020

Valentina, R, et al.: An integrated multi-media approach to cultural heritage conservation and documentation: from remotely sensed lidar imaging to historical archive data. In: Earth Resources and Environmental Remote Sensing/GIS Application VI, vol. 9644, p. 96440C. International Society for Optics and Photonics (2015)

Varady, T., Martin, R.R.: Cox, J: Reverse engineering of geometric models – an introduction. Comput. Aided Des. **29**(4), 255–268 (1997)

Wenderlich, T., Niemeier, W., Wujanz, D., Holst, C., Neitzel, F.: Khulmann, H: A real deformation analysis from TLS points clouds – the challenge. Allgemeine VermessungsNachrichten (AVN) **123**, 340–351 (2016)

Zan, G., Caifa, Z., Jan D.W., Andreas, W.: The perfect match: 3D point cloud matching with smoothed densities. In: IEEE Conference on Computer Vision and Patters Recognition. In: IEEE/CVF Conference on Computer Vision and Pattern Recognition (CVPR), pp. 5545–5554. IEEE, Long Beach (2019). https://doi.org/10.1109/CVPR.2019.00569.

Zhou, W., Guo, H., Hong, T.: Fine deformation monitoring of ancientbuilding based on terrestrial laser scanning technologies. IOP Conf. Ser.: EarthEnviron. Sci. **17**(1), 012166 (2014). https://doi.org/10.1088/1755-1315/17/1/012166.

Wrap-Up Synthesis Model from High-Quality HBIM Complex Models, and Specifications, to Assess Built Cultural Heritage in Fragile Territories (Arquata Del Tronto, Earthquake 2016, the Church of St. Francesco, IT)

Raffaella Brumana[1] , Chiara Stanga[2(✉)] , Mattia Previtali[1] ,
Angelo Giuseppe Landi[2] , and Fabrizio Banfi[1]

[1] Department of Architecture, Built Environment and Construction Engineering (ABC),
Politecnico di Milano, via Ponzio 31, 20133 Milan, Italy
{raffaella.brumana,mattia.previtali,fabrizio.banfi}@polimi.it
[2] Department of Architecture and Urban Studies (DAStU),
Politecnico di Milano, via Bonardi 3, 20133 Milan, Italy
{chiara.stanga,angelogiuseppe.landi}@polimi.it

Abstract. The paper intends to define the different levels of quality models achieved to assess architectural heritage in fragile contexts as the earth quaked territories, proposing to reverse the BIM logic 'simple-to-complex' in favor of a complex-to-simplex one targeted to HBIM. In order to perform a preservation plan, given the complexity of a damaged heritage, the simplification can't be the starting point, but the synthesis of the detailed levels of understanding obtained: the case study of St. Francesco church, damaged by the earthquake occurred in 2016, is presented to highlight the deliverables submitted as part of the support to the preliminary preservation design project and decision-making process carried out by the research group of the Politecnico di Milano for the Municipality of Arquata del Tronto. The high level of geometry description acquired by the surveying (TLS, MMS, Photogrammetry) has been finalized to analyze the out-of-plumbs and structural behavior, enriched by the diagnostic analysis detecting the materials and construction techniques, supported the recognition of the stratigraphic volume units and construction phases to better understand the transformations across the centuries integrating the direct data sources with the indirect ones (documents, archives). While in the traditional BIM logic the level of enrichment progressively crosses the Level of Development phases (LOD100-500) by adopting a progressive parallel Level of Geometry (LOG100-500), the paper proposes scales model definition (GOA100-50-20-10) and LOG specifications adapted to the LOD (Design Development, Preservation Plan) reversing the logic and introducing a synthesis model that collects the different analysis, a wrap-up model, to be used together with the detailed high scale models (LOG200-300-400-100), for BIM-to-FEA or BIM energetic analysis, and within LOD600 VR.

Keywords: Level of geometry · Level of development · Arquata del Tronto · High-resolution models · Construction techniques

© Springer Nature Switzerland AG 2021
M. Ioannides et al. (Eds.): EuroMed 2020, LNCS 12642, pp. 100–111, 2021.
https://doi.org/10.1007/978-3-030-73043-7_9

1   Introduction

When dealing with Built Cultural Heritage damaged by catastrophic events, such as earthquakes, flooding, or wars, the representation of the current building status becomes a useful tool for analyzing the damage mechanisms and understanding what has been lost, assessing the structural behavior, which also depends on the transformations occurred in the past. The paper illustrates the different GOAs LOGs and LODSs generated in support of the preliminary preservation project, adapting the 3D model to the architectural design process, progressively embodying the different analyses, starting from the territorial scale up to the 3D modeling of the elementary block components (i.e., bricks block, stones) and their arrangements. Such concepts have been applied to the case study of St. Francesco church in the municipality of Arquata del Tronto (Ascoli Piceno, Italy), damaged by the earthquake that struck central Italy between August and October 2016 (Fig. 1). The work is the result of the study developed between May and June 2019, when the Municipality of Arquata commissioned the group of the Politecnico di Milano, coordinated by Prof. A. Grimoldi (guidelines and preservation plan research) and Prof. R. Brumana (scantoBIM survey research) to draw the preliminary design project. It included 3D model HBIM-oriented analysis and VR support to the decision making and communication phases.

Fig. 1. Arquata del Tronto and St. Francesco church after the earthquake and the architectural survey (Photo credit AgCult, Arquata del Tronto Municipality, and DABClabGIcarus).

2   GOA, LOG, and LOD Specifications for Built Cultural Heritage at Risk for the Preliminary Assessment and Design Phases

The accuracy of 3D models is an issue that still needs to be addressed appropriately to get a consensus and compromise among the knowledge and the user needs. For this matter, there is not the possibility to pre-fix a model scale; there is not a model right and a model wrong in absolute. In the digital era of HBIM and sharing platform, it becomes mandatory the proper communication of the intrinsic geometric qualities of the models adopted in the function of the different uses: the definition of different Grade of Accuracy (GOA100-50-20-10) in the model generation based on the standard representation scale goes in that direction [4]. GOGs guidelines for the model generation becomes necessary to optimize the procedures for representing complex objects and irregular elements coherent with the adopted GOA [6]. The 3D model could also result from components realized with different Grades of Accuracy, depending on the diverse documentation (i.e., a façade modelled on 3D laser scanner data, or furniture from a standard object library). Depending on the available documentation and finalization, different Grade of Accuracy can be adopted for each building component. Starting from the results obtained from different guidelines proposal on the LOG and LOD [3, 6], the paper shows how the application of different Grade of Accuracy in the modeling scales (GOA-50-20-10 and 100) can support different Levels of Geometry and analysis from the complex one to assess state of the art and to understand the structural behavior till to the simplified ones (Figs. 2 and 3): LOG 200 Appropriate geometric model, LOG300 Accurate BIM-enabled model and LOG400 BIM-use (here precisely the conservation plan with the diagnostics, material, stratigraphic analysis together with the decay mapping) together with the LOG100 Conceptual model used as a wrap-up model enriched by the different analysis adopted for the case study are illustrated.

Grade of Accuracy (GOAs) and model scale parameter (tolerance)				
GOA 200 (t80÷120mm)	**GOA100** (t40÷60cm)	**GOA50** (t20÷30mm)	**GOA20** (t8÷12mm)	**GOA10** (t4÷6mm)

LOGs	GOA*	Data collection-acquisition	Output
LOG200 **Appropriate** **Geometry** As found model, Surveying and Multi-temporal data collection	GOA50, 20, 10	TLS&MMS laser scanning, 2D-3D photogrammetry, Historical drawings, postcards, images across the time, archives data.	2D-3D profiles and meshes, Rectified images across time, Orthoimages
LOG300 **Accurate BIM** **enable model** Scan-to-BIM, Model object	GOA50, 20, 10	Multiscale Multipurpose Geometric analysis and Object generation	3D Model BIM-enabled (interoperable modeller tools to parametric tools), BIM-based analysis
LOG400 **HBIM uses** Diagnostic analysis, Preservation design project, FEA, Energetic analysis	GOA50, 20 (and GOA10)	Diagnostic analysis (Material Mapping, Decay Mapping), Construction techniques reading and interpretation, Preservation project	Stratigraphic Units detection, Material and decay Mapping and analysis, Preservation plan, Automatic computing
LOG100 **Concept wrap-up** **model**		Historical drawings, archives data, construction techniques reading and interpretation, 2D drawings, and building archaeology	Thematic models (building construction phases; 3D building Archaeology; preservation works)
LOG500-600	GOA turned to 100 (and 50-20)	HBIM model, HBIM Object Database	Toward co-working Common Data Environment and VR
		* It can be selected more than one GOA in the function of the needing.	

Fig. 2. GOAs scales followed for the model's generation (upper) and the proposed LOGs specifications addressed to the Preservation plan.

As explained in the following paragraphs, different Grade of Accuracy and Level of Geometry in the models' generation and analysis have been realized to tackle the architectural project's steps (Level of Developments): the work-in-progress Design phase (LOD300), here the preliminary Preservation Plan, that will be followed by the definitive and executive phases, in preparation of the LOD400 (Construction site management), LOD500 (Life Cycle Management, Maintenance and Facility Management) and LOD600 (Information Sharing). The process allowed us to adapt the 3D model to the architectural design process and different analyzes, starting from the territorial scale up to the 3D modeling of small building components (i.e. stones) and their arrangements. It supported the analytical phases to the preservation plan and design project following the best-practices suggested by the Basilica di Collemaggio conservation site closed in December 2013 at L'Aquila, Earthquake 2011 [3] awarded by Europa Nostra (2020) [2].

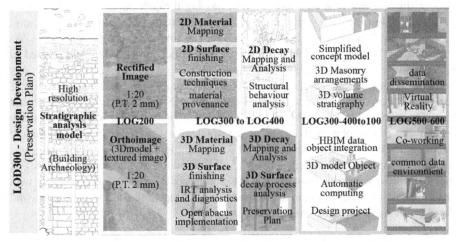

Fig. 3. LOD300 – Design Development and high detailed LOGs in the specific case of the Stratigraphic analysis model. The appropriate geometry (LOG200) supports the accurate high resolution HBIM enabled geometric model (LOG300), and the material and decay analysis addressed to the stratigraphic model for the preservation plan (LOG400 HBIM uses), feeding the synthesis model (LOG100) and LOG500-600 for data communication in view of LOD600.

3   Morphological-Constructive Analysis of St. Francesco Façade (GOA 20, 10 and 100) and LOGs (200–300)

The different Grade of Geometry made it possible to study the church as the preservation plan took shape, starting with first elementary modeling to analyze out-of-plumb and geometric irregularities due to the earthquake. However, the following are preliminary analysis and hypothesis that will be deepen as the research goes ahead.

LOG200 – Appropriate geometry. As found model, Surveying and Multi-temporal data collection: GOA50-20 Surveying for punctual geometric analysis. Restorations over the centuries till the 2016 earthquake: multitemporal data analysis, rectification of the main façade for the analysis of the stratigraphic units. The geometrical analyzes are based on the architectural survey performed through laser scanner, total station, together with photogrammetric datasets where possible due to the scaffolding (i.e. west and east façade, June 2019). Further data integration has been performed thanks to a portable MMS (Mobile Mapping System) GEOSLAM based data acquisition to cover the lack of data in some portions hidden by the temporary provisional scaffolding. It helped get fast feedback in few ground floor rooms of the cloister with limited accessibility, allowing to chain the clouds through the MMS path, reconstruct the 3D models, including the north wall and bell tower. The LOG200 level has been obtained integrating the current surveying with the precious past data collection and documentation (pictures, drawing, documents) according to the BIM NBS specification. In particular, it has been beneficial for the time-lapse 3D model's reconstruction (LOD300, Par. 3.2) and structural behavior understanding for the preservation plan (LOD400, Par. 3.3) to compare the current situation with the past one (Fig. 4), passing through the intermediate shocks, thus highlighting the cracks, the crashed portions and damages logics of the structural sequences and behavior, and beneficial also for the future recommendation. The 'As found model, Surveying and Multi-temporal data collection (LOG200)' was used to understand the church's architectural changes over the last century, such as restorations and maintenance plans. Some damages due to earthquakes are better understanding if one knows the previous architectural works. In August 2016, a first shock caused several damages to the church, which was still accessible. The situation worsened with the second shock in October 2016, while a heavy snowfall caused the roof collapse, ruining the interior. The safety measures involved strengthening the walls with hydraulic lime mortar and strips of galvanized steel or basalt fiber mesh (west-east-south façade). A metal profile structure was built to support the arches of the dividing wall, together with scaffoldings. It was set a system to limit the arches' thrusts and connect the walls, avoid the overturning of the main (west), and east façade.

Fig. 4. LOG200-Appropriate Geometry: 'time lapse-comparison' of the main façade using current and past image collection: a) after the provisional safety works (Othoimage, DMS, 2019); b) after the first shock in August 2016 (rectified image); c) before the earthquake (rectified image).

3.1 LOG300 – Accurate Geometry (HBIM Enabled Model) to Generate 3D Models Derived from LOG200 Out-of-Plumbs, Irregular Geometry, and Structural Deformations. GOA 20 (High Resolution Model).

The geometric data obtained for LOG200 2D drawings of horizontal and vertical wall sections (Fig. 5) has been exploited for LOG300 High Resolution 3D HBIM enabled model reconstruction (Fig. 6), embodying the complexity of the geometry resulting from the past transformation and the damages of the earthquake. A GOA 20 high resolution model of the main façade made it possible to observe the planar deviations of the façade through horizontal and vertical sections (out-of-plumbs).

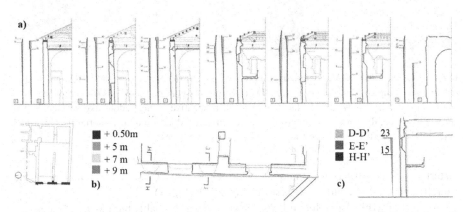

Fig. 5. LOG200 – main façade (west front): a) out-of-plumb analysis of the main façade; b) wall horizontal sections overlapping and c) wall vertical sections overlapping comparison.

The deviation from the plane of the façade is perhaps due also to the thrusts of roof and wall-dividing arches, which are not linked to the west wall (main façade). Pillars and arches were built when the church was enlarged with the second nave, between the 16th and 17th centuries. The 3D model highlighted the greatest out-of-plumb of the main façade corresponding to the dividing wall. The out-of-plumb is about 15 cm on the arches' spring-line and about 23 cm on the arches' key. The survey shows that, in general, the façade is subject to overturning and bulging (*spanciamento*). However, it must be noticed that measures include the reinforcement strips and mortar. The variable geometry of cracks and deformations – while referring to general phenomena already described – must be supported by further diagnostic investigations to define the masonry features, clamping, historical repairs, or deformations. This model provides essential information for structural analysis (i.e., FEM, BIM-to FEA).

3.2 LOG400 – BIM Uses: Preservation Plan, Mapping Material and Construction Technologies, Building Archaeology, and Diagnostic

The preliminary study for the preservation plan has been carried out through different analyses performed on the previous data models. The in-depth study of the building's

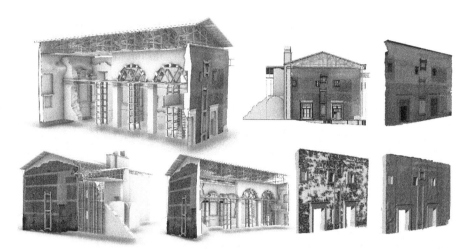

Fig. 6. LOG300. 3D GOA20 detailed wall (West front). NURBS based model HBIM enabled to manage the complexity of the geometry. 3D out-of-plumb, curvature analysis (red color, positive Gaussian curvature, bowl-like surface; blue color, a negative value, saddle-like surface; green color, zero value, flat surface in at least one direction – the added strengthen mortar was included in the analysis) textured by the orthophoto. (Color figure online)

materials and construction techniques made it possible to clarify some phases of the church's construction, alongside historical research (Fig. 7).

According to bibliographic sources, the church was probably built in the 13th century [1]. It was enlarged starting from the 16th century when a second nave was added on the south side. The arrangement of the stones on the main façade shows the two building phases of the church. The material mapping and stratigraphic analysis on the orthophoto show how some masonry portions on the left side of the main façade, corresponding to the older church, are built with squared stones with homogeneous horizontal mortar beds. It is different from the right side, which presents an irregular arrangement of stones. The same arrangement discrepancies are visible on the east wall. The stones placed along the line that divides the first and the second nave were measured and modelled. It helped to understand the alignment of the older church on the horizontal section, so if there was correspondence between the stones of the east façade and the walls of the dividing wall at the church's interior. Starting from the material mapping it has been carried out a preliminary crack analysis (Fig. 8) for the preservation plan.

LOG400 - GOA 10 Close-Up: CONSTRUCTION Techniques Analysis with the 3D Arrangement of the Block Sample Units (Sandstone and Travertine)

GOA 10 allows representing how the walls were realized. It helped understand their construction techniques in three dimensions at the intersection of the different stratigraphic units highlighted by the previous level, modelling the stone elements of the west and east façades. The close-up construction techniques focused on the "line" that marks two different building phases on the east façade: the church's first layout and the second nave (Fig. 9). The focus was on one sample of travertine stones of the church's first construction phase. The aim was to study the vertical alignment between the east façade

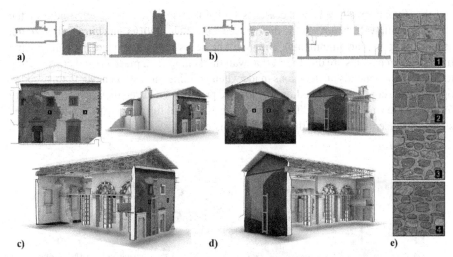

Fig. 7. LOG400. First hypothesis about the construction sequence. Top: on the main facade, the former layout in red matches the north wall (a), while the added nave in beige matches the south wall (b). Centre: church rectified image before the earthquake (c). Stone arrangements are highlighted in different colors. Red area: uneven travertine stones masonry, horizontal (older church layout, one nave); Sand area: rough sandstone masonry (16th–17th centuries, second nave); Dark gray: squared quoin sandstones (1940s restorations). Similar stone arrangements are found on the east wall (rectified image before the earthquake (d). Bottom: the two different stone arrangements of the west and east façades: 1–2) regular stone masonry; 3–4) irregular stone masonry. This scheme does not take into consideration the numerous and minute maintenance and repairs (i.e. the repointing of mortar joints) that has been mapped in the material analysis. (Color figure online)

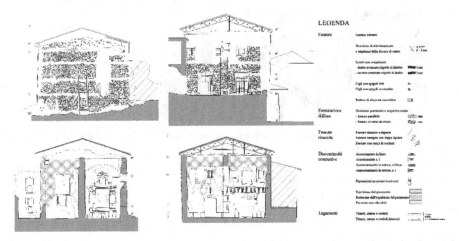

Fig. 8. LOG400, Preliminary Preservation Plan, Material decay mapping, cracks on the west and east façades and counter-façades.

and the dividing wall. Where the arches built following the former alignment of the church's south wall, or not? Some differences are visible at different church's horizontal sections (Fig. 9, plan alignments), and it will be necessary further studies to understand if those discrepancies are due to internal wall thickening (i.e., plasters) and construction techniques, or depends on decisions made when building the second nave. In this second option, some construction needing would have probably occurred that made it necessary to change the wall alignment. The orthoimage 3D model further helps to understand the stones' surface finishing and the working tools used.

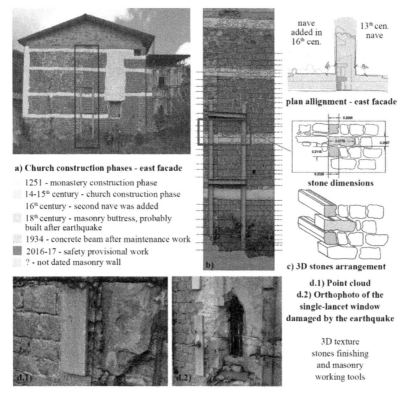

Fig. 9. LOG400-GOA10 construction technique close-up: a) east façade and the different construction phases; b) focus area, see the "line of discontinuity" between the first church phase (green, uneven travertine stones masonry) and the second church phase (yellow, rough sandstone masonry), visible on the mortar bed joints that are not aligned; c) 3D arrangement of the stone block sample: 2D plan (gray horizontal section at +0.7 m; green horizontal section +1.9 m; blue horizontal section +6.75 m; orange horizontal section +9.65 m; light blue horizontal section + 12 m) and front view with stones dimensions; 3D model and 3D material mapping, stones surface finishing. (Color figure online)

3.3 LOG100 and GOA 100: 'Wrap Up' Conceptual Models Summarizing the Detailed Analysis and Models (GOA10-20-50) Implemented in the LOGs200-300-400

The paper proposes to use the LOG100 and GOA100 as a synthesis model inheriting the richness of the knowledge gained (Figs. 7, 8 and 9) in the LOG200-300-400 with the higher scale models (GOA50-20-10). This stage initially used for a territorial scale study and was a prerequisite for the subsequent steps, is here enriched (Fig. 10) with the church's geometric-morphological-stratigraphic detailed data of the LOG300-400 (Figs. 7, 8 and 9); but it can also be enriched by the structural data or energetic analyses to be implemented in the BIM uses. It poses the accent on the aspects connected to define a methodology to entailing the richness of the information coming from the 3D complex model (i.e., managing the out of plumbs in the LOG300 and its interpretations contained within LOG400) toward a simplified, reliable version. These simplified 'enriched' models go in the direction to be used within other environments and tools, including VR, as n the following paragraphs with linked the detailed LOG300-400 models.

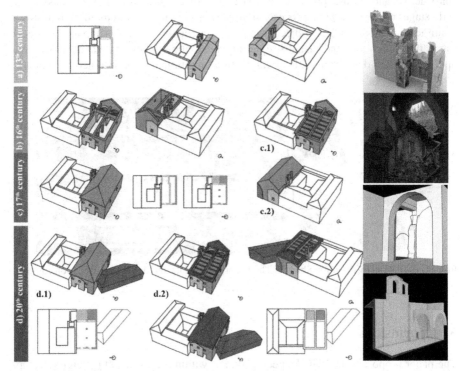

Fig. 10. Left: the wrap-up synthesis model summarizing the stratigraphic analysis models (LOG200-300-400): a) church first construction phase; b) church enlargement (south nave); c.1) wooden altar and coffered ceiling (1615): c.2) east-façade buttress: d.1) casa Bucciarelli (1910): d.2) restorations works (1934). Right: HR volume analysis (GOA 100-LOG100) summarizing the LOGs analysis results at different resolution levels (GOA 50–20-10).

4   Towards LOD600: VR to Sharing Immaterial and Material Heritage and Risk Awareness Among Citizens

Nowadays, the growing need to share information during the life cycle of the building, from the first survey campaigns up to scheduled maintenance, requires a system capable of increasing the level of communication between the actors involved. For this reason, the achievement of a LOG 600 (Information sharing) was proposed with the aim of increasing the level of communication of the previous phases. Thanks to novel cutting edge software application and methods has been possibile to develop an opne VR project able to share tangible and intagible valures of the research case study such historical, cultural and geographic values. It was fond that residents were discouraged by the impossibility of accessing the church. They want the building to be restored and religious services to be resumed. Thanks to new development logics and scan-to-BIM-to-VR requirements [5] based on an open platform, reviving the church has been possible. Its digital version allows an immersive and interactive use where any user (virtual tourist, residents, students, professionals) can discover tangible and intangible values from a historical, constructive, and cultural point of view. The VR project has inherited the richness of the early stages of the generative process, giving the possibility (even remotely) to discover multimedia archives and 3D objects capable of interacting with user inputs. Figure 11 shows the church's virtual-visual storytelling, recounting the events that have occurred up to the present day through historical, cultural, multimedia, and interactive contents.

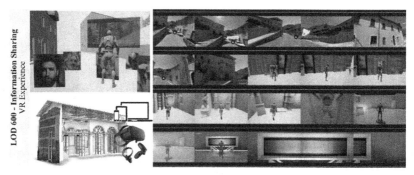

Fig. 11. LOD600, Information Sharing. The VR project and its interactive dissemination contents.

5   Conclusions

The paper proposes LOG-GOA specifications - within the LOD300 (Design development, preservation plan) - to be integrated into the scan-to-BIM process starting from surveying (LOG200) to HBIM geometric detailed models (LOG300) addressed to preservation plan models (LOG400), ensuring a reliable 3D model methodology able to manage the complexity. The proposed approach LOD-LOG-GOA makes it possible to address the preservation plan adopting the proper restitution scales (GOAs 10-20-50) of the HBIM enabled models with respect to the research's needs and purposes, guaranteeing more transparent data sharing of the 'content model' (in term of scales and enriched information) among the users and operators. Moreover, the complex models obtained in the sequence LOG200-300-400 integrating the current surveying with the past data collection and documentation (pictures, drawing, documents), have been progressively enriched by the stratigraphic analysis embodying the architectural changes occurred over the centuries, boosting the geometric-structural behavior comprehension in support of the preservation plan. Simplified time-lapse wrap up 3D models (LOG100) generated after the complex chain - entailing the richness of the LOG300-400 levels - supported the comparison of the current situation with the past ones, passing through the intermediate shocks, and helped to highlight the damages logics of the structural sequences and 3D interpretation useful for the future recommendation. The potential of feeding LOD600 - as resulting from the augmented level reached by the previous steps - can help the building's maintenance data management (i.e., digital twins monitoring) through VR/AR, as well as the dissemination of the content models knowledge gained, for a more in-formed and immersive tourism.

Acknowledgments. The authors thank the Municipality of Arquata del Tronto (RUP Mauro Fiori and arch. Davide Olivieri). Preliminary Restoration Design, Scientific Responsible Manager: A. Grimoldi and A. G. Landi. Collaborators: E. Facchi, E. Zamperini (POLIMI DAStU).

Surveying and SCANtoBIM process, Scientific responsible: A. Brumana. Laser scanning responsible: M. Previtali, F. Roncoroni. 2D drawings and 3D modelling: F. Banfi, C. Stanga, M. Petrone (POLIMI DABC, Lab. GIcarus). Thanks to the graduate students Andrea Rusconi and Luca Rovelli for the VR implementation. Thanks to the SSBAP students (POLIMI) for the LOD stratigraphic analysis, 2019 workshop, prof. R. Brumana, A. Grimoldi, and F. Doglioni.

References

1. Ortolani, C.: La provincia riformata delle Marche nel 1837. Picenum Seraphicum **I**(2), 237–246 (1915)
2. European Heritage Award/Europa Nostra Award 2020 The Basilica of Santa Maria di Collemaggio 07 May 2020 I Conservation I Italy I L'Aquila.
3. Brumana, R., Della Torre, S., Previtali, M., Barazzetti, L., Cantini, L., Oreni, D., Banfi, F.: Generative HBIM-Modeling to embody complexity: surveying, preservation, site intervention. The Basilica Di Collemaggio (L'Aquila). Applied Geomatics 10, 545–567 (2018)
4. Brumana, R., Banfi, F., Cantini, L., Previtali, M., Della Torre, S.: HBIM Level of Detail-Geometry-Accuracy and survey analysis for architectural preservation. Int. Arch. Photogramm. Remote Sens. Spatial Inf. Sci. XLII-2/W11, 293–299 (2019)
5. Banfi, F., Brumana, R., Stanga, C.: Extended reality and informative models for the architectural heritage: from scan-to-BIM process to virtual and augmented reality. Virtual Archaeol. Rev. **10**(21), 14–30 (2019)
6. Banfi, F.: HBIM, 3D drawing and virtual reality for archaeological sites and ancient ruins. Virtual Archaeology Review **11**(23), 16–33 (2020)

Project Papers: Remote Sensing for Archaeology and Cultural Heritage Management and Monitoring

Cultural Master Plan Bamiyan (Afghanistan) – A Process Model for the Management of Cultural Landscapes Based on Remote-Sensing Data

Georgios Toubekis[1]([📧]) [iD], Michael Jansen[2,3], and Matthias Jarke[1,4] [iD]

[1] Fraunhofer Institute for Applied Information Technology – FIT, Sankt Augustin, Germany
georgios.toubekis@fit.fraunhofer.de
[2] Research Center Indian Ocean, [RIO] Heritage, Maskat, Oman
michael.jansen@rio-heritage.org
[3] German University of Technology, GUTech, Maskat, Oman
[4] Information Systems, RWTH Aachen University, Aachen, Germany
jarke@dbis.rwth-aachen.de

Abstract. The Cultural Landscape and Archaeological Remains of the Bamiyan Valley are inscribed on the UNESCO World Heritage List since 2003. An international safeguarding campaign is active for its preservation, including the remains of the Buddha figures destroyed by the Taliban in 2001. Efforts are underway to set up an effective management system for the historical areas within a wider landscape approach balancing conflicting uses and demands. Based on detailed high-resolution satellite imagery and accompanying ground surveys, a comprehensive inventory of vernacular settlements, traditional water systems, and historic cultural remains was compiled. The Bamiyan Cultural Masterplan has been elaborated as a zoning proposal to support future planning processes in Bamiyan. A GIS System has been set up to manage planning and monitoring activities in the future. The current condition of the archaeological remains of Bamiyan has been documented with different remote sensing and high precision 3D documentation methods. Within cultural heritage management, Virtual Reality technologies are an innovative approach for documentation and presentation of complex architectural objects, especially in landscape settings. The project includes a digital reconstruction of the destroyed Small Buddha (38 m) Figure of Bamiyan integrated into the high-resolution 3D model of the niche and the cliff. The composite model of previous and actual conditions serves as a communication and planning tool for future consolidation for experts and the interested public.

Keywords: UNESCO world heritage · Remote sensing · Heritage management · Geographical Information Systems (GIS)

1 Introduction

The World Heritage Convention of 1972 puts forward the concept of protection of the cultural heritage of outstanding universal value as a collective effort in international assistance and collaboration of humankind as a whole. It has since been the most successful

© Springer Nature Switzerland AG 2021
M. Ioannides et al. (Eds.): EuroMed 2020, LNCS 12642, pp. 115–126, 2021.
https://doi.org/10.1007/978-3-030-73043-7_10

policy instrument on cultural issues at the international level adopted by all countries in the world.

Therefore, the protection of World Heritage properties in countries like Afghanistan is well suited to exemplify the implementation of the World Heritage Convention as a best practice of the United Nations' efforts to support education, environmental conservation, and sustainable development in communities all over the world. Negative impacts arising from natural and human-made factors are an increasing threat to heritage sites worldwide. Integrated approaches are required that translate preservation activities into broader sustainable planning efforts, in particular to cultural environments at a landscape scale.

This paper will present the achievements of a broader international cooperation project including experts from Japan, Italy, France, Germany, and Afghanistan that collaboratively work together for more than fifteen years addressing technical and societal challenges to mitigate these threats. The results achieved are motivating to serve as best practice examples for countries under similar austere societal conditions. It is argued that the new use of advanced information and communication technology is crucial for the success of such efforts, as the role of emerging tools for conservation practice and heritage management goes beyond mere functional requirements driven by cultural heritage preservation objectives. An important aspect is the enhancement of the human aspect of the collaboration of people with diverse cultural and professional backgrounds in such projects that require systems that can intelligently augment the collective knowledge, diverse approaches, and different viewpoints in solving the tasks.

Furthermore, the paper addresses the responsibility of large international institutions such as UNESCO to ensure the longevity of efforts in advocating and promoting the centrality of cultural heritage as a universal value and human right in the implementation of the principles of the rule of law and the promotion of a culture of peace [1].

The following section two will give a brief overview of the significance of the Bamiyan site and the background on the international safeguarding campaign following the UNESCO nomination as World Heritage in 2003. Section three outlines the methodology for the proposed landscape protection approach based on remote sensing data. A focus lies here in the creation of accurate map material for the World Heritage property based on high-resolution satellite imagery as a foundation for the proposed monitoring system for the cultural landscape. The use of Information and Communications Technologies (ICT) is presented for monitoring the condition both at object and at landscape scale, assisting in the mitigation of threats. Section four will present the results so far, and the suitability of the system to perform basic monitoring tasks. In the last section, an outlook is given on the possible impact of future information systems that combine both visualization and interpretation approaches trough the contextualization of different pieces of information expressed by the diverse range of media artifacts.

2   Significance of the Site and the UNESCO Safeguarding Campaign

The Bamiyan Valley in Afghanistan is located around 200 km north-west of the capital Kabul at the height of about 2500 m above sea level. The valley is backed by the massive 4000–5000 m peaks of the Hindu-Kush mountain range along the seismically active

Bamiyan-Herat fault with a semi-arid mountainous climate and intense winter periods. A prominent cliff located at the confluence of minor tributaries from the west and the south marks the center of the valley. The site where once the Giant Buddha figures stood extends for approximately 1500 m in east-west direction comprising more than one thousand caves. These caves line up for several kilometers on the north side of the entire valley, leaving the fertile valley plane open for agriculture. In the Buddhist period, they served as monastic cave sanctuaries, and many are in use till today as dwelling opportunities for some part of the population.

Fig. 1. View of the Bamiyan Valley from the hill of Shahr-e Gholghola with the main cliff

The ensemble of the Giant Buddha figures of Bamiyan was known as the world's largest depiction of a standing Buddha figure. Carved deeply into the soft cliff conglomerate, the "Big" Western Buddha measured 55m, and in a distance of 800 m to the east, the so-called "Small" Eastern Buddha raised to 38 m. International intervention and protest could not prevent the destruction of the Giant Buddha figures ordered by the Taliban leadership in March 2001. Situated within the crossroads of the civilizations of the East and the West, these valleys served as a passageway for the intercontinental trade routes of the Silk Road between India and China. Due to the artistic expression of its mural paintings, Bamiyan became a genuine center for Buddhist art in the Hindu Kush region in the course six to ninth century CE (Fig. 1).

At the beginning of the 20th century, French archaeologists prepared extensive photographic documentation, a first map of the valley, and emergency restorations on the figures [2], contributing to the first phase of the valley's international recognition before

WWII. Bamiyan and its particular artistic expression came into focus again in the second half of the 20th century [3–5] when international aid assistance by the Government of India prepared the site as a major national tourist attraction [6].

By the end of 2003, the empty niches, the cave complexes of the main cliff, as well as the ruins of the medieval historic city of Shahr-e Gholghola and the fortification complex of Shahr-e Zohak from the Islamic period have been nominated a UNESCO World Heritage property. The Cultural Landscape and Archaeological Remains of the Bamiyan Valley is a serial nomination property of eight individual larger and smaller areas representing artistic and religious developments from the 1st to the 13th century CE. Due to its too delicate state of conservation, the property was also inscribed on the World Heritage List of Endangered Sites in order to underline the responsibility of the State Party to pursue emergency preservation activities.

Within the UNESCO campaign for the preservation of the Bamiyan site funded by the Japanese government, a first detailed topographic map of the central valley based on high-resolution satellite imagery analysis and from aerial images from the 1970s was prepared, including a first 3D laser scan of the central cliff façade and the empty niches was prepared by the Japanese expert team. They initiated a comprehensive conservation intervention in selected caves in order to prevent further deterioration of the murals and conducted non-destructive ground prospection to determine the underground extension of the archaeological areas in front of the cliff. The scientific analysis revealed many new findings that are discussed in detail in [7]. The lateral sides of the niches in which once the Buddha figures stood were in danger to collapse entirely due to the impact of the detonations. Therefore, emergency consolidations have been realized by Italian rock-climbers from RODIO Inc. [8]. German restorers from ICOMOS are active to salvage the remaining rock fragments exposed to the forces of wind and water. They stabilize the rear wall of the empty niches and have consolidated loose original mud plaster surfaces in situ [9] that have survived the detonations. High-resolution laser scans of the niches have been executed to generate detailed site plan material in support of the work of rock engineers and restorers. Based on these plans, rock mechanical stabilization works could be planned and executed.

3 Recording, Mapping, and Zoning – A Landscape Approach for the Management Framework of the World Heritage Property

The establishment of an effective management framework for a UNESCO World Heritage property also includes the inventory of the cultural elements that convey the property's Outstanding Universal Value (OUV) in order to fulfill the requirements for effective management as defined in §110 and §111 of the Operational Guidelines (OG)[1] to the World Heritage Convention. In our case, it was necessary to identify the specific cultural assets, characteristics of the cultural landscape, and the threats from ongoing development to anticipate adverse impacts on authenticity and integrity on the inscribed property.

Based also on the findings from the international archaeological teams, RWTH Aachen University conducted a mapping of historic settlement and cultural landscape

---

[1] https://whc.unesco.org/en/guidelines/ (last accessed September 2020).

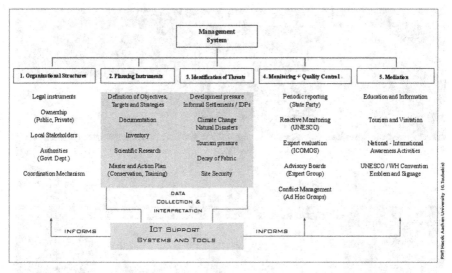

Fig. 2. Management Framework of a World Heritage property adapted after [10].

assessment in 2005. As a result, an inventory of the cultural assets of the valley could then be elaborated as the Cultural Master Plan of the Bamiyan Valley, forming the basis for all future planning activities [11]. The envisioned management framework builds upon several interrelated components of guiding principles, the integration of initial assessments into planning decisions, and continuous monitoring. To ensure the sustainability of the management efforts, continuous capacity building in techniques, as well as governance issues, is indispensable [12], which requires adapted information system support for data collection and interpretation to inform the overall management system (Fig. 2).

All works are embedded in the recommendations[2] of the UNESCO Expert Working Group for the Preservation of the Bamiyan Site, which is coordinating the efforts of the different international teams in close collaboration with the Afghan authorities.

4   Remote Sensing as Foundation for the Landscape Management System

Continuous monitoring is an essential instrument of the World Heritage Convention (Article 29), and State Parties are required to report to the World Heritage Committee regularly on the conditions of listed World Heritage properties.

Since the overall tense security situation does not allow long-lasting field missions, a survey approach based on remote sensing technologies using stereo high-resolution satellite imagery was used to obtain precise 3D spatial information of the area covered by the Cultural Master Plan.

---

[2] All events and recommendations of the Bamiyan Experts Working Group are documented at the UNESCO Website https://whc.unesco.org/en/list/208/

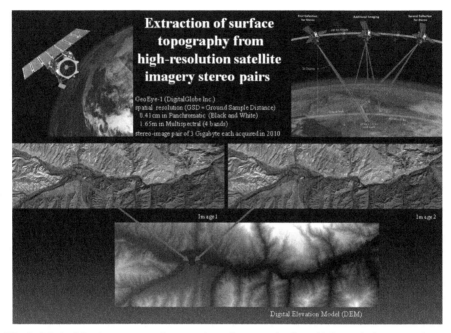

Fig. 3. Method for the stereoscopic extraction of topography from high-resolution stereo-image pairs, resulting in a DEM with a spatial resolution of 2m (Images courtesy DigitalGlobe).

A Digital Elevation Model (DEM) is a digital dataset of elevations in XYZ coordinates of which topographic information can be derived by photogrammetric means from the analysis of images acquired under different viewing geometries. Image matching algorithms detect identical points in two images, referred to as a *stereo pair*. For the generation of the topographic map of Bamiyan, a GeoEye stereo image pair from November 2010 in an orbit of 681 km altitude provided imagery with a ground sampling distance of 41 cm (GSD) in panchromatic (b/w) mode and 2 m in multispectral (4 bands) mode[3] (Fig. 3).

4.1   Processing of High-Resolution Stereo Imagery for Topography Generation

The identical points which are identifiable in both stereo images, called homologous points, form the basis for the DEM since their height can be calculated directly from their different spatial positions. Flat areas show little visual distortions in the images, and many points are available. In areas with moderate or high relief, the number of points to be found is more or less reduced, as the terrain is imaged differently due to the different viewing angles of the sensor. The lack of homologous points is also a problem in areas that are not covered in both images, for example, areas in front of steep cliffs, which overlay the surrounding terrain and in areas that are not illuminated at all,

---

[3] In summer 2013 the orbit altitude of the GeoEye-1 Satellite sensor was raised to 770 km with new nadir ground sample distance (GSD) of 46cm compared to the previous GSD of 41cm.

because shadowing is too severe. Additional information about the exact geo-location is necessary to get an absolute geographical position of the points. This information can be derived from the orbit parameters of the satellite leading to a referencing accuracy of a few meters or improved with the help of ground truth data. In this work, Differential GPS (DGPS) measurements from two different field campaigns were used to archive significantly higher geo-coding accuracy. Altogether 2.8 million homologous height points (on average one point per 7mx7m) were detected by the software system in a supervised automatic extraction with the manual alignment of the geo-coded height points from the field campaigns.

4.2 Digital Elevation Model (DEM) and Relief Model

The DEM has a horizontal resolution of less than 2 m and covers an area of about 22 km × 7,2 km with elevation values ranging from 2353 m to 3130 m. The elevation values correspond to the EGM96 geoid model and therefore represent local height. The georeferencing of the satellite imagery is based on the field survey and the orbital parameters from GeoEye. The DEM represents the elevation, including vegetation and buildings, not only the bare ground. If buildings or vegetation are present in the DEM depends on their size. Small objects tend to be omitted, and large objects are more likely included in the DEM. A relief for visual interpretation can be calculated from the DEM.

4.3 Orthophoto Base Map and Validation of the Results

The acquired satellite images were projected onto the processed DEM to generate a geometrically correct image of the area, which can be used to derive high precision map information at a resolution of 50 cm/pixel. Validation was performed via a visual comparison of all DPGS points from the 2003 and 2010 field campaigns. Horizontal accuracy has shown to be better than 1m. This very high accuracy is not quoted for the complete area, and will probably be lower for terrain with stronger relief. All datasets are included in a GIS system that was set up as a reference for any future survey related work in Bamiyan. Besides the purpose of documentation of spatial entities, the aim is to track, visualize, and compare changes over time. The challenge here is the integration of survey material originating from different sensor sources and the user and access management to the system.

5 Remote-Controlled Monitoring System

In the initial phase of the UNESCO safeguarding campaign, international support assistance concentrated on the consolidation of the cliff niches where once the figures stood. Following the recommendation of the Bamiyan Expert Working Group detailed documentation of all the other World Heritage areas has to be accomplished as well in order to determine the state of conservation of these areas that have been little studied in the past. To overcome the lack of expertise and experience on the national side, we proposed a monitoring approach that could be executed by local staff that was in constant communication with experts assisting the campaign remotely. Communication was enabled by regular briefings using various channels via smartphone and chat-messaging, even in the field.

5.1 GPS Based Photo Documentation for Time-Efficient Damage Assessment

In order to ensure consistency of the photographic documentation in the field, GPS enabled cameras and smartphones were used geo-coding photo positions directly into the EXIF information tag of the digital images. Images were printed on the spot, and observations from the field were directly noted on the image prints, which were scanned and added to a geo-referenced database. The entire field survey was supervised remotely by the expert based at RWTH Aachen University (Germany), who obtained survey results daily via the internet and ensured the quality of the data collection. The information thus can be consulted remotely by experts and already proved to be very helpful as necessary evaluation in the preparation of more comprehensive conservation activities at a later stage. The method was elaborated further and proved to be successful even in more challenging environments in Afghanistan [13].

5.2 Geographical Information Systems for Land-Use Planning, Zoning, and Management

The basic usage of the established Geographical Information Systems (GIS) for Bamiyan and regular use of remote sensing technology may serve to ensure observation of broader areas for the Cultural Landscape of Bamiyan also over more extended periods. It is the aim to identify the effects of development projects (e.g., road construction) on the World Heritage property well in advance and to examine alternatives in the initial phases of a

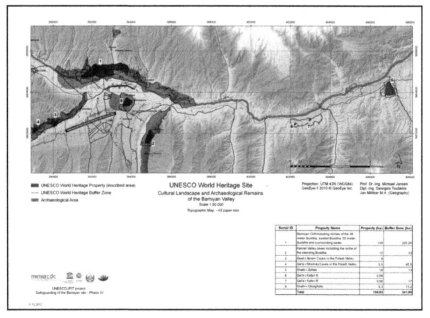

Fig. 4. New topographic map indicating the current extent of the World Heritage property and culturally sensitive areas derived from the various information sources

project. For such an integrated planning approach, it is vital to indicate culturally sensitive areas within the territory of the Cultural Master Plan. Important here is that assessment guidelines need to be specified to clarify between "World Heritage compatible" and "non-World Heritage compatible" development projects within the central Bamiyan Valley and that it requires efficient technical support to achieve mutual understanding on such decisions among the different stakeholders using a variety of media and communication channels. After several years it has now become clear that national authorities can not maintain access to this information, although national and international planning agencies require this material (Fig. 4).

5.3 New Digital Technologies for Visualizing and Experiencing Heritage Values

Contemporary digital visualization technologies are proposed to complement the interpretation strategy. The entire cliff has been digitized with 3D laser scanners in the context of the engineering consolidation measures, and the Small Buddha Figure has been digitally reconstructed in 3D [14, 15]. From the remote sensing imagery, digital 3D landscape models have been generated that can be combined with the 3D information from the individual high-resolution scans of the individual areas allowing for an extraordinary level of detail in the resulting digital 3D models. At the current stage, the ICT applied is primarily intended to serve as a communication tool for representation and interpretation – to serve as a visual exploration tool for the different results obtained up to this point by the project. While these tools have up to now served mainly the needs

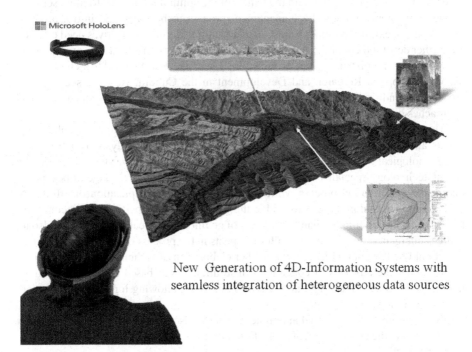

Fig. 5. Future systems will be based on a profound understanding of context information

of engineers and restorers, they hold the potential to engage and communicate with a broader public as well. New Virtual and Augmented Reality technologies allow for a completely new way of interaction with digital models through an interactive exploration of virtual environments [16]. Augmented Reality (AR) applications combine real and virtual scenes (2D or 3D visuals) and other information in the user's perception of the environment [17]. This can be done in large virtual reality labs such as the AixCAVE[4] located the IT Center of RWTH Aachen University, in museum environments as immersive full 3D projection [18] and in the near future also with native 3D Apps on consumer smartphones. The integration of contextual information of data sources for providing meaningful usage within the related digital communities is the research challenge of the future (Fig. 5).

6 Conclusion and Outlook

Based on high-resolution remote sensing imagery, a set of tools was presented, serving the management of the Cultural Landscape and Archaeological Remains of the Bamiyan Valley. The approach presented is suited to create agreement among key stakeholders on the cultural values based on a thorough and shared understanding of the significance of the property. The toolbox presented with the creation of the Cultural Master Plan Bamiyan is regarded as an example of an integrated Cultural Heritage management system that includes technologies for monitoring, surveying, documentation, and evaluation of the cultural landscape. The focus on technical tools here is to support the management process and give guidance to retain the values of the cultural landscape. Remote sensing is one component to allow the management process to be integrated into a broader landscape context. It is our understanding that Cultural Heritage objectives need to drive the further development of these emerging tools so they can consolidate the preservation efforts. From an epistemic point of view, use cases like Bamiyan offer a challenging testbed for applied Research and Development in the Cultural Heritage sector since the austere conditions ask for adaptation of practices in which innovative technological approaches demonstrate their potential.

The methodological foundation lies in the accuracy, reliability, and verifiability of results allowing for comparative and qualitative geographical analysis over time. On the technological level, the theoretical and methodological objectives have to be shared among technology specialists and heritage experts to ensure the exchange of best practice in the conservation process while seeking to avoid the duplication of efforts. A challenge for the future here is to bridge the gap of lack of expertise within countries like Afghanistan after more than thirty years of conflict. Technical assistance has also to address intergenerational and intercultural aspects in the process of knowledge transfer; this should be the guiding idea in the further elaboration of technical support systems, ideally under the auspices of educational institutions. Web-based collaborative information systems have the potential to address this issue, allowing for global access and exchange of views on local matters.

Furthermore, it is expected that remote sensing landscape monitoring will contribute significantly to the enforcement of protection initiatives and international rules since it is

---

[4] For details on the aixCave see < https://vr.rwth-aachen.de/page/10/ >

suited to support planning policies and improve legislation procedures. The discussion process initiated with the Cultural Master Plan Bamiyan is, therefore, ongoing and, at the moment, the only platform to bring the various stakeholders together. From the perspective of cultural heritage management, VR and AR technologies are here an innovative approach for documentation and presentation of complex architectural contexts, especially in landscape settings. AR applications can have here considerable impact on how different stakeholders perceive tangible cultural heritage sites because they allow for augmenting the perception both indoors in exhibition contexts but as well as outdoors, such as on the archaeological site itself.

As stated in the *Florence Declaration on Heritage and Landscape as Human Values* of ICOMOS [19], the efforts are to create inclusive and transparent management processes shaped by dialogue and agreement since successful management contributes to a sustainable and peaceful society. It is acknowledged that landscapes are an integral part of heritage as they are the living memory of past generations and they can provide tangible and intangible connections to future generations.

References

1. UNESCO ed: From a culture of violence to a culture of peace. UNESCO Publishing, Paris (1996)
2. Hackin, J., Carl, J. (eds.): Nouvelles Recherches Archéologiques à Bamiyan. Les Editions G. Van Ouest, Paris (1933)
3. Miyaji, A.: Wall paintings of Bamiyan Caves: stylistic analysis. In: Japan-Afghanistan Joint Archaeological Survey in 1974, pp. 17–31. Kyoto University Archaeological Mission to Central Asia, Kyoto (1976)
4. Tarzi, Z.: L'architecture et le décor rupestre des grottes de Bāmiyān. Impr. Nationale, Paris (1977)
5. Klimburg-Salter, D.: The Kingdom of Bamiyan - Buddhist Art and Culture of the Hindu Kush. Istituto per il Medio ed Estremo Oriente (ISMEO), Naples and Rome (1989)
6. Sengupta, R.: Restoration of the Buddha Colossi at Bamiyan 1969–1973. ASI, New Delhi (1973)
7. Yamauchi, K., Suzuki, T., Kondo, H. (eds.) Documentation of the Bamiyan Sites 1-4. Japan Center for International Cooperation in Conservation. National Research Institute for Cultural Properties Tokyo, Tokyo (2012)
8. Margottini, C. (ed.): After the destruction of giant Buddha statues in Bamiyan (Afghanistan) in 2001: A UNESCO's emergency activity for the recovering and rehabilitation of cliff and niches. Springer, New York (2014)
9. Petzet, M. (ed.): The Giant Buddhas of Bamiyan. Safeguarding the Remains. Bäßler, Berlin (2009)
10. Ringbeck, B.: Management Plans for World Heritage Sites. A practical guide. German Commission for UNESCO, Bonn (2008)
11. Jansen, M.: Presentation of the Cultural Master Plan Bamiyan (Kabul, 31 July/Bamiyan, 2 August 2006). In: Petzet, M. (ed.) The Giant Buddhas of Bamiyan, pp. 123–124. Bäßler, Berlin (2009)
12. Mitchell, N.J., Rössler, M., Tricaud, P.-M. (eds.): World Heritage Cultural Landscapes: A Handbook for Conservation and Management. UNESCO World Heritage Centre, Paris (2009)
13. Toubekis, G., Ley, K., Jansen, M.: The Ghazni City wall restoration project: latest technology on remote sensing. In: From the Past and For the Future: Safeguarding the Cultural Heritage of Afghanistan; Jam and Herat, pp. 89–92. UNESCO, Pari (2015)

14. Toubekis, G., Mayer, I., Döring-Williams, M., Maeda, K., Yamauchi, K., Taniguchi, Y., Morimoto, S., Petzet, M., Jarke, M., Jansen, M.: Preservation and management of the UNESCO world heritage site of bamiyan: laser scan documentation and virtual reconstruction of the destroyed buddha figures and the archaeological remains. In: Stylianidis, E., Patias, P., Santana, M.Q. (eds.) CIPA Heritage documentation: best practise and applications; series 1, 2007 & 2009, pp. 93–100. CIPA (2011)

15. Toubekis, G., Jansen, M., Jarke, M.: Long-term preservation of the physical remains of the destroyed Buddha figures in Bamiyan (Afghanistan) using Virtual Reality technologies for preparation and evaluation of restoration measures. ISPRS Annals. Photogramm. Remote Sens. Spat. Inf. Sci. **IV-2/W2**, 271–278 (2017). https://doi.org/10.5194/isprs-annals-IV-2-W2-271-2017.

16. Canciani, M., Conigliaro, E., Del Grasso, M., Papalini, P., Saccone, M.: 3D Survey and Augmented Reality for Cultural Heritage. The Case Study of Aurelian Wall at Castra Praetoria in Rome. ISPRS - Int. Arch. Photogramm. Remote Sens. Spat. Inf. Sci. **XLI-B5**, 931–937 (2016). https://doi.org/10.5194/isprsarchives-XLI-B5-931-2016.

17. Forte, M.: Virtual Reality, Cyberarchaeology, Teleinmersive Archaeology. In: 3D Recording and Modelling in Archaeology and Cultural Heritage, pp. 115–129 (2014)

18. Pietroni, E.: Virtual Museums for Landscape Valorization and Communication. ISPRS - Archives. (2017). https://doi.org/10.5194/isprs-archives-XLII-2-W5-575-2017

19. ICOMOS ed: The Florence Declaration on Heritage and Landscape as Human Values (2014)

Monitoring Marine Areas
from the International Space Station: The Case
of the Submerged Harbor of Amathus

Daniele Cerra[1]([✉]), Peter Gege[1], Evagoras Evagorou[2,3], Athos Agapiou[2,3],
and Raquel de los Reyes[1]

[1] German Aerospace Center (DLR), Remote Sensing Technology Institute, Münchnerstr. 20,
82234 Weßling, Germany
daniele.cerra@dlr.de

[2] Remote Sensing and Geo-Environment Lab, Department of Civil Engineering and Geomatics,
Faculty of Engineering and Technology, Cyprus University of Technology,
Saripolou 2-8, 3036 Limassol, Cyprus

[3] Eratosthenes Centre of Excellence, Saripolou 2-8, 3036 Limassol, Cyprus

Abstract. The submerged harbor of Amathus in Cyprus is a sensitive cultural
heritage requiring special attention in the frame of Marine Spatial Planning. The
monitoring of water depth in the surrounding area can raise awareness on effects,
such as shoreline erosion, which could lead to a deterioration of the relics.

This paper assesses the quality of bathymetric maps around the site derived
from the DESIS hyperspectral sensor mounted on the International Space Station. The depth values are compared to products derived from traditional multispectral sensors, and assessed with LiDAR measurements acquired in situ. An
imaging spectrometer such as DESIS would be able to derive additional water
quality parameter such as phytoplankton concentration, assessing at the same
time eutrophication and pollution in this sensitive area.

Keywords: Bathymetry · Remote sensing · Imaging spectrometry · DESIS ·
Marine spatial planning · Cultural heritage · Amathus · Cyprus

1 Introduction

Marine Spatial Planning (MSP) is defined in the EU Directive (2014/89/EU) [1] as 'a
process by which the relevant Member State's authorities analyze and organize human
activities in marine areas to achieve ecological, economic and social objectives [2]. Various local, regional projects and initiatives are currently implemented at a European level.
The European MSP platform [3] summarizes these efforts made by several European
countries towards the implementation of the Directive. Among other EU MSP projects,
a cross-border cooperation program is currently running in Cyprus (more information
in [4]), aiming to better coordinate actions regarding the MSP policy.

In general, the MSP goal is to study and plan the use of the coastal and sea space
in line with societal goals, values and targets towards future sustainability. The MSP

M. Ioannides et al. (Eds.): EuroMed 2020, LNCS 12642, pp. 127–137, 2021.
https://doi.org/10.1007/978-3-030-73043-7_11

policy is not an easy task, rather a very complex one integrating land (coastal) and sea activities, taking into consideration the problems raised from the interaction of these activities, as well as future potentials and opportunities derived from these activities in the given economical and societal context of the country. In order to do this, minimum requirements are needed to identify the interactions of the various activities in the coastal and sea zones, as well as to identify and use available and updated data.

The role of Earth Observation sensors to support MSP policy has been already acknowledged in the past in several studies [5–7]. Satellite sensors are able to provide reliable and up to date information over large areas, covering in the same time land and sea, providing an important informative tool to local stakeholders and other interested parties. Among other activities, the historical and cultural aspects of an area should be taken into consideration during the design and implementation of an MSP policy. The role of Earth Observation sensors for heritage management has been highlighted in [8–10], providing information regarding the context of a site. A critical aspect of heritage managements refers to sites that are nowadays partially covered by water. Several examples can be found where archaeological sites, once established in the coast, are nowadays partially or fully covered by water due to sea level changes through the millennia [11, 12].

The utility of bathymetry maps derived from remote sensing analysis in the field of underwater archaeology is presented in [13] for the EU-funded project ITACA. Results on the prehistoric settlement at Metohi Greece, and analysis of the modern shipwreck Elphis I, place the archaeological sites in a spatial context of the surrounding underwater and surface features, and help in estimating anthropogenic hazards to the site.

In this paper, we study the ancient town of Amathus or Amathous, an important archaeological site situated on the south coast of the island of Cyprus, in close proximity to the modern town of Lemesos (Limassol). During the Archaic period the town acquired special wealth as one of the Kingdoms of Cyprus, and had remarkable commercial relations both with the Aegean and the Syropalestinian coast. The agora, baths and palace on the archaeological site attract a large number of visitors and tourists every year. Of special interest for this paper is the external port of the city, the ruins of which are preserved today under the sea [14].

Due to the proximity of the site to the modern town of Lemesos, as well as its location just a few meters from the coastline, with the ancient harbour now submerged, Amathous requires a special attention in the frame of the MSP implementation. In this paper we aim to showcase how new sensors can support such actions in better understanding the context of an archaeological site, even if this is partially submerged. In contrast to the use of very high resolution multispectral sensors, which have been widely used in the last years in the literature for monitoring archaeological sites [15, 16], this study uses data acquired from DESIS (DLR Earth Sensing Imaging Spectrometer), a recently launched hyperspectral sensor mounted on the International Space Station (ISS) [17]. An imaging spectrometer measures the reflected solar radiation for a target on ground across narrow and contiguous spectral bands, allowing identifying and characterizing Earth surface materials, such as minerals in rocks and soils, vegetation types and stress indicators, and water constituents.

This paper assesses the quality of bathymetric maps derived from the DESIS sensor around the Amathus Cultural Heritage site. We show how small variations in the water level covering the submerged harbor can be observed, along with spatial and temporal changes due to tidal activities and long term phenomena. Such information is important for the management of the site, as changes in the surroundings, such as shoreline erosion, may lead to the deterioration of the relics. The accuracy of the depth values is assessed by comparing them to LiDAR measurements acquired in situ. In addition, bathymetric maps are useful for the better understanding of the topography of the site as a whole, connecting thus the land and sea information; furthermore, these are necessary for shallow and underwater geophysical prospections, such as the application of electric resistivity, which may be carried out in the area in the future. These non-invasive remote sensing technologies can penetrate the seafloor, and indicate geophysical anomalies that can be linked with archaeological proxies.

Finally, the advantages of using an imaging spectrometer with respect to a multispectral sensor are demonstrated by comparing the depth values with bathymetrical maps derived from Sentinel-2 data. This is not the only application for which DESIS can outperform traditional multispectral sensors in coastal environments, of interest for MSP in critical sites such as Amathus: an imaging spectrometer would be able to yield several additional physical parameters, in order to help monitoring both water quality and vegetation and soil characterization in the area. These can greatly improve the characterization of submerged habitat compositions [18], the assessment of water quality [18], and the monitoring of environmental threats. Some examples will be shortly discussed in the conclusions to highlight the value of imaging spectrometry in the frame of MSP.

2 Batyhmetry Analysis

2.1 The DESIS Sensor

The DESIS sensor was installed on the Multi-User System for Earth Sensing (MUSES) platform of the ISS in 2018, and represents one of the few spaceborne sensors of this kind being operative in the last few years, especially after the decommissioning of the EO-Hyperion sensor on March 2017. Imaging spectrometry, also known as hyperspectral remote sensing, enables the quantification of chemical and physical parameters by a dense sampling of the solar electromagnetic energy reflected by the Earth's surface. DESIS operates in the spectral range from 400 and 1000 nm, with a spectral sampling distance of 2.55 nm and a Full Width Half Maximum (FWHM) of about 3.5 nm. The ground sampling distance is 30 m with 1024 pixels across track. For a comprehensive review of the data products, quality and validation of DESIS, the reader is remanded to [17].

Imaging spectroscopy represents a powerful tool for analysis and monitoring of sensitive marine areas, as water quality parameters such as concentration of phytoplankton and suspended matter can be reliably derived, along with bathymetrical maps in coastal areas, which are accurate up to a water depth in which the light reflected at sea floor is still detectable at the surface. The DESIS sensor can derive such parameters more accurately than multispectral sensors characterized by broad spectral bands with large gaps between them, with a decrease in spatial resolution as tradeoff. Nevertheless, the hindrances posed by the decrease in ground sampling distance can be mitigated by the use of spectral unmixing techniques, which allow performing analysis at sub-pixel level for specific applications such as target detection and constituents mapping.

2.2 Dataset

The ISS flies on a non-sun-synchronous orbit, with an inclination of 51.6° from west to east, approximately 400 km above the Earth surface. In the case of the island of Cyprus, around 40 acquisitions per year are possible with a sun elevation angle of 30° or larger, with acquisition possibilities well distributed along the year [20]. This number increases when taking into account the MUSES/DESIS tilting capabilities of 40°.

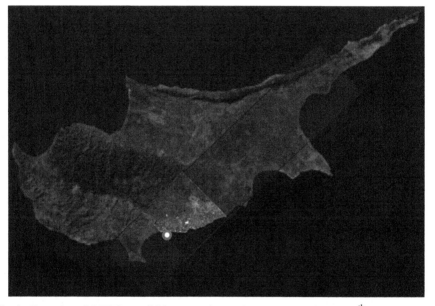

Fig. 1. Footprint of DESIS acquisition over the southern coast of Cyprus (9ᵗʰ of June 2020), covering most of the island's southern coast. A sample DESIS quicklook depicted as a true color combination for a single tile including the Amathus harbor is overlaid. The location of the submerged harbor is indicated by a blue circle. (Color figure online)

Given the inclined orbit of the ISS, a single DESIS acquisition, having an approximate width of 30 km, can cover most of the southern coast of Cyprus with a single pass (Fig. 1). In this paper, we analyse a DESIS image acquired over the southern coast of Cyprus on the 9ᵗʰ of June 2020 at 8:28 am local time. The image is acquired in rolling shutter mode, which acquires the spectral bands sequentially. The resulting spatial and spectral shifts in the acquisitions are compensated in the DESIS DLR ground segment processing chain, along with the usual geometric, radiometric and spectral corrections. The final output is in Bottom-of-atmosphere reflectance, corresponding to a Level 2A product.

A subset of the strip in Fig. 1 is analyzed. In the figure, the location of the submerged Amathus harbor is shown. A quicklook for a single DESIS tile is overlaid on the image in a true color combination (R: band 24 at 636 nm, G: band 16 at 554 nm, B: band 8 at 472 nm). The derived bathymetrical maps are compared to the ones generated from Sentinel-2 data. For this multispectral sensor, a cloud-free acquisition from the 13th of June 2017 is used, in the same period of the year as the DESIS acquisition. Validation is performed using a set of official water depth records.

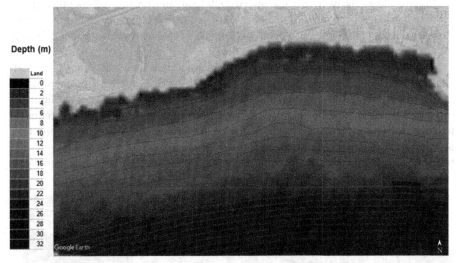

Fig. 2. Batyhmetrical map on the Amathus harbor area, derived from DESIS data, with overlaid contour lines of depth values measured in situ, depicted in black. The contour lines are spaced 2 m and are used to assess the results. Pixels depicted with the same color have a depth within a range of 2 m. For depths up to approximately 15 m, the estimated depth matches well the contour lines. The map is overlaid on an archive image on the site (Google Earth,© 2020 Maxar Technologies). (Color figure online)

2.3 DESIS-Derived Bathymetry

We used the 2D module [21] of the WAter color SImulator WASI [21, 23] for processing the DESIS data. WASI is a Windows-based software that is available free of charge [24]. By applying inverse modeling to the measured reflectance spectra, the water depth was derived for each DESIS pixel together with two further parameters that were assumed to vary across the image, i.e. the brightness of sand and the reflections at the water surface. The underlying algorithm is a physically based, so-called bio-optical model for shallow waters of Albert [25, 26]. The reflectance of the sea floor was approximated using an albedo spectrum of sand from the WASI data base, which was measured at the Baltic Sea. The reflections at the water surface were simulated using the three-component model of Gege [27] for the sky radiance that is reflected in the viewing direction. This model also compensates to some extent for errors from atmospheric correction. Because inverse modeling of DESIS pixels in adjacent deep water areas indicated very low concentrations of water constituents, the model parameters for the concentrations of phytoplankton, total suspended matter and colored dissolved organic matter were set to zero.

The derived water depths are validated by comparison with depth measurements carried out by the Department of Land Surveyors of Cyprus (DLS), the country's official cartographic provider. The dataset covers water depths up to 50 m and was collected in three phases, in 2012, 2014 and in 2018 using multi-beam echo sounders and airborne LiDAR. The horizontal and vertical accuracy of the data is ± 0.1 m and ± 0.5 m, respectively.

Figure 2 shows the bathymetrical map with the contour lines for water depth overlaid. The depth map has been mapped to a false color image in discrete intervals, with a color change indicating an increase in depth of 2 m. This depth interval is the same spacing the contour lines in the overlaid reference data.

A detail reported in Fig. 3 on the Amathus harbor area shows how the subtle variations around the harbor are captured by the DESIS-derived bathymetric map, which are smoothed out in the depth contour lines of the reference data set. This indicates that accurate maps could be obtained on the site, and the variations in depth accurately monitored, helping the management of the site by continuously observing long term phenomena such as shoreline erosion and changes in tidal effects. The DESIS-derived bathymetric map is shown in Fig. 4 for a larger area including the Amathus harbor site.

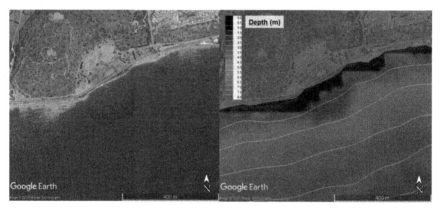

Fig. 3. Left: The submerged Amathus harbor, visible under water close to the coastline, and surroundings (Google Earth, © 2020 Maxar Technologies). Right: comparison of contour lines derived from in situ measurements and overlaid bathymetric map derived from DESIS data. Local variations around the harbor are lost in the contour lines.

As illustrative validation, a scatter plot comparing estimated and reference depth values is reported in Fig. 5. The locations of the points used for the validation are reported as circles in Fig. 4. In total, 37 points could be used for this purpose.

The plot confirms the reliability of the derived map, showing that the depth values derived from DESIS match very well the measured depth values in the area of interest.

2.4 Comparison with Sentinel-2 Analysis

In order to further compare the bathymetrical results of DESIS, we rely on a recent work by Evagorou et al. [28] which performs a multi-temporal analysis in the wider

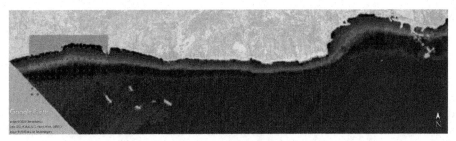

Fig. 4. Estimated depth values for a subset of the image depicted in Fig. 1 including the Amathus harbor. The black dots represent the locations of points where LiDAR depth measurements have been collected, which are used to assess the accuracy of the results (see Table 1 and Fig. 5). The area reported in Fig. 2 is highlighted on the left side of the image (ref. Legend therein). The map is overlaid on an archive image on the site (Google Earth, © 2020 Maxar Technologies).

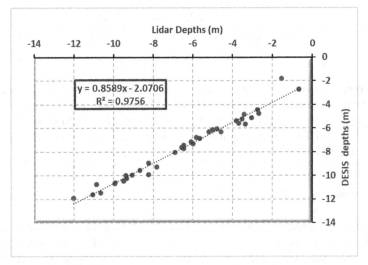

Fig. 5. Scatter plot of 37 depth values as measured in situ with LiDAR instruments vs. Values estimated from spaceborne DESIS data, up to a depth of 12 m.

area of Amathus using the Sentinel-2 sensor. More specifically, we use a bathymetrical map derived by applying the ratio transform algorithm on a Sentinel-2 image of Level 2A which includes radiometric, geometric, cloud masking, and atmospheric corrections, obtained through the Copernicus Hub, with a sensing period of the 13th of June 2017.

An offset and scaling were then applied using different factors to the two depth maps in order to find a best fit to the measured values, regarded as ground truth. Both sets of values fit the measured depths very well, with a correlation index (R^2) above 0.96 for the depth ranging from 0 to 12 m. The figure of merit for the comparison is the Root

Mean Squared Error, defined as.

$$RMSE(X, Y) = \sqrt{\frac{\sum_i (x_i - y_i)^2}{N}}, \tag{1}$$

where x_i and y_i represent the i-th estimated and reference depth value present in both data collections, respectively, and N the total number of comparable points. Results are summarized in Table 1.

Table 1. Comparison between depth values derived from DESIS and Sentinel-2 for the depth range from 0 to 12 m. The RMSE is computed with respect to the reported number of validation points available in the area, measured in situ with LiDAR instruments.

Sensor	Date	RMSE (m)	R^2
DESIS	09/06/2020	**0,41**	**0,98**
Sentinel-2	13/06/2017	0,72	0,96

The comparison of DESIS and Sentinel-2 shows that the former can produce more accurate bathymetrical results, in spite of the worse ground sampling distance characterizing the sensor (30 m of DESIS against 10 m of Sentinel-2). An RMSE value of 0.41 m was estimated for DESIS, resulting in an approximate twofold increase in accuracy with respect to Sentinel-2.

3   Conclusions

In this paper we assessed the capabilities of the DESIS imaging spectrometer mounted on the ISS to derive accurate bathymetric maps: the area of interest are the shallow waters in which the submerged harbor of Amathus lies, just outside the southern coast of the Cyprus area nearby Limassol. Results show that the bathymetric maps derived from the DESIS imaging spectrometer are quite accurate, with a Root Mean Squared Error below half a meter with respect to a series of approximately 40 points measured in situ with LiDAR instruments. The error approximately doubles when using instead traditional satellite data characterized by a higher spatial resolution and broader spectral bands, such as Sentinel-2.

The use of imaging spectrometer data on the site goes well beyond the production of bathymetric maps. The frequent possible acquisitions of the DESIS sensor can be employed to derive water quality parameters such as turbidity, and suspended and dissolved water constituents such as chlorophyll-a and Colored Dissolved Organic Matter (CDOM). In turn, these can help in estimating the phytoplankton concentration and assess eutrophication and pollution in this sensitive area.

Furthermore, the sensor would be optimal to map the distribution of Mediterranean seagrass meadows, such as the Posidonia Oceanica which is abundant in this area, and protected by legislation, among other conventions, also under the EU Habitat Directive

(92/43/CEE). This will be included in our future analysis on the site. At the same time, relevant soil and vegetation parameters could be derived for the emerged lands in a single acquisition, yielding a complete picture on the surroundings and the context of a site of interest. This highlights the important role that remote sensing can play in the frame of MSP, as this technology provides frequent, inexpensive and accurate information on large areas.

Acknowledgements. The authors would like to acknowledge the 'ECXELSIOR' H2020 Teaming project (www.excelsior2020.eu). This paper is under the auspices of the activities of the 'ERATOSTHENES: Excellence Research Centre for Earth Surveillance and Space-Based Monitoring of the Environment'—'EXCELSIOR' project that has received funding from the European Union's Horizon 2020 research and innovation programme under Grant Agreement No. 857510 and from the Government of the Republic of Cyprus through the Directorate General for the European Programmes, Coordination, and Development.

Part of this research was supported by the project entitled: "Cross-Border Cooperation for Implementation of Maritime Spatial Planning" referred as "THAL-CHOR 2" ("ΘΑΛ-ΧΩΡ 2" in Greek) and co-funded by the European Regional Development Fund (ERDF), under the Cross-Border Cooperation Programme "INTERREG V-A Greece-Cyprus 2014–2020". Also, acknowledgements are given to Department of the Land Survey of Cyprus, for providing soundings of bathymetry.

References

1. Directive 2014/89/EU of the European Parliament and of the Council of 23 July 2014, "Establishing a Framework for Maritime Spatial Planning". https://eur-lex.eur opa.eu/legal-content/EN/TXT/?uri=uriserv:OJ.L_2014.257.01.0135.01.ENG MSP Project Cyprus. https://www.msp-platform.eu/projects/cross-border-cooperation-maritime-spatial-planning-development. Accessed 11 Sep 2020
2. MSP Platform, https://www.msp-platform.eu/msp-eu/introduction-msp. Accessed 11 Sep 2020
3. MSP Projects. https://www.msp-platform.eu/msp-practice/msp-projects. Accessed 11 Sep 2020
4. MSP Project Cyprus. https://www.msp-platform.eu/projects/cross-border-cooperation-mar itime-spatial-planning-developmentAccessed 11 Sep 2020
5. Valentini, E., Filipponi, F., Nguyen Xuan, A., Passarelli, F.M., Taramelli, A.: Earth observation for maritime spatial planning: measuring, observing and modeling marine environment to assess potential aquaculture sites. Sustainability **8**, 519 (2016)
6. Ouellette, W., Getinet, W.: Remote sensing for marine spatial planning and integrated coastal areas management: achievements, challenges, opportunities and future prospects. Remote Sens. Appl. Soc. Environ. **4**, 138–157 (2016). ISSN 2352–9385, https://doi.org/10.1016/j.rsase.2016.07.003.
7. Hadjimitsis, D., et al.: Maritime spatial planning in cyprus. Open Geosci. **8**(1), 653–661 (2016). https://doi.org/10.1515/geo-2016-0061
8. Agapiou, A., Lysandrou, V., Hadjimitsis, D.G.: The Cyprus coastal heritage landscapes within Marine Spatial Planning process. J. Cult. Herit. **23**, 28–36 (2017). https://doi.org/10.1016/j.culher.2016.02.01
9. Agapiou, A., Lysandrou, V., Hadjimitsis, D.G.: Earth observation contribution to cultural heritage disaster risk management: case study of eastern mediterranean open air archaeological monuments and sites. Remote Sens. **12**, 1330 (2020)

10. Cerra, D., Plank, S., Lysandrou, V., Tian, J.: Cultural heritage sites in danger—towards automatic damage detection from space. Remote Sens. **8**, 781 (2016)
11. Mogstad, A.A., et al.: Mapping the historical shipwreck figaro in the high arctic using underwater sensor-carrying robots. Remote Sens. **12**, 997 (2020)
12. Guyot, A., et al.: Airborne hyperspectral imaging for submerged archaeological mapping in shallow water environments. Remote Sens. **11**, 2237 (2019)
13. Guzinski, R., Spondylis, E., Michalis, M., Tusa, S., Brancato, G., Minno, L., Hansen, L.: Exploring the Utility of Bathymetry Maps Derived With Multispectral Satellite Observations in the Field of Underwater Archaeology, Open Archaeology **2**(1) (2016). https://doi.org/10.1515/opar-2016-0018
14. Amathous, Department of Antiquities. https://www.mcw.gov.cy/mcw/DA/DA.nsf/All/D20ED526826AB796C225719B00374A92Accessed 11th Sept 2020
15. Masini, N., Lasaponara, R.: Sensing the past from space: approaches to site detection. In: Masini, N., Soldovieri, F. (eds.) Sensing the Past. From Artifact to Historical Site. Springer, Dordrecht, The Netherlands, pp. 23–60 (2017)
16. Luo, L., Wang, X., Guo, H., Lasaponara, R., Zong, X., Masini, N., Wang, G., Shi, P., Khatteli, H., Fulong, C., et al.: Airborne and spaceborne remote sensing for archaeological and cultural heritage applications: A review of the century (1907–2017). Remote Sens. Environ. **232**, 111280 (2019)
17. Alonso, K., Bachmann, M., Burch, K., Carmona, E., Cerra, D., de los Reyes, R., Dietrich, D., Heiden, U., Hölderlin, A., Ickes, J., Knodt, U., Krutz, D., Lester, H., Müller, R., Pagnutti, M., Reinartz, P., Richter, R., Ryan, R., Sebastian, I., Tegler, M.: Data Products, Quality and Validation of the DLR Earth Sensing Imaging Spectrometer (DESIS). Sensors **19**, 4471 (2019)
18. Pinnel, N.: A Method for Mapping Submerged Macrophytes in Lakes Using Hyperspectral Remote Sensing. Ph.D. thesis, Technische Universität München, München, Germany (2007)
19. Hestir, E.L., et al.: Measuring freshwater aquatic ecosystems: the need for a hyperspectral global mapping satellite mission. Remote Sens. Environ. **167**, 181–195 (2015)
20. Huemmrich, F., Campbell, P., Gao, B., Flanagan, B., Goulden, M.: ISS as a platform for optical remote sensing of ecosystem carbon fluxes: a case study using HICO. IEEE J. Sel. Top. Appl. Earth Observations Remote Sens, 16 (2017). https://doi.org/10.1109/JSTARS.2017.2725825.
21. Gege, P.: WASI-2D: a software tool for regionally optimized analysis of imaging spectrometer data from deep and shallow waters. Comput. Geosci. **62**, 208–215 (2014). https://doi.org/10.1016/j.cageo.2013.07.022
22. Gege, P. The water colour simulator WASI: An integrating software tool for analysis and simulation of optical in-situ spectra. Comput. Geosci. **30**, 523–532 (2004)
23. Gege, P., Albert, A.: A tool for inverse modeling of spectral measurements in deep and shallow waters. In: Richardson, L.L., LeDrew, E.F. (eds.) Remote Sensing of Aquatic Coastal Ecosystem Processes: Science and Management Applications. Kluwer book series: Remote Sensing and Digital Image Processing, 2006, pp. 81-109. Springer (2006). ISBN 1-4020-3967-0
24. Gege, P. WASI (Water Colour Simulator). (2020) https://www.ioccg.org/data/software.html. Accessed 24 Sept 2020
25. Albert, A., Mobley, C.D.: An analytical model for subsurface irradiance and remote sensing reflectance in deep and shallow case-2 waters. Opt. Express **11**, 2873–2890 (2003)
26. Albert, A.: Inversion Technique for Optical Remote Sensing in Shallow Water, Ph.D. thesis, University of Hamburg, Hamburg, Germany (2004)

27. Gege, P.: Analytic model for the direct and diffuse components of downwelling spectral irradiance in water. Appl. Opt. **51**, 1407–1419 (2012). https://doi.org/10.1364/AO.51.001407
28. Evagorou, E., Mettas, C., Agapiou, A., Themistocleous, K., Hadjimitsis, D.: Bathymetric maps from multi-temporal analysis of Sentinel-2 data: the case study of Limassol, Cyprus. Adv. Geosci. **45**(1988), 397–407 (2019). https://doi.org/10.5194/adgeo-45-397-2019

A GIS and Remote Sensing Approach for Desertification Sensitivity Assessment of Cultural Landscape in Apulia Region (Italy)

Mattia Previtali[(⊠)] ⓘ

Department of Architecture, Built Environment and Construction Engineering (ABC),
Politecnico di Milano, Via Ponzio 31, 20133 Milan, Italy
mattia.previtali@polimi.it

Abstract. Climate change is posing new challenges to cultural landscapes. Indeed, rapid climate modifications can significantly interfere with the link existing between natural and man work, typical of cultural landscapes. This problem is even more fundamental for areas characterized by accelerated climatic changes, like the Mediterranean one. For those regions the definition of a proper methodology for sensitivity evaluation to land degradation is a key element to promote new conservation/valorization strategies and policies. This work presents a new methodology integrating GIS and Remote Sensing with environmental models to simulate land degradation processes and to provide a comprehensive index (Integrated Desertification Index, IDI) of desertification for the Apulia region in Southern Italy. After an extensive analysis of both the conditions and the evolution of natural features in the study area, through spatial data investigation, a set of appropriate indicators of land degradation have been identified on the basis of their applicability and sensitivity to environmental processes. The following five indicators were considered: overgrazing pressure, drought pressure, water erosion, vegetation condition and soil salinity. To evaluate them both existing Open GIS and statistical data, as well as Remote Sensing images have been combined into a unique indicator to evaluate the most vulnerable areas to land degradation in the Apulia region.

Keywords: GIS · Integrated desertification index · Land erosion · Land degradation

1 Introduction

The concept of "Cultural landscape", defined by the UNESCO [1] as the "cultural properties [that] represent the combined works of nature and of man [that] are illustrative of the evolution of human society and settlement over time, under the influence of the physical constraints and/or opportunities presented by their natural environment and of successive social, economic and cultural forces, both external and internal", is revolutionizing the concept of cultural and natural heritage as the combination of both natural and human factors, as well as tangible and intangible values. In that sense, due to the

© Springer Nature Switzerland AG 2021
M. Ioannides et al. (Eds.): EuroMed 2020, LNCS 12642, pp. 138–149, 2021.
https://doi.org/10.1007/978-3-030-73043-7_12

mutual interaction existing between natural and man action, threads to natural elements are significantly affecting the cultural landscape as a whole, suddenly becoming threats also for tangible and intangible values (e.g., cultivation practices, social values, etc.).

Due to this strict connection between natural elements and human factors, global warming and climate change phenomena are a major threats for cultural landscapes all over the world [2]. Indeed, changes connected to climate change are significantly altering the relationship with natural elements in a way, and with a velocity, that has never experienced before. For this reason, areas that are characterized by rapid changes due to climate change are also the ones experiencing the highest stress to cultural landscapes.

In particular, most of arid and semi-arid Mediterranean areas are affected by land degradation and desertification phenomena and the strong connection existing in this areas between natural/cultivated environment and man work has the risk of being lost. For example, more than 1/5 of the Italian territory is at risk of desertification involving over 40% of the South. Critical areas, amounting to 9.1% of the country surface, are mainly localized in Sardegna, Sicilia, Puglia, Basilicata and Calabria regions, where environmental conditions are more unfavorable and agriculture and grazing activities strongly affect the territory settings [3]. Taking into consideration these factors, it is evident the need of a careful selection of key-variables and indicators that should describe the current state of the system, highlight the degradation processes and related effects. Mapping the more vulnerable areas is of primary importance for defining adequate mitigation measures.

The Apulia region, in Southern Italy is a typical example of a very diversified Mediterranean cultural landscape. In fact, the Salento region is characterized by typical farmhouses, oil mills, old aquaculture systems and olive groves with centuries-old olive trees. In province of Taranto, the so called "Gravina system" is characterized by an important concentration of rock-cut settlements as well as archaeological sites. In addition, natural wealth and karst phenomena are creating a peculiar landscape [4]. Climate change and land degradation is significantly threating this cultural landscape and the need of specific tools for evaluating desertification sensitivity is fundamental for definition of proper policies and management practices.

This paper presents a new methodology integrating GIS and Remote Sensing with environmental models to simulate land degradation processes and to provide a comprehensive index (Integrated Desertification Index, IDI) of desertification. After an extensive analysis of both the conditions and the evolution of natural features in the study area a set of appropriate indicators of land degradation has been identified on the basis of their applicability and sensitivity to environmental processes. The following five indicators were considered: overgrazing pressure, drought pressure, water erosion, vegetation condition and soil salinity. This research will study the five indicator models of the IDI model, and finally synthesize a map of land desertification through the Apulia Region.

2 Related Work

Given the multi-faceted and multi-disciplinary aspects of desertification, the interest of political institutions and research communities has supported the development of different methods of analysis. The Environmentally Sensitive Areas (ESAs) approach, developed within the framework of MEDALUS projects and financed by the European Commission from 1991 to 1999, has become one of the most used methodologies to monitor land sensitivity to degradation and desertification all over the world [5, 6]. Evan if this method has been efficiently adopted in different researches it is taking into consideration a set of parameters that may not be the one influencing desertification and land degradation phenomena in the study area.

It is also important to mention other significative models for assessment of desertification or land degradation, GLASOD [7], and recently LADA [8].

The Global Assessment of Human-induced Soil Degradation (GLASOD) [7] was the first global evaluation of soil degradation. Despite its known limitations, it remains an impressive evaluation, and it has been the most influential global appraisal of land quality in terms of environmental policy. However, its expert judgments were never tested for their consistency and could not be reproduced at unvisited sites, while the relationship between the GLASOD assessments of land degradation and the social and economic impact of that degradation remains unclear [9]. GLASOD in fact was limited to soil degradation assessment and did not include degradation of the full land resource in its climate, vegetation and water resources aspects.

LADA has been set up by FAO, UNEP-GEF and various other partners to assess land degradation in dryland areas [8]. The LADA project used indicators obtained through traditional data collection and remote sensing, set in the larger context of the Driving Forces – Pressures – States – Impacts – Responses (DPSIR) framework, with the need for stratification, interpretation and monitoring. Main objective of the LADA project was developing tools and methods to assess and quantify the nature, extent, severity and impacts of land degradation on ecosystems, watersheds and river basins, and carbon storage in drylands. The LADA approach has only been used in the LADA project context, with few applications in the current literature, pointing out the problems occurring in adapting this methodology for the assessment of soil erosion process at a local scale [10].

The method presented in this paper is taking inspiration form the LADA concept identifying the driving forces and pressures that can influence the desertification and land degradation phenomena in the Apulia Region. The identification and the selection of the affecting parameters was carried out making an in-depth analysis of the study area and by identifying the main pressures working on it as well as the main ongoing phenomena (e.g., land degradation and land productivity loss, overgrazing, etc.) that can determine desertification vulnerability. The different parameters have been evaluated by using available Open GIS Data provided by the local and national PAs within their Geoportal, as well as European datasets. For the evaluation of the vegetation and salinity Remote Sensing data have been used by processing Sentinel-2 data over the study area.

3 Study Area and Method Overview

3.1 Study Area

Apulia (Fig. 1) is an Italian region of approximately 4 million inhabitants, with capital Bari. It borders to the north-west with Molise and to the west with Campania and Basilicata and is bathed by the Adriatic Sea to the east and north and the Ionian Sea to the south. Its territory is flat for 53%, hilly for 45% and mountainous for only 2% which makes it the least mountainous region of Italy. Throughout the Apulia the climate is typically Mediterranean: coastal and low-lying areas have summers hot, windy and dry and winters mild, are not rare snowfall in the plains. The temperature variations between summer and winter are very noticeable in the internal plains: in the Tavoliere you can go from over 40° C in summer to −3° C/−4° C in winter mornings.

Fig. 1. Study area-Puglia region with municipality highlighted.

3.2 Desertification Sensitivity Assessment with a Comprehensive Methodology

In the Puglia region, land degradation is caused by a series of complex processes that can be attributed to: overgrazing, climate variability, water erosion, vegetation degradation, soil degradation. To take into account that complex set of phenomena a methodology has been developed (see Fig. 2) to study them separately first and then combining them into a unique indicator. In this way an overall evaluation to sensitivity to desertification is provided.

Overgrazing was studied considering the CAIA model [11] that takes into consideration the pressure of different livestock into a specified areas normalized to a standard Fully-Grown Unit. This pressure is then considered with respect a specified reference area. Information about the livestock in Apulia are available at municipal level and are classified according to the specific livestock unit (e.g., cows, sheep and goats, pigs and poultry).

Drought was studied by using the Reconnaissance Drought Index (RDI) [12] evaluated in the study area taking into consideration average monthly temperatures and precipitation evaluated in a period of time ranging from 2009–2019. Punctual information concerning precipitation and temperatures were derived from the climatologic station network of the region and their spatialization over the entire region was carried out by using Kriging interpolation [13].

Soil degradation due to water erosion was evaluated taking into consideration the RUSLE [14] methodology and by using the dataset provided by the European Union of the RUSLE indicator in Europe.

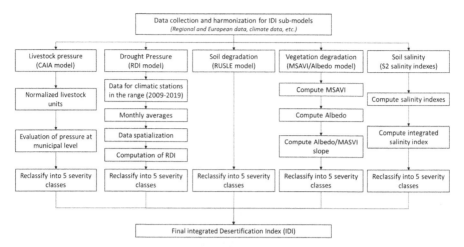

Fig. 2. Flowchart representing the scheme followed to implement IDI method.

Vegetation degradation was quantified by using the approach presented by Wu et al. [15] for the evaluation of areas characterized by high stress in vegetation by adopting an approach based on the evaluation of Albedo and MSAVI starting from Remote Sensing data. However, in contrast to the approach followed in [15] Sentinel-2 data were used for the evaluation.

Soil salinity was modeled using indexes derived from Sentinel-2 data of the area [16].

The different parameters were then reclassified into 5 severity classes which were finally combined into a unique Integrated Desertification Index (IDI) to provide a sensitivity map for the entire region.

4   Computation of the Integrated Desertification Index (IDI)

This section presents the different parameters taking into consideration a specific pressure in the Apulia Region, used for the computation of the Integrated Desertification Index (IDI).

4.1   Overgrazing Pressure

Overgrazing is one of the main factors of land degradation observed in the Mediterranean region. In Puglia, an excessive livestock pressure affects the lands by compacting the soil and reducing the vegetation cover, both of which lead to decreased soil structure and stability. The model CAIA [11] formulates the land degradation as a function of grazing intensity and land carrying capacity. Effect connected with grazing pressure can be evaluated from 20 sub-coefficients, measuring animal (bovine, ovine and sheep) vegetation consumption and trampling on soil, animal productivity (low, medium or high productive level) and grazing management (extensive or intensive). CAIA could be calculated as:

$$CAIA = \frac{b_1X_1n_1 + b_2X_2n_2 + b_3X_3n_3}{S} * \frac{1}{500} \qquad (1)$$

where X is the weight of a fully grown unit; n is the number of the unit on the territory; b is a matrix of the twenty sub-coefficients; S is the total surface area (in Ha). The sum of these sub-coefficients identifies the b coefficient which represents a weighing factor for the live weight X of the Fully-Grown Unit (FGU) of a given species present in a territory with surface area S. For the Apulia region livestock information are available at municipal level for which the CAIA index has been computed and categorized in 5 classes of overgrazing severity (Fig. 3).

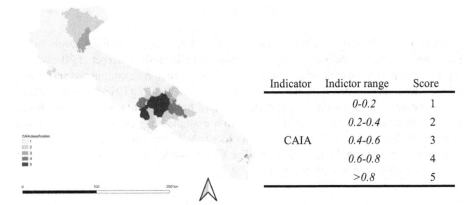

Indicator	Indictor range	Score
	0-0.2	1
	0.2-0.4	2
CAIA	*0.4-0.6*	3
	0.6-0.8	4
	>0.8	5

Fig. 3. Spatial distribution of CAIA index.

4.2 Drought Pressure

The Reconnaissance Drought Index (RDI) can be characterized as a general meteorological index for drought assessment. The RDI can be expressed in three forms: the initial value a_k, the normalized RDI (RDI$_n$), and the standardized RDI (RDI$_{st}$).

The initial value (a_k) is presented in an aggregated form using a monthly time step and may be calculated on monthly, seasonal or annual basis. The a_k, for the year i and a time basis k (months) is calculated as:

$$a_k^{(i)} = \frac{\sum_{j=1}^{k} P_{ij}}{\sum_{j-1}^{k} PET_{ij}}, i = 1\ to\ N\ and\ j = 1\ to\ 12 \qquad (2)$$

where P_{ij} and PET_{ij} are the precipitation and the potential evapotranspiration of month j of year i and N is the total number of years of the available data. To calculate the PET, the Thornthwaite equation [17] is used:

$$PET = 16\left(\frac{L}{12}\right)\left(\frac{N}{30}\right)\left(\frac{10T_d}{I}\right)^{\alpha} \qquad (3)$$

Where T_d is the average daily temperature of the month being calculated; N is the number of days in the month being calculated; L is the average day length (hours) of the month being calculated as:

$$\alpha = \left(6.75 * 10^{-7}\right)I^3 - \left(7.71 * 10^{-5}\right)I^2 + \left(1.792 * 10^{-2}\right)I + 0.49239 \qquad (4)$$

$$I = \sum_{i=1}^{12} \left(\frac{T_{mi}}{5}\right)^{1.514} \qquad (5)$$

Where I is a heat index which depends on the 12 monthly mean temperature T_{mi}.

The initial formulation of RDI_{st} used the assumption that a_k values follow a lognormal distribution and RDI_{st} is calculated as:

$$RDI_{st}^{(i)} = \frac{y^{(i)} - \bar{y}}{\vartheta_y} \qquad (6)$$

in which y is the $\ln(a(i))$, $\bar{y}$ is its arithmetic mean and ϑ_y is its standard deviation. In the presented case the temperature and precipitation were derived from a set of 30 climatologic station present in the territory of Apulia. In ordered to have a continuous set of data all over the area, punctual information were interpolated by using Kriging interpolation. In the presented analysis computation of the RDI_{st} has taken into consideration using average monthly temperatures and precipitation evaluated in a period of time ranging from 2009–2019. This choice was made in order to take into consideration the average situation of drought in the last 10 years. The final classification of RDI in 5 classes of drought severity is presented in Fig. 4.

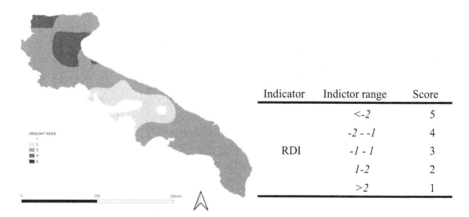

Indicator	Indictor range	Score
	<-2	5
	-2 - -1	4
RDI	-1 - 1	3
	1-2	2
	>2	1

Fig. 4. Spatial distribution of drought index.

4.3 Water Erosion

The Revised Universal Soil Loss Equation (RUSLE) [14] was chosen because it is widely used for scientific studies, as applied and verified for different landscape scenarios, even in very complex topographies. In this model, each variable influencing erosion is associated to an index representing the effect of the variable on erosion according to the magnitude of the specific index.

RUSLE is expressed as follows:

$$A = R*K*LS*C*P \tag{7}$$

Where A is the computed soil loss per unit area, R is the rainfall-runoff factor, K is the soil erodibility factor, LS (unitless) is the slope length/steepness factor, C (unitless) is the soil cover and management factor and P (unitless) is the support practice factor, accounting for the management of protection of soil against erosion. In this work the RUSLE dataset provide by EUROPEAN SOIL DATA CENTRE (ESDAC) was used and reclassified into 5 classes of water erosion severity (Fig. 5).

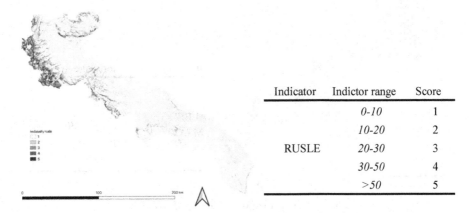

Indicator	Indictor range	Score
	0-10	1
	10-20	2
RUSLE	*20-30*	3
	30-50	4
	>50	5

Fig. 5. Spatial distribution of RUSLE index.

4.4 Vegetation Condition: Albedo-MSAVI

The Puglia region has a large diversity of vegetation cover across various regions and seasons. Within this semi-arid region, it is difficult to distinguish desertified land from other land cover types using low-quality vegetation information. Research shows that the Albedo-MSAVI model is suitable for assessment of areas with relatively low vegetation cover. The formula for MSAVI is as follows:

$$MSAVI = \frac{2*NIR+1-\sqrt{(2*NIR+1)^2-8(NIR-RED)}}{2} \tag{8}$$

where NIR is near infrared band and RED is red band.

The formula for albedo computation by using Sentinel 2 image is as follows:

$$Albedo = 0.356*BLUE + 0.13*RED + 0.373*NIR + 0.085*SWIR1 + 0.072*SWIR2 - 0.0018(9) \tag{9}$$

The computation of both MSAVI and Albedo for the presented area was carried out by using a set of Sentinel-2 images collected in the period July/August 2019.

According to the research conclusions made by Wu et al. [15], different desertification lands can be effectively separated by dividing the Albedo-MSAVI feature space in the vertical direction into changing trends of desertification. In addition, the location of the vertical direction in Albedo-MSAVI feature space can be well fitted by a simple binary linear polynomial expression as follows:

$$DDI = K \times MSAVI - Albedo \tag{10}$$

where "DDI" was the desertification divided index and K was determined by the slope of the straight line fitted in the feature space. Figure 6 shows the spatial distribution of the Albedo-MSAVI reclassified into five classes of vegetation condition.

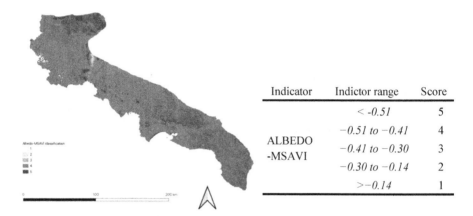

Indicator	Indictor range	Score
	< -0.51	5
	-0.51 to -0.41	4
ALBEDO -MSAVI	-0.41 to -0.30	3
	-0.30 to -0.14	2
	> -0.14	1

Fig. 6. Spatial distribution of Albedo-MSAVI index.

4.5 Soil Salinity

Salinity is one of the most important factors affecting soil degradation and desertification is caused by natural or human-induced processes. Sentinel 2 satellite images are used to calculate the Soil Salinity Index (SI). In particular, four salinity index according to different band are chosen to calculate the final salinity map.

$$SI1 = \sqrt{B * R} \tag{11}$$

$$SI2 = \sqrt{G * R} \tag{12}$$

$$SI3 = \sqrt{G^2 + R^2 + NIR^2} \tag{13}$$

$$SI4 = \sqrt{G^2 + NIR^2} \tag{14}$$

The comprehensive salinity equation is:

$$SI = \sqrt{SI1 * SI2 * SI3 * SI4} \tag{15}$$

The final salinity map was reclassified into five severity classes (Fig. 7).

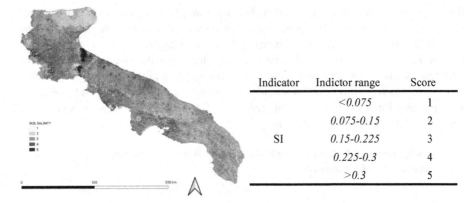

Indicator	Indictor range	Score
	<0.075	1
	0.075-0.15	2
SI	*0.15-0.225*	3
	0.225-0.3	4
	>0.3	5

Fig. 7. Spatial distribution of soil salinity index.

4.6 Integrated Desertification Index (IDI)

Starting from the previously computed parameters, each one classified into 5 class of severity are combined into a unique final indicator named Integrated Desertification Index (IDI) by using the following formula:

$$IDI = (CAIA * RDI * RUSLE * Albedo|MSAVI * SI)^{1/5} \qquad (16)$$

The final indicator presents 5 classes of desertification sensibility (Fig. 8).

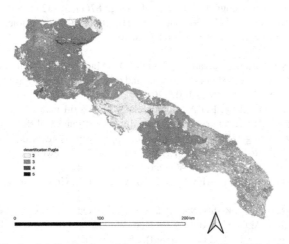

Fig. 8. Spatial distribution of desertification sensibility (IDI) in Puglia

5 Discussions and Conclusions

Climate change is a pressure that can significantly threaten cultural landscapes in the Mediterranean area. The availability of systems for identification of vulnerable areas and the development of monitoring systems become fundamental to develop new policies and management systems. This paper presented a new methodology, integrating GIS and Remote Sensing, to evaluate land sensitivity degradation and desertification through the definition of a comprehensive index, named Integrated Desertification Index (IDI) taking into consideration five indicators considering overgrazing pressure, drought pressure, water erosion, vegetation condition and soil salinity. In future works results obtained with presented method will be compared with ESA-MEDALUS ones to evaluate the accuracy of the developed methodology.

Acknowledgements. I'd like to acknowledge Mengdie Wang for preparing the maps presented in this paper as part of her internship.

References

1. UNESCO. Operational Guidelines for the Implementation of the World Heritage Convention. UNESCO World Heritage Centre. Paris (2012)
2. Sabboni, C., Cassar, M., Brimblecombe, P., Tidblad, J., Kozlowski, R., Drdacky, M., et al.: Global climate change impact on building heritage and cultural landscapes. In: de Buergo, A., Heras, G., Calvo, V. (eds.) Heritage, Weathering and Conservation - Fort (2006)
3. Salvati, L., De Angelis, A., Bajocco, S., Ferrara, A., Barone, P.M.: Desertification risk, long-term land-use changes and environmental resilience: a case study in Basilicata. Italy Scott. Geogr. J. **129**(2), 85–99 (2013)
4. Mørch, H.: Rural landscapes in Puglia—on the functional relationship between agriculture and natural resources. Geogr. Tidsskr.-Dan. J. Geogr. **87**(1), 36–42 (1987)
5. Kosmas, C., Danalatos, N.G., Gerontidis, S.: The effect of land parameters on vegetation performance and degree of erosion under Mediterranean conditions. Catena **40**(1), 3–17 (2000)
6. Ferrara, A., Kosmas, C., Salvati, L., Padula, A., Mancino, G., Nolè, A.: Updating the MEDALUS-ESA framework for worldwide land degradation and desertification assessment. Land Degrad. Dev. **31**(12), 1593–1607 (2020)
7. Oldeman, L.R., Hakkeling, R.T.A., Sombroek, W.G.: World map of the status of human-induced soil degradation: an explanatory note. In: International Soil Reference and Information Centre, Wageningen, UNEP, Nairobi, vol. 27, p. +3 maps, revised edition (1991)
8. Ponce-Hernandez, R., Koohafkan, P.: Methodological framework for land degradation assessment in Drylands (LADA). FAO report: Rome (2004)
9. Sonneveld, B.G., Dent, D.L.: How good is GLASOD? J. Environ. Manage. **90**(1), 274–283 (2009)
10. Slavko, V.D., Kust, G.S., Rozov, S.Y., Andreeva, O.V., Kegiyan, M.G.: Experience in testing and adapting the LADA methodology for land degradation assessment and mapping in arid regions at the local level. Arid Ecosyst. **4**(4), 259–269 (2014)
11. Pulina, G., Zucca, C.: Un nuovo indicatore territoriale per la valutazione dell'impatto del pascolamento. Informatore Agrario **55**, 105–110 (1999)
12. Tsakiris, G., Pangalou, D., Vangelis, H.: Regional drought assessment based on the Reconnaissance Drought Index (RDI). Water Resour. Manag. **21**(5), 821–833 (2007)
13. Trochu, F.: A contouring program based on dual kriging interpolation. Eng. Comput. **9**(3), 160–177 (1993)
14. Renard, K.G.: Predicting soil erosion by water: a guide to conservation planning with the Revised Universal Soil Loss Equation (RUSLE). United States Government Printing (1997)

15. Wu, Z., Lei, S., Bian, Z., Huang, J., Zhang, Y.: Study of the desertification index based on the albedo-MSAVI feature space for semi-arid steppe region. Environ. Earth Sci. **78**(6), 232 (2019)
16. Taghadosi, M.M., Hasanlou, M., Eftekhari, K.: Retrieval of soil salinity from Sentinel-2 multispectral imagery. Eur. J. Remote Sens. **52**(1), 138–154 (2019)
17. Thornthwaite, C.W.: An approach toward a rational classification of climate. Geogr. Rev. **38**(1), 55–94 (1948)

'EXCELSIOR' H2020 Widespread Teaming Phase 2 Project: Earth Observation and Geoinformatics Research and Innovation Agenda for Cultural Heritage

Diofantos Hadjimitsis[1,2]([✉]) [iD], Georgios Leventis[1,2], Daniele Cerra[3],
Kyriacos Themistocleous[1,2], Phaedon Kyriakidis[1,2], Athos Agapiou[1,2],
Despina Makri[1,2], Nikoletta Papageorgiou[1,2], Chris Danezis[1,2], Vasiliki Lysandrou[1,2],
Marios Tzouvaras[1,2], Christodoulos Mettas[1,2], Evagoras Evagorou[1,2],
Nicholas Kyriakides[1,2], Evangelos Akylas[1,2], Silas Michaelides[1,2], Gunter Schreier[4],
Thomas Krauss[3], Haris Kontoes[5], and Georgios Komodromos[6]

[1] Department of Civil Engineering and Geomatics, Faculty of Engineering and Technology,
Cyprus University of Technology, Limassol, Cyprus
[2] ERATOSTHENES Centre of Excellence, Limassol, Cyprus
d.hadjimitsis@cut.ac.cy
[3] German Aerospace Center, Remote Sensing Technology Institute,
Oberpfaffenhofen, Weßling, Germany
[4] German Aerospace Center, German Remote Sensing Data Center, Oberpfaffenhofen, Germany
[5] National Observatory of Athens, Beyond Centre of Excellence, Athens, Greece
[6] Department of Electronic Communications, Deputy Ministry of Research,
Innovation and Digital Policy, Cyprus Government, Nicosia, Cyprus

Abstract. This paper presents how the EXSELSIOR H2020 Teaming project will support the management and monitoring of the cultural heritage domain through its research and innovation agenda within the Eastern Mediterranean, Middle East, and North Africa (region known as EMMENA). The pressing need for protecting the cultural heritage assets is highlighted throughout the document by reviewing the conducted research work in key funded projects attained in the past by the Cyprus University of Technology team in collaboration with EXCELSIOR's partners.

Keywords: EXCELSIOR · Geoinformatics · Earth observation · Cultural heritage

1 Introduction

The study of human activity has always been an important and challenging task for the experts of the field in understanding the past and the bonds tied upon a civilization's origins. Archaeology is heavenly dependent on surveying, excavating and data collection for the archaeologists and researchers to acquire a glimpse at their ancestor's way

© Springer Nature Switzerland AG 2021
M. Ioannides et al. (Eds.): EuroMed 2020, LNCS 12642, pp. 150–161, 2021.
https://doi.org/10.1007/978-3-030-73043-7_13

of living, while several-from time to time- hypotheses build the conceptual framework behind. Such hypotheses are usually validated through the discovery of possible patterns derived from the analysis of in-situ findings during the excavation process. Due to excavations being considered invasive techniques causing severe deteriorations of ancestral findings, modern archaeology has shifted towards a more sustainable approach ([1, 2]), where non-invasive techniques (e.g. surface survey, limited test excavation, GIS, Remote Sensing, LiDAR, etc.) are used to study and better analyse the human past. An exponential increase was observed during the last decades in the use of Geoinformatics and, more specifically, in leveraging the advances in Spatial Analysis (SA) and Remote Sensing (RS) within the field of archaeology, where several geospatial tools (GIS, Satellite images were considered valuable for the collection, integration and management of spatial data ([3]) thus offering a representational approach to the study of the past. However according to ([4]) the past should not be interpreted in a static and definitive way but instead be regarded as a dynamically changed constant that affects both the present and the future, hence it is transforming from a social and theoretical science to a more spatially-aware ([5]), where-among others- performing exploratory spatial data analysis (ESDA) one may discover meaningful trends/patterns ([6]).

1.1 Cultural Heritage Within EMMENA Region

Eastern Mediterranean, Middle East, and North Africa (known as EMMENA) is a broad geographical area spanning in 3 continents (Europe, Asia, and Africa). Not only does the region has a high strategic importance for political and military forces, but also archaeological and cultural significance due to the vast amount of cultural wealth, as a result of being an important crossroad in archaic times for several civilizations [7]. Monuments, burial places, artefacts, etc. are remnants from another era to remind us that once civilizations prospered and declined during several periods of the archaic history in the region. As the region is strategically well-placed, many war conflicts have taken place resulting to severe and catastrophic consequences at its archaeological sites, with most recent example being the war atrocities in Palmyra's ancient city that eventually led to its destruction.

In an attempt to raise awareness and protect at a global scale the cultural and natural heritage sites, the United Nations Educational, Scientific and Cultural Organization (UNESCO) adopted in 1972 an international treaty called "Convention concerning the Protection of the World Cultural and Natural Heritage" [8], defining what the terms "Cultural Heritage" and "Natural Heritage" encapsulate, along with the nomination process that is being followed for the cultural heritage properties. Adopting such treaty, UNESCO demarcates the sites as protected areas by granting them international recognition and legal protection, while governments and administrative authorities may request to obtain the necessary funding aid to ensure their integrity in time. Towards that end, UNESCO developed an interactive map (available on http://whc.unesco.org/en/list) that depicts the sites of great cultural and natural importance (Fig. 1) enriched with additional information (map, images, documents, etc.), and indicating which of these are endangered (Fig. 2) in order for immediate conservation actions to be taken by the involved stakeholders and the scientific community.

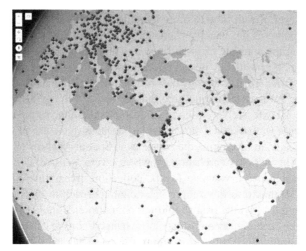

Fig. 1. UNESCO Cultural Heritage Sites in EMMENA region. Category of sites: ◇Cultural site ◓Natural site ◑Mixed site. Sources: Esri, HERE, Garmin, FAO, NOAA, USGS, © OpenStreetMap contributors, and the GIS User Community.

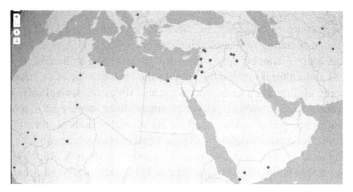

Fig. 2. UNESCO Endangered Cultural Heritage Sites in EMMENA region. Category of sites: ◆Cultural site ●Natural site. Sources: Esri, HERE, Garmin, FAO, NOAA, USGS, © OpenStreetMap contributors, and the GIS User Community.

2   The EXCELSIOR H2020 Teaming Project

Through the 'ERATOSTHENES: Excellence Research Centre for Earth Surveillance and Space-Based Monitoring of the Environment (EXCELSIOR)' Horizon 2020 Widespread Teaming Phase 2 project (www.excelsior2020.eu), a new, autonomous and self-sustained Centre of Excellence entitled 'ERATOSTHENES Centre of Excellence (ECoE)' will be created, as a result of upgrading the existing Remote Sensing and Geo-Environment Lab (Eratosthenes Group), operating within the Department of Civil Engineering and Geomatics, Faculty of Engineering and Technology of the Cyprus University of Technology (CUT) since 2007. Within the next 7 years, the ECoE aspires to become a world-class

Digital Innovation Hub (DIH) for Earth Observation (EO) and Geospatial Information and a point of reference within the EMMENA region as well [9]. The EXCELSIOR project aims also at creating an inspiring environment for conducting basic and applied research and innovation in in the thematic clusters of Environment and Climate, Resilient Society, and Big Earth Data Analytics through the integrated use of remote sensing and space-based techniques.

EXCELSIOR is a team effort between the Cyprus University of Technology (CUT, acting as the coordinator), the German Aerospace Centre (DLR), the National Observatory of Athens (NOA), the German Leibniz Institute for Tropospheric Research (TROPOS) and the Deputy Ministry of Research, Innovation and Digital Policy of Republic of Cyprus, through the Department of Electronic Communications (DEC).

3   Other CH Related Projects from EXCELSIOR Members

Over the years, the scientific personnel of the Department of Civil Engineering and Geomatics at CUT (currently involved in the ERATOSTHENES Group) participated in numerous projects concerning the documentation and the analysis of the past. The following subsection briefly presents these efforts, while highlights few (out of many) research works that were conducted.

3.1   ATHENA Twinning Project

Through the Horizon 2020 ATHENA Twinning Project (https://athena2020.eu/) the scientific team aspired to support the current cultural heritage needs through the systematic exploitation of earth observation technologies, while its core element was the knowledge transfer, achieved primarily through intense training activities (including virtual training courses, workshops and summer schools) with an ultimate scope to: enhance the scientific profile of the research staff as well as to accelerate the development of research capabilities of the ERATOSTHENES research center for CH, promoting at the same time the earth observation knowledge and best practices intended for CH. Active and passive remote sensing data for archaeology, SAR for change and deformation detection, satellite monitoring for archaeological looting, hyperspectral image analysis for crop marks detection, integration of remote sensing data for protection and preservation of cultural heritage were also highlighted during its running years. The scientific strengthening and networking achieved in Cyprus through the ATHENA project proved to be of great benefit for the entire Eastern Mediterranean Region, highlighting the need for monitoring and safeguarding [10] of the archaeological sites and monuments. In this work [11], the author exploited the benefits of remote sensing along with the advantages of the Big Data platform (Earth Engine) to apply orthogonal equations in the area of Thessalian plain, hence identifying more than 50% of the Neolithic sites from the visual representation of the crop, surrounded vegetation and soil components in the designated study area. In this paper [12], the synergistic effort to detect, quantify, and visualize the presence of the deterioration patterns on a monument's surface (Paphos Harbour Castle, Cyprus) was presented. This effort was achieved by combining both destructive material analysis and non-destructive DIP analysis for the digital mapping of the alterations. The results of the visual investigation and recording of the various deterioration patterns were successfully correlated to the analytical methods used and detected through the non-destructive DIP analysis. The supervised classification of the results of the images treated by unsupervised techniques demonstrated the potential of providing results that can be verified by laboratory analysis and the DIP procedure. The visualization of these patterns was represented through color variation intensity, and the results comprise indices for those parts of the monument requiring conservation interventions.

Through the collaboration formed between DLR, CUT and the National Research Council (CNR) in Italy within the ATHENA project, the research personnel defined a framework for the automatic damage detection to endangered CH sites, based on the extraction of textural information and robust differences of brightness values related to pre- and post-disaster satellite images [13]. A map highlighting potentially damaged buildings is derived, which could help experts assessing in due time the damages in inaccessible areas. Results were reported for all sites destroyed by the Islamic State in the ancient city of Palmyra in Syria. The work conducted by [14] estimates for the first time objectively the suitability of maps derived from hyperspectral images for the detection of buried archaeological structures in vegetated areas. This is achieved by computing the statistical dependence between the extracted features and a digital map indicating the presence of buried structures using information theoretical notions. Based on the obtained scores on known targets, the features can be ranked and the most suitable can be chosen to aid in the discovery of previously undetected crop marks in the area under similar conditions. Three case studies are reported: the Roman buried remains of Carnuntum (Austria), the underground structures of Selinunte in the South of Italy, and the buried street relics of Pherai (Velestino) in central Greece.

3.2 NAVIGATOR Project

The main objective of the project NAVIGATOR (http://web.cut.ac.cy/navigator/overview/) is the exploitation of Earth Observation datasets in addressing CH needs, capitalizing on the European Copernicus space program. Furthermore, Copernicus gathers data from satellites and ground sensors which after processing are available to users through a set of services related to environmental and security issues.

Within the context of protecting the CH assets, [15] used Sentinel-1 and Sentinel-2 data to estimate the proportion of vegetation cover at the vicinity of archaeological site(s) which afterwards were supplemented by crowdsourced OpenStreetMap geodata to better locate the vegetated and non-vegetated areas. Since the monitoring of the vegetation dynamics and long-term temporal changes of vegetation cover is of great importance for assessing the risk level of a hazard, authors selected a particular area at the western part of Cyprus in Paphos, that holds important open-air archaeological sites and monuments like the UNESCO enlisted archaeological sites of "Nea Paphos" and "Tombs of the Kings" while several historical buildings are found near the downtown. Their overall findings indicate that Sentinel-1 and-2 indices can provide a useful pattern only over vegetated areas, which can be further elaborated to estimate temporal changes using integrated optical and radar Sentinel data.

Leveraging on the advantages that new technologies have to offer towards the monitoring and protection of the CH, members of the ERATOSTHENES team focused on detecting displacements within the archaeological sites in Cyprus after a 5.6 magnitude scale earthquake event using the Hybrid Pluggable Processing Pipeline (HyP3) Cloud-Based System and Sentinel-1 Interferometric Synthetic Aperture Radar (InSAR) Analysis [16]. Authors acquired Sentinel-1 data, which contained information on the orbits (ascending and descending), as well as for each one they used one image to examine and better compare the before/after status. Afterwards, they applied the InSAR GAMMA algorithm of the HyP3 to generate a wrapped interferogram, an unwrapped one as well as a displacement map to visualize any ground deformations and changes in distance from the sensors. However, it was considered important to evaluate their accuracy using coherence maps. The results showed that relative displacements have occurred in the areas of the UNESCO Heritage sites (Nea Paphos, Tombs of the Kings and Paphos Historic Town Centre).

3.3 PLACES Project

The project "Synergistic Use of Optical and Radar data for cultural heritage applications", in short PLACES (https://ktisis.cut.ac.cy/cris/project/pj00387), aims at investigating the potentials of earth observation and space technologies for cultural heritage. Despite the availability of sensors providing a range of different spatial and spectral characteristics, research is sometimes restricted by the mismatch observed between the individual sensors' characteristics related to their spatial, spectral, radiometric, and temporal resolution. Since each sensor operates on a specific wavelength range and is sensitive to specific environmental conditions, the acquisition of all the required information is not feasible to be acquired by a single sensor. It is essential therefore to capitalize on the capacity of existing sensors and understand potential synergies between them, expanding thus the scope of space-based Earth system science in order to meet the needs of a particular domain area such as cultural heritage. The various activities planned in the project, follow the general trend in the field towards the fusion and synergistic use of heterogeneous satellite datasets (i.e., optical and radar images), especially satellite datasets which have nowadays become open and freely distributed. The activities of the project include multi-temporal analysis of satellite images, image processing and fusion of remote sensed datasets.

A recent study by [17] that falls under the scope of the PLACES project, investigates the potential of open access EO images for the detection of large-scale looted areas. Moreover, the author performed an analysis using Landsat 7 ETM + images over the archaeological site of Apamea, Syria that was repeatedly looted from the beginning of the Syrian war. The multi-temporal analysis of the Landsat images (period: January 2011 to April 2012), completed through the interpretation of pseudo-color temporal composites, investigation of the multi-temporal spectral profiles, correlations between the spectral bands, and the application of principal component analysis (PCA). The overall findings were compared with available images from Google Earth Digital Globe and published articles and reports related to the Apamea archaeological site. It was found that the high revisit temporal resolution of the Landsat sensor was able to detect and map the looting activity in the area as a result of the spectral change in the archaeological landscape, despite its 30 m spatial resolution.

3.4 RESEARCH MSCA-RISE H2020 Project

The project RESEARCH (REmote SEnsing techniques for ARCHaeology, https://www.re-se-arch.eu/) tests risk assessment methodology, by examining soil erosion, land movement and land use change threatening archaeological sites. The project uses an integrated system of documentation and research in the fields of archaeology and environmental studies, combining advanced remote sensing technologies with GIS application for the mapping and the long-term monitoring of archaeological heritage. This work [18] concentrated on the land movement estimation, and the potential hazard that such ground displacement might have on cultural heritage sites. Concerning the land movement estimation in Amathus archaeological site (Limassol, Cyprus), Sentinel-1A SAR (Synthetic Aperture Radar) observations were used with a spatial resolution of 5×20 m and coverage 250 km. Subsequently, the authors generate the interferogram, followed by the subtraction of its topographic phase using a Digital Elevation Model (DEM), as well as they accomplish the phase unwrapping, which finally is converted to displacement.

Soil erosion is one of the most significant environmental issues, as it seriously threatens archaeological sites and monuments. The present study [19] calculates average annual soil erosion in terms of spatial and temporal patterns based on the Revised Universal Soil Loss Equation (RUSLE) model, combined with Geographic Information Systems (GIS) in Paphos District. In this study, the authors also considered satellite remote sensing images (Landsat TM) and available data sources such as meteorological data, a digital elevation model (DEM), land use and soils maps for soil erosion analysis. The methodology is based on the estimation of soil loss per unit area and considers specific parameters such as rainfall factor, steepness and slope length factor, cover management, practice factor as well as soil erosion factor. The results indicate that the estimated mean annual soil erosion varied from 0 to 235.532 t/ha. The rate differs due to the topography and land use-land cover.

3.5 SaRoCy Project

Project SaRoCy (http://sarocy.cut.ac.cy/) – "Delineating probable sea routes between Cyprus and its surrounding coastal areas at the start of the Holocene: A simulation approach" – seeks to offer novel insights, based on physical/environmental modelling and computer simulation, into the possible prehistoric maritime pathways between Cyprus and other Eastern Mediterranean coastal regions at the boundary between Terminal Pleistocene/early Holocene (Epipaleolithic/early Neolithic), a critical period for understanding the origins of the early visitors in Cyprus in connection with the Neolithic transition.

In this work [20], ocean circulation modeling and particle tracking are employed for characterizing drift-induced sea-borne connectivity for that period, using data and assumptions to approximate prevailing paleo-geographical conditions (re-constructed coastline from global sea level curves), and rudimentary vessel (rafts, dugouts) characteristics, as well as present-day weather conditions. The Regional Ocean Modeling System (ROMS, [21]), forced by Copernicus Marine portal hydrological data, with wave and wind forcing derived from a combination of global reanalysis data and regional-scale numerical weather predictions (ERA5 and E-WAVE project products), are employed to provide the physical domain and atmospheric conditions. Particle-tracking is carried out using the OpenDrift model [22] to simulate drift-induced (involuntary) sea-borne movement. The sensitivity of the results on the hydrodynamic response (e.g. drag) of rudimentary vessels, such as rafts of postulated shape, size, and weight, that are believed to have been used for maritime travel during the period of interest, is also investigated. The simulation results are used to estimate the degree of maritime connectivity, due to drift-induced sea-borne movement, between segments of Cyprus coastline as well as its neighboring mainlands, and identify areas of both coastlines where landing/departure might be most favorable.

4 EXCELSIOR Contribution in Advancing the Field of Cultural Heritage

One of EXCELSIOR's main research areas (at the Resilient Society cluster, see Fig. 3) is the study and analysis of region's CH for the benefit of the public, education, stakeholders, researchers, and other countries in the region. Towards that end, the activities that will be implemented under ECoE's umbrella will focus on the use of advanced geospatial computation methods and EO techniques to support and drive the actions needed and decisions as well as to ensure the integrity of CH assets in the EMMENA region. An important activity expected to find fruitful ground through the exploitation of the research outcomes is the societal impact, as an effective and timely CH monitoring will offer crucial benefits (e.g. decision of suitable conservation efforts) to national authorities and stakeholders, which are self-identified through the cultural domain, while at the same time raising awareness of the public (either in local or international level) proved to be a supportive shaft throughout modern history in times of global CH looting and destruction (e.g. NewPalmyra repository [23], Rebuild of citadel's fortified entrance of Aleppo from photos [24], etc.); an important aspect that ECoE intends to take advantage of.

Performing and fostering top-tier research and innovation within its Resilient Society cluster, the ECoE is expected to funnel the research results in entrepreneurship, thus granting opportunities for spin-offs in its capacity as DIH, facilitating at the same time the opening of new CH related jobs for researchers and new markets as well. Through the capitalisation of existing networks, the ECoE will reach significant innovation ecosystems to foster the conditions needed to unleash the potential of EO and geospatial solutions in relation to the protection of cultural assets. Conditions that will benefit indirectly the human communities at global level, however in order for this to become more feasible, citizens need to have been given the necessary education so to better understand the importance the cultural concept plays in their lives, which forms their common identity. To that end, the ERATOSTHENES Center of Excellence plans to offer several CH modules/lessons jointly with higher academic institutions thus covering every education aspect (from bachelor to postdoctoral studies).

The research Agenda of the EXCELSIOR H2020 funded project, identifies cultural heritage (both tangible and intangible) as a strategic resource for Europe that is high in cultural, social, environmental, and economic value. To maximise the benefits that derive from the application of digital technologies to the CH field, important challenges and obstacles need to be addressed through research, thus developing a holistic approach

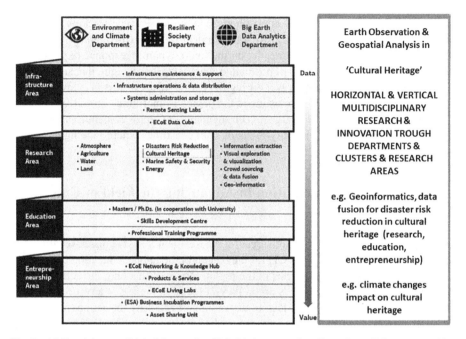

Fig. 3. (a) Excelsior as a Digital Innovation Hub (b) An example of how CH will be supported by the 2-axis approach

that meets the needs of all existing and potential future user/experts groups. In that way, the social and economic value of Digital Cultural Heritage (DCH) increases, while it reinforces and expands partnerships and networking, exploiting the unique strategic position of Cyprus in the region; an island that connects Western countries with East and South continents. Towards that end, the involvement of the UNESCO Chair in DCH, held by the director of the DHR Lab at CUT, will address a full range of key aspects in research and development such as:

– The creation of a regional hub for the EMMENA, bridging the collaboration between the region and the EU, whilst continuing to actively contribute and act as a focal point at European level,
– The documentation and analysis of cultural heritage data for both its tangible and intangible aspects,
– Monitoring of CH sites for damages from looting, geo-hazards, etc.

Based on the two-axis approach of the digital innovation hub [25], it is noteworthy that the scientific actions related to the CH domain will be implemented through EXCEL-SIOR's Resilient Society department, while the remaining two departments (Environment and Climate, Big Earth Data Analytics) and 4 clusters (Infrastructure, Research, Education, Entrepreneurship) will also support the CH research area (see Fig. 3a and b)

The current capabilities along with the prospects that derive through the integration of EO and geospatial analysis in the management and monitoring of CH sites are focused on:

– Protecting and managing the cultural heritage sites through systematic information flow and monitoring,
– Our ability to store RS data properly in limited space,
– Retaining data in a more economically efficient way and recovering them faster,
– Correlating simultaneously the heterogeneous information (e.g., spatial, and descriptive data)
– Performing temporal data analysis of the CH sites (either are accessible or not),
– Creating the conditions for the achievement of an integrated process of collection, analysis and decision making,
– Responding efficiently to the analysis of the Big Data that are expected to be produced from the Satellite Ground Receiving station that will be installed in Cyprus (e.g., collection of near real time satellite data both passive and active).

5   Conclusions

The use of geospatial technology and EO methods in the cultural sector plays a crucial role in offering not only a spatial view and understanding of the archaeological remains, but also the opportunity to discover important details (depending on case study) that often are not easily distinguishable. Fostering and building upon such developments, the proposed ECoE envisions to become an inspiring environment for conducting basic and applied research and innovation in the thematic area of Cultural Heritage in the EMMENA region, strategically important and known for its cultural wealth. Leading the research developments, the scientific team through its participation in several projects showcased its proven experience in applying new technologies to important aspects that define CH's nature (e.g. protection, valorization, promotion and documentation), while it is anticipated that the ECoE will attract highly-skilled professionals and researchers to work in the forthcoming years within the cultural domain, thus making Cyprus a research and innovation hub that will drive the developments in the particular thematic area of the region.

Acknowledgments. The authors would like to acknowledge the 'ECXELSIOR' H2020 Teaming project (www.excelsior2020.eu). This paper is under the auspices of the activities of the 'ERATOS-THENES: Excellence Research Centre for Earth Surveillance and Space-Based Monitoring of the Environment' — 'EXCELSIOR' project that has received funding from the European Union's Horizon 2020 research and innovation programme under Grant Agreement No. 857510 and from the Government of the Republic of Cyprus through the Directorate General for the European Programmes, Coordination, and Development.

References

1. Ferris, N., Welch, J.: Beyond archaeological agendas: in the service of a sustainable archaeology. In: Atalay, S., Rains Claus, L., McGuire, R.H., Welch, J.R. (eds.) Transforming Archaeology: Activist Practices and Prospects, pp. 215–237. Left Coast Press, Walnut Creek, California (2014)
2. Glencross, B., Warrick, G., Eastaugh, E., Hawkins, A., Hodgetts, L., Lesage, L.: Minimally invasive research strategies in huron-wendat archaeology: working toward a sustainable archaeology. Adv. Archaeol. Pract. **5**(2), 147–158 (2017)
3. McCoy, M.D., Ladefoged, T.N.: New developments in the use of spatial technology in archaeology. J. Archaeol. Res. **17**(3), 263–295 (2009)
4. Haciguzeller, P.: GIS, critique, representation and beyond. J. Soc. Archaeol. **12**(2), 245–263 (2012)
5. Smith, M.E., Feinman, G.M., Drennan, R.D., Earle, T., Morris, I.: Archaeology as a social science. Proc. Natl. Acad. Sci. **109**(20), 7617–7621 (2012)
6. Conolly, J., Lake, M.: Exploratory data analysis. In: Geographical Information Systems in Archaeology, pp. 112–148. Cambridge University Press (2006)
7. Longuet, R.: Encyclopaedia of the History of Science, Technology, and Medicine in Non-Western Cultures. Springer, Netherlands, Dordrecht (2008)
8. Unesco: Convention concerning the protection of the world cultural and natural heritage. Heritage, p. 17 (1972)
9. Hadjimitsis, D.G.: On the pathway to success: becoming a leading earth observation centre through the EXCELSIOR project. In: Ioannides, M., et al. (eds.) EuroMed 2018. LNCS, vol. 11196, pp. 648–653. Springer, Cham (2018). https://doi.org/10.1007/978-3-030-01762-0_57
10. Hadjimitsis, D.G., et al.: Earth observation technologies and cultural heritage needs through the 'Athena Twinning Project'. In: CAA 2018: Human History and Digital Future, pp. 1–199 (2018)
11. Agapiou, A.: Remote sensing heritage in a petabyte-scale: satellite data and heritage Earth Engine© applications. Int. J. Digit. Earth **10**(1), 85–102 (2017)
12. Lysandrou, V., Agapiou, A., Ioannides, M., Kantiranis, N., Charalambous, E., Hadjimitsis, D.: Integrated investigation of built heritage monuments: the case study of paphos harbour castle, cyprus. Heritage, vol. 1, no. 1 (2018)
13. Cerra, D., Plank, S., Lysandrou, V., Tian, J.: Cultural heritage sites in danger—towards automatic damage detection from space. Remote Sens. **8**(9), 781 (2016)
14. Cerra, D., Agapiou, A., Cavalli, R., Sarris, A.: An objective assessment of hyperspectral indicators for the detection of buried archaeological relics. Remote Sens. **10**(4), 500 (2018)
15. Agapiou, A.: Estimating proportion of vegetation cover at the vicinity of archaeological sites using sentinel-1 and-2 data, supplemented by crowdsourced openstreetmap geodata. Appl. Sci. **10**(14), 4764 (2020)
16. Agapiou, A., Lysandrou, V.: Detecting displacements within archaeological sites in cyprus after a 5.6 magnitude scale earthquake event through the Hybrid Pluggable Processing Pipeline (HyP3) cloud-based system and Sentinel-1 Interferometric Synthetic Aperture Radar (InSAR) analysis. IEEE J. Sel. Top. Appl. Earth Obs. Remote Sens. **13**, 6115–6123 (2020)
17. Agapiou, A.: Detecting looting activity through earth observation multi-temporal analysis over the archaeological site of apamea (Syria) during 2011–2012. Journal of Computer Applications in Archaeology (2020)
18. Makri, D., Agapiou, A., Hadjimitsis, D., Papoutsa, C.: Land movements estimation in Amathus archaeological site in Limassol district with In- SAR DIn-SAR methodologies. In: EuroMed 2020 Online Conference on Digital Heritage, p. 8 (2020)

19. Papageorgiou, N., Hadjimitsis, D.G.: Evaluation of soil loss by water in archaeological landscapes by using the (R)USLE Model and GIS. The case study of Paphos district, Cyprus. In: EuroMed 2020 Online Conference on Digital Heritage, p. 13 (2020)

20. Nikolaidis, A., et al.: Modeling drift-induced maritime connectivity between Cyprus and its surrounding coastal areas during early Holocene. In: EGU General Assembly 2020 (2020)

21. Shchepetkin, A.F., McWilliams, J.C.: The regional oceanic modeling system (ROMS): a split-explicit, free-surface, topography-following-coordinate oceanic model. Ocean Model. **9**(4), 347–404 (2005)

22. Dagestad, K.-F., Röhrs, J., Breivik, Ø., Ådlandsvik, B.: OpenDrift v1.0: a generic framework for trajectory modelling. Geosci. Model Dev. **11**(4), 1405–1420 (2018)

23. Busta, H.: An Open-Source Project to Rebuild Palmyra, Architect Technology (2015). https://www.architectmagazine.com/technology/an-open-source-project-to-rebuild-palmyra_o. Accessed 10 Nov 2020

24. Barreau, J.-B., Lanoë, E., Gaugne, R.: 3D sketching of the fortified entrance of the citadel of aleppo from a few sightseeing photos. In: Kremers, H. (ed.) Digital Cultural Heritage, pp. 359–371. Springer, Cham (2020). https://doi.org/10.1007/978-3-030-15200-0_24

25. Hadjimitsis, D., et al.: The ERATOSTHENES Centre of Excellence (ECoE) as a digital innovation hub for Earth observation. In: Detection and Sensing of Mines, Explosive Objects, and Obscured Targets XXV, p. 29 (2020). https://doi.org/10.1117/12.2567070

Project Papers: Modelling and Knowledge Management

Project Papers: Interactive Environments and Applications

Route Generator for Integrating Cultural Heritage to Smart City: *Ontheroute*

Özge Ceylin Yıldırım[1] ⓘ, Derya Güleç Özer[2(✉)] ⓘ, and Aslı Sungur[1] ⓘ

[1] Department of Architecture, Faculty of Architecture,
Yıldız Technical University, İstanbul 34349, Turkey
[2] Department of Architecture, Faculty of Architecture,
Istanbul Technical University, İstanbul 34367, Turkey
dgulec@itu.edu.tr

Abstract. The city is an entity with both tangible and intangible cultural heritage values. It is impossible to think of cultural heritage values independently of the city in smart cities designed to overcome the challenges that arise for all stakeholders and elements of the city from global urbanization, technological innovations, and various urban policies. Cities that transform rapidly should aim to change without becoming detached from their cultural context. In this study, a route planning proposal based on individual preferences will be developed on how "smart city" strategies can be implemented to strengthen, ensure and protect the interaction between cultural heritage and visitors. To transform cultural heritage values into the "smart" state, their interactions with cultural heritage should be improved through advanced infrastructures in Smart City applications. With this study, the aim is to develop a user-oriented route generator integrated with city transportation data to improve the visitor experience. The Istanbul Esenler District was chosen as the field of study given its important historical and cultural values from the Byzantine and Ottoman periods. Also, the area has strategic importance as becoming a smart city in Turkey. With the proposed application, the plan is to provide simultaneous information on all cultural heritage values available to the visitor, convey visual information, and provide verbal explanations. At the same time, the route generator enables interaction with cultural heritage by allowing the user to design routes using smart city transportation data for the bus and metro, current location, and travel times.

Keywords: Smart city · Cultural heritage route generator · Mobile applications · Esenler

1 Introduction

Urbanization in the 21st century is defined by the global economy, social development, and information and communication technologies (ICT). It is estimated by the United Nations (UN) [1] that 68% of the world's population will live in urban areas by 2050. This situation creates many problems with dense urban populations and globalized economic and social activities [2]. In particular, there is a risk to the integrity of the cultural heritage

© Springer Nature Switzerland AG 2021
M. Ioannides et al. (Eds.): EuroMed 2020, LNCS 12642, pp. 165–177, 2021.
https://doi.org/10.1007/978-3-030-73043-7_14

that constitutes a reference to the past, present and future of the city and includes its socio-cultural values. While innovative proposals have been developed for many aspects of the physical and functional structure of the city with the increase in perception, information, data analysis, communication and network technologies [2–4], cultural heritage values are generally given less importance [5, 6]. Smart cities tend to represent the heritage values of the city only with information and communication technologies (ICT) without considering their cultural and historical profiles [7].

By challenging urban planning principles and practices, smart cities change their understanding of urban planning with sustainable urban development agendas and concepts of efficiency, standardization, and corporate control [8–11]. Smart city initiatives can be adapted to the local context, building on the city's existing assets and the identity of the location [12]. Tangible, intangible, and natural heritage values take place in varying proportions and values in urban areas and form the identity of cities. In the protection and monitoring of heritage values, the potential and difficulties inherent in using smart city applications are discussed [7, 13, 14], and studies are carried out on the use of technological tools such as AR and VR [15, 16]. In addition, there is research aimed at protecting cultural heritage on different scales and increasing the participation of visitors with smart city strategies [17, 18]. That cultural heritage be included in the digital ecosystem of smart cities becomes increasingly important [19]. In addition, mobile systems and applications are ongoing study areas for protecting heritage, interacting with visitors, and raising awareness. However, the studies are technology-centered, and cultural heritage values in smart cities do not go beyond the use of ICT in infrastructure, management, and monitoring. From the studies, it is clear that efforts to increase the access of cultural heritage to cultural heritage values and scientific knowledge using digital technologies have been limited to small-scale solutions. Tangible and intangible cultural heritage values, which include socio-economic and cultural components, should be protected in integration with the urban structure and included in urban planning.

Smart cities developed as a solution to current and future challenges and opportunities of cities on an international, national, regional, and local scale. However, the cultural heritage values of cities have not been considered in the context of the smart city applications that are just beginning in Turkey. Even though smart city projects emphasize the need for heritage conservation, there is much uncertainty as to how they can be integrated and used to support urban development. The study aims to reveal the potential of information and communication technologies to help city dwellers develop their relationship with the city, create awareness of heritage values and transfer them to the future.

There is increasing demand for digital tools to establish a deeper relationship with the cultural heritage visitor and to discover heritage values within the city according to their interests. Heritage values are increasingly transferred to the digital domain [20]. Online and mobile applications provide opportunities for the visitor who encounters, discovers and interacts with the heritage to convey a higher level of knowledge, engagement, and differentiation and create added value. The major problem is the limited Point of Interest (POI) coverage and the lack of tools to enhance the user experience. The availability and importance of real-time data such as sensors, open data, and IoT provided by the smart city to collect these data and create the algorithm are increasing. In this context, the data of cultural heritage values are collected and spatialized with the help of digital tools. Next, the study aims to increase the relationship between the visitor and cultural heritage by proposing a route planning system (see Fig. 1). For the proposed route generator we chose the Esenler district, whose history goes back to Byzantium and which has important cultural heritage values with its barracks, water structures, and religious buildings. Also, plans to implement sample implementations for the strategies and actions of the 2019–22 National Smart City Strategy and Action Plan within the borders of Esenler district is another reason for choosing this area.

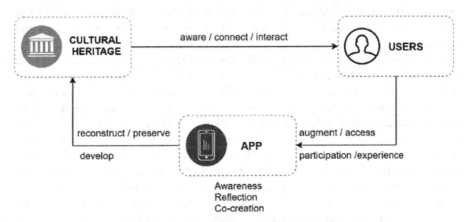

Fig. 1. Concept diagram of the study

This paper's structure consists of (1) the importance of cultural heritage values in smart city strategies; (2) changing behaviors and demands in experiencing urban space; (3) mobile applications related to current route planning and cultural heritage; (4) the overall system of the *"ontheroute"* application including general information about the Esenler district and POIs and the user interface design of the application. The application is a prototype and the studies required for the route generation algorithm are not the focus of this paper. However, as a result of the ongoing project, an application will be developed for Android and iOS users that creates thematic routes according to location, duration, and personal preferences. It is predicted that this will increase interaction with the user and the quality of the experience of the urban space.

2   New Approaches in Experiencing the City

The multi-dimensional character of the city, which covers political, economic, social, cultural, and spatial contexts with different parameters, includes interdisciplinary dynamics such as daily life, cultural context, collective memory, and psychology. Lefebvre [21] suggests a theoretical view of the space "designed abstractly by architects, planners (space representations)", "living through symbols and meanings (spaces of representation)" and "perceived in everyday life (spatial practice)". He directs us to think of the social production of urban space as a trilogy. People who take an active role in the production of the city space undergo changes in the continuity of time, and therefore the change of the city becomes inevitable. Every changing value is constructed, renewed and transformed in the historical accumulation of the city. Change on the urban scale refers to the change in the experiential nature rather than the change of the physical environment. The city dweller and the visitor interact by experiencing the city through the senses and make the city meaningful from their perspective by developing a sense of belonging. The phenomenological assumption of the relationship that man establishes with his environment forms the concept of place. To belong to the city and to be a local, it is necessary to be exposed to the place in a cultural sense [22]. The city is the individual experience area of people. To understand, define and perceive the city, which has different time layers, functionalities and trends, is only possible by experiencing and reading it.

City dwellers desire to discover the unknowns of the city, which they perceive in the network of business life, cultural life, leisure time, and residence, in the continuity of "daily life" and to participate in the process of experiencing it. This experience can take various forms: walking, living, getting lost, wandering, and exploring with the help of virtual media and digital tools. In particular, walking means realizing urban life; it means experiencing and interacting with the city. The concept of the "Flaneur", developed by Walter Benjamin [23], refers to the traveler who feels at home in the public spaces of the city and tries to analyze the meanings related to the city. The potentials of the city offer the opportunity to meet and experience its concrete and abstract cultural values. "Through the act of walking, new connections are made and re-made, physically and conceptually over time and through space… Walking is a way of at once discovering and transforming the city" [24]. He emphasizes that it is a basic way of experiencing the city. During the walk, different perceptions and experiences are gained in the urban space with rich associative and sensory impressions. Sensory interaction with the environment while walking in the urban area involves the concentration of emotions, images and metaphors that we associate with spaces [25, 26]. It is important to perceive the social, cultural and historical values of the city by walking, to be an active participant in the values of the city, to experience the city and to belong to it.

In experiencing the city, the ability of residents and visitors to perceive and understand [27] have evolved into a search for authenticity and active participation [28]. Today, when experiencing the city, there is a desire to discover new experiences that differ from daily habits. In addition, beyond consuming the location-specific values visually, there is a desire to perceive values through all the senses. Residents and visitors experience fishing in authentic boats, while fishermen work in supermarkets [29]. Today, technological tools house the potential to increase and convey urban experiences. The usage rates of digital media where we can share the location of the place and our thoughts and feelings about it are increasing rapidly. We can learn not only about individual sharing with these tools but also about a place we see while walking on the street with "QR codes", one of the smart city applications developed by institutions and organizations. With the help of digital tools, it can be much easier and faster to read, analyze, and evaluate the cultural, social, and relational values of the urban space. While passively walking in the city, there is new potential to experience, perceive and understand the city with physical and digital tools.

3   Overview of Current App Functions

Smart city development is not only a technological facilitator, it also requires all stakeholders to adapt to changing and evolving roles in public-private sector cooperation in which city dwellers participate [30]. It should be considered not only as a technological entity but also as a dynamic system that interacts with the existing city and its people through information and communication technologies. As a result, the interaction between the city and the user with mobile applications increases and urban life becomes "smarter" [31]. The development of mobile applications allows the promotion of heritage values and information exchange with visitors, enhances the travel route experience, and increases the visitor's participation in the route planning process [32]. These make flexible and experience-enhanced route planning possible.

Cultural heritage information such as monuments, photographs, and written material can be given a geographical reference. Many websites include cultural heritage content on maps containing mobile applications and geographical location information [33]. However, many of these applications contain pure information and are limited to map exploration. To solve this problem, there are multimodal and thematic route planning suggestions and tendencies that try to make sense of the data related to the location and content of cultural heritage [34–36].

For routes combining cultural heritage with a distinct theme specific to personal preferences [37], route-planning suggestions are carried out with routing algorithms according to the location and interest rates of POIs with data collected from various geo-based web resources [38]. Personalized thematic routes considering the sustainability of using digital technologies in cultural heritage areas serve education, entertainment and aesthetics. They aim to increase the user's experience of digital heritage and heritage tourism, making it more interesting and diversified [39]. In addition, the Council of Europe supports common European programs such as the Cultural Routes Program.

This study focuses on both geographical multimodal and personalized thematic route generators in the use of mobile applications, which are an important part of Smart Cities for the exploration of cultural heritage. In this section, current mobile applications that allow cultural heritage visitors to connect while traveling will be examined.

3.1   Mobile Route Planner App

Mobile route planning applications ensure that the visitor has access to the right information before and during the trip. In these applications, there is information on popular destinations, automated route planning and personal profile creation possibilities. These applications range from simple and more general route planning, in which a digital map of the city is provided, to calculating the most appropriate route based on current location and context information in line with personal interests over a particular area. However, there is no mobile application integrated with the city's transport infrastructure, the personal preferences of the visitors, and the unknown multifaceted and multi-layered cultural values of the city.

Applications with downloads between 3,000 and 57,000 in the App Store and Google Play were compared (see Table 1). The analyzed applications provide routes that support the tourist experience according to time, location, and other criteria. However, none of

Table 1. Comparison between the different mobile route planner applications.

PLATFORM CRITERIA	Visit a city	Trip It	Culture Trip	VisitIn	İzi	Piri	TripTrend	GeziManya	Ontheroute
Route personalization	-	-	-	-	-	-	-	-	+
Audio guides	-	-	-	-	+	+	-	+	+
Real Time Location Detection	+	+	+	+	+	-	+	-	+
Probability of Discovering the Unknown	+	-	+	+	+	+	+	+	+
Directions	+	+	+	+	+	-	+	-	+
Information about each POI	+	+	+	+	+	+	+	+	+
Profile creation	+	+	+	+	+	+	+	-	+
Adding participants	-	-	-	-	-	-	-	-	+
AR technology	-	-	-	-	-	-	-	-	+

the applications provide information on the cultural heritage of the city, audio narration, or ar technologies, and none allow the visitor to determine the route with personal preferences through different transportation modes and cultural heritage values. Nor can they suggest a different route by adding new participants during the trip. In the study, a route generator application that supports all criteria will be developed.

4   *"ontheroute"* Mobile Application

In the first step, data containing the values of the city were created. For each POI, a title, description, location, picture, details of opening hours and links giving more detailed information were developed. Moreover, transportation data for the city were also included. Next, personal information, location data and preference information about travel time are received from the user. Then, the user is asked to choose among the routes determined according to different theme categories in the city. Finally, from POIs classified according to these categories, the most appropriate route is suggested according to the location and time information of the person. The user can access the details of the POIs on this route and make route previews, additions and subtractions. As a result, a personalized route is created (see Fig. 2).

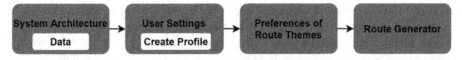

Fig. 2. *"ontheroute"* system

This application has been designed as the most accurate route generator for the user with an interface design that is fast, simple and integrated with urban transportation. The flow chart for the user of the application, which aims to increase the interaction of the user with the city and to present the city's unknowns visually and audibly, is given in Fig. 3. For the directions provided by the application to the user, detailed information is accessed with city transportation data, comments made by visitors on each POI, historical explanations, time to spend and budget information, audio narration, and AR technologies. The route is completed with the experience process and the photos and comments of the user.

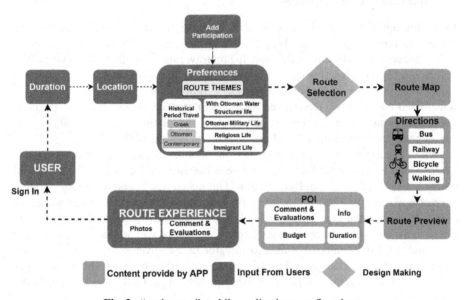

Fig. 3. *"ontheroute"* mobile application user flowchart

4.1   Case Study: Esenler in Istanbul

There were numerous rural settlements outside the Istanbul city wall in the 16th century and there remain historical layers of two settlements named Avas and Litros. There are church and school ruins in these areas where Greeks settled. In addition, Esenler is rich in water facilities. It has two arches, spirit-levels, cisterns, and fountains. Schools and public buildings with different functions were built by Davut Pasha, the grand vizier of Ottoman Emperor Beyazıt II. In the 17th century, the area gained military importance and began to be used as a residence in the summer months. The Davutpaşa campus, which is part of the Yıldız Technical University campus today, was built in 1827 [40].

The ethnic, demographic and socio-economic structure of Litros and Avas, which witnessed two waves of migration between Turkey and Greece after the Balkan Wars (1912–13), has changed [40]. These two settlements, which were merged as Esenler with the declaration of the Republic, developed rapidly with industrialization after the 1950s. Uncontrolled development occurred in Esenler, whose population increased quickly. [41]. This situation negatively affected the historical and cultural layers within Esenler. In recent years, conservation efforts have been carried out by institutions and organizations to protect cultural heritage values.

In this study, a route generator application is developed that will provide guidance for the visitor to the site and increase interaction with cultural heritage values. In Fig. 4, POIs, locations and photographs of religious, military and water structures and routes on the themes "Ottoman Military Life" and "Ottoman Water Structure Life" are shown.

4.2 Application User Interfaces

The mobile application user interface should be simple, follow an easy flow that appeals to every user and be quick to use [42]. Groth and Haslwanter [43] examined efficiency, effectiveness and satisfaction while searching for travel and route information via mobile applications. In their experiments with two different mobile applications, they found that the application with a simple and understandable flow performed better. In addition, the voice-based interface is a feature that increases interaction with its user. In situations that appeal to more than one sense while traveling, the quality and memorability of the experience increase by listening and seeing at the same time [44].

When visiting the Esenler district with the mobile application, the experience is improved by increasing the interaction between the user and the historical and cultural values that have survived from Byzantine and Ottoman times. Users enter the application by creating the user profile in Fig. 5. In Fig. 6, route maps are created over the database that include the user's real-time location, travel time and personal preferences, and heritage values in the area. In addition, the user is told how long he will need according to route times and transportation types. Consequently, the user is given historical explanations about the unknown or unseen values of a city under urban pressure, reviews of other visitors and directions for transportation. The application guides the user throughout the experience (see Fig. 7).

A pilot application is planned to evaluate the usability of the interface and acceptance by the user. After analyzing, it will be possible to work on the usability of the application and how the route suggestion algorithm should be developed. The application developed with a user-centric approach is still in the design phase. By increasing the functionality with experiments still to be carried out, it is anticipated that the application, which was initially started in Esenler, will be developed first for the entire city of Istanbul and then for other cities.

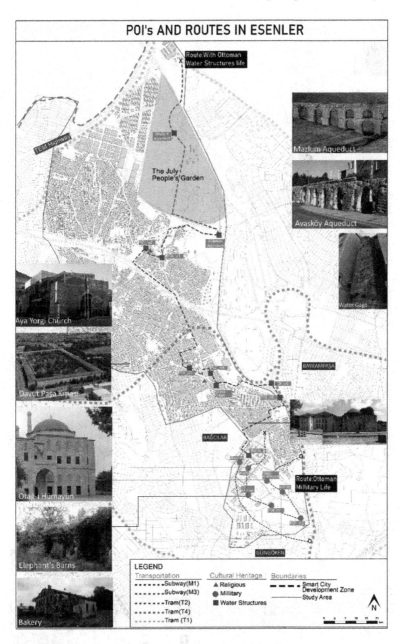

Fig. 4. POI's and routes in study area

Fig. 5. Creating user profile

Fig. 6. User information and preferences

Fig. 7. Route generator and experience

5 Conclusion and Future Work

Developed to provide route proposals for the integration of smart city and cultural heritage values, "ontheroute" aims to increase visitor interaction with cultural heritage, create awareness for the discovery and protection of cultural heritage values and provide a wide range of uses to make it suitable for commercial and non-commercial purposes. User assessments of the application;s functionality and cultural heritage will extend the life cycle of the route generator. The application suggests a route based on personal preferences. these consist of four main components: (1) the collection and spatialization of data to create a database; (2) integration with urban transport data; (3) ar studies of values that have not survived to the present day; (4) creation of route planning with location, time and route themes with the user interface. Although it has not yet been fully implemented in the mobile application, the routes have been tested by processing esenler cultural heritage and city data through the system.

As a future study, the routes could be expanded from one area to the entire city and route planning could be carried out in many areas based on location-specific themes and user preferences. With the application, which can be a network that renews and develops itself with feedback from users, cultural heritage data will be collected and access to visitors will be facilitated. It might support the potential of smart city applications and tools to increase visitor participation and to create a database to be included in urban planning.

References

1. BM World Urbanization Prospects: The 2018 Revision, https://population.un.org/wup//Publications/Files/WUP2018-KeyFacts.pdf , last accessed 2020/09/10.
2. Bibri, S.E., Krogstie, J.: Smart sustainable cities of the future: An extensive interdisciplinary literature review. Sustain. Urban Areas **31**, 183–212 (2017)
3. Mora, L., Deakin, M., Reid, A.: Combining co-citation clustering and text-based analysis to reveal the main development paths of smart cities. Technological Forecasting and Social Change 142 (SI), 56–69 (2018).
4. Ojo, A., Dzhusupova, Z., Curry, E.: Exploring the nature of the smart cities research landscape. In: Gil-Garcia, J.R., Pardo, T.A., Nam, T. (eds.) Smarter as the New Urban Agenda: A Comprehensive View of the 21st Century City, pp. 23–47. Springer International Publishing, Cham (2016)
5. Sindhu, S., Reshmi, M. K., Cultural Infrastructure and the Planning of Future Cities. IN E3S WEB OF CONFERENCES (Vol. 170). EDP Sciences (2020).
6. Jara, A.J., Sun, Y., Song, H., Bie, R., Genooud, D., Bocchi, Y. Internet of Things for cultural heritage of smart cities and smart regions. In: 2015 IEEE 29th International Conference on Advanced Information Networking and Applications Workshops, pp. 668–675 (2015)
7. Allam, Z., Newman, P.: Redefining The Smart City: culture, metabolism and governance. smart. Cities 1(1), 4–25 (2018)
8. Späth, P., Knieling, J.: How EU-funded smart city experiments influence modes of planning for mobility: observations from Hamburg. Urban Transf. 2(1), 1–17 (2020)
9. Martin, C., Evans, J., Karvonen, A., Paskaleva, K., Yang, D. ve Linjordet, T.: Smart-sustainability: a new urban fix? Sustainable Cities Soc. **45**, 640–648 (2019)
10. Haarstad, H.: Constructing the sustainable city: examining the role of sustainability in the 'smart city'discourse. J. Environ. Planning Policy Manage. **19**(4), 423–437 (2017)

11. Parks, D., ve Rohracher, H.: From sustainable to smart: Re-branding or re-assembling urban energy infrastructure? Geoforum **100**, 51–59 (2019)
12. Angelidou, M.: Four European smart city strategies. Int. J. Soc. Sci. Stud. **4**, 18–25 (2016)
13. Gambardella, C., Pisacane, N., Avella, A., Argenziano, P.: Pompei knowledge factory cultural heritage and ICT for a smart city. In: 2014 International Conference on Virtual Systems & Multimedia (VSMM), pp. 132–139. IEEE (2014)
14. Diego, F.J.G., Esteban, B., Merello, P.: Design of a hybrid (wired/wireless) acquisition data system for monitoring of cultural heritage physical parameters in smart cities. Sensors **15**(4), 7246–7266 (2015)
15. Garau, C.: From territory to smartphone: Smart fruition of cultural heritage for dynamic tourism development. Plan. Pract. Res. **29**(3), 238–255 (2014)
16. McKenna, H.P.: Adaptive reuse of cultural heritage elements and fragments in public spaces: the internet of cultural things and applications as infrastructures for learning in smart cities. In: 2017 13th International Conference on Signal-Image Technology & Internet-Based Systems (SITIS), pp. 479–484. IEEE (2017)
17. Alkhafaji, A., Cocea, M., Crellin, J., Fallahkhair, S.: Guidelines for designing a smart and ubiquitous learning environment with respect to cultural heritage. In: 2017 11th International Conference on Research Challenges in Information science (RCIS), pp. 334–339. IEEE (2017)
18. Wang, Q., Shen, S.: digital inheritance strategy of intangible cultural heritage and big data model-taking the southern liaoning province as an example. In: 2018 International Conference on Intelligent Transportation, Big Data & Smart City (ICITBS), pp. 295–298. IEEE (2018)
19. Chianese, A., Piccialli, F., Valente, I.: Smart environments and cultural heritage: a novel approach to create intelligent cultural spaces. J. Location Serv. **9**(3), 209–234 (2015)
20. Economou, M. Heritage in the Digital Age, pp. 215–228. John Wiley & Sons Inc., Chichester, West Sussex (2015)
21. Lefebvre, H.: The Production of Space. Blackwell, Malden (2012)
22. Canella, C.: Experiencing the city by walking. Mobile Culture Studies, Basel (2011)
23. Benjamin, W.: Passages. DABAA Publishing (1995)
24. Rendell, J.: Art and Architecture: A Place Between. I. B. Tauris, London (2006)
25. Lynch, K.: The Image of the City, 11th edn. MIT Press, Cambridge (1960)
26. Banerjee, T., Southworth, M.: City Sense and City Design: Writings and Projects of Kevin Lynch. MIT Press, Cambridge (1990)
27. Boorstin, D.J.: The Image: A Guide to Pseudo-Events in America. Atheneum, New York (1961)
28. Urry, J.: The Tourist Gaze: Leisure and Travel in Contemporary Societies. Sage Publication, London (1990)
29. Paul, B.D.: The impacts of tourism on society. Ann. Faculty Econ. **1**(1), 500–506 (2012)
30. Lom, M., Pribyl, O., Svitek, M.: Industry 4.0 as a part of smart cities. In: 2016 SMART Cities symposium prague (SCSP), pp. 1–6. IEEE (2016)
31. Greenfield, A.: Against the Smart City: A Pamphlet. This is Part I of "The City is Here to Use". Do projects, New York (2013)
32. Oh, S., Lehto, X.Y., Park, J.: Travelers' intent to use mobile technologies as a function of effort and performance expectancy. J. Hosp. Market. Manag. **18**(8), 765–781 (2009)
33. Kauppinen, T., Paakkarinen, P., Mkela, E., Kuittinen, H., Vtinen, J., Hyvnen, E.: Digital Culture and E-Tourism: Technologies, pp. 48–64. Applications and Management Approaches. IGI Global Publisher, Hershey (2011)
34. Luo, J., Joshi, D., Yu, J., Gallagher, A.: Geotagging in multimedia and computer vision—a survey. Multimed. Tools Appl. **51**(1), 187–211 (2011)
35. Zheng, Y., Zha, Z., Chua, T.: Research and applications on georeferenced multimedia: a survey. Multimed. Tools Appl. **51**(1), 77–98 (2011)

36. Baker, K., Verstockt, S.: Cultural heritage routing. J. Comput. Cult. Herit. **10**(4), 1–20 (2017)
37. Nagy, K.: Methodology of heritage-based tourism product development—Thematic routes as new and special possibilities. Doctoral Students Forum, pp. 104–110. University of Miskolc, Hungary (2011)
38. Sanders, P., Schultes, D.: Engineering fast route planning algorithms. In: Demetrescu, C. (ed.) WEA 2007. LNCS, vol. 4525, pp. 23–36. Springer, Heidelberg (2007). https://doi.org/10.1007/978-3-540-72845-0_2
39. Nagy, K.: Heritage Tourism, thematic routes and possibilities for innovation. Theory Methodol. Pract. (TMP) **8**(1), 46–53 (2012)
40. Güldal, F., Uçar, A.: Esenler'in Tarihi (History of Esenler). Esenler Municipality Cultural Publications, Istanbul (2013)
41. Tümertekin, E.: İstanbul çevresinde sanayinin yeni yayılma alanları (New spreading areas of industry around Istanbul). Tarih Vakfı Yurt Yayınları, İstanbul (1997)
42. Nilsson, E.G.: Design patterns for user interface for mobile applications. Adv. Eng. Softw. **40**(12), 1318–1328 (2009)
43. Groth, A., Haslwanter, D.: Efficiency, effectiveness, and satisfaction of responsive mobile tourism websites: a mobile usability study. Inf. Technol. Tourism **16**(2), 201–228 (2015). https://doi.org/10.1007/s40558-015-0041-0
44. Wörndl, W., Herzog, D.: Mobile applications for e-Tourism. In: Handbook of e-Tourism, pp. 1–21(2020)

Development of a Virtual CH Path on WEB: Integration of a GIS, VR, and Other Multimedia Data

A. Scianna[1]([⊠]), G. F. Gaglio[1], M. La Guardia[2], and G. Nuccio[1]

[1] ICAR-CNR (High Performance Computing and Networking Institute - National Research Council of Italy) At GISLab, Via Ugo La Malfa 153, 90146 Palermo, Italy
andrea.scianna@cnr.it

[2] Department of Engineering, Polytechnic School of University of Palermo, Viale delle Scienze, Edificio 10, 90128 Palermo, Italy
marcellolaguardia87@libero.it

Abstract. Recent advances in computer science allowed people to explore new possibilities for the fruition of CH all around the world. The development of Geographic Information Systems (GIS) in the field of territorial systems and the evolution of Virtual Reality (VR) solutions opened new scenarios for the valorization of cultural goods. At the same time, recent advances in digital photogrammetry and 3D interactive navigation models on WEB-based on WebGL technologies offered new opportunities of digital fruition of CH. Considering this panorama, the presented work shows how the integration of these technologies gives a precious added value to the virtual fruition of CH. In particular, it has been considered a cultural path in the La Loggia district, located into the historic centre of Palermo. This area is rich in monuments, many of them not accessible to the public, within the I-ACCESS European Project. The starting idea was to enlarge and diffuse, as much as possible, the accessibility to the knowledge of cultural goods in a virtual way, stimulating at the same time their real fruition. The developed solution implemented a GIS platform HTML 5 based and freely available online from desktop and mobile devices. In the virtual tour, everyone could navigate inside the cultural path, accompanied by touristic information, and come and visit the indoor environments of the main monuments. This work offers a new approach to accessibility and represents an example of how new technologies could support the diffusion of knowledge of CH.

Keywords: CH · VR · GIS · WebGL · SfM · TLS

1 Introduction

This paper regards a work on the application of GIS systems and the virtual world to the enhancement of Cultural Heritage. The advances achieved on the potential of these technologies are today increasingly promising. Even more interesting is the union of several technologies that, born in different contexts and for various purposes, allow users a better use of what surrounds them. Considering the field of territorial information

© Springer Nature Switzerland AG 2021
M. Ioannides et al. (Eds.): EuroMed 2020, LNCS 12642, pp. 178–189, 2021.
https://doi.org/10.1007/978-3-030-73043-7_15

services, the use of the GIS platform is almost widely diffused for providing the necessary information linked to the geographic position. It allows users to connect the geographic elements (points, lines and polygons) with semantic data stored in a Relational Database Management System (RDBMS) server (Zlatanova and Stoter 2006). In fact, today the implementation on WEB of this kind of technology (WEBGIS) is typical in many sectors, because users have the possibility to remotely connect their devices to GIS platforms through Web Map Services (WMS) and Web Feature Services (WFS). In this field, the collaboration between developers and researchers all over the world created a free and open-source standard protocol share geographic information in free repositories distributed on the WEB (Brovelli et al. 2012). The implementation of this technology to CH allows achieving a further level of accessibility to monuments and cultural sites, for touristic and scientific aims.

Advances in technologies related to photogrammetric reconstruction allow obtaining very accurate models both in geometry and in the application of realistic textures. The point clouds generated by the Structure from Motion algorithm (SfM) can be obtained today in a relatively short time and with a surprising quality using not expensive cameras. The use of low/medium range Unmanned Aerial Vehicles (UAVs) also offers new solutions in surveying and image acquisition operations, thanks to the possibility to acquire aerial nadir and oblique images with high-resolution cameras (Pepe et al. 2019). The 3D data obtained by these means can then be used in various applications in the field of CH valorization, from monitoring and conservation purposes (Dominici et al. 2017) to documentation (Guarnieri et al. 2017) or virtual representations finalized to virtual fruition (Scianna et al. 2020; Scianna et al. 2016). In Virtual Reality applications, in particular, 3D models of architectural heritage can be freely explored by users from any point of view. This makes this technology, mainly applied to the world of video games, very captivating in a higher context such as the cultural one. Furthermore, virtual environments can now be accessed at any time and in any place, thanks to mobile devices such as smartphones and tablets. Just downloading a particular app or accessing a webpage it is possible to gain new levels of knowledge. The virtual exploration of an environment also allows eliminating, at least in part, some problems related to accessibility to CH. Many cultural sites are inaccessible today both due to problems associated with the disability of some users and because they are located in places that are difficult to reach or, more simply, because they are closed to the public. Another interesting aspect is, as mentioned previously, the possibility of sharing virtual reconstructions through the WEB. The WebGL libraries, based on the HTML5 standard, allow users to load three-dimensional virtual environments within .html pages that can be opened in the most common browsers. With a simple click, it is possible then to quickly access a large number of visual information on CH. All of these technologies connected together allow enhancing the possibility of sharing CH information, useful for conservation, documentation and accessibility purposes (Dhonju et al. 2018; Themistocleous et al. 2015). In fact, recent studies focus the attention on the experimentation of the integration of augmented, virtual and mixed reality finalized to the improvement of CH accessibility (Bekele et al. 2018).

In the following sections of this article, therefore, the level of advancement and the potential offered by the technologies mentioned above, in the context of the CH, will be analysed. This will then be followed by the presentation of the case study regarding the creation of a virtual path inside the historic centre of the city of Palermo in which different technologies and different types of data will be combined to offer a complete exploration of some architectural jewels present in the site.

2   GIS and WEBGIS Finalized to Fruition and Conservation of CH

The fast diffusion of desktop and mobile electronic devices and the diffusion of portable internet connection enlarged the possibilities offered by GIS-based territorial services. In fact, if before the use of these technologies was almost limited to only specialists like architects, engineers and archaeologists, today GIS applications are commonly used by everyone simply through the activation of georeferencing of proper devices. Considering the world of CH, the development of GIS platform accessible by clients on the WEB, called WEBGIS, strongly supported in recent times the accessibility of monuments and archaeological sites. Indeed, it's possible to connect the geographical localization of the place of interest with semantic documentation regarding history, conditions and characteristics, connecting the GNSS positioning of the considered places with a proper relational database (Pelcer-Vujačić and Kovačević 2016). This is the case of Spatial Information System (SIS), where specialists that came from different fields work together for the construction of a platform available through a WEBGIS implementation useful for the fruition and the conservation of cultural goods (Vacca et al. 2018). The making of this kind of structure also needs the integration of different kinds of data to be acquired (Scianna and Villa 2011). For instance, considering the archaeological sites it's necessary to connect raster and vectorial data, semantic RDBMS information and 3D models in the same system. The possibility of associating geometrical 3D datasets with semantic information stored in a proper database approaches the GIS structure based on CityGML (Geographic Markup Language) standard with the BIM architecture based on IFC (Industry Foundation Classes). In particular, this affinity could result useful for developing multiscale methodologies for the territorial analysis (Noardo et al. 2020; Colucci et al. 2020).

Sometimes the use of SIS applied to the world of CH could be also strategic for the monitoring of monuments and archaeological sites threatened by anthropogenic hazards. In this case, the integration of remote sensing acquisitions integrated with GIS analysis is necessary (Agapiou et al. 2015). A similar approach could be used for discovering possible archaeological remains hidden by vegetation in impervious landscapes (Gennaro et al. 2019). Considering the GIS visualization, recent advances in computer graphics allowed specialists to develop 3D Globe platforms (Brovelli et al. 2013; Scianna and La Guardia 2018), where every kind of data could be loaded and projected over the terrain surface. However, the 2D visualization for some applications remains more accessible and more user-friendly in navigation.

3   3D Environments for CH Valorization: VR and AR

The speed and accuracy with which, today, the technologies related to the architectural survey allow the digital reconstruction of CH elements are surprising. An important strength is, in fact, the possibility of obtaining complete point clouds of an architectural complex with an adequate level of geometric accuracy. In particular, digital photogram-metry has the great advantage of allowing rapid acquisition of images with not too expensive equipment. The scanned images acquired from different points and from different angles of view achieved a good level of quality and definition. This, combined with the automatic reconstruction based on the SfM algorithm, allows obtaining aligned point clouds of external and internal environments in a relatively accurate way. The use of high-quality images also guarantees a good result in the creation of textures to be applied to 3D models. Obviously, it is always necessary to take into account the size of the object to be detected, the lighting conditions, the number of photos needed and the processing times. These are all elements that influence, in different ways, the final result aimed at creating navigable virtual environments. The point clouds generated through digital photogrammetry procedures can be transformed into meshes and used in virtual and augmented reality applications.

The use of VR, already widespread in various fields, has recently also involved the world of CH. Thanks to the availability of new media, the digitisation of CH qualifies as a new way of transmitting knowledge. It is, therefore, possible to provide information in different forms and for various purposes, quickly and with a user-friendly approach. In particular, the VR application to the world of CH has proved to be an interesting tool for the reconstruction, preservation and safeguarding of artistic works. Huge advantages can be obtained in the digital reconstruction of damaged parts or in supporting restoration interventions. Furthermore, three-dimensionality and virtuality are capable of giving particular emotions to the observer. For this reason, it has been experimented in museums to enrich the real experience (Carrozzino and Bergamasco 2010). Moreover, the images enjoy a more immediate degree of understanding than reading. This makes visualization-based applications very effective in cultural dissemination and documentation (Koeva et al. 2017). Archaeological sites, museums and art collections (Fineschi and Pozzebon 2015) can also rely on these technologies to increase the involvement of the viewer, offering a further level of knowledge of what is observed in reality (Becattini et al. 2016). Interactive monitors, consoles with three-dimensional reconstructions and AR applications increase and renew interest in culture. By making use of virtuality, it is, therefore, possible to interact with objects in the collection even at a distance, thus involving a greater number of users, including the disabled and students. The new scenarios opened by the application of VR to the world of CH led researchers to produce several experimentations in the field of heritage education, coming proper in the world of serious games (Luigini et al. 2020; Skarlatos et al. 2016).

4   The Virtual Path Through the La Loggia District of Palermo

Within the I-Access European Project, the choice to enhance the monumental heritage in the part of the city of Palermo named La Loggia or Castellammare was inspired by the extraordinary cultural, artistic and architectural value of the district (Fig. 1). From the Norman period, the district became the favourite place of settlement for merchants of different origins. Genoes, Venetians, Pisans, Amalfitans, Catalans built their lodges for commerce, their high houses and their churches.

With their decline, the craft corporations settled and the heart of the district became the largest food market in the city, still known today with the name of Vucciria. The

Fig. 1. The cultural goods considered in the virtual tour in the historical centre of Palermo.

term comes from the French "boucherie" meaning butchery and in the Sicilian dialect indicates the confusion and shouts typical of the popular market.

In the minute and winding urban context of the shops, examples of monumental churches stand out. Most of these are the result of the political, economic and spiritual commitment of religious orders and confraternities. Rarely accessible to the public, these buildings constitute and preserve, within them, examples of significant artistic value that the virtual path aims to make accessible by the means of augmented reality applications.

Starting from the point closest to the sea, the route intercepts the church of San Giorgio dei Genovesi, an example of a sixteenth-century church on columns.

Its peculiarity consists in the tetrastyle pillars that divide the three naves, a characteristic that united the church to the cathedral of Palermo where these were replaced in the eighteenth century. The second step of the virtual path consists in the XVII century church of Santa Cita or Santa Zisa, severely damaged by the bombings of World War II and by carelessness; now restored and returned to worship (Mendola 1998). The church preserves one of the first works by the sculptor Antonello Gagini in Palermo, the external arc of the altar, sculpted in Carrara marble in 1504 and completed by the altar in 1516-17 (Nobile 2010; La Barbera 1998).

On the right side of the apes opens the chapel of the SS. Rosario, burial place of the Brotherhood of SS Rosario, built between 1635 and 1641. The colourful marble inlays, covering its wall entirely, are an early example of this kind of decoration in Palermo, inspired by the chapel of Santa Rosalia inside the cathedral, and by some chapels in the Jesuit's church of Casa Professa. Attributed to Nicolò Travaglia and Gaspare Guercio the decoration was accomplished between 1696 and 1722 by sculptural reliefs of the ten Mysteries of the Rosary, realized by Giocacchino Vitagliano on models by Giacomo Serpotta (Piazza 2007).

The rich monumental site of Santa Cita also includes the oratory with the same name. It was entirely decorated at the end of the XVII century by Giacomo Serpotta, master in the creation of complex decorative sculptural patterns in white stucco, polished with marble dust. The rectangular oratory features sculptures of personifications of the Mysteries and Virtues on the major sides, while the main theme is represented in the entrance wall: the battle of Lepanto, celebrating the victory of the Christian fleet over the Turkish fleet in 1571 (Palazzotto 2016; Grasso et al. 2015).

Moving forward the market, the path intercepts another extraordinary example of baroque decoration with marble inlays, the church of Santa Maria in Valverde of the Carmelite nuns, work of the architect of the Senato of Palermo Paolo Amato. The decorative setting was structured by Amato articulating the walls with imposing and hyper-decorated marble altars, framed by giant Solomonic columns (Piazza 2007). The sixteenth-century church of Santa Maria la Nova dominates a small square at crossroads between the via Giovanni Meli street and the Materassai street. The architect, Antonio Peris, designed a three naves basilica supported by columns with a large transept-sanctuary, basing on the example of the late-gothic Church of Santa Maria della Catena at the ancient port of Cala (Nobile 2009). The facade, based on the same model, took inspiration from the fifteenth-century front porch with three arches of the cathedral of Palermo. Continuing towards the sea you can come across the baroque facade of the church of San Sebastiano, attributed to Gaspare Guercio. Behind the facade hides a sixteenth-century church with characteristics similar to that of Santa Maria la Nova.

The project is modular, other partners must provide textual information through the general project website. Information hotspots present on facades of monuments call links to the project website pages (https://www.i-access.eu/ - under construction). The information will be provided at different levels of detail depending on the users and their level of interest. The work described here is an accomplished part of the larger platform that will provide web services, geoservices, textual information and other multimedia information.

5   The Construction of the WEB Platform

The first study of the work has been the choice of the best solution to guarantee user-friendly navigation of the considered historical path. The idea has been the creation of a reference map of the site, where it's possible to visualize the touristic path and the main monuments of the area. Navigating inside the map, users can click and navigate along the path or inside the cultural goods.

Hence, the proper virtual navigation starts, where users could make a virtual walk along the path, where it's possible directly to come inside the monuments and to read the related historical documentation (Fig. 2). In this way, the tourist is immersed inside the environment such as a serious game and is motivated to continue the visit and discover new places. An important requirement of this platform should be the free and the simple access on the WEB from any kind of device, in order to be totally user-friendly.

5.1   The Main Map

In light of these requirements, the main visualization has been a 2D map of the considered area of the historic center of Palermo. This visualization is based on a WEBGIS connected to the Open Street Map Site and to server folders, in order to load georeffered elements like maps, rasters and vectorial data. The coordinate system used in the platform is EPSG 4326 WGS 84. The main visualization of the map consists of a.html file, where an Open Layer structure has been set up through the implementation of javascript strings. In this way it's possible to insert in the map further layers called from remote servers through WMS service. The touristic path is indicated with a series of points, where each one is located in correspondence with the spherical panorama associated with it. Users could start the navigation simply clicking on any point of the path. Along the path the main monuments are indicated with proper popups, allowing direct access to the virtual navigation models.

5.2   The Virtualization of the Monuments: From Survey to WEB Navigation

The process of virtualization of historical constructions is very complex. First of all, it's necessary to define the final use of the 3D representation. In this case, the final aim is to allow the online navigation of the 3D environments. Hence, it's necessary to find the true balance between the weight of the 3D models and the necessary level of detail and realism to achieve. In fact, to guarantee good performance on web-browsing of virtual monuments, it's necessary to limit the file extension of the models strongly. It's essential to take care of these requirements in all the phases of the process, starting from the survey. The monuments considered for the virtual navigation along the La Loggia district path of Palermo were chosen based on their historical relevance and their difficult accessibility. In particular, the considered monuments have been the church of San Giorgio dei Genovesi, focusing the attention on the internal pillars, the church of

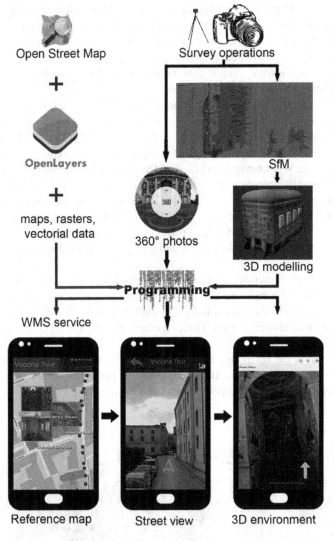

Fig. 2. Application development workflow.

Santa Cita, considering the altar of Gagini, the chapel of SS. Rosario and the indoor environment of the oratory, the church of Santa Maria La Nova.

Survey operations started with the geometrical acquisition of the environments with Terrestrial Laser Scanner (TLS) instrumentation and then to acquire several chunks of photos from different angles and with different cameras for the further photogrammetric reconstruction.

In particular, a Faro Focus 3D 150 laser scanner has been used for geometric acquisition. The photo acquisition has been obtained with three different instrumentations, a Single Reflex Camera (SLR) Canon EOS 550 D with 18 megapixels for shootings on the ground, an SLR Camera Sony Alpha 6000 with 24 megapixels for shootings taken with an extendable pole at different levels, and the micro UAV equipment DJI Tello with 5 mpx camera for shootings on flight of not accessible surfaces. The digital photogrammetric reconstruction based on SfM algorithm has been carried out with Agisoft Photoscan software, creating the point clouds of the considered environment and subsequently generating the 3D meshes.

The 3D models obtained from the photogrammetric processing have been properly simplified and refined in Blender, an opensource modelling software. In this phase, the geometric shape and the texture map have been modified to be loaded into a WebGL environment. In particular, considering the strong limitation on geometric dimension to guarantee effective WEB navigation (15–20 MB), a good level of texture definition has been a fundamental requirement to obtain a realistic online virtual visualization. Once refined, the Blender file has been loaded into the Verge3D application to proceed with programming the WebGL application. Verge3D, in fact, consists of two parts: a plug-in, in Blender, that allows the export of the project in.glTF and an application that reads this file together with the original Blender file and allows it to be modified visually through a puzzle template.

To carry out the first-person navigation, a capsule-shaped object was created to which physical properties of a rigid body were associated. A camera was attached to it at a height corresponding to the human head. Physical properties of a rigid body have also been associated with church models. This procedure, also used in the creation of the most common first-person video games, is necessary to prevent the user from going across the walls and objects of the 3D model. Through the Verge3D visual programming system, it was then possible to add movement to the capsule-shaped object which, moving, drags the camera with it following a specific input from the user (Fig. 3).

Fig. 3. WebGL app visualization from the browser. Particular of the church of S. Cita.

6   Conclusions

This paper describes an example of how digital technologies could be implemented in a unique structure for the development of an immersive experience on CH. WEBGIS implementation, 3D modelling, Virtual Reality and WebGL navigation are integrated for a unique goal: adding an advanced level of accessibility to a network of cultural goods. The created structure could be further enriched, adding semantic descriptions, 3D models, and linking AR applications connected to the main path. The project is promoted and publicized through public initiatives aimed at the various public and private stakeholders by the municipalities of Palermo and Valletta. The impact on users will be verified through some indicators by other project partners. The developed work allows simple navigation with the main browsers (Chrome, Firefox, Safari) for desktop and mobile devices, and is completely free. In this way, it's possible to freely navigate inside the path, visiting the considered monuments independently from any obstacle to their real accessibility. The virtual navigation grows not only the knowledge about cultural goods but also the interest and the desire to visit the real ones. In fact, the virtual tourist path is a complementary source of knowledge to the real visit of the monuments, and couldn't be never seen as a substitute for it. The diffusion of this kind of applications could be strategic in the future to disseminate the CH knowledge embracing the interest of the new generations and, at the same time, offering a further opportunity of accessibility complementary to the real fruition.

References

Dhonju, H.K., Xiao, W., Mills, J.P., Sarhosis, V.: Share our cultural heritage (SOCH): worldwide 3D heritage reconstruction and visualization via web and mobile GIS. ISPRS Int. J. Geo-Inf. **7**, 360 (2018)

Pelcer–Vujačić, O., Kovačević, S.: A GIS database of Montenegrin Katuns (Kuči Mountain and Durmitor). In: Ioannides, M., et al. (eds.) Digital Heritage. Progress in Cultural Heritage: Documentation, Preservation, and Protection. Lecture Notes in Computer Science, vol. 10059, pp. 72–80. Springer, Cham (2016). https://doi.org/10.1007/978-3-319-48974-2_9

Vacca, G., Fiorino, D.R., Pili, D.: A spatial information system (SIS) for the architectural and cultural heritage of Sardinia (Italy). ISPRS Int. J. Geo-Inf. **7**, 49 (2018)

Brovelli, M., Hogan, P., Minghini, M., Zamboni, G.: The power of Virtual Globes for valorising cultural heritage and enabling sustainable tourism: NASA World Wind applications. Int. Arch. Photogram. Remote Sens. Spatial Inf. Sci. **XL-4/W2**, 115–120 (2013). https://doi.org/10.5194/isprsarchives-XL-4-W2-115-2013

Scianna, A., Villa, B.: GIS applications in archaeology. Archeologia e Calcolatori **22**, 337–363 (2011). ISSN 1120-6861

Agapiou, A., et al.: Cultural heritage management and monitoring using remote sensing data and GIS: the case study of Paphos area, Cyprus. Comput. Environ. Urban Syst. **54**, 230–239 (2015). https://doi.org/10.1016/j.compenvurbsys.2015.09.003

Gennaro, A., Candiano, A., Fargione, G., Mussumeci, G., Mangiameli, M.: GIS and remote sensing for post-dictive analysis of archaeological features. A case study from the Etnean region (Sicily). Archeologia e Calcolatori **30**, 309–328 (2019)

Scianna, A., La Guardia, M.: Globe based 3D GIS solutions for virtual heritage. In: International Archives of the Photogrammetry, Remote Sensing and Spatial Information Sciences, vol. XLII-4/W10, pp. 171–177 (2018)

Colucci, E., De Ruvo, V., Lingua, A., Matrone, F., Rizzo, G.: HBIM-GIS integration: from IFC to CityGML standard for damaged cultural heritage in a multiscale 3D GIS. Appl. Sci. **10**, 1356 (2020)

Noardo, F., et al.: Tools for BIM-GIS integration (IFC georeferencing and conversions): results from the GeoBIM benchmark 2019. ISPRS Int. J. Geo-Inf. **9**, 502 (2020)

Bekele, M.K., Pierdicca, R., Frontoni, E., Malinverni, E.S., Gain, J.: A survey of augmented, virtual, and mixed reality for cultural heritage. J. Comput. Cult. Herit. **11**(2), 1–36 (2018). https://doi.org/10.1145/3145534

Pepe, M., Fregonese, L., Crocetto, N.: Use of SfM-MVS approach to nadir and oblique images generated throught aerial cameras to build 2.5D map and 3D models in urban areas. Geocarto Int., 1–22 (2019). https://doi.org/10.1080/10106049.2019.1700558

Guarnieri, A., Fissore, F., Masiero, A., Vettore, A.: From TLS survey to 3D solid modeling for documentation of built heritage: the case study of porta savonarola in Padua. Int. Arch. Photogram. Remote Sens. Spatial Inf. Sci. **XLII-2/W5**, 303–308 (2017). https://doi.org/10.5194/isprs-archives-XLII-2-W5-303-2017

Dominici, D., Alicandro, M., Massimi, V.: UAV photogrammetry in the post-earthquake scenario: case studies in L'Aquila. Geomat. Nat. Haz. Risk **8**(1), 87–103 (2017). https://doi.org/10.1080/19475705.2016.1176605

Scianna, A., Gaglio, G.F., La Guardia, M.: Digital photogrammetry, TLS survey and 3D modelling for VR and AR applications in CH. Int. Arch. Photogram. Remote Sens. Spatial Inf. Sci. **XLIII-B2-2020**, 901–909 (2020). https://doi.org/10.5194/isprs-archives-XLIII-B2-2020-901-2020

Scianna, A., La Guardia, M., Scaduto, M.L.: Definition of a workflow for web browsing of 3D models in archaeology. In: Ioannides, M., et al. (eds.) Digital Heritage. Progress in Cultural Heritage: Documentation, Preservation, and Protection. Lecture Notes in Computer Science, vol. 10059, pp. 41–52. Springer, Cham (2016). https://doi.org/10.1007/978-3-319-48974-2_6

Brovelli, M.A., Mitasova, H., Neteler, M., Raghavan, V.: Free and open source desktop and Web GIS solutions. Appl. Geomatics **4**(2), 65–66 (2012)

Zlatanova, S., Stoter, J.: The role of DBMS in the new generation GIS architecture. In: Rana, S., Sharma, J. (eds.) Frontiers of Geographic Information Technology, pp. 155–180. Springer-Verlag, Heidelberg (2006). https://doi.org/10.1007/3-540-31305-2_8

Carrozzino, M., Bergamasco, M.: Beyond virtual museums: experiencing immersive virtual reality in real museums. J. Cult. Herit. **11**(4), 452–458 (2010). https://doi.org/10.1016/j.culher.2010.04.001

Fineschi, A., Pozzebon, A.: A 3D virtual tour of the Santa Maria della Scala Museum Complex in Siena, Italy, based on the use of Oculus Rift HMD. In: 2015 International Conference on 3D Imaging (IC3D), Liege, pp. 1–5 (2015). https://doi.org/10.1109/IC3D.2015.7391825

Becattini, F., Ferracani, A., Landucci, L., Pezzatini, D., Uricchio, T., Del Bimbo, A.: Imaging Novecento. A mobile app for automatic recognition of artworks and transfer of artistic styles. In: Ioannides, M., et al. (eds.) Digital Heritage. Progress in Cultural Heritage: Documentation, Preservation, and Protection. Lecture Notes in Computer Science, vol. 10058, pp. 781–791. Springer, Cham (2016). https://doi.org/10.1007/978-3-319-48496-9_62

Luigini, A., Parricchi, M.A., Basso, A., Basso, D.: Immersive and participatory serious games for heritage education, applied to the cultural heritage of South Tyrol. Interact. Des. Archit. J. IxD&A **43**, 42–67 (2020)

Skarlatos, D., et al.: Project iMARECULTURE: advanced VR, iMmersive Serious Games and Augmented REality as Tools to Raise Awareness and Access to European Underwater CULTURal heritagE. In: Ioannides, M., et al. (eds.) Digital Heritage. Progress in Cultural Heritage: Documentation, Preservation, and Protection. Lecture Notes in Computer Science, vol. 10058, pp. 805–813. Springer, Cham (2016). https://doi.org/10.1007/978-3-319-48496-9_64

Koeva, M., Luleva, M., Maldjanski, P.: Integrating spherical panoramas and maps for visualization of cultural heritage objects using virtual reality technology. Sensors **17**, 829 (2017)

Themistocleous, K., Ioannides, M., Agapiou, A., Hadjimitsis, D.G..: The methodology of documenting cultural heritage sites using photogrammetry, UAV, and 3D printing techniques: the case study of Asinou Church in Cyprus. In: Proceedings of the SPIE 9535, 3rd International Conference on Remote Sensing and Geoinformation of the Environment (RSCy2015), vol. 9535, 19 June 2015. https://doi.org/10.1117/12.2195626

Piazza S.: I colori del Barocco. Flaccovio, Palermo (2007)

Nobile, M.R..: Antonello Gagini Architetto. Flaccovio, Palermo (2010)

Nobile, M.R.: Chiese colonnari in Sicilia (XVI secolo). Caracol, Palermo (2009)

Mendola, G.: La chiesa di Santa Cita. In: Di Natale, M.C. (ed.) La chiesa di Santa Cita. Ritorno all'antico splendore, Palermo, pp. 33–60 (1998)

La Barbera, S.: Antonello Gagini a Santa Cita. In: Di Natale, M.C. (ed.) La chiesa di Santa Cita. Ritorno all'antico splendore, Palermo, pp. 61–92 (1998)

Palazzotto, P.: Giacomo Serpotta. Gli oratori di Palermo. Guida Storico artistica. Edizioni d'arte Kalós, Palermo (2016)

Grasso, S., Mendola, G., Scordato, C., Viola, V.: Giacomo Serpotta. L'oratorio di Santa Cita. Eunoedizioni, Palermo (2015)

Kirini: An Interactive Projection-Mapping Installation for Storytelling About Mediterranean Beekeeping Heritage

Nikolaos Ioakeim, Petros Printezis, Charalampos Skarimpas,
Panayiotis Koutsabasis⃝, Spyros Vosinakis⃝, and Modestos Stavrakis⁽⊠⁾⃝

Department of Product and System Design Engineering, University of Aegean,
84100 Syros, Greece
{dpsd16036,dpsd16095,dpsd16100,kpg,spyrosv,modestos}@aegean.gr

Abstract. Project Kirini is an autonomous interactive indoor exhibit, which utilizes the technologies of projection mapping and physical computing to highlight the cultural heritage of beekeeping in the island region of Cyclades in Greece. The team members researched and collected material on the tradition and the techniques of beekeeping from the ancient times until today through bibliographies and physical interviews. After the completion of the research and organization of the information, the team designed four different types of interactive scenarios. Through a set of formative evaluations, several issues comments and ideas emerged and iteratively implemented to enhance the prototype. Having gathered the results and the conclusions from the evaluations an interactive exhibit was produced and installed in public space.

Keywords: Interactive exhibit · Storytelling · Projection mapping · Physical computing · Beekeeping · Apiculture · Cultural heritage · Cyclades

1 Introduction

Project Kirini is an autonomous interactive indoor exhibit, which utilizes the technologies of projection mapping and physical computing to highlight the cultural heritage of beekeeping in the Cycladic islands located at the Aegean Sea in Greece. It is based on beekeeping's history, techniques and practices that have been used in the past and continue to exist in the present, as well as current testimonials. The project idea is presented by an interactive documentary based on a large-scale projection installation with physical interaction. It has an educational and entertaining character. Users have the ability to interact with a room that is fully mapped with projections (walls, floor). The users are involved in various tests/tasks that are presented throughout the scenario. Each task is related to a specific part of the scenario and is dubbed by a voice over narration.

The project belongs to the category of interactive exhibits. It can stand on its own as part of a museum, in an exhibition area related to beekeeping or independent in a suitable room. Depending on the installation space it would require appropriate adjustments in association with the audience and its duration, as well as to the installation itself. In this

M. Ioannides et al. (Eds.): EuroMed 2020, LNCS 12642, pp. 190–201, 2021.
https://doi.org/10.1007/978-3-030-73043-7_16

project we approach Kirini as an autonomous exhibit, intended for ages 12 and above, while its chapters aim to approach all ages.

Today, we experience an increase in interest from the audience for exhibits rich in content, quality and interaction. Interactive systems are the solution as they more easily capture the viewers' interest and expose them directly to information with which they come in physical contact and therefore assimilate them faster and easier. When it comes to exhibits with an extensive narrative character, viewers need even more motivation to stay focused. In such a case, a system rich in audiovisual material and interactions becomes essential [1]. A system with a narrative character can more effectively strike at the emotion of the audience and therefore transmit ideas, information and raise awareness [2]. Research supported by this paper aims at proving the technological means to raise awareness on the importance of bees for the environment, inform users about the value of beekeeping practices as exercised in the past and today and thus promote interest and educate people to understand the necessity of the protection of these cultural assets.

2 Related Work

In recent years technology has allowed us to acquire experiences of cultural content in new and exciting ways. A number of methods, techniques and design approaches where presented in literature to prove this fact [3–10]. In this section we provide a short review of the most important projects, similar to our work. The following projects are independent examples of smart applications of today's technology, for the entertainment of people or even for a new experience of visiting an art museum. Immersive Interactive Ltd. is a system that uses Kinect motion sensing controller, projectors, and projection mapping software to display video and images within a space with which a user can interact. The user can solve quizzes given by the system itself and do various actions by simply waving his/her hands or touching the projection. The big difference with the project Kirini is the technology that is used, the absence of narrative flow in the form of a documentary as well as that the user has to read the system usage instructions. RoomAlive is a concept project that uses projection mapping in a room setting. It achieves it by using projectors and depth sensing cameras, thus turning the room into a projected surface. By simultaneously using projection software, Kinect and motion sensors, users can interact with the space around them by leaning against the walls and the floor. It offers many possibilities for interaction in the form of a virtual game. It has similarities with project Kirini, although it does not entail physical contact with surface areas or tangible objects in the given space. It focuses on providing an entertaining rather than an educational character. Vincent Van Gogh The Experience is a touring exhibit on the works of the famous post-impressionist painter. Using multiple projection mapping technologies, an entire museum wing (or an exhibition space respectively) including many different rooms, halls and big objects is mapped. On the surfaces, animated versions of the artist's works are projected. This layout makes a lifelike environment and thus immerses the visitors to the content presented. The project is not an interactive installation and therefore it does not provide any means of direct involvement through action to the users.

3 Research, Design and Prototyping

To complete this project we followed an iterative design approach based on the methodology presented in the Interactive Systems Design Studio course [11] and it can be described with the following intertwined phases: Research and inquiry (R&I), Design and prototyping (D&P) and Evaluation and testing (E&T).

3.1 Research

This phase concerned the research that had to be conducted. The stage lasted three to four (3–4) weeks. It was focused on beekeeping's history and techniques in the Mediterranean and Aegean areas from antiquity to the present [12, 13]. At first a quick pre-panning of our research took place in identifying potential sources and securing their availability. Some basic information was found on bibliographic sources about beekeeping, honey production, problems that beekeepers were faced through times, historical facts, characters and people's testimonies [14, 15]. This material arranged and our research was planned accordingly. We identified three main areas of interest about the beekeeping practices and history of apiculture: Antiquity, Middle Ages and Present time. Each member of the research team undertook the task of finding further material for each research topic. Materials found in books, as well as information from relevant conferences and living testimonies were used besides the information from the internet. It's important to note that live testimonies from experienced beekeepers were used in this paper/work as non-disputed information. A big part of this data has been used but not to their entire extent.

When all the available material had been collected, the team started filtering the information and organizing the most useful and important parts of it. For antiquity, we used ancient Greek myths about beekeeping that show the importance of the bees and their honey information about the beehive's form and techniques that were used back then to extract the honey from the hives [14]. In the Middle Ages, we paid attention to Cyclades and beekeeping active islands [13, 14]. It mentions each beehive's variation of the form and functionality as well as each beekeepers' techniques. For today, our research was focused mainly on current beekeeping techniques. Important information was gathered through our interview with an experienced Syrian beekeeper and his personal history with the art. Having collected the desired material, the team started creating the structure of the script which would communicate the most important elements of the information to the users in a more understandable and simplistic form.

3.2 Design

The general idea of the exhibit is an interactive room with a control center in the middle. All four (4) walls of the room are video projected with content. The user, by utilizing the controllers from the control center as well as touching the projected walls, can interact with the main scenario and complete specific tasks after following the guidelines provided from the voice-over narration.

This phase included an eight-week-long design phase, including designing the prototype, writing the script, choosing the technologies and developing the audiovisual content. Having completed the research and the organization of information, the design team proceeded to design four different types of interaction with the system, as indication of the system's potential. We ended up with the following four: Games, Trivia questions, Control of narrative's flow and Interaction with tangible objects and the video projection (Fig. 1).

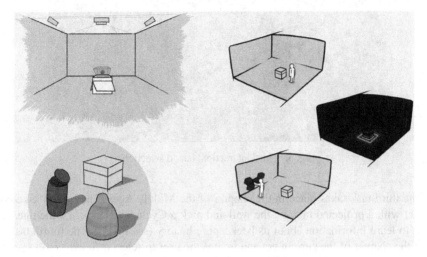

Fig. 1. Concept ideas of the exhibit

The first task regards the chapter of Antiquity, in mythology. It consists of a simple digital obstacle game where the user is asked to control a digital character. As presented in Fig. 2, the goal is to avoid the lightnings of Zeus that comes towards him/her, until the designated time passes, and the character is saved.

Fig. 2. The first interaction, digital obstacle game

The second task is also about Antiquity. The user, based on acquired knowledge provided by the installation, is asked to answer a set of multiple-choice questions. The representation of the questionnaire is provided by an ancient honeycomb. The user is asked to pick the right answer by touching one of the four different options (respective honeycomb cell) on the wall.

Fig. 3. Third interaction, island selection

The third task takes place in the chapter of the Middle Ages. The user is asked to interact with a projected map on the wall and pick a Cycladic island for which he/she wants to learn information about its beekeeping history (see Fig. 3). The fourth task is about the chapter of the current era and invites the user to select a "honeycomb frame" and place it in the right hive. For this reason, the system provides three (3) tangible objects that represent a honeycomb frame and ask the user to place them in an appropriate socket. Every honeycomb frame prob has unique physical and visual characteristics in order to be distinguishable from the rest (see Fig. 4).

Fig. 4. Fourth interaction, interaction with tangible objects

After the ideation of these four interactions, we created use case scenarios, the semi-final script of the documentary (with room for small content changes) and some indicative storyboards describing the entrance of the user in the room, his first contact with the system and how it's operation will proceed. At the same time, task analysis diagrams were created and were corrected and made more detailed in the design process that followed.

The control center was the last piece of the Design. It would represent a beehive in shape (and in particular the "warm construction" that was designed by the monk Stephen de la Rocca [12]) and through this the user could interact to some extent with the system. It would include projections in a form of holograms, which would represent the three of our narrators as well as it would show some indications for the user about the operation and interaction with the system (Fig. 5).

Fig. 5. Left: Our final prototype of the control center, right: De la Roca's "warm construction" [12]

3.3 Prototyping

The technologies tested and used for prototyping include hardware and software platforms. For hardware we used Arduino, Bare Conductive Touch Board and a variety of sensors and actuators. Software used includes Unity, Qlab and MadMapper. Since we concluded that we could make use of these technologies, we performed technology tests and focused in identifying potential problems and incompatibilities with our scenarios. One useful conclusion that came up was that Arduino Uno did not meet our needs. More specifically, the Midi and Keyboard libraries were not functioning as expected, to trigger events on Qlab. For this reason we chose to continue with two of the Care Conductive Touch Boards which also provided core libraries for Midi and keyboard interaction (Fig. 6). In parallel to this design task we completed the script direction and the graphic design and animations of the exhibit using frame by frame technique. The graphics where designed to represent real objects and locations of the Cycladic area, except for the part of Mythology in the chapter of Antiquity that were loosely based on reality and were mostly conceptualized by the graphic artist/animator.

The first prototype was based on the task of 'island selection' of the third chapter. It consisted of a small-scale model, and the projector. For the control center and its hologram, we built a miniature physical model made from paper and utilized a tablet as a projector of the visuals.

After several design iterations the final prototype was an actual full-scale room. The prototype was built by using three wooden frames covered with cloth for the room

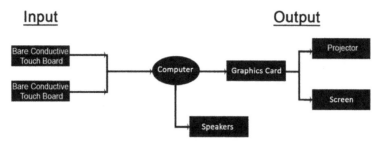

Fig. 6. The structure of the whole system

walls, the contact points on the fabric were created with copper threads which passed through one side of the cloth to the other where the wiring existed while in the control center the corresponding contact points were created with conductive paint provided by Bare Conductive. In terms of interactivity, these touch points provided the user with a tangible interface to control the Trivia questions, and Control of Narrative's flow. The control center was created with an actual 1:1 scale. On its top surface the physical controls/buttons where placed: one to initiate the application of the exhibit, another to start the game and finally a skip button for advancing to the next task. On the right and left sides respectively the buttons that control the character of the game where placed, while on the lower left side a drawer that contained the three tangible honeycombs of the fourth task where placed. At the center of the construction an opening was created to support the displays of the hologram. All individual pieces of the control center operated through a Bare Conductive Touch Board and touch interaction based on conductive sensors. A second Touch Board was also used for the cloths covering the walls. These included eight (8) contact points for the island selection and four (4) other points for the multiple choices used on the honeycomb tasks (Trivia question). The video wall projection was developed with a wide-angle projector, mounted on a tripod (stand) at the right side of the room. The following Fig. 7 provides a schematic of the various components used and the general layout of the installation.

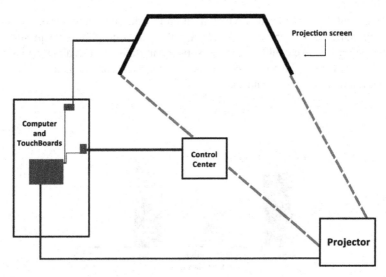

Fig. 7. Room's layout with components

4 Evaluation

The evaluation took place after the installation of the prototype and it lasted two days. Its purpose was to expose aspects of the system that needed improvements, simulating the experience that a person would have with the final system. The information that we would extract through this process would help us improve the system to a more ideal form, in the evolution of the interactions and in the functionality of the whole structure.

Twelve (n = 12) people were divided in six (6) teams of two (2). By design this is considered the ideal number of people for the simultaneous use of the system. The volunteers were university students through the ages of 19 and 23 years of age and professors 35 to 45 years of age. Most of them were not familiar with such systems. Each evaluation lasted about 30 to 40 min. Each team was requested before the start of the process to externalize their thoughts, while some important instructions were given to familiarize them with the subject and understand what they were about to experience. The users then came in contact with the system itself. They experienced a complete simulation of the final project/exhibit. During this process the reviewers (we) had the role of a passive observer and acted only if user aid was needed. However, every user's move and action was observed and then recorded for later evaluation of the system's use. At the end of the process, the users were given a twenty (20) part questionnaire to answer, with questions relative to the theme, the interactions, the aesthetics of the graphic elements and generally the experience and the construction of the system.

Via the evaluation, many problems and aspects that needed improvement were recorded. Some of the most basic problems and discoveries were: a) that the users didn't know where to stand during the test, b) didn't know when they should leave and/or return at the control center or walk toward the projection surface, c) we found some issues with the clarity of the interactions, d) some of the users said that they would like to see more interactions to feel more engaged throughout the whole experience and e) an issue was discovered about the control center which didn't allow the smooth use of the system for every height (taller users were unable to observe the hologram). From the questions that were made at the end, we could proceed to some quantitative results about which of the three chapters was more favored from the users in terms of content, and which was the most liked interaction (Figs. 8 and 9).

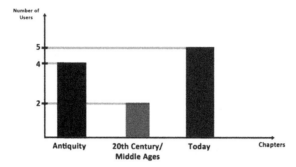

Fig. 8. Diagram showing which chapter the users preferred most

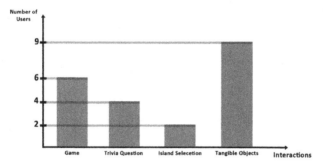

Fig. 9. Diagram showing user's most preferred interaction

All the users expressed learning things about beekeeping after this experience as well as it was made really engaging by presenting information in the form of animation and live narration. One of the things that was requested by users when they were asked "what they would change in this system", was to be able to choose one of the three chapters and the option to repeat the instructions of the interactions again in case they missed some information.

4.1 Evaluation Results and Future Directions

The evaluation of the early prototype led to the collection and modeling of the evaluation data. In the following list we summarize the most important findings:

- Interaction with video projected content in large rooms is a current design trend.
- The system is expensive to implement and needs specialized staff for installation.

- Information overload is not ideal for all users, especially for children.
- The user of hologram narrator and animated projection better engage users.
- Interaction mechanisms capture users' attention but also distract them.
- The design physical components must consider ergonomic factors.
- The animations should be rich and not static to keep the interest of the children.
- Interactions should be explained in detail to be understood by all users.
- Users need time comparative to amount of information in order to grasp data.
- Upon physical interaction, audio feedback is considered important.

5 Summary

Although there were areas for improvement and pieces in the design that we had not calculated from the beginning, we managed to accomplish our main goals, which were raising awareness and informing users about beekeeping culture, while entertaining them throughout the exhibit.

The need for interactive narrative exhibits and its usefulness would be assessed by performing the evaluations in a complete room, in a relevant space such as a museum or an exhibition and with the participation of people who really show interest in learning about the relevant issue. The evaluations would be in the form of a study of use by visitors in the field, as they were performed in our prototype, letting users externalize their thoughts throughout the exhibit, following a series of targeted questions. Our prototype's purpose was the "proof of concept" and that is why the evaluation of these objectives would follow in it's later generations.

Having the results and coming up with our conclusions from the evaluations, we proceeded in the implementation of the final form of the exhibit. Bearing in mind the difficulties the users encountered, we came up with a different design for the control center (Fig. 10).

Fig. 10. Renders of the control center's final concept

Initially we changed it's form to accommodate more users regardless of their height and position in the room. Then we changed the position of the screen and the glass that reflected the projection from the screen to create the hologram. Now the glass is placed in the front of the structure, while the screen was placed just in front of the glass having a 45° inclination between them. Now, the users can see the hologram clearly by standing in front of the controls (from the reflection of the glass), as well as standing on the opposite side (by looking through the glass to the screen). Also, the drawer that contained the "honeycomb frames" for the fourth interaction was moved to the front part so it could be more easily detectable by the users. Finally, one more projector will be added to achieve projections on the four walls of the room thus having five in total (4 projections for the walls and 1 for the floor) (Fig. 11).

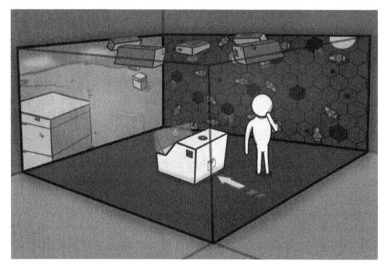

Fig. 11. Final concept of the project Kirini

References

1. Khalaf, M.: Smart cultural heritage: technologies and applications, vol. 10, pp. 1–6 (2019). https://doi.org/10.1049/cp.2019.0183
2. Beltrán, M.E., et al.: Engaging people with cultural heritage: users' perspective. In: Stephanidis, C., Antona, M. (eds.) UAHCI 2014. Lecture Notes in Computer Science, vol. 8514, pp. 639–649. Springer, Cham (2014). https://doi.org/10.1007/978-3-319-07440-5_58
3. Dimitropoulos, A., et al.: The Loom: Interactive weaving through a tangible installation with digital feedback. In: Ioannides, M. (ed.) Digital Cultural Heritage. Lecture Notes in Computer Science, vol. 10605, pp. 199–210. Springer, Cham (2018). https://doi.org/10.1007/978-3-319-75826-8_17
4. Gkiti, C., et al.: i-Wall: a low-cost interactive wall for enhancing visitor experience and promoting industrial heritage in museums. In: Ioannides, M., et al. (eds.) EuroMed 2018. Lecture Notes in Computer Science, vol. 11196, pp. 90–100. Springer, Cham (2018). https://doi.org/10.1007/978-3-030-01762-0_8
5. Ronchi, A.M.: eCulture: Cultural Content in the Digital Age. Springer, Heidelberg (2009). https://doi.org/10.1007/978-3-540-75276-9
6. Hu, J., Bartneck, C.: Culture matters: a study on presence in an interactive movie. Cyberpsychol. Behav. **11**, 529–535 (2008). https://doi.org/10.1089/cpb.2007.0093
7. Márkus, Z.L., et al.: Interactive game development to assist cultural heritage. In: Digital Presentation and Preservation of Cultural and Scientific Heritage, vol. 8, pp. 71–82 (2018)

8. Legrady, G.: Intersecting the virtual and the real: space in interactive media installations. Wide Angle **21**, 105–113 (1999). https://doi.org/10.1353/wan.1999.0005
9. Saleh, F., Badawi, M.: Cultural interactive panorama (culturama) (2007). https://patents.goo gle.com/patent/US20070139626A1/en
10. Hagebölling, H., Lling, H.H.: Interactive Dramaturgies New Approaches in Multimedia Content and Design. Springer, Heidelberg (2004). https://doi.org/10.1007/978-3-642-186 63-9
11. Koutsabasis, P., Vosinakis, S., Stavrakis, M., Kyriakoulakos, P.: Teaching HCI with a studio approach: lessons learnt. In: Presented at the Proceedings of 22nd Pan-Hellenic Conference on Informatics Conference, PCI 2018, Athens, Greece (2018)
12. Rocca, D.: Traité complet sur les abeilles, avec une méthode nouvelle de les gouverner, telle qu'elle se pratique à Syra, île de l'Archipel; précédé d'un précis historique et économique de cette île. Par M. l'abbé Della Rocca. Chez Bleuet père, Paris (1790). https://doi.org/10.5962/ bhl.title.36423
13. Hatjina, F., Mavrofridis, G., Jones, R., (eds.): Beekeeping in the Mediterranean, from antiquity to the present. Division of Apiculture Hellenic Agricultural Organization "Demeter", Nea Moudania, Greece (2017)
14. Hatjina, F., Mavrofridis, G., Jones, R.: Beekeeping in the mediterranean, from antiquity to the present. Bee World **91**, 28 (2014). https://doi.org/10.1080/0005772X.2014.11417587
15. Prost, P.J., Medori, P., (eds.): Apiculture. Intercept Ltd., Andover (1994)

Project Papers: Reproduction Techniques and Rapid Prototyping in CH

Digital Humanities: Prototype Development for Balinese Script

Cokorda Pramartha[1]([✉]) [iD], I. B. Ary Indra Iswara[2] [iD], I. P. G. Hendra Suputra[1] [iD], and I. B. Gede Dwidasmara[1]

[1] Udayana University, Bali 80361, Indonesia
cokorda@unud.ac.id
[2] STIKI Indonesia, Bali 80225, Indonesia

Abstract. In Indonesia there are more than 600 ethnic groups and 719 mother-tongue languages spoken. A significant 13 Indonesian mother-tongue languages have vanished and been forgotten as they are no longer used for daily communication. When a language is forgotten, not only is the structural aspect of the language lost, which becomes the main focus of the linguistic domain, but also the cultural and historical knowledge that is attached to the language. The Balinese language is a mother-tongue spoken on the islands of Bali and Lombok, and the Balinese script (*Aksara Bali*) is a traditional script that is used to write the Balinese language in the form of Balinese short stories, history (*itihasa*), proverbs, poetry, music, and spells (*mantra*) on the top of palm leaves (*lontar*). Recently, fewer members of the young generation of Balinese are able to speak this language due to its complexity and the widespread use of the national language (Bahasa Indonesia) in all levels of formal education. This study aims to preserve, protect, and continue the use of Balinese language and script by adopting modern technology that can be utilized by the younger Balinese generation. In this study, a physical non-QWERTY keyboard specifically for Balinese script has been designed, developed, and tested to work for multiple devices (e.g., computer, tablet, and smartphone), diverse operating systems (e.g., Windows, macOS, iOS, and Android), and various applications (e.g., Word processor, instant messenger, and social media applications). Through consultation with professors from Udayana University with expertise in Balinese language and script, a total of 89 out of 185 Balinese scripts are included in our IT artefact that can be utilized for daily use.

Keywords: Balinese language · Balinese script · Digital humanities · Heritage erosion · Non-QWERTY keyboard

1 Introduction

Bali is one of the thousands of islands in Indonesia. Bali and Indonesia are recognized internationally for their rich, diverse, and deep cultural heritage. In Indonesia, there are more than 600 ethnic groups and 719 mother-tongue languages spoken. The latest study by the Summer Institute of Linguistics (SIL) found that a significant 13 Indonesian mother-tongue languages have vanished and been forgotten as they are no longer used

© Springer Nature Switzerland AG 2021
M. Ioannides et al. (Eds.): EuroMed 2020, LNCS 12642, pp. 205–214, 2021.
https://doi.org/10.1007/978-3-030-73043-7_17

for daily communication [1]. In a mother-tongue language, the beliefs, philosophical values, rules, and traditions of a community can be understood and learned by the next generations and others [2]. When a language is forgotten, the loss is not only of the structural aspect of the language, which is the main focus of the linguistic domain, but also the cultural and historical knowledge attached to the language.

The Balinese language is one of 719 living languages spoken in Indonesia, and is mainly used on the islands of Bali and Lombok. People in Bali practice three different levels of Balinese language: high tongues (*Basa Bali Alus*), common tongues (*Basa Bali Madya*) and low tongues (*Base Bali Sor*). In the Balinese social system there are four hierarchy levels that are highly related to how the Balinese language is used: common people (*Sudra*), traders or government officials (*Waisya*), the royal family (*Kshatriya*), and high priests (*Brahmana*). "The high and low tongues are distinct, unrelated languages with separate roots, different words, and extremely dissimilar character" [3]. Up until today, many of the Balinese people have learned and transferred their cultural knowledge through socialization, where the Balinese let others experience the culture in order to understand it [4]. This can be seen from every traditional practice, such as the *banjar adat* and costume village (*desa adat)* ceremonies, which always involve a large number of people from the community [5].

Out of this diverse range of mother-tongue languages, Indonesia practices 12 traditional scripts that are commonly used to write letters, namely: Javanese script, Balinese script, Ancient Sunda, Bugis/Lontara, Rejang, Lampung, Karo, Pakpak, Simalungun, Toba, Mandailing, and Kerinci/Rencong [6]. The Balinese script (*aksara bali*) has a unique characteristic that distinguishes it from other scripts in Indonesia. Furthermore, Balinese script has mainly being used to write Balinese short stories, history (*itihasa*), proverbs, poetry, music, and spells (*mantra*) on the top of palm leaves (*lontar*). Recently, fewer and fewer Balinese practice these scripts and the scope of usage has become narrow.

Balinese people usually learn Balinese language and script from their family and community by practising it in daily communication. The teaching of Balinese language is also accommodated in formal education (elementary and high school). According to the Balinese Province statistics, there are 3,216 schools available in Bali, comprising 2,728 public schools and 488 private schools [7]. These schools are distributed to eight regencies and one multiplicity. Most of the schools now have computer labs, and some of them have a limited Internet connection, provided by central or state government. The computer labs are mainly used for learning specific units of study, such as information technology, mathematical modelling, English training, and so forth. However, none has been used to learn Balinese language or script.

Many areas in Indonesia have experienced an erosion of traditional heritage, especially in the use of mother-tongue language, due to the influence of the national language of Bahasa Indonesia in all levels of education. Also, for some ethnic groups, Bahasa Indonesia is flatter and free caste or hierarchy levels. Unfortunately, the preservation of Balinese language and script faced a significant challenge in 2013 due to the Balinese language and script unit of study being excluded from the Balinese school curriculum [8, 9]. However, in 2018 the Bali province released a new regulation about Balinese cultural preservation and protection [10], to ensure the preservation and protection of

Balinese language and script, not only in the school domain but in all organisations and communities in Bali.

This study aims to preserve, protect, and continue the use of Balinese language and script by adopting modern technology that can be utilized by the younger Balinese generation. Currently, it can be understood that there is no physical Balinese keyboard available as an input device to digital technology, such as a computer, tablet or smartphone, that can be used to learn Balinese language and script in digital form by people who want to learn, and preserve the language and script. Furthermore, this study also highly supports the Bali Governor Regulation number 80 of 2018 concerning Protection and Use of Balinese Language, Scriptures and Literature and the Implementation of Balinese Language Month.

2 Balinese Script (*Aksara Bali*)

The Balinese script, or *Aksara Bali*, is one of 12 scripts available in Indonesia. This script is used for writing the native Balinese language known as *Basa Bali*. The Balinese script is derived from the Pallava and Devanagari scripts of India, and it has many similarities with modern scripts of South Asia and Southeast Asia. The Balinese script is mainly used for writing Kawi, or Old Javanese, which had a strong influence on the Balinese language [11, 12].

Though everyday use of the script has largely been supplanted by the Latin alphabet, the Balinese script has a significant prevalence in many of the island's traditional ceremonies and is strongly associated with the Hindu religion. The script is mainly used today for copying *lontar* or palm leaf manuscripts containing religious texts.

The Balinese script is also known as *Hanacaraka*, and has been used since the 11th century AD [13]. The complex structures and rules for writing the script are known as *pasang aksara*. Due to the complex structure of the *pasang aksara*, other academics have researched the development of digital tools for auto-correction for Balinese script on Android operation systems [14].

In total there are 185 unique characters to represent Balinese script, which are categorized into 18 basic syllables, 5 vowels, 10 numbers and punctuation [15]. Balinese script is written from left to right, and there are no spaces between words or sentences, which means that those who would like to read Balinese script should understand Balinese words.

Balinese script can be divided into two major classifications:

1. Vowel script (*Aksara Suara*)
2. Consonant script (*Aksara Wianjana*), a Balinese script that represents consonants and numbers. This *Aksara Wianjana* is further divided into four main subcategories:

   a. *Aksara Wreastra* is a Balinese script that use to write common Balinese language, which consists of Ha Na Ca Ra Ka Da Ta Sa Wa La Ma Ga Ba Nga Pa Ja Ya Nya (ᬳ ᬦ ᬘ ᬭ ᬓ ᬤ ᬢ ᬲ ᬯ ᬮ ᬫ ᬕ ᬩ ᬗ ᬧ ᬚ ᬬ ᬜ)
   b. *Aksara Swalalita* is a Balinese script used to write letters for Balinese spiritual verses and chorus (*kekawin* and *kidung*) and ancient Javanese language music.

c. *Aksara Modre* is a Balinese script is used to write mantra (*rerajahan*).
d. Numbers. 1 2 3 4 5 6 7 8 9 0 (ᬧᬩᬨᭆᬙᬕᬗᬱᬲᬳᭀ)

3 Methodology

The design science research methodology (DSRM) [16] offers a useful approach to our research in that it aims to develop and evaluate Information Technology artefacts to address humanity problems. We chose the DSRM method as the object of our study is an IT artefact. There are five major processes in the DSRM (Fig. 1): (1) problem identification and motivation; (2) objectives for solutions; (3) design and development; (4) demonstration and evaluation; and (5) communication [17].

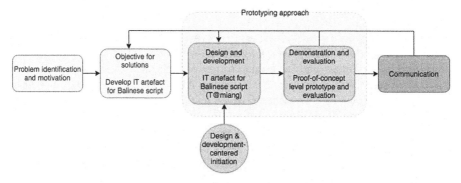

Fig. 1. Research methodology

The process of DSRM is usually depicted in sequential order. However, in our project, we decided the starting point was the design and development stage, as shown in Fig. 1, where we improved an initial IT artefact that had been developed by Pramartha and Dwidasmara [18] to become a solution for the existing humanity problem.

The design and development phase involves planning in detail how the IT artefact will be modelled, designed, constructed and the kind of system development methodology used when developing the artefact. We employed the prototyping approach for our system development methodology. In this stage, we focused on defining the functional requirement of our IT artefact and produced a proof-of-concept level prototype. A prototype is a tangible artifact, not an abstract description that requires interpretation. Designers, developers, and users can utilize the IT artefact to envision and reflect upon the final system [19].

We modeled the system with a prototype and then refined the system in several iterations based on users' feedback. Prototyping is an important activity in most new product development processes; whether the aim is to explore new opportunities or refine existing solutions, prototyping can be a valuable tool [20]. The prototyping approach consists of three components (Fig. 2): system analysis, system design, and programming and testing. These three phases work iteratively until all the requirements and outcomes are satisfied.

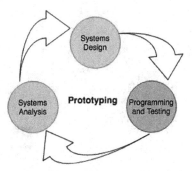

Fig. 2. Prototyping approach

The demonstration and evaluation step is a crucial component of the design science research process. The evaluation includes assessment of functionality, usability, performance, and any relevant characteristic dealing with the actual research problem. To obtain rapid feedback, the IT artefact was demonstrated to and tested by the relevant users.

After refining the IT artefact using rapid feedback from the relevant users, the outcome of the study is communicated to the non-technology-oriented and technology-oriented audience. This communication can be in the form of a published academic article in a journal, academic conference proceedings, and media such as newspapers or TV.

4   Design, Development, and Evaluation

In our previous work, we designed a non-QWERTY computer keyboard (see Fig. 3) for Balinese Script that is supported and funded by the Denpasar City Council of Bali. The keyboard composition approach was designed based on the character extraction of available Balinese digital datasets. The keyboard was designed to work on the top of the QWERTY physical keyboard, and we developed a driver that translates the Unicode generated from the QWERTY keyboard. Unfortunately, our keyboard only works on the word processor application that we developed, and cannot be used for other applications.

When our work was demonstrated to the relevant community, it gained a lot of attention and feedback. Many people gave positive feedback on our work and expected us to release the device for public consumption, so that students and schools could use it for teaching Balinese script in a modern way.

A semi-structured interview was conducted with relevant users in the community to capture the user requirements and needs. The aim of this interview was to gain information about the functional and non-functional requirements of the system. Some of the interviewees suggested making the keyboard suitable for multiple devices (e.g., computer, tablet, and smartphone), operating systems (e.g., Windows, macOS, iOS, and Android), and applications (e.g., word processor, instant messenger, and social media applications). To enable use with multiple devices, we designed our keyboard to work with two types of wireless connection: 1) Wi-Fi, by attaching a USB dongle for computer and laptop use; and 2) Bluetooth connection for mobile devices.

Fig. 3. First T@miang keyboard design and layout

In addition to getting feedback from relevant users, we also conducted a similar type of interview with experts in Balinese language and script. This type of interview aimed to clarify whether the number of characters of Balinese script shown on the keyboard was enough to accommodate the daily use and needs of students and schools from elementary to high school level. We involved two professors who are acknowledged experts in Balinese language and script from Udayana University. Both professors agree that the number of characters designed in our previous work was enough, and they suggested adding the additional character of *Ongkara* 🕉 to our design, due to this character commonly being used in writing a welcome banner during a spiritual ceremony, which represents God in Balinese beliefs.

As previously mentioned, the total number of characters in the Balinese script is 185. For our keyboard design, we only included 89 characters that are commonly used for writing Balinese script in the community. The composition and structure of our layout can be seen in Fig. 4 and Fig. 5. Starting in 2005, the Balinese script has been encoded in Unicode, with the range of U+1B00–U+1B7F [11]. The advantage of having Balinese script in the Unicode standard is that it enables Balinese script to work in many applications, as long as the fonts associated with Balinese script are available on the system. In Fig. 4 we give a number for every keyboard keystroke and map it with the Unicode for Balinese script (see Table 1). Due to the limitations of Unicode, for Balinese script some characters are a combination of two Unicodes: for instance, *Ongkara* on stroke number 15 is a combination of Unicode 1B12+1B01. In our design, the maximum number of characters on every stroke is four. Each stroke represents one to four related characters shown in the colours black, green, purple, and red, which are selected using combination keys: Gantasuri, Gantapa, and Gatacem (see Fig. 6). For example, stroke number 54–57 represents the character T with four different combinations, and each combination is used for a different word specified in *pasang aksara*.

To enable our Balinese script keyboard to work on computers, such as desktops and laptops, a Balinese font should be installed on the system. By default, no Balinese fonts such as Vimala[1], Pustaka Bali, and Kadiri are installed on operating systems such as Windows, macOS, and Linux. We designed our systems to install the Balinese script font with two options: 1) Install embedded Balinese script fonts from the USB dongle

---

[1] https://github.com/longnow/bali-fonts

Fig. 4. Balinese script composition structure

Fig. 5. Balinese script keyboard layout

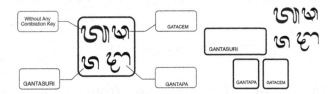

Fig. 6. Keystroke and color order combination of T in Balinese script

provided with our Balinese keyboard, or 2) Download fonts from a specific website that we recommend, as seen in Fig. 7. On the other hand, if the keyboard is utilized on a mobile device, such as those using iOS and Android systems, a Bluetooth connection will be used, and no Balinese script font installation is required because a noto sans Balinese font is already included on those mobile systems unless a specific font such as Vimala or Pustaka Bali is needed.

Table 1. Unicode mapping to the keyboard

Master Key	OnKeyPress	Balinese Script	Unicode
15	15	OngKara	1B12 + 1B01
16	16	Cekcek	1B02
17	17	Nya	1B1C
18	GANTASURI+ 18	Gant. Nya	1B44 + EA2C
19	19	Nga	1B17
20	GANTASURI+ 20	Gant. Nga	1B44 + EA26
21	21	Ca	1B18
22	GANTASURI+ 22	Gant. Ca	1B44 + EA27
23	GANTAPA + 23	Ca Laca	1B19
50	50	Sa	1B32
51	GANTASURI+ 51	Gant. Sa	1B44 + EA33
52	GANTAPA + 52	Sasapa	1B31
53	GATACEM + 53	Sasaga	1B30
54	54	Ta	1B22
55	GANTASURI+ 55	Gant. Ta	1B44 + EA32
56	GANTAPA + 56	Ta Latik	1B1D
57	GATACEM + 57	Ta Tawa	1B23

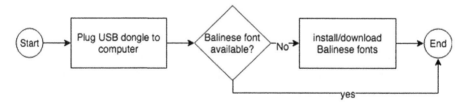

Fig. 7. Balinese font installation via USB dongle

Our IT artefact was designed for users who would like to learn about writing Balinese script in a natural way, which means auto-correction for *pasang aksara* was not included, as it was not the main focus of our study. Also, on our keyboard we did not display any Latin characters, to minimize the need for users to see Latin characters rather than the Balinese script.

Currently, initial testing of our approach has been conducted among the researchers. We tested the logical process of the system, including whether the Unicode embedded in the keyboard gives the correct output of Balinese script on the user's screen. We also tested it with different Balinese script fonts, such as Vimala, Pustaka Bali, Kadiri, and noto sans Balinese. We plan to conduct a larger scale evaluation by involving actual users such as students, Balinese language and script teachers, professors with expertise in Balinese language and script, and the Balinese community. The evaluation will seek to determine whether the functionality and non-functionality requirements have been met by the actual IT artefact. Moreover, we have communicated with local governments, such as Bali Province and Denpasar City Council. The Denpasar City council planned to be involved in our project this year; however, due to COVID19 pandemic, their collaboration has been postponed.

5 Conclusion and Future Work

We have presented the details of our research dealing with Balinese language and script. Our contribution includes the design and development of a physical non-QWERTY keyboard for Balinese script. The design and development process included targeted users, the Balinese community, and Balinese cultural experts. A rapid iteration process through a prototyping approach was applied to receive rapid feedback from actual users.

We are currently producing a number of physical Balinese script keyboards that will be tested with users on a large scale to evaluate the functionality and non-functionality of the final product. After receiving feedback from users, improvements will be made to the IT artefact. Finally, we will produce a large number of IT artefacts and, in collaboration with the state government (Bali Province and Denpasar City council), distribute the IT artefact to 3,216 schools around Bali.

Acknowledgements. This project received funding from the 2020 Udayana University Innovation research grant [grant no. B/20-78/UN14.4.A/PT.01.05/2020].

References

1. Widiyanto, N.: Badan Bahasa Petakan 652 Bahasa Daerah di Indonesia, 24 July 2018. https://www.kemdikbud.go.id/main/blog/2018/07/badan-bahasa-petakan-652-bahasa-daerah-di-indonesia. Accessed 01 Nov 2019
2. Dixon, R.M.: The Rise and Fall of Languages. Cambridge University Press, Cambridge (1997)
3. Covarrubias, M.: Island of Bali. Periplus Editions (HK) Ltd., Singapore (2008)
4. Pramartha, C., Davis, J.G.: Digital preservation of cultural heritage: Balinese kulkul artefact and practices. In: Ioannides, M., Fink, E., Moropoulou, A., Hagedorn-Saupe, M., Fresa, A., Liestøl, G., Rajcic, V., Grussenmeyer, P. (eds.) 6th International Conference on Digital Heritage. Progress in Cultural Heritage: Documentation, Preservation, and Protection, EuroMed 2016, pp. 491–500. Springer, Cham (2016). https://doi.org/10.1007/978-3-319-48496-9_38
5. Pramartha, C., Davis, J.G., Kuan, K.K.Y.: A semantically-enriched digital portal for the digital preservation of cultural heritage with community participation. In: Ioannides, M., Fink, E., Brumana, R., Patias, P., Doulamis, A., Martins, J., Wallace, M. (eds.) 7th International Conference on Digital Heritage. Progress in Cultural Heritage: Documentation, Preservation, and Protection, EuroMed 2018, pp. 560–571. Springer, Cham (2018). https://doi.org/10.1007/978-3-030-01762-0_49
6. Damanik, C.: 12 Aksara Lokal Bukti Kebinekaan, Jakarta. Kompas.com (2017)
7. Bali, B.P.P.D.: Data Bali Membangun 2013. Pemerintah Provinsi Bali, Bali (2014)
8. Rohmat, Bahasa Bali Tak Masuk Kurikulum, Gubernur Susun Pergub. Okezone.com (2013)

9. Hasanudin, M.: Bahasa Bali Tak Masuk Kurikulum, Ratusan Mahasiswa Demo. Kompas (2013)
10. Bali, G., Peraturan Gubernur Bali No 10 Tahun 2018 Tentang Perlindungan dan Penggunaan Bahasa, Aksara, dan Sastra Bali serta Penyelenggaraan Bulan Bahasa Bali, Indonesia (2018) https://doi.org/10.1007/978-981-10-7653-4_4
11. Everson, M., Suatjana, I.M.: Proposal for encoding the Balinese script in the UCS (2005). https://www.unicode.org/L2/L2005/05008-n2908-balinese.pdf. Accessed 02 Jul 2020
12. Sudewa, I.B.A.: Contemporary use of the Balinese script (2003). https://www.unicode.org/L2/L2003/03118-balinese.pdf
13. Nala, N.: Aksara Bali dalam Usada. Pāramita, Surabaya (2006)
14. Iswara, I.B.A.I., P.P. Santika, Wijaya, I.N.S.W.: An algorithm for auto-correction in PaTik Bali using Pasang Pageh Aksara Wianjana. In: 2019 5th International Conference on New Media Studies (CONMEDIA) (2019)
15. Suwija, I.N.: Ngiring Nulis Bali. Wineka Media, Denpasar (2012)
16. Peffers, K., et al.: A design science research methodology for information systems research. J. Manag. Inf. Syst. 24(3), 45–77 (2007)
17. Pramartha, C., Davis, J.G., Kuan, K.K.Y.: Digital preservation of cultural heritage: an ontology-based approach. In: The 28th Australasian Conference on Information Systems, Hobart, Australia (2017)
18. Pramartha, C., Dwidasmara, I.B.G.: The composition approach non-QWERTY keyboard for Balinese script. In: 2014 IEEE Canada International Humanitarian Technology Conference (IHTC), Montreal, Canada (2014)
19. Beaudouin-Lafon, M., Mackay, W.: Prototyping tools and techniques. In: Sears, A., Jacko, J.A. (eds.) Human Computer Interaction: Development Process, pp. 122–142. CRC Press, Boca Raton (2009)
20. Elverum, C.W., Welo, T., Tronvoll, S.: Prototyping in new product development: strategy considerations. Procedia CIRP 50, 117–122 (2016)

Look Behind You! – Using a Face Camera for Mobile Augmented Reality Odometry

Jan Čejka[1(✉)] and Fotis Liarokapis[2]

[1] Faculty of Informatics, Masaryk University, Brno, Czech Republic
xcejka2@fi.muni.cz
[2] Research Centre on Interactive Media, Smart Systems and Emerging
Technologies (RISE), 1011 Nicosia, Cyprus
f.liarokapis@rise.org.cy

Abstract. Augmented reality applications provide new ways of presenting cultural heritage assets thanks to the recent advancement in the field
of smart devices. Unfortunately, the construction of the hardware and
lower computational power of mobile processors limit the potential of
these applications. Namely, almost all current visual-inertial odometry
libraries employed in smartphones require the real tracked objects to be
close and contain distinguishable features, which is an issue when observing large virtual structures outdoors like historical buildings or objects
on plain walls of halls or museums. This paper exploits the possibility of
using the face cameras available in mobile devices for augmented reality
tracking. It designs a prototype composed of iPhone and iPad devices
and evaluates its contribution in two scenarios that current systems cannot handle. The results reveal the clear benefit of this approach for the
cultural heritage, allowing it to operate in situations when users look up
in the sky to see the roof of virtual buildings, or when they move closer
to a white wall to perceive details of a virtual painting. In the end, the
paper discusses the system's limitations and proposes solutions to them.

1 Introduction

Augmented reality (AR) is on its way to become a part of our everyday lives.
It has the capability not only to enhance the existing objects and visualize the
future, but it also allows us to observe lost artefacts and understand our history.
Increased computational power of mobile devices allows them to process input
images in real time, and with the aid of inertial measurement units (IMU),
smartphones are able to precisely track users position, which is essential for AR
applications. Operating systems now include libraries that simplify development
of such applications with features like estimation of the reflection map and of
environmental lighting, recognition of basic objects with artificial intelligence
(AI), cooperation between users, and other [1,11].

Despite the vast capabilities, limited resources of these devices constrain the
algorithms to utilize only the data of the rear camera, IMUs, and ambient light
sensors. This restricts the applications, because they must force users to aim the

© Springer Nature Switzerland AG 2021
M. Ioannides et al. (Eds.): EuroMed 2020, LNCS 12642, pp. 215–227, 2021.
https://doi.org/10.1007/978-3-030-73043-7_18

device at nearby distinguishable objects, usually at tables or down at the ground. When the user rotates its view and the device cannot see any of such objects, the tracking stops working and the AR experience is weakened. This can be partially compensated with other localization technologies like global navigation satellite systems (GNSS), but their precision is not sufficient to closely examine virtual objects. For these reasons, it is still very hard to provide AR tools for observing virtual objects on clear walls like virtual paintings in digital museums, or to create electronic guides displaying non-existing cultural heritage structures over their remains at archaeological sites.

Mobile devices are equipped with a front camera (face camera) and a set of one or more rear cameras, but hardware limitations disallowed developers from using the face camera and any of the rear cameras at the same time. Fortunately, recent developments indicate that this is no longer an issue, and the latest hardware is capable of processing both image streams from the face and the rear camera at the same time, which can be used in video conversations [2]. However, this also opens new options for localizing the device in the environment.

This paper enhances the abilities of AR at cultural heritage sites and investigates the possibility of using the face camera to maintain the tracking when the data from the rear camera is insufficient. It presents a system that tracks the device position by processing the visual information in front of the device as well as behind it. This system is tested with a prototype consisting of two joined mobile devices oriented in opposite directions, and evaluated in two experiments, one with participants observing a non-existing historical church, and one with them examining a virtual painting on a clear white wall. To our knowledge, this is the first tracking system designed for mobile AR applications that utilizes the data from behind the user to improve tracking in situations when the rear camera is not sufficient.

The main contributions of this paper are:

- a design of a system that builds the tracking on a combination of the data in front of the device with the data behind the device;
- an evaluation of this system in two experiments: an outdoor experiment with users walking around a non-existing historical building, and an indoor experiment with users observing a virtual painting on a clear white wall.

2   Related Work

Odometry algorithms solve the problem of localization, which includes feature detection and matching for the purpose of finding the viewer in a known area and updating its location. This is often combined with the problem of mapping, which is building a map of the surrounding area that is used for the localization. Algorithms that incorporates and optimizes both parts together are denoted as simultaneous localization and mapping (SLAM).

Many algorithms for single-camera visual-only SLAM are based on the work of Klein et al. [15] presenting an algorithm that separates the tracking and mapping into two parallel components that are updated at different rates.

Various natural features are exploit for fast detection and matching, like ORB features [20] or line features [10,26,37]. Some authors decide not to use features and perform a direct evaluation of intensity changes between subsequent frames of the video [6–8,29]. Benefits of stereo cameras were explored in works of Park et al. [24] or Hsieh et al. [13]. SLAM algorithms based only on the visual data are prone to blurred images, caused especially by large rotational movements of the cameras. This can be compensated very well by incorporating data from inertial sensors, combined with feature trackers [17,19,21,27] or direct trackers [3,4], and optimized for mobile devices [18]. Visual-inertial odometry (VIO) SLAM systems with a pair of stereo cameras were exploit in the work of Leutenegger et al. [17] or Usenko et al. [32]. Non-stereo multiview VIO SLAM systems were exploit mostly in the field of robotics and used various distribution of cameras, e.g., multiple pairs of stereo cameras [12,23], cameras directed forward and down [5,36], and cameras with non-overlapping views [31]. Karrer et al. presented a system for collaborative AR [14], which combined maps of several mobile AR systems into a large shared map. All of these systems were designed for the general problem of mapping, however, and none of them were tested in situations when one of the cameras could not track its surrounding.

There are many commercial libraries for indoor AR applications developed for common mobile devices like smartphones or tables [25,35], and some of them are also integrated directly into the mobile operating systems [1,11]. They support markerless VIO SLAM, estimation of the environment lighting conditions, detection of vertical and horizontal surfaces, and recognition of predefined 2D images. They can also share the tracking data between multiple devices to create a collaborative AR experience. There are also open-source libraries for building AR applications [28]. Outdoor AR systems are often related to applications for sites with cultural heritage importance [34]. Galatis et al. [9] described KnossosAR, a system designed for ancient sites that handled occlusions of real objects on the virtual scenery. Some mobile AR systems were also aimed at underwater environments [22] and underwater cultural heritage sites [33]. Other systems [16,30] showed historical buildings in existing cities, but none of them tackled the problem of insufficient amount of features to track.

3   System Description

Our system is designed for Apple devices and bases its tracking on the ARKit library, which is available for the general public. Unfortunately, this library can use only the rear camera to track the environment, using the face camera for tracking in AR applications is not supported. For this reason, our system consists of two mobile devices, the iPad device (iPad Pro, 2nd generation, 10.5-inch, iPadOS 13.4), which tracks the world in front of the user, provides additional tracking data with its IMU, displays the augmented reality content, and receives the user input, and the iPhone device (iPhone XS, iOS 13.4), which uses its rear camera to track the scenery behind the user (see Fig. 1).

The iPhone is placed in the lower left corner on the iPad with its screen facing the screen of the iPad. The iPhone is secured with a wedge, pressed to

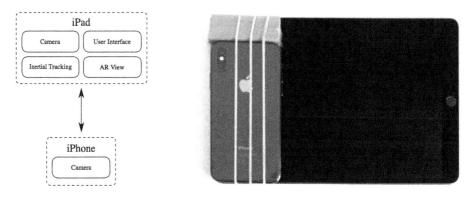

Fig. 1. Left: The tracking system consists of two components: an iPad (receives the data from its rear camera, its IMU, and the user, and displays the AR content), and an iPhone (receives the data from its rear camera). Right: The iPhone being placed on the iPad device with its rear camera directed behind the user, and together, the devices work as one stable unit.

the iPad with rubber bands, and separated with a soft pad to protect the screens. Despite the simplicity, this setup was found to be compact, stable, firm, and easy to manipulate, and the iPhone's camera is very close to the actual position of the iPad's face camera. Relative position between the devices was measured with a precision lower than one centimeter, and their relative orientation was estimated from the setup.

The devices communicate via Apple's Multipeer Connectivity framework. The iPhone tracker sends updates in measured position and orientation, status of tracking, number of tracked features, and a timestamp of each data. In the opposite direction, the iPad tracker sends commands to reset the tracking at the start of each user test. For testing purposes, the iPhone also sent the image stream from its rear camera in a low quality, which was then presented in the lower right corner of the iPad.

3.1 Tracking

The system is composed of three tracking units: an iPad tracker, an iPhone tracker, and a Core Motion tracker. The first tracking unit, the iPad tracker, is realized with the ARKit library and tracks the objects located in front of the user. The iPhone tracker is similar and tracks the objects behind the user. The last tracker, the Core Motion tracker, is based on Apple's Core Motion framework and uses the inertial sensors to track the orientation of the iPad.

The tracker state is derived from four states of ARKit mapping. When the ARKit library reports that it is in a *mapped* environment or *extending* its internal map, the tracking provides good estimates of device location. The *limited* state indicates that the system can provide some estimates of the position, but the area is not sufficiently mapped. If the mapping has just started or is not consistent,

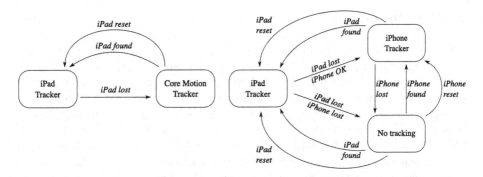

Fig. 2. Left: The orientation is tracked by switching between iPad tracker and Core Motion tracker. Right: The position is tracked by switching between iPad tracker and iPhone tracker, when they are capable of tracking.

the tracking is *not available*. Our system accepts the *mapped* and *extending* tracking, and includes also the *limited* tracking if the number of features is at least 100. In other cases, it still uses the position obtained from ARKit for one second, since the preliminary tests found that the error in position is tolerable and the library often relocates itself. After this second, the tracker is considered lost.

The system switches between the tracking units according to their ability to track their location, see Fig. 2. Computing the orientation is easier; the system uses ARKit and iPad data, and if the library cannot track the location, it switches to the Core Motion tracker (denoted as *iPad lost*). When the iPad tracker relocates itself (*iPad found*), the system drops the orientation from the Core Motion tracker and continues using the iPad tracker. When ARKit decides to reset the tracking session (*iPad reset*), the system aligns the last known orientation with the new ARKit session and continues tracking.

The position is computed differently. The system again uses the position from the iPad tracker, and when it becomes lost, it starts using the iPhone tracker (*iPad lost, iPhone OK*). If the iPhone tracker cannot measure the position, the system stops updating the position and updates only its orientation (*iPad lost, iPhone lost*). This also happens when the iPhone stops tracking the position (*iPhone lost*). When the iPhone tracker successfully relocates itself (*iPhone found*), the system continues with updating the position. Similarly, if the iPhone tracker resets the tracking session (*iPhone reset*), the system aligns the new session and continues tracking. When the iPad tracker successfully locates itself in its environment (*iPad found*), the system drops the position updated by iPhone and uses the iPad position. If the iPad tracker is reset (*iPad reset*), the system aligns the new session and continues tracking.

4   Experiment

Our solution was evaluated in two experiments. The first experiment focused on users observing large objects in outdoor environments, as illustrated in Fig. 3. A virtual model of a historical church was placed in the city center where it stood before it was demolished. The model of was unlit, textured, and consisted of approximately 19000 triangles. It spanned the area of $32 \times 30\,\mathrm{m}$, and was 26 m high. The shape of the city square is approximately a triangle of length $130 \times 150 \times 170\,\mathrm{m}$. In this experiment, five users (three males and two females; one participant in age category 18–25, two participants of age 26–33, and two participants more 50 years old) walked around the church and observed how it fit the square. They were not limited by time and were instructed to look up to see its upper floors and its roof. The application logged the tracking status, the orientation, and the time at which the frame was recorded.

Fig. 3. A participant observing a historical church

The second experiment focused on people observing objects on surfaces with no features to track, like white walls. The users were asked to see a virtual painting on a real wall and search the painting for specific small details. The virtual model of the painting was realized with a simple textured rectangle of size $1.35 \times 0.9\,\mathrm{m}$ and located in a room of size of $4.2 \times 5.0\,\mathrm{m}$. This test was completed by four users (two males and two females; two participants of age 26–33, and two participants more than 50 years old). Again, they were not limited by time or distance at which they should search the painting. As they moved closer, the rear camera it saw only the wall and could not track the user's position. The application logged similar data as in the first experiment, but in this test, the device recorded the distance from the virtual object instead of its orientation.

In the beginning of both experiments, the participants were familiarized with the procedure, and they were instructed to tilt the device to avoid being in the field of view of the face (iPhone) camera. The supervisor then initialized the system and placed the virtual object at its correct location. The participants attended a single session of each experiment and spent from 3 to 6 min with the first part and from 1 to 2 min with the second part.

5 Results

Evaluation of the experiments was based on the comparison of the number of frames in which our system and sole face and rear trackers provide position data. The results include the one-second interval of accepting the estimated location in insufficient conditions as described in Sect. 3.1, which is sufficient for presenting the AR content.

Figure 4 presents the results of the first test evaluating the system in the outdoor environment. It shows that when the pitch is negative (the users look down), the rear camera tracker (iPad) is able to track the user without any significant issues. The face camera tracker (iPhone) cannot accurately follow the user and tracks the user in rare parts when there is a static object to track, like a lamp. The users spent most of their time looking ahead or slightly down (in range from $-20°$ to $10°$), and in these situations, the combined system provided the tracking sufficient for AR applications in more than 50% of frames. It should be noted that the graphs show only the results of position tracking; the orientation is always available, thanks to the Core Motion tracker. When the pitch is around zero, the view of users is directed ahead, and both trackers have the ground in their field of view. Thanks to this, the number of tracked frames increases for the front-camera tracker. The performance of the rear camera tracker is lower, since the frames contain fewer close features to follow than when the view of users is directed down.

When the pitch is positive, users look up and the usability of the rear camera tracker is very low. The system compensates this with the data of the face camera tracker, which is now directed down. However, the performance of the face tracker is still very low when compared to the rear tracker. The reason is that the users

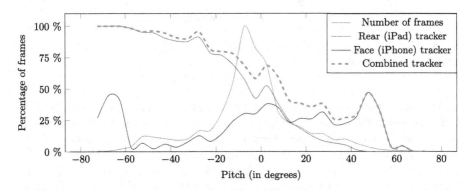

Fig. 4. The performance of the tracking solutions when users observed the virtual model of the church

were fully immersed in the experience and forgot to tilt the device to be out of the iPhone's field of view. The presence of both moving and static objects in the camera stream confused the tracker, which could not provide any data. The figure also shows an unexpected peek in performance at the beginning of the graph when the pitch is negative and the device is directed to the ground. We assumed that this represents some very rare occasions when users asked for a help during the testing, stopped walking, and thus they became the static object that the iPhone camera required for tracking.

Figure 5 shows the results of the experiment with users observing details of a virtual painting on a real clear wall. Performance of the rear-camera (iPad) tracker was decreasing as the users moved closer to the wall, since the camera started losing recognisable objects to follow. The face-camera (iPhone) tracker had no problem with tracking, as it continued to track the room behind the user. In this experiment, the participants focused more on being out of the field of the view of the iPhone camera than in the previous experiment, which allowed the tracker to operate in most of the frames. The figure confirms that our system utilized the data from both trackers and provided the tracking in more than 50% of frames, and more than 75% of all frames except a peak at around 0.7 m. The users spent most of their time at a distance between 1.1 and 1.4 m, at which they started the experiment, and at the distance of around 0.2 m, at which they searched the painting for the objects.

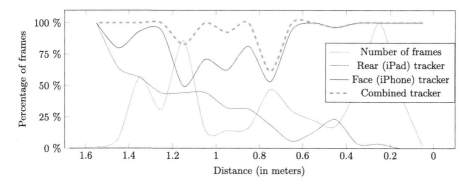

Fig. 5. The performance of the tracking solutions when users observed the virtual painting on a clear wall

The participants enjoyed the first experiment very much, especially the possibility of seeing the non-existing historical church at is former place. They mentioned that in some situations, they had problems with walking around the church as it was moving with them – this happened when the system lost the tracking from both cameras and could use only the data from the inertial unit. Regarding the second experiment, the participants reported that the resolution of the painting was very low, they saw individual pixels of the image and had difficulties to recognize the object they were supposed to find. Despite this, none of them reported the impossibility of moving closer to the painting, which indicates that the system had no problems with tracking the user's position.

5.1   Discussion

The ARKit library assumes that the tracked environments is static and objects do not move. This was found to be a major issue of the face-camera (iPhone) tracker, since the participants were in the field of view of this camera, which confused the tracker. Although the users were asked to slightly rotate the device during the experiments, this was more successful in the second test. Additionally, the preliminary tests found that the automatic focus caused blurring of the background and a loss of tracking when the users accidentally got into the field of view, so it was disabled for the iPhone and fixed at 2 m (however, the automatic focus was enabled on iPad). Another possibility is to detect the person in the image, mask it out, and use only the background for tracking, but this is not supported by ARKit, which does not allow the developers to change the camera image before it is processed.

When the individual trackers got lost, it took a few seconds to create a new map of the area and restart tracking. This time could be decreased if the trackers shared the map of the surroundings. Although ARKit supports sharing the maps with *collaborative sessions*, the preliminary tests found that the relative position between the devices was erroneous, and sharing a map of the environment did not decrease the time to initialize the tracking, so this feature was removed from the final version of the system.

The experiments did not evaluate the precision of the tracking, which we expect to be comparable to the precision of individual trackers, because the system has no effect on the mapping capabilities of individual trackers. The precision of the whole system is affected by inaccuracies in the measured relative position and orientation between the devices and will influence the final position if the distance travelled without tracking is large, but this was not an issue. Our system accumulated large errors in position only in situations when it lost the tracking from both devices, which occurred only during the outdoor experiment when one device lost the tracking and the second device was building its map of the environment. It was observed by just a few users only for brief moments, and since the evaluation of this experiment was not based on the position of the user, this problem was ignored. Such error in position can be reduced by adding additional points of reference into the environment (like markers) or by incorporating GNSS. Errors in the orientation were vary rare and happened at the beginning. In such situations, the test was restarted and the measured data was ignored. These problems could be avoided by incorporating the magnetometer, but preliminary experiments showed that it can easily start reporting invalid data due to the presence of artificial objects that deform the magnetic field of the Earth, so it was not integrated into the system.

The system requires the area behind the user to contain features to track when observing virtual paintings on clear walls, but this can be an issue in two scenarios. The problem appears in corridors when the user is surrounded by clear walls, since the system cannot find any distinguishable features in front of the users as well as behind them. It is also observed in large halls, since the objects behind the user are not sufficiently close. These limitations can be overcome only by incorporating GNSS.

Modern smart devices are equipped with time-of-flight sensors, which allow them to measure the distance of close objects. Such devices were not tested in our experiments, but despite the fact that they can obtain the distance to clear walls, we assume they will have problems with tracking changes in the user's position when moving along the wall, because the grid that is projected and recorded by such sensors travels as well. Also, they will not help outdoors, since there are no close objects when users look up. Despite this, these sensors can still help with tracking, as they are able to decrease the time required to initialize the trackers.

6   Conclusion

This paper focused on enhancing the capabilities of AR in digital museums and cultural heritage sites. It presented a system for mobile AR applications that tracked the position of users also in situations with no recognizable objects in front of them. Unlike the state-of-the-art systems that use only the rear camera of the device, our system added the face camera oriented behind the user to provide the data when the information obtained from the rear camera was insufficient. A prototype of this system consisted with two devices, an iPhone and iPad, and was tested in two use cases – one with participants observing a virtual model of a historical church at its formal location, and the other with participants examining a virtual painting on a clear white wall. The results showed that the combination of both data sources increased the number of tracked frames and allowed the system to work when the rear camera could not continue tracking.

The future work is aimed at utilizing both the rear and face cameras of the same device. Adapting a state-of-the-art library that provides the visual-inertial tracking will allow us to solve the main issues of our system, namely, a faster initialization of the tracking by utilizing the information from the other camera, and removing user's face from images obtained by the front camera. This will be followed by investigating which camera provide the best data for tracking, and optimizing the computation by removing the other camera from processing.

Acknowledgments. The authors wish to thank David Střelák for providing us with the model of the church, and all participants for evaluating the system. Part of this project has received funding from the European Union's Horizon 2020 Research and Innovation Programme under Grant Agreement No. 739578 and the Government of the Republic of Cyprus through the Directorate General for European Programmes, Coordination and Development.

References

1. Apple: ARKit3 - Augmented Reality - Apple Developer (2019). https://developer.apple.com/augmented-reality/arkit/

2. Apple: Introducing multi-camera capture for iOS (2019). In: Presented at Worldwide Developer Conference, WWDC 2019 (2019)
3. Bloesch, M., Omari, S., Hutter, M., Siegwart, R.: Robust visual inertial odometry using a direct EKF-based approach. In: 2015 IEEE/RSJ International Conference on Intelligent Robots and Systems (IROS), pp. 298–304 (September 2015). https://doi.org/10.1109/IROS.2015.7353389
4. Concha, A., Loianno, G., Kumar, V., Civera, J.: Visual-inertial direct SLAM. In: 2016 IEEE International Conference on Robotics and Automation (ICRA), pp. 1331–1338 (May 2016). https://doi.org/10.1109/ICRA.2016.7487266
5. Eckenhoff, K., Geneva, P., Bloecker, J., Huang, G.: Multi-camera visual-inertial navigation with online intrinsic and extrinsic calibration. In: 2019 International Conference on Robotics and Automation (ICRA), pp. 3158–3164 (May 2019). https://doi.org/10.1109/ICRA.2019.8793886
6. Engel, J., Schöps, T., Cremers, D.: LSD-SLAM: large-scale direct monocular SLAM. In: Fleet, D., Pajdla, T., Schiele, B., Tuytelaars, T. (eds.) ECCV 2014. LNCS, vol. 8690, pp. 834–849. Springer, Cham (2014). https://doi.org/10.1007/978-3-319-10605-2_54
7. Forster, C., Pizzoli, M., Scaramuzza, D.: SVO: fast semi-direct monocular visual odometry. In: 2014 IEEE International Conference on Robotics and Automation (ICRA), pp. 15–22 (May 2014). https://doi.org/10.1109/ICRA.2014.6906584
8. Forster, C., Zhang, Z., Gassner, M., Werlberger, M., Scaramuzza, D.: SVO: semidirect visual odometry for monocular and multicamera systems. IEEE Trans. Robot. 33(2), 249–265 (2017). https://doi.org/10.1109/TRO.2016.2623335
9. Galatis, P., Gavalas, D., Kasapakis, V., Pantziou, G., Zaroliagis, C.: Mobile augmented reality guides in cultural heritage. In: Proceedings of the 8th EAI International Conference on Mobile Computing, Applications and Services, MobiCASE 2016, pp. 11–19. ICST (Institute for Computer Sciences, Social-Informatics and Telecommunications Engineering), Brussels, Belgium (2016). https://doi.org/10.4108/eai.30-11-2016.2266954
10. Gomez-Ojeda, R., Moreno, F.A., Zuñiga-Noël, D., Scaramuzza, D., Gonzalez-Jimenez, J.: PL-SLAM: a stereo SLAM system through the combination of points and line segments. IEEE Trans. Robot. 35(3), 734–746 (2019). https://doi.org/10.1109/TRO.2019.2899783
11. Google: ARCore - Google Developers (2019). https://developers.google.com/ar
12. Heng, L., Lee, G.H., Pollefeys, M.: Self-calibration and visual SLAM with a multi-camera system on a micro aerial vehicle. Auton. Robot. 39, 259–277 (2015). https://doi.org/10.1007/s10514-015-9466-8
13. Hsieh, C.H., Lee, J.D.: Markerless augmented reality via stereo video see-through head-mounted display device. Math. Probl. Eng. 2015, 1–13 (2015). https://doi.org/10.1155/2015/329415
14. Karrer, M., Schmuck, P., Chli, M.: CVI-SLAM - collaborative visual-inertial SLAM. IEEE Robot. Autom. Lett. 3(4), 2762–2769 (2018). https://doi.org/10.1109/LRA.2018.2837226
15. Klein, G., Murray, D.: Parallel tracking and mapping for small AR workspaces. In: 2007 6th IEEE and ACM International Symposium on Mixed and Augmented Reality, pp. 225–234 (November 2007). https://doi.org/10.1109/ISMAR.2007.4538852
16. Lee, G.A., Dünser, A., Kim, S., Billinghurst, M.: CityViewAR: a mobile outdoor AR application for city visualization. In: 2012 IEEE International Symposium on Mixed and Augmented Reality - Arts, Media, and Humanities (ISMAR-AMH), pp. 57–64 (November 2012). https://doi.org/10.1109/ISMAR-AMH.2012.6483989

17. Leutenegger, S., Lynen, S., Bosse, M., Siegwart, R., Furgale, P.: Keyframe-based visual-inertial odometry using nonlinear optimization. Int. J. Robot. Res. **34**(3), 314–334 (2015). https://doi.org/10.1177/0278364914554813
18. Li, P., Qin, T., Hu, B., Zhu, F., Shen, S.: Monocular visual-inertial state estimation for mobile augmented reality. In: 2017 IEEE International Symposium on Mixed and Augmented Reality (ISMAR), pp. 11–21 (October 2017). https://doi.org/10.1109/ISMAR.2017.18
19. Mourikis, A.I., Roumeliotis, S.I.: A multi-state constraint Kalman filter for vision-aided inertial navigation. In: Proceedings 2007 IEEE International Conference on Robotics and Automation, pp. 3565–3572 (April 2007). https://doi.org/10.1109/ROBOT.2007.364024
20. Mur-Artal, R., Montiel, J.M.M., Tardós, J.D.: ORB-SLAM: a versatile and accurate monocular SLAM system. IEEE Trans. Robot. **31**(5), 1147–1163 (October 2015). https://doi.org/10.1109/TRO.2015.2463671
21. Mur-Artal, R., Tardós, J.D.: Visual-inertial monocular SLAM with map reuse. IEEE Robot. Autom. Lett. **2**(2), 796–803 (2017). https://doi.org/10.1109/LRA.2017.2653359
22. Oppermann, L., Blum, L., Lee, J.Y., Seo, J.H.: AREEF multi-player underwater augmented reality experience. In: 2013 IEEE International Games Innovation Conference (IGIC), pp. 199–202 (2013). https://doi.org/10.1109/IGIC.2013.6659137
23. Oskiper, T., Zhu, Z., Samarasekera, S., Kumar, R.: Visual odometry system using multiple stereo cameras and inertial measurement unit. In: 2007 IEEE Conference on Computer Vision and Pattern Recognition, pp. 1–8 (June 2007). https://doi.org/10.1109/CVPR.2007.383087
24. Park, J., Seo, B.K., Park, J.I.: Binocular mobile augmented reality based on stereo camera tracking. J. Real-Time Image Process. **13**, 571–580 (2017). https://doi.org/10.1007/s11554-016-0640-9
25. PTC: Vuforia: Market-Leading Enterprice AR (2020). https://www.ptc.com/en/products/augmented-reality/vuforia
26. Pumarola, A., Vakhitov, A., Agudo, A., Sanfeliu, A., Moreno-Noguer, F.: PL-SLAM: real-time monocular visual SLAM with points and lines. In: 2017 IEEE International Conference on Robotics and Automation (ICRA), pp. 4503–4508 (5 2017). https://doi.org/10.1109/ICRA.2017.7989522
27. Qin, T., Li, P., Shen, S.: VINS-Mono: a robust and versatile monocular visual-inertial state estimator. IEEE Trans. Robot. **34**(4), 1004–1020 (2018). https://doi.org/10.1109/TRO.2018.2853729
28. Romero-Ramirez, F.J., Muñoz-Salinas, R., Medina-Carnicer, R.: Speeded up detection of squared fiducial markers. Image Vis. Comput. **76**, 38–47 (2018). https://doi.org/10.1016/j.imavis.2018.05.004
29. Schöps, T., Engel, J., Cremers, D.: Semi-dense visual odometry for AR on a smartphone. In: 2014 IEEE International Symposium on Mixed and Augmented Reality (ISMAR), pp. 145–150 (September 2014). https://doi.org/10.1109/ISMAR.2014.6948420
30. Seo, B.K., Kim, K., Park, J., Park, J.I.: A tracking framework for augmented reality tours on cultural heritage sites. In: Proceedings of the 9th ACM SIGGRAPH Conference on Virtual-Reality Continuum and its Applications in Industry, VRCAI 2010, pp. 169–174. ACM, New York (2010). https://doi.org/10.1145/1900179.1900215
31. Tribou, M.J., Harmat, A., Wang, D.W., Sharf, I., Waslander, S.L.: Multi-camera parallel tracking and mapping with non-overlapping fields of view. Int. J. Robot. Res. **34**(12), 1480–1500 (2015). https://doi.org/10.1177/0278364915571429

32. Usenko, V., Engel, J., Stückler, J., Cremers, D.: Direct visual-inertial odometry with stereo cameras. In: 2016 IEEE International Conference on Robotics and Automation (ICRA), pp. 1885–1892 (May 2016). https://doi.org/10.1109/ICRA.2016.7487335

33. Čejka, J., Zsíros, A., Liarokapis, F.: A hybrid augmented reality guide for underwater cultural heritage sites. Pers. Ubiquit. Comput. (2020). https://doi.org/10.1007/s00779-019-01354-6

34. Vlahakis, V., et al.: Archeoguide: an augmented reality guide for archaeological sites. IEEE Comput. Graph. Appl. **22**, 52–60 (September 2002). https://doi.org/10.1109/MCG.2002.1028726

35. Wikitude: Wikitude Augmented Reality: the World's Leading Cross-Platform AR SDK (2020). https://www.wikitude.com

36. Yang, S., Scherer, S.A., Zell, A.: Visual SLAM for autonomous MAVs with dual cameras. In: 2014 IEEE International Conference on Robotics and Automation (ICRA), pp. 5227–5232 (May 2014). https://doi.org/10.1109/ICRA.2014.6907627

37. Zhang, N., Zhao, Y.: Fast and robust monocular visua-inertial odometry using points and lines. Sensors **19**(20) (2019). https://doi.org/10.3390/s19204545

A Comparative Analysis of Different Software Packages for 3D Modelling of Complex Geometries

Styliani Verykokou[1]([⊠]), Sofia Soile[1], Fotis Bourexis[1], Panagiotis Tokmakidis[2], Konstantinos Tokmakidis[2], and Charalabos Ioannidis[1]

[1] School of Rural and Surveying Engineering, NTUA, 9 Iroon Polytechniou, 15780 Athens, Greece
st.verykokou@gmail.com, {ssoile,cioannid}@survey.ntua.gr,
fotis.bourexis@gmail.com
[2] School of Rural and Surveying Engineering, AUTH, 54124 Thessaloniki, Greece
ptokmaki@gmail.com, ktok@auth.gr

Abstract. The purpose of this paper is the investigation of the performance of four well-established commercial and open-source software packages for automated image-based 3D reconstruction of complex cultural and natural heritage sites, i.e., Agisoft Metashape, RealityCapture, MicMac and Meshroom. The case study is part of the inaccessible giant rock of St. Modestos, in the archaeological site of Meteora. In terms of computational time, the commercial software packages were the most time-efficient solutions, with Metashape being the fastest one. They also have a friendlier user interface, which makes them adoptable even by non-photogrammetrists. All four solutions yielded approximately comparable results in terms of accuracy and may be used for generation of 3D dense point clouds of complex sites. With the exception of Meshroom, they may produce georeferenced results. Also, with the exception of MicMac, which did not yield satisfactory results in terms of textured mesh, they may be used for generating photorealistic 3D models. The comparative analysis of the results achieved by the tested software will serve as the basis for establishing photogrammetric pipelines that may be generally used for 3D reconstruction of complex geometries.

Keywords: 3D model · Geometric documentation · Software evaluation

1 Introduction

The importance of 3D documentation of cultural and natural heritage sites is well-understood at an international level and experts attempt to use modern technologies to produce highly accurate and detailed 3D models of such sites. Several works have been conducted in recent years, showing promising results achieved via photogrammetric methods, using images [1] or combination of images and laser scanning techniques [2]. Some cultural and natural sites correspond to complex geometries, either because they are inaccessible or because of their magnitude and geometric characteristics. Thus, their

© Springer Nature Switzerland AG 2021
M. Ioannides et al. (Eds.): EuroMed 2020, LNCS 12642, pp. 228–240, 2021.
https://doi.org/10.1007/978-3-030-73043-7_19

3D modelling requires specific attention. Such a site is the UNESCO world heritage site of Meteora, characterized by inaccessible giant rocks with morphological peculiarities and challenging topographical features. The 3D geometric documentation of Meteora, which is dealt with within the ongoing "METEORA" project [3], is a highly demanding task, accomplished using images from unmanned aerial vehicles (UAVs) and manned aircrafts, terrestrial images, LiDAR data and ground control points (GCPs) [4].

The purpose of this paper is the investigation of the performance of well-established commercial (Agisoft Metashape [5] and RealityCapture [6]) and open-source (MicMac [7] and Meshroom [8]) software packages for the automated 3D reconstruction of complex cultural and natural sites. The study area is part of the rock of St. Modestos, known as "Modi", located in the Meteora site. On top of this rock, ruins of the old monastery of St. Modestos exist. It is of great height (about 200 m) and the ascent to this rock is of increased difficulty, so it was covered by UAV images. Its topographic features are representative of complex cultural and natural sites, so it was selected as the study area.

2   Image-Based 3D Modelling

The reconstruction of the 3D scene geometry from images is a problem that has occupied the photogrammetric community for more than 40 years. Advances in photogrammetry and computer vision have led to the development of automated structure from motion (SfM) and multi-view stereo (MVS) approaches that have seen tremendous evolution over the years. SfM refers to the process of estimating the camera poses corresponding to a 2D image sequence and reconstructing the sparse scene geometry [9]. MVS is the general term given to a group of methods using stereo correspondences as their main cue in more than two images [10]. The combination of SfM and MVS provides automated workflows for generating dense 3D point clouds and surface models.

The first step of SfM is the extraction of features in each image [11]; SIFT-based algorithms are the most commonly used ones. The matching of the descriptors is the next step, using the criterion of a minimum distance measure, followed by outlier rejection techniques. The correspondences are then organized into tracks [9]. An incremental, hierarchical or global method follows. Incremental methods register one camera at each iteration; hierarchical ones gradually merge partial reconstructions; and global methods register all cameras simultaneously [12]. In case of incremental and hierarchical methods, intermediate bundle adjustment processes are necessary to ensure successful camera pose estimation and sparse 3D point cloud extraction, in addition to a final bundle adjustment, as required by global methods. Georeferencing of the SfM results is generally performed via a 3D similarity transformation between the arbitrary SfM system and the world reference system using GCPs and/or GPS measurements.

The generation of a dense point cloud is the next step within a MVS scheme, through a dense image matching (DIM) algorithm, using either a stereo (via a local, global or semi-global algorithm) or a multi-view approach. Local methods compute the disparity at a given point using the intensity values within a finite region, thus trading accuracy for speed. Global ones are more accurate but time consuming; they solve a global optimization by minimizing a cost function based on the whole image. Semi-global methods perform a pixel-wise matching, allowing to shape efficiently object boundaries and details, and represent a good trade-off between accuracy and speed [13]. The conversion of dense cloud into mesh and its texturing are the final steps of the MVS pipeline.

3 Experiments

3.1 Test Dataset

A dataset consisting of 238 UAV images depicting part of the giant rock of St. Modestos, known as Modi, was used in the experiments. The rock is located in the archaeological site of Meteora, in central Greece, near the town of Kalambaka. Meteora hosts one of the largest and most precipitously built complexes of Eastern Orthodox monasteries. Modi features a complex geometry, being a giant inaccessible rock with challenging topography. The images were captured by a DJI camera using a DJI Phantom 4 Pro UAV. They correspond to a size of $5,472 \times 3,648$ pixels, a focal length of 8.8 mm and a pixel size of 2.41 μm. They are accompanied by GPS/INS information.

The ground coordinates of 6 GCPs were computed via Agisoft Metashape using a georeferenced model of the Meteora site. The latter was generated using aerial images of Meteora and GCPs in the wider area. The geometry of Modi did not permit the on-site measurement of GCPs, so the computed coordinates of these 6 GCPs were used for georeferencing. All experiments were performed using a 64-bit Intel Core i7-8700 CPU 3.2 GHz computer with 24 GB of RAM and MS Windows 10 Pro operating system.

3.2 Agisoft Metashape

Agisoft Metashape [5], developed by Agisoft LLC., is a commercial software that generates 3D models from images. Its pipeline consists of four fully automated steps, i.e., SfM, DIM, meshing and texturing, which let the user set various parameters, along with some optional steps, e.g., manual measurement of GCPs or tie points, manual or semiautomatic definition of masks, etc. It has a very simple graphical user interface and offers a high degree of automation, making it usable even by less experienced users.

The first was the alignment of the images. It is a SfM process that uses the available GPS/INS data to generate a georeferenced sparse point cloud of the scene and compute the camera poses and optionally their interior orientation. A modification of SIFT is used for feature extraction. The feature points were extracted in images of original size. Thresholds of 30,000 features and 15,000 tie points per image were specified, so that the sparse point cloud does not consist of too many points and the alignment process is not computationally intensive. The image pairs used for matching were selected using the GPS/INS data, to avoid matching of all possible pairs. Camera calibration was performed during the alignment step, using a frame camera model. A distortion model encompassing 11 degrees of freedom (DoF) was used: 1 for focal length, 2 for principal point, 2 for affinity and skew transformation coefficients, 4 for radial distortion coefficients and 2 for tangential distortion coefficients. The alignment time was 16 min.

6 GCPs were measured in the corresponding images, resulting in 129 image measurements, and their ground coordinates were inserted (modified, up to a translation transformation, to overcome a visualization issue in the derived point clouds in case of big coordinates). The points were added manually as "markers". The optimization of the cameras took place, via auto-calibrating bundle adjustment for exterior orientation estimation and sparse cloud generation in the reference system defined by the GCPs.

DIM was the next step. Metashape calculates depth information for each camera and combines it into a single dense point cloud. DIM was performed using the "medium" quality setting, which implies image downscaling by a factor of 16 (4 times by each side). The "aggressive" depth filtering mode was used to sort out most of the outliers. The computational time of the dense point cloud generation process was 2 h 36 min.

The dense cloud was then transformed into mesh. The "arbitrary" surface type was chosen and the maximum number of polygons was set to 1/5 of the number of dense cloud points, via the "high" setting. Image downscaling by 4 (2 times by each side) was selected via the "high" quality setting. In order to automatically fill holes in areas without points, interpolation mode was enabled, according to which Metashape interpolates some surface areas within a circle around every point. The meshing lasted 17 min.

The generation of texture was the last step. The "generic" mapping mode, which does not make any assumptions on the scene type, and the "mosaic" mode, which performs blending of the low frequency component for overlapping images and uses the high frequency one from one image, were used. Hole filling and ghosting filter were disabled. The texture size was set to 15,000 × 15,000 pixels. This step lasted 10 min.

3.3 RealityCapture

RealityCapture [6] is a commercial software package developed by Capturing Reality s.r.o., which generates 3D models from images, laser scans or combination of both. Its pipeline consists of alignment, reconstruction and texturing. By the term reconstruction, RealityCapture implies both the DIM and meshing processes.

The alignment was the first step. Although its documentation is limited, probably a modified SIFT algorithm is used. The alignment mode was set to "high", i.e., a setting targeted to highly overlapping images; RealityCapture was set to detect 60,000 features per image and keep 10,000 of those for further matching and processing. This initial alignment was completed in 4 min, using the GPS/INS metadata for georeferencing.

The same GCPs measured within Metashape were added in the corresponding images within RealityCapture. Then, using the update alignment tool, information about the reprojection error of each GCP was available. Running the final alignment was much faster, because there was no need for running SIFT again; RealityCapture keeps this information from the initial alignment. The estimated values of exterior and interior orientation were more precise, compared to the corresponding values of the initial alignment. The distortion model used was "Brown3 with Tangential2" that has 8 DoF: 1 for focal length, 2 for principal point, 3 for radial distortion coefficients and 2 for tangential distortion coefficients. The final alignment was completed in 2 min.

Reconstruction was the next step for creating a 3D mesh of the surveyed area. "Normal" mode was selected, without any downscaling of the images, and specifying a maximum of 5,000,000 vertices per part and a detail decimation factor of 1, indicating no decimation for smoothing details when creating the mesh. The unwrapping style was set to "maximal texture count"; unwrapping parameters were set to: 8,192 × 8,192 pixels; optimal texel size was calculated to 0.0083 m and set to 0.016 m for processing. A decimation took place within RealityCapture using the "simplify" command to reduce the number of triangles from 153.2M to 50M (21.5M vertices). The processing times were as follows: depth mapping: 1 h 9 min; meshing: 2 h 46 min; post-processing: 9 min.

RealityCapture provides a set of tools for selecting vertices and filtering them out, i.e., the reconstruction region bounding box, a lasso, rectangle and box tool for 3D selection, and the "Advanced" selection tool, which calculates the average edge length and provides four different selection options: marginal triangles; largest connected component; small triangles; and large triangles using a given threshold by (times × average edge length). Those tools were used to clean up the model and the topology of the model was checked (check topology tool) before proceeding to texturing.

The final step was texturing. The model was textured using multiple texture files (18 texture images) of 8,192 × 8,192 pixels resolution and the processing time was 21 min.

3.4 MicMac

MicMac [7] is a free open-source photogrammetric suite developed by IGN, France, which can be used for image-based 3D reconstruction. It consists of a set of command line tools, permitting a high degree of parameterization. Some visual interfaces are also provided, by calling the appropriate command, to facilitate parameter tuning. The target users are rather professionals, with a basic knowledge of photogrammetry.

The SfM procedure was completed using eight MicMac commands and seven of its tools. Initially, the OriConvert tool was used for transformation of the GPS/INS data accompanying the images from text format to MicMac's orientation format and generation of a file with the pairs of overlapping images. This task was completed in 1.5 min.

The Tapioca tool was used for computation of tie points using SIFT in images of original size. The file exported by OriConvert was used as input in Tapioca, so that tie points are extracted only in overlapping images. A first experiment was applied in images of original size, resulting in 13 h 30 min of computational time. Due to the extremely long processing time of Tapioca for full-resolution images, a second experiment was conducted for extracting feature points in images downscaled by 16, i.e., 4 times by each side (1,368 × 912 pixels). The processing time was dramatically different, as it took only 27.5 min. The fact that Tapioca does not provide the possibility of adjusting SIFT thresholds to extract a maximum number of features per image, e.g., like Metashape, makes it computationally ineffective in case of full-resolution images. For instance, about 750,000 features were extracted per image in the first experiment, while the maximum number of features per image in Metashape was set equal to 40,000.

The Tapas tool was used for camera calibration and relative orientation. "RadialStd" mode was selected, indicating an 8DoF distortion model: 1 for focal length, 2 for principal point, 2 for distortion center and 3 for coefficients of radial distortion. The processing time was 23 h 57 min using the tie points of the first test, whereas the Tapas command was completed in 14 h 28 min using the tie points of the second test.

A sparse cloud of the scene including the camera poses, in an arbitrary coordinate system, was created via AperiCloud in 23.5 min for the first test and 3.5 min for the second one. Whereas the output of this step is not used in any subsequent tool, it is useful for visualization reasons. Until this step, the GPS/INS values by MicMac are only used for image pairs determination, without being used for georeferencing reasons.

Whereas MicMac has a tool for measuring GCPs (SaisieAppuisInitQT), it was not used, in order to apply the same measurements made via Metashape. The coordinates of the GCPs, exported by Metashape, were converted in formats readable by MicMac.

The transformation of the relative orientation, as computed by Tapas, into absolute orientation was performed via the GCPBascule tool, using as input the image and ground coordinates of the GCPs. This command was completed in 5 s for both tests.

The bundle adjustment of the whole block of images was conducted via Campari. Self-calibration was not performed within the block adjustment. Whereas Campari provides the option of using GPS values within the adjustment, they were not used in the experiments. This step lasted 2 h 43 min for the first test and 11 min for the second one.

The creation of a sparse cloud of the scene including the camera poses in the ground reference system was implemented via AperiCloud. The processing times were similar to the ones achieved before absolute orientation and bundle adjustment, i.e., 25 min for the first test and 2.5 min for the second one. This was the last step of the SfM procedure.

The dense point cloud was created through automated DIM via the C3DC tool. The "BigMac" option was used, according to which the 3D coordinates of 1 point per 4 pixels are computed through DIM. A color point cloud was the output of this process. DIM lasted 18 h 21 min for the first test and 2 h 15 min for the second one.

In order to visualize the point cloud and crop it, so that it depicts the geometry of the area of interest, the MeshLab software [14] was used, as MicMac does not provide any tool for visualization and editing of 3D models. MeshLab is a free open-source 3D mesh processing software, developed by the ISTI-CNR institute of Italy. The cropping process was manual and was applied for the dense clouds generated by both tests.

The generation of a 3D mesh was implemented via the MicMac tool TiPunch, using the cropped dense cloud of each test via the Poisson reconstruction algorithm. The maximum reconstruction depth was set to 8, as any higher setting regarding a bigger reconstruction depth was too computationally ineffective. Meshing took 4 min for each test.

The Tequila tool was used for texturing, using the "Stretch" criterion for selecting the best image for each triangle, i.e., the best stretching of triangle projection in the image. The "Angle" criterion that takes into account the angle between the triangle normal and image viewing direction was also tested but was discarded, as it produced worse results. "Basic" mode was used, according to which all images are stored in the texture map. The maximum texture dimension was set to 15,000 pixels. It lasted 5 min.

3.5 Meshroom

Meshroom [8] is a free open-source 3D reconstruction software based on the AliceVision framework that produces textured models and provides its users with the possibility of parameterizing each of its steps. Once the parameterization is specified, the whole processing may be automatically completed. Meshroom permits input of additional images, while the processing is ongoing. Also, it can perform a live reconstruction. However, it does not provide the possibility of adding GCPs. It requires CUDA-enabled GPU, with a computing capability of at least 2.0. Its photogrammetric pipeline includes two main stages, i.e., SfM and MVS, and eleven basic steps, referred to as nodes.

Within the SfM stage, the camera intrinsic parameters were loaded from the image metadata and SIFT feature extraction took place. "Low quality" was selected, taking into account the quality and viewing angles of the cameras. This process took 3 min. A quick (<10 s) image matching preprocessing step was applied for determining the image pairs, without the cost of resolving all matches in detail, through tree classification. Then, the main process of image matching took place, followed by RANSAC for outlier rejection. This process took 3 min. An incremental SfM method was used for computing the camera poses and generating a sparse point cloud, which was completed in 2 min.

The undistortion of the images through the PrepareDenseScene node was then implemented in less than 5 min. The DepthMap and DepthMapFilter nodes were two of the most time consuming procedures (38 h without image downscaling); they were applied in order to retrieve the depth value of each pixel for all cameras and force depth consistency, respectively. As soon as these steps were finished, the dense point cloud and the arbitrary polygon mesh were generated through the Meshing node in 2 h. Values such as the maximum number of points of the point cloud, observation angle and factor, etc. were specified. The noise of the primary polygon mesh was largely eliminated by the MeshFiltering node, in which a smoothing operation took place (1.5 min), preparing the polygon mesh for texturing. Attribute values, such as the unwrapping mode, the resolution, etc. were user-specified. A maximum texture size of 8,192 pixels was specified for texturing, which took no more than 20 min without image downscaling. The dense point cloud and mesh model were cropped via the Meshlab software.

Table 1 outlines the tools of the tested software concerning each stage of 3D modelling and the basic parameterization selected. Table 2 indicates the computational time for each test.

Table 1. Tools of the tested software and parameterization used in each one

Stage	Metashape	RealityCapture	MicMac	Meshroom
Search for pairs	**Align Photos** (GPS/INS use; full-resolution images; feature point limit: 30,000; tie point limit: 15,000; 11DoF distortion model)	**Align** (GPS/INS use; alignment mode: high; max features per image: 60,000; preselector features: 10,000; 8DoF distortion model)	**OriConvert** (GPS/INS use)	**Image Matching**
Feature extraction and matching			**Tapioca** (test 1: full-resolution images; test 2: images downscaled by 16)	**Feature Extraction** (downscaled by 16); **Feature Matching**
Interior and relative orientation			**Tapas** (8DoF distort. Model)	**Structure-from-Motion**
Sparse point cloud			**AperiCloud**	
Measurement of GCPs	**Markers** (6 GCPs measured: 129 image measurements in total)	**Markers** (the GCPs measured in Metashape were used)	**SaisieAppuisInitQT** (the GCPs measured in Metashape were used)	-
Absolute orientation	**Optimize Cameras** (autocalibration)	**Align** (alignment before and after GCPs input)	**GCPBascule**	
Bundle adjustment			**Campari** (no autocalibration)	
Sparse point cloud			**AperiCloud**	

(*continued*)

Table 1. (*continued*)

Stage	Metashape	RealityCapture	MicMac	Meshroom
DIM	**Build Dense Cloud** (downscaled by 16; aggressive depth filtering)	**Reconstruction** (detail level: normal; no image downscaling; max vertices count per part: 5,000,000; no decimation; no editing of dense point cloud)	**C3DC** (the 3D coordinates of 1 point per 4 pixels are computed)	**PrepareDenseScene; DepthMap; DepthMapFilter; Meshing**
Cropping of dense point cloud	**Free-form selection**		**MeshLab** (no editing tools)	**MeshLab** (no editing tools)
Generation of 3D mesh	**Build Mesh** (arbitrary surface; high face count; interpolation enabled)		**TiPunch** (Poisson reconstruction; max reconstruction depth = 8)	**Meshing**
Cropping of 3D mesh	**Free-form selection**	**Selection toolbox; Simplification tool**	**MeshLab** (no editing tools)	**MeshLab** (no editing tools)
Generation of textured 3D model	**Build Texture** (mode: generic, mosaic; size: 15,000)	**Texture** (visibility-based; size: 8,192; max count: 40)	**Tequila** (criter.: Stretch; mode: Basic; size: 15,000)	**Texturing** (mode: basic; max size: 8,192)

Table 2. Computational time of the tests implemented using the four software packages

	Metashape	RealityCapture	MicMac test 1	MicMac test 2	Meshroom
SfM	0 h 16 min	0 h 6 min	41 h 0 min	15 h 14 min	0 h 8 min
DIM	2 h 36 min	1 h 8 min	18 h 21 min	2 h 15 min	38 h 0 min
Meshing-texturing	0 h 27 min	3 h 24 min	0 h 9 min	0 h 9 min	2 h 18 min
Total time	3 h 19 min	4 h 38 min	59 h 30 min	17 h 38 min	40 h 26 min

4   Results

The main results are summarized in Table 3. Meshlab does not provide any information concerning the number of tie points (matches). The number of tie points per image was set to be fixed in the case of RealityCapture. In the other two software packages, the average, maximum and minimum number of matches were different. The average number of tie points was too big in the case of the first MicMac test using the full-resolution images for feature extraction, as it does not provide the possibility of defining an upper threshold. Thus, the only available solution to reduce the computational time was to downscale the images, as implemented in the second test. Metashape displays the number of matches per image but may not export them. Hence, whereas such statistics could also be estimated for Metashape as well, they require a great deal of manual processing, so their extraction was discarded. The maximum number of tie points per image was quite similar for the case of Metashape, RealityCapture and the second test of MicMac.

Table 3. Main results of the experiments conducted using the tested software solutions

Metric	Metashape	RealityCapture	MicMac test 1	MicMac test 2	Meshroom
Avg tie points per image	n/a	10,000	181,295	11,030	n/a
Max tie points per image	11,200	10,000	283,023	13,991	n/a
Min tie points per image	n/a	10,000	49,845	3,584	n/a
Avg residual of tie points	0.58 pix	0.38 pix	0.40 pix	0.83 pix	1.10 pix
Max residual of tie points	43.45 pix	0.99 pix	0.46 pix	1.03 pix	4.00 pix
Avg GCPs residual	0.57 m	n/a	0.52 m	0.53 m	n/a
Max GCPs residual	0.69 m	n/a	0.74 m	0.71 m	n/a
Avg GCPs residual in axial components X, Y, Z (m)	0.21, 0.25, 0.43	0.22, 0.25, 0.38	0.24, 0.25, 0.34	0.23, 0.24, 0.37	n/a
Max GCPs residual in axial components X, Y, Z (m)	0.40, 0.36, 0.60	0.42, 0.45, 0.55	0.46, 0.56, 0.56	0.42, 0.53, 0.60	n/a
RMS error of GCPs in axial components X, Y, Z (m)	0.23, 0.30, 0.45	n/a	0.27, 0.30, 0.38	0.25, 0.29, 0.41	n/a
Sparse cloud points	0.65M	4.7M	35.6M	2.7M	0.018M
Dense cloud points	24.2M	81.9M	24.4M	24.8M	24.0M
Dense cloud points (cropped)	21.2M	25.1M	21.9M	21.9M	12.8M
Vertices of final 3D mesh	1.4M	25.1M	0.07M	0.07M	8.2M
Faces of final 3D mesh	2.9M	50.0M	0.15M	0.11M	13.4M

The smallest average residual of tie points was observed for RealityCapture and the biggest one for Meshroom. The first MicMac test yielded the smallest worst residual. The worst residual of tie points for Metashape was quite big, indicating that at least an outlier was not removed. However, this does not generally influence the rest Metashape results, which are satisfying.

Regarding the average residual of GCPs in axial components $[X, Y, Z]$, approximately equivalent results were reported by Metashape, RealityCapture and MicMac. The X and Y residuals and RMS errors were similar for Metashape and MicMac, whereas the Z residual and RMS error were the worst for Metashape. Similar results were reported for the RMS errors of GCPs in axial components for Metashape and MicMac, while this kind of information was not available for RealityCapture and Meshroom.

The sparse cloud density was significantly lower for Meshroom and Metashape. This number for the first MicMac test was too big, due to lack of any tie points threshold. The dense cloud density of Metashape, MicMac and Meshroom was comparable. Whereas the number of dense cloud points after editing within RealityCapture was equivalent with the other solutions, its initial dense cloud included 3 times more points. The meshing and texturing MicMac tools are still under development, so the textured MicMac meshes were not satisfactory, as shown in Fig. 1. The rest textured models are visually satisfying. The numbers of mesh vertices and faces are significantly lower for MicMac. The biggest numbers of vertices and faces were reported by RealityCapture.

The computational time of these software packages differs a lot. Metashape is the quickest option, as the total processing time was less than 3.5h, while RealityCapture is also very fast, completing the 3D reconstruction process in a little more than 4.5h.

Furthermore, comparisons in the derived dense point clouds were made using the free open-source CloudCompare software [15], via its "Cloud to Cloud Distance" tool. The Metashape dense cloud was assumed to be the reference one. While the RealityCapture and MicMac point clouds were georeferenced, the Meshroom cloud was in an arbitrary system; hence, it was aligned to the reference one via measurement of common points, followed by the ICP algorithm. The mean and standard deviation of distances are presented in Table 4. The smallest mean difference was observed for the first test of MicMac (full-resolution images for alignment) and the biggest one for its second test. Comparable results are derived using all software packages, as verified by the mean differences between these dense clouds, which do not exceed 7.5 cm. The order of magnitude of these differences is quite smaller than the uncertainty of the models in the reference system, which is quite big, due to the quality of GCPs (see Sect. 3.1) An interesting aspect is the fact that the MicMac dense clouds derived using different alignment parameterization yield comparable differences from the reference Metashape cloud; hence, a computationally intensive full-resolution matching via MicMac is not generally needed, taking into account the time parameter. Figure 2 provides a visualization of the absolute differences (m) between the Metashape dense cloud and each one of the four compared clouds. The largest differences are observed in the edges of all dense clouds, due to the insufficient number of overlapping images depicting these regions.

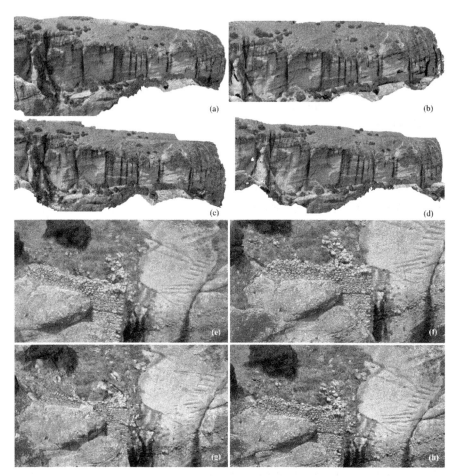

Fig. 1. Textured 3D models and zoom-in views derived using Metashape (a, e), RealityCapture (b, f), MicMac - test 2 (c, g) and Meshroom (d, h)

Table 4. Distances between the reference (Metashape) dense cloud and the compared ones

Metric	RealityCapture	MicMac - test 1	MicMac - test 2	Meshroom
Mean (cm)	6.9	5.8	7.4	6.7
Std. Dev. (cm)	9.4	6.4	7.5	8.5

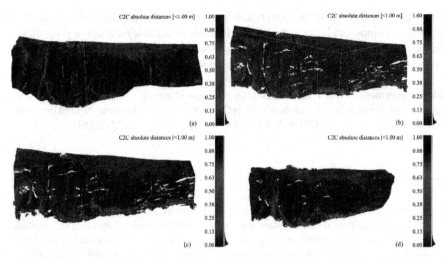

Fig. 2. Absolute differences (m) between the reference (Metashape) and the compared dense point clouds, i.e., RealityCapture (a), MicMac - test 1 (b), MicMac - test 2 (c) and Meshroom (d).

5 Discussion and Conclusions

Within this paper, the performance of four well-established commercial and free software solutions was evaluated for image-based reconstruction of complex cultural and natural heritage sites. Regarding bundle adjustment results, all solutions produced comparable outputs in terms of accuracy (taking into account tie points and GCP residuals as well as RMS errors, where applicable). The mean distance of the derived dense point clouds is almost negligible, whereas biggest differences are observed in the edges of the dense clouds. A major disadvantage of Meshroom was the fact that it does not provide the possibility for measuring GCPs; hence, its results refer to an arbitrary coordinate system. MicMac produced satisfactory results in terms of dense point cloud; however, its final textured mesh model was not satisfactory, as the corresponding tools are still under development. The investigation of the use of the MicMac dense cloud for mesh generation via another software solution, e.g., MeshLab, and its texturing either using MicMac or another software using the orientation of images produced by MicMac would be interesting. In terms of computational time, the commercial software packages were the most efficient solutions, with Metashape being the fastest one. The commercial software have a friendlier user interface, which makes them adoptable even by non-photogrammetrists. Also, Meshroom is quite user-friendly, giving the possibility of quite wide parameterization. On the other hand, MicMac consists of command line tools which can be used by experts in photogrammetry, thus not being easy to use.

In conclusion, in cases of geometric documentation of complex sites in a ground system defined by GCPs, Metashape and RealityCapture are suitable for generating a textured 3D surface model, while MicMac is suitable for generating a 3D dense point cloud, which may be inserted in another software for the meshing and texturing process. Meshroom may only be used for generating a 3D model in an arbitrary coordinate system. On the other hand, Metashape and RealityCapture are commercial software, so if the budget of an organization or project does not permit a purchase of their licenses, both free solutions yield acceptable results in terms of accuracy and dense point clouds. Their combination with a mesh processing software would probably produce satisfactory results; this is an issue that will be investigated within our future research.

Acknowledgements. This research has been co-financed by the European Union and Greek national funds through the Operational Program Competiveness, Entrepreneurship and Innovation, under the call RESEARCH–CREATE–INNOVATE (project code: T1EDK02859).

References

1. Verykokou, S., Doulamis, A., Athanasiou, G., Ioannidis, C., Amditis, A.: Multi-scale 3D modelling of damaged cultural sites: use cases and image-based workflows. In: Ioannides, M., et al. (eds.) Digital Heritage. Progress in Cultural Heritage: Documentation, Preservation, and Protection, vol. 10058, pp. 50–62. Springer, Cham (2016). https://doi.org/10.1007/978-3-319-48496-9_5
2. Jo, Y., Hong, S.: Three-dimensional digital documentation of cultural heritage site based on the convergence of terrestrial laser scanning and unmanned aerial vehicle photogrammetry. ISPRS Int. J. Geo-Inf. **8**(2), 53 (2019). https://doi.org/10.3390/ijgi8020053
3. METEORA project. https://www.meteora.net.gr/. Accessed 01 Sept 2020
4. Ioannidis, C., Verykokou, S., Soile, S., Boutsi, A.-M.: A multi-purpose cultural heritage data platform for 4D visualization and interactive information services. Int. Arch. Photogramm. Remote Sens. Spatial Inf. Sci. **XLIII-B4-2020**, 583–590 (2020). https://doi.org/10.5194/isprs-archives-XLIII-B4-2020-583-2020
5. Agisoft Metashape. https://www.agisoft.com/. Accessed 01 Sept 2020
6. Capturing Reality. https://www.capturingreality.com/. Accessed 01 Sept 2020
7. MicMac Wiki. https://micmac.ensg.eu/index.php/Accueil. Accessed 01 Sept 2020
8. AliceVision. https://alicevision.org/. Accessed 01 Sept 2020
9. Verykokou, S., Ioannidis, C.: A photogrammetry-based structure from motion algorithm using robust iterative bundle adjustment techniques. Int. Arch. Photogramm. Remote Sens. Spatial Inf. Sci. **IV-4/W6**, 73–80 (2018). https://doi.org/10.5194/isprs-annals-IV-4-W6-73-2018
10. Furukawa, Y., Hernández, C.: Multi-view stereo: a tutorial. Found. Trends Comput. Graph. Vis. **9**(1–2), 1–148 (2015). https://doi.org/10.1561/0600000052
11. Tareen, S.A.K., Saleem, Z.: A comparative analysis of SIFT, SURF, KAZE, AKAZE, ORB, and BRISK. In: iCoMET 2018, pp. 1–10. IEEE (2018)
12. Verykokou, S., Ioannidis, C.: Exterior orientation estimation of oblique aerial images using SfM-based robust bundle adjustment. Int. J. Remote Sens. **41**, 7217–7254 (2020)
13. Nalpantidis, L., Christou Sirakoulis, G., Gasteratos, A.: Review of stereo vision algorithms: from software to hardware. Int. J. Optomechatron. **2**(4), 435–462 (2008)
14. MeshLab. https://www.meshlab.net/. Accessed 01 Sept 2020
15. CloudCompare. https://www.danielgm.net/cc/. Accessed 01 Sept 2020

Robotic Fabrication in Conservation: Digital Workflows and Skills Evaluation

Sara Codarin$^{(\boxtimes)}$ (iD) and Karl Daubmann

College of Architecture and Design, Lawrence Technological University,
Southfield, MI 48075, USA
{scodarin,kdaubmann}@ltu.edu

Abstract. The paper describes a laboratory experiment carried out at Lawrence Technological University - College of Architecture and Design. The project assumes that the ubiquity of digital technologies in the framework of the Fourth Industrial Revolution has an important potential for the conservation of Cultural Heritage. The enhancement of digital resources, the possibility to access data simulation, and the availability of new construction tools such as robots allow for restoration methods to be augmented by digital data. In the current technological ecosystem, Cultural Heritage can benefit from digital information and digital fabrication, to achieve both digital and tangible conservation. The experiment simulates an on-site robotic fabrication process by imagining an integration of machines in the conservation building site. An industrial robot was used to operate within vertical and horizontal constraints on irregular surfaces to fabricate the missing volume of a wall gap. An abandoned church in Detroit downtown was used as a test case. A methodological workflow emerged from the research process and was evaluated as a proof of concept.

Keywords: Robotic fabrication · Cultural Heritage · Digital workflows

1 Introduction

1.1 Technological Framework in Architecture and Manufacturing

Today, many technological sectors and disciplines are intertwined within a wide digital infrastructure. In the present era, defined by the term Anthropocene [1] different technologies are increasingly evolving towards the definition of an interconnected ecosystem, which characterizes the global artificial layer called Technosphere. The systemic evolution in the productive culture is framed in terms of the Fourth Industrial Revolution [2]. It is a socio-technical change that comes from manufacturing and includes advances in big data, augmented reality, artificial intelligence, machine learning, social networks, analytics, and cloud storage in the postindustrial society[1]. Compared to previous revolutions, the Fourth Industrial Revolution is occurring more quickly and is characterized

---

[1] The concept of postindustrial society emerges in countries that experienced the Industrial Revolution (i.e. United States, western Europe, and Japan). It is characterized by a transition from a manufacturing-based to a service-based economy. For further information, see: https://www.britannica.com/topic/postindustrial-society (accessed: October 25th, 2020).

© Springer Nature Switzerland AG 2021
M. Ioannides et al. (Eds.): EuroMed 2020, LNCS 12642, pp. 241–253, 2021.
https://doi.org/10.1007/978-3-030-73043-7_20

by ubiquity and communication of the means of production, which are able to create a direct relation between the virtual and physical world.

The ongoing digital transfer between manufacturing and design opens unexplored possibilities for design at all scales, from the construction unit to the technological system, with consequences throughout the decision-making phases. Narrowing this discussion to the architecture sector, the results of the Fourth Industrial Revolution have been theorized as the Second Digital Turn [3], which refers to the introduction of automated tools for customized production within the design process. The Second Digital Turn assumes that a previous phase change occurred. This previous change happened in the 1980's, when the architectural design sector began to absorb digital workflows from the naval and aeronautic industries. With the Digital Fabrication Revolution, design is not separated from construction and the translation between one and the other becomes nearly instantaneous. The resulting digital continuum defines an opportunity to bring back the master-builder, as an expression of digital complexity and dexterity. Digital manufacturing technologies (robotic arms, 3D printers, smart-assembly or combined tools, to name a few) occupy a fundamental role in this scenario [4]. These technologies are the foundations for mass-customization and performative architecture.

1.2 Customized Production for the Conservation of Cultural Heritage

The context of the Fourth Industrial Revolution highlights the current lack of innovation within the building process, where the construction site continues to refer to methods strongly rooted in building traditions and narrow technological choices. While the construction industry must manage risks based on economics, labor, and safety, new technologies [5] highlight the need to identify new practices to enhance construction roles.

In the current age of automation, it is possible to imagine continuity between design and manufacturing in a single workflow that aims at bringing smart industrial robots to the conservation-site. The protection of existing buildings would entail customizing the on-site operations in a responsive way through the compartmentalization of automated tools. The creation of a workflow [6] is therefore intended not as a standardization of the design outcomes, but as an update of the culture of making that combines technological and cultural instances.

However, rapid technological development is not always followed by the same rate of acceptance; there is an increasing divide between the devices that we use and the culture of their use. It's hard for organizations to absorb change. Within a change/time equation, technologies evolve exponentially (Moore's Law) while organizations change at a logarithmic rate, much slower (Martec's Law). If it's hard for the construction industry to accept change, which is not technologically driven, it's even harder for the conservation sector. The conservation building-site is a very specific context that requires non-standard construction components. It is a context where risk should be managed with a particular care. Indeed, restoration traditions are strongly linked to craftspeople on-site that interrupt the digital continuum in the realization of projects.

Given the inevitable digital transformation, a new conception of the master-builder might represent a balance between the current technological advancement in architectural construction methods and the artisanal approach that characterizes interventions on Cultural Heritage. The new master-builder constitutes a figure that links the various actors operating in a complex building process. This professional (or multidisciplinary team of professionals) could be also the promoter of the project culture and the supervisor of all the design - construction - management activities that take place in the digital continuum. Digital technologies and fabrication tools such as additive manufacturing could support the decision-making phases for innovative interventions on Cultural Heritage and be exploited to support design outcomes.

2 Methodology

This paper investigates the relationship between the Fourth Industrial Revolution and the consequences on Cultural Heritage. It describes the definition of an experimental workflow, or methodological strategy, to hypothesize the use of on-site automation for Cultural Heritage conservation. The outcome is a laboratory experiment to support the case, as a means of prototyping the proposed workflow. The work was carried out by the main investigator Sara Codarin in coordination with a research group at Lawrence Technological University - College of Architecture and Design (LTU-CoAD)[2].

2.1 Phases of the Experimentation

The laboratory experiment addressed technical problems and gave theoretical insight. The experimental phases, unpacked in the following paragraphs, required an academic year of work and were structured as listed below:

Phase 1. Identification of a test case, that was a significant architecture in a state of damage, located in Detroit downtown - the Woodward Avenue Church (see Fig. 1). Formulation of a hypothesis of intervention supported by a critical approach to the topic;

Phase 2. Qualitative photographic survey of the building, selection of a specific case of damage (a wall gap) used as a basis to study a possible robotic process for the reconfiguration of the lost geometry;

Phase 3. Quantitative survey of the building, carried out by a work group at LTU-CoAD. Collection of digital data such as point cloud of the interior spaces and texture mesh of the wall gap;

Phase 4. Elaboration of the survey data to define a digital model of the damaged architectural element under study. Definition of a 3D model. Conversion of the 3D model into compatible input to be processed by different tools for digital fabrication;

---

[2] The experiment was developed during the second doctoral year within the program International Doctorate in Architecture and Urban Planning (IDAUP) at the Department of Architecture – University of Ferrara for the development of the dissertation "Innovative construction systems within building processes. An approach to large-scale robotic Additive Layer Manufacturing for the conservation of Cultural Heritage".

Phase 5. Selection of significant portions of the 3D model, to realize a physical mock-up at 1:1 scale. Elaboration of the robot's work cell (reachability area for the axis extension). Set up of the experiment and creation of the digital twin (see Fig. 2);

Phase 6. Feasibility checks in accordance to budget[3]. Selection of the material used for additive manufacturing: raw clay;

Phase 7. Tool making. Design and digital fabrication of the end-effector (extruder and customized robot's head). Preparation for large-scale robotic additive manufacturing;

Phase 8. Robo-scripting: a) generation of toolpaths; b) conversion of toolpaths to a robot code; c) digital simulation of the robot code[4];

Phase 9. Set to zero the wall mockup (matching the digital and physical origin of axis);

Phase 10. Definition of the project outcome (three-dimensional customized volume created by additive robotic manufacturing within the geometrical limits of a pre-existing irregular geometry).

2.2 Outcome: A Robot Fabricated Wall Gap

The quantitative data collected during the survey of the Woodward Avenue Church were turned into matter through the full-scale realization of a partial wall. The process simulated possible on-site operations of additive manufacturing for the production of large-scale architectural elements within complex geometrical constraints such as a wall gap. Specific equipment for testing the digital manufacturing process was provided. A six-axis Kuka robot was used to accomplish the kinematic sequences. A do-it-yourself end-effector (a nozzle connected to a hose) was installed on the robot, for the extrusion of the 3D printing material. A pipe was used to push the raw clay, by a compressed air system, into the end-effector. Clay was chosen as a base material for the experiment because it is recyclable, inexpensive, and allows iterations.

The robot script (a Grasshopper definition, obtained using the plug-in Kuka|Prc) was used to simulate and validate the robot movements. After validation, the robot code was uploaded to the robot controller. Once the kinematics were verified, the additive manufacturing process was tested. The responsiveness of the material (viscosity, hardening

---

[3] The activity was funded by the Italian Ministry of Education with the Research Grant for Doctoral Activities Abroad (3,500 €). The budget covered the purchase of 3D printing material and the equipment needed to build a customized robot end-effector.

[4] A common workflow used to program Kuka robots consists of drawing the robot motions (tool-path) in Rhinoceros and turning the geometry (usually splines or polylines) into target points using Grasshopper. Finally, the plug-in Kuka|Prc is used to translate target points (defined by a plane and a normal vector) into coordinates and polar rotations in relation to the origin (x, y, z = a, b, c = 0, 0, 0) that corresponds with the robot's base. Moreover, Kuka|Prc allows for the interpolation of target points to densify the toolpath and avoid approximation during the robot motion in the physical world. The input is a geometry; the output is a system of coordinates. The script can be validated digitally before running the program on the robot.

Fig. 1. Interior space of the Woodward Avenue Church in Detroit, selected as a test case. It was designed by architect Sidney Badgley and built in 1911 in Gothic Revival. It is a national landmark since 1982. The last religious service in 2005 marked the beginning of its abandonment.

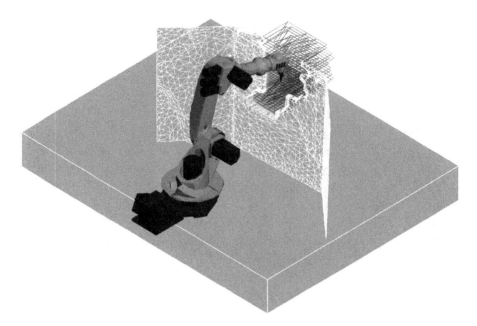

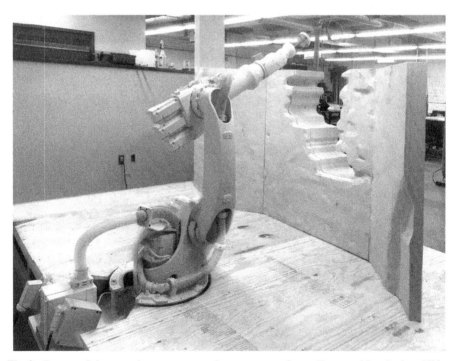

Fig. 2. Set up of the experiment – create the geometry of a wall gap with robotic additive manufacturing. Creation of a digital twin to simulate the process before testing.

rapidity, and compressive strength) was a key point in relation to the different surface slopes deposited with the extruder. During the experimental phases, certain aspects were monitored. They were investigated to evaluate precision, replicability, and measurability of the performance.

The experiment was carried out in an interior lab environment, given the access to available robotic equipment. The robot at LTU-CoAD works within a static work cell – a set up that is commonly used in fab labs. This means that a dynamic support system would be needed to use such a machine on-site. Additionally, an array of sensors would be required for real-time feedback, due to the complexity of a restoration building site.

For the experiment, an industrial robot decommissioned by the automotive industry was used. However, in the state of the art, robotic tools have been developed further to achieve more flexibility. An example of this approach is the Digital Construction Platform[5], a mobile system capable of on-site design, sensing, and fabrication of large-scale structures that combines a large hydraulic boom arm and a smaller electric 5-axis robotic arm. The result is a mobile stand potentially able to produce or install customized technological units directly on-site.

The outcome of the additive manufacturing robotic test to repair a building crack is shown in the photographic documentation (see Fig. 3). The digital construction phases to fill a gap through large-scale robotic additive layer manufacturing were simulated. The extrusion process needed to be divided into four sessions; the volume was created in four days. This four-day process allowed the material to dry overnight to prevent a collapse under the weight of the subsequent layers. Moreover, the script generated by the Grasshopper script (containing the robot's toolpath) was exported in two parts, due to the limit of the embedded robot software to read files with maximum 703 lines of code, within a disk space of 65 KB. This limitation was expected because industrial robots need to perform short repetitive tasks only.

Circumstantial conditions such as: budget, timeframe for setting up the experiment, availability of the people involved in this research, and laboratory tools informed the outcome. However, all the improvements and technical optimizations that can be made in a possible future development will be taken into consideration, to improve the 3D print resolution and the effectiveness of the end-effector to reach all the target points defined in the project objective in the digital simulation phase.

3 Validation of the Experimental Results

The applied research took place in a low-cost and low-risk work context. To maximize the experimental results, decisions were made to operate under specific constraints, to simulate the building site environment. Mapping the constraints and disclosing the complexities served to share the phases of the process, so that other research groups could benefit from this "workflow prototype". Moreover, the proposed digital construction phases could encourage research to manage robotic construction processes with low capitalization costs. The evaluation was carried out by elaborating a matrix that associated low/medium/high level of expertise for the completion in terms of labor

---

[5] For further information, see: https://www.media.mit.edu/projects/digital-construction-platform-v-2/overview/ (accessed: October 25th, 2020).

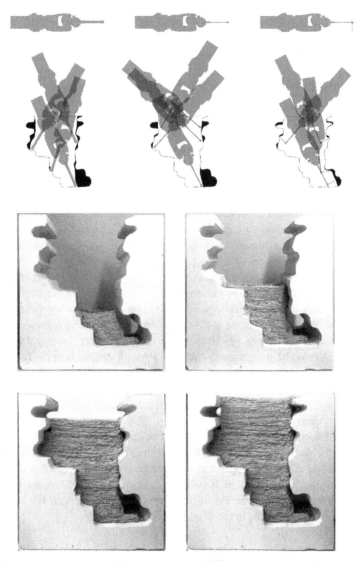

Fig. 3. The outcome of the workflow is a result of different extrusion sessions. It is a narrow application on a technological unit as a proof of concept informed by advanced ways of making. This realization allowed for a speculation on how to advance the experiment by optimizing the end-effector and extend the reachability of target points.

involved in the phases, equipment available, and material used. The overall work, a low-budget entry-level process, was mapped as "low" in all categories, due to the following conditions:

1. no previous exposure in robotics and large-scale additive manufacturing;

2. implementation of students' skills with a background in architecture: grad and undergrad research assistants with experience on desk-3D printing only;
3. use of equipment provided by the university fab lab equipment: a used industrial robot - with not particularly advanced mechatronic technology - to be customized for architectural design purposes;
4. use of low engineered material, necessary to synchronize the kinematics with the theoretical building production. This means that the principal investigator/author, personally worked for the first time in this type of process.

The inexperience was considered an opportunity to understand how a background in architecture could help creating a "computational though" to control advanced machines that could soon appear on construction/conservation sites. A lot is yet to come in terms of widespread of robotics in construction. Until national and international regulations and guidelines are elaborated, robotic fabrication process will be continuously hacked with do-it-yourself strategies (especially in academic research) and adapted to different construction needs. The evaluation of the experiment provides insights for alternative scenarios (see Table 1) for the development of the proposed methodology. The different scenarios could depend on how work groups are organized and skills are balanced to complete a project.

Table 1. Evaluation of the experiment and insights for alternative scenarios in a rating scale low/medium/high for the development of the proposed methodology. The different scenarios depend on how work groups are organized to complete a project.

Expertise	Labor	Equipment	Material
Low	Low	Low	Low
Alternatives:			
High	Medium	Medium	Low
Medium	Low	High	Medium
Low	Low	High	High

The validation of the experiment allowed for a comparison between phases (see Fig. 4 and Fig. 5) and skills embedded in: hypothesis (premise and expectations), actual experiment (carried out work), and future scenarios informed by the acquired knowledge. For instance, by reading horizontally the workflows: in the hypothesis, the main investigator considered to buy an off-the-shelf end-effector to turn the industrial robot into a customized tool for additive production; the experimental phase created specific lab conditions that required to operate with a do-it-yourself strategy, the end effector was designed and digitally fabricated; in the future, it is expected that sensors and end-effectors will be integrated on robots for architecture to collect data in real-time adopting the feedback-loop strategy. In between the present state of the art and future application, it is foreseeable the possibility to carry out interim, low cost, realization of the workflow, before reaching increasingly high levels of sophistication.

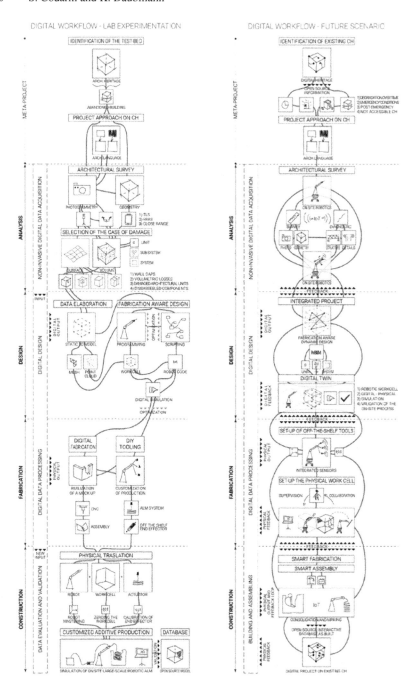

Fig. 4. Diagram that compares experiment and future workflows. The systematization of the workflows allowed the identification of the different skills needed to carry out the proposed working methodologies. These professional skills overlap at various phases and, potentially, they will be fully integrated in a foreseeable scenario.

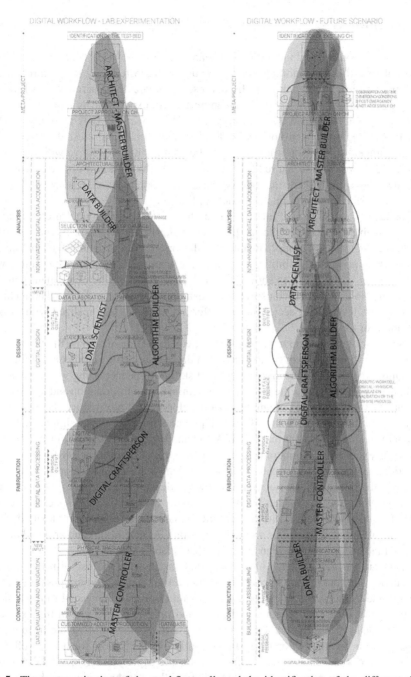

Fig. 5. The systematization of the workflows allowed the identification of the different skills needed to carry out the proposed working methodologies. These professional skills overlap at various phases and, potentially, they will be fully integrated in a foreseeable scenario.

4   Conclusions

Process validation resulted in a Minimum Viable Process (MVP). According to the definition of Eric Ries, a minimum viable product is the fastest way to get through the build-measure-learn feedback loop. In this research context, the acronym MVP represented a "minimum viable product" meaning that an experiment is more than just a theoretical inquiry it is also a first prototype [7]. Moreover, not only the outcome, but the whole workflow is a prototype. Its fundamental goal was to test the hypotheses and encourage the interest toward the scientific community to continue with feasibility studies to achieve more structured goals in the future. The workflow prototype could be replicated, deployed in different contexts, and transformed; the concept test of the wall repair is a starting point for much broader application.

The lack of technological literacy related to robotic programming in conservation made it possible to identify all the complexities related to technical aspects and organizational assets of the work group. The intent of this project was to simulate a construction process. Among other possibilities as subtractive or mixed techniques, 3D printed was selected as an explicit way to show data in reality. However, the experiment was not able to refer to any real previous full-scale example because none exist. The technology readiness level in the sector did not offer any cases already realized with on-site innovation for restoration.

The experiment - a temporary coalition of people and organizations [8] - is a starting point of a working culture in compliance with the requirements of the Fourth Industrial Revolution. In the future, the dissemination of skills will be increasingly accelerated by the reduction of the costs of the tools. The dissemination of information and open source software that rely on open communities of developers will also reduce the investment necessary for the software and for the development of the emerging design tools. Future development trends indicate that the ToA (technology of architecture) discipline will witness an exponential democratization of software and hardware allow for innovative educational paths. Higher education plays a fundamental role in developing a learning model for the future [9]. This underlines how the designers are in the right position to lead these processes. Architects stands to potentially become the prime operators of the Fourth Industrial Revolution, and will be able to manage: the digital complexity derived by tools, software, and methods 4.0; the transition CAD/CAM (computer-aided design and manufacturing) with a design approach that is fabrication-aware.

There are various elements of analysis that suggest that the use of robots on the construction site for building interventions can occur in the near future, possibly in less than a decade. This scenario can be either on-site or off-site. In special time-sensitive situations, the need to accelerate production and operate with a just-in-time strategy can be defined [10], so that various components arrive at the building site from different production facilities. Moreover, digital workflows will allow for a more efficient use of resources and robots will compensate for the expected increase in labor costs. The management of new and scaled-up tools-workflows-technologies will be up to an expert/master controller/operator able to: understand the dynamics of digital complexity; modify the operational sequences of work flows and verify optimization opportunities; synthesize the various collaborative technologies emerging in Industry 4.0; balance the technical-theoretical contribution in a project; organize multidisciplinary work groups and collaboration.

This professional could be described as the operator of the Fourth Industrial Revolution who coordinates all experts involved in design and construction processes. In the future, construction procedures will be leveraged intellectually, creating a work environment based on high-level knowledge. With this premise, the architecture discipline will become a driving force for other sectors, as it is the perfect synthesis between theory – practice – culture – social organization and work.

References

1. Crutzen, P.J.: The "Anthropocene." In: Ehlers, E., Krafft, T. (eds.) Earth System Science in the Anthropocene, pp. 13–18. Springer-Verlag, Berlin/Heidelberg (2006). https://doi.org/10.1007/3-540-26590-2_3
2. Schwab, K.: The Fourth Industrial Revolution. Crown Business, New York (2017)
3. Carpo, M.: The Second Digital Turn: Design Beyond Intelligence. MIT press, Cambridge (2017)
4. Gallozzi, A., Senatore, L.J., Strollo, R.M.: An overview on robotic applications for cultural heritage and built cultural heritage. SCIRES-IT-Sci. Res. Inf. Technol. 9(2), 47–56 (2019)
5. Ceccarelli, M., Blanco-Moreno, F., Carbone, G., Roig, P., Cigola, M., Regidor, J.L.: A robotic solution for the restoration of fresco paintings. Int. J. Adv. Rob. Syst. 12(11), 160 (2015)
6. Marble, S. (ed.): Digital Workflows in Architecture: Design–Assembly–Industry. Birkhauser, Basel (2012)
7. Ries, E.: The Lean Startup. How Today's Entrepreneurs Use Continuous Innovation to Create Radically Successful Businesses. Crown Books, New York (2011)
8. Groak, S.: The Idea of Building: Thought and Action in the Design and Production of Buildings. Taylor & Francis, New York (2002)
9. Ford, M.: Rise of the Robots: Technology and the Threat of a Jobless Future. Basic Books, New York (2015)
10. Burry, M.: Robots at the Sagrada Família Basilica: a brief history of robotised stone-cutting. In: Reinhardt, D., Saunders, R., Burry, J. (eds.) Robotic Fabrication in Architecture, Art and Design 2016, pp. 2–15. Springer, Cham (2016). https://doi.org/10.1007/978-3-319-26378-6_1

Towards a Building Information Modeling System for Identification and Retrofit Planning of Stone Damages

Klaus Luig[1]([✉]), Dino Mustedanagic[1], Dieter Jansen[1], Sebastian Fuchs[2],
Robert Schülbe[2], Peter Katranuschkov[3], Al-Hakam Hamdan[3], Christoph Franzen[4],
Kristin Hiemann[4], and Raimar Scherer[3]

[1] 3L Architekten, Horlecke 46, 58706 Menden, Germany
klaus.luig@3-l.de
[2] TragWerk Software, Prellerstraße 9, 01309 Dresden, Germany
[3] TU Dresden, Faculty of Civil Engineering, Institute of Construction Informatics,
01062 Dresden, Germany
[4] Institut für Diagnostik und Konservierung an Denkmalen in Sachsen und Sachsen-Anhalt e.V.
Schlossplatz 1, 01076 Dresden, Germany

Abstract. Nowadays building works, especially of historic buildings with facades out of natural stone, require continuous maintenance, repair and retrofit works. In order to fulfill the needs for a completely digitized natural stone retrofit process, works are to be projected, planned, conducted and cleared with instrumentation of Building Information Modeling (BIM). Due to this need, a novel knowledge-based stone damage identification system focused on natural stone damage on the basis of BIM is developed, which will present implicitly existing knowledge and information from the building survey explicitly and objectively by using semantic data structures. BIM-SIS is an adaptive damage identification system for natural stone, which allows to virtually merge different natural stone damages, recorded by different information systems and with different procedures, into a holistic damage model. This model is used to assess the damages integrative and in detail, supported by knowledge-based methods, and to develop a uniform and cost-stable remediation strategy. Therefore, the BIM-SIS methodology consists of BIMification for information processes, Ontologies for knowledge representation and Multimodels for data interoperability. The so formed continuous interoperable digital construction representation consists of separate but interlinked domain models. This model structure is then extended for remediation execution management and allows to simply incorporate subsequently detected defects during execution. The complete damage profile is the basis for all further retrofit-creation and calculation processes in BIM-SIS which will automatically lead to user customized retrofit variants presented in VR and AR.

Keywords: BIM · Cultural heritage · Stone damage · Retrofit · Digitalization

M. Ioannides et al. (Eds.): EuroMed 2020, LNCS 12642, pp. 254–261, 2021.
https://doi.org/10.1007/978-3-030-73043-7_21

1   Stone Damages on Facades

Natural stone as well as other porous building material is altered when exposed to the natural environment. Weathering, erosion and degradation of the stone takes place in several dimensions and orders of magnitude. These weathering related changes define the life cycle of a natural stone facade. Compared to other branches of industry, construction products are fundamentally renewed several times in their life cycle and are often used for a different purpose. On average the life span of a building is 100 years with a renovation period of 25 years. Monument-protected buildings as part of our cultural heritage are to be preserved indefinitely and must therefore be continuously renovated at appropriate intervals. Therefore, an up-to-date condition and damage assessments is an increasingly frequent task in the construction industry. A large proportion of digital planning work for damage assessment and remediation measures is not standardized. Today mostly analogue methods are used in companies and in the public sector. Data is passed on as a non-processable file (e.g. documents, pictures, etc.) or as processable files that follow no standard (e.g. tables). This leads to information loss or incorrect facts due to misinterpretation, data loss and inconsistencies. With regular maintenance and repair a natural stone facade can be very durable, as proven by the cultural heritage stock. However, referring to stone damages one should always distinguish between the damage phenomena, damage processes and damage factors. Damage factors are the outer circumstances and parameters necessary to cause the damaging processes. That is for example the exposition to water, the atmosphere, wind, chemical agents etc. While the treatment of those damage factors will be partially referred to in the retrofit action, the actual damaging weathering processes have no relevance in the context here. However, the stone damage phenomena are of main importance, as they are the most visible exposure of the damage on the stone (see Fig. 1). The assessment of the natural stone facade starts with recognition of those damage phenomena. The damages have to be noticed first and then recorded and inspected. Most of such kind of stone damages can be easily noticed and recorded by non-trained people using photos. Here the foundation for the digital assessment and a workflow towards a treatment plan is laid. The damage of the stone is identified and classified, which ultimately defines the need and way of repair. Connected to the BIM-model of the corresponding building the retrofit can be planned. With advancing digitalization in the construction industry, the entire building stock will eventually be digitalized for BIM, which will enable the BIM-based renovation planning as envisioned by the BIM-SIS project. Knowledge about stone damage is well developed and builds an important basis for knowledge-based damage assessment systems. Fitzner et al. (1995) introduced a damage classification and mapping methodology on a graphic basis and tabular calculation for the actual damage assessment of stone buildings. The exactly defined visual appearance of stone damages were collected and logically classified by Vergès-Belmin el al. (2008). In BIM-SIS, this classification is converted and transferred into an ontology knowledge base. Using this database and the geometric representation of the building and stone geometry, the user can map their analysis of the damage phenomena into the BIM-model and thus creating a semantically enriched damage-, and ultimately renovation-, multi-model.

Fig. 1. Damage phenomena of deposits

2 The BIM-SIS Project

The Building Information Modeling - Damage Identification System (BIM-SIS) is a three year lasting German research project. Four German project partners aim to develop a new type of integrative damage identification system for stone materials with a focus on natural stone. BIM-SIS targets to change the process of building renovation with innovative methods. Combining three areas – intelligent information management, knowledge-based methods as well as technically separated and semantically linked data models – an innovative semi-automatic damage identification system is created. The cost of determining damages increases with the degree of accuracy of the damage identification method while the uncertainty of the remediation concept and the remediation costs increase disproportionately with the blurring of the damage identification. Accordingly, the aim is to determine the damage as accurately as possible at a reasonable financial cost before concluding the contract. To this end, a system is created that enables an assessment of the potential range of damage based on the extensive knowledge about damages resulting from completed remediation cases. The imprecision of the extent of damages is quantified by a simple risk management using confidence intervals, i.e. for the extent of damage, a maximum and a minimum damage system is created based on the input data from which recovery and renovation concepts are determined and offers are designed. These are created with a high grade of automation in order to keep the subsequent costs within a limited acceptable framework. The integrative information system is created as an interoperable knowledge-based platform based on BIM that can easily be extended to cover any sort of damage- or renovation-scenario of buildings. For this end the project employs the highly flexible multi-model-method, which is based on data structures standardized in (ISO-21597). Within the framework of the BIM-SIS project a software platform for damage identification and mapping procedures that are particular suitable for stone is developed (see Fig. 2). The developed platform is intended to ensure that the information of any new measurement and damage identification methods can be integrated into the BIM system. Accordingly, the platform of the BIM damage identification system is designed for data and information management tasks, such as complex model views, model mapping and model variation formation (e.g. for sensibility and variant investigations), which are universally applicable and support the BIMification process and building process for a BIM model, as defined by Scherer et al. (2017). A strong focus is given to the structuring of the multidimensional information into explicitly and dynamically linked technical and factual models using the multi-model method (Scherer and Fuchs 2017) based on OWL ontologies as well as model filtering (views), model images (mappings) and model validation in order to clearly separate facts from observations, damage assessment decisions and remediation consequences, thus improving interaction and flexibility in the information process chain and cooperative work. In particular it is intended to enable better feedback in the process chain and to update the individual models when new information is gained. Using interoperable information flows and knowledge-based support, remediation concept models, cost models and supplementary models can then be derived from this damage outcome model, which can be flexibly adapted to the current and dynamically changing context. Technical solutions in the realm of virtual and augmented reality are important in order to penetrate the complex information space consisting of data for damage, the deconstruction, the restoration and the new construction. This ensures high accuracy and transparency for the costs between contractor and client and enables to users to recognize dependencies.

3 BIMification

A large portion of the data created during the inspection and assessment of stone facades and their damage are record in formats that are not machine readable and therefore cannot be automatically processed or digitally managed. Consequently, this increases the risk of data loss and incorrect information due to human misinterpretation. Therefore a multi-model based approach has been developed in which stone facades of existing building are digitized as IFC-model by using proxy entities, which are then linked with web ontologies for semantic enrichment. By utilizing additional rules and inference mechanisms, the anomalies can be classified, and a knowledge-based damage assessment can be processed. In order to ensure the safe continuation of a stone facade that consists of damaged stones, its structure must be evaluated considering any occurred damage. For a computer-based damage evaluation, machine-readable data about the affected construction and their inspected damages are mandatory. Therefore, (Scherer and Katranuschkov 2018) propose a process called BIMification, where a BIM-model of an existing building is created based on the standardized BIM specification Industry Foundation Classes (IFC) (ISO-16739). This new method ensures a continuous, structured and interoperable flow of information, starting from variety of heterogeneous sources of information on the phases anamnesis and diagnosis and subsequent BIM phase of therapy (see Fig. 3). The BIMification approach, ensures an objective separation into three phases, which are based on each other, in such a way that information is not lost, erroneously classified or interpreted as a result of premature decisions. The BIMification approach, directly results in the individual specialist models, which can be managed separately and thus contribute to a clear structuring of the information. At the moment the research efforts

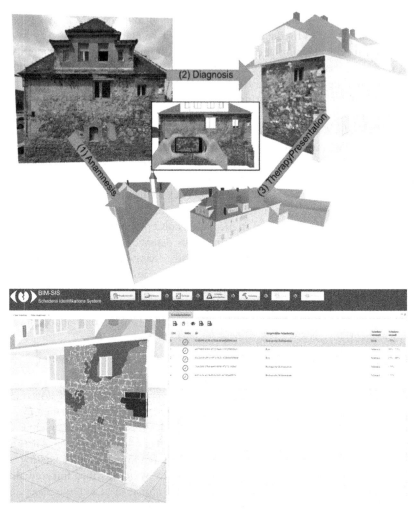

Fig. 2. Screenshot of the BIM-SIS platform showing the process (top), the 3D model of the building and the facade in question (left) and the associated damage types of its stones (right)

in the BIM-SIS project have developed a concept that covers the Anamnesis for natural stone components, which is the first major stage of the BIMification and dedicated to the survey and collection of facts about the building. The Anamnesis stage includes several subtasks, which are processed through the creation of various data models. The geometrical BIMification involves the production of a pure geometric model and therefore is realized in this approach through creating an IFC model for the building components and their aggregated parts, respectively stones and joints. For detailed, local system identification, it is also important to know the current damage per single brick or joint element, as well as a type-specific damage system, so that a type- and stone-specific system identification can be performed. This requires special methods of computer science, since the observed facts must first be brought together and consolidated into a context, then divided into stone elements and interpreted, in order to then be reorganized and reconsolidated into a consistent overall damage system. Here, much information is blurred and requires variation considerations and readjustments. Due to this the Multimodel, which has a strong informational structure, has a particularly important role to play.

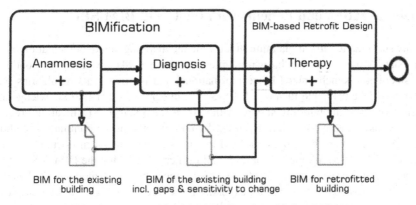

Fig. 3. 3-stage method for BIM-based retrofitting design.

4   Multi-model-Method

The multi-model method, which was developed from 2009 to 2012 in the BMBF's flagship project Mefisto of TUD for use in construction operations, i.e. Production planning, which was evolved and standardized in DIN-SPEC 91350 for bidding and award and is currently in very generic form in ISO standardization (ISO-21597). This method is adapted in the BIM-SIS project towards damage identification and remediation processes. This allows the diverse information to be modeled explicitly and separately in functionally structured, separate models. These domain models are then connected with each other through link-models, which link individual sets of model-elements with each other. The multi-model is structured in such a way that it optimally supports the BIMification process without losing information dependencies between the subject models. Furthermore, the link information can be addressed directly and dynamically, by a supporting ontological framework. This is particularly important in case of a damage update. The link information is contained in separate link models, so that the subject models do not need to be changed or supplemented and thus remain readable for the application programs with which they were created. Furthermore, the links between the many subject models can be managed separately and dynamically, i. e. are created, modified, deleted and evaluated separately. This allows damage assessments to be dynamically improved, modified and cost models to be propagated semi-automatically. Supplemented by context-specific filters, generated from a filter toolbox, and managed by a multi-model generation and management system, information can be filtered out of the complex information space, updated, modified and semi-automatically propagated and merged into the renovation concept and the cost model. This in turn results in higher interoperability as well as a high, technically significant structuring of the information. In particular, the technical models and parts (views) can be superimposed and negative models (demolition models) can also be created and managed. All multi-model methods and tools are further developed according to the project requirements.

5   Digitalization and Benefits with the Use of BIM-SIS

For any sustainable retrofit planning of a façade the mapping and documentation of the actual state is one of the most basic principles (Assmann 2014). Inventory and condition assessments are synchronized by several national and internationals regulations (e.g. EN 16096). The principle idea of BIM-SIS is to integrate the existing knowledge and information from the building survey, with help of the 3 staged BIMification process, explicitly and objectively in a modern BIM environment using a continuous methodology. As a result of the process, a BIM-model is created for each documented and analyzed part of the building as a basis for all further steps within the BIM-SIS system. In order to achieve realistic and practicable results the aimed BIM-model has to be modeled as precise as possible. To reduce expenditures for the maintenance of building stock in future the entire digital treatment for all the buildings is essential. It has to be taken into account that for modern buildings, where architectural imagination and application already starts digital, the planning and construction period is based digital anyway, the challenges are to transmit the existent data pool into the operating and maintenance phase of the building. For the older building inventory including the cultural heritage stock the situation to date is different. All digital information to feed the model have to be recreated, in wide parts previously determined by measuring and then gathered to build them up into a digital model. These processes have already started - but just on a single project basis covering discrete buildings. However, future developments have to overcome the lack in data knowledge on every building. BIM-SIS facilitates the steps beyond. The stone damage, recorded with any digital tool is referred to the model and processed and leads semi-automatically to an integrative procedure of damage identification and planning of retrofit actions. The principal goal of BIM-SIS is to create automatically a damage analysis with variable renovation variants presented in 5D (3D model + construction costs + time) as cost-effectively and precisely as possible, thus ensuring cost security in the preliminary calculation and tender. The renovation process is initially specialized in natural stone walls, but can easily be adapted to other expert areas. Beside the need of the BIM building model for the retrofit planning it is a highly valuable tool for every works of maintenance and facility management. The BIM model provides a permanently updated database of the real building, with which almost all kind of repair work can be significantly supported and improved. The advantages of BIM-SIS are also in damage assessment using digital methods, in the identification and analysis of damage patterns, in the possibility of easily deriving alternative, maximum and minimum damage, remediation and cost scenarios and in decision support in the remedial concept. In addition, the created BIM model can be used as a communication platform for further measures.

6   Conclusion

With regards to the future development and improvement of building digitalization BIM-SIS has provided the basis for processing retrofit cases in a continuous approach from the obtainment of fundamental information to retrofit variants including cost and time considerations. The focus of the project is on objects of natural stone but it can be easily adapted to different materials and damage-systems as long as the knowledge about the material specific damages is well-classified. Currently, BIM-SIS has been tested on natural stone facades of two different buildings. To this purpose precise and linked BIM-models based on the elements *IfcWall* and *IfcBuildingElementProxy* had to be created. This process is mandatory for any further steps in BIM-SIS and is still an obstacle to overcome in order to digitize the building stock and its related tasks. However, future developments have to address this lack of existing digital information on every building.

Acknowledgement. The project BIM-SIS is funded by the German Federal Ministry of Education and Research (BMBF) KMU-innovativ 01 | S18017.

References

Vergès-Belmin, V., el al.: Illustrated glossary on stone deterioration patterns. In: ICOMOS-ISCS (2008). English-French version 78 p. ISBN 978-2-918068-00-0

Fitzner, B., Heinrichs, K., Kownatzki, R.: Verwitterungsformen – Klassifizierung und Kartierung. In: Snethlage, R. (ed.) Denkmalpflege und Naturwissenschaft, pp. 41–87. Verbundforschungsprojekt Gesteinszerfall und Gesteinskonservierung, Natursteinkonservie-rung I (1995)

Fuchs, S., Scherer, R.J.: Multimodels-instant nD-modeling using original data. Autom. Constr. **75**, 22–32 (2017). https://doi.org/10.1016/j.autcon.2016.11.013

Hamdan, A., Bonduel, M., Scherer, R.J.: An ontological model for the representation of damage to constructions. In: 7th Linked Data in Architecture and Construction Workshop (2019)

Scherer, R.J., Katranuschkov, P.: BIMification: how to create and use BIM for retrofitting. Adv. Eng. Inform. **38**, 54–66 (2018)

Seeaed, M.K., Hamdan, A.: BIMification of stone walls for maintenance management by utilizing Linked Data, 31. Forum Bauinformatik, Berlin (2019)

Aßmann, M.: Bauwerkskartierung als Grundlage für eine Ausführungsplanung am Bestandsobjekt; Fachvortrag zum DENAK – Natursteinforum 2014, Kaisersesch (2014)

Cacciotti, R., Blaško, M., Valach, J.: A diagnostic ontological model for damages to historical constructions. J. Cult. Herit. **16**, 40–48 (2015)

EN 16096: Conservation of cultural property - Condition survey and report of built cultural heritage (2012)

ISO 16739-1:2018: Industry Foundation Classes (IFC) for data sharing in the construction and facility management industries—Part 1: Data schema, ICS 25.040.40, 1474 p.

DIN SPEC 91350:2016-11: Linked BIM data exchange comprising building information model and specified bill of quantities. Beuth Verlag. https://doi.org/10.31030/2581152

ISO 21597-1:2020: Information container for linked document delivery—Exchange specification—Part 1: Container, ICS 35.240.67, 41 p.

Project Papers: Preservation and Use and Re-use

Project Papers: e-Libraries and e-Archives in Cultural Heritage

PAGODE – Europeana China

Valentina Bachi[1]([✉]), Antonella Fresa[2], and Maja Veselič[3]

[1] Photoconsortium, Via della Bonifica 69, 56037 Peccioli, PI, Italy
valentina.bachi@photoconsortium.net
[2] Promoter Srl, Via della Bonifica 69, 56037 Peccioli, PI, Italy
fresa@promoter.it
[3] University of Ljubljana, Aškerčeva cesta 2, 1000 Ljubljana, Slovenia
maja.veselic@ff.uni-lj.si

Abstract. PAGODE is a new project started on the 1st of April 2020, which proposes a thematic approach for aggregation, curation and presentation of Chinese cultural content hosted in European museums and Cultural Heritage Institutions (CHIs). The project aims to offer an innovative experience by making this content available in Europeana, the European digital library. PAGODE will aggregate to Europeana more than 10,000 newly digitised objects, annotate more than 2,000 digital objects that are already in Europeana, enrich automatically the metadata of more than 20,000 records, and activate a wide range of CHIs to plan new digitization and curation of relevant content from their collections. Focusing on the various forms of the presence of Chinese culture in Europe, the overall objective of PAGODE is to add further value to CHIs that own Chinese collections, to reach new end users, and to encourage creative use and reuse of cultural content in the domains of multicultural integration, cultural tourism, education and research.

Keywords: Chinese cultural heritage · Digitized photography · Metadata · Linked thesauri · Europeana

1 Introduction

In the frame of the effort to leverage digital Cultural Heritage (CH) in answering the new challenges posed by the globalization of cultures and the creation of new cultural connections, a new project was recently awarded by the European Union named PAGODE Europeana China. The project focuses on highlighting the CH held by European institutions, which represent the flows of people, objects and knowledge between Europe and China. The exchanges that took place across time, along the Silk Road and over the seas, established cultural, economic and societal relationships that are still relevant nowadays. Those relationships and their history are attested by the artefacts, photos, books, archival records and other types of cultural heritage items preserved in European museums, libraries, galleries and archives. This rich heritage can find now its route to a digital enhancement via the PAGODE project.

The main concept of PAGODE is to allow Chinese heritage preserved in Europe to be showcased in digital form, generating rich user experiences and high audience engagement, targeting researchers, students, scholars and the general public.

© Springer Nature Switzerland AG 2021
M. Ioannides et al. (Eds.): EuroMed 2020, LNCS 12642, pp. 265–277, 2021.
https://doi.org/10.1007/978-3-030-73043-7_22

The main channel used by PAGODE to give access to this heritage is Europeana, the European digital library [1].

The project is co-funded by CEF Connecting Europe Facility Programme of the European Union [2], responding to the call for Generic Services dedicated to the improvement and enrichment of Europeana. For this scope, public and private institutions that preserve content related to Chinese CH are working together to digitise photos, artefacts and books, enrich metadata and crowdsource annotations.

It is very significant that the coordinator of this project is the Italian Ministry for Economic Development. This highlights that heritage is not only a matter of culture and scholars, but it represents also a huge potential to be unlocked in the overall process of development of nations and societies, and of their economies.

PAGODE participates in the effort of lowering cultural barriers across and beyond Europe, creating unique cross-border perspectives and leveraging the benefits of digitized cultural heritage. This is achieved by connecting existing digital historical resources and by creating new digital collections, sourced both from the institutional content of archives, museums, galleries and libraries, and from personal materials collected by citizens (for example exploring family albums).

PAGODE promotes expressions of cultural diversity, engaging with a wide range of audiences, giving access to the richness of extra-European cultures, generating new multi-disciplinary knowledge, and facilitating research in the multi-faceted culture and history of Europe entering in contact with the world. In doing so, the whole Europeana concept and its surrounding environment of users and content providers is challenged to play a core and novel role.

Two main content providers are involved in the project as partners: KIK-IRPA and United Archives. KIK-IRPA is the Royal Institute for Cultural Heritage [3], based in Brussels, a Belgian federal research institute of the Belgian Federal Science Policy Office (BELSPO). The institute studies and conserves artistic and cultural assets of Belgium and is a major contributor of Europeana since its establishment. United Archives [4] is a private company based in Cologne (Germany). The company owns a large photo library that offers professional image content for editorial usage. It has a wide running digitization program and participates actively with its collections to Europeana. The two content providers are members of Photoconsortium, the international association for valuing photographic heritage, based in the area of Pisa (Italy).

Photoconsortium [5] is partner of PAGODE with the role of content coordinator. The association represents a centre of expertise and knowledge on photography, digitization, aggregation of content, metadata standards, indexing, cataloguing, controlled vocabularies, sharing best practices for management of digital archives and being acknowledged as expert hub for photography. Photoconsortium is an accredited aggregators of Europeana and, in this role, it participates in the Digital Service Infrastructure initiative of the European Commission, which supports the operations of the Europeana core service platform [6]. Through Photoconsortium, a number of associate partners from all over Europe are joining the PAGODE network to support the project and to contribute with their collections. The association was established in 2014 as a spin off of a successful digitisation project named Europeana Photography. Its members include: museums, archives, professionals and amateurs of vintage photography. In addition to aggregate content to Europeana, the main areas of research of Photoconsortium are storytelling and curation of photographic heritage. It is active in the domains of multilingualism and linked data to improve searchability and interlinking of digital CH resources. Projects like PAGODE are in the core business of Photoconsortium, to deploy and build up new expertise, and to act as a multiplier of knowledge transfer from and towards the network of its members.

Two highly active SMEs participate in the consortium with specific technical roles: Promoter S.r.l. in Italy and Postscriptum Ltd. in Greece. The former is the technical coordinator of the whole project, steering the implementation towards its general objectives. Furthermore, Promoter leads the project's communication activities and the dissemination initiatives that aim to prepare for the future sustainability and exploitation of the project's results. The latter is in charge of developing the liaison of PAGODE with Chinese CHIs, benefitting of its role of official representative of the Europeana initiative in China. The two SMEs collaborate in the EastMeetsWest initiative, whose first instance is the EastMeetsWest in Greece initiative [7], coordinated by Postscriptum, with the participation of Promoter.

The Department of Asian Studies of the University of Ljubljana [8] completes the PAGODE consortium. Its expertise enables a critical understanding of the main cultural determinants of the Chinese culture in their social and historical context, and supports the creation of a scientifically sound semantic background for the whole project.

Fig. 1. A trip to China, Carl Simon, 1920, © United Archives.

2   A New Project for Cross-Cultural Exchanges

PAGODE proposes a thematic approach for the aggregation, curation and presentation of the Chinese culture related content that is hosted in European museums and CHIs, ranging from societal topics, to fine arts, science, and applied arts.

The project will aggregate more than 10,000 newly digitised objects to Europeana, including photographic collections, digital representation of artworks and paintings, books and manuscripts. Furthermore, it will annotate and enrich the metadata associated with more than 2,000 digital objects that are already in Europeana, experimenting with new forms of crowdsourced annotations and interlinking in a dedicated pilot that involves scholars, researchers, curators and non-professionals practitioners. Finally, it will enrich automatically the metadata of more than 20,000 digital objects that are in the Europeana database, by adopting Artificial Intelligence and Natural Language Processing technologies.

PAGODE team members are already at work since April 2020, tackling the following six main objectives.

First objective: To aggregate new content of Chinese cultural heritage to Europeana and to hook up with data that are already in Europeana. New collaborations are established with content providers and Europeana aggregators, at different levels, national, thematic and domain ones. New technical information is integrated in the curation processes of the existing datasets, highlighting links between Europeana content and Chinese culture.

Second objective: To increase discoverability of Chinese content and collections in Europeana. This is achieved via an annotation methodology, based on crowdsourcing, to be validated in a real-life pilot.

Third objective: To bring more Chinese collections into Europeana, according to the requirements of the Europeana Publishing Framework [9]. In particular, new content is provided in compliance with the technical and rights conditions of the so-called 'Tier 4' specification that requires that digital objects are available in high-resolution and for free use and re-use.

Fourth objective: To reach the professionals of the CH sector with a rich program of dissemination, awareness raising and capacity building activities, including organization of workshops, participation in professional events, and the organisation of an international conference in Brussels planned for the end of September 2021.

Fifth objective: To promote user engagement in multiple forms, on the social media, through crowdsourcing and with exhibitions. This aims to facilitate cultural exchanges among European and Chinese CHIs, encouraging professionals and non-professionals to become users of Europeana, for education, research, social integration and cultural tourism purposes. In particular, a virtual exhibition will be published in Europeana in September 2021, and a series of online events organized across Spring-Summer 2021 in collaboration with the Museo della Grafica [10] will engage with culture lovers and general audience.

Sixth objective: To open cultural connections to China. Encounters and debates will discuss how a richer reciprocal knowledge of our cultures can support profitable economic exchanges. Sino-European dialogue is necessary to support the development of a harmonious Sino-European political and economic relationship and needs to be fostered through mutual understanding of cultural notions [11].

Focusing on the various forms of the presence of Chinese culture in Europe, PAGODE is adding further value to CHIs that own Chinese collections. PAGODE promotes further understanding of the cultural values of China and the cultural exchange between China and Europe. This allows CHIs to connect and share their collections and metadata across new sectors and borders and, in this way, to increase awareness and usage of Europeana to a wider audience, internationally.

The project's originality lies in the creation of a framework for a holistic overview of all Chinese collections within the scope of the pan-European area. As such, it offers the foundations for further scholarship in this field. Even more important, PAGODE is developing instruments for the reinterpretation of questions about circulation, trade, collection and display of Chinese art in modern Europe. Offering novel interpretations of Europe-China relationship from the historical and contemporary perspectives, the results of the project can accompany the reality of the present economic exchanges.

The project naturally wants to engage with Chinese CHIs and will do this by exploiting the power of the digital technologies. Discussions are ongoing, among professionals in the field, both in Europe and in China, about how digital technologies, high quality digitization and 3D visualization can help in allowing Chinese artefacts preserved in Europe to come back to China, "virtually", for all Chinese people to enjoy such gems. There is a strong interest from Chinese and European institutions to find new ways of collaboration in this domain. Europeana can play a fundamental role in this process, offering a platform made of millions of CH digital objects accompanied by rich and constantly growing thematic collections. 'Europeana China' is the title of a new thematic collection foreseen to be published in Europeana in 2021, where the visitors will find virtual exhibitions, stories, curated digital galleries and much more. Digital galleries have already started to become available online, namely: 'Mandarins of China' [12] and 'Rice cultivation in China' [13].

The potential of digitization is also considered as a solution for challenges that CHIs experience and that are particularly relevant for China. In such a large country, with communities in hard-to-reach regions, where inhabitants often have no possibility to journey to big cities to visit museums and cultural sites, access to CH is a major issue. Moreover, remote areas often lack reliable internet access. As citizens cannot travel to meet CH, it is possible that CH travels to meet citizens, with the support of digital technologies! An interesting example of this approach dates back to 2013, when the "Mobile Digital Museum" project was launched by the Inner Mongolia Museum [14]. The Mobile Digital Museum started as a response to three main challenges: the inaccessibility of physical museums; the lack of the connection between visitors and artefacts; and, the safety of physical relics when travelling outside the museums. Most of the biggest museums are located in the centre of the big cities, and visiting them becomes both a time-consuming and an expensive activity, even for people living in the outskirts, let alone those who live in the countryside. This situation conflicts with the museums' mission of transferring knowledge, empowering all people and inspiring citizens to embrace and respect country's diverse heritage. Furthermore, museums serve also as knowledge and creativity centres, but, although museums engage with the use of verbal and visual aids (e.g. brochures and audio guides), visitors are often left with unanswered queries or pass through exhibitions without being truly engaged. Due to the fact that every visitor is peculiar in their interest and preferences, it is difficult to develop a comprehensive offer able to provide all the information, histories and stories, or other content that each visitor would like to get. The Mobile Digital Museum is conceived as a futuristic truck, equipped with the most advanced digital technologies, with a custom made exterior and interior to cater to various digital requirements. It measures 13 m in length and 2.5 m in width, but by the push of a button it can extend to 5.3 m in width, thus creating a space of 45 m^2. A central computerized system is designed to control all the advanced interactive screens and contents of the museum. CH items are displayed on screen and accompanied with compelling interactive features such as interactive games, quizzes to increase knowledge, surveys and in-depth information. Additionally, interactive platforms allow visitors to manipulate the digital artefact freely, viewing it from all angles, zooming in to discover details, exploring how it functions, and even "holding" the 3D printing of valuable artefacts in their hands, which would never be possible with the actual physical relics. By traveling to remote areas, addressing schools and underprivileged communities, the Mobile Digital Museum approached visitors in an innovative way. This is just one example of how high-quality digitization and 3D visualization can help engagement with CH and access without borders.

3   Past and Future of a Collection

One typical story of a Chinese collection preserved in Europe is that of the Slovene Ethnographic Museum, one of the PAGODE associate partners. The Museum houses the largest number of Chinese objects in Slovenia. Among these, the Skušek collection is the most notable for its size, variety and prestige. It contains around 500 objects ranging from paintings, figurines, ceramics and porcelain, lacquered objects, textiles, musical instruments, coins, fans, snuff bottles, to larger items such as furniture and architectural models, to photographs, books and postcards.

Ivan Skušek jr. (1877–1947), an Austro-Hungarian navy officer, obtained these objects during his nearly 6-year stay in Beijing between 1914 and 1920. He arrived in China onboard of the cruiser SMS Kaiserin Elisabeth at the start of the World War I. The ship was sent to help defend the German concession in Qingdao, but they were overpowered by the Japanese and the British navies. While most crew members were transported as prisoners of war to Japan, some were put in confinement in China. As the chief supply officer, Skušek, who was sent to Beijing, was nevertheless able to freely move around the city, slowly developing appreciation for the culture and people of China, and making contacts that allowed him to purchase, store and eventually transport the 75 crates of objects back to Ljubljana. During his sojourn he also met his future wife Tsuneko Kondō Kawase (Marija Skušek) (1893–1963), who likely helped shape the collection. Upon his return, Ivan Skušek planned to open a museum in the style of traditional Chinese architecture, where he and his wife could educate their compatriots about the cultural and technological achievements of China, dispelling the negative stereotypes widely circulating in the press at the time. While this project never materialized due to financial constraints, the Skušek's apartment became the center of cultural and social life of the Ljubljana's intellectual and art elites [15]. Within the PAGODE project, the Museum is digitizing several visually attractive items from Skušek collection that portray the early 20th century Beijing: a souvenir photo album with 450 images of the city and its surroundings and two lavishly illustrated studies of the imperial architecture and decorations of the palaces published by the famous Japanese photographer Ogawa Kazumasa in 1906 [16].

The case of the collection of Ivan Skušek is just an example of the impact of the PAGODE project, which offers the opportunity to content holders to enable valuable collections to be discovered and showcased to a general European public. These are highly relevant collections with equal appeal to the most famous holdings of big museums, preserved in institutions that have specialist knowledge and skills, but are less visible in the panorama of European museums. Digitization and online access are the key to expanding the outreach and thus to empower the statutory mission of sharing knowledge.

Other interesting cases are those of the valuable collections of ancient books, maps and music sheets held by Leiden University Libraries [17], and the interesting photos of Missionaries in China in the Manneheim's collections held by the PhotoArchive of the Finnish Heritage Agency [18]. Furthermore, even if more accessible to visitors, the digitization of the Chinese collections of the National Museum of World Cultures in the Netherlands [19] and of the Benaki Museum in Greece [20], and their access via Europeana, is making possible to have on display precious artefacts and documents that otherwise would have still to find their place in a digital showcase, allowing more people to engage with these collections.

In addition to the above mentioned content holders, the group of associate partners to PAGODE project includes the experts of the Digital Humanities Lab at the University of Basel, and a number of associate cultural institutions in China. Contributing their expertise in the digital transformation in the CH field, heritage and the many stories it tells are becoming more accessible to people.

4 Embarking on a Journey

The launch of PAGODE was originally intended as a double event in Rome, hosted by the coordinator at the prestigious venue of the Italian Ministry of Economic Development in via Molise. The plan was to first hold an operative meeting reserved for project partners, which was to be followed by an open event for associate partners and other stakeholders, with invited guests from Europe and China. Due to the unprecedented circumstances of the COVID-19 pandemic, the consortium was forced to change the plans. Both meetings were preserved, but eventually took place online. Already during the initial discussions, the question of "what is Chinese Heritage in Europe" became predominant. The sinologists and experts from the University of Ljubljana began defining themes and keywords that depict the concept of "Chinese cultural heritage". To devise a suitable semantic background, the project started defining what can be considered as Chinese CH in Europe, distinguishing between "Chinese" versus "made in China" and analysing the (dis)connection between materiality and cultural connotations. Another aspect considered were the various (ex)changes related to cross-cultural contact. Travel and migration are of particular importance as Europeans in China and Chinese in Europe have contributed significantly to mutual cultural influences between the two regions. The discussion then extended to the types of objects that represent Chinese CH - tangible, intangible, natural (especially landscapes) - and which are the examples of these types of heritage that can be found in PAGODE's partners archives. The final and crucial step has been the definition of metadata specification on which rests the correct representation of the digitized objects in online environments, especially in Europeana. Correct metadata are necessary to grant the best user experience in the search and retrieval of content, and to meet various search purposes. The project originally foresaw a dedicated workshop to be held in Ljubljana in July 2020, with the aim of finalizing the methodology and the metadata specifications for the curation of PAGODE digital content in Europeana. Due to travel restrictions, the meeting had to be reorganized in virtual format, which nevertheless did not prevent from reaching interesting outcomes.

The metadata requirements and guidelines for curation need to be integrated in the process of digitization and indexing that happens in the rooms of cultural institutions. The task of digitization is guided by KIK-IRPA in collaboration with the Digital Humanities Lab of the University of Basel, true experts about all the secrets of high-quality CH digitization. All this expertise is complemented by a Content Quality Plan, developed in the frame of the project. The Plan establishes the process for the review, improvement and enrichment of the content to be delivered to Europeana. The coordination of the entire work on content selection, digitization and delivery to Europeana is managed by Photoconsortium that makes use of the MINT mapping tool [21] developed by the Digital Cultural Heritage group at the National Technical University of Athens, to perform the conversion from content providers' data structure to the Europeana Data Model [22].

A robust program of communication, dissemination and visibility is undertaken under the coordination of partner Promoter s.r.l. Besides an appealing project website [23], a sound planning for outreach has been developed, even if limited in scope because of the pandemic. A dense editorial calendar of blogs, galleries and social media actions have been set to engage with users. The work to develop the PAGODE exhibition has been initiated. PAGODE was presented at the Europeana Aggregators Forum on 6–7 May 2020. The forum is a gathering event, where, twice a year, the community of Europeana's most trusted partners meet to review strategies and collaborations, and make plans for the future. All the aggregators work with CHIs to gather authentic, trustworthy and robust cultural data and make them accessible through Europeana. Through the Europeana Aggregators Forum, partners exchange the knowledge and best practices that support the digital transformation of CHIs. In the most recent gathering, PAGODE was enthusiastically presented by Photoconsortium to colleagues, with a video and a short pitch. The invitation to participate in the project was extended to other aggregators and CHIs, with the intention to use PAGODE as a seed for a new community around Chinese CH in Europe. The project is promoted also by the European Commission on its channels, on twitter, LinkedIn and in the newsroom of the Innovation and Networks Executive Agency INEA [24].

Fig. 2. Lion of Fo, or Lion of Buddha, c. 1800 © KIK-IRPA, Brussels, Belgium

5 Chinese Cultural Heritage Content in PAGODE

Photographic heritage is just one kind of Chinese CH in Europe, but it represents an important share of the content digitized in the PAGODE project. The past photographs of China provide a wealth of information about a civilization that has undergone so profound change over the last century. Yet, in addition to the knowledge embedded in the images, waiting to be discovered through their analysis and study, photography is also an important element for storytelling. This is, for example, the case of the photographic collection by Carl Simon (1873–1952), which was acquired by United Archives in March 2012 [25]. The Carl Simon Archive was a sleeping treasure of photos for 60 years. In 2011 the sensational life work of this visionary man was finally rediscovered in an old storage room in Unterbilk, in the city of Düsseldorf, Germany – a treasure trove of approximately 23,000 wonderful glass slides (9.5 × 8.5 cm and 8.5 × 8.5 cm), for the most part hand-coloured and well-assorted in 200 wood boxes. There were also 2 original projectors, accessories, 15 lenses as well as countless scripts for slide lectures. Carl Simon first worked as procurator at the German photo company Liesegang in Düsseldorf. He founded his own company Lichtbild-Anstalt Carl Simon & Co. in 1907, which offered services for the upcoming photo industry. He constructed cameras, rented slide projectors, and began to collect wonderful hand-coloured glass slides. The most important part of his activities were live slide performances. Carl Simon had the ambition to show the big world to many people and to that end he gave about 300 slide performances to amazed spectators all over Germany. During these events, whilst showing the photos, an actor read a special text for each image and, last but not least, a small orchestra was playing background music. Until 1945 Carl Simon collected 80,000 images. Over the years, more than 23,000 survived. After his death Karl-Heinz Simon (1920–2002), his son, carried on with the tradition of slide shows performances up to the 1960s. The end came with the introduction of television. There are several beautiful photographic trips within this marvellous collection, that showed far and strange countries to people who never had the opportunity to visit them, for example of Rome, life in East Africa, Asia, a journey through France, earthquakes and volcanic activity, Japan, Tibet, the sinking of the Titanic and many more "highlights" of glass slide photography. China has a great role in the collection. Part of the Carl Simon Archive is already available in Europeana, under the umbrella of Photoconsortium aggregated content [26]. Thanks to PAGODE, United Archives will offer more content from this wonderful collection. Furthermore, another more recent relevant photography collections of United Archives will be made available in PAGODE, with images taken during the Cultural Revolution.

Many representations of Chinese and China-related artefacts in various collections held by museums and libraries in Europe are also part of the PAGODE content, in addition to photographs. These collections include decorative objects, clothes and accessories, porcelain, furniture, Chinoiserie, paintings, musical instruments, books, engravings and much more. All these different kinds of objects have their own peculiar requirements for digitization. A common simple way is to take a picture - or more pictures - of the object from different angles, and just show the images. Technologies and standards, such as the International Image Interoperability Framework IIIF [27], help a deeper interaction with the image allowing for zooming and navigating the various part of the pictures in high detail. 3D digitization is a more complicated solution, especially for porcelain due to light reflections in the object's surface, even though this technique provides a much better user experience user experience than a set of plain photographs. This, however, opens a question on technology and accessibility as not all institutions, particularly not the smaller ones, have access to or resources for 3D production facilities. Currently, several initiatives [28] are making technological efforts to develop tools and solutions for 3D content. Also, Europeana established a dedicated task force [29] for increasing the support for 3D cultural heritage and the availability of 3D content for education, research and by the creative industries. The expertise of KIK-IRPA on digitization and 3D representation of CH is vast and in PAGODE is applied to the digitization of Chinese artefacts from European museums.

Chinese books are another hard nut to crack, because of the challenges connected with the digitisation of texts in Chinese language: although Optical Character Recognition technologies are mature enough nowadays, their application to Chinese book requires to recognise the characters in both traditional and simplified form, and with orientations that differ from the one used for Latin languages - especially, but not only, older books are written vertically and from right to left. This means that offering a meaningful digital experience with an old Chinese book requires much more than just scanning the pages and putting them online one after the other [30, 31].

Finally, the world of music heritage: China has a long and influential musical tradition based on the philosophy and culture of ancient China. Confucians embraced a correct use and form of music that was to match social and cosmological conceptions, so to discover traditional Chinese music helps understanding Chinese culture. There are still a number of barriers to online access for audio and audio-related materials, including the need of appealing content display to support user-friendly search and engagement, which is a difficult task also in the physical museums: but this will be the subject for future projects.

6 Conclusions

PAGODE is just the beginning of a long journey. Partners and associate partners are currently digitizing interesting and varied collections of CH items that including artefacts, photos, books, and much more. These digital collections aim to represent a meaningful selection of the Chinese heritage preserved in Europe and Europeana is a fundamental channel to reach a plethora of audiences who can access, use and re-use these collections. Contacts established with Chinese CHIs indicate a very strong potential for future collaborations: Chinese institutions show a strong interest in the project and in Europeana, and this is creating a basis for renewed collaborations and connections.

The project is expected to deliver its major outcomes in 2021. These include a bulk of new records published in Europeana in the form of open access CH materials, compelling stories and narratives to enable users' engagement. A virtual exhibition will be published in Europeana in September 2021 to target general public, and a final conference will be organized to target professionals from CHIs and disseminate the project's knowledge.

The hope and aim is that PAGODE becomes a seed for the establishment of a network of common interest for CHIs that have a stake in Chinese CH. This will allow the legacy of PAGODE to not only be kept alive, but also to continue to grow, beyond the end of the project's EU funding period, promoting more actions to enable collaborations among European and with Chinese institutions.

References

1. Europeana Homepage. https://www.europeana.eu/en. Accessed 08 Jun 2020
2. CEF Connecting Europe Facility Programme Website. https://ec.europa.eu/inea/en/connecting-europe-facility. Accessed 29 Oct 2020
3. KIK-IRPA, for Koninklijk Instituut voor het Kunstpatrimonium - Institut Royal du Patrimoine Artistique, is a federal scientific institute responsible for the documentation, study and conservation-restoration of the cultural and artistic heritage of Belgium. https://www.kikirpa.be/EN/. Accessed 08 Jun 2020
4. United Archives Homepage. https://united-archives.de/. Accessed 08 Jun 2020
5. Photoconsortium Homepage. https://www.photoconsortium.net/. Accessed 08 Jun 2020
6. Europeana Digital Service Infrastructure initiative. https://pro.europeana.eu/page/europeana-a-digital-service-infrastructure. Accessed 29 Oct 2020
7. EastMeetsWest in Greece is a new initiative to link the countries of Asia with Europe in Greece under a digital cultural heritage umbrella. https://emwg.site/. Accessed 08 Jun 2020
8. Department of Asian Studies at University of Ljubljana. https://as.ff.uni-lj.si/english/english. Accessed 28 Oct 2020
9. The Europeana Publishing Framework. https://pro.europeana.eu/post/publishing-framework. Accessed 28 Oct 2020
10. Museo della Grafica is a joint venture of the University of Pisa, the Municipality of Pisa and the Tuscany Region. https://museodellagrafica.sma.unipi.it/. Accessed 29 Oct 2020

11. EU-China: Silk Road Cultural Dialogues, Networking Session, ICT2018, 5th of December Austria Centre Vienna
12. Mandarins of China digital gallery on Europeana. https://www.europeana.eu/it/galleries/mandarins-of-china. Accessed 29 Oct 2020
13. 'Rice cultivation in China' digital gallery on Europeana. https://www.europeana.eu/it/galleries/rice-cultivation-in-china. Accessed 28 Oct 2020
14. Mobile Digital Museum post on DigitalMeetsCulture magazine, https://www.digitalmeetsculture.net/article/mobile-digital-museum-the-frontier-for-cultural-heritage-exhibitions/, last accessed 2020/06/08.
15. Vampelj Suhadolnik, N.: Collecting Chinese objects in Slovenia at the turn of the twentieth century. Ming Qing Yanjiu **24**(2), 161–180 (2020). https://doi.org/10.1163/24684791-12340047
16. About VAZ - Vzhodnoazijske zbirke v Sloveniji/East Asian Collections in Slovenia. https://vazcollections.si/predmeti/album-the-imperial-city-of-peking-china/; https://vazcollections.si/predmeti/album-the-decoration-of-the-palace-buildings-in-peking/. Accessed 28 Oct 2020
17. Chinese Special Collections of Leiden University Libraries. https://www.library.universiteitleiden.nl/subject-guides/chinese-special-collections. Accessed 28 Oct 2020
18. Manneheim's China photos are preserved in the Ethnographic Picture Collection of Finnish Heritage Agency. https://www.museovirasto.fi/en/collection-and-information-services/the_picture_collections/collections/ethnographic-collection. Accessed 28 Oct 2020
19. Museum Volkenkunde's website. https://www.volkenkunde.nl/en; its permanent exhibition about China: https://www.volkenkunde.nl/en/whats-on-0/exhibitions/china; the digital China collection: https://collectie.wereldculturen.nl/Default.aspx?collectionid=42328#/query/440fba9c-c006-4e38-ba0c-24113400dcd5. Accessed 28 Oct 2020
20. Benaki Museum's Chinese and Korean Collection of porcelain: https://www.benaki.org/index.php?option=com_collections&view=collection&id=41&Itemid=540&lang=en. Accessed 28 Oct 2020
21. MINT is the tool that provides users the ability to perform a mapping of their own metadata schemas to reference domain models. The tool is used by several aggregators of Europeana to map the content providers metadata schema to the model of Europeana. The tool is published as open source. https://mint.image.ece.ntua.gr/redmine/projects/mint/wiki/Mapping_Tool. Accessed 08 Jun 2020
22. Europeana Data Model EDM is the model used by the Europeana Core Service Pltaform to as the basis for the implementation of the aggregation process. https://pro.europeana.eu/page/edm-documentation. Accessed 08 Jun 2020
23. PAGODE Homepage. https://photoconsortium.net/pagode/. Accessed 08 Jun 2020
24. The Innovation and Networks Executive Agency INEA of the European Commission is appointed to run the monitoring and assessment of the progresses of the PAGODE project. The newsroom of INEA promoting the PAGODE project. https://ec.europa.eu/inea/en/news-events/newsroom/pagode-project-brings-chinese-heritage-europe-europeana. Accessed 08 Jun 2008
25. TV report about the discovery of Carl Simon's archive. https://www1.wdr.de/mediathek/video/sendungen/lokalzeit-duesseldorf/video-dia-schatz-hinter-der-tuer-100.html. Accessed 28 Oct 2020
26. Blog about Carl Simon photographs in Europeana. https://www.photoconsortium.net/discovering-carl-simon-a-storyteller-who-used-photography-to-engage-people/. Accessed 28 Oct 2020
27. The International Image Interoperability Framework™ is driven by a community of research, national and state libraries, museums, companies and image repositories committed to providing access to high quality image resources. https://iiif.io/. Accessed 08 Jun 2020. Europeana is implementing the support to the IIIF standard.

28. Initiatives on the use of 3D technology to represent CH include several research projects (relevant references are: 3D-ICONS about digitisation of architectural and archaeological heritage, VI-MM about virtual multimodal museums; INCEPTION.eu time-dynamic 3D reconstruction of artefacts, built and social environments) and Generic Services supporting Europeana (such as the new Share3D project).

29. The Europeana task force on 3D. https://pro.europeana.eu/project/3d-content-in-europeana. Accessed 28 Oct 2020

30. Sturgeon, D.: Large-scale optical character recognition of pre-modern Chinese texts. Int. J. Buddhist Thought Cult. **2**(2), 11–44 (2018). https://dsturgeon.net/papers/large-scale-chinese-ocr.pdf

31. Sturgeon, D.: Digitizing Premodern text with the Chinese text project. J. Chin. Hist. **4**(2), 486–498. https://doi.org/10.1017/jch.2020.19

On the Digital Road: A Case of Stecci

Meliha Handzic[✉]

International Burch University, Sarajevo, Bosnia and Herzegovina
meliha.handzic@ibu.edu.ba

Abstract. This paper explores the work done so far on creating and using digital data regarding stecci – UNESCO-listed world heritage from medieval Bosnia. Firstly, the paper reveals a slow, but steady progress towards creating a wholistic digital catalogue of all existing stecci necropolises and tombstones. Secondly, it discovers an encouraging trend of innovative research methods for analysing these digital data, as well as for production of digital art inspired by these important monuments. Finally, the paper identifies the main problem that hinders faster progress towards 'digital stecci' in the costly and somewhat piecemeal approach evidenced in individual endeavours of scholars, professionals and/or artists. More coordinated effort and teamwork is recommended as a way forward.

Keywords: Digital humanities · Cultural heritage · Stecci

1 Introduction

Modern information and communication technologies have profoundly transformed the research and practice of the humanities and social sciences over the past decade. New forms of digital data, tools, and methods have enabled new ways of working across academic disciplines for scholars and professionals, as well as the wider public. Most recently, various digital humanities (DH) projects have attracted attention and gained substantial financial support from EU funding agencies such as COST [1]. These projects cover a wide range of DH topics at the intersection of computing and traditional humanities disciplines (e.g. history, archaeology, literature, linguistics etc.).

Of special interest to this study is the reach and value of 'going digital' in the context of Bosnian cultural heritage. It is suggested that digital developments may play an important role in safeguarding and promoting cultural heritage by fostering digital curation, reuse of digital data, as well as inspiring new research questions and attracting new audiences.

The main objective of current study is to examine these issues in the case of stecci – the medieval Bosnia's monumental tombstones inscribed on the UNESCO world heritage list [2]. Specifically, the study aims to trace past work done on creating and using digital data regarding stecci, assesses its success so far and recommends potential directions for the future.

© Springer Nature Switzerland AG 2021
M. Ioannides et al. (Eds.): EuroMed 2020, LNCS 12642, pp. 278–286, 2021.
https://doi.org/10.1007/978-3-030-73043-7_23

2   Digital Data Creation

So far, only a few projects have been found to be dedicated to the creation of digital repositories of stecci. One of the earliest identified projects involved experimenting with 3D models of stecci for the National Museum of Bosnia and Herzegovina by computer science students from the University of Sarajevo. Their final product represents an interactive digital catalogue of stecci that can be explored via website [3].

A completely different approach, focusing solely on metadata, was taken by two scholars who created a spreadsheet file from the available UNESCO documentation on stecci for the purpose of their later spatial, temporal and stylistic analysis [4]. Therefore, the file included only data items of authors' research interests.

Going beyond the UNESCO list, a much larger digital project was started by the 'Mak Dizdar' Foundation. The foundation managed to mobilise local teams of volunteers for the purpose of digital mapping of stecci in their municipalities. The outcome of this project is an interactive map of necropolises registered so far with related photos and basic descriptions [5].

Most recently, a very important initiative proposing a systematic approach to creating digital records of stecci was offered by the team of archaeologists from the University of Sarajevo. Their approach was successfully tested in several municipalities [6] and can serve as a reference for all other municipalities until all of the estimated 3,000+ necropolises with over 70,000 tombstones are digitally recorded, stored and preserved for future reuse. Figures 1, 2, 3 below show a series of proposed and tested templates for creating digital fieldwork records.

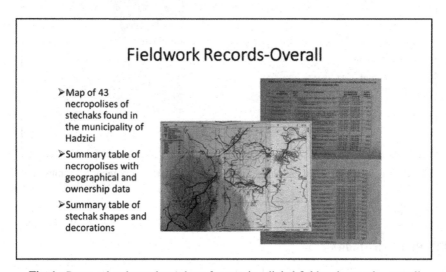

Fig. 1. Proposed and tested templates for creating digital fieldwork records - overall

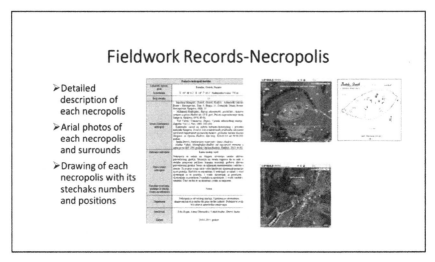

Fig. 2. Proposed and tested templates for creating digital fieldwork records - necropolis

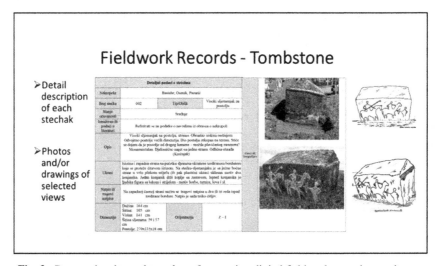

Fig. 3. Proposed and tested templates for creating digital fieldwork records - tombstone

3   Digital Data Usage

3.1   Research Studies

One of the suggestions put forward in the introductory section of this paper is that digital developments may inspire new research questions and attract new audiences. With respect to research, this author carried out a series of empirical studies using the existing limited pool of digital data about stecci. These studies were conducted mostly as part of the COST action ARKWORK [7].

Using a conceptual model of digital humanists' knowledge space [8, 9] as a theoretical basis for investigation, these studies discovered and visualised various novel spatial, temporal and relational patterns from data [4, 10–12]. Figures 4, 5, 6 below present selected results of the representative analyses of sample stecci data. More detailed information about these studies has been shared with the wider scholarly community via ResearchGate [13].

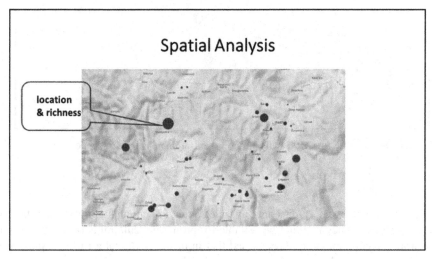

Fig. 4. Results of spatial analysis and visualisation of sample stecci

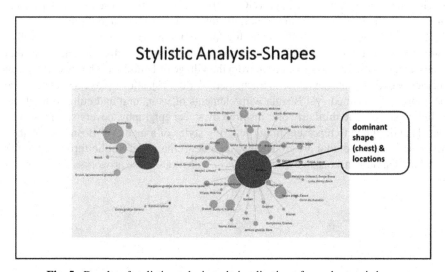

Fig. 5. Results of stylistic analysis and visualisation of sample stecci shapes

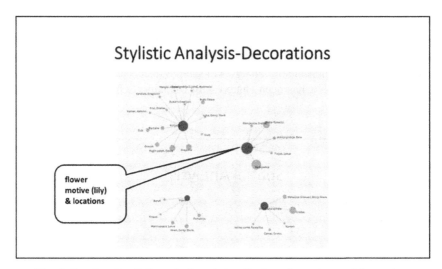

Fig. 6. Results of stylistic analysis and visualisation of sample stecci decorations

3.2 Art Projects

While the above research studies have attracted a fair amount of attention from scholars and professionals, they may not be suitable for promoting cultural heritage to a wider non-professional community. It is argued that in that case digital art using innovative visual techniques and tools may be more helpful. Thus, a special session on visual approaches for digital humanities was organised as part of the Eurographics Workshop on Graphics and Cultural Heritage (GCH 2019) in order to showcase local Bosnian talents and achievements [14] in promoting cultural heritage through digital art.

The following three contributions all addressed some aspects of stecci. The first contribution, inspired by stecci iconography, is the animated film 'Azdaja' [15] that retells a well-loved legend of a dragon from the village of Umoljani. The second one, an interactive digital game named 'The Enchanted World' [16], allows players to experience the atmosphere of medieval Bosnia with elements of its natural and cultural heritage, including stecci. The third artwork, inspired by stecci epigraphy, covers several usable fonts [17] designed to represent major lettering styles of a medieval Bosnian alphabet. All these works of digital art are freely available to the wider public through popular social media. Screenshots shown in Figs. 7, 8, 9 illustrate these artworks.

Fig. 7. Screenshot from the animated movie 'Azdaja'

Fig. 8. Screenshot from the digital game 'The Enchanted World'

Fig. 9. Four font designs from 'Bosancica Catalogue'

4 Discussion

The advent of ubiquitous computing has created a perfect opportunity for cultural heritage researchers and the participating public for developing a great variety of digital data formats along with complex ways of data reuse in order to better understand and promote cultural resources. Responding to the above challenge, this study traced significant initiatives undertaken over the past decade in regard to the creation and/or usage of digital data about one specific UNESCO world heritage case, medieval Bosnia's monumental tombstones - stecci [2].

The main findings indicate a slow, but steady progress towards building a wholistic digital catalogue of the existing necropolises and tombstones. The study identified several interesting projects undertaken towards this end by individual researchers and/or volunteers. But more importantly, the study identified one especially promising development in terms of a systematic approach to the creation of relevant digital records. This approach was proposed by a group of archaeologists and was successfully tested in several municipalities. However, given the large number of necropolises and tombstones scattered all over Bosnia and Herzegovina, coupled with the lack of necessary human and financial resources, the project is progressing rather slowly.

With respect to data usage, the main study findings indicate a growing research interest for analysing these digital data, as well as for the production of digital art inspired by stecci. With respect to research, the use of the 'distant reading' method for the analysis of digital data enabled the discovery of interesting novel spatial, temporal and relational patterns. With respect to art, several award-winning visual, performing and literary artworks have been identified. They address different aspects of stecci by using innovative digital methods and tools that are particularly attractive to the young technology-savvy audience. Collectively, these works enhance our understanding of the nature and importance of stecci for the Bosnian national identity.

5   Conclusions

This paper makes a significant contribution to research of digital cultural heritage through a study of a specific heritage case (stecci) on its digital road. The evidence of a systematic approach adopted for creating digital data in multiple forms, as well as innovative research and art generated by using these data is encouraging. Such findings imply a huge potential of digital approaches for better understanding and promoting cultural resources. However, the task is not without problems, as evidenced in the reported lack of human and financial resources that slow down the current progress. More conversations and collaborations between interested parties, as well as greater institutional support is needed to deal with these limitations. Overall, it is hoped that going digital will help stecci become a commonly accepted instrument for conveying knowledge of the most important aspects of Bosnian culture worldwide.

References

1. COST Homepage. https://www.cost.eu/. Accessed 03 Sept 2020
2. UNESCO World Heritage List. https://whc.unesco.org/en/list/1504/. Accessed 03 Sept 2020
3. Stecaks Digital Catalog Homepage. https://h.etf.unsa.ba/dig-katalog-stecaka/index_eng.htm. Accessed 03 Sept 2020
4. Handzic, M., Dizdar, S.: Picturing the past: a case of knowledge management application in Archaeology. In: Proceedings of the 12th International Forum on Knowledge Asset Dynamics – Knowledge Management in the 21st Century: Resilience, Creativity and Co-creation, IFKAD 2017, 7–9 June, St. Petersburg, Russia, pp. 1251–1261 (2017)
5. Stecak.map: Interactivna karta stecaka Homepage. https://stecakmap.info/. Accessed 03 Sept 2020
6. Bujak, E., Aladuz, V., Jasika, D., Dzemidzic, A.: Stechaks of Hadzici-Inventory of stechaks in the municipality of Hadzici. Municipality of Hadzici & Stanak (Society for Medieval Bosnian History), Hadzici (2016)
7. ARKWORK Homepage. https://www.arkwork.eu. Accessed 04 Sept 2020
8. Handzic, M., Heuvel, C.: Digital humanists' knowledge space: a conceptual design. In: Proceedings of the 13th Forum on Knowledge Asset Dynamics – Societal Impact of Knowledge and Design (IFKAD 2018), 4–6 July, Delft, Netherlands, pp. 1815–1823 (2018)
9. Handzic, M., Heuvel, C.: Virtual research environments for the digital republic of letters. In: Hotson, H., Wallnig, T. (eds.) Reassembling the Republic of Letters in the Digital Age: Standards. Systems, Scholarship, pp. 433–445. Gottingen University Press, Germany (2019)
10. Handzic, M., Ismajloska, M.: Transferring cultural knowledge through arts: two digital stories. In: Handzic, M., Carlucci, D. (eds.) Knowledge Management, Arts, and Humanities. KMOL, vol. 7, pp. 77–96. Springer, Cham (2019). https://doi.org/10.1007/978-3-030-10922-6_5
11. Handzic, M., Zulic, H., Guja, Z.: Knowledge discovery from arts data: a case of distant listening. In: Proceedings of the 14th Forum on Knowledge Asset Dynamics – Knowledge Ecosystems and Growth, IFKAD 2019, 5–7 June, Matera, Italy, pp. 256–263 (2019)
12. Handzic, M.: Archaeology in contemporary arts: a case of Stecci. In: COST ARKWORK Conference: On Shifting Grounds, 3–5 October, Rethymno, Crete (2019). https://www.ark work.eu/archaeology-in-contemporary-arts-a-case-of-stecci/
13. ResearchGate Homepage. https://www.researchgate.net/profile/Meliha_Handzic. Accessed 04 Sept 2020

14. Handzic, M.: Preface, Proceedings of the Special Session on Visual Approaches for Digital Humanities, Eurographics Workshop on Graphics and Cultural Heritage (GCH 2019), 8 November, Sarajevo, Bosnia and Herzegovina, pp. 6–7 (2019)
15. Ramadan, I.: Azdaja. https://www.youtube.com/watch?v=9yWaXsjDPkQ. Accessed 04 Sept 2020
16. Zubcevic, A., Ramadan, I.: The Enchanted World. https://apps.apple.com/us/app/the-enchanted-world/id1459917958. Accessed 04 Sept 2020
17. ulupubih, Pisem ti bosancicom. https://issuu.com/milamelank/docs/bosancica_katalog_3 6_str. Accessed 04 Sept 2020

Project Papers: Virtual Museum Applications (e-Museums and e-Exhibitions)

The Diary of Niels: Affective Engagement Through Tangible Interaction with Museum Artifacts

Mette Muxoll Schou and Anders Sundnes Løvlie[✉] [iD]

IT University of Copenhagen, Copenhagen, Denmark
asun@itu.dk

Abstract. This paper presents a research through design exploration using tangible interactions in order to seamlessly integrate technology in a historical house museum. The study addresses a longstanding concern in museum exhibition design that interactive technologies may distract from the artifacts on display. Through an iterative design process including user studies, a co-creation workshop with museum staff and several prototypes, we developed an interactive installation called *The Diary of Niels* that combines physical objects, RFID sensors and an elaborate fiction in order to facilitate increased visitor engagement. Insights from the research process and user tests indicate that the integration of technology and artifacts is meaningful and engaging for users, and helps introduce museum visitors to the historic theme of the exhibition and the meaning of the artifacts. The study also points to continued challenges in integrating such hybrid experiences fully with the rest of the exhibition.

Keywords: Affective design · House museum · Experience design · Tangible interaction

1 Introduction

In recent years, there has been increasing interest in the role of emotion and affect in the design of visitor experiences for museums [6,11,24]. However, along with the increasing use of digital technology to facilitate engaging visitor experiences in museums, many have voiced concern that such use of technology may be a detriment and distraction as much as a benefit [13,22,25,28]. Such concerns from museum professionals often focus on the risk that visitors' attention may be drawn away from the museum artifacts [2]. Concepts such as hybrid design and tangible interactions are offered in response [3,7,8,12,14–16,18,21,29]. A recent user study indicates that museum visitors prefer tangible interaction formats over smartphone apps [19].

This paper presents a research through design exploration of affective design with tangible interactions in a historical house museum: Greve Museum in Denmark. Historical museums face a difficult balancing act as they need to facilitate engaging visitor experiences, while also respecting their commitment to historical

M. Ioannides et al. (Eds.): EuroMed 2020, LNCS 12642, pp. 289–299, 2021.
https://doi.org/10.1007/978-3-030-73043-7_24

accuracy and authentic preservation and presentation of artifacts [11]. Furthermore, house museums have a particular set of challenges, such as the fact that not just the objects on display but also the house itself is considered an historic artifact, meaning that "content and container are one" [9]. Since the historical authenticity of the house is at the heart of the museum's identity, when introducing technology it is considered important to "maintain the spirit of the house" and to design for seamless experiences [9].

We explore the following research question: *How can we design for affective engagement through tangible interactions with museum artifacts, while accommodating the museum's need to communicate historical and cultural knowledge?* The study contributes with a case that is comparable to the one discussed in [9], but with some key differences in addition to country and local context. In particular, the museum's requirements regarding historic accuracy demanded a design in which the technology was integrated seamlessly into the house, centering the interaction entirely on original historic artifacts, in a narrative presenting a historic, rather than fictional character.

2 Background

Affect has been discussed in fields such as art history [20] and literature [17] as well as design [5]. In recent years, there has also been increasing interest in the role of affect in the design of museum experiences [23,24]. This development is sometimes seen as part of a broader "affective turn" [4] in social sciences and HCI. For Gregory and Witcomb affect is "an important means to achieve audience participation in the process of making meaning" [11, p. 263]. Witcomb sees affect as an element in developing a critical pedagogy for history museums, and has suggested that the traditional museum concept of a "pedagogy of walking" be replaced with a "pedagogy of feeling" [26,27].

History museums pose challenges for experience design, as the need to facilitate audience engagement must be balanced against the museum's mission to exhibit authentic historical artifacts and knowledge. In museum studies, there is a long-standing concern that using mobile devices for interpretive artwork information will lead users to focus only on their mobile screens rather than the exhibited artifacts in front of them (cf. [13,25]). In the words of Woodruff et al. [28], interactive museum experiences require visitors to engage in a "sophisticated balancing act", dividing their attention between different information sources. Recent work suggests that the tension inherent in these concerns continue to be a challenge for hybrid design in museums [2].

Particular challenges apply to house museums: museums that were once houses or homes but which have been transformed into museums displaying and communicating the original interior and functions of the house. Because the house itself is considered a historic artifact, it is challenging to introduce technological installations in such houses because they might conflict with the presentation of an authentic historic interior. Claisse et al. [9] formulate four central considerations for the design of experiences for house museums, based on interviews with museum experts:

1. Maintaining the spirit of the house.
2. Building on the domestic nature of historic houses.
3. Telling stories about, for and by people.
4. Designing for a seamless experience of technology.

Claisse suggests the demands of house museums make them "an interesting and relatively underexplored context for the integration of 'tangible interaction"' [8]. Furthermore, Ciolfi and McLoughlin [7] have formulated some lessons for design of tangible interactions in a museum setting:

1. Both digital and physical components must fit well within an overall storyline.
2. Tangible artifacts need to be place-sensitive, in order to avoid distracting from the museum setting.
3. The tangible artifacts should be limited to a simple and straightforward functionality, in order to work as "bridging" components between the digital and physical, rather than "high-tech gimmicks".

3   Approach

The study at hand was conducted as a Research through Design project [30] from February till December 2018. The process included observations and interviews with visitors at the museum and a co-creation workshop with employees and volunteers at the museum, followed by an iterative design process in which several prototypes were built and tested. Initial prototypes were tested in lab facilities of the university, while the last prototype was integrated and tested in the museum from 27 October to 1 December. The lab tests were done with invited test users as "think aloud" tests with observations and interviews. Data from the observations and interviews were summed up, themed and analyzed in order to form the base of further iterations towards the next prototype. Evaluation of the final prototype was done through observations of the museum's visitors using the prototype in situ.

4   Context: Greve Museum

Greve Museum is a small local museum exhibiting the historic evolution of Greve village on the outskirts of Copenhagen, Denmark. The museum is located in an old farmhouse furnished and arranged as a farm in this area would be in the 1800s. Our study focuses on a redesign of one of the rooms in the museum, the old storage hall Øverstuen (Fig. 1). In the 1800s this room had an interesting combination of functions: It was originally used for storage, but was also the room for celebrations as well as for mourning. Being the coldest room on the farm, it was used to lay dead family members on display for mourning, before carrying them out of the "Death Door" - a door specifically used for the dead, as superstition prevented dead bodies from being carried through the door used by the living. However, as museum representatives explained to us at the start of the project, the existing exhibition of the room had failed to engage audiences to any large degree. Guests did not seem to understand this room, or find it interesting enough to spend much time exploring. The museum had decided to redesign the room, removing display cases with old documents and refocusing attention on the room and the artifacts belonging to it, in an attempt to better convey the original functions of the room. As part of this endeavour they asked us to design an interactive experience that could help to better engage the visitors while at the same time providing knowledge about life on the farm in the 1800s. In particular, the museum was hoping to engage interest among younger audiences.

Fig. 1. Øverstuen before the redesign.

5   Design

Our design process started with observations and interviews with visitors in Øeverstuen, which confirmed the assessment of the curators: Most visitors barely stepped into the room before turning around and leaving, and few if any engaged with the educational material on display. Subsequently we arranged a co-creation workshop with a group of museum employees and volunteers. Through a structured ideation process we developed a narrative about a ghost haunting the room. Exploring different technologies which could be used to bring this ghost to life, we decided against solutions that would involve smartphones or tablets, as the museum already had a tablet-based experience which was rarely if ever used by visitors. Based on the ideal of seamless integration of technology into the authentic interior we also discarded ideas involving sophisticated display techniques such as augmented reality or Pepper's Ghost.

Fig. 2. The diary of Niels.

Instead we took inspiration from a scene in a Harry Potter movie [10], in which a ghost communicates with Harry by writing on the blank pages of a diary. Through an iterative process we developed a concept consisting of a diary - a physical book with blank pages - lying on a table, with a projector in the ceiling above it (Fig. 2). This is the diary of Niels, a historic person who lived at Greve Farm from 1797 to 1870. Writing in the pages of his old diary, the ghost of Niels asks visitors to show him three specific everyday objects from the farm. For each object, Niels responds by sharing a memory from his diary in which this object played a role. This meant combining the physical context of the objects and the room with the digital installation of the diary, thus exploring the opportunities of tangible technology in combination with the potential affective response to the fiction of a ghost in an old farmhouse. Though the diary entries were fictions they were based on the museum's documentation of life on the farm, describing scenarios tied to the everyday objects and how they were used by the farm people. These objects consisted of the following (Fig. 3):

1. A hymnbook which was an important decorational part of the lit de parades in Øeverstuen.

2. An ike beater, a wooden tool used by the locals to process fibers when making cloths.
3. A rummelpot (or friction drum), which was a traditional homemade musical instrument used by farm children on festive occasions.

While the rummelpot used in the installation was a copy, the hymnbook and ike beater were authentic historical objects, that we were allowed to use due to the fact that they were not registered as archival material in the museum collection.

5.1 Prototyping

To create the sensation of a ghost writing in the diary, the text of the diary was animated and projected down upon the blank pages of a physical book from a projector in the ceiling (Fig. 4). Using a font that looked like handwriting, the letters would appear one at a time, giving the impression that Niels was writing on the pages in real time. The work on our first prototype revolved around building and testing this "magic" diary and projecting it on blank pages. Testing this in a lab setting on two young users (10 and 15 years old), the users found the overall concept entertaining but wanted more variety in interaction forms and questioned the historical authenticity.

In our second prototype we focused on varying the forms of interaction as well as elaborating the historical memories for the diary. Next to the book was now placed a push button which guests were asked to press when they wanted to move forward with the reading. Hidden under a tablecloth, a radio frequency identification (RFID) reader was placed. Three artifacts were each equipped with a set of RFID tags that, when held close to the RFID reader, would trigger a corresponding memory to appear on the pages of the diary. The RFID reader was hidden in order to support the fiction of a supernatural presence in the room. When we tested the second prototype in our lab on three new test users aged 10–11, the test users found the experience engaging and mostly easy to use, in spite of some technical and usability problems. When we asked the users about the contents of the diary, 2 of the 3 were able to recall parts of the content, whereas the third had struggled too much with the readability of the "handwritten" font to remember any of the content. Given that we were aiming to engage children at an age where reading skills are variable, we decided to change the font in order to improve the readability, as well as adjusting the language used in the diary.

6 Evaluation

The Diary of Niels was implemented in Øeverstuen at Greve Museum as a fully functional prototype in November 2018. This "in the wild" deployment gave us the chance to observe how the prototype was used by visitors who had not received any prior instructions or explanations about the prototype. We spent one day in Øeverstuen observing how visitors engaged with the installation, interviewing some of them after the experience.

Fig. 3. The Diary of Niels and the three artifacts used with the diary: A hymn book, an ike beater and a rummelpot.

6.1   Overall Reception

There was a marked difference from our initial observations at Øeverstuen before the implementation of the diary. Visitors quickly discovered the diary and started interacting with it, and spent more time exploring the room compared to earlier observations. It should be noted that the entire room had been redesigned in the meantime, so it is impossible to say how much of this improvement was due to *The Diary of Niels*. However, in interviews with the guests they were all able to recall and explain the function of at least one of the three historical objects, indicating that they had engaged sufficiently with the prototype to learn a little about the exhibition.

6.2   Group Experience

While the installation had been designed with a single user in mind, visitors actually came to the exhibition and approached the installation in groups (typically families). Thus an adult would do the reading, while the children engaged with the physical objects. This may have helped the educational function of the installation, as the children remembered more about each object than users in the earlier lab test scenarios which had to read themselves. Approaching the diary as families also enabled collective reflection on the exhibition. Visitors discussed the age of the objects, and one visitor approached the adjoining rooms

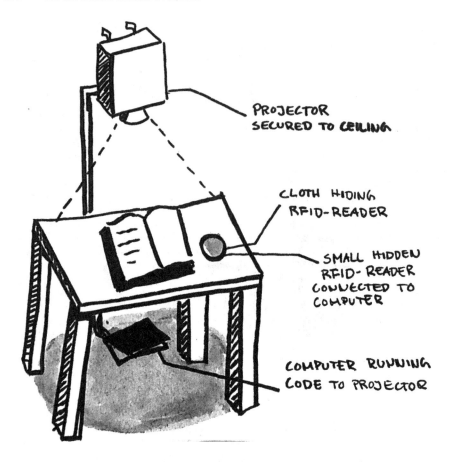

PROJECTOR
SECURED TO CEILING

CLOTH HIDING
RFID-READER

SMALL HIDDEN
RFID-READER
CONNECTED TO
COMPUTER

COMPUTER RUNNING
CODE TO PROJECTOR

Fig. 4. Overview of the physical and technical setup of the final prototype.

of the farm house, wondering aloud which of the furniture and pictures were Niels' old belongings. This indicates that the diary installation could be used to spark conversations between parents and children, helping them reflect and learn about the exhibition.

6.3 Place-Sensitivity

Interviews with the visitors revealed a surprising failure of the installation. While the visitors had understood and engaged with much of the content of the diary, recalling events taking place in Øeverstuen, they were not aware that they were standing in that very same room in which the events had taken place. This oddity can be explained by the fact that the museum curators had wanted to avoid explanatory texts and signposts on the walls when redesigning the room, so the only text stating the name of the room and explaining its function was an easily overlooked sign posted by the entrance. Meanwhile, while the diary speaks about

Øeverstuen it does not actually point out that this is the very room the diary is placed in. This illustrates that the design strategy of this installation, aiming to blend in as seamlessly as possible with the historic interior, puts increased demands on the overall exhibition design of the whole room: Curators must consider how much extradiegetic information is needed, and how and where this should be presented to visitors, in order to avoid confusion.

7 Conclusions

The setting at Greve museum offered a fertile opportunity for experimenting with tangible interaction, as the museum allowed us to use authentic historic objects in our prototype. This allowed us to use the objects not only as a bridge between the physical and the digital, but also as a material connection between the past and the present. This will not always be possible in other contexts - similar projects have used replicas [16]. However, as many house museums do allow visitors to touch and pick up many of their artifacts, there may be possibilities to explore tangible interactions with authentic artifacts by using non-invasive techniques, e.g. visual object recognition.

The problem we encountered with the place-sensitivity of our prototype points to a need for designers to look holistically at the information provided to visitors, not just through the interactive system but also the rest of the room and the museum as a whole. In our design process we had explored the possibility of integrating the installation more extensively with the rest of the room by turning it into a scavenger hunt, in which the objects belonging to the diary installation would be hidden around the room. This would have required users to search and explore the room in order to unlock the diary entries, thus extending the interaction into the entire room rather than just the tabletop. However, this idea had to be discarded due to limitations set by the museum. Further effort could be made to connect the diary with the room, for instance by installing other personal traces of Niels in the room so that the narrative of the diary would be conveyed through several different means in different parts of the room. These traces could e.g. be "micro-augmentations" [1] such as sound installations of Niels whispering when a visitor approached certain objects. Future research should explore opportunities for further integrating artifact interactions with the experience of the rest of the museum space.

Acknowledgments. The project has received funding from the European Union's Horizon 2020 research and innovation programme under grant agreement No 727040 (the GIFT project: gifting.digital).

References

1. Antoniou, A., O'Brien, J., Bardon, T., Barnes, A., Virk, D.: Micro-augmentations: situated calibration of a novel non-tactile, peripheral museum technology. In: Proceedings of the 19th Panhellenic Conference on Informatics, PCI 2015, pp. 229–234. ACM, New York (2015). https://doi.org/10.1145/2801948.2801959. http://doi.acm.org/10.1145/2801948.2801959

2. Back, J., et al.: GIFT: hybrid museum experiences through gifting and play. In: Antoniou, A., Wallace, M. (eds.) Proceedings of the Workshop on Cultural Informatics co-located with the EUROMED International Conference on Digital Heritage 2018, EUROMED 2018, Nicosia, Cyprus, vol. 2235, pp. 31–40. CEUR Workshop Proceedings (2018)

3. Bannon, L., Benford, S., Bowers, J., Heath, C.: Hybrid design creates innovative museum experiences. Commun. ACM **48**(3), 62–65 (2005)

4. Blackman, L.: Immaterial Bodies: Affect, Embodiment, Mediation. SAGE, Newbury Park (2012)

5. Boehner, K., DePaula, R., Dourish, P., Sengers, P.: Affect: from information to interaction. In: Proceedings of the 4th Decennial Conference on Critical Computing: Between Sense and Sensibility, CC 2005, pp. 59–68. ACM, New York (2005)

6. Boehner, K., Sengers, P., Gay, G.: Affective presence in museums: ambient systems for creative expression. Digit. Creativity **16**(2), 79–89 (2005)

7. Ciolfi, L., McLoughlin, M.: Physical keys to digital memories: reflecting on the role of tangible artefacts in "reminisce", p. 10 (2011)

8. Claisse, C.: Crafting tangible interaction to prompt visitors' engagement in house museums. In: Proceedings of the 10th International Conference on Tangible, Embedded, and Embodied Interaction, TEI 2016, pp. 681–684. ACM (February 2016)

9. Claisse, C., Petrelli, D., Dulake, N., Marshall, M., Ciolfi, L.: Multisensory interactive storytelling to augment the visit of a historical house museum. In: Proceedings of the 2018 Digital Heritage International Congress. IEEE (August 2018)

10. Columbus, C.: Harry Potter and the Chamber of Secrets (2002)

11. Gregory, K., Witcomb, A.: Beyond nostalgia: the role of affect in generating historical understanding at heritage sites. In: Museum Revolutions: How Museums Change and are Changed, pp. 263–275 (2007)

12. Hornecker, E., Buur, J.: Getting a grip on tangible interaction: a framework on physical space and social interaction. In: Proceedings of the SIGCHI Conference on Human Factors in Computing Systems, CHI 2006, pp. 437–446. ACM, New York (2006)

13. vom Lehn, D., Heath, C.: Displacing the object: mobile technologies and interpretive resources. In: International Cultural Heritage Informatics Meeting: Proceedings from ichim03. Archives & Museum Informatics, Paris (2003). http://www.archimuse.com/publishing/ichim03/088C.pdf

14. Løvlie, A.S., et al.: The GIFT framework: Give visitors the tools to tell their own stories. In: Museums and the Web 2019. In: Museums and the Web, MW18, Boston, MA, USA (April 2019). https://mw19.mwconf.org/paper/the-gift-framework-give-visitors-the-tools-to-tell-their-own-stories/

15. Løvlie, A.S., Eklund, L., Waern, A., Ryding, K., Rajkowska, P.: Designing for interpersonal museum experiences. In: Black, G. (ed.) Museums and the Challenge of Change: Old Institutions in a New World. Routledge, London (2020)

16. Marshall, M.T., Dulake, N., Ciolfi, L., Duranti, D., Kockelkorn, H., Petrelli, D.: Using tangible smart replicas as controls for an interactive museum exhibition. In: Proceedings of the 10th International Conference on Tangible, Embedded, and Embodied Interaction, TEI 2016, pp. 159–167. ACM, New York (2016). https://doi.org/10.1145/2839462.2839493. http://doi.acm.org/10.1145/2839462.2839493

17. Meskin, A., Weinberg, J.M.: Emotions, fiction, and cognitive architecture. Br. J. Aesthetics **43**(1), 18–34 (2003)

18. Pedersen, T., Andersen, E.T., Løvlie, A.S.: Designing a "no interface" audio walk. In: Museums and the Web 2019. Museums and the Web, Boston, MA, USA (April 2019). https://mw19.mwconf.org/paper/designing-a-no-interface-audio-walk/
19. Petrelli, D., O'Brien, S.: Phone vs. tangible in museums: a comparative study. In: Proceedings of the 2018 CHI Conference on Human Factors in Computing Systems, CHI 2018, pp. 112:1–112:12. ACM, New York (2018)
20. Prown, J.D.: Style as evidence. Winterthur Portf. **15**(3), 197–210 (1980)
21. Risseeuw, M., et al.: Authoring augmented digital experiences in museums. In: Proceedings of the International Working Conference on Advanced Visual Interfaces, AVI 2016, pp. 340–341. ACM, New York (2016). https://doi.org/10.1145/2909132.2926064. http://doi.acm.org/10.1145/2909132.2926064
22. Rudloff, M.: Det medialiserede museum: digitale teknologiers transformation af museernes formidling. MedieKultur: J. Media Commun. Res. **29**(54), 22 (2013)
23. Ryding, K., Fritsch, J.: Play design as a relational strategy to intensify affective encounters in the art museum. In: Proceedings of the 2020 ACM Designing Interactive Systems Conference, DIS 2020, pp. 681–693. Association for Computing Machinery, New York (2020). https://doi.org/10.1145/3357236.3395431. https://doi.org/10.1145/3357236.3395431
24. Smith, L., Wetherell, M., Campbell, G.: Emotion, Affective Practices, and the Past in the Present. Routledge, London (June 2018)
25. Wessel, D., Mayr, E.: Potentials and challenges of mobile media in museums. Int. J. Interact. Mob. Technol. (iJIM) **1**(1) (October 2007). http://journals.sfu.ca/onlinejour/index.php/i-jim/article/view/165
26. Witcomb, A.: Understanding the role of affect in producing a critical pedagogy for history museums. Mus. Manage. Curatorship **28**(3), 255–271 (2013). https://doi.org/10.1080/09647775.2013.807998. https://doi.org/10.1080/09647775.2013.807998
27. Witcomb, A.: "Look, Listen and Feel": the first peoples exhibition at the Bunjilaka gallery, Melbourne museum. In: Thema La revue des Musées de la civilistion, vol. 1, pp. 49–62 (2014)
28. Woodruff, A., Aoki, P., Hurst, A., Szymanski, M.: Electronic guidebooks and visitor attention. In: Bearman, D., Garzotto, F. (eds.) International Cultural Heritage Informatics Meeting: Proceedings from ichim01. Archives & Museum Informatics, Milano, Italy (2001). http://www.archimuse.com/publishing/ichim01_vol1/woodruff.pdf
29. Zancanaro, M., et al.: Recipes for tangible and embodied visit experiences. In: Museums and the Web 2015, MW2015, Chicago, IL (2015). https://mw2015.museumsandtheweb.com/paper/recipes-for-tangible-and-embodied-visit-experiences/
30. Zimmerman, J., Forlizzi, J., Evenson, S.: Research through design as a method for interaction design research in HCI. In: Proceedings of the SIGCHI Conference on Human Factors in Computing Systems, pp. 493–502. ACM (April 2007)

Digital Transformation Strategy Initiative in Cultural Heritage: The Case of Tate Museum

Vassiliki Kamariotou[1]([⊠]), Maria Kamariotou[2], and Fotis Kitsios[2]

[1] School of History and Archaeology, Aristotle University of Thessaloniki, Thessaloniki, Greece
[2] Department of Applied Informatics, University of Macedonia, Thessaloniki, Greece
mkamariotou@uom.edu.gr, kitsios@uom.gr

Abstract. Museums have now changed their intent and embraced a more "visitor-oriented" approach to provide this unforgettable experience for visitors. Digital museum strategy plays a decisive role in how museums want to use technology to promote innovation network growth, competitive advantage, and economic efficiency. However, it is worth noting that there are still significant gaps in technical equipment between museums. This paper draws on the Museum of the Tate and aims to examine its transformation from a conventional museum to a museum of the 21st century. The case of Tate museum is of particular interest because of its obvious intention to be regarded as a leading museum in Europe, expressed in its current strategic planning policies. This paper also highlights some of the advantages and problems associated with this program and its future directions. This paper examines how Tate has introduced technological systems to turn itself into a virtual museum and succeed in the global economy. This paper aims at examining and explaining a museum's transformation into a virtual museum. The findings of the case study show that the Tate museum has successfully applied the digital strategy with the goal of being a model for the world of virtual museums. This paper helps cultural practitioners draw more lessons from the proposed key drivers of digital museum strategies and reach conclusions on digital museum planning today.

Keywords: Cultural heritage · Virtual museum · Digital strategy · Digital transformation · Visitor experience

1 Introduction

Cultural organizations are locations where visitors have learning and unforgettable experiences, take part in events and exchange ideas on exhibits [6, 23, 30]. Museums have now changed their intent and embraced a more "visitor-oriented" approach to provide this unforgettable experience for visitors. By using emerging technology, existing museums have been changed to "digital/ virtual museums" [23, 30]. This transition has helped heritage industry professionals transform museums into a more creative and visitor-oriented approach [6, 12]. Cultural institutions need to build a sustainable future and make efforts to provide digital access to more cultural heritage data for all. This digitization process has a high cost to museum management and they have to look after their key properties

M. Ioannides et al. (Eds.): EuroMed 2020, LNCS 12642, pp. 300–310, 2021.
https://doi.org/10.1007/978-3-030-73043-7_25

and collections. They must also ensure that museums remain important and meaningful to future generations by allowing public engagement and improving audience experience. Museums have succeeded in moving from one-way communication to two-way communication in which they allow audiences to engage [24].

At the time, the Internet was considered a groundbreaking technical and social breakthrough, even though a website was merely a museum display, displaying works of art, various cultural and educational tools, and practical information aimed at promoting the visit and access to the museum [17]. However, it is worth noting that there are still significant gaps in technical equipment between museums. These variations depend on their scale, venue, funding or even management: many museums do not yet benefit from high-level technology. For financial and technological reasons and the lack of specialized technical expertise, only large and medium-sized museums can afford a full collection of digital devices (multimedia tools, apps, website), allow them to digitize cultural resources, build tools for interpretation, develop business activities and allow the processes and activities associated with the so-called portion to be implemented [3, 4, 10, 13]. A big and challenging problem for the future of museums in the digital age is the real/ virtual connection. Museum digital strategy is sadly not a priority for museum strategists [21–23].

This paper draws on the Museum of the Tate and aims to examine its transformation from a conventional museum to a museum of the 21st century. The case of Tate museum is of particular interest because of its obvious intention to be regarded as a leading museum in Europe, expressed in its current strategic planning policies. This paper also highlights some of the advantages and problems associated with this program and its future directions. This paper examines how Tate has introduced technological systems to turn itself into a virtual museum and succeed in the global economy. This paper aims at examining and explaining a museum's transformation into a virtual museum while answering the following research questions: How does museum handle transformation? What are the required conditions for the transformation? What assets/ infrastructures are essential to become a virtual museum? The findings of the case study show that the Tate museum has successfully applied the digital strategy with the goal of being a model for the world of virtual museums.

The paper is structured accordingly. Section 2 describes the influencing powers of the idea of a "digital museum". It discusses museum advances in the digital transformation and digital strategy. It also reveals how recent technological changes have influenced museum transformation, and how the digital museum concept is turned into a reality thanks to these innovations. Section 3 presents examples of integrated modern museum techniques on the basis of previous findings, and explores the basic concepts of what it means to be "digital" in a museum context. Section 4 of the paper addresses the findings of the preceding study.

2   Literature Review

2.1   Digital Transformation in Museums

The shift from cultural collections themselves to data streams and services, across different platforms (mobile, personalized), is certainly one of the defining developments that will shape digital culture in the coming decades [25]. This development has to do with both the production of data and their use and access to it. Everyday user, armed himself as a content producer, through the capabilities of mobile devices (digital photography and video, sensors, geographical location), seeks access to cultural content not in a specific place or from a single source but from a combination of media and in different forms [3, 14]. At the same time, the volume of data generated opens up for the first time the possibilities of pattern detection and knowledge mining in cultural ensembles and large-scale digital collections. The shift to data flows and services frees cultural objects from the place of collection and diffuses them through different means into knowledge environments or into "information-space museums", museums outside the walls that function as channels of information flow [1, 27].

Cultural organizations, meanwhile, are sharing new, more frequent interactions with users and are both part of the same process, as, for the first time in history, users and the information management institutions share a common information space through Internet. This opens up new opportunities for cultural organizations to research, connect and leverage cultural information to the global online audience. The use of digital technologies and networks can significantly increase the public value of cultural heritage collections [5, 25].

In this changing environment, cultural organizations and cultural heritage managers in general are called upon to develop new models of harnessing digital opportunities that address their specificities and priorities. Publicly interconnected digital information (data) is the means of reaching out to users and creating new products, services and value at multiple levels [9, 17, 25].

Potential applications in the field of culture, following the above trends, include the user's interaction with the exhibit, space or cultural object through an inexhaustible number of combinations, which are limited only by human creativity [1]. As the Internet and Information and Communication Technology (ICT) have penetrated our everyday lives profoundly, virtual exhibits have become readily accessible and popular [29]. The proliferation of technical advances in the virtual exhibition arena has opened up a new frontier for more productive communication and interaction with visitors. Owing to their ability to transcend the geographic, economic, and accessibility limitations of physical exhibits, the scale and function of these exhibits have expanded rapidly through remarkable technological advances. Digital exhibits such as Google Arts & Culture are not only websites that provide basic information such as opening hours, locations and event schedules, but also vast online data sets that offer rich user experiences that have become integral to the activities of museums [18, 19].

Recent years' technological developments such as Virtual Reality, Artificial Intelligence, Cloud Computing, Big Data, 3D models, have made the creation of a vast array of technologies and products that aim to make the digital museum possible. These items use ICTs to enhance the experience and interaction, learning and knowledge of the travelers. A series of problems have arisen in the economies and needs of the museums in recent years, promoting the popularization of the concept of the digital museum. The first relates to communication. Digital exhibits are used in museums as the primary means of contact with the public, and the focus of the museum has shifted from collecting and preserving artifacts primarily to presenting information and engaging with visitors [18].

Visitor motivation awareness is a key element in exhibition contact, which is contact between museum and visitors. This is because museums in both physical and virtual exhibits have rich and dynamic settings and free-choice learning environments, and visitor enthusiasm affects their behaviors and communication. Another critical aspect of exhibition communication is the awareness of visitor behaviors because visitor behaviors decide what they will see; where they concentrate their attention; and eventually what they will learn and experience [8]. A significant communication element in the virtual exhibition is interaction with the virtual guide, museum staff or other users. In addition, virtual visitors and museum professionals can interact openly and exchange information movement through the creation of a group or forum in a virtual exhibition setting. Provided that multiple users can connect to the virtual exhibition simultaneously via a chat system or in the form of avatars, visitors can exchange information and have discussions about exhibitions [18, 25].

The second one is information. Visitors have become literate about information and are not content with restricted access to the material in the collection of a museum [18]. Social media should be used as a means to inform the public about history, traditions, and development, not just to encourage exhibitions and any occurring events. Nowadays also the educational process is focused on everything online.

It is also only safer if the museums continue to use this medium by offering the valuable knowledge of traditional and modern histories and cultures as a resource of references. This can be done if only the members of the organization are committed enough from time to time to update the details online. In this new globalizing world, the information can be easily transmitted just as quickly as lightning. It is therefore only resourceful if the museum institutions continue to take ever more seriously the steps of being the platform for educating the public. In addition to captioning or marking material in physical exhibits, interactive exhibits may provide considerably more detail on artefacts, such as ownership history, episodes and other related details. A virtual museum may also provide relevant information on objects in other museums or institutions to take it one step further, allowing cross-collection and cross-institutional searches. Similar knowledge can also be provided in different languages [7, 18, 26].

Managers use social media, blogs, wikis, Facebook and YouTube to connect with their visitors in a way that enhances the relationships the modern museum wants to have with its visitors. They could, for example, improve the online learning experience, the interaction between people with different interests, and the use of virtual reality to enable museum artifacts to be examined [23, 30]. In addition, in museum exhibits, cultural practitioners incorporated immersive electronic media, presentations, storytelling, theater, dance and musical performances, and hands-on experiences to improve educational engagement through the use of emerging technologies [9, 15, 16, 25].

Overall, museums will need to deliver enhanced and flexible facilities to gain and maintain critical recourse. This phenomenon explains the broad diffusion over recent years of interest in digital museums. Recent technical advancements and pressing technology drive have advanced the opportunity to realize these visions of technology [25]. We now have the potential to realize concepts as previously often were ideas, instead of admiring them in the form of small-scale pilots. Advanced technology and its wide-ranging application are no longer a concept of idea; rather, they are a fact and something possible, and "the main problem is no longer technological; it is organizational as ever" [2].

2.2 Digital Museum Strategy

In 1947 André Malraux first proposed the concept of virtual museum. He put forward the idea of an imaginary museum, a museum without walls, place or spatial boundaries, such as a virtual museum with its content and details about the objects could be made available throughout the world [31]. The use of technology in museums dates back to the late 1960s, during which most of the technologies were used for museum collection recording and management. The growth of information and communications technology in the decades to come saw a paradigm change in the museum landscape, the essence of museums moving from providing "object centering" to visitor experience. This change is a catalyst for a debate on the relationship between newly developed technologies, understanding of museums and visitor experience [5, 20]. Since the mid-2000s, the use of ICT has fundamentally changed the mode of development and even the purpose of Cultural Heritage exhibitions, shifting rapidly from an old vision, presenting visitors with static information consisting of a large number of "cultural signs" to new, customized services that fulfill the personal desires of visitors by working together to fulfill their cultural needs and expectations [1, 25]. The transition in the cultural heritage world has meant that museums have shifted from being seen as safe-keepers of collections to gradually becoming centers of education, learning, and entertainment, expected to provide a varied audience with different types of experiences [7, 11].

However, a new term, the "museum digital strategy" was implemented during the last quarter of the 20th century regardless of museology. Over the course of these decades, museums from all over the world have experienced a remarkably significant shift in which they are confronted with the digital age, witnessing the museums as pure institutions that concentrated only on audience-oriented strategic approaches to the collections [1, 9, 30]. The museum managers strive to increase the number of visitors, so they try to prove museum atmospherics, including pleasure, attraction and friendliness towards others, attendance, time spent browsing, and spending money. These activities can influence the decision of a person to stay, repeat the visit and spend money in a given environment, as well as the actions of the visitor [7, 28]. The digital strategy for culture moves in two dimensions, the cultural and the digital, and on the basis of these a unified business approach is formed. It is located at national, local and regional level but is also in direct relation and relevance to the respective policy trends at European level. These two dimensions are then supplemented by a third horizontal level which concerns the formulation of policies for the creation, management and utilization of the intellectual and cognitive capital of the country and is directly related to the policies of research, development and innovation.

The three objectives of the digital strategy set the framework for creating value through the digital culture of the country. These three objectives are: the protection and promotion of cultural heritage and identity through new digital channels, the creation of conditions and infrastructure and the development of skills for the future sustainability of digital culture, and sustainable development through interconnection of culture with local communities, entrepreneurship and tourism [32].

ICT offers great ease in the use of innovative and personalized solutions for the implementation of digital strategy by cultural heritage management bodies. The sustainability of information, the development and utilization of national facilities and infrastructure and the development of a variety of digital services must therefore be a top priority of a national strategy and an essential support tool for the sustainable management of digital cultural heritage, as well as provide the framework for the development of exhibits and cultural organizations in general [25].

An important digital priority is the one that concerns the overall management of the user experience regarding the cultural content through advanced services. This experience should be defined in terms of its core values by quality standards, but in terms of the way in which it will be presented to the public a mixed model can be followed: the cultural organization that has the content sets quality criteria and maintains control over the distribution of content, but should be the - thus regulated - market that will offer content distribution channels to the public. This is something we already see with services like Google Arts & Culture, social networking platforms but also through other digital storytelling platforms or games that just hold the overall quality level, but have the freedom to create applications and overall the environment that is optimal for the user [7, 20, 25].

3   Digital Strategy in Tate Museum

An example of an integrated strategy for the digital museum is the one that is being implemented in the Tate museum in Britain. Tate is an organization that houses the UK's national collection of British art, as well as international modern and contemporary art, in a network of four art museums. It is not a government agency but the UK Department for Digital, Culture, Media and Sport.

In 2010 Tate established its digital strategy. Digital started emerging in the company in 2012 as a component of departmental and divisional plans, outlining goals to produce new digital content and create new digital communities. Digital-focused positions arose in departments outside the Tate Marketing department to promote these emerging initiatives and broader use of blogs, social media, third-party websites and related "community manager" positions, as well as the need for new mechanisms to facilitate these activities. Thus, distinctions between organizational roles and activities blurred within digital spaces resulting in the need for more collaborative working practices putting the visitor at the middle.

Digital is no longer the remit of a single museum technologists group. As part of their plans, both agencies currently have digital activity and are planning to pursue even more digital activity in future years. Software and hardware resources, training, recruiting, induction, career growth and performance management are part of the organization's necessary transformation. New governance frameworks are being implemented to align digital expectations with available resources, ensure the implementation of sustainable practices and set the path for change.

Tate's vision is to use digital platforms and networks to provide rich content for existing and new art audiences, build and grow a dedicated arts community and optimize the associated revenue opportunities. Tate's visitors will have interactive experiences that enhance their enjoyment and appreciation of art, provoke their thoughts and invite them to participate, promote the gallery programme, give them easy access to knowledge, encourage them to explore deeper content, encourage them to purchase items, join Tate and make donations, provide an elegant and usable interface whatever their needs might be. To accomplish this, the Tate Museum embraced an approach that is audience-centered and insight-driven, constantly assessed and improved, well-designed and architecturally spread across multiple channels, open and sharable, sustainable and scalable, and centrally controlled and devolved across the organization.

In particular, Tate has published digital publications such as Tate Kids, Tate Shots, Tate Papers, Tate Etc. as well as the online tools for collecting and learning. Having digitized the art collection, Tate plans to digitize the collections of the museum and special library, including Tate's stock of artist books. In the Art & Artists section of the website, digitized archive objects are incorporated with the artworks to allow user travel between related content. This approach seeks greater curatorial interaction with the online art and archive collection as there is a major opportunity in digital spaces to manifest enhanced curatorial activity. Now the keystone of Tate's multimedia communications is editorial material in the form of short videos and blog posts. They are increasingly able to tell their stories effectively through their own media platforms – website, social media, email, etc., as well as communicating the program through high-quality content of lasting value. To optimize this con tent's capacity, an editorial center was set up to organize and produce content around the program of the museum.

Digital innovations have changed gallery experience for visitors. Wi-Fi is available in all galleries, and mobile website extensions designed for in-gallery use allow access to a wealth of information and interpretation about the museum's works on display. Information professionals are able to use tablet computers to view and exchange information with visitors. Digital learning studios provide facilities for new types of learning experiences and interaction. Artist sketchbooks and Tate Archive scrapbooks are made available via Tate Britain's touchscreens. Interactive comment walls connected to social media have been successfully prototyped at Tate Modern and are being deployed more widely.

Tate has a large presence on social media, and the plan is for it to expand only to continue. Tate's website has grown considerably over the past decade, from a very static one. Network containing visiting details and an event calendar on a social website where users can take part in online discussions and debates. Also there are inter-active areas such as Tate Kids and Tate Collectives that allow users to upload their own content. Also added to the site were social features such as sharing buttons, real-time Twitter stream widgets, comments, and a feature that enables users to create their own online galleries of artworks and archive objects. This feature allows users to upload their own photos, and then tag and post it.

The website has not only become more social, but Tate has also opened regularly updated profiles on various social networking sites such as Instagram, Facebook, Tumblr, Twitter and Pinterest. The number of accounts and the number of people from various departments participating in these activities has been increasingly growing and the usage of these social media has been significantly diversified. The scope of social media initiatives undertaken is very large, ranging from announcements announcing the opening of an exhibition to an interpretation tool used in galleries. In these sites, new posts are frequently posted, including promotion of exhibitions and activities, tournaments, links to website material such as blogs or videos, news updates, or information visiting.

Tate has many active community projects including Tate Kids, turbine generation, blogs, online social media accounts, and Tate Collectives. Curators are often regularly writing about their shows, and workers involved in training and learning programs are now starting to blog more often. Looking forward, blogging is a considered aspect of most departments' job activity. Employees around the company have become communicators and the museum has many voices – a transition that needs to be controlled and that involves a relaxation of the external controls that talk from Tate. The new project Archives and Access brings social learning tools into the array of online art and archives. User-generated content brings user voices and suggestions to the digitized set. Creation ensures these do not overshadow the online collection's other uses, such as study.

The social value of Tate's expertise and properties is limited by the approach of the institution to its public reuse. Using more permissive software licenses – such as Creative Commons – unlocks the freedom and enables learners to repurpose and use Tate-generated material in their own projects as long as their intent is non-commercial. In this way, the material of Tate joins the broader digital world and is found across the network, amplifying interaction with art in line with the mission of Tate.

Digital products and services also provide income opportunities which have not been utilized. Tate seeks to raise sales by launching new goods and changing the way it speaks to its customers. The implementation of a paperless, self-service ticketing service – now a trend in many industries – presents some challenges and serves as an important step towards an integrated suite of ticketing services such as personalization and access to paid content. In order to raise sales the online shop is marketed through all digital platforms. When digital visitors use free content they are promoted with related items from the online store. Tate Enterprises and Tate have also created various digital products for purchase through the iTunes newsstand, such as online courses, games, ebooks and a version of Tate Etc. It is evident that this is a field of tremendous organizational potential and digital media are projected to be a major revenue source in the future. Tate and Tate Enterprises work together through the newly formed Digital Publishing Group to make business opportunities decisions within the digital sphere. Figure 1 summarizes the main pillars of Tate's digital strategy.

To achieve sustainable growth, a coherent plan for digital museums needs to draw on both technology and culture. Technology, generally speaking, underpins the cultural development and vice versa; the two of them. Unfortunately this influence is not recognized by many of today's strategies. This is why strategic planning needs to draw on both technical innovation and cultural growth for the development of digital museums. Most "digital" strategies are not something that can be done here and there, but suggest a systematic approach to long-term goal fulfillment. Thus, the museum's vision of the future is an integral component of the interactive museum's debate, be it within or out of immediate reach.

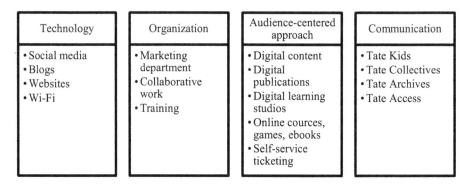

Fig. 1. Tate's digital strategy.

4   Conclusion

Digital museum strategy plays a decisive role in how museums want to use technology to promote innovation network growth, competitive advantage, and economic efficiency. They still pursue answers to many digitization challenges and the experience of visitors. Despite being innovative, it stands in essence for very concrete and critical policies on digital museums that require substantial investments and have significant implications for the years ahead. For this purpose, it is important to research them methodically and in a coherent manner, both in terms of policy design and policy implementation. Digital museums can and should be designed strategically for achieving results in economic and social growth. Therefore more research in this direction is required. Future researchers could conduct in-depth interviews with museum managers in order to discuss about the impact of ICT on museums as well as opportunities opened by the digital revolution experienced in the last decade.

In terms of comprehension, this paper helps cultural practitioners draw more lessons from the proposed key drivers of digital museum strategies and reach conclusions on digital museum planning today. Such research will help academics have a more comprehensive understanding of the role of technology and functions in the heritage field, and help cultural organization professionals realize the potential engagement techniques for visitors to incorporate them in increasing the competitive advantage. The practical contribution of this paper is that it provides curators with guidance on the interactive techniques which can be implemented to include visitors in the overall museum experience and make visits more enjoyable.

Professionals use emerging technology to influence the actions of visitors and develop an intimate relationship that stretches well beyond a physical location. They strive to meet changes in the needs and desires of visitors, so they adjust the mission and orientation of the museum by using modern museum technology, and turning them into interactive museums. Becoming more open, entertaining, enriching content and increasing revenue is obviously what museums focus on based on their digital strategies, and luckily, thanks to digital technologies, there are so many resources available in these areas.

The idea of digital museums in Tate is used as a strategic tool to incorporate digital transformation factors within a common context and encourage museum competitiveness. Digital services have been successfully adopted as the key outputs of the digital transformation model, to promote collaboration, innovation and growth. In the hope that this will result in successful heritage management, a prerequisite of every the museum, Tate introduced the digital transformation model. To maintain an efficient heritage management framework, network technologies are needed to drive economic development, support a sustainable museum and provide better service quality.

There are also important lessons to be gained by dealing with more analytical aspects on what the digital can bring and how its application will improve heritage interactions' cultural value. Bridging the activities of both heritage practitioners and their audiences as well as theory remains not merely a realistic possibility, but a requirement if we are to fully understand whether visitors are becoming more comfortable with digital technologies, and if so, what is the meaning of this contribution to their heritage experience.

References

1. Amato, F., et al.: Big data meets digital cultural heritage: design and implementation of scrabs, a smart context-aware browsing assistant for cultural environments. J. Comput. Cult. Heritage (JOCCH) **10**(1), 1–23 (2017)
2. Bertacchini, E., Morando, F.: The future of museums in the digital age: new models of access to and use of digital collections. Int. J. Arts Manage. **15**(2), 60–72 (2013)
3. Cassidy, C.A., et al.: Digital pathways in community museums. Mus. Int. **70**(1–2), 126–139 (2018)
4. Champipi, E., Kitsios, F., Kamariotou, M.: Innovation management and new service development strategy: a case study in cultural heritage institutions. In: Proceedings of the 8th International Symposium & 30th National Conference on Operational Research, Patras, Greece, pp. 115–119 (2019)
5. Ch'ng, E., Cai, S., Leow, F.T., Zhang, T.E.: Adoption and use of emerging cultural technologies in China's museums. J. Cult. Heritage **37**, 170–180 (2019)
6. Conway, T., Leighton, D.: Staging the past, enacting the present: experiential marketing in the performing arts and heritage sectors. Arts Mark. Int. J. **2**, 35–51 (2012)
7. Damala, A., Ruthven, I., Hornecker, E.: The MUSETECH model: a comprehensive evaluation framework for museum technology. J. Comput. Cult. Heritage (JOCCH) **12**(1), 1–22 (2019)
8. Daniela, L.: Virtual museums as learning agents. Sustainability **12**(7), 1–24 (2020)
9. Dragoni, M., Tonelli, S., Moretti, G.: A knowledge management architecture for digital cultural heritage. J. Comput. Cult. Heritage (JOCCH) **10**(3), 1–18 (2017)
10. Evrard, Y., Krebs, A.: The authenticity of the museum experience in the digital age: the case of the Louvre. J. Cult. Econ. **42**(3), 353–363 (2018)
11. Gil-Fuentetaja, I., Economou, M.: Communicating museum collections information online: analysis of the philosophy of communication extending the constructivist approach. J. Comput. Cult. Heritage (JOCCH) **12**(1), 1–16 (2019)
12. Gofman, A., Moskowitz, H.R., Mets, T.: Marketing museums and exhibitions: what drives the interest of young people. J. Hosp. Mark. Manage. **20**, 601–618 (2011)
13. Greffe, X., Krebs, A., Pflieger, S.: The future of the museum in the twenty-first century: recent clues from France. Mus. Manage. Curatorship **32**(4), 319–334 (2017)

14. Ioannides, M., et al.: Immersive digital heritage experience with the use of interactive technology. In: Ioannides, M., et al. (eds.) EuroMed 2016. LNCS, vol. 10059, pp. 265–271. Springer, Cham (2016). https://doi.org/10.1007/978-3-319-48974-2_30

15. Kamariotou, V., Kamariotou, M., Kitsios, F.: Strategies for increasing visitors' interaction: the case of virtual museum and exhibitions. In: Sakas, D.P., Nasiopoulos, D.K., Taratuhina, Y. (eds.) IC-BIM 2019. SPBE, pp. 409–414. Springer, Cham (2021). https://doi.org/10.1007/978-3-030-57065-1_42

16. Kamariotou, V., Kamariotou, M., Champipi, E., Kitsios, F.: Moving towards museum digital strategy: a transformational framework. In: Sakas, D.P., Nasiopoulos, D.K., Taratuhina, Y. (eds.) IC-BIM 2019. SPBE, pp. 397–402. Springer, Cham (2021). https://doi.org/10.1007/978-3-030-57065-1_40

17. Karp, C.: Digital heritage in digital museums. Mus. Int. **56**(1–2), 45–51 (2014)

18. Kim, S.: Virtual exhibitions and communication factors. Mus. Manage. Curatorship **33**(3), 243–260 (2018)

19. Kim, S., Lee, H.: Visitor attention and communication in information-based exhibitions. Int. J. Des. **10**(2), 15–30 (2016)

20. King, L., Stark, J.F., Cooke, P.: Experiencing the digital world: the cultural value of digital engagement with heritage. Heritage Soc. **9**(1), 76–101 (2016)

21. Kitsios, F., Champipi, E., Grigoroudis, E.: Cultural and creative industries innovation strategies for new service development using MCDA. In: Grigoroudis, E., Doumpos, M. (eds.) Operational Research in Business and Economics. SPBE, pp. 69–84. Springer, Cham (2017). https://doi.org/10.1007/978-3-319-33003-7_4

22. Kitsios, F., Champipi, E., Grigoroudis, E.: New service development: strategy and innovation process in cultural and creative industries using MCDA. In: Proceedings of 4th International Symposium & 26th National Conference on Operational Research, Chania, Crete, Greece, pp. 36–42 (2015)

23. Lehman, K., Roach, G.: The strategic role of electronic marketing in the Australian museum sector. Mus. Manage. Curatorship **26**, 291–306 (2011)

24. Lo Turco, M., Calvano, M.: Digital museums, digitized museums. In: Luigini A. (ed) Proceedings of the 1st International and Interdisciplinary Conference on Digital Environments for Education, Arts and Heritage. EARTH 2018. Advances in Intelligent Systems and Computing, vol. 919, pp. 387–398. Springer, Cham (2019)

25. Marty, P.F.: Museum websites and museum visitors: digital museum resources and their use. Mus. Manage. Curatorship **23**(1), 81–99 (2008)

26. Münster, S.: Digital heritage as a scholarly field—topics, researchers, and perspectives from a bibliometric point of view. J. Comput. Cult. Heritage (JOCCH) **12**(3), 1–27 (2019)

27. Münster, S., Ioannides, M.: A scientific community of digital heritage in time and space. In: 2015 Digital Heritage, Granada, Spain, pp. 267–274. IEEE (2015)

28. Perry, S., Roussou, M., Economou, M., Young, H., Pujol, L.: Moving beyond the virtual museum: engaging visitors emotionally. In: 23rd International Conference on Virtual System & Multimedia (VSMM), Dublin, Ireland, pp. 1–8. IEEE (2017)

29. Russo, A., Watkins, J., Groundwater-Smith, S.: The impact of social media on informal learning in museums. Educ. Media Int. **46**(2), 153–166 (2009)

30. Shaharir, S.A., Zanuddin, H.: museum institutions in the digital age: the insights of Malaysian museums' use of facebook. J. Soc. Sci. Res. 357–366 (2018)

31. Sylaiou, S., Liarokapis, F., Kotsakis, K., Patias, P.: Virtual museums, a survey and some issues for consideration. J. Cult. Heritage **10**(4), 520–528 (2009)

32. Zhou, Y., Sun, J., Huang, Y.: The digital preservation of intangible cultural heritage in china: a survey. Preserv. Digit. Technol. Cult. **48**(2), 95–103 (2019)

Time-Layered Gamic Interaction with a Virtual Museum Template

Erik Champion[1,2(✉)], Rebecca Kerr[3], Hafizur Rahaman[3], and David McMeekin[3]

[1] University of Western Australia, 35 Stirling Highway Perth WA6907, Perth, Australia
erik.champion@uwa.edu.au
[2] Australian National University, Sir Roland Wilson Building, 120 McCoy Circuit, Acton, ACT2601, Australia
erik.champion@anu.edu.au
[3] Curtin University, GPO Box U1987l, Perth 6845l, Australia
david.mcmeekin@curtin.edu.au

Abstract. This paper discusses a simplified workflow and interactive learning opportunities for exporting map and location data using a free tool, Recogito into a Unity game environment with a simple virtual museum room template. The aim was to create simple interactive virtual museums for humanities scholars and students with a minimum of programming or gaming experience, while still allowing for interesting time-related tasks. The virtual environment template was created for the Oculus Quest and controllers but can be easily adapted to other head-mounted displays or run on a normal desktop computer. Although this is an experimental design, it is part of a project to increase the use of time-layered cultural data and related mapping technology by humanities researchers.

Keywords: Time-Layered culture map · Recogito · Virtual museums · Unity · Interactive simulation · Immersive and multimedia experiences

1 The Aims of the Time Layered Cultural Map

This project is part of a larger overall project (Time Layered Cultural Map, http://tlcmap. org/) run by a national consortium of digital humanities academics. Our objectives are not only to produce mini-projects that use mapping and related technologies to collate, demonstrate and solve time and space-related cultural datasets challenges, but also to provide examples and workflows for Australian humanities researchers with limited programming experience to modify and extend. Our part of the project involves developing exemplars and a workflow for humanities scholars to import locational data from Recogito, create clickable maps in a virtual environment, and provide a clear demonstration of interactive elements to display time-related and spatially-dynamic cultural heritage assets, as well as related information from other media sources.

M. Ioannides et al. (Eds.): EuroMed 2020, LNCS 12642, pp. 311–322, 2021.
https://doi.org/10.1007/978-3-030-73043-7_26

2   Design Problems: The Vanishing Virtual

Real-world museums provide artifacts and art pieces for education, conservation, for reflection (to muse on), and for research. Studies of real-world museums and how they use images on their website reveal that the aims of visitors include more than just experiencing the art collection: they also wish to experience the museum's actual physical space and to enjoy the presence of others. Hadley [1] surveyed 24 museum websites and found "three strong trends" for images: depictions of the buildings or grounds; the collection and its "treasures"; and photos of the visitors (and "how will I feel when I get there?") Strong branding of museums through their web presence emphasize their spatial grandeur (and setting); the explorative nature of the collection experience; and the shared social sense of expectation and atmosphere. One or more of these evocative elements is typically missing from a virtual museum experience.

According to Parry and Huhtamo [2], virtual museums are vaguely defined. Baldwin has argued that museums, and by extension, virtual museums, emphasize perfection over risk and experimentation [3]. Virtual museums [4] have seldom managed to capture and retain worthwhile visitor numbers [5]. The technology of VR is often impressive, the expense, expertise required, and dynamic and volatile market-driven supply of software and hardware create implementation and preservation challenges for smaller GLAM (Galleries Libraries Archives and Museums) organizations, as well for academic fields not heavily experienced with either such technology or the programming required to develop and maintain content. In virtual heritage, this has been called the "Vanishing Virtual" as few virtual heritage models survive and prosper [6].

What were the main features and attractions of virtual museums? Why have they gone in and out of fashion and have they been of any benefit to real-world museums? Or could they become important again? The ViMM - Virtual Multimodal Museum project investigators [7] suggested that virtual museums "…may add value in ways not possible in the physical museum such as enhanced cultural 'presence', immersive experiences, and vivid narratives by means of animation, and virtual functionalities." And now, with the COVID 19 virus, there is an urgent need to engage the public with museum collections through remote participation and engagement [8]. For instance, in May 2020 UNESCO [9] undertook a survey and stated that more than 1 in 10 museums could stay closed permanently and that "In Africa and Small Island Developing States (SIDS), only 5% of museums have developed online content for their audiences.

2.1   Freedom, Movement, and Constraints

Some writers promote virtual museums as being free of the limitations of real museums. Klaus Müller [10], said virtual museums no longer need walls, and "… Virtual museum 'spaces' can take on any shape they want, but they lack the conventional authority and emotion a museum building evokes." In the article, *The Uses of Virtual Museums: The French Viewpoint*, Roxane Bernier [11] provided more reasons for virtual museums: newfound freedom [12] from awkward display spaces; freedom from "limitations on objects"; and "indefinite storytelling." Mokre (1998) and Davallon (1998) also stress there are no physical constraints.

Klaus Müller [13] had an opposite view: "Virtual museum 'spaces' can take on any shape they want, but they lack the conventional authority and emotion a museum building evokes." Do participants wish to change the interactive experience? Art is often created to form a mental gestalt based on an observer's movement around it. We argue a virtual museum implies a spatial, immersive experience, that can be spatially navigated, traversed with intent, or wandered through. A question worthy of investigation is to examine how different participants prefer to experience virtual museums.

2.2 Engaging Interaction

Do virtual museums leverage the ability of digital media to include interaction, real-time data, and other information with the intentions or performance of the visitors? Unfortunately, interaction is limited in virtual museums, according to Wazlawick [14] and where it is possible, it is usually trivial and unexciting: Petridis noted [15], "Usually, interaction is confined to reading labels with little information on the exhibits, shop booklets, and audio guided tours." Virtual museums do not need to offer physical protection from the elements, real-live preservation, a procession of set spatial narratives, or adherence to causality and the laws of nature. Virtual artworks could transition into each other based on the physiology of the user or the way the viewer navigates the work could influence the way the art presents itself.

There are online "virtual museums" with useful content. For example, http://3D. si.eu (Smithsonian Institute). Smaller museums and galleries also use https://sketchfab. com/ to create guided audio tours of 3D interior and exterior models. Collections in 3D UK (https://www.collectionsin3d.co.uk/) are seeking more feedback and two-way interaction on curation but in the main virtual museums are single 3D-model hosting sites.

They can however educate and allow people to peruse and examine artistic context. They can provide access to art as purchasable (and downloadable) commodities, pre-visit experiences, or information on the background or development of artworks and artifacts. They can also overlay the virtual collection with visualization of who remotely visited and why. An advantage of virtual museums over real-world equivalents is that digital artefacts with time-related layers can be re-organized in interesting and educational ways. A second research question is how to provide suitable reconfigurable assets and interaction methods and examine which are most useful, usable, and engaging.

2.3 Contextual Evaluation

How would we assess the success of virtual museums? Sylaiou et al. [16] argued that an important criterion of virtual museums is a sense of presence, of being there. Unless the virtual museum's main aim is to simulate the placeness of a real-world place this is secondary to the primary aim of a virtual museum: to understand more about the artefacts, media, and gathered information, separate to but also related to the outside world. Can a virtual museum can provide multimodal, contextual information, that thematically addresses the participant's curiosity and explorations?

3   Design Solution

COVID-19, has created compelling reasons for virtual museums to help rather than compete with real-world museums. However, there are many failed examples, in terms of engagement, usefulness, or longevity. A potential solution to the sterility short-term value, and rigidity of many virtual museums is to create a reconfigurable simple virtual environment as a base template. This template would allow the import of various media formats connected to data sets that can be selected, ordered, and repositioned based on the personal and variable interactions chosen by participants in a virtual reality environment, or via time layers. It could also provide for simple game-like interaction.

However, resource-poor museums may also require lower-cost and less complex virtual solutions. We provided example assets and workflows so that non-programmers could customize the collections, interaction, and output mode (either virtual environment via HMD (head-mounted display) VR, or via a conventional desktop digital 3D environment). As we also had a goal of educating digital humanities researchers on the value of maps and related cultural data, we decided to convey techniques for providing locational data of cultural heritage via a game engine functioning as a virtual museum.

3.1   Workflow

We created a simple workflow (Fig. 1) that shows others how they can import assets into a Unity scene then incorporate interactive elements within the assets. The prototype created has been designed for use on an Oculus Quest or Rift, however, it can easily be

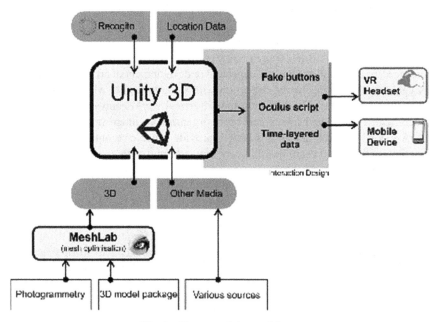

Fig. 1. Diagram of the workflow.

transferred to any desktop version of VR hardware, and to be playable on the desktop. Unity also can export to smartphones, but that is beyond the scope of the paper.

With little to no programming, but a basic understanding of Unity, a person can create a museum showcasing a mixture of media: digitally created artifacts; architecture; images; maps; and videos. Assets were deliberately modeled and rendered so as not to discourage beginners but higher quality assets can also be imported. The basic unity game environment is a four-walled virtual museum-type display space. We chose Unity as it is an effective tool for making simple immersive and interactive environments. In front of or behind the participant is a 3D model. On the three walls in front of the participant is a picture-map with clickable locations, a video wall that plays video clips, and an image wall that can display a variety of images.

The media (3D model, picture-map, video clips, and images) can all be changed or reconfigured. The aim is to create a fully flexible game-like 3d template that showcases, demonstrates, and can be easily adjusted to show different time and place-data relationships that can be explored in a desktop virtual environment, or ideally, through a head-mounted display VR environment with controllers. The project can be deployed to engage participants via interactive elements such as showing the progression of time, solving puzzles, or answering questions.

3.2   3D Software: MeshLab and Unity

MeshLab is a free, open-source system for processing and editing 3D triangular meshes. It can be used for editing, refining rendering, texturing, or converting meshes (including into printable 3D objects). Unity is an effective tool for making simple immersive and interactive environments and is free to use if the project is earning less than $100,000 USD. Even though Unity is most known as a game engine, this application has a variety of uses. This tutorial will show the steps required to create a scene within Unity.

With only a basic understanding of Unity, a person can create a museum that showcases a mixture of media such as digitally created artifacts, architecture, images, maps, and videos. This environment can then be used to engage the user via interactive elements such as showing the progression of time, solving puzzles, or answering questions. We created a simple workflow that shows others how they can import assets into a Unity scene then incorporating interactive elements within the assets. The prototype created has been designed for use on an Oculus Quest, however, it can easily be transferred to any desktop version of VR hardware, and to be playable on the desktop.

3.3   Display: Head-Mounted Display (Oculus Quest) or Desktop 3D

Although some HMDs have eye-tracking, they are relatively expensive, so we aimed for an HMD that was robust, well-supported, reasonably priced, and had interesting additional features. We chose an Oculus Quest for this experimental project but we also provided a desktop 3D digital environment version (for Windows PC or Mac OS).

The imported media types possible are maps, images, video clips, and 3D models. The display hardware used was an Oculus Quest; with a cable to connect to the computer and also a desktop computer capable of running Unity at a reasonable framerate. The software we used and provide tutorials and asset examples for was Unity, MeshLab, a

3D modelling program (Blender or Photogrammetry), and Recogito. We used Recogito and a national gazetteer dataset to extract latitude and longitude data for historical place names so that we could create an interactive 2D map in Unity that could be used as an interface to change the other media elements.

In the example we provided, each virtual wall displays a different media type, one wall shows videos, one wall displays images, one wall contains the clickable map, and behind the participant is a 3D model that can sit anywhere in the virtual space. Each media element can be changed, which in turn changes the media on the other walls depending on the narrative thread chosen. The model can also change (to other models, to other levels of resolution or completeness) depending on the time and space related to the narrative thread selected by the participant.

3.4 Generic Options

The overall options we provided in our tutorials were:

1. 3D: Develop a 3D model from Photogrammetry or 3D software (e.g. Blender). Reduce 3D mesh in MeshLab.
2. Other media: Source archival images, related atmospheric sound, movie clips (may have to splice video files), and a related thematic map (picture-map) with key locations, and textual information about the places and their related time periods.
3. Text: Import text document into Recogito. Recogito creates locational coordinates from text documents for KML export etc.
4. Location Data: Import and position location data onto picture-map, into Unity. Also import 3D mesh, images, and movie clips.
5. Interface: Create fake buttons that connect hot points of locations on the map to different images, frames of movie clips, or 3D model in Unity (Unity can create desktop, phone-based, or VR-suitable 3D environments.
6. Setup options: We provided instructions to calibrate an Oculus Quest headset and thematically relate Oculus Quest controllers to time-interaction in Unity so that selection and movement of objects create new configurations.

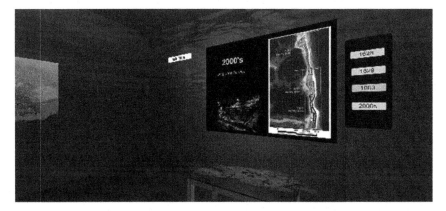

Fig. 2. Virtual museum seen with oculus quest or rift (time periods can be clicked).

7. Learning Component: We also provided an example of a quiz-style serious game. It requires the player to select, move, rotate, scale, and place or orient objects (image, map points, frames of the movie clips, or elements of the 3D mesh) to reveal missing information or conflicting time-layered data.

3.5 The Demo Room

The above example (Fig. 2) was inspired by the historic and famous shipwreck, the Batavia wreck of 1629. The below figure (Fig. 3) shows the room from the opposite side, the table, and the 3D model is placed beyond or in front of the participant, depending on where they virtually enter the room. The sourced content was: 3D photogrammetry models; still images; and video.

Fig. 3. Overview of the box museum space with 3D ship model.

3.6 Assets Used for the Tutorials

For this project, we extracted images (Fig. 4) of the famous shipwreck, the Batavia, wrecked in 1629 in the Houtan Abrolhos, off Western Australia. Images were sourced from the Western Australian Museum website (https://museum.wa.gov.au/), from an Australian shipwrecks database, and a Sketchfab-sourced 3D model (but we did not have access to a 3D model of the original 17th century Batavia so used a placeholder model). We also provided a tutorial explaining how MeshLab can be used to reduce the poly count of the 3D objects while preserving Normals, before exporting to Unity. Please note that to implement many photogrammetric objects in a game engine, the polygon count needs to be reduced, although this will also affect the visual fidelity.

Fig. 4. Assets supplied.

Below are the types of media assets we provided:

- *Buttons with dates* - selecting these dates changes the content displayed in the scene. Within this example, selecting a date will change the photo/art images on the top right and the 3D object in the bottom right.
- *Map with an animated ship*: An example of how the map could be used. Currently, the animation is on loop however it can be tied to move with the selection of buttons.
- *Interactive diary*: A diary or information panel can be used and scrolled through by the user. In this example, we took two images from the diary of a historic shipwreck, the user can switch between the two by pressing the green or white arrow buttons.
- *Animated 3D object*: This example shows a 3D object that is animated and changes when a date is selected. Users can change the orientation of the 3D object.
- *Photo/art images*: Images can be displayed in a variety of different ways. In this example, the images are placed together in the top right and change when different dates are selected.

The prototype showcased three 3D interactive scenes that can be used for an interactive desktop experience. In scene examples one and two, a participant can move about the room and interact with a book and image, one version allows a participant to walk around freely, while the other uses teleporting pads. These two versions allow for accessibility for different needs, as the virtual reality-walking option may be uncomfortable or unnerving for some users. The third version was a 2D environment to display media assets up close, allowing for detailed information. The participant can solve puzzles by moving objects or by teleporting between a virtual museum room to a simulation of the ship outside as a wreck (Fig. 5), and in its past condition (Fig. 6), moored at a simplified version of Beacon Island, populated with Non-Playing Characters.

Fig. 5. Explorative outside world.

3.7 Formative Assessments

We asked three people at a university makerspace to provide formative comments on the first HMD VR version, and then we ran both this version and an improved HMD VR version with three more people (Fig. 6). Four of the six were experienced VR users. We used an Oculus Rift environment and allowed the participants to explore freely.

The questions were: whether the gamification (discovering artefacts to win badges) was a hinderance or desirable; if they appreciated the ability to turn on fog to add to the atmosphere; if sound improved navigation; if the underwater scene added to the experience; if they noticed in the "Box Museum" they could change time periods; and if they had any ideas for improvement.

They all enjoyed the gamification; mostly enjoyed the fog option (two did not notice it); all but one enjoyed the sound; enjoyed the underwater scene but wanted more direction; all but one noticed they could change the time periods on the map in the Box Museum; they suggested more instructions and one person in particular said to encourage more exploration and gameplay but not in a way that suggested there was a right or a wrong way. The historian in particular saw great opportunities for using the template in workshops with historians to discuss how to present and explore different types of collections and historical data.

4   Next Steps

4.1   Automatic Data Visualisation Possibilities

Our colleague Drew Fordham [https://github.com/drewfrobot/more-unity-and-data] created a tutorial with QGIS, R/RStudio, SQLite ("free in the public domain and runs locally without servers") and Unity assets so that students and less experienced programmers can create data visualizations with Unity. The code allows Unity to create global landscapes with data from RStudio datasets, to generate contours (heightmaps). We tested this process with two groups of students but for humanities staff and students a simplified process is needed to create 3D terrain maps from datasets.

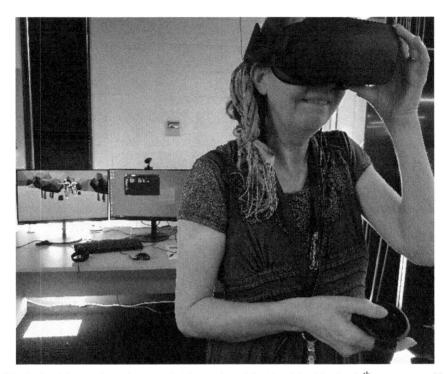

Fig. 6. Participant teleporting to a simple version of Beacon Island in the 17th century, outside the virtual museum, with NPCs (her view is also cast to the left monitor).

4.2   Related Collaborative Mixed Reality Project

A Ph.D. student has also been developing collaborative mixed reality projects using two Microsoft HoloLenses [17], and has created walkable mixed reality maps with interactive objects and 3D models that appear only when the participant is near or walks over that point in the mixed reality 3D map. Map data is sent using a special GeoJSON format, to handle time-related data. Alternative historical interpretations can be viewed and interacted with and the results shared by speaking to the other participant.

5   Conclusion

We demonstrated a workflow using free software (Recogito, the personal/low-customer Unity game engine version, and MeshLab). We developed the workflow and the exemplar in a 3D Unity game environment, with video, images, 3D mesh, and picture-map. We undertook preliminary comparisons of tools, interaction, and VR versus desktop 3D versions. We also built a simple artefact-finding game in the HMD-version. From preliminary discussions with our national colleagues, there is interest in using free tools like Recogito and exporting locational data to 3D environments and game engines for cultural heritage, but participants would appreciate more streamlined online tutorials and videos.

Our local formative test participants preferred gamification to less interactive virtual environment. Our simple evaluation also indicated that embodiment and gamification appear to improve the desirability of virtual museums, but we would like to formally evaluate this and filter for demographic factors. The third element mentioned at the start of this paper: sociability, still needs to be investigated.

The last design component to be completed is developing more engaging microgames to convey different time and space dimensions without resorting to sliders or other simple but non-thematic interface elements. We will explore how VR controller-based interaction can change time-layered data related to the media assets (and therefore the configuration, display, and behavior) of the media assets. We also intend to run a formal evaluation study to compare the desktop and head-mounted VR versions and to assess whether potential museum-goers find the separation of media on four walls useful for understanding archival data and whether they find it an engaging experience.

References

1. Hadley, P.: What do the best museum websites all do?: Cogapp, Online (2017)
2. Huhtamo, E.: On the origins of the virtual museum. In: Parry, R. (ed.) Museums in a Digital Age, pp. 121–135. Taylor & Francis, London, UK (2013)
3. Baldwin, J.: Saying What You Mean & Getting Better at What You Do. Leadership Matters Thoughts on 21st Century museum leadership by Anne Ackerson and Joan Baldwin, vol. 2017 (2017)
4. Huhtamo, E.: On the Origins of the Virtual Museum Virtual Museums and Public Understanding of Science and Culture, pp. 121–135. Nobel Foundation, Stockholm, Sweden (2010)
5. Sylaiou, S., Liarokapis, F., Kotsakis, K., Patias, P.: Virtual museums, a survey and some issues for consideration. J. Cult. Heritage **10**, 520–528 (2009)
6. Rahaman, H., Champion, E.: The scholarly rewards and tragic irony of 3D models in virtual heritage discourse. In: Haeusler, M., Schnabel, M.A., Fukuda, T. (eds.): 24th Annual Conference of the Association for Computer-Aided Architectural Design Research in Asia (CAADRIA 2019). CuminCAD, Wellington NZ, pp. 695–704 (2019)
7. Ioannides, M., Davies, R.: ViMM-virtual multimodal museum: a manifesto and roadmap for europe's digital cultural heritage. In: Ricardo, J.-G., Mendonça, I.P., Jotsov, V., Marques, M., Martins, J., Bierwolf, R. (eds.): Proceedings of 9th International Conference on Intelligent Systems 2018 Theory, Research and Innovation in Applications (IS 2018) Conference, Funchal - Madeira, Portugal, pp. 343–350. IEEE (2018)
8. Kahn, R.: Corona as curator: how museums are responding to the pandemic. Elephant Lab (2020)
9. UNESCO: COVID-19: UNESCO and ICOM concerned about the situation faced by the world's museums. vol. 2020. UNESCO, Online UNESCO website (2020)
10. Müller, K.: Museums and virtuality. In: Parry, R. (ed.) Museums in a Aigital Age, pp. 295–305. Routledge, Abingdon Oxford (2013)
11. Bernier, R.: The uses of virtual museums: the French viewpoint. In: Sixth International Conference of Museums and the Web, Boston, Massachusetts USA, pp. 17–20 (2002)
12. Champion, E., Rahaman, H.: 3D digital heritage models as sustainable scholarly resources. Sustainability **11**, 1–8 (2019)
13. Müller, K.: Museums and virtuality. Curator Mus. J. **45**, 21–33 (2002)

14. Wazlawick, R.S., et al.: Providing more interactivity to virtual museums: a proposal for a VR authoring tool. Presence Teleoperators Virtual Environ. **10**, 647–656 (2001)
15. Petridis, P., et al.: Exploring and interacting with virtual museums. In: Figueiredo, A., Velho, G.L. (eds.): Proceedings of Computer Applications and Quantitative Methods in Archaeology (CAA), Tomar, Portugal, pp. 73–82 (2005)
16. Sylaiou, S., Mania, K., Paliokas, I., Killintzis, V., Liarokapis, F., Patias, P.: Exploring the effect of diverse technologies incorporated in virtual museums on visitors' perceived sense of presence. In: Intelligent Environments (Workshops), pp. 493–506 (2013)
17. Bekele, M., Champion, E.: Redefining mixed reality: user-reality-virtuality and virtual heritage perspectives. In: Haeusler, M., Schnabel, M.A., Fukuda, T. (eds.): 24th Annual Conference of the Association for Computer-Aided Architectural Design Research in Asia (CAADRIA 2019). CuminCAD, Wellington, New Zealand, pp. 675–68 (2019)

Virtual Museum 'Takeouts' and DIY Exhibitions–Augmented Reality Apps for Scholarship, Citizen Science and Public Engagement

Sandra Woolley[1]([⊠]) [ID], James Mitchell[1] [ID], Tim Collins[2] [ID], Richard Rhodes[1] [ID], Tendai Rukasha[1] [ID], Erlend Gehlken[3] [ID], Eugene Ch'ng[4] [ID], and Ashley Cooke[5]

[1] Keele University, Staffordshire, UK
s.i.woolley@keele.ac.uk
[2] Manchester Metropolitan University, Manchester, UK
[3] Goethe-Universität, Frankfurt am Main, Germany
[4] Nottingham Ningbo University, Ningbo, China
[5] National Museums Liverpool (World Museum), Liverpool, UK

Abstract. This paper presents an Augmented Reality (AR) project for the curation of virtual museum 'takeouts' and DIY exhibitions. The project's outputs include novel AR app technology demonstrators to support co-design with museum users and stakeholders - the goal being to create useful and easy-to-use AR apps for scholars, citizen scientists and the interested public.

The apps were designed for users to create, display, animate and interact with exhibitions of selected 3D artefacts that could, for example, reflect academic specialisms for sharing with fellow researchers, support curators in exhibition planning or enable friends and students to share eclectic favourites from museum visits. The overarching project ambition was to create AR apps to support research, engagement and education, and to enable interactive and personalized visualizations of individual artefacts as well as reconstructed forms. As presented in the paper, these forms are exemplified in the AR apps with 3D models of a cuneiform envelope and its tablet contents, viewable either as i) separate artefacts or ii) in their reconstructed enveloped form, with the AR apps enabling animated opening and 'X-ray views' of the contents within. In this way, the apps can enable users to visualize individual objects and reconstructions that could, for example, incorporate artefacts held in different museums.

Keywords: Augmented reality · Digital heritage · Virtual reconstruction

1 Introduction

Augmented Reality (AR) offers new and exciting opportunities to enrich museum and art gallery visits and provide additional interactions and experiences for visitors [1–4]. AR can also provide digital heritage visualization opportunities, for example, for archaeological finds [5] and reconstructed artefacts such as glass plates [6], as well as

© Springer Nature Switzerland AG 2021
M. Ioannides et al. (Eds.): EuroMed 2020, LNCS 12642, pp. 323–333, 2021.
https://doi.org/10.1007/978-3-030-73043-7_27

affording the potential for engaging educators and student learners in cultural heritage experiences [7].

Notable museum AR examples include Saltzburg's Museum of Celtic Heritage 'Speaking Celt' historical AR avatar [8], Cleveland's Museum of Art ArtLens AR app that provides enriched tour experiences of displayed artworks [9] and The Franklin Institute's AR app that enables visitors to interact with virtual 3D models of Terracotta Warriors [10]. These AR apps enrich the in-museum experiences of displayed artefacts [11, 12] but, like other heritage AR apps, they do not support interaction with artefacts that are not on display or enable the creation of virtual exhibitions. More broadly, amongst art and digital heritage AR apps, there is scope for improved personalization and better ways of revealing non-visible components and communicating artefact information [13].

The Virtual Museum 'Takeouts' and DIY Exhibitions project [14] evolved from The Virtual Cuneiform Tablet Reconstruction Project [15] whose original ambitions included support for virtual access to museum artefacts and the creation of tools to support artefact reconstruction [16] as exemplified by the virtual reconstruction of the Atrahasis cuneiform tablet [17–19]. The aims of the Virtual Museum 'Takeouts' and DIY Exhibitions project were (i) to create technology demonstrators that could supplement the co-design of useful and easy-to-use AR apps aimed at benefiting diverse user groups that include scholars, citizen scientists and the interested public, and (ii) to provide interactive, informative and personalized views of individual artefacts and virtual reconstructions. The creation of technology demonstrators was important because co-design improves technology outcomes [20] and functional technology demonstrators can support the process by helping to inspire ideas [21]. In addition, technology demonstrators are useful when some user groups may be unfamiliar with a new technology.

2   AR Apps for Museum 'Takeouts' and DIY Exhibitions

The requirements for the AR apps were to incorporate functionality to demonstrate:

- virtual presentations of museum artefacts that may or may not be on physical display,
- the collection and arrangement of virtual life-sized artefacts in augmented reality exhibitions,
- alternative point cloud and wire mesh views of artefacts for interest and for educational insights into the structure of 3D models,
- the optional display of artefact information,
- artefact rotation to provide all-around views,
- the option to display individual artefacts or to view them in their assembled or reconstructed forms.

2.1   3D-Model Acquisitions

The models for the AR apps were acquired in 2018 and 2019 from National Museums Liverpool (World Museum), UK using the Virtual Cuneiform Tablet Reconstruction Project photogrammetric turntable system [22] and an Einscan-SP 3D scanner with Discovery Pack. The models included a 'shabti' figurine and cuneiform tablets.

Shabtis are small funerary figurines that were placed in Egyptian tombs to act as servants for the deceased. The shabti scanned for use in the app is over 2,500 years old and was once owned by Florence Nightingale who spent several months in Egypt in 1849–50.

Cuneiform tablets are early written records from Mesopotamia, created by making impressions in clay tablets. The tablets scanned for the app included one with an accompanying envelope bearing cylinder seal impressions. This envelope originally secured a silver purchase recorded on a tablet within (which had been removed and the envelope resealed). The scanned cuneiform tablets are included in the collection of World Museum Liverpool tablets published in [23] and in the Cuneiform Digital Library Initiative (CDLI) database [24].

2.2 AR App Development

The Android AR app was developed using the Processing for Android AR Java library, which itself uses the Google ARCore library. The iPhone AR app was coded in Swift with Xcode using ARKit. The apps were tested in development by researchers and testers accessing pre-release versions in Google Play test track and the Apple App Store Test Pilot. Both apps require minimum device specifications; Android's ARCore, at the time of writing, requires Android 8.1 or later [25] and the iPhone app requires iOS11 and an A9 or later processor [26]. Example screenshots of the Android and iPhone apps are shown in Fig. 1.

ARKit and Swift for iOS

ARKit is Apple's library for iOS device augmented reality development, supporting motion tracking, surface detection and light estimation. It uses the smartphone's camera to identify and track features in the environment and estimate ambient light so that it can position and illuminate selected objects in the camera view of the environment. When running, ARKit extracts features from the camera images and builds a topographic map of the real world.

Xcode is Apple's iOS Operating System Integrated Development Environment (IDE) [27]. Xcode (IDE) version 11.7 (11E801a) was used to create the prototype application with Swift being the predominant coding language. The app was developed using SwiftUI (iOS 13). This allows for the building of user interfaces for any Apple device using just one set of tools and APIs

ARCore and Processing for Android

ARCore [28] is Google's library for Android smartphone augmented reality development, supporting motion tracking, surface detection and light estimation. It uses the smartphone's camera to identify and track features in the environment and estimate ambient light so that it can position and illuminate selected objects in the camera view of the environment. When running, ARCore extracts features from the camera images and builds a 3D map of the real world. A collection of features located on a horizontal or vertical plane is known as a 'trackable' and can have virtual objects attached to it using an 'anchor'. The Android AR app was created using 'Processing for Android'

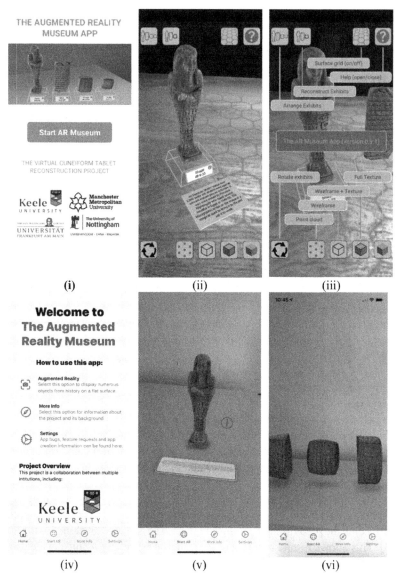

Fig. 1. Android and iPhone AR app screen examples. For Android: (i) initial Android splash screen, (ii) a positioned shabti and (iii) help menu explaining interface buttons. Below for iPhone: (iv) the splash screen, (vi) positioned shabti artefact with information display ON and (v) a screenshot from the opening/closing animation of the cuneiform envelope that reveals the cuneiform tablet within.

[29] which enables the creation of Processing 'sketch' programs for Android devices and includes support for 'AR in Processing' [30] via the ARCore library.

Processing for Android has an advantage over development using Android Studio in terms of ease-of-use and the simplicity of the code. A rudimentary demonstration AR

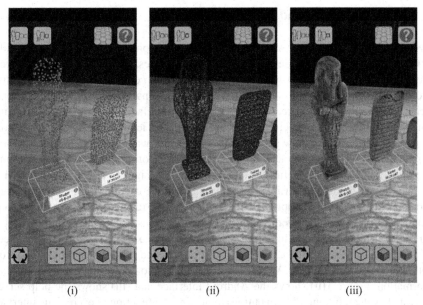

| (i) | (ii) | (iii) |

Fig. 2. 3D model views. (i) low-fidelity point cloud view, (ii) wire mesh view and (iii) 3D photographically rendered view.

Processing app can be produced using less than 30 lines of code whereas an equivalent Android Studio project would require the creation and navigation of a folder structure containing 50 or more different files. However, the ease of getting started in Processing for Android should not trivialize the coding required of full app development. At the time of writing, the current version of the AR Museum app comprises six files that add up to approximately 1200 lines of code (much of which is required for the loading and interpretation of 3D object files).

There are also limitations to the Processing for Android approach; not all of the features of the ARCore library are exposed to programmers by the Processing interface. For example, depth mapping, augmented images and cloud anchors [28] cannot (at the time of writing) be utilised in Processing. Additionally, the multiple 'activities' made available by Android Studio are not available in Processing for Android. For example, implementation of an initial 2D splash screen could be easily achieved in Android Studio by creating a new activity. In Processing, however, an overlay is needed to obscure the main activity. The Processing splash screen screenshot is shown in Fig. 1(i).

To enhance the functionality of the app, user interface control buttons overlaying the 3D display were added. No library functions for this are provided. Normally, implementing a 2D overlay on a 3D view in Processing would simply require the 'camera' to be placed in its default position meaning a 3D coordinate of $(x, y, 0)$ would correspond to a screen coordinate of (x, y); then, the controls can be drawn using standard 2D graphics functions. When using the AR library, however, camera positioning is disabled so a lower level approach was required. Instead of utilizing Processing's camera placement function, the OpenGL projection matrix coefficients were directly reset to achieve the same effect.

3   Design Decisions and View Options

Several design decisions were required during app development. For example, Android's ARCore library enables the detection of *any* flat surfaces, which would allow objects to be impossibly attached to walls or suspended from ceilings. To simplify the surface detection process, only horizontal surface detections were permitted. Additional decisions were required to create a functional user interface. This was achieved using intuitive icon designs based on past research [16]. The icons were placed away from the centre of the camera view and artefact information was placed so that it remained in view of its ON/OFF control. Improving the usability of user experience of AR apps [31] is an important goal of further research and co-design. In addition to improving the interface to the objects, it is also important to guide users in the basics of getting started with the use of AR apps. For example, making recommendations on ambient light levels, smartphone movement and surface selections because dim lighting, rapid camera movement and smooth featureless surfaces all make surfaces difficult to detect.

As shown in Fig. 1, artefacts were placed on labelled plinths with clickable information '*i*' buttons in both the Android and iPhone apps to toggle the display of artefact information. Figure 1(ii) shows the Android interface and (iii) shows the help screen (activated by the top right '?' help button) indicating the function of each of the interface buttons.

3.1   3D Model Views

One of the education goals of the apps included insights about the underpinning 3D graphics of virtual objects. For this purpose, we implemented alternative artefact view options to enable users to see low-resolution point cloud views of models and wire mesh views, as well as photographically rendered views, as shown in Fig. 2.

For the iPhone AR app, which did not implicitly support point cloud and mesh views of objects, 3D models were created comprising small 3D sphere 'points' and meshes made from narrow cylinder 'wires', respectively, to give the appearance of the views. An additional supporting webpage multi-view interface [32, 33] was also created for viewing from desktop computers and other devices, as shown in Fig. 3. The web page also provides links to 3D file downloads for artefact models as both.ply and.stl formats and in low- and medium-resolutions, for example, for printing artefacts at different sizes as shown by the 3D printed shabti models in Fig. 4. Models were also made available for the cuneiform tablet [32].

3.2   Exhibition Views and Interactions

As shown in the example screenshots in Fig. 5, users can (i) arrange artefacts on detected surfaces (with or without information display) and (ii) select an automated positioning format to arrange artefacts in line with each other.

The apps also support interaction with the artefacts, for example, with a toggle artefact "rotate" function in the Android app.

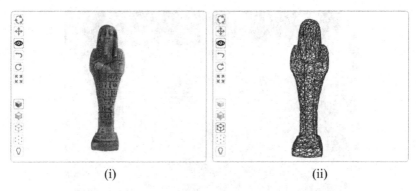

(i)   (ii)

Fig. 3. Interactive desktop browser interface with 3D multi-view options [33].

Fig. 4. 3D prints of the shabti figurine. Transparent clear resin prints at full and reduced sizes.

3.3 Individual and Reconstructed Artefact Views

Fragmented artefacts can be separated within collections or between museum collections that may be many kilometres apart [17]. For example, joining pieces of cuneiform tablets have been found separated by 1,000 kilometres, in the British Museum and the Musée d'Art et d'Histoire in Geneva [18, 19]. AR apps can enable the viewing of individual fragmented or component artefacts or their constructed forms. For example, as shown in Fig. 6, cuneiform envelopes and their tablet contents can be shown separately or assembled with the contents (as it would have originally been) inside the envelope. In Fig. 6 (i) the iPhone app animation opens and closes the envelope to reveal the contents, in (ii) the Android app, on close inspection, reveals the enveloped contents to the user.

(i)

(ii)

Fig. 5. Views of eclectic Android app exhibition arrangements (i) user-positioned artefacts with information display ON and background grid OFF and (ii) Exhibits viewed with automatic line-up ON, information display OFF and background grid ON.

4   Opportunities and Future Development

4.1   Opportunities

3D models of artefacts offer new opportunities for curators in museum exhibition planning and design. Models provide accurate data for the arrangement of artefacts within the fixed space of a showcase, giving a greater visual impression before installation, conceivably reducing the need for last-minute changes in the days before opening. This is of particular advantage when creating exhibitions that bring together artefacts from numerous institutions and private collections. There is a greater call on museums to extend the legacy of short-lived temporary exhibitions beyond the usual publication of a catalogue. 3D models could be used to enhance a virtual tour of the gallery with inscribed artefacts such as cuneiform and shabtis, offering greater intellectual stimulation for virtual visitors.

(i)   (ii)

Fig. 6. Reconstructed views showing animated and 'X-ray' inside views, respectively for the cuneiform tablet envelope contents in (i) the iPhone AR app and (ii) the Android AR app.

4.2 Future Development

The apps and their 3D models make demands of smartphone storage space and, in the current apps, the example models are downloaded as part of the app installation. Ideally, the app and models would be separate downloads and new models would be downloadable individually when selected. This would speed up updates to the app and allow for new models to be downloaded more efficiently. In museum contexts this could be via a local Wi-Fi service to reduce the burden on mobile data transfer limits.

In physical exhibition spaces, QR codes could reveal the details and locations of available AR 'takeout' artefacts, enable easy selection and download, and provide links to more information and multimedia resources. To engage and incentivize visitors, the app could support social media sharing of artefacts, and user achievements could be recognised for artefact collection milestones.

Achieving the functionality of the AR app with a minimal and uncluttered interface was one of the main challenges of the app development. Further work and co-design with different users and stakeholder groups is needed to evolve the apps from technology demonstrators to fully functioning apps. Ideally, the apps would be supported by infrastructure and data repositories to enable the download of 3D artefacts at appropriate scale and resolution, and in suitable formats. Ideally, the apps would also support language options, for example, from Google Translate, so that exhibit information displays could be shown in the user's chosen language. A further enhancement to this would include the option for text to speech delivery of the information.

Acknowledgements. The development of the app was supported by Keele University Faculty of Science Awards. The authors thank Ash Leake, from the School of Computing and Mathematics at Keele University, for the 3D printing of artefacts. The authors also wish to thank National Museums Liverpool for permissions and support in achieving the acquisitions and apps.

References

1. Ding, M.: Augmented reality in museums. Mus. Augmented Reality Collect. Essays Arts Manage. Technol. Lab. 1–15 (2017)
2. Morozova, A.: How to use augmented reality in museums: examples and use cases. https://jasoren.com/how-to-use-augmented-reality-in-museums-examples-and-use-cases/. Accessed 13 Sep 2020
3. González Vargas, J.C., Fabregat, R., Carrillo-Ramos, A., Jové, T.: Survey: using augmented reality to improve learning motivation in cultural heritage studies. Appl. Sci. **10**(3), 897 (2020)
4. Challenor, J., Ma, M.: A review of augmented reality applications for history education and heritage visualisation. Multi. Technol. Interact. **3**(2), 39 (2019)
5. Fernández-Palacios, B.J., Rizzi, A., Nex, F.: Augmented reality for archaeological finds. In: Euro-Mediterranean Conference, pp. 181–190. Springer, Berlin, Heidelberg October 2012
6. Abate, A.F., et al.: An augmented reality mobile app for Museums: virtual restoration of a plate of glass. In: Ioannides, M., et al. (eds.) EuroMed 2018. LNCS, vol. 11196, pp. 539–547. Springer, Cham (2018). https://doi.org/10.1007/978-3-030-01762-0_47
7. Tzima, S., Styliaras, G., Bassounas, A.: Augmented reality applications in education: teachers point of view. Educ. Sci. **9**(2), 99 (2019)
8. Breuss-Schneeweis, P.: The speaking celt": augmented reality avatars guide through a museum - case study. In Proceedings of the ACM International Joint Conference on Pervasive and Ubiquitous Computing: Adjunct, pp. 1484–1491 (2016)
9. Alexander, J.: Gallery one at the cleveland museum of art. curator: Mus. J. **57**(3), 347–362 (2014)
10. Terracotta Warriors meet augmented reality at The Franklin Institute. https://www.wikitude.com/showcase/terracotta-warriors-augmented-reality-at-the-franklin-institute/. Accessed 13 Sep 2020
11. Serravalle, F., Ferraris, A., Vrontis, D., Thrassou, A., Christofi, M.: Augmented reality in the tourism industry: a multi-stakeholder analysis of museums. Tourism Manage. Perspect. **32**, (2019)
12. Damala, A., Stojanovic, N., Schuchert, T., Moragues, J., Cabrera, A., Gilleade, K.: Adaptive augmented reality for cultural heritage: ARtSENSE project. In: Ioannides, M., Fritsch, D., Leissner, J., Davies, R., Remondino, F., Caffo, R. (eds.) EuroMed 2012. LNCS, vol. 7616, pp. 746–755. Springer, Heidelberg (2012). https://doi.org/10.1007/978-3-642-34234-9_79
13. Čopič Pucihar, K., Kljun, M.: ART for art: augmented reality taxonomy for art and cultural heritage. In: Geroimenko, V. (ed.) Augmented Reality Art. SSCC, pp. 73–94. Springer, Cham (2018). https://doi.org/10.1007/978-3-319-69932-5_3
14. The augmented reality museum app homepage. https://virtualcuneiform.org/ARMuseum.html. Accessed 13 Sep 2020
15. The Virtual Cuneiform Tablet Reconstruction Project homepage. https://virtualcuneiform.org/index.html. Accessed 13 Sep 2020
16. Woolley, S.I., et al.: A collaborative artefact reconstruction environment. In: Proceedings of the British HCI Conference. BCS. Sunderland, UK, 3rd–6th July (2017)

17. Woolley, S.I., Gehlken, E., Ch'ng, E., Collins, T.: Virtual archaeology: how we achieved the first long-distance reconstruction of a cultural artefact, The Conversation, UK (Art and Culture), 28 Febuary 2018. https://theconversation.com/virtual-archaeology-how-we-achieved-the-first-long-distance-reconstruction-of-a-cultural-artefact-91725. Accessed 2 Sep 2020
18. Gehlken, E., et al.: Searching the past in the future - joining cuneiform tablet fragments in virtual collections, 63rd Rencontre Assyriologique Internationale (2017)
19. Collins, T., Woolley, S., Gehlken, E., Ch'ng, E.: Computational aspects of model acquisition and join geometry for the virtual reconstruction of the Atrahasis cuneiform tablet. In: 23rd International Conference on Virtual System & Multimedia (VSMM), pp. 1–6 (2017)
20. Steen, M., Manschot, M., De Koning, N.: Benefits of co-design in service design projects. Int. J. Des. **5**(2) (2011)
21. Ciolfi, L., et al.: Articulating co-design in museums: reflections on two participatory processes. In: Proceedings of the 19th ACM Conference on Computer-Supported Cooperative Work & Social Computing, pp. 13–25 (2016)
22. Collins, T., Woolley, S.I., Gehlken, E., Ch'ng, E.: Automated low-cost photogrammetric acquisition of 3D models from small form-factor artefacts. Electronics, **8**(12), 1441 (2019)
23. Cripps, E.L.: Sargonic and presargonic texts in the World Museum Liverpool. Archaeopress (2010)
24. Cripps, E.L.: Short history of the cuneiform collection in the World Museum Liverpool. https://cdli.ucla.edu/collections/liverpool/liverpool_intro.pdf. Accessed 13 Sep 2020
25. ARCore supported devices. https://developers.google.com/ar/discover/supported-devices. Accessed 13 Sep 2020
26. Apple Augmented Reality. https://www.apple.com/uk/augmented-reality/. Accessed 2020
27. Apple, 2020. Xcode - Apple Developer Apple Developer. https://developer.apple.com/xcode/. Accessed 14 Sep 2020
28. ARCore Overview. https://developers.google.com/ar/discover. Accessed 13 Sep 2020
29. Processing for Android. https://android.processing.org/index.html. Accessed 13 Sep 2020
30. https://android.processing.org/tutorials/ar_intro/index.html. Accessed 13 Sep 2020
31. Dey, A., Billinghurst, M., Lindeman, R.W., Swan, J.: A systematic review of 10 years of augmented reality usability studies: 2005 to 2014. Front. Robot. AI **5**, 37 (2018)
32. D interactive cuneiform tablet. https://virtualcuneiform.org/tellohModels.html. Accessed 13 Sep 2020
33. D interactive shabti model. https://virtualcuneiform.org/shabtiModels.htm. Accessed 13 Sep 2020

EPANASTASIS-1821: Designing an Immersive Virtual Museum for the Revival of Historical Events of the Greek Revolution

Georgia Georgiou$^{(\boxtimes)}$ ⓘD, Eleftherios Anastasovitis ⓘD, Spiros Nikolopoulos ⓘD, and Ioannis Kompatsiaris ⓘD

Centre for Research and Technology Hellas, 6th Km Charilaou-Thermi Rd., 57001 Thermi, Thessaloniki, Greece
{georgiou_georgia,anastasovitis,nikolopo,ikom}@iti.gr

Abstract. Recent technological advances have greatly affected the museum practice, introducing new and innovative technological solutions for the creation of more interactive, multisensory and experiential museum exhibitions. Virtual reality applications allow museums' visitors to be fully immersed in interactive adventures and consequently, many museums are focusing their digital strategy on that direction. Meanwhile, the use of serious games technology in museum environments set new perspectives in the educational and the entertaining impact of museums' experiences. This contribution describes the principles and the guidelines that defined the digital museological design process of the Virtual Museum EPANASTASIS-1821, the development of which is based on the technologies of virtual reality and serious games. The paper indicates how the use of virtual reality and serious games in exhibition design can strengthen designers' creativity, enhance the interpretation dynamic of the exhibition and the memorization potential and lastly, create memorable museum experiences.

Keywords: Virtual museum · Digital museology · Exhibition design · Virtual reality · Immersive technologies

1 Introduction

In the era of digital transformation, Cultural Heritage (CH) is a representative sector where the cutting-edge technological achievements are applied, offering innovative solutions to their visitors, as well as to CH professionals. Interdisciplinary cooperation is imperative during this evolutionary process. Historians, archivists and museologists need to actively get involved in the creative team for the design and implementation of a virtual museum that communicates a specific historical period, especially when it introduces new types of full-immersive virtual experiences, for better understanding and revival of the past.

Virtual museums are a predominant tendency of contemporary museum practice. Although, there is not a generally accepted definition for virtual museums, they can be characterized as the digital counterparts of the physical museums, as their development

© Springer Nature Switzerland AG 2021
M. Ioannides et al. (Eds.): EuroMed 2020, LNCS 12642, pp. 334–345, 2021.
https://doi.org/10.1007/978-3-030-73043-7_28

is also based on a collection of artefacts, with the mission to be communicated to an audience with the purpose of both knowledge and entertainment. One commonly used definition for virtual museums is that given by Virtual Museum Transnational Network, which describes a virtual museum as "a digital entity that draws on the characteristics of a museum, in order to complement, enhance, or augment the museum experience through personalization, interactivity and richness of content" [1]. Apart from the richness of the exhibiting material virtual museums may display, they offer at least two more potentials: firstly, their virtual exhibition space can host a collection of artefacts that come from an unlimited source of institutions, museums and exhibition spaces from all over the world. Secondly, virtual museums are not a static entity, they are continuously evolving, as they adapt to the technological developments in information communication [2]. This is a valuable asset for the museum curator, as it gives him flexibility and the freedom to apply his creativity in the exhibition design process, through innovative exhibition solutions and the embodiment of hi-tech representation means.

The evolution of creative industries such as virtual reality and videogames has a universal effect in every section of daily life. From the obsolete two-dimensional (2D) digital games in early 90's, nowadays the increased level of player's immersion into three-dimensional (3D) virtual environments offers breathtaking experiences [3, 4]. By adding and enhancing the educational perspective, a game is converted into a serious one (SG), which can simultaneously be an entertaining and an interpretive tool [5–7]. The better the design of such an application, the more effective it is [8, 9]. Cultural Heritage and History is an inexhaustible source that provides interesting and meaningful stories for the creation of game scenarios for digital applications.

Meanwhile, during the last years, Greek cultural and educational institutions are getting prepared for the celebration of the 200 years of the Greek revolution war against the Ottomans, which led to the independence of part of the Greek territory from the Ottoman empire and the establishment of Greece as independent, sovereign state. In 1821, after almost 400 years under the Ottoman rule, Greek revolutionaries waged war against the Ottoman Empire vindicating their independence. Since then, Independence Day is celebrated every year on March 25th. In 2021, Greeks will celebrate the 200 years of the beginning of the war that set the foundation for the formation of modern Greece. Nowadays, countless museums all over Greece hold cultural assets from the period of Greek revolution war. Their collections include weapons, paintings, drawings, flags, maps, archives, among others. The plurality and diversity of the available cultural material offer an exhaustible source for digital museology for the production of virtual applications.

In this contribution we present the design of *EPANASTASIS-1821*; a full-immersive virtual museum for the revival of historical events of the Revolution, under the prism of digital museology. In section two the context of museology and the challenges of digital museology are depicted. Section three describes the detailed museology plan of the experiential virtual museum, in full alignment with the proposed immersive technologies of virtual reality and serious games. An extended discussion for the impact of well-designed and full-immersive virtual experiences for better understanding and communication of History and Cultural Heritage takes place in section four, while in the last section the conclusion and future work are being presented.

2   Related Work

2.1   Cultural Heritage in the Digital Era

CH becomes gradually more digital and virtual. Nowadays, advanced technological tools are being widely used in the cultural sector for a variety of purposes. In archaeology, virtual reconstructions of archeological sites with the use of innovative technological tools (Virtual Archaeology) help the researchers to study, analyze, better understand, document and interpret their findings, and often make them accessible to the public [10].

In the field of museology, technology shares a great merit of nowadays museums' publicity. Museums develop their digital strategy according to technological advances, in order to retain their audience's interest and engage new visitors, especially among the younger generations. Museum professionals, and their multidisciplinary colleagues take advantage of the technology achievements nearly in every aspect of the cultural management and museum function. Designers create virtual reconstructions of cultural assets for the purposes of documentation, study and presentation. Museums develop productions incorporating AR, VR, MR technologies to support their educational programs and the exhibition design. Museum professionals exploit the technological advances to make cultural heritage accessible, through open databases and online resources or to enhance the accessibility by all, breaking the barriers of age, distance and physical disabilities.

One aspect of how technology is used in museum practice is that of the exhibits' presentation. In order to tell the story of Mytilene Treasure, a group of precious Byzantine objects, a multidisciplinary collaboration at the Byzantine and Christian Museum of Athens displayed holograms inside showcases side by side with the real artefacts, creating intentionally an engaging blurring of reality, which involves the visitor into a sensory interaction with the objects. The designers achieved, with the use of holograms, their intentions to enhance the scenography and the dramaturgy of the exhibition, to engage the visitors' attention, to keep them engaged during the narration, to exacerbate their senses and enhance the memorization of the museum experience [11].

Moreover, one aspect of digital museology, not very well known, is the use of technological tools borrowed by architecture and urban design in the exhibition design phase. Having in mind that spatial layout influences the museum experience, museum experts turned their interest on how to study visitors' flow inside the museum space and evaluate their interaction with the exhibition plan. Space Syntax is a tool that uses graphic data to analyze the spatial behavior of buildings, such as museums. CH professionals use it to study their museum's visitors' space–use patterns and evaluate the correlation developed between spatial layout and museum experience [12].

2.2   Museums in the Virtual Era

However digital museology goes a step further and with the help of technological advances, museums can transfer visitors in space and time or virtually transfer them inside their own museum space. Thus, virtual tours, virtual exhibitions and virtual museums have overwhelmed the internet and consequently, a wide amount of literature resources deal with the aspects of theory, the practices, the potentials and the development of the current virtualization of the cultural heritage [13]. Although the term *virtual museum* has become an all-encompassing term [14], referring to all the aforementioned practices of museums' virtuality, in this paper is discussed the case of the virtual museums that are created with no physical counterparts and they embody digital material and storytelling. *MEDWINET* is a virtual museum and edutainment application that narrates the story of the wine trade in the Eastern Mediterranean areas in ancient times. The application was designed for the Museum of Ancient Agora of Athens, which is housed in the Attalos Stoa. Its development was based on a group of ancient amphorae, wine trade vessels, that were digitized and reconstructed as 3d models. The developers created a virtual museum, which incorporates a virtual museum environment, an exhibition plan, the exhibition material of the vases and storytelling [15].

Although virtual museums are, even in their simple form, appealing and engaging, digital museology is continuously working towards more interactive potentials. In full alignment with current digital museology's direction, the research questions of the suggested museology design of VM *EPANASTASIS-1821* are:

Q1: How virtual museums can be more participatory, more edutaining, more interactive and more experience-oriented?

Q2: How virtual museums can offer a museum experience that is both educational and experiential?

Virtual museum *EPANASTASIS-1821* ventures towards that direction, by implementing a three-goal strategy (see Fig. 1). In VM *EPANASTASIS-1821*, the visitor can: a) learn about the history of the Greek revolution war, through the exhibits and the interpretation material, b) experience the historical environment through his engagement in full-immersive experiences and c) act, as a historical figure, in accomplishing missions in games, developed on the basis of famous paintings.

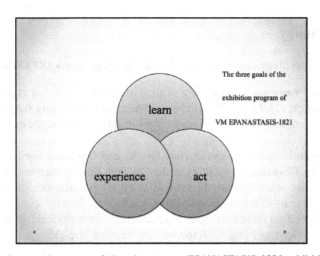

Fig. 1. The three-goal strategy of virtual museums *EPANASTASIS-1821* exhibition program.

2.3 Virtual Museum *EPANASTASIS-1821*

The virtual museum *EPANASTASIS-1821* is being created from scratch, with no given exhibition material or exhibition program. Its development followed the exhibition planning process of a physical museum, nonetheless this is adjusted to the needs, restrictions and requirements of the virtual museum space. Yet the advantages of creating a museum for a virtual space are numerous and they have all been taken into consideration in the development process.

Before proceeding to the development process, the preliminary issues the exhibition design must address are in short [16]; to define the purpose of the museum exhibition, to specify the exhibition's target visitors, to whom intend to communicate its story, and to delineate the most suitable means of communicating this story to its audience, that will keep it engaged throughout the whole course of the exhibition program. The answers to these questions formulated the concept idea of the Virtual Museum *EPANASTASIS-1821*.

The purpose of the virtual museum *EPANASTASIS-1821* is to communicate important events of the Greek Revolution and to highlight aspects and personalities of the Nation's revolution, through the exhibition of a variety of digitised archival material, books and artistic representations, like paintings. The museum will be accessible by the general public and aims, through the use of innovative educational tools of high-immersion virtual reality (full-immersive) and serious games, to enhance the user's experience and to create a more effective understanding of the impact these events had on people, the evolution of the Greek state and its influence in the European world.

A meaningful exhibition starts with a striking idea, but the effectiveness of the exhibition depends on how the story is told. It is the thematic framework and the exhibition means the museum uses to narrate the story that keep the audience engaged. In Virtual Museum *EPANASTASIS-1821*, the exhibition design was structured on the basis of three verbs/goals: learn- experience - act.

3 Methodology

3.1 Digital Museology Design of the Virtual Museum *EPANASTASIS-1821*

The Thematic Framework. The story of the Greek revolution war is not easy to be narrated in a single exhibition. Thus, it became necessary to identify the three thematic objectives that reflected the three primary stages of information in the exhibition plan:

- The pre-revolution thematic circle. How Greeks and Ottomans lived in Rum Millet (the Orthodox Christian Community of the Ottoman Empire) before the revolution?
- The circle of the war. What are the main military and political facts that describe the story of the 9 years of the Greek revolution war?
- The after-revolution thematic circle. What are the main historical topics of the years after the war (Governor Ioannis Kapodistrias' thematic circle)?

This core thematic framework is structured in chronological period of about 9 years (1821−1830), yet it is clustered by an array of sub-themes that support the exhibition meaning and thus, help the audience acquire a broad but comprehensive perception of the historical period of the Greek independence war. To sum up, the exhibition program of museum *EPANASTASIS-1821* has 8 main thematic units with their sub-themes (see Fig. 2). On the whole, the structure of the thematic framework, with its main themes and sub-themes, is designated on the basis of two principles: thematic autonomy, so each thematic unity has its own meaning that can be acquired separately, which gives the user the flexibility to skip thematic units that is not interested in, and continuous narration flow, which helps visitor understand the sequence of the historical events.

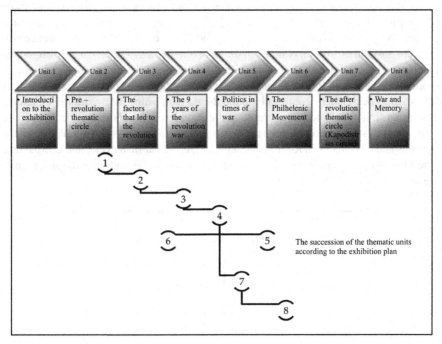

Fig. 2. The core thematic structure of virtual Museum *EPANASTASIS-1821* with the succession of the thematic units.

Experience the Exhibition. Creating a virtual museum environment where the visitor is able to experience history and not only view the exhibits, was one of the primary goals of VM *EPANASTASIS-1821*. This aim is addressed with a twofold museological option. The first refers to the architectural and spatial design of the exhibition plan and the second to the creation of full - immersive virtual reality experiences.

VM *EPANASTASIS-1821* used an existing historical building as a basic form to design the virtual museum space. The historical building of the *Ellinomouseio* in Zagora of Pelion, in Thessaly, which used to function as a school during 18th and 19th century and is famous now as the *School of Rigas Feraios*, because this renown writer of Greek Enlightenment and pioneer of the Greek revolution used to study there as a child, was digitised and 3d modelled. The building is characteristic of the traditional architecture of the area in the Ottoman period. The out walls and the general architecture plan were transformed into the virtual space, so when the visitor starts his tour in the museum, he gets the feeling of entering a historical building. This feeling is very common to the Greek museum visitors, as many historical buildings have gone under adaptive reuse, so as to host historical museum collections. Consequently, the first level of engagement has been achieved by connecting the visitor with something familiar.

In the exhibition design process, the possibilities offered by the virtual reality design tools were fully exploited, so as the inner exhibition space to be adapted to and support the objectives and the philosophy of the museological plan. Taking into consideration that the museum space is being experimented and influences the subjective perception and interpretation of the exhibition meaning [17], in the inner space of the adapted virtual building, the partitions walls were removed, and a free of stable hindrances space was formed to host the exhibition plan. Each of the seven thematic units, that are designed to be displayed in the two floors of the museum space (the eighth thematic unit is displayed outside the virtual building, in an outdoor environment), has its own contextual display plan, which is designated accordingly to the thematic meaning. The exhibition meaning works as an archetypal and it is mirrored in the exhibition plan. For instance, the second thematic unit, that refers to the pre-revolution period and narrates the mutual life of the Ottomans and the Greeks in Rum Millet, symbolizes a historical cycle, and is organized in the plan of cycle, where the visitor can stand in the center and view the sub-themes been displayed around him (see Fig. 3).

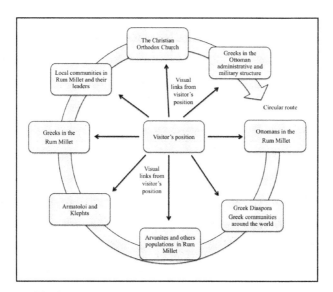

Fig. 3. The exhibition design of the second thematic unit.

On the exhibit level, the museum offers the visitors two options for experimental interaction with the digitised artefacts. Firstly, the visitor is invited to touch and interact with certain exhibits, as archive material or weapons. Furthermore, selected exhibits will trigger full immersive experiences, transferring the user in place and time, where he could experience a historical environment. As an example, in the full-immersive experience

"The captain's cabin" the visitor will experience the environment of a captain's cabin, and while sitting in his office, he will be able to interact with a selected number of archives, which are thematically related to naval history.

The Active Visitor. In virtual museum EPANASTASIS-1821 the visitor has an active role that is not limited to his interaction with the artefacts. The virtual museum is embedding serious games, making the museum experience more participatory, experiential and edutaining. Selected paintings, as Nikiforos Lytras painting "Kanaris Burning the Turkish Flagship" (1832–1927)[1] will trigger a full-immersive game, where the user will have a mission related to the historical event of the painting, for example to be the one who sets the Turkish ship on fire. Thus, the visitor becomes the protagonist of the story, he is transferred in an artificial historical environment and he is invited to be part of the story, to act himself, or more specifically, to revolutionize.

3.2 Technologies

For the implementation of the aforementioned museology plan for the virtual museum of *EPANASTASIS-1821*, various cutting-edge technologies from the sector of creative industry and applied informatics will be used.

Content Creation. The 3D representations of the exhibits and artifacts of the virtual museum that are not digitized will be created from scratch using various techniques such as polygon, revolution, and Boolean modeling. The *Cinema4D* software package by *Maxon* [18], will be used for the accurate design of 3D models according to blueprints and real images from physical exhibitions. In combination with the open-source image editor *GIMP* [19], the photorealism will be succeeded through *UV-mapping* and *baking* techniques for texturing and materials. In the same way, the selected paintings that represent historical events from the Greek War for Independence will gain their third dimension and will take their place into the exhibition. Regarding the 3D animation that will be embedded on *FBX* file format, the *rigging and bones* procedure of *Cinema4D* will be applied. Furthermore, for the needs of 3D character animation, the use of *Smartsuit Pro* motion capture system by *ROKOKO* [20] is the most suitable solution.

Game Platform. The defined scenarios for the user's navigation in the virtual museum and in full-immersive experiences will be developed in a game platform that supports the generated content and is compatible with advanced virtual reality equipment. *Unity* [21] game engine will be the basis for the virtual environmental designs, not only for the virtual museum, but also for the virtual places that battles and battleships will take place. All interactions between the user and virtual cosmos' elements will be scripted in *C#* and *JavaScript* languages. Moreover, the addition of physics, dynamics and visual effects in Unity will increase the feeling of presence for the player in the designed 3D virtual environments.

---

[1] https://commons.wikimedia.org/wiki/File:Lytras-nikiforos-pyrpolisi-tourkikis-navarhidas-apo-kanari.jpeg.

Virtual Reality. User's immersion is a crucial factor for the virtual museum of *EPANAS-TASIS-1821*. The player needs to be convinced that is present in the virtual environment, with most of the senses. The more physical the user interacts, the more immersive the player feels. In this direction, *Oculus Rift S* Head Mounted Display *with touch controllers 2nd generation* offers the higher level of immersion [22]. This combination of virtual reality equipment provides a resolution of 1280×1440 pixels per eye with a refresh rate of 80 Hz, and simulates the movements of human's hand up to the level of the fingers. Furthermore, *Oculus Rift S* is fully compatible with *Unity* game engine and can be obtained at an affordable price.

4 Discussion

During the first months of the coronavirus pandemic, when almost all the cultural institutions around the world were closed, according to *ICOM*'s survey "*Museums, Museum professionals and COVID-19: survey results*" [23] museums reconsidered their digital strategy and made efforts to enhance their digital activities, in order to maintain their visitors. Under these circumstances, that demand social distancing and remote, more personalized experiences, virtual museums set the new perspectives of contemporary digital museology. What is expected is that museums will turn their focus on their digital identity and they will implement new strategies to retain public accessibility to their collections and their social activities, through virtual solutions. The operation of virtual exhibitions and programs inside the museum's walls, that can function remotely and as more personalized user experiences, is a future potential to address the current situation.

The development process of virtual museum *EPANASTASIS-1821* made clear the distinctive differences between digital and virtual museums. Given that there is not a defined and widely accepted definition for virtual museums, what is considered to be a virtual museum varies from a presentation of digitised material of its collection in a museum's website to the creation of a realistic museum space, where the users, with the use of hi-tech hardware equipment, feel as if they are inside the museum, staring at the real artefacts. In this paper, a line is drawn between the two terms. The term virtual museum is considered to reflect an immersive experience in a three-dimensional virtual world, that can both be reconstructed by an existing physical space or be a newly created one. In any case, a virtual museum experience, as it is applied in the design process of VM *EPANASTASIS-1821*, requires interaction with space and objects and multi-sensory involvement in experiential activities.

One of the most important assets of the virtual museums is the ability of virtual space to concentrate and display digitised material originated from an unlimited amount of resources. Although, it is beyond doubt that in virtual exhibitions the artefacts lose in terms of authenticity, no matter how realistic the virtual exhibit looks, it is of great significance that what is lost in authenticity, it may be compensated in terms of plurality. In VM *EPANASTASIS-1821* a consolidated museological narrative of the story was structured in a large number of exhibits that originate from about twelve different cultural institutions, that include museums, archives, libraries and galleries. The practice of displaying artefacts from different sources, as in temporary exhibitions, enhance the correlation of the artefacts and the interpretation process, strengthens the exhibition's dynamic and breaks down the limitations of distance, as it gives visitors the ability to view artefacts that may never see in real.

The key aspect in the philosophy of VM *EPANASTASIS-1821* is the way it answers to the initial questions of its conception of how the story of the Greek revolution war will be narrated in a conceivable, interactive and experiential way. In VM *EPANASTASIS -1821*, the answer to this question is expressed with three goals: learn – experience – act. The visitor is invited to learn the history of Greek revolution through a consolidated museological narration, to experience the museum's story by interacting with the virtual space and the virtual exhibits and finally, to act or, as it may be better to say, revolutionize through his engagement in gamified full immersive virtual experiences. The conjunction of these three factors is what characterizes the VM *EPANASTASIS 1821* as experiential and differentiates it from digital museums.

5   Conclusion and Future Work

The purpose of this contribution is to present the implementation of cutting-edge technology in the virtual design process of VM *EPANASTASIS-1821*. With the description of the museological program, the current potentials of digital museology are highlighted, as also the contribution of the technologies of virtual reality and serious games in the production of engaging full-immersive museum exhibitions. Even if the development of the museum is still in progress, this paper is an opportunity to recall the principles and the guidelines that defined the research team's vision of an innovative virtual museum. It became clear that the exploitation of advanced technology in museum practice reflects the fundamental shift of current museology from object-oriented exhibitions to experience-oriented ones. This paper aims to outline the framework of digitization, virtualization and gamification of museums today and their impact to the creation of more participatory, interactive and experiential museum experiences. With the description of the methodology adopted in the development phase of the virtual museum, this contribution examines the aspects of virtual space management and of the exhibition design, the correlation of which determines the perception of the museum meaning.

Above all, this contribution indicates the potentials of the embodiment of serious games in a virtual museum environment, which could, in a nutshell, redefine the way people experience virtual museums of the future. The further development of the museum and the subsequent evaluation of its performance, will give the opportunity to reconsider the principles and the values of narrating a historical issue in a virtual gamified museum environment. For this reason, VM *EPANASTASIS-1821* will be presented in various of the collaborating cultural institutions, in order the research team to evaluate its effectiveness and usability.

Acknowledgements. The project *EPANASTASIS-1821*: *"Communication and Promotion of Revival of Historical Events of the Revolution through Virtual Reality-1821"* is supported by the *Hellenic Foundation for Research and Innovation* (H.F.R.I.) under the First Call for H.F.R.I. "Science and Society" - "200 years since the Greek Revolution" (Project Number: 134) (http://www.epanastasis1821.gr/).

References

1. V-MUST Homepage. http://www.v-must.net/. Accessed 15 Sep 2020
2. Schweibenz, W.: The virtual museum: an overview of its origins, concepts, and terminology. Mus. Rev. **4** (1), 1–29 (2019)
3. Anastasovitis, E., Roumeliotis, M.: Virtual museum for the Antikythera mechanism: designing an immersive cultural exhibition. In: 2018 IEEE International Symposium on Mixed and Augmented Reality Adjunct (ISMAR-Adjunct), pp. 310–313. IEEE, Munich (2018). https://doi.org/10.1109/ismar-adjunct.2018.00092
4. Anastasovitis, E., Nikolopoulos, S., Kompatsiaris, I.: Experiencing the impossible through virtual and augmented reality. In: Proceedings They are not silent after all… Human remains in archaeological museums: Ethics and displays, submitted for publication, Hellenic Ministry of Culture and Sports, 31 October-01 November 2019, Athens (2020)
5. Susi, T., Johannesson, M., Backlund, P.: Serious games: An overview (IKI Technical Reports). Institutionen för kommunikation och information, Skövde (2007)
6. Bellotti, F., Kapralos, B., Lee, K., Moreno-Ger, P., Berta, R.: Assessment in and of serious games: an overview. Adv. Hum-Comput. Interact. 136864, 11 (2013). https://doi.org/10.1155/2013/136864
7. Anastasovitis, E., Ververidis, D., Nikolopoulos, S., Kompatsiaris, I.: Digiart: building new 3D cultural heritage worlds. 2017 3DTV Conference: The True Vision-Capture Transmission and Display of 3D Video (3DTV-CON), pp. 1–4. IEEE, Copenhagen (2017)
8. Anastasovitis, E., Roumeliotis, M.: Designing an edutainment serious game for the Antikythera mechanism in virtual reality. In: Helin, K., Perret, J., Kuts, V. (Eds.) (2019). The application track, posters and demos of EuroVR: Proceedings of the 16th Annual EuroVR Conference - 2019 VTT Technical Research Centre of Finland. VTT Technology, Tallinn, no. 357, pp. 94–97. IEEE (2019). https://doi.org/10.32040/2242-122X.2019.T357
9. Tsita, C., Satratzemi, M.: A serious game design and evaluation approach to enhance cultural heritage understanding. In: Liapis, A., Yannakakis, G., Gentile, M., Ninaus, M. (eds.) GAMES AND LEARNING ALLIANCE - GALA 2019. LNCS, vol. 11899, pp. 438–446. Springer, Cham (2019). https://doi.org/10.1007/978-3-030-34350-7_42
10. Tasić, N.T.: Introduction to virtual reconstructions. In: Tasić, N., Novaković, P., Horňák, M. (eds.) Visual Reconstructions and Computer Visualisations in Archaeological Practice, CONPRA Series, vol. IV, pp. 13–22. University of Ljubljana Press, Faculty of Arts, Ljubljana (2017)
11. Pietroni, E., Ferdani, D., Forlani, M., Pagano, A., Rufa, C.: Bringing the illusion of reality inside museums – a methodological proposal fo an advanced museology using holographic showcases. Informatics, **6**(1), 2 (2019)
12. Tzortzi, K.: Museum building design and exhibition layout: patterns of interaction. In: Kubat, E. et al. (eds.) 6th International Space Syntax Symposium, 12–15 June 2007, Instabul (2007)
13. Povroznik, N.: Virtual museums and cultural heritage: challenges and solutions. In: Mäkelä, E., Tolonen, M., Tuominen, J. (eds.) Proceedings of the Digital Humanities in the Nordic countries, 3rd Conference, Helsinki, Finland, 7–9 March 2018, pp. 394–402. University of Helsinki, Faculty of Arts, Helsinki (2018)
14. Perry, S., Roussou, M., Economou, M., Young, H., Pujol, L.: Moving beyond the virtual museum: engaging visitors emotionally. In: 23rd International Conference on Virtual Systems & Multimedia (VSMM), Dublin, pp. 1–8. IEEE (2017). https://doi.org/10.1109/vsmm.2017.8346276

15. Kazanis, S., Kontogianni, G., Chiverou, R., Georgopoulos, A.: Developing a virtual museum for the ancient wine trade in eastern Mediterranean. In: 26th International CIPA Symposium 2017: The International Archives on the Photogrammetry, Remote Sensing and Spatial Information Sciences, vol. XLII-2/W5, Ottava, Canada, pp. 399–405 (2017). https://doi.org/10.5194/isprs-archives-xlii-2-w5-399-2017

16. Lord, B., Lord, G.D.: The Manual of Museum Exhibitions. Altamira Press, Walnut Creek, CA (2001)

17. Sfintes, A.I.: The architecture of virtual space museums. In: 1st Annual International Interdisciplinary Conference, AIIC 2013, 24–26 April, Azores, Portugal (2013)

18. MAXON Homepage. https://www.maxon.net/en/. Accessed 15 Sep 2020

19. GIMP Homepage. https://www.gimp.org/. Accessed 15 Sep 2020

20. ROKOKO Homepage. https://www.rokoko.com/en. Accessed 15 Sep 2020

21. Unity Homepage. https://unity.com/. Accessed 15 Sep 2020

22. Oculus Homepage. https://www.oculus.com/rift-s/. Accessed 15 Sep 2020

23. ICOM Homepage. https://icom.museum/en/. Accessed 15 Sep 2020

Virtual Museums and Human-VR-Computer Interaction for Cultural Heritage Application: New Levels of Interactivity and Knowledge of Digital Models and Descriptive Geometry

Fabrizio Banfi$^{(\boxtimes)}$ (iD)

Department of Architecture Built Environment and Construction Engineering (ABC),
Politecnico di Milano, via Ponzio 31, 20133 Milan, Italy
`fabrizio.banfi@polimi.it`

Abstract. Open and advanced real-time 3D creation tools are continuously evolving, offering new cutting edge solutions to support the creation of immersive virtual experience-oriented to different purposes, devices and users. In recent years, different Virtual and Augmented reality (VR-AR) projects have clearly shown how 3D modelling and Building Information Modelling (BIM) can be the proper bases to enhance the new paradigm of interactivity of 3D informative systems, moving from static models to virtual objects able to interact with the user's input. For those reasons, this study proposes a method able to give life to 3D survey data and static models, transforming them into interactive virtual objects (IVO) able to enhance the virtual-visual storytelling (VVS) of heritage buildings. This was made possible by the use of novel scan-to-BIM modelling requirements based on the values of scientific drawing, descriptive geometry, historic documentation and digital proxemics. The combination of all these factors has made it possible to achieve new levels of communication and human-VR-computer interaction, favouring documentation, education and learning of tangible and intangible values of our built cultural heritage.

Keywords: Interactive virtual object (IVO) · Virtual-Visual storytelling (VVS) · Virtual museum · Visual scripting · Scan-to-BIM · Digital cultural heritage · Descriptive geometry

1 Introduction

Nowadays, the advent of the second digital era is transforming the way we interact and communicate. Latest generation software and tools are used more and more to increase our level of virtual and digital interactivity [1]. The construction sector has benefited from a profound digital transformation in recent years. In particular, the disciplines and software relating to architectural representation have been able to align themselves with the needs of the market, favouring increasingly detailed (geometric accuracy) and information (level of content) representations. Just think of the operational transition

© Springer Nature Switzerland AG 2021
M. Ioannides et al. (Eds.): EuroMed 2020, LNCS 12642, pp. 346–357, 2021.
https://doi.org/10.1007/978-3-030-73043-7_29

between the drafting machine, two-dimensional CAD software, and the various nuances of BIM (Building Information Modeling). The latter in recent years has made it possible to reach, connect, and improve disciplines and sectors, from restoration to advanced 3D prototyping. At an international level, BIM (created for the management of new buildings) has been oriented to the representation and management of historic buildings, exponentially expanding tangible and intangibles values of the artefact. In this specific field of application, interesting studies and developments allowed users to properly manage 3D survey data (laser scanning and digital photogrammetry outputs), transforming simple points into models informative [2]. As is well known, point clouds represent one of the main outputs of 3D survey tools and cannot be considered as real models. For this reason, in recent years the author's research has focused on improving the automation process of point cloud modelling, proposing new scan-to-BIM requirements [3]. These new requirements, known as Grades of Generations (GOG) and Accuracy (GOA) have made it possible to identify the gaps in tools and functions within BIM software and propose novel guidelines for the transformation of point clouds into BIM objects via Non-Uniform Rational Basis-Splines (NURBS) algorithms. The paradigms of uniqueness and complexity of the architectural and structural elements of heritage buildings represented the first obstacle for a correct 3D representation. It has been demonstrated how the GOGs and the GOAs have made it possible to improve the reliability of parametric models both from the geometric (value of the measurement, accuracy, and level of detail) and the informative point of view (transmission of information).

Nevertheless, the management of 3D information platforms and architectures are not always easy to use and understand for users who have not undertaken long-term training courses. Software such as Autodesk Revit, Graphisoft Archicad, MC Neel Rhinoceros and Autodesk Autocad require months of practice to be able to manage them independently and correctly in their full function. Accordingly, this study proposes a digital process able to support the user (creator of the model and the VR project) during the digitization process of the buildings surveyed, from the point cloud to its transformation into interactive virtual objects (IVO), where the end-user can discover the artefact and its tangible and intangible values without having a high level of knowledge of computer development language. In this specific context, the author proposes a research method aimed at inheriting and transmitting the richness of the scan-to-BIM model to open VR platforms such as Unreal Engine. Consequently, the study of digital proxemics and IT development through visual scripting have allowed the creation of virtual-visual storytelling (VVS) and favoured the transformation of static models into a new type of virtual museum [4].

The case study implemented for this research is the Arch of Peace in Milan. The heterogeneity of its architectural, structural and decorative elements has allowed the author to give life to a varied range of IVOs, works of art, unique architectural elements of their kind, making them remotely accessible and increasing their communicative value through the new paradigms of interactivity and digital learning.

2 Research Objectives

Digital Cultural Heritage (DCH) now represents an acronym recognized worldwide, where different disciplines are intertwined with the common goal of documenting, preserving and passing on to future generations historical artefacts of undisputed cultural, historical and social value [5]. On a digital level, software and methods implemented in recent years must be considered tools to support the digitization process of buildings in which the scientific drawing, descriptive geometry, measurements, historic documentation are the foundations for the proper 3D representation [6]. In this context, the scan-to-BIM process represents the only method capable of holistically representing those values and at the same time increasing the informative value of the models for different types of analysis [7]. In particular, as is well known, starting from a point cloud it is possible to achieve the creation of an informative parametric model. This process is structured on the identification of geometric primitives from point clouds and thanks to conversion procedures (semi-automatic or automatic) it is possible to transform simple points into digital models, where the relationship between object and information is bidirectional. By changing the parameter, the update of the 3D model is automatic. In summary, through this process, a BIM model with levels of detail (LOD) and grade of accuracy (GOA) is obtained according to the project objectives.

Furthermore, thanks to the benefits demonstrated in various application fields, BIM has been subject to national and international regulations, where bodies, governments and institutions have proposed their hierarchy through the various LODs and information LOIs [8]. On the other hand, methods, protocols and guidelines are not yet present for the world of Mixed Reality for Cultural Heritage Application (DCH), where virtual and augmented reality (VR-AR) can collect the wealth of information of these digital architectures and transmit it to a wider audience such as virtual tourists, students, and non-experts in the field of construction.

Consequently, one of the main objectives of this research is to propose a digital workflow able to synthesize the transformation phases of scan-to-BIM models, from the simple point cloud to the creation of interactive objects, facilitating their understanding and use through a scientific proposal able to explain the pros and cons of the various digital tools used. Figure 1 shows the research proposal, trying to pay attention to the relationship that is established among the tool used, the input and output formats and the final goals of each phase. The main phases identified are:

- **Data collection**: Documentation, Historical archives, 2D CAD drawings, multimedia data;
- **Scan-to-BIM process**: 3D survey, Modelling by GOGs, Automatic Verification System (AVS);
- **Information Mapping**: Historic Building Information Modeling (HBIM), granular HBIM objects, HBIM parameters, stratigraphic units, schedules, databases;
- **Information Sharing**: Interoperability, Exchange formats, Mixed reality (VR-AR), Devices, Virtual Visual storytelling, Virtual Museums.

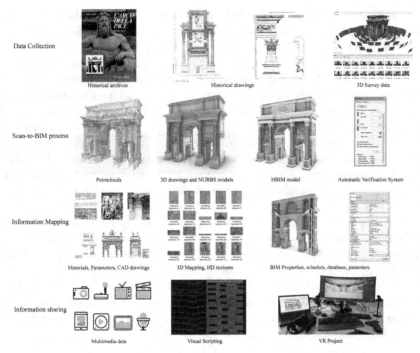

Data Collection
Historical archives   Historical drawings   3D Survey data

Scan-to-BIM process
Pointclouds   3D drawings and NURBS models   HBIM model   Automatic Verification System

Information Mapping
Materials, Parameters, CAD drawings   3D Mapping, HD textures   BIM Properties, scheduls, database, paramters

Information sharing
Multimedia data   Visual Scripting   VR Project

Fig. 1. The research method: from point clouds and historical drawings to new levels of interactivity and knowledge of digital models and virtual museums.

3 The Value of Descriptive Geometry and Historical Archives in the Scan-to-BIM Process: From Tangible to Intangible Values

The exponential development of methods, tools, software applications has allowed the author to investigate the main generative techniques of three-dimensional scan-to-BIM models characterized by architectural, structural, and decorative elements with a high level of complexity such as ancient wall traces, partition damaged walls, and variable section, stratigraphic units, vaults, arches, columns, historical decorative elements, mosaics, paintings, sculptures and works of art in general. The next step was to be able to transmit all those intangible values in an interactive virtual environment

1. deriving from studies and discoveries from recognized historical sources,
2. cultural and social insights through interviews and statistics,
3. collection and production of multimedia files capable of providing a 360-degree virtual story,
4. development/testing of devices aimed at improving the level of interactivity and digital proxemics (VR headset, joystick, laptop, mobile, and desktop) between 3D objects and user (first and third person).

For these reasons, the enhancement of interactive virtual objects (IVOs) has made it possible to transmit information of a historical, social and cultural nature to a specific type of users such as students and virtual tourists. The monument of the Arch of Peace of Milan does not have a vast historical archive and reference bibliography. Due to the various historical vicissitudes, the historical-cultural heritage of the monument is gradually being lost over the years. The collection of multimedia data and historical texts was fundamental for describing the history hidden behind its decorative apparatus. In particular, the Arch of Peace of Milan presents geometric characteristics that derive directly from neoclassical elements rich in decorative elements and architectural details with high levels of detail [9, 10]. This excess of detail and the high number of sub-elements such as low reliefs, decorations and friezes, required the study of descriptive geometry and a large amount of two-dimensional historical representations able to better explain the constructions and geometric proportions. Furthermore, the limited historical bibliography has been entirely digitized in its entirety and transformed into a digital historical archive where the user in a digital environment can browse and discover specific descriptions of the entire decorative apparatus having the possibility to interact with the IVOs of the monument at the same time. Figure 2 shows the digitization process of different types of data, from point clouds, historical archives, drawings to detailed HBIM objects. Thanks to the integrated use of the main GOGs and GOAs with traditional representation techniques such as descriptive geometry, it was possible to obtain an HBIM model capable of accommodating different types of information using different modes such as schedules, databases, BIMcloud and 3D exchange formats such as e57, pts dwg, dwf, 3 dm, rcs, rcp, rvt, rcp, fbx, dae, and obj.

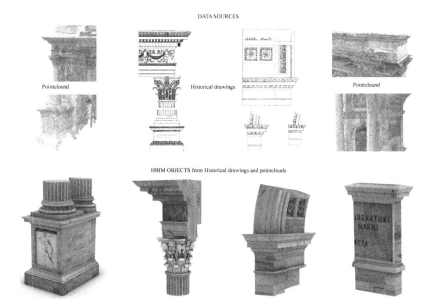

Fig. 2. Descriptive geometry and historical archives were crucial for the correct geometric interpretation of each architectural element during the scan-to-BIM process.

4 Human-VR-Computer Interaction, Digital Proxemics and Visual Scripting: From Static Models to Interactive Virtual Objects (IVO)

4.1 Communication, Digital Proxemics and the Human-VR-Computer Interaction

The extreme flexibility of the project developed for the monument has made it possible to develop computer codes capable of attracting the user to information content through 3D animation and correct digital proxemics. The latter has been interpreted as a fundamental element for the improvement of communication in a 3D environment. Man, by his nature, is a communicating being, immersed in an environment that sends us continuous signals. Communication, for the most part, can be defined as a transmission of thoughts and sharing of meanings between interacting subjects, whatever the conscious and unaware purposes of the passage of information, it necessarily presupposes a relationship and therefore of one exchange [11, 12].

Communication should therefore not be considered as simply a tool, but as a constitutive psychological dimension of the subject. He does not choose whether to be communicating or not, but he can choose whether and in what way to communicate. For this reason, the relationship between space and distances created between IVOs and user [13, 14] has been carefully investigated through visual, perceptual and sensory tests. In this particular context, it should be emphasized that for the most part human interaction in the digital environment can essentially take place via various devices such as VR headsets, workstations, laptops, and mobile phones. Accordingly, four modes have been undertaken to maximize the interactions that can be created between the user and different types of devices. Figure 3 relates the device and the user (virtual or real), explaining the pros and cons of the four methods investigated and developed for the research case study.

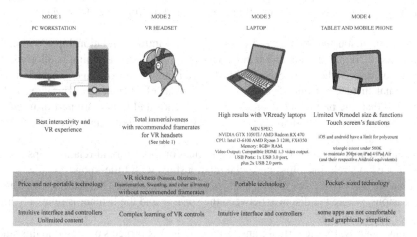

Fig. 3. The main pros/cons of four modes investigated for the creation of the VR project.

From the tests conducted (Fig. 3 & Fig. 4), the first method was found to be the most flexible to accommodate a large number of interactive content, models, and objects. The creation of a workstation-oriented VR project allows users to have the maximum possibilities in terms of processing, power and memory of the various hardware and software components. It should also be noted that the use of a keyboard compared to a joystick allows any type of user to assimilate the rules of use and digital interaction in a very short time. The second mode was found to be a way to maximize user immersion. Thanks to the 3D viewer and the transposition of user gesture in a virtual environment through motion sensors and joysticks capable of grabbing, activating and turning off objects and information panels, it was possible to offer a more immersive alternative solution than the previous one. On the other hand, the rules of interaction between the user and the digital environment are not easy to learn for users who are not familiar with these types of devices. Where the keyboard can support the discovery of the 3D environment through the use of the right-left-up-down arrows, VR headsets such as Oculus Quest (or similar) require a phase of adaptation and learning by the user. In this context, the study of body movements, kinetics, and digital proxemics were crucial for the correct proportioning of the distances between IVOs and user. The way in which individuals relate based on this non-verbal signal follows very precise rules that vary in relation to the relationship established between the two or more subjects. It has been found that the distance that an individual adopts towards another person (or VR object) is proportional to the relationship or existing links between the two participants in the interaction. Numerous experimental studies have highlighted that the proxemic distance is also regulated by another very important factor: the hierarchical relationships established in the group/environment. How an individual inserts himself into space has communicative value and can be indicative of the relationships of collaboration, intimacy, or hierarchy that are established between the subjects. According to T. Hall [11] for the individual, the boundary of his own body does not correspond to the physical one, but there is a "personal space", beyond which one cannot go without explicit request. The author speaks of a hidden dimension with which he defines the interpersonal distance, the one that the person puts between himself and others, and distinguishes four types:

- Minimum distance (from 0 to 45 cm.): Typical of intimate relationships. Within this distance there are friends and family with whom almost everything is allowed: one caresses, approaches, you can smell and there is a mutual exchange of emotions.
- Personal distance (from 45 to 120 cm.): Typical of friendships. This area is less limited than the previous one and less close friends and family are part of it, but the distance between individuals is sufficiently limited to capture and perceive emotions and sensations.
- Social distance (from 120 to 3.60 m.): Typical of more formal relationships. In this area, we have relationships and social relationships with little-known people.
- Public distance (over 4 m.): Typical of public circumstances. This is the area of official occasions, where the distance between the speaker and the listener is relatively high.

Consequently, for the virtual transposition of the VR projects proposed in this study, connections and networks were created capable of intertwining the four typologies identified by T. Hall and the four modes identified in Fig. 3. From these tests and studies

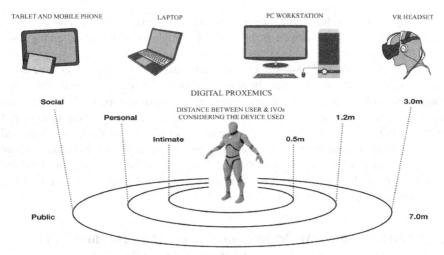

Fig. 4. Digital proxemics concerning specific objects: the schemas adopt to reduce VR sickness for the virtual visual storytelling of the arch of Peace

on digital proxemics in relation to specific devices, a preference has emerged for the mode which excludes the VR viewer and favors the direct use of work-stations and laptops. Beyond all the PC hardware, sensors, processing power, and controllers that VR demands, this VR headset has shown some limitations such as VR sickness (dizziness, nausea, disorientation, sweating, and others). One of the main factors that can affect this cause is the framerate dropping too low. For this reason, developers must be constantly aware of our game's performance on the chosen platform. In Table 1 is reported the recommended framerates for several of the VR headsets that Unreal Engine 4 supports [15]:

Table 1. The recommended framerates for several of the VR headsets.

Vive	90 FPS
Gear VR	60 FPS
PSVR	Variable up to 120 FPS
Rift retail	90 FPS
DK1	60 FPS
DK 2	75 FPS

Some established methods of locomotion that have arisen from development in VR techniques include cockpit-based, natural, artificial, physical, and teleportation. Other methods of controlling VR sickness include avoiding 3D animation effects (cinematic cameras) that alter the user's vision, such as motion blur and using dimmer lighting. Blurring effects and bright colours cause players nausea as a result of eye strain. Finally, it is also worth noting that medical science has still not thoroughly studied the effects of the prolonged use of VR, as well as the issues that might arise from children regularly using the VR headset.

Finally, the mobile and tablet versions proved to be crucial to complete the experience and the virtual story. In particular, the migration of the VR project to a mobile phone takes place via an automatic function that allows the user to transform the VR project into a real app. The limit found is a low number of polygons and content that can be managed by the mobile device compared to the workstation. For this reason, the main augmented reality (AR) techniques have been investigated using mobile phones and tablets, where by creating a digital library it is possible to recall objects and information of any kind and view them three-dimensionally on-site or at distances, visualizing objects that would be impossible or impractical to see otherwise.

5   From Scan-to-BIM Projects to Virtual Museums and Game Technologies for Cultural Heritage Application

5.1   The Process of Creating Virtual Interactive Objects (IVO)

The process of creating interactive virtual objects (IVO) has been oriented to the logic of virtual scripting which represents one of the main values that have emerged in recent years in the field of IT development oriented to the creation of interactive digital environments. This development technique allows developing codes capable of giving life to a wide range of elements such as 3D objects, solids and surfaces, hyper-realistic environments, textures, lights, 3D animations, avatars, menus, and digital archives. The integration of this development technique with the management and creation of digital models within a single open gaming platform such as Unreal Engine has allowed optimizing the usefulness of scan-to-BIM models in the field of Mixed Reality (VR-AR) oriented to DCH. In this context, the Information Sharing phase (see Fig. 1) has been enhanced thanks to the development of the first three previous phases and the definition of guidelines capable of supporting the creation of virtual museums and VVS with high levels of information, interactivity and resolution. Thanks to the development of a method based on consolidated scan-to-BIM modelling requirements and exchange formats, it was possible to increase the human-VR-computer interaction using key principles for a good design of the VVS of the monument.

The use and identification of 3D exchange formats, useful for the conversion and transfer of scan-to-BIM objects from the first three to the fourth phase, required the definition of new conversion schemes. Table 2 shows the model conversion concerning the four phases identified in Fig. 1.

5.2   Virtual-Visual Storytelling (VVS) and the Virtual Museum of the Arch of Peace of Milan

Virtual-visual storytelling (VVS) and VR projects have a greater predisposition to sharing than words and figures. Using VVS to convey content makes our messages more visible since it is possible to reach a wider audience. VVS is intended as a cross-disciplinary

Table 2. 3D exchange formats used for the conversion and transfer of scan-to-BIM objects from the first three phases to the VR project of the research case study.

Phase	Subject	Import file format	Export file format
From data collection (1) to Scan-to-BIM process (2)	Point clouds, Historical Drawings, Pictures, and CAD drawings	Jpg, png, pdf, TIFF	E57, pts, xyz, rcs, rcp, DWG, 3 dm
From 2 to information mapping (3)	NURBS Model, BIM Model	DWG, 3 dm, rvt, rvp	Fbx, obj
From 3 to information sharing (4)	VR project, VIO, AR objects	Fbx, 3ds, 3 dm, dwg	UEpf, Obj, dae

approach to teaching visual narratives and digital documentation through motion capture, visual effects, digital proxemics and VR simulated experiences [4].

VVS is more effective than words because:

- communicates immediately by simplifying concepts which, if expressed in text form, are more complex.
- excites: with the same content, it is more likely to be moved in front of a movie, rather than reading a book made up of text only.
- when faced with content that we consider exciting, relaxing or useful, we tend to want to show it to others.

It has been found that exploiting the 'power of the virtual' and the latest generation VR tools has allowed amplifying the experience of any form of communication by adding non-real content. The strategy adopted for the definition of the VVS of the monument is summarized in Fig. 5. Through the various steps, the main idea was to transform the starting point of the VVS by creating two interactive menus, which in turn they contain different levels of detail, virtual rooms, content and IVOs. The first menu (historical memories) is composed of nine themes of a general, historical, cultural, and geographical nature, which allow users to discover information of a general nature, immersing him in the history of the monument, while the second menu is characterized from 9 themes oriented to tell the richness of the decorative apparatus of the monument and its artworks of inestimable value. To make everything more interactive and immersive as possible, ideal museum rooms have also been created where the user can increase his knowledge of the arch through a large number of interactive objects. Thanks to visual scripting it has been possible to create different types of IVOs: museum rooms, historical archives, browsable books and drawings, descriptions, decorations, paintings, historical and cultural context, geographical context, 3D animation, videos, audios, and 360 pictures, characters able to interact according to user input.

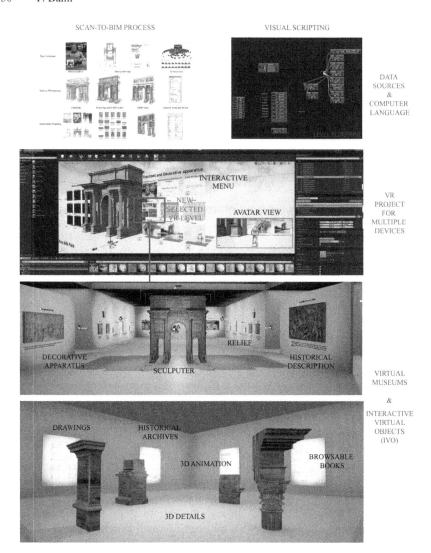

Fig. 5. The virtual museum of the Arch of Peace of Milan.

6 Conclusion

The case study of the Arch of Peace showed how a scan-to-BIM process must make use not only of digital tools but also of architectural representation techniques such as descriptive geometry. In-depth research of different types of documents and data made it possible to correctly interpret the complex forms of the monument and transfer them to the latest generation software aimed at creating a VR project. The latter thanks to the use of a computer language known as visual scripting, has been enriched with interactive virtual objects (IVO) capable of increasing the interactivity of the virtual-visual storytelling (VVS) of the monument. Thanks to a sustainable process characterized by new levels of interoperability and communication it has been possible to tell the tangible and intangible values of one of the most complex and historical monuments of the city of Milan and to define a scan-to-BIM-to-VR method sustainable and usable for any type of building.

References

1. Wujec T.: The Future of Making. Autodesk Inc. Mechel Media (2017)
2. Oreni, D., et al.: Survey turned into HBIM: the restoration and the work involved concerning the Basilica di Collemaggio after the earthquake (L'Aquila). ISPRS Ann. Photogrammetry Remote Sens. Spat. Inf. Sci. **2**(5) (2014)
3. Banfi, F.: BIM Orientation: Grades of generation and information for different type of analysis and management process. Int. Arch. Photogrammetry Remote Sens. Spat. Inf. Sci. 42.2/W5 (2017)
4. Bennett, G., Kruse, J.: Teaching visual storytelling for virtual production pipelines incorporating motion capture and visual effects. In: SIGGRAPH Asia 2015 Symposium on Education, pp. 1–8 (2015)
5. Caffo, R.: Digital cultural heritage projects: opportunities and future challenges. Procedia Comput. Sci. **38**, 12–17 (2014)
6. Ioannides, M., Nadia, M.T., George, P. (eds.): Mixed reality and gamification for cultural heritage, vol. 2. Springer, Cham, Switzerland (2017)
7. Brumana, R., et al.: Survey and scan to BIM model for the knowledge of built heritage and the management of conservation activities. Bruno Daniotti Marco Gianinetto (2020)
8. Latiffi, A.A. et al.: Building information modeling (BIM): exploring level of development (LOD) in construction projects. In: Applied Mechanics and Materials. vol. 773. Trans Tech Publications Ltd, (2015)
9. Giani, G.: L'Arco della pace di Milano. Di Baio Editore, Italy (1988)
10. Sacchi, D.: L'Arco della pace a Milano. Manini (1838)
11. Hall, T., et al.: Proxemics [and comments and replies]. Current Anthropol. **9**(2/3), 83–108 (1968)
12. Hall, T.: Proxemics and design. Des. Environ. (1971)
13. Lepouras, G., Vassilakis, C.: Virtual museums for all: employing game technology for edutainment. Virtual Reality **8**(2), 96–106 (2004)
14. Carvajal, D.A.L., Morita, M.M., Bilmes, G.M.: Virtual museums. captured reality and 3D modeling. J. Cult. Heritage, **45**, 234–239 (2020)
15. Unreal Engine. 'Virtual Reality Best Practices Information about developing for VR'. https://docs.unrealengine.com/en-US/Platforms/VR/DevelopVR/ContentSetup/index.html

Project Paper: Visualisation Techniques (Desktop, Virtual and Augmented Reality)

COSMOS. Cultural Osmosis – Mythology and Art

A Data Organization and Visualization Platform, with the Use of AI Algorithms

Stelios C. A. Thomopoulos[1(✉)], Panagiotis Tsimpiridis[1], Eleni-Ino Theodorou[1], Christos Maroglou[1], Efstathios Georgiou[1], and Christiana Christopoulou[2]

[1] NCSR "Demokritos"-IIT-ISL, P.O. Box 60037, 15310 Agia Paraskevi, Greece
`{scat,ptsimpiridis,itheodorou,cmaro,`
`stgeorgiou}@iit.demokritos.gr`
[2] Ekdotike Athenon S.A, Solonos 27, 10672 Athens, Greece
`c.christopoulou@ekdotikeathenon.gr`

Abstract. The richness of Greek mythology, combined with the need to preserve and spread the intangible and tangible cultural heritage, constitute the incentives towards the exploration of new ways to narrate these fascinating "stories" and to display their artistic depictions. COSMOS offers the opportunity to record Greek mythology, both in its written and visual forms.

COSMOS is developed in two interrelated units, *Myths* and *Art*. Each one is organized in three dynamic windows, that visualize the correlations among their basic elements, thus offering a complete picture to the user. Myths include: a) the myths as stories, b) the participating characters and c) the places these stories are set in, whereas, Art includes: a) the portrayals of myths in artworks, b) the depicted characters and c) their original and present location.

The implementation is realized by the Knowledge Management System and the Knowledge Presentation System, that make use of state-of-the-art technologies in the fields of Machine Learning, Natural Language Processing and 3D Imaging, in order to visualize myths, artworks and their connections, in an appealing and comprehensible way.

The final product addresses to a vast audience and it can be used: a) as a study aid for anyone interested, b) for educational purposes, by teachers and students, c) as a reference tool in the field of the Social Sciences and the Humanities, for the production of research projects, and d) as a scientific documentation tool, for exhibition curating purposes.

Keywords: AI · Linked data · Nodes · Mythology · Artworks · Cultural heritage · Education

© Springer Nature Switzerland AG 2021
M. Ioannides et al. (Eds.): EuroMed 2020, LNCS 12642, pp. 361–373, 2021.
https://doi.org/10.1007/978-3-030-73043-7_30

1 Introduction

1.1 Project Overview

Greek mythology, a topic of international interest with influences on many aspects of modern western culture [1], comprises a rich collection of stories with numerous characters, evolving in different locations of the known and/or the mythical ancient world [2]. This collection, including the myths variations, is a voluminous and expensive work, recorded in the unique, perhaps, scientifically sound and complete work, *The Greek Mythology* of I.T. Kakridis, by Ekdotike Athenon [2]. The richness of Greek mythology, combined with the need to preserve and spread the intangible and tangible cultural heritage [3], constitute the incentive towards the exploration of new ways to narrate these fascinating "stories" and to display their artistic depictions. COSMOS [4] is a platform that offers a new, non-linear approach to encoding Greek mythology in both its written and visual forms.

The project identifies three basic elements for myths and artworks respectively. The myths' narratives comprise: (a) the myths as stories (b) the participating characters and (c) the places these stories are set in. Artworks consist of: (a) the portrayals of the myths (b) the depicted characters and (c) their original (if known) and present location. In order to display Greek myths and relevant artworks, COSMOS is composed of two interrelated units, *Myths* and *Art*, each one organized in three distinct categories, based on the aforementioned elements (see Fig. 1).

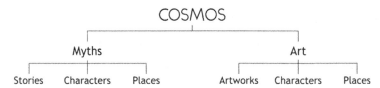

Fig. 1. COSMOS concept diagram

COSMOS achieves to overcome the usual practice of linear narration and highlights the links between various myths, based on common entities. At the same time, it connects the myths to their depictions in works of art that originate from different places and eras, and are now physically located across the world.

The project partners are Ekdotike Athenon [5] (Project Coordinator) and the Integrated Systems Laboratory [6] of the National Centre for Scientific Research "Demokritos", Institute of Informatics & Telecommunications (Scientific Coordinator).

1.2 Project Objectives

The development of the COSMOS project seeks to achieve the following objectives:

1. Dissemination of Greek mythology, as well as its various representations in ancient artworks, as important forms of Greek tangible and intangible [7] cultural heritage.

2. Development of a dynamic application, that will offer the possibility to further enrich its content after the completion of the project with: (a) various forms of art, relevant to Greek mythology, dating from antiquity to the present (b) stories and artistic creations from mythologies of other cultures (e.g. Celtic, Nordic), while revealing the connections between these works [8], thus expanding the project internationally.
3. Better understanding and supervision of the complex and massive work of Greek mythology, as well as the relevant art.
4. Development of an easy-to-use reference and search tool for educational and research purposes.
5. Easy access to the popular content of Greek mythology, through the distribution of the application in desktop and mobile versions.
6. Linking the research of NCSR "Demokritos" with the work of Ekdotike Athenon, for the development of an innovative application that will increase the domestic added value of cultural products and will boost the company's digital transformation [9], responding to its customer needs and enhancing the company's competitiveness in international markets.

1.3 Inspiration and Other Applications for Greek Mythology

In terms of data visualization, COSMOS has drawn inspiration from *The Museum of the World* [10], a collaboration between the Google Cultural Institute and The British Museum, with the purpose of creating an interactive experience for remote museum visitors. The project is a WebGL desktop application, showcasing exhibits of the British Museum collections aligned on a timeline, while at the same time drawing their connections to each other. Taking a step further, COSMOS adopted an approach that includes three dynamic windows of parallel data visualization, for the basic elements of Myths and Art units (see Fig. 1).

In the bounds of the COSMOS project, a Feasibility Study was conducted, in order to better evaluate the position of the application in the market. In this study, 22 applications about Greek mythology (e.g. *Greek Mythology- Gods & Myths* [11], *Greek Mythology & Gods Offline* [12], *Greek Mythology* [13]) were examined, on the basis of their features. The outcome was that they are mainly limited to an index of the most important mythical characters, by means of which the user can access and read myths related to them. Any connections among myths and participating characters are offered as hyperlinks in the texts, while none of them provides connections with the locations, nor with relevant works of art. As a result, the afore-mentioned applications do not achieve to present mythology in a dynamic way, and remain restricted in a linear reading of the story.

2 COSMOS: Information Organization and Presentation

The two main functions of COSMOS are (a) the organization of the knowledge that derives from Greek mythology texts and artworks, and (b) the presentation of the information to the user, through a dynamic environment (see Fig. 2). The system makes use of state-of-the-art technologies in the fields of Machine Learning (ML), Natural Language Processing (NLP) and 3D Imaging, in order to visualize myths, artworks and their connections, in an appealing and comprehensible way.

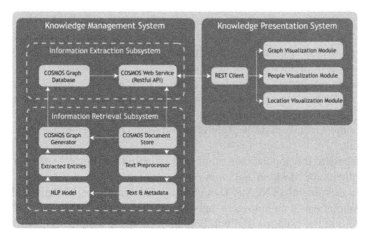

Fig. 2. COSMOS system architecture diagram

2.1 Knowledge Organization System (KOS)

KOS is responsible for the automated extraction of structured and machine-readable information from unstructured sources (e.g. mythology texts). This information is subsequently organized into correlation graphs, by means of which the myths are connected to each other, according to common attributes (e.g. characters, locations, artworks). KOS comprises the following two, independent, subsystems.

Information Extraction Subsystem (IES). IES uses the unstructured mythology texts as input, and creates the correlations between the myths, based on certain entities mentioned in the texts (e.g. characters, locations, other keywords). IES consists of:

- COSMOS Document Store: A MongoDB [14] database which contains the mythology texts in English and Greek, and the entities (locations, persons) in them.
- Text Preprocessor: Takes the texts and entities stored in the Document Store and produces the annotated dataset to be used for the training and evaluation of the Named Entity Recognition (NER) [15, 16], NLP model.
- NLP Model: This was developed using the NLP framework spaCy [17]. While spaCy provides pre-trained models for many languages, the Named Entity Recogniser's performance was insufficient. The pre-trained English model was further trained using the project's annotated dataset and evaluated against the gold standard. Table 1 illustrates the model's performance.
- COSMOS Graph Generator: Takes the entities extracted from each text by the NLP model and generates a Neo4j graph database which contains the links between each mythology text.

Model Development Methodology. For the development of the NLP model a corpus of 129 Stories was used for training and testing and is currently included in COSMOS. Half of the mythology texts were used for the NLP model development and the other half was

Table 1. Performance metrics per entity type of the pre-trained model versus the trained model.

Model type	Precision (Person)	Recall (Person)	F1 (Person)	Precision (Location)	Recall (Location)	F1 (Location)
Train dataset						
Pre-trained model	86.70	48.35	62.08	23.42	10.48	14.48
COSMOS model	100	100	100	100	100	100
Test dataset						
Pre-trained model	89.54	49.62	63.85	37.50	15.51	21.95
COSMOS model	94.43	98.23	96.29	79.41	93.10	85.71

automatically processed by the trained model. The first half of the raw mythology texts were manually processed, in order to extract the relevant metadata (entities, tags) and build the ground truth. Then, the raw texts, as well as the extracted metadata, were stored in the COSMOS Document Store database. To generate the corpus, the Text Preprocessor (a script in Python) was developed, which takes the raw texts and the metadata from the COSMOS Document Store and then produces the corpus in the format spaCy requires. For example, in order to train the Named Entity Recognizer, the training dataset must be in the following format:

```
(
    'At a time when Minos was trying to establish himself as king of
Crete, he asked Poseidon to send a sign revealing that the gods favored
Minos and his ascent to the throne.',
    {'entities': [(15, 20, 'PERSON'), (64, 69, 'LOC'), (80, 88,
'PERSON'), (136, 141, 'PERSON')]}
)
```

After generating the dataset, Transfer Learning was applied by starting from existing pre-trained representations (e.g. word vectors) and training them on the Greek mythology corpus. An amount of 80% of the dataset was used for training and the rest 20% for testing. A 20% dropout rate was applied to features to reduce overfitting. The results exhibit that the COSMOS model-trained specifically on the Greek mythology texts domain- performs better than the pre-trained model-trained on the OntoNotes 5 corpus [18]- (see Table 1), which was an expected outcome, as the COSMOS model has learnt to recognize specific language patterns occurring in Greek mythology texts. At the same time, the Location identification is not as accurate as the Person identification, because, the raw texts contain significantly more references to Persons than Locations, making the Location identification harder to train.

Information Retrieval Subsystem (IRS). IRS is responsible for searching and retrieving the information that the end-user is looking for and consists of:

- COSMOS Web Service: A RESTful API developed in NodeJS [19] using the Fastify framework [20]. The API provides endpoints to query and retrieve data stored in the COSMOS Document Store and the COSMOS Graph Database.
- COSMOS Graph Database: A Neo4j graph database [21] which contains the links between each mythology text. The entity relationship queries to the graph database are implemented in Cypher, Neo4j's own query language.

When a system component, such as the Knowledge Presentation System, wants to access the linked information stored in the graph database, it performs an http request to the appropriate endpoint of the COSMOS Web Service. The service queries the graph database through the Cypher API [22] and returns the results to the system component.

2.2 Knowledge Presentation System (KPS)

KPS is the interface, via which the user interacts with the KOS. The KPS makes use of 3D graphic technologies, in order to present the connected information in an original and interactive way. The available data is offered in two interrelated units, Myths and Art. Each unit is organized in three separate visualization windows, according to the unit's categories (see Fig. 1), that contain complementary information. The user can swift between the two units, directly relating the myths' narratives to their visual representations and vice versa. In order to organize the large amount of available information (129 Stories, 329 Characters, 124 Locations)-and therefore the visualized nodes in the three windows- a dynamic system of nodes connection has been developed, based on their degree of correlation.

Unit Myths. Unit Myths aims at recording, digitizing and promoting the narratives of Greek mythology, as an important part of the intangible cultural heritage. It offers an overview of the flow of events in a mythical time sequence, while at the same time, it discovers and highlights connections among stories, characters and places-with the help of artificial intelligence algorithms- which are not easily perceived otherwise.

Stories. The Stories window (see Fig. 5, window 1) includes the narratives of all the myths that are registered in the application. By means of a character-centered approach, COSMOS structures Greek mythology into Thematics that revolve around gods' and heroes' lives and achievements, e.g. Athena's Thematic, Heracles' Thematic, etc. The Thematics are divided into subsections (Stories) and each Story is visualized as a node in a three-dimensional space.

Since there are no specific dates in mythology, the time sequence, referred to as a mythical timeline, has been created through the "chronicle" relations between Stories of different Thematics, with the use of Landmark-Stories. The rest of the Stories have been set on the timeline on the basis of whether they took place before or after the Landmark-Stories. Consequently, the Story nodes' placement between the Landmark-Stories, as well as the distance between the Story nodes, is relative rather than accurate.

For example, in the diagram below (see Fig. 3), the Story *The Search for Medusa* of the Perseus Thematic, in which Pegasus is born, is characterized as a Landmark-Story and chronologically identifies the Story *Taming of Pegasus* of the Bellerophon Thematic, as well as its latter ones.

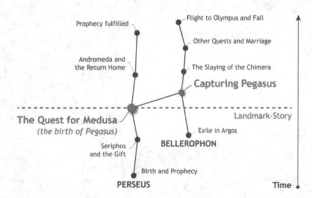

Fig. 3. Temporal location of Story nodes on the mythical timeline, based on Landmark-Stories

In the Stories window there are three types of node connections (see Fig. 4):

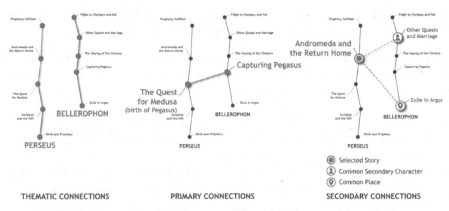

Fig. 4. Story nodes connection types (Thematic, Primary and Secondary)

1. Thematic Connections are the ones that connect nodes along the same Thematic
2. Primary Connections are those between nodes of different Thematics (a) with common entities (e.g. characters, notions, objects) that play an important role in the evolution of the story or (b) narrate related events.
3. Secondary Connections are the ones between nodes of different Thematics with (a) common secondary characters or (b) common places.

Characters. The Characters window (see Fig. 5, window 2) includes all the mythical characters participating in the registered Stories, categorized as (a) Olympian gods (b) gods (c) minor gods (d) heroes and (e) mythical creatures. They are visualized as color coded nodes, according to the category they belong.

Fig. 5. Unit Myths: information visualization (1. Stories, 2. Characters and 3. Places)

Places. The Places window (see Fig. 5, window 3) includes the locations where the Stories evolve. The Places nodes are visualized on a two-dimensional map.

Node Selection. When a node is selected, the KPS queries the graph database through the COSMOS Web Service for relevant linked information. Depending on the node type, the relevant linked information is retrieved and presented in the three windows:

1. Story node selection (see Fig. 5). The characters that participate in the Story are presented in the Characters windows and the locations of the Story in the Places window.
2. Character node selection. The Stories, which this character takes part in, are highlighted in the Stories window and the locations of these Stories in the Places window.
3. Place node selection. The Stories that take place in the specific location are highlighted in the Stories window and the characters of these Stories in the Character window.

Node selection in each window offers additional options to the user.

1. Story node selection (see Fig. 5). (a) Presentation of the Story (text and illustration) and (b) access to the unit Art, where the nodes of artworks related to the specific Story are highlighted.
2. Character node selection. (a) Presentation of a short biography text about the selected Character, enriched with personality traits and additional analysis where available

(e.g. name origin) and (b) access to the unit Art, where the nodes of artworks related to the specific Character are highlighted.
3. Place node selection. (a) Presentation of a short descriptive text about the selected Place (e.g. its role in Greek mythology) and (b) access to the unit Art, where the nodes of artworks with origin or current location in the specific Place are highlighted.

Unit Art. Unit Art aims at recording and showcasing ancient works of art that draw inspiration from the stories of Greek mythology. At the same time, it offers a visualization of the geographical densities or dispersions of these artworks, along with the depicted characters.

Artworks. The Artworks window (see Fig. 7) includes works of art from antiquity, that portray registered Stories. Accordingly, each Story node (unit Myths) may correspond to one or more visual representations, of different typology and/or period. Each artwork is visualized as a node arranged along a three-dimensional chronological timeline. Artworks are further categorized, color-coded, based on their typology (Metalwork, Pottery, Sculpture, Mosaic), while each typology is divided into its known chronological periods. In the Artworks window there are two types of node connections:

1. Story Connections are the ones between artwork nodes that have a common theme and depict the same Story,
2. Secondary Connections (see Fig. 6) are the ones between artwork nodes that have a common (i) creator or (ii) depicted character or (iii) location of origin or exhibition (e.g. archaeological site, museum).

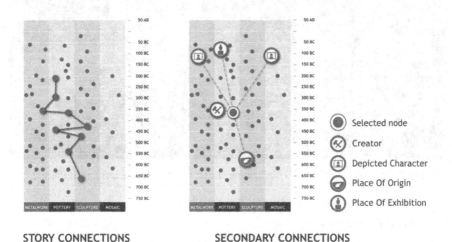

STORY CONNECTIONS   SECONDARY CONNECTIONS

Fig. 6. Unit art. Secondary connections

Characters. The Characters window includes all the mythical characters that are depicted in the registered Artworks. The visualization is similar to the one in the unit Myths.

Places. The Places window, (see Fig. 7), includes the place of origin or/and current location of the artifact on a two-dimensional map.

Node Selection. Node selection in each window offers additional options:

1. Artwork node. (a) Presentation of information about the selected Artwork (typology, place of origin, present location, date of creation, artistic period, artist, depicted characters, brief description, visual material) and (b) access to the unit Myths. In Myths, the Story node related to the specific Artwork is highlighted.
2. Characters node. (a) Presentation of a short biographical text about the Character (similarly to the unit Myths) and (b) access to the unit Myths. In Myths, the Story nodes where the selected Character participates (or has a leading role) are highlighted.
3. Places node. (a) Presentation of information about museums (place of exhibition) and archeological sites (place of origin and/or exhibition), with registered artifacts, located in the specific area and (b) access to the unit Myths, where the Story nodes that take place in the selected Place are highlighted.

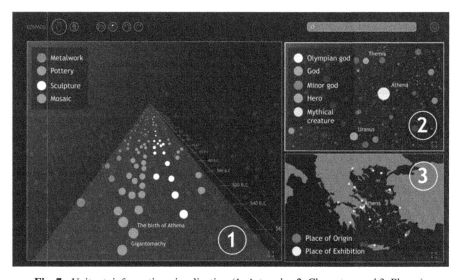

Fig. 7. Unit art: information visualization (1. Artworks, 2. Characters and 3. Places).

2.3 Prototype Evaluation

A two-day event was organized in February 2020, aiming to assess the features, the content and the overall experience of the application. The survey group comprised 42 participants, divided into the following age groups: 10–17 (2.38%), 18–29 (2.38%), 30–39 (42.86%), 40–49 (30.95%), 50–59 (2.38%), 60 and above (19.05%), with 90.48% holding a higher education degree, whereas, 9.52% has attended secondary school. Their familiarity with digital applications ranged from medium (15.38%) to extensive

(84.62%), while their knowledge regarding Greek Mythology spanned from limited (23.81%), medium (57.14%), to extensive (19.05%).

The audience was invited to use and evaluate -by means of a questionnaire- a functional prototype of COSMOS. The provided answers validated that, for the vast majority of users (97.62%) the application is easy to use, the operation is original and pleasing (97.62%), the information search is simple (88.10%) and the switching among the three windows is straightforward and interesting (76.19%). The feature that drew the audience's attention the most, reaching a percentage of 68.29%, was the innovative way of presenting the available information, whereas, 19.51% was more interested into the texts; moreover, while they evaluated the available graphics positively (85.71%) they also suggested that they would like for myths and characters illustrations to be additionally included (66.67%). The above-mentioned was taken into account and the application is further enriched with illustrations (see Fig. 5). The most competitive features of the COSMOS application (multiple choice question) were the parallel visualization of the myths' three elements - stories, characters, places- (80.95%), the non-linear reading (59.52%), the visualization of the myths (stories) correlations (54.76%) and the easy knowledge acquisition (54.76%). Finally, all the participants considered the application to be suitable for educational purposes.

3 Expected Results

The development and distribution of the COSMOS application aims at a wide range of results with social, economic and cultural impact. First and foremost, it is a unique opportunity for a combined recording and digitization of the Greek mythology, both in its written and visual forms. At the same time, there is realized a worldwide identification, localization and interconnection of ancient Greek artworks, related to the specific thematic. Moreover, an opportunity emerges for the wide dissemination of an important part of the Greek cultural heritage, and for the better understanding and overview of this complex and massive work, by means of an attractive, user-friendly and easily accessible product.

The above-mentioned, result in a potential increase of the interest around Greek cultural heritage, by expanding the audience in a worldwide level, and by attracting younger age groups that are more familiar with digital applications and technology in general. Educational and cultural tourism are respectively encouraged, by means of showcasing the registered artworks, the places (e.g. Archaeological sites) and the museums that host relevant collections or individual exhibits. In addition, the establishment of an international digital network of sites and institutions is favoured, encouraging new cultural collaborations (e.g. exchange of knowledge and exhibits, collaboration in the organization of exhibitions, research and publications production). The outcomes of these partnerships can prove beneficial in further expanding and feeding the COSMOS content and its narrative branches anew.

Apart from focusing on Greek mythology, COSMOS can also be expanded to linking mythologies in an intercultural level, thus resulting in an even wider audience. On top of the traditional research process, the data interconnection will be performed automatically, based on the knowledge organization subsystems. This will facilitate the comparative study of mythologies from geographically and/or chronologically distant cultures.

The final product is intended to address to a vast audience and it can be used: a) as a study aid for anyone interested, b) for educational purposes, by teachers and students, c) as a reference tool in the field of the Social Sciences and the Humanities, for the production of research projects (a tool produced by Research, to be offered to Research anew), and d) as a scientific documentation tool, for exhibition curating purposes.

The COSMOS project offers the opportunity to foster new interdisciplinary collaborations between the social sciences, the ICT sector and the cultural and creative industries, in order to develop an innovative product. The COSMOS platform could be used after the completion of the project, for the development of corresponding applications, in order to revive, exhibit and disseminate other forms of intangible cultural heritage (e.g. history, fairy tales and folk tales).

Acknowledgements. COSMOS is co-financed by the European Union and Greek national funds through the Operational Program Competitiveness, Entrepreneurship & Innovation (EPANEK), in the framework of the RESEARCH – CREATE – INNOVATE Action (project code T1EDK-04283). Project duration: 30 months.

References

1. Chami, A.: The influence of the Greek mythology over the modern Western society. University of Tlemcen (2015)
2. Kakridis, I.T.: Greek Mythology (5 volumes). Ekdotike Athenon, Athens (1986)
3. UNESCO: Basic Texts of the 2003 Convention for the Safeguarding of the Intangible Cultural Heritage (2018). https://ich.unesco.org/doc/src/2003_Convention_Basic_Texts-_2018_version-EN.pdf
4. COSMOS homepage. https://cosmosapp.gr. Accessed 27 Oct 2020
5. Ekdotike Athenon homepage. https://www.ekdotikeathenon.gr. Accessed 23 Oct 2020
6. ISL homepage. https://www.iit.demokritos.gr/labs/isl/. Accessed 23 Oct 2020
7. Intangible Cultural Heritage of Greece. http://ayla.culture.gr/en/introduction. Accessed 26 Oct 2020
8. Baldick, J.: Homer and the Indo-Europeans. Comparing Mythologies. Bloomsbury Publishing, London (1994)
9. Buchmesse. https://www.buchmesse.de/files/media/pdf/whitepaper-industry-leaders-perspectives-frankfurter-buchmesse.pdf
10. The Museum of the World. https://britishmuseum.withgoogle.com. Accessed 23 Oct 2020
11. Internet Projects Ltd.: Greek Mythology-Gods & Myths, Version 2.7.2 (2016) [Mobile application software]. https://play.google.com/store/apps/details?id=com.internetprojects.greekmythology
12. Chiko_tzu: Greek Mythology & Gods Offline, Version 1.0.0 (2019) [Mobile application software]. https://play.google.com/store/apps/details?id=com.expos.offline.greekmythology
13. Elisav, A.: Greek Mythology, Version 1.0 (2017) [Mobile application software]. https://play.google.com/store/apps/details?id=com.andromo.dev609633.app600895
14. MongoDB homepage. https://www.mongodb.com. Accessed 26 Oct 2020
15. Sang, E.: Introduction to the CoNLL-2002 shared task: language - independent named entity recognition. In: Roth, D., Van den Bosch, A. (eds.) Proceedings of CoNLL-2002, Taipei, Taiwan (2002). https://doi.org/10.3115/1118853.1118877

16. Kapetanios, E., Tatar, D., Sacarea, C.: Natural Language Processing: Semantic Aspects. CRC Press, Boca Raton (2013). 10.1201/b15472
17. spaCy homepage. https://spacy.io. Accessed 26 Oct 2020
18. Onto Notes homepage. https://catalog.ldc.upenn.edu/LDC2013T19
19. Nodejs homepage. https://nodejs.org/en/about. Accessed 26 Oct 2020
20. Fastify homepage. https://www.fastify.io. Accessed 26 Oct 2020
21. Neo4j Graph Database. https://neo4j.com/neo4j-graph-database. Accessed 26 Oct 2020
22. Cypher, The Graph Query Language. https://neo4j.com/cypher-graph-query-language. Accessed 26 Oct 2020

Project Papers: Storytelling
and Authoring Tools

Learning About the Heritage of Tinian Marble Crafts with a Location-Based Mobile Game and Tour App

Panayiotis Koutsabasis$^{(\boxtimes)}$ ⓘ, Anna Gardeli, Konstantinos Partheniadis,
Panayiotis Vogiatzidakis, Vassiliki Nikolakopoulou, Pavlos Chatzigrigoriou,
and Spyros Vosinakis ⓘ

Department of Product and Systems Design Engineering,
University of the Aegean, Syros, Greece
kgp@aegean.gr

Abstract. The paper presents a mobile location-based app that promotes learning and sensitization about the Tinian marble craftsmanship, which is enlisted to the Representative List of the Intangible Cultural Heritage of Humanity of UNESCO. It consists of a location-based game and a tour that provide semantic connections to visitors of the museum of Marble Crafts and the settlement of Pyrgos, Tinos island, Greece. The paper presents the game design which emphasizes exploratory learning and storytelling. Furthermore, an evaluation of the game has been conducted with playtesting at the field, with the participation of ten expert users: interaction and game designers, technology developers and cultural heritage professionals.

Keywords: Location-based game · Cultural heritage · Tinian marble crafts · Role-playing · Storytelling · Evaluation · Playtesting · Usability · User experience · Experts

1 Introduction and Related Work

Over the last few years, we are witnessing the development of several mobile apps that promote the digital preservation and learning about cultural heritage with engaging ways like tours and games.

Examples of tour apps include the Dramatric [5] which interweaves fiction and reality to engage museum visitors, as well as the Viking VR [22] which allows the visitors of the British Museum and York Museum to make a Virtual Reality tour into a Vikings camp. Mobile tour apps are often atomic experiences and may be combined with some elements of gamification and storytelling. Some tour apps may also have additional goals, including to enhance the accessibility of museum exhibits like in [3], who present a mobile tour app for blind users who can touch museum replicas to enable audio descriptions from their mobile phone.

Examples of mobile games that promote cultural heritage (CH) include the 'Gossip at the Palace' [19] which can be played at a historic Italian residence to convey stories

© Springer Nature Switzerland AG 2021
M. Ioannides et al. (Eds.): EuroMed 2020, LNCS 12642, pp. 377–388, 2021.
https://doi.org/10.1007/978-3-030-73043-7_31

about the people that have lived there in the past; Gocha [7] addresses children who take the role of a group of archaeologists and search and collect (replicas of) fragments of antiquities (connected with location sensors). These games may be played indoors and outdoors and are especially addressed to young visitors of cultural sites who are better acquainted with interactive technology and prefer playful ways of learning. Location-based games for cultural heritage are evolving into a game genre with several unique features [12].

In this paper, we present a mobile app that combines a tour and a game with the aim to promote learning about the cultural heritage of Tinian Marble Crafts. The mobile app connects a small village with important heritage: the settlement of Pyrgos, island of Tinos, Greece, to its peripheral Museum of Marble Crafts. The mobile app provides users with a virtual tour to several POIs (points of interest) located in the museum and the settlement. The location-based game is intended to be played by visitors while in the museum or the settlement.

We first present the local context and heritage of Tinian marble crafts. Then, we emphasize on the mobile game design, which interweaves exploratory learning and storytelling. Finally, we discuss the evaluation of the game that has been conducted with playtesting at the field, with the participation of ten expert users.

The research is part of the work conducted in the project Mouseion Topos: http://www.mouseion-topos.gr/.

Fig. 1. Aspects of the settlement of Pyrgos, Tinos, Greece; the use of marble works in the settlement is omnipresent.

Fig. 2. Aspects of the Museum of marble crafts.

2   The Tinian Marble Craftsmanship and the Museum of Marble Crafts

Tinian marble craftsmanship has been recognized globally, and since 2015 it is inscribed at the Representative List of Intangible Cultural Heritage of Humanity (UNESCO). Tinian marble-craftsmen acquire unique knowledge concerning marble and its properties, such as the handling of its veins. Moreover, they have developed the relevant skills for the making of the tools used both in marble-crafting and marble-mining [6]. The transmission of marble craftsmanship is based on a master-apprentice model through informal education, where the apprentice, after long and tough training, finally receives complete expertise. Built heritage is the consequence of craftsmanship that has been transmitted by craftspeople throughout the centuries and embodies the predominant knowledge and practices concerning nature and the universe [13].

One of the most delegate villages of such rich and exceptional tradition of marble craftsmanship is the village of Pyrgos. Pyrgos is located at the western part of the island, about 27 km from the town of Tinos. The village experienced growth during the 18th and 19th century due mainly to shipping and marble. Marble trade gave an economic outlet to the Tinian people that is reflected upon renovated houses with the engraved dates on marble signs upon doors. From the involvement of the inhabitants with the marble craftsmanship, Pyrgos also created a remarkable artistic tradition and highlighted some of the greatest Greek artists. The settlement is declared traditional and has maintained the image it had in the past as well as its local character. The settlement has a strong robust Cycladic essence physiognomy and can be characterized as an open-air museum of folk art. The juvenile engravings on the marble-paved streets of the settlement testify the engagement of the local craftsmen habitants with this material since their early childhood (Fig. 1).

The Respective List of UNESCO classifies the products of Tinian marble craftsmanship based on their use and many of them can be identified inside the settlement. There are tools and utensils of everyday life (such as mortars, stone crushers, sinks), etc., architectural applications such as (paving, columns, frames, porches, balconies, church facades), etc. and marble sculptures or stone carvings such as (coats of arms, skylights, fountains, tombstones, children engravings) etc. The carvings' decoration bears symbols that draw from religious, magical and oral traditions. Such ornamental carvings on the skylights of the houses (Fig. 1), church facades, fountains, and tombstones at the local cemetery, represent basic essential elements of the physiognomy of the settlement.

Local heritage is exhibited by the Museum of Marble Crafts. The museum describes in detail and vividly, through mini-documentaries with testimonies of the local people, the tool equipment and the techniques used in order to mine, manipulate, design, artistically create, and merchandise Tinian marble during the pre-industrial age (Fig. 2), when Tinos was the most important center for the production and commerce of marble crafts in Greece. Nonetheless, the scope of the museum's scope is not only to present the developed technology around Tinian marble but also to connect and reveal the social and economic context from which the craftspeople advanced their workshops and contributed, through their work, to the overall image of their place.

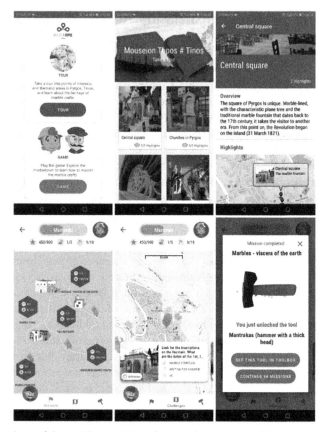

Fig. 3. Screenshots of the mobile app. Upper images show aspects of the tour and lower images aspects of the game about marble crafts.

3 Design of the Mobile App

3.1 Combining Tour and Game

The mobile app (Fig. 3) aims to enhance learning and experience of visitors of Tinos in two ways. Firstly, the app provides users with a virtual tour to several POIs (points of interest) located in the museum and the settlement. The tour functionality is intended to be used before the visit to help visitors better prepare and plan. The location-based game is intended to be played by visitors while in the museum or the settlement. While visitors walk through the sites, they can locate places where specific questions are asked that require from them to explore the place, locate answers and ultimately learn about local heritage.

3.2 Location-Based Game Design

At the heart of the mobile app is the location-based game, entitled 'Exploring the Marble Town'. The goal of the mobile game is to enhance visitors' experience by engaging them into exploration and learning activities in the settlement of Pyrgos and the museum.

Educational Affordances. The educational goals are not explicitly provided to the users; instead they are indirectly conveyed in a playful way. The aim is to create awareness and sensitization about the tangible and intangible cultural heritage of the place. We do not pursue in-depth learning of a specific educational subject, but rather the transfer of knowledge, understanding and awareness in relation to issues of tangible and intangible culture.

Exploratory learning [18] is generally about the activities of observation and exploration, which happen naturally to all people, especially in previously unknown situations. In the case of our mobile game, many visitors of the cultural site (i.e. many tourists and pupils or students in educational visits) will be visiting the museum and the settlement for the first time.

The player of the game is motivated to observe carefully, to explore and discover information and elements that exist in the physical world, but also to process and combine them in order to complete the challenges. As a result, they are able to construct new knowledge through action (constructivist approach), instead of receiving it passively.

Storytelling and Game Design Elements. Storytelling creates an imaginary context in which the discovery takes place, combining real (e.g. historical information related to context) and imaginary elements (e.g. role-playing and script). It is an important element of games as it can give meaning to the goals, challenges and rules of the game as well as motivate the players. Additionally, it enhances engagement and empathy with strangers/places/situations, as the player feels that he can participate or influence the story.

We have adopted the Mechanics-Dynamics-Aesthetics (MDA) approach [8] to organize the main design directions about the mobile game. According to MDA, the consumption of games is based on three elements: rules, system and fun; these are based on three elements of game design: mechanics, dynamics and aesthetics.

- Mechanics are essentially the rules of the game at the level of data representation and algorithms. In our game, the main mechanics are missions, challenges, player levels, experience points, player inventory (or toolbox, about marble tools), hints, answers and more information.
- Dynamics refers to the "behavior" of the elements of engineering, at the level of interaction with the player. Dynamics update some of the mechanics of the game (e.g. experience points, player level, missions and challenges completed, etc.) with respect to user location and provided answers to challenges.
- Aesthetics refers to the desired emotional responses of the player while engaging in the game. We have selected the following aesthetics of MDA that we consider suitable for the specific activity, technology and target group: Discovery, Challenge, and Narration.

○ The discovery aspect i.e. the player's sense of discovering unknown and interesting elements, is supported through the semi-structured space tour and the observation in the physical world, where players explore aspects of the settlement which are unknown to them.

○ Challenge, i.e. the feeling that one has to make an effort to solve a puzzle that makes sense to him and is rewarded along the way, is inherent in the game through the need to combine elements and information of the physical and digital world to solve a puzzle.

○ Narrative is the feeling that the game is guided by a story that gives meaning to the player's challenges and goals. This emerges through the design of roles and digital characters that the players engage with; as well as the revelation of correct answers to the puzzles, from which data for the respective point of interest emerge as parts of the general story.

4   Evaluation

4.1   Method: Experts' Playtesting with Constructive Interaction

We conducted the evaluation at the stage where the mobile app was developed and tested in the lab, but not yet in the field. We were especially interested to test the playability of the game, which is a composite concept that is mainly concerned with issues of gameplay, usability and functionality [17]. So, the goal of the evaluation was to play the game in the field and discover various issues that could not be possibly identified in laboratory testing.

Furthermore, we wanted to recruit experts from the domains of CH, game design and development and interaction design, to play the game in order to predict issues before end user testing. As noted in [15], it is important for digital heritage projects to consider the opinions and knowledge of local CH experts early and often during the design and development process, along with the opinions of other experts about design and technology development. Several aspects of mobile games for cultural heritage can be reviewed by experts before recruiting end-users that include, but are not limited to,

- the quality of cultural content (selection, fidelity, representativeness, etc.),
- the gameplay (i.e. the rules, mechanics, and dynamics of the game),
- mobile usability and design including guidelines (e.g. Android Material Design), and technical issues.

Therefore, we have constructed a practical method of evaluation, which requires from experts to play the game in pairs, as they would do if they were visitors of a CH site. Thus, the experts engage in constructive interaction or co-discovery learning [16] about the game and the place. The experts-players are continuously observed by two researchers, who do not intervene in the process but record each player's comments, questions (to one another) and actions. During the process, researchers may further identify corrections that must be made, redesign ideas and other improvements. The researchers take notes about performance indicators, findings on playability and possible recommendations, preferably with digital devices that can also record videos of interactions and voice comments. At the end of the playtesting, a discussion with experts can summarize findings and yield more general remarks; additionally, benchmarking questionnaires about the usability or user experience can be completed.

The proposed method makes a purposeful synthesis of known methods and concepts from HCI (Human-Computer Interaction) evaluation and game design:

- It is a design review method (rather than an inspection), since that it does not rest on heuristics or guidelines, but on expert opinion.
- It is an empirical method, which unfolds as experts experience the game, in contrast to typical design reviews or juries that examine presentations or demonstrations of artefacts or systems. In comparison to heuristic evaluation where 3–5 double experts are proposed [14], a larger pool of experts is assumed. We do not propose employing game design experts only (e.g. as in [9]); we find essential the participation of CH professionals, interaction designers and software developers.
- It requires playtesting, a standard approach to game evaluation that emphasizes playability, i.e. a composite concept that includes (at least) aspects of gameplay, usability, and functionality [9].
- It requires from experts to actively play the game following the approach of constructive interaction, which has proved very productive in other contexts, (e.g. [1, 10],), in contrast to other expert-based approaches that rest on inspection or review.

Regarding the documentation and notes taking, we propose the following taxonomy of issues about mobile games for cultural heritage, for which researchers can keep notes of player cooperative actions:

- Performance indicators, which are average values of player performance, which can be approximately anticipated from real users.
- Playability findings, which are concerned with qualitative statements about identified problems or issues that fall into the dimensions of gameplay, usability functionality, as well as about cultural content and location context (which are specific to a location-based game for cultural heritage).
- Recommendations for improvement, which fall into corrections (immediate, easy), bug fixes, actions for redesign (minor), actions for redesign (major/considerable), actions for creation of cultural content.
- Questionnaires for benchmarking: At the end, we ask experts to benchmark the quality of the mobile game by filling-in standardized questionnaires.

4.2 Participants

Ten experts were recruited in playtesting of the mobile game, average age 41 years, four women. Four of them were CH experts: the museum director, two museum staff and a local heritage expert. Other experts were: two game designers and developers, two interaction designers, one graphics and 3D content developer, and one from IT (Information Technology) and CH project management.

Fig. 4. Photos from playtesting with experts.

Table 1. Performance indicators collected during playtesting with experts

Performance indicators	Values
Game completion time	107.6 min
— *Gameplay time*	54.7 min
— *Time in-between gameplay*	52.9 min
Distance covered	3.3 km
Challenge time to complete	3 min
Experience points gained	790 (max 900)
Challenges not answered correctly	2.9 (total 18)
Challenges' difficulty	4 hard; 9 medium; 5 easy

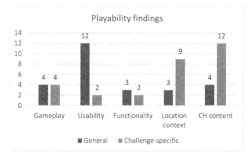

Fig. 5. Playability findings (on general and challenge-specific functions)

The playtesting sessions (Fig. 5) took place during a two-day project meeting at the Museum of Marble Crafts. For each playtesting session, a pair of expert players was formed as well as with a pair of researchers. Each researcher was focusing on the movements, comments and behavior of a particular player. After each researcher recorded findings on his/her own, they cooperatively processed and characterized them.

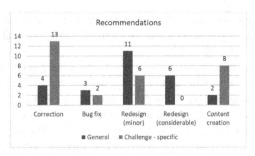

Fig. 6. Recommendations (types of).

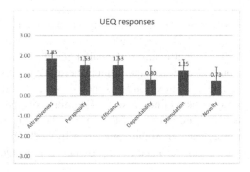

Fig. 7. Responses to the user experience questionnaire.

4.3 Results

We report on evaluation results in terms of performance indicators, playability findings and recommendations, and benchmarking questionnaires.

Performance Indicators. As shown in Table 1, the game lasted for a total of 107.6 min in total (average for all five pairs of players). We note that most challenges (13 from 18) were to be discovered outdoors (in the settlement), which also reflects the average distance covered by each pair of players (3.3 km).

The game was played at players' pace as would players normally do in a visit: they continuously interweaved gameplay with walking around the museum or the settlement to see the sites and discuss about them.

All player pairs undertook all challenges with a high level of success, and they failed to answer correctly to a few of them.

The researchers retrospectively assessed the difficulty of the challenges with characterizations easy, medium, hard.

These data about performance indicators could not be safely estimated beforehand. These are valuable data that can be used to further enhance the UX of the game by introducing them in the gameplay, e.g. to the reward system or to add indications or warnings.

Playability Findings. Figure 5 shows the number of playability findings for general aspects of the game (onboarding screens, mission information, tools earned, user profile, etc.), and for challenge-specific aspects (questions of multiple formats that require from the user to find the answer in the location), in terms of: gameplay, usability, functionality, location context, CH content.

Regarding general playability findings, most issues were about usability. Examples include: "It is not perceived by users that the helper character icon can be clicked"; "Missions accomplished are not highlighted onto the mission map", etc. Furthermore, a considerable number of findings are about functionality of the games; e.g. "The app crashes in Android versions close to the minimum version", "The player must be given the option to download offline maps", etc. Another considerable number of issues are about gameplay, for example: "Missions (and challenges) must be illustrated in the (suggested) order in which they can be undertaken", "Messages about user success/failure must first reveal the correct answer (consistent structure of messages)".

Regarding challenge-specific playability findings, issues about CH content and location context prevail. Regarding CH content, findings include several corrections to texts and photographs as well as identification of challenges that were not conveying an important takeaway about cultural heritage (which therefore needed to be replaced or reworked). Regarding location context, findings include several corrections on guiding users where to navigate or look to find answers. Examples of findings about location context include: "Some users are not sure if they are at the right spot in order to start looking for the answer (they wander around unnecessarily)", "Some users cannot locate the answer, despite on the spot (they need to be provided with a guideline, e.g. read the sign)".

Recommendations. Figure 6 presents recommendations for general aspects of the game as well as for challenge-specific aspects, in terms of: corrections (immediate, easy to make), bug fixes, redesign (minor), redesign (major/considerable), content creation.

Regarding general recommendations, most of them fall into minor redesign actions required, like for example "Add short animation to the character icon to denote that he is a helper to the user and that it is clickable"; "Redesign the map to illustrate the shortest route that includes game challenges", etc. There were also some redesign issues that will require considerable effort like that "Add more onboarding screens about characters of the game". These redesign actions are mostly about usability and gameplay findings. We also identified some actions for bug fixes and additional software testing, like "Upgrade minimum version of the app".

When we look at recommendations about the challenges of the game, we can see that most actions are corrections that must be made, mainly to CH content, for example "Fix naming of the player levels", "Ensure consistent English terminology with the signs of the museum", "Add explanation to reward message (challenge-specific)", etc. Another major area of recommendations is about the need to create new CH content, mainly new challenges to replace or supplement existing ones. The need to add a new challenge arose during playtesting with the experts, who often suggested alternatives, additions, or corrections. Since, we were in the field, we rapidly drafted the required information and took required photos.

Benchmarking Questionnaires. At the end of each playtesting session, we asked the participants to fill-in benchmarking questionnaires about perceived usability and user experience (UX).

Perceived usability was measured with the SUS (System Usability Scale) questionnaire [11]. The SUS score is satisfactory (81.8), although it implies room for improvement. According to [1] the SUS usability score is very satisfactory when above 80, it is fairly satisfactory when between 60 and 80, and not satisfactory when below 60.

Perceived UX was measured with the UEQ (User Experience Questionnaire) [21]. The results are shown in Fig. 7. All dimensions of UX are positively ranked and range in [0.73, 1.85]. According to [20] "it is extremely unlikely to observe values above +2 or below -2... the standard interpretation of the scale means is that values between -0.8 and 0.8 represent a neural evaluation of the corresponding scale, values> 0.8 represent a positive evaluation and values < -0.8 represent a negative evaluation."

The responses on benchmarking questionnaires are positive. The game was rated high in perceived usability and UX which implies that a first good design was achieved. However, there are still several qualitative issues that have been identified that must be addressed in another design and development iteration.

5 Summary and Conclusions

The paper presented the design and evaluation of a location-based mobile game and tour app that promotes the cultural heritage of Tinian marble crafts. The design of the mobile app is original because it combines a tour and a game which emphasizes storytelling and exploratory learning. We have constructed a novel method for the evaluation of the mobile app (experts' playtesting with constructive interaction) that emphasizes playing the game at the location by experts from the domains of cultural heritage, game design and development and interaction design. We envisage the human-centered and iterative approaches and methods presented in this paper can be adopted by researchers and practitioners in other digital heritage projects that involve mobile games and tour apps for cultural heritage.

Acknowledgements. This research has been co-financed by the European Union and Greek national funds through the Operational Program Competitiveness, Entrepreneurship and Innovation, under the call RESEARCH – CREATE – INNOVATE (project code:T1EDK-15171).

References

1. Albert, W., Tullis, T.: Measuring the User Experience: Collecting, Analyzing, and Presenting Usability Metrics. Newnes, London (2013)
2. Als, B.S., Jensen, J.J., Skov. M.B.: Comparison of think-aloud and constructive interaction in usability testing with children. In: Proceedings of the 2005 Conference on Interaction Design and Children, pp. 9–16. ACM (2005)
3. Anagnostakis, G., et al.: Accessible museum collections for the visually impaired: combining tactile exploration, audio descriptions and mobile gestures. In: Proceedings of the 18th International Conference on Human-Computer Interaction with Mobile Devices and Services Adjunct, pp. 1021–1025 (2016)

4. Android Developers. Guide to app architecture. Online document. https://developer.android. com/jetpack/guide. Accessed 12 Sept 2020

5. Callaway, C., Stock, O., Dekoven, E.: Experiments with mobile drama in an instrumented museum for inducing conversation in small groups. ACM Trans. Interact. Intell. Syst. (TiiS) **4**(1), 2 (2015)

6. Florakis, A.: Museum of Marble Crafts, Guidebook. Piraeus Bank Group Cultural Foundation, Athens (2009)

7. Georgiadi, N., et al.: A pervasive role-playing game for introducing elementary school students to archaeology. In: Proceedings of the 18th International Conference on Human-Computer Interaction with Mobile Devices and Services Adjunct, pp. 1016–1020. ACM (2016)

8. Hunicke, R., LeBlanc, M., Zubek, R.: MDA: A formal approach to game design and game research. In: Proceedings of the AAAI Workshop on Challenges in Game AI, vol. 4, no 1 (2004)

9. Korhonen., H.: Comparison of playtesting and expert review methods in mobile game evaluation. In: Proceedings of the International Conference on Fun and Games, Leuven, Belgium, pp. 18–27 (2010)

10. Koutsabasis, P., Spyrou, T., Darzentas, J.: Evaluating usability evaluation methods: criteria, method and a case study. In: Jacko, J.A. (ed.) HCI 2007. LNCS, vol. 4550, pp. 569–578. Springer, Heidelberg (2007). https://doi.org/10.1007/978-3-540-73105-4_63

11. Lewis, J.R.: The system usability scale: past, present, and future. Int. J. Hum.-Comput. Interact. **34**(7), 577–590 (2018)

12. Malegiannaki, I., Daradoumis. T.: Analyzing the educational design, use and effect of spatial games for cultural heritage: a literature review. Comput. Educ. **108**, 1–10 (2017)

13. Mergos, G., Patsavos, N.: Cultural heritage and sustainable development: Economic Benefits, Social Opportunities and Policy Challenges. Technical University of Crete Chania. (2017)

14. Nielsen., J.: Finding usability problems through heuristic evaluation. In: Proceedings of the SIGCHI Conference on Human Factors in Computing Systems, pp. 373–380 (1992)

15. Nikolakopoulou, V., Koutsabasis, P.: Methods and practices for assessing the user experience of interactive systems for cultural heritage. In: Applying Innovative Technologies in Heritage Science, pp. 171–208. IGI Global (2020)

16. O' Mailey, C., Draper, S., Riley, M.S.: Constructive interaction: a method for studying user-computer-user interaction. In: IFIP INTERACT'84 First International Conference on Human-Computer Interaction (1984)

17. Paavilainen. J.: Playability: a game-centric definition In: CHI PLAY 2017 Extended Abstracts: Annual Symposium on Computer-Human Interaction in Play, pp. 487–494 (2017)

18. Rieman, J.: A field study of exploratory learning strategies. ACM Trans. Comput.-Hum. Interact. (TOCHI) **3**(3), 189–218 (1996)

19. Rubino, I., Barberis, C., Xhembulla, J., Malnati, G.: Integrating a location-based mobile game in the museum visit: evaluating visitors' behaviour and learning. J. Comput. Cult. Heritage (JOCCH) **8**(3), 15 (2015)

20. Schrepp. M.: User Experience Questionnaire Handbook. https://www.ueq-online.org/ Material/Handbook.pdf (2018)

21. Schrepp, M., Hinderks, A., Thomaschewski, J.: Construction of a benchmark for the user experience questionnaire (UEQ). Int. J. Interact. Multi. Artif. Intell. **4**, 40–44 (2017)

22. Schofield, G., et al.: Designing a virtual reality experience for a museum. In: Proceedings of the 2018 Designing Interactive Systems Conference, pp. 805–815. ACM (2018)

"Narration": Integrated System for Management and Curation of Digital Content and Production of Personalized and Collaborative Narratives

Stelios C. A. Thomopoulos$^{(\boxtimes)}$, Konstantinos Dimitros$^{(\boxtimes)}$, Konstantinos Panou$^{(\boxtimes)}$ ⓘ, Giorgos Farazis$^{(\boxtimes)}$ ⓘ, Sofia Mitsigkola$^{(\boxtimes)}$ ⓘ, and Korina Kassianou$^{(\boxtimes)}$ ⓘ

NCSR "Demokritos"-IIT-ISL, P.O. Box 60037, 15310 Agia Paraskevi, Greece
{scat,k.dimitros,kpanou,gfarazis,sofmits}@iit.demokritos.gr

Abstract. The objective of this paper is to illustrate the common social need for preservation of Cultural Heritage (CH), through innovative and interactive processes of curation of exhibits and events in places of cultural interest or remotely [1]. Through the project "Narration" we are demonstrating ways for specialized and non-specialized users to create and curate narrations of various extents based on the content available, and share them with the general public. To this extent, the main focus can remain the research of adding an impact in providing a historical and cultural significance by enhancing the understanding and appreciation of cultural values. "Narration" proposes an innovative integrated platform for curating digital exhibitions and cultural content. Through a complex schema of interconnected narrative formations, "Narration" aims to contribute to a better understanding of the cultural and artistic relationships between exhibited objects and cultural heritage collections. Aiming at enhancing the preexisting apprehension on the way cultural heritage items carry valuable and explicable meanings, Narration suggests innovative and holistic curatorial solutions which enrich cultural heritage analysis and experience.

Keywords: Cultural heritage · Narration platform · Digital curation · AR/VR technology · Integrated system · Interactive experience · Digitization · Storyline creation · Digital museum

1 Introduction

CH is a common good passed from previous generations as a legacy for those to come. [2] CH assets carry significant historical and cultural information, back from their time of existence, to next generations. It is a fact that Museums remain among the main institutions which promote, demonstrate and preserve CH Artefacts [3]. However, they currently face a growing need of finding alternative ways of approaching and attracting wider audiences [4]. What is partially missing from their program are contemporary approaches to digital CH. While this may seem at odds with our technologically advanced society, it cannot be ignored. Current research in the field of museology has demonstrated

© Springer Nature Switzerland AG 2021
M. Ioannides et al. (Eds.): EuroMed 2020, LNCS 12642, pp. 389–399, 2021.
https://doi.org/10.1007/978-3-030-73043-7_32

growth in new directions enhancing visitors' experiences. One of the key ways museums attract new visitors can be achieved by enriching the tools and means through which museum professionals use interactive ways of retrieving information while transforming museum visits into a whole new experience [5, 6]. Digital tools have been a way of disseminating knowledge and research of CH artefacts. These tools are perfect means for everyone to share information and knowledge across different areas of interest. They are also proving to be valuable to museum professionals particularly in establishing a new era in sharing their collections and connecting with other groups of society. Through digitization which is being developed and used extensively for more than two decades now, museums are engaging in sharing their wide range of collections. Storytelling is an extension of how museums are dealing with ways to create connections between visitors and content and thus is a valuable tool [5]. Additionally, the reusability of CH assets in their digital form, and a greater degree of involvement from users contribute to the better understanding of the importance of our common cultural history [7] and thus in their preservation through time.

"Narration" project [9. Acknowledgments] addresses this need facilitating the management, interlinking and presentation of digital CH assets, by creating a tool accessible for all, specialists, non-specialists as well as the general public. "Narration" is co-developed by the Integrated Systems Laboratory (I.S.L.) [0] of National Centre for Scientific Research "Demokritos" (N.C.S.R.D), MUSEOLOGYLAB [9] of the Department of Cultural Technology and Communication [10], and Aegean Solutions S.A. [11] The Scientific Responsible of the project is Dr Stelios C.A. Thomopoulos, head of the ISL NCSRD.

2 Related Work

In the Cultural field, the use of educational methods in providing information about stories related to exhibits has become increasingly attractive [12]. The use of AR technology offers experiences by enhancing educational skills and approaching valuable knowledge coming from CH institution's data collection. Cultural institutions leverage digitization methods towards the preservation, representation and accessibility of their content. However, due to the increasing numbers of digital archives, curators still struggle to manage and demonstrate the significance of digital cultural assets. "Collections contain large amounts of data and semantically rich, mutually interrelated metadata in heterogeneous distributed databases. Facing the large amount of metadata with complex semantic structures, it is becoming more and more important to support users with a proper selection of information or giving serendipitous reference to related information" [13]. In fact, in many cases, the value of digital cultural assets is not being realized [14]. Furthermore, the meaning of a cultural asset is understood as either a single object when studied separately or in a more holistic way, when studied as part of a bigger system, when connected to a whole CH collection.

Applications addressing the above-mentioned issues exist for some time in the field of CH. From typical audiovisual cultural guides in AR, VR or in physical space, to systems that support the management of digitized cultural content, CH application's popularity is evident in the research sector by a multitude of projects. *The Museum*

Platform [15] creates online exhibitions mainly in the form of linear representations of digitized pictures or items uploaded by the user. They are managed through exhibition builder tools that enable the creation of predetermined connections. Collections display as relevant pictures of specific search results and they prioritize written details rather than actual multisensory experiences.

Furthermore, apart from the fact that it possesses the first position of the five pillar policy of the EU [16], significance in the inclusion of all to cultural activities is profound by the work that has been done in areas of public participation in CH. *Pluggy* is Europe's first social networking platform for CH, and it's focused on creating communities interested in CH. The *Pluggy* [17] social platform and the pluggable applications (*PLUGGY3D, PLUGGY Pins, PlugSonic Suite* and *Games Hunter*) were built upon the idea of empowering European citizens to be actively involved in CH activities, encouraging them to "transform their stories into experiences". Moreover, the employment of popularized mediums and technologies in CH, such as VR and AR seem to facilitate accessibility of cultural activities. *Pluggy 3d* [18] invites the public to start creating their own AR/VR exhibitions and project CH assets to their physical space, while *Pluggy Pins* [19] allow the creation of and provide access to cultural geolocation tours. *i-guide Knossos* [20] is an immersive 3D, Virtual Reality guide for the Knossos complex, based on Arthur Evans work, enriched with storytelling elements (video, audio, interactions, overlaying layers) that serve to inform the visitor of various aspects of the myth, culture and history. [20–22].

Narration and storytelling are adopted in some works concerning CH dissemination. *"Emotive uses emotional storytelling to dramatically change how we experience heritage sites"* [23]. *Emotive* uses drama-based narratives referencing a cultural space as means to enhance one's experience and encourage to repeat his/her visit there. *Artsteps* [24], on the other hand, allows the design of virtual environments, the creation of virtual exhibitions and storytelling through guide points across the VR space. It offers a full VR experience and utilizes images, videos, sounds and three-dimensional assets. The user is being offered a complete set of tools to build the exhibition space, place the artifacts, create and share narrations. At the same time, *Ortelia* [25] provides curators with an exhibition design software that enables users to archive important exhibitions in 3D space as well as designing narrative driven environments. *Ortelia* not only brings the opportunity to galleries to convert their floor plan into a 3D virtual gallery but also provides theater professionals with the designing tools to visualize theater settings and lighting.

The *Narration* project scopes to facilitate the management, interlinking and presentation of digital CH assets, by creating a tool accessible for all, specialists and the public. The platform offers a holistic approach to the access, creation, processing and preservation of cultural heritage content establishing a personalized approach to the interlinking of cultural assets. Visitors can experience the proposed narrative and navigate from one exhibit to the next, both by being in the physical space of the museum and virtually, through VR, by their smart device.

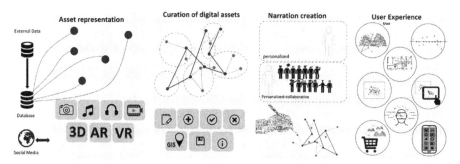

Fig. 1. Narration, graph of functions

3 Narration Concept

CH artefacts are inherited from the past to societies that intend to preserve and transmit them to the next generations [26]. Thus, it is important that CH artefacts themselves will remain physically unaltered while adapting to new digital practices. The *Narration* Project encourages curators to pass on knowledge and engage with non-specialised museum visitors on-site or remotely. By engaging CH assets through digital applications, curators can use and re-use CH asset's digital form, while creating new correlations through interlinking, which can lead to additional connections and renewed value which amplifies CH significance. The "Narration" system reassures CH inheritance to modern societies in a way that its significance is protected and preserved while also adapted to the digital culture.

Narration content originates from digital collections of distinct institutions and organizations of cultural interest which is eventually enriched with additional user-created content that addresses all the above-mentioned issues by the creation of the *Narration* platform, an integrated system to facilitate the management, support and promotion of cultural digital content in cultural institutions (CH sites, museums, exhibition spaces, etc.). Thus, the *Narration* platform offers curators tools to reuse CH content widely by using them in multiple ways and through digital media. Digitization substantially impacts CH management. Initially the digital image of the artefact can increase public awareness of the physical asset, and gradually increase interest in accessing knowledge of the context and narratives relating to this CH artefact and relating artefacts. This can be part of a creative process and dynamic methodology decision makers in the museum context can adopt in their curatorial approach [27]. Through the *Narration* platform (see Fig. 1)a (a) cultural specialist or a curator, manages, interlinks and associates digital CH assets, in order to create collections, or design a series of cultural experiences. Moreover, through this system, they can collect and use all the available information (blueprints, plans, assets, data, stories) and present the outcome in the form of interaction narratives, delivering a presentation on subjects of their choosing. This is one of the benefits of curating digital CH assets. Visitors can then navigate the physical space of the museum through their smart device (smartphone, tablet, headset etc.) using advanced technologies of Virtual and Augmented Reality, and experience the multiple narrations created by the curator through the platform. Throughout this use of the *Narration* Platform, both in the stages of research and presentation of the exhibition, a wide range of records relating to CH artefacts can constantly be added, enriching the available repository and providing a dynamic documentation of connections made regarding the artefacts both between themselves and the narratives associated to them. (b) The system is designed to be addressed to non-specialized users as well, aiming to further their understanding of CH and provide the adequate tools in order to explore and create narrations that will deliver valuable insights according to their interests and relative to spatial and digital content. The concept is based on the offering of an innovative set of tools and services for curator professionals in order to enable them to create narratives and enhance storytelling buildup processes having as final goal the immersive visualization of these narratives through digital media. For this purpose, hereby the definition of some terms which will be mentioned in the following chapters is provided. Core term in the current scope is the "Curator". "Curator" is the main professional user of the *Narration* project solution and the one to create narratives and build up the storytelling processes. The term "exhibit" is also introduced. Every digital asset which is either uploaded to the platform or ingested from 3rd party databases is related to a specific "exhibit" which will potentially be part of a digital narrative. Finally, the term "Narration" (warning: not the project name) is introduced. Every narrative or storytelling process created by the Curator is referred to with the term "Narration". What is more, *Narration* is a collection of several rich content Exhibit objects interconnected (forming a graph), with accompanying narrative text over these connections having as a final goal the creation of a coherent story. The following image depicts conceptually the narration graph creation process (see Fig. 2).

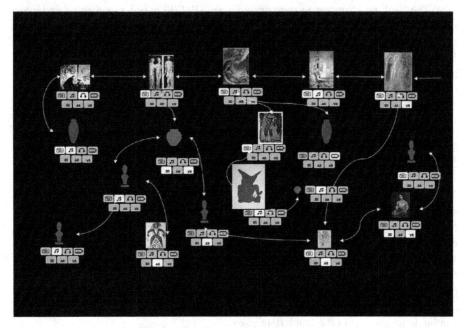

Fig. 2. Narration graph creation process

4   Overall System Architecture

Narration solution follows a three-tier System Architecture that is composed of three main layers: Data, Business and Presentation Layer. The Data Layer is the layer concerned with the ingestion of information and the storage and retrieval of data from the Database systems of the platform. The Data Layer contains the 3rd party database (Artplus), the Graph database and the User Management database. The Business layer is responsible for the main processing of available information, coming from the Data Layer, in order to transform it and make it available for visu-

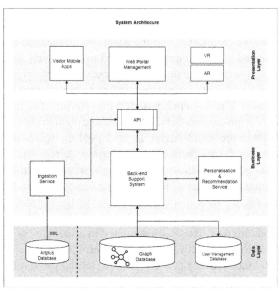

Fig. 3. Narration system architecture

alization at the Presentation Layer. The Business Layer contains the main Back-end Support System, the Ingestion service and the Personalization & Recommendation service. The Back-end Support System provides an API [28] in order to abstract and make transparent the internal operations and processes. Presentation layer comprises the different front-end applications that interface with Backend services (residing within the Business Layer), visualize the processed information in a user-friendly manner and allow the end-user to query and analyze information available. The Presentation Layer contains the *Narration* Web Portal Management, the Mobile Applications and AR/VR Applications. The Overall System Architecture is depicted in the following diagram (see Fig. 3).

5   Storage Solution

The *Narration* platform employs a multi-modal storage solution that makes use of two different types of database systems, the relational and the graph database. This architectural decision was made after researching several state-of-the-art approaches of holding digital artifacts and semantically maintaining them in diverse types of repositories ranging from simple storage file systems to more organized query able relational databases [29]. This allows for a flexible approach where storage of data takes place in each database according to the nature of data. A clear example of this are Narrations which can be deduced to graphs with interconnections between them which makes them a great candidate for storage in the graph database.

6 Backend System

The Backend System Services provides users and applications with a series of services for accessing, storing and managing data on the platform with the responsibility of abstracting users from the storage layer and implementing the necessary business logic to fulfill the requirements of the *Narration* platform. The services provided can be broken down into five high level categories: User management, Exhibit and Rich content services, Narration services, Geolocation services and Recommendation services.

User management services are responsible for providing a secure framework for authentication and authorization of users. The *Narration* platform supports three different types of users with different sets of capabilities:

Administrators. - Highest privilege type, can create and manage users.

Curators. - Users with advanced capabilities such as creation of Exhibits and Narrations.

Viewers. - Simple users that can only preview allowed Exhibits and Narrations.

Curators for instance are able to create new Exhibits and enrich their content as well as being able to create new narrations. On the contrary Viewers are only allowed to view public Exhibit and Narrations while Administrators provide the most capabilities.

Exhibit and Rich content services provide the necessary capabilities for creating and managing Exhibits along with Rich content. The platform supports rich metadata for Exhibits and a wide range of media types regarding media content ranging from simple text and images to sound, video and 3D files.

Narration services are concerned with providing capabilities to create and manage narrations. Narrations are structured as a graph where nodes are represented by Exhibits and directed edges that define the flow of the narration. Curators and Administrators can create and edit Narrations by using available Exhibits.

Geolocation services provide features regarding storage of spaces in the form of geometry along with the means to geolocate Exhibits in space. The services allow for the creation and management of existing spaces and locations. In the diagram depicted in (Fig. 4) the physical locations on the map are depicted along with their representation using GeoJSON [30] format. (see Fig. 4).

Recommendation services form part of the recommendation engine where users can rate Exhibits and Narrations and depending on their preferences the recommendation system suggests further interesting Exhibits or Narrations. The recommendation engine is using the Biased SVD algorithm where user ratings are estimated by the following formula:

$$\tilde{r} = \mu + b_u + b_i + q_i^T p_u$$

Where μ: mean of the users' ratings
b_u: difference between the mean rating of user u and the mean rating of all users
B_i: difference between the mean rating of exhibit i and the mean rating of all users.

```
{
 "type": "FeatureCollection",
 "features": [
  {
   "type": "Feature",
   "properties": {},
   "geometry": {
    "type": "Polygon",
    "coordinates": [
     [
      [26.575222983956337, 39.075272064228066],
      [26.575353741645813, 39.0751570199022],
      [26.575312167406082, 39.07512890949545],
      [26.575381234288216, 39.07506800357568],
      [26.57542079687118, 39.07509403175293],
      [26.575452983379364, 39.075063318502735],
      [26.575544849038124, 39.075125786116224],
      [26.575310155749317, 39.07533140828663],
      [26.575222983956337, 39.075272064228066]
     ]
    ]
   }
  }
 ]
}
```

```
{
 "type": "FeatureCollection",
 "features": [
  {
   "type": "Feature",
   "properties": {},
   "geometry": {
    "type": "Point",
    "coordinates": [26.575379893183708,
39.0751986649287]
   }
  }
 ]
}
```

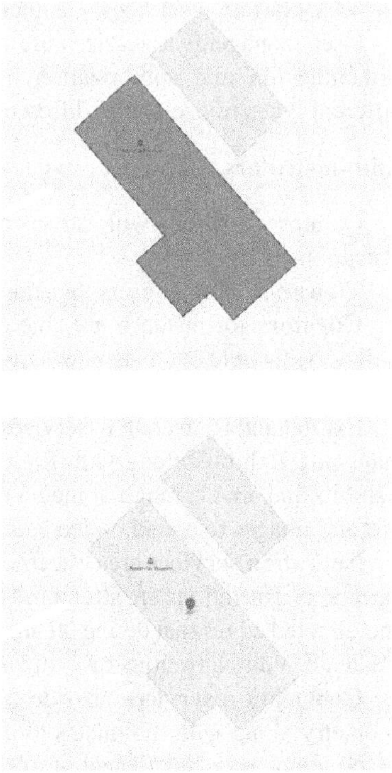

Fig. 4. Geometry representation using GeoJSON

The calculation of r is done by minimizing the following cost function J by applying the Stochastic Gradient Descent algorithm setting and in case of users who have not rated and in case of exhibits who were not rated. Below the cost function J:

$$J = \sum_{r_{ui} \in R_{train}} (r_{ui} - \tilde{r_{ui}})^2 + \lambda\left(b_i^2 + b_u^2 + \|q_i\|^2 + \|p_i\|^2\right)$$

7 Integration with Existing Systems

"Narration" project provides seamless integration with 3rd party repositories for importing cultural digital artifacts and enriching the available items collection which the platform offers to end-users - in this case, the curators. This is a very important and vital feature that *Narration* solution offers because it is highly expected for such systems to exploit and reuse the plethora [31, 32] of digital information which is already available in several cultural repositories around the world. Therefore, instead of offering yet another digital tool with which the user - curators, mostly, in this case - needs to create and digitize from scratch content to use for storytelling, by importing already rich content from 3rd party repositories, curators are offered a wide collection of diverse digital objects to select from in order to build their own unique storyline.

Within the scope of *Narration* project, an ingestion use case was followed regarding the importing of available digital artifacts in a collaborative platform - used by the museum -, named Artplus [33]. Artplus offers the capability to export available digital artifacts in XML format in order for 3rd party systems, such as the *Narration* platform to consume. XML exported files from the Artplus database are processed using Python and open source parsing libraries available while information is finally inserted in the *Narration* database using the available exposed API. Ingestion service (see System Architecture above) is responsible for the orchestration and implementation of the ingestion process. The ingestion flow is depicted in the following diagram (see Fig. 5).

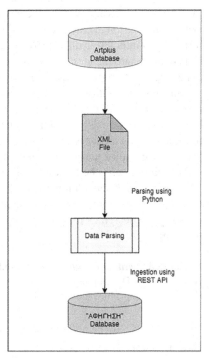

Fig. 5. Ingestion flow of 3rd party data

8 Summary and Future Work

As digitization of CH artifacts is developing into a common practice among institutions, the need to explore innovative ways of interpreting, correlating and distributing digital content becomes imperative. This paper highlights the rising need for the development of an effective integrated system for managing and displaying digitized CH artifacts and presents a concrete example through the creation of the *Narration* platform.

While Museums and Cultural Institutions play a catalyst role in maintaining, displaying and contextualizing artworks principally in the form of physical exhibitions, in the digital world cultural objects appear deprived of time, scale and space limitations. They can be manipulated, enriched, rearranged and clustered into meaningful entities as never before revealing unique artistic and cultural perspectives.

On this basis, successful storytelling has to be adapted to the implementation of alternative and creative procedures which would allow institutions to distribute CH values to wider audiences and provide them with unprecedented experiences of digital content. With the utilization of enhanced narrative design solutions, CH collections are to be transformed into interactive digital structures, gain interchangeable content, become accessible to third parties, be supplemented with advanced material and, therefore, contribute to the preservation of enriched CH information.

Shifting the mindset of conventional and linear interpretation of the narrative process, the project *Narration* offers vast possibilities for experimentation and creativity both for professionals and non-specialized users. Through a sophisticated system of innovative tools and services, *Narration* platform facilitates both curators and viewers in creating complex narrative formations and storytelling processes as well as organizing and developing enriched VR and AR interactive experiences. Furthermore, the system offers an extended evaluation layout to allow users and visitors to review the experienced narratives. In the long term, the evaluation results will be used for the improvement of the storyline design as it is communicated to the curators through the operation of the platform.

Acknowledgments. *Narration* is co-funded by Greece and the European Union- European Regional Development Fund (ERDF) within the operational program Competitiveness-Entrepreneurship-Innovation (EPAnEK).

References

1. Aslan, Z., Court, S., Teutonico, J.M., Thompson, J. (eds.): Protective Shelters for Archaeological Sites. Proceedings of a Symposium, Herculaneum, Italy, 23–27 September 2013. https://www.academia.edu/37090131/ Protective_Shelters_for_Archaeological_Sites
2. Directorate-General for Education, Youth, Sport and Culture (European Commission), LNCS, p. 4. https://op.europa.eu/en/publication-detail/-/publication/5a9c3144-80f1-11e9-9f05-01a a75ed71a1. Accessed 27 May 2019
3. ICOM. Russian National Committee, Kochelyaeva, Nina, Social and Educational Role of Museums in Promoting the Principles of the UNESCO Convention on the Protection and Promotion of the Diversity of Cultural Expressions, Unesco publication (2015). https://une sdoc.unesco.org/ark:/48223/pf0000233565.locale=en
4. Bertacchini, E., Morando, F.: The Future of Museums in the Digital Age: New Models of Access and Use of Digital Collections, p. 2. https://iris.unito.it/retrieve/handle/2318/105581/ 58394/bertacchini_morando_ijam_paper-revised-final_reading.pdf
5. Bertacchini, E., Morando, F.: The Future of Museums in the Digital Age: New Models of Access and Use of Digital Collections, p. 20. https://iris.unito.it/retrieve/handle/2318/105581/ 58394/bertacchini_morando_ijam_paper-revised-final_reading.pdf
6. Bedford, L.: Storytelling: the real work of museums. Curator Museum J. **44**(1), 27–34 (2001). https://doi.org/10.1111/j.2151-6952.2001.tb00027.x
7. Liarokapis, F., Petridis, P., Andrews, D., de Freitas, S.: Multimodal serious games technologies for cultural heritage. In: Ioannides, M., Magnenat-Thalmann, N., Papagiannakis, G. (eds.) Mixed Reality and Gamification for Cultural Heritage, pp. 371–392. Springer, Cham (2017). https://doi.org/10.1007/978-3-319-49607-8_15
8. I.S.L. https://www.iit.demokritos.gr/labs/isl/. Accessed 14 Sep 2020

9. Museology lab. https://museologylab.ct.aegean.gr. Accessed 12 Sep 2020
10. University of the Aegean. https://www.ct.aegean.gr/En/En_Index. Accessed 12 Sep 2020
11. Aegean Solutions. https://www.aegeansolutions.com/en/. Accessed 12 Sep 2020
12. Craig, A., et al.: Educational applications. In: Developing Virtual Reality Applications (2009). https://doi.org/10.1016/B978-0-12-374943-7.00006-9
13. Wanga, Y., et al.: Recommendations based on semantically enriched museum collections. Web Semant. Sci. Serv. Agents World Wide Web. (2008). https://doi.org/10.1016/j.websem. 2008.09.002
14. Hampson, C., et al.: Metadata-enhanced exploration of digital cultural collections. Int. J. Metadata Semant. Ontol. 9(2), 155–167 (2014). https://doi.org/10.1504/IJMSO.2014.060342
15. The Museum Platform. https://themuseumplatform.com/. Accessed 14 Sep 2020
16. Directorate-General for Education, Youth, Sport and Culture (European Commission): European framework for action on cultural heritage (2019). https://doi.org/10.2766/949707
17. The *Pluggy* project. https://www.pluggy-project.eu. Accessed 12 Sep 2020
18. The *Pluggy 3D*. https://www.pluggy-project.eu/pluggy3d/. Accessed 12 Sep 2020
19. The *Pluggy Pin*. https://www.pluggy-project.eu/pluggypins/. Accessed 12 Sep 2020
20. Iguide KNOSSOS: An immersive Virtual Reality Guide for the Archaeological site of KNOS-SOS. Press release. https://isl.iit.demokritos.gr/news/iguide-knossos-immersive-virtual-rea lity-guide-archaeological-site-knossos. Accessed 12 Sep 2020
21. Farazis, G., et al.: Digital approaches for public outreach in cultural heritage: the case study of *iGuide Knossos* and *Ariadne's Journey*. Digit. Appl. Archaeol. Cult. Heritage 15, e00126 (2019). https://doi.org/10.1016/j.daach.2019.e00126
22. Thomopoulos, S., et al.: DICE: digital immersive cultural environment. In: Ioannides, M., et al. (eds.) EuroMed 2016. LNCS, vol. 10058, pp. 758–777. Springer, Cham (2016). https:// doi.org/10.1007/978-3-319-48496-9_61
23. *Emotive* project. https://emotiveproject.eu. Accessed 15 Sep 2020
24. artsteps | Make your own Virtual Exhibitions. https://www.artsteps.com/. Accessed 14 Sep 2020
25. Ortelia Interactive - Exhibition Design Software for Galleries .... https://ortelia.com/. Accessed 14 Sep 2020
26. Ioannides, M., Alonzo, A., Georgopoulos, A., Kalisperis, L.: Documenting, archiving, preserving and visualising digital cultural heritage: from concept to reality. Int. J. Archit. Comput. 7(1), 2 (2009). https://doi.org/10.1260/147807709788549385
27. King, L., Stark, J.F.: Experiencing the digital world: the cultural value of digital engagement with heritage. https://doi.org/10.1080/2159032X.2016.1246156
28. API stands for Application Programming Interface. https://en.wikipedia.org/wiki/API
29. Nishanbaev, I.: A web repository for geo-located 3D digital cultural heritage models. Digit. Appl. Archaeol. Cult. Heritage 16, e00139 (2020). https://www.researchgate.net/publication/ 339560541_A_web_repository_for_geo-located_3D_digital_cultural_heritage_models
30. More information about GeoJSON: https://geojson.org/
31. Rosa, C.A., Craveiro, O., Domingues, P.: Open source software for digital preservation repositories: a survey. Int. J. Comput. Sci. Eng. Surv. (IJCSES) 8(3) (2017). https://arxiv.org/ftp/ arxiv/papers/1707/1707.06336.pdf
32. Elias, C.: Whose digital heritage? Contemporary art, 3D printing and the limits of cultural property, pp. 687–707, October 2019. https://doi.org/10.1080/09528822.2019.1667629
33. Artplus. https://artplus.com/

Wandering in the Labyrinth - Enhancing the Accessibility to the Minoan Past Through a Visitor-Sourced Approach

Thérèse Claeys[1](✉) and François Clapuyt[2]

[1] Department of Archaeology and Art History, Université Catholique de Louvain,
Louvain-la-Neuve, Belgium
therese.claeys@uclouvain.be
[2] Earth and Life Institute, Université Catholique de Louvain, Louvain-la-Neuve, Belgium
francois.clapuyt@uclouvain.be

Abstract. Arising on the island of Crete around 2700 BC, the Minoans are traditionally regarded as the first advanced civilization on the European continent in its modern meaning. The safeguarding of this primordial heritage faces multiple challenges. Besides extrinsic natural and anthropic threats, Minoan remains are also jeopardized by some of their own intrinsic properties. This paper aims to address two of these hazards: first, the preservation state of Minoan sites, leading to their restricted comprehension; secondly, their complex, "labyrinthine", architecture, further limiting this intelligibility but also challenging the physical access to the remains. The on-going research presented here intends to instrumentalize pathways as a solution to these drawbacks: it seeks to demonstrate that paths can not only be used as mobility vectors to guide and control visitors' movement but also, when context-aware, as interpretation media to improve on-site experience. Drawing upon phenomenological theories, this paper focusses in particular on the integration of the visitors' interaction with their surrounding as an innovative approach in the design of such well-informed paths. Based on the outcome of an original experiment conducted among 73 participants on the archaeological site of Malia, this study explores the possibilities of a combined qualitative and quantitative analysis of the visitors' movement in informing recommendations to increase the visitors' understanding and orientation abilities on site. The visitors-based approach discussed in this paper is only but one of the three axes to be combined in the general workflow advocated for the formalization of curated visitors' paths on Minoan archaeological sites.

Keywords: Archaeological site management · Minoan crete · Visitor behaviour · Human movement analysis · GPS-tracking · GIS spatial analyses

1 Introduction

1.1 Preservation vs. Presentation: Dichotomy or Complementarity?

One of the major challenges in the present-day cultural heritage management sector (CHM) is to find a proper balance between the imperatives of both preservation and

© Springer Nature Switzerland AG 2021
M. Ioannides et al. (Eds.): EuroMed 2020, LNCS 12642, pp. 400–411, 2021.
https://doi.org/10.1007/978-3-030-73043-7_33

presentation of archaeological and historical heritage sites: sites need to be open, displayed and explained to the large public while the impact of visitors' presence should be mitigated. This responsibility towards visitors has been progressively integrated in heritage discourse since the beginning of the postmodern era [1]. It was not until 2008, however, that the role of public communication and education in heritage preservation received an official international acknowledgement with the ratification of the ICOMOS Charter on the Interpretation and Presentation of Cultural Heritage [2]. This new paradigm in cultural heritage management stems from the belief, already expressed in the 1950s by Tilden, the "father of heritage interpretation" [3], that "through interpretation, understanding; through understanding, appreciation; through appreciation, protection" [4].

However, few archaeological sites show demonstrated concern for effective interpretation and communication strategies that could benefit their visitors. As noted by Williams, "it seldom articulates a holistic vision of the site, recognizing different voices or the complexity of visitors" [5]. One of the by-products of this deficiency is the lack of engagement of the visitors with archaeological sites. From Tilden's quote, one can easily understand this feeling of disconnection is likely to pave the way for neglecting attitude or misuse of those heritage places.

1.2   Through the Visitors' Eyes and in Their Shoes

To overcome these pitfalls, the present study advocates a visitor-centred approach. Such perspective used to be sceptically considered, or at least, undervalued by some scholars in the past because of the elusive character of the visitor experience and the difficulty of its conceptualization [6]. However, in the last two decades, visitors' spatial behaviour has started to receive more attention and has hence opened new venues for the quantitative study, and thus for a more objective approach, of the visitors' perception in heritage places. Arising from phenomenological theories and spatial cognition considerations, the movement of visitors can be interpreted as the expression of the interaction between the visitor and the cultural heritage space [7].

The study and understanding of general human mobility patterns covers a wide range of applications aimed at adapting different types of environment to a society's needs: from urban planning to traffic forecasting, or, to cite a much topical example, the tracking of the spread of biological and mobile viruses [8]. In the cultural sector in particular, the role of the visitors' behaviour in exhibition design and planning was acknowledged by museum institutions as early as the 1990s [9]. In parallel to these museum studies, there has been an ever-growing body of literature on recording techniques (from basic pen and paper, to complex satellite technologies) and analytic methodologies for tracking visitors' movement in heritage spaces [10]. However, most of these studies were mostly driven by economic agendas or primarily interested in the regulation of tourist flows.

1.3   Bridging the Gap with Visitors' Paths

From this brief literature review, Chrysanthi [7, 11, 12]'s research was pioneering in specifically applying the study of visitors' spatial behaviour to archaeological sites, and for the purpose of interpretation planning. The benefits of the visitor-centred approach she advocated in her PhD thesis [11] is twofold. On the one hand, it allows for multiple readings and understandings of the archaeological space. On the other hand, it provides insights to design presentation strategies at a conceptual and practical level, including context-informed walking paths respectful of the visitors' interests, their preferences and their emotional experience.

Indeed, in combination with other interpretative strategies such as information panels, visitors' itineraries constitute the main vehicle through which archaeological remains are displayed to the public. Despite their mention as "formalized walking tours" in the ICOMOS Charter on Interpretation and Presentation of Cultural Heritage the potential of visitor's paths as an interpretative tool has been so far largely under-investigated. While visitors' circulation paths are traditionally regarded as a preventive conservation strategy to monitor visitors' flow on fragile archaeological sites, this paper argues that curated paths may also be instrumentalized as an active interpretation medium to stimulate optimal cultural heritage experiences.

2 Methodology

2.1 Background and Case Study

The Minoan civilization flourished on the island of Crete between ca. 2700 – 1450 BCE. Besides their great age, the remains of this brilliant protohistoric civilization are characterized by their vulnerable fabric and their relatively poor state of preservation, not only threatening their safeguarding but also limiting their visibility. The legibility of Minoan ruins is further hindered by the labyrinthine architectural layout of their monumental court-centred buildings, commonly called "palaces". Considering these characteristics, already outlined by Platon in 1961 [13], there is a crucial need for proper interpretation supports and Minoan sites therefore offer an optimal environment for the development, implementation and evaluation of our innovative methodology aimed at designing curated paths. The archaeological site of Malia was selected as the main case study of this research for its historical importance, as it is the third largest "palace" on the island, and because of the variety of its preservation and presentation infrastructure.

Malia is located in a coastal plain on the north-east coast of central Crete. The settlement, occupied from the Early Minoan II period (around 2700 BCE) until the Late Minoan IIIB period (around 1200 BCE), saw the construction of a court-centred building ('palace') and several administrative, industrial and housing quarters during its long history. There were also port installations and cemeteries to the north close to the seashore. This northern section as well as some residential quarters are located outside the fenced area that is accessible by the public. To accommodate the almost 80 000 annual visitors [14], a master plan aimed at the valorization of the site was designed by M. Schmidt of the French School at Athens in close concertation with the Greek Archaeological service in 1985 and implemented in the early 90s. It entailed landscaping interventions, the construction of visitors' amenities and an exhibition centre, the installation of orientation and identification panels, the re-roofing of earth-based remains using protective shelters and some stabilization and restoration work [15]. Contrary to the 1990s conservation interventions, which have been punctually replaced when severely damaged, the presentation supports have been left as they were, despite their gradual decay.

2.2 Data Collection

The visitor data were collected over a period of nine days spread over two field sessions: the first in late August 2018 (three days of pilot tests conducted with archaeology students) and the second in late September (six days). Attention was paid to two crucial parameters during the survey.

The first was diversity: visitors with the most diversified profiles regarding age, gender, origin and companionship were preferably approached. Of course, the dataset could have certainly benefited from longer study seasons, but it became impossible to expend it due to time constraints. Potential sources of bias in the dataset hence need to be acknowledged before further detailing the methodology:

- Some visitors profiles will be misrepresented because of the restricted schedule of the survey (in particular, families with children avoid the September period which falls outside the school holidays, while it is the predilection holiday period for retired people).
- Some visitor types will be absent from the dataset due to the context of the visit. In particular, visitors accompanied by a tour guide were not surveyed since they usually have a tight-schedule, which would not have allowed them to participate in the entire experiment.
- The representation of nationalities will be biased too because of some language barriers, further detailed later in this section.

Besides the diversity, obtaining visitors' consent was another critical point. The rare opportunity to contribute to a participatory study that was interested in their opinion probably explains the high participation rate of visitors (reaching almost 95%).

The tracking of the visitors' movement was performed by means of four handheld Garmin eTrex touch 35 (interval time: 2 s; accuracy reading: 4 m) in order to collect good resolution data. Participants were given the GPS at the entrance of the site. They were asked to carry it with them whether in their hand, their bag or their pocket to avoid touching it so that the device could record both visitors' moves and stops. Participants were also assigned with the mission of taking pictures as they would normally do whether with their camera or smartphone. The collection of the pictures was aimed at informing visitors' decisions to stop or slow down in particular areas of the site. This method appeared to us as the least intrusive.

At the end of their visit, participants were asked to fill in a questionnaire specifically designed for the purposes of the study. It was translated into five languages (French, English, German, Italian, and Greek). It is beyond the scope of this paper to develop the conceptual framework behind the creation of this original questionnaire but it is worth briefly describing its outline. The survey started with some basic demographic questions about the visitors' profile and their level of knowledge of Minoan civilization prior to their visit to Malia. Following these, the questions were structured in a way that would allow visitors to express their views on four main axes:

1. What they learned and understood from the ruins;
2. What they valued the most and the least;

3. What they would advise for future management decisions;
4. Their degree of satisfaction from both a cognitive perspective based on quality evaluation and from an affective perspective based on mood evaluation.

2.3 Data Processing

The answers of the questionnaires were converted into numeric values for enabling standard statistical analyses performed in IBM's Statistical Package for Social Sciences (SPSS Statistics 22). The GPS data were converted from a GPX XML format to shapefiles (Geographic Coordinate System: GCS_WGS_1984) to enable a series of spatio-temporal analyses performed on ArcGIS and presented here below.

3 Preliminary Results

This paper strictly focusses on the characterization of the visitors' spatial behavior as given by the analyses conducted within ArcGIS. A more detailed and comprehensive study combining the outcome of the spatial analyses together with the results of the statistical processing of the questionnaires and the georeferencing of the pictures taken by the survey participants will be published elsewhere (Table 1).

Table 1. Metadata of the experiment conducted in Malia

Data type	Quantity recorded
GPS track	66
Questionnaires	73
Pictures	813

3.1 Density Analyses

We first conducted line density analyses of all the visitors' tracks. The aim was to try visualizing overlapping visitor movement in order to identify some patterns. As shown by the heat map (see Fig. 1a), the data were classified according to a color ramp: from dark blue indicating lower values of density to dark red indicating higher values. From Fig. 1a, we can see how the visualized outputs allow to immediately emphasize the areas with increased accessibility and/or attraction, and those, on the contrary, failing to attract visitors and/or remaining inaccessible to them.

Alongside the line density analyses, we also conducted point density analyses. The main difference between a point density analysis and a line density analysis lies in the presence of a time component only in the first case. Instead of characterizing visitors' flow, the heat map obtained through the point density analyses thus enables to detect those areas on the site where visitors stopped or slowed down (see Fig. 1b). In other words, while line density analyses can inform the accessibility potential and /or the "attraction power" of specific Points of Interest (POI), point density analyses are helpful for defining the "holding power" [16] of those POI, that is to say the ability of these POI in holding the interest of a visitor for a certain time, as discussed later on in this paper. By comparing the two heat maps, some differences appear in the distributions of the higher density values. For instance, we can observe on Fig. 1b a higher density of points to the south of the south-wing of the palace (framed in white). This corresponds with one of the rare resting areas on the site where a bench is located under a tree.

Fig. 1. Density maps overlapping an aerial picture of the site of Malia (© Google Earth): (a) Heat map showing the results of the line density analysis; (b) Heat map showing the results of the point density analyses (Color figure online)

3.2 Linear Directional Mean

The intention behind the calculation of the linear directional mean of the recorded tracks was to understand the direction of visitor flows in some selected areas on the site. Figure 2 proposes an insight in the general direction followed by visitors on the busiest passageways and the narrowest ones within the ruins of the palace.

In order to assess the potential impact of visiting Minoan sites prior to a tour at Malia, we conducted a new set of linear directional mean analyses discriminating between participants visiting a Minoan site for the first time and participants already familiar with similar sites. These comparative analyses revealed that visitors who had already been to other Minoan sites prior to their visit to Malia (65% of them) were most likely to start their visit by turning east towards the court-centered building, the most emblematic expression of Minoan architecture and a focal point of the Minoan town. The difference in the itinerary (starting whether to the north or to the east) followed by visitors who discovered Malia and hence a Minoan site for the first time was not significant.

4   Interpretation

These two types of spatial analyses can be performed to answer a plethora of questions related to interpretation planning purposes. They can also leverage other spatial analyses. For the sake of this paper, we limit the interpretation of the visualization of the dataset to test the following three hypotheses.

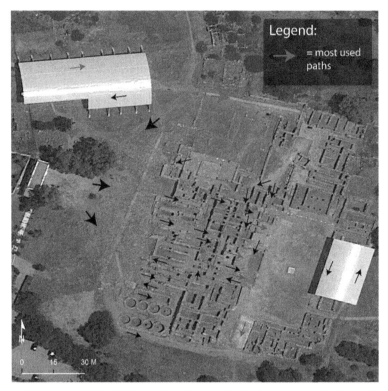

Fig. 2. Aerial picture of Malia (© Google Earth) overlaid with the outcome of the linear directional mean analyses.

Hypothesis 1: High density areas correspond to the so-called Points of Interest. Since interpretation supports are expected to target the most remarkable archaeological features that should attract visitors' attention, these supports should correspond to the POIs revealed by the heat map.

If we overlay the heat map with the location of the interpretation media (see Fig. 3), this hypothesis seems to be true in the case of information boards and most identification signs. However, some exhibits are still completely missed out by visitors (such as the Kappa quarter sign framed in white on Fig. 3).

These conclusions can be further specified using two other indicators often used in museum studies to identify where production of meaning takes place [17].

Firstly, we can calculate the frequency rate, or "attraction power" of each existing interpretation support by creating a buffer zone around them, intersecting this buffer with the visitors' tracks and then dividing the number of intersected tracks by the total number of recorded tracks (66). Considering the unavoidable GPS inaccuracies, this measure actually provides us less with a clear idea of the attraction power of the implemented interpretation strategies than with an indication of their maximum visibility or accessibility potential for visitors.

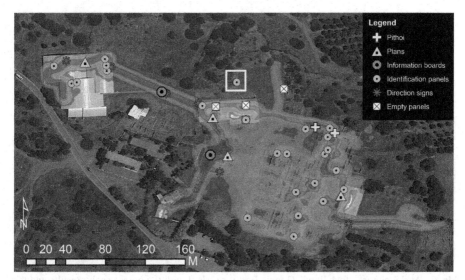

Fig. 3. Aerial picture of Malia (© Google Earth) overlaid with the line density results and the location of the interpretation infrastructure.

Secondly, the efficiency of the site exhibit equipment can be assessed by measuring their "holding power", that is to say the average time spent by visitors around each interpretation medium, applying and automating the following workflow: 1) creating a buffer zone around each exhibit; 2) using GPS track points rather than track lines, defining the entry and exit time of each track within the buffer based on the time code; and 3) with all the data, running a standard frequency analysis in SPSS. This "holding power" can also be measured by overlaying the location of the interpretative infrastructure with the outcome of the movement suspension analysis based on clustering techniques (Fig. 4). Such an analysis, aimed at detecting the location of visitors' stops, also allows to identify new and crowdsourced Points of Interest, thus far overlooked by site managers, but that would be worth integrating in site planning decisions.

The presence on the heat map of high density values in areas other than those targeted by the interpretation supports already gave an initial ideal of these POIs (see Fig. 3). The on-going processing of the images captured by visitors should help the accurate identification of these POIs before conducting Hotspot analyses.

Considering these interpretations, it can be argued that the assessment of visitors' spatial behavior can advise the implementation of interpretation supports and their orientation as well as the installation of much appreciated resting areas to enhance both the site understanding and comfort of visitors.

Hypothesis 2: Visitors' behavior is respectful of the safeguarding of the site.

By overlaying the heat map with the location of the modern pathways and dissuasive fences, we can observe that visitors tend to respect the security perimeters defined by these measures to keep them away from the most fragile remains. However, it is striking to notice that in some areas where the height of the walls is rather low, visitors might still step on them (Fig. 5).

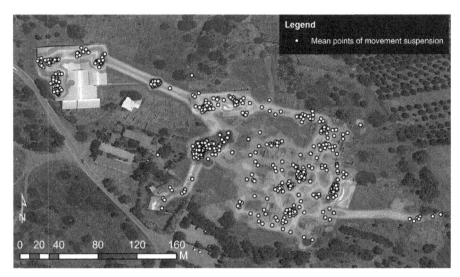

Fig. 4. Aerial picture of Malia (© Google Earth) overlaid with the point density results and the location of the clustered points of movement suspension.

We can thus argue that the assessment of visitors' spatial behavior can also be used as a detector of visitors' misbehavior that can help prevent anthropogenic damages to the archaeological fabric.

Fig. 5. Aerial picture of Malia (© Google Earth) overlaid with the density results and the location of fences and areas endangered by wall climbing.

Hypothesis 3: Visitors intuitively follow ancient circulation patterns

This hypothesis can be tested by overlaying the heat map with the location of known and assumed ancient street networks, derived from archaeological evidence [18] and space syntax studies [19]. From the visualization of the dataset, it appears that our initial statement needs to be nuanced: for example, the original west entrance to the "Palace" seems ignored by most visitors (as framed in white on Fig. 6).

We can thus argue that the assessment of visitors' spatial behavior can provide valuable insights into the visitors' perception of the integrity and authenticity of a site.

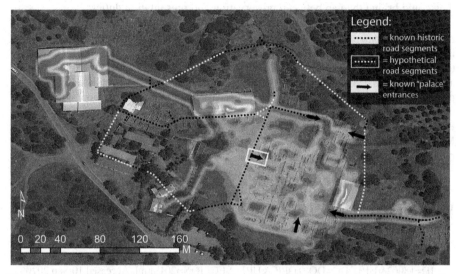

Fig. 6. Aerial picture of Malia (© Google Earth) overlaid with the density results and the location of known and hypothetical historic circulation paths

5 Conclusion and Future Perspectives

The main conclusions to infer from our hypotheses can be summarized as follows:

- Regarding hypothesis 1, spatial analyses based on visitors' tracked movements in Malia have demonstrated that some interpretation media are not optimally used while new ones could be added to the overall management plan;
- Regarding hypothesis 2, spatial analyses confirmed the efficiency of the current preventive conservation measures. However, special care should be afforded to sensitive passages with high values of visitors' flows such as low-preserved walls or narrow passages between high-preserved walls;
- Regarding hypothesis 3, spatial analyses stressed the need to provide visitors with more circulation instructions, on the one hand, and the ancient circulation patterns with more visibility, on the other hand.

Of course, these results need to be completed by further exploring the spatial data and by cross-referencing them with the two other types of data collected, namely visitors' pictures and the answers from the questionnaires.

In conclusion, this study has argued that visitors-sourced data bring a valuable approach in the creation of well-informed, secured and enjoyable itineraries on site. We defend this approach as complementary to two other types of assessment: that of ancient circulation patterns, on the one hand, and, on the other hand, that, diagnostic, of the fragility of the remains. In this way, we claim that curated visitors' paths could be used as effective and sustainable measures for the management of archaeological sites since they could bridge the gap between preservation and presentation duties.

Acknowledgements. This research was supported by a F.R.S.-FNRS FRESH grant. We would like to thank Prof. Alexandre Farnoux, then director of the French School at Athens, for permission to conduct our research at Malia, as well as the staff of the archaeological site for their support and warm welcome. We are also greatly indebted to the 73 visitors who kindly accepted to take part in this survey. Finally, we address special thanks to Dr. Athanasios Argyriou, at the Institute of Mediterranean Studies (IMS) – FORTH, for his guidance in processing the data and to our PhD supervisors, Prof. Jan Driessen, at the UCLouvain, Dr. Eleni-Eva Toumbakari, at the Greek Ministry of Culture, for their continuous help and valuable comments on early versions of this paper.

References

1. See, for instance, Art. 11 in the 1956 UNESCO Recommendation on International Principles Applicable to Archaeological Excavations. https://portal.unesco.org/en/ev.php-URL_ID=13062&URL_DO=DO_TOPIC&URL_SECTION=201.html. Accessed 10 Sep 2020
2. Charter on the Interpretation and Presentation of Cultural Heritage Sites, ICOMOS. https://www.icomos.org/charters/interpretation_e.pdf. Accessed 10 Sep 2020
3. Sansom, E.: Peopling the past: current practices in archaeological site interpretation. In: McManus, P. (ed.) Archaeological Displays and the Public. Museology and Interpretation, pp. 125–144. Routledge, New York (2016). https://doi.org/10.4324/9781315434575
4. Tilden, F.: Interpreting Our Heritage. The University of North Carolina Press, Chapel Hill (1977)
5. Williams, T.: The conservation and management of archaeological sites. A twenty-year perspective. Conserv. Perspect. GCI Newslett. **33**(1) (2018). https://www.getty.edu/conservation/publications_resources/newsletters/33_1/feature.html. Accessed 10 Sep 2020
6. Packer, J., Ballantyne, R.: Conceptualizing the visitor experience: a review of literature and development of a multifaceted model. Visitor Stud. **19**(2), 128–143 (2016)
7. Chrysanthi, A., Caridakis, G.: The archaeological space via visitor movement and interaction. A hybrid computational approach. In: Archaeological Research in the Digital Age. Proceedings of the 1st CAA-GR Conference, pp. 168–175. Institute for Mediterranean Studies – Foundation of Research and Technology, Rethymno (2014)
8. Toch, E., Lerner, B., Ben-Zion, E., Ben-Gal, I.: Analyzing large-scale human mobility data: a survey of machine learning methods and applications. Knowl. Inf. Syst. **58**(3), 501–523 (2018). https://doi.org/10.1007/s10115-018-1186-x
9. Yalowitz, S.S., Bronnenkant, K.: Timing and tracking: unlocking visitor behavior. Visitor Stud. **12**(1), 47–64 (2009). https://doi.org/10.1080/10645570902769134
10. Toha, M.A.M., Ismail, H.N.: A heritage tourism and tourist flow pattern: a perspective on traditional versus modern technologies in tracking the tourists. Int. J. Environ. Sustain. **2**(2), 85–92 (2015)

11. Chrysanthi, A.: Augmenting archaeological walks. Theoretical and methodological considerations. Ph.D. thesis, University of Southampton, Southampton, U.K. (2015)
12. Chrysanthi, A., Earl, G.P., Pagi, H.: Visitor movement and tracking techniques. A visitor-sourced methodology for the interpretation of archaeological sites. Int. J. Heritage Digit. Era 1(1), 33–37 (2012). https://doi.org/10.1260/2047-4970.1.0.33
13. Platon, N.: Problèmes de consolidation et de restauration des ruines minoennes. In: Atti del settimo congresso internazionale di Archeologia Classica 1, pp. 103–111. L'Erma di Bretschneider, Roma (1961)
14. The site welcomed 79.837 visitors in 2019 according to the Hellenic Statistical Authority. https://www.statistics.gr/en/statistics/-/publication/SCI21/. Accessed 10 Sep 2020
15. Schmid, M.: Aménagement, sauvegarde et protection des monuments minoens. Bulletin de correspondance hellénique 114(2), 908–939 (1990)
16. Alexandridis, G., Chrysanthi, A., Tsekouras, G.E., Caridakis, G.: Personalized and content adaptive cultural heritage path recommendation: an application to the Gournia and Çatalhöyük archaeological sites. User Model. User-Adap. Interact. 29(1), 201–238 (2019). https://doi.org/10.1007/s11257-019-09227-6
17. Lanir, J., Kuflik, T., Sheidin, J., Yavin, N., Leiderman, K., Segal, M.: Visualizing museum visitors' behavior: where do they go and what do they do there? Pers. Ubiquit. Comput. 21(2), 313–326 (2016). https://doi.org/10.1007/s00779-016-0994-9
18. Gomrée, T.: La voirie des villes minoennes en Crète orientale et à Cnossos (Minoen Moyen I – Minoen Récent I). Ph.D. thesis, Université Lumière Lyon 2, Lyon, France (2013)
19. Haciguzeller, P.: Modeling human circulation in the minoan palace at Malia? In: Posluschny, A., Lambers, K., Herzog, I. (eds.) Layers of Perception. Proceedings of the 35th International Conference on Computer Applications and Quantitative Methods in Archaeology (CAA), pp. 336–341. Rudolf Habelt Verlag, Bonn (2007)

The REACH Project Contribution to Protecting, Preserving and Valuing Tangible and Intangible Heritage Through Participation

N. Alfarano[1], E. Debernardi[1], A. Fresa[1(✉)], F. Melani[2], and E. Pardini[2]

[1] Promoter srl, Pisa, Italy
{alfarano,debernardi,fresa}@promoter.it
[2] Gogate srl, Pisa, Italy
{francesca.melani,elena.pardini}@gogate.it

Abstract. This paper aims to demonstrate how social participation in culture contributes fostering the resilience of tangible and intangible heritage, and to enhance its preservation and conservation. The REACH Social Platform brings together a wide community of relevant heritage stakeholders' representatives. They include research communities, heritage practitioners from public and private cultural institutions and organisations as well as policy-makers at European, national, regional and local levels. Based on a focused, critical mapping of existing research and practice, the objective of the Social Platform is to develop a better understanding of the challenges and opportunities for research and innovation in the participatory preservation, (re-)use and management of cultural heritage. The project identifies theoretical participatory models and tests them in practice through four thematic pilots. Final aim of the Social Platform is to propose the adoption of an integrated model of resilient European cultural heritage milieux.

Keywords: Participatory approaches · Cultural heritage · Social innovation · Resilience · Minority heritage · Small towns heritage · Institutional heritage · Rural heritage

1 Introduction

In the context of radical social changes taking place at global levels, Europe faces the need for its citizens to live together in peace and mutual respect and to value and enjoy the diversities, which they bring to their respective societies. In this light, protecting, preserving and valuing tangible and intangible cultural heritage plays an important role in contributing to social integration in Europe. Identifying and assessing participatory methodologies for enhancing and unlocking the potential of cultural heritage for social good is discussed in this paper.

The ability to link participatory approaches with capacity of resilience is the focus of the REACH Social Platform. The Social Platform is developed by the REACH project, 'RE-designing Access to Cultural Heritage for a wider participation in preservation,

© Springer Nature Switzerland AG 2021
M. Ioannides et al. (Eds.): EuroMed 2020, LNCS 12642, pp. 412–424, 2021.
https://doi.org/10.1007/978-3-030-73043-7_34

(re-)use and management of European culture' [1]. REACH is a Coordination and Support Action funded by the Horizon 2020 programme of the European Commission in the frame of its call about participatory approaches and social innovation in culture, as part of the Societal Challenge 6 'Europe in a changing world – Inclusive, innovative and reflective societies' [2].

The scope of the REACH Social Platform is to identify good practices of participation based on a bottom-up approach and demonstrate how this approach is the most suitable for facilitating the resilience of communities as well as the resilience of heritage (tangible and intangible) as it takes into account the needs of local populations and it alerts to the complex interactions between people and places.

The largest number of participants has been a priority along the whole process of establishment of the Social Platform and the pre-condition for its sustainability on a longer period, well beyond the conclusion of the project funded by the European Union.

2 The REACH Project Proposal for a Resilient Cultural Heritage

From a wider point of view, resilience is the capacity of a system to renew and reorganize itself after disturbance, offering strategies for the management of change and for social and economic development. Resilience is investigated in the REACH project from the perspective of the capacity of the cultural heritage system (including tangible and intangible heritage) to survive and readapt to political, social, historical and economical changes.

In this respect, REACH has designed a rich programme of activities to support and coordinate pilot initiatives in the area of participation in cultural heritage. These initiatives include online and on site activities that contribute to develop a sustainable Social Platform. The Social Platform is a community space that aims to offers a forum for debate, a network of research and cultural organizations, a collection of innovation projects, a database of good practices and a range of hand-on experiences of collaboration between institutions and local interest groups. Through these experiences, a large number of research and cultural heritage partners, from all over Europe has worked to broaden citizen engagement in the cultural sector and to strengthen the consciousness and awareness of the importance of culture and cultural heritage for communities and societies.

The project carried out two complementary objectives.

The first objective is to support the research on cultural heritage from the point of view of the adoption of participatory approaches. The work of four leading edge European Universities and of the Institut für Museumsforschung of Prussian Cultural Foundation (Stiftung Preußischer Kulturbesitz, SPK) was to map and to provide analysis of research results achieved in previous programmes. With a particular focus on the research and innovation programmes of the European Union, Coventry University (the Coordinator of the REACH Project), Granada University, ELTE University in Budapest, Charles University in Prague and SPK identified current and emerging research trends to offer authoritative new knowledge of the cultural heritage field of investigations to European, national and regional policy makers.

The second objective is coordination and communication about the research and innovation initiatives in the domain of cultural heritage, carried out by European organisations. The efforts of the REACH Social Platform aim to offer benefits to its participants, expanding knowledge of complementary research domains and of new research methodologies, generating opportunities for cooperation, offering pathways to wider user engagement with research outputs. This objective was achieved through the communication and dissemination work carried out by Promoter S.r.l., leader of the Communication and Dissemination work-package of the REACH project, in collaboration with all the project's partners and with very appreciated voluntary contributions from associate partners and in particular Gogate S.r.l..

All inputs received by the REACH Social Platform from its various contributors – institutions, academies, civic interest groups, business and public administrations, etc. - have been addressed to give culture and cultural heritage a greater, more relevant and even transformative role in the economy, communities and territories.

In this respect, REACH has worked on the development of an integrated model of resilient European cultural heritage milieux based on a two-step process: while the first step is the construction of participatory models based on the theoretical understanding of resilient European cultural heritage, the second step consists in testing and applying this model in a series of participatory pilots. The two steps are proceeding in parallel. Preliminary milestones have been achieved and are documented in the public deliverables published on the project's website [10], while final results are expected by the end of 2020.

3 Participatory Models

In times of growing xenophobia and extremist nationalism the involvement and participation of local communities throughout Europe seems more important than ever and the need for an effective model of participatory heritage practices seems crucial [3].

Starting by the assessment of the work carried out by current and completed projects, the REACH Social Platform aimed to gather understanding and lessons about the reasons of their successes and failures.

This analysis leaded to discover and evaluate a wealth of information that the REACH project used for a twofold scope. On one hand, it allowed a critical consideration on how participatory work is able to deliver effective results in terms of research investigation and innovation implementation. On the other hand, it created the basis for the elaboration and definition of a set of theoretical models for management, preservation and (re-)use of cultural heritage. In addition, the analysis presented options of the formation of practical participatory models, consisting of a flexible protocol that can be adapted to different cultural heritage contexts.

The proposed models were tested into four participatory pilots of a diverse nature, working with different types of communities and stakeholders, in different situations and political climates. In this way, the models have been assessed in varied circumstance to establish a level of robustness, ahead of being finalised and presented by the project.

The REACH participatory models aim to provide indications to the cultural heritage actors to develop participatory activities, being them researchers, cultural managers, curators, civic interest groups, administrators and policy makers. These models should be dynamic and resilient, to become easily adaptable to social, cultural and economic changes. On the basis of the concept of 'extended epistemology' elaborated by Heron and further developed in collaboration with Reason [4], two underlying methodologies were identified by the REACH project and adapted for the definition of its models, namely: 'Participatory Action Research' (PAR) and 'Plan-Do-Check-Act Management' cycle (PDCA).

The scope of the definition of the REACH participatory models has been to draw a level of legitimacy to research approaches that, integrating theory and action, explore practical ways able to generate new knowledge. Adopting the REACH models, different actors are engaged in the investigation on cultural heritage, including the targets of the research, i.e., in the case of the REACH pilots, visitors and curators of museums, minority or rural communities and small towns heritage managers.

The work conducted in the REACH project for the definition of its proposition of participatory models included an emphasis on social assessment and ethics, with a particular regard to the themes of gender, age and identity, offering a theoretical and practical basis for starting, conducting, adjusting and evaluating participatory project.

The REACH project noted that, often, participatory cultural heritage activities, despite their intrinsic, economic and societal benefits, are considered as add-on activities, receiving short-term funding. It is a lesson learnt that for a participatory project to be successful, it is essential to incorporate also long-term strategies that involve planning and decision-making processes, as they are needed to maximise the advantages of public engagement.

4 Participatory Pilots

The REACH project carried out for experimental pilots to assess the models for participatory research in cultural heritage.

Each pilot assessed and validated the models in different thematic and geographic areas. The pilots focused on strengths and challenges, discussing opportunities and threads, and how these occur throughout different regions in Europe. They considered participatory approaches within their respective communities, even if sharing areas of commonality, interacting with stakeholders to test ideas through a series of local encounters.

With the aim to advocate the socio-economic value of civic participation in preservation, (re-)use and management of cultural heritage, the pilots gathered and discussed best practices in the development of resilient policies in community building, education, data management and protection of intellectual rights. Furthermore, the pilots demonstrated successful cases in cultural tourism and provided examples of improved public services for cultural heritage management.

The REACH pilots covered four thematic areas of the European heritage: (1) minority heritage in collaboration with Roma community in Hungary, (2) institutional heritage in collaboration with museums of different size in Germany, (3) rural heritage in collaboration with local associations in Andalusia and Italy, (4) small towns heritage in collaboration with local interest groups in Czech Republic, Poland and Italy.

A special focus is deserved in the REACH pilots to the case of intangible cultural heritage and its preservation through participatory practices. As said in the UNESCO website: *"The term 'heritage' has evolved considerably over time. Initially referring exclusively to the monumental remains of cultures, the concept of heritage has gradually been expanded to embrace living culture and contemporary expressions. As a source of identity, heritage is a valuable factor for empowering local communities and enabling vulnerable groups to participate fully in social and cultural life."* [6] These are the concepts adopted by the REACH partners in a kind of 'circular' investigation triggered through the pilots. An initial research (mostly desk research, supported by daily practices of the participating cultural heritage institutions) highlighted how intangible heritage is at the basis of all the four thematic areas. Further, in the pilots, intangible heritage demonstrated its fundamental role in valuing and preserving cultural heritage, such as for the cases of: the Roma heritage in Hungary, the historical irrigation system on Sierra Nevada (Spain), the various stories connected with collections, including personal stories, as a mean to engage visitors with the museums, and last but not least witnesses of people living in the small towns and the memories from their ancestors. Eventually, evidences gathered within the pilots went back to the researchers of REACH as an enriched basis to plan new investigations and to advocate new policies and innovation programmes for preservation, (re-)use and management of cultural heritage.

4.1 Participatory Pilot on Minority Heritage

The Minority Heritage pilot, coordinated by ELTE University in Budapest, focused on marginalized minorities and, in particular, on Roma communities mostly based in Hungary but also in other European Countries [7].

It studied heritage practices aiming at establishing a Roma minority heritage. The analysis of case studies, mostly based on empirical work have shown the importance of social aspects of the cultural activities in this particular context, focusing on social cohesion that Roma heritage-related institutions, organisations or individual actors maintain. In most cases, this aspect is realised in the form of education, even if are other options were also found in the pilot. Cultural rights were investigated, examining participatory methods and community-involvement from the perspective of gaining equal rights in cultural recognition.

The experience demonstrated how the institutionalisation of Roma (re-)appropriated cultural heritage has resulted in economic and social revival and has reinforced social inclusion, contributing to create more tolerant societies in Central Europe (Fig. 1).

4.2 Participatory Pilot on Institutional Heritage

The Institutional Heritage pilot, coordinated by SPK (Prussian Cultural Heritage Foundation) in Berlin, compared the effects of participatory approaches in the case of large cultural heritage institutions with international audiences as opposed to the case of smaller institutions targeting local users [8].

The pilot carried out a comparison of three museums of different types, describing their concepts of participatory engagement, areas of activities, approaches, methodologies, gaps and impacts. The three museums are: the Industrie- und Filmmuseum

Fig. 1. Pictures from a local encounter of the Roma heritage pilot, Pécs, May 2019

(Industry- and Film Museum) in Wolfen, the Haus der Geschichte (House of History) in Wittenberg and the Museum für Islamische Kunst (Museum for Islamic Art) in Berlin. Using these three case studies, it has been possible to examine their options for participatory work, highlighting needs, difficulties, limits and gaps of this type of activity.

The activities of the pilot aimed at evaluating the complexity of involvement, inclusion and engagement of citizens in institutional cultural heritage, exploring possibilities and limitations of participation. It concluded that collaborative and participatory activities can only be implemented and consolidated if all parties involved (museums, politicians, wider society) work together. The pilot mapped common requirements for these collaborative activities in order to identify successful approaches and lessons learnt while fostering a constructive dialogue and building mutual awareness between people, museums and their cultural heritage (Fig. 2).

Fig. 2. "Bilderschau", March 2019 (Photography by Friederike Berlekamp)

4.3   Participatory Pilot on Rural Heritage

The Rural Heritage pilot, coordinated by the University of Granada, promoted participation in cultural and environmental protected natural areas as a way to solve conflicts between preservation of historical sites and exploitation of touristic and economic activities.

The case study focused on the preservation of rural areas of Sierra Nevada (Spain) by the engagement of local communities in the restoration and recovery of historical irrigation systems (Fig. 3).

Fig. 3. Cleanliness of Fuente de los Caños, Sorbas, Almería, February 2020 (Photography by E. Aramburu and R. Corselli)

The result of this pilot is the implementation of a co-governance initiative for the territorial safe-keeping as the best way to protect agrarian landscapes and promote a more resilient rural heritage (tangible and intangible).

A second focus of the pilot, carried out by the Italian Ministry of Economic Development in collaboration with Politecnico of Milan, concerned the case study of the *marcita* meadow and highway project at Ticino Park [9], in the North of Italy, an area recognised - as for Sierra Nevada - as a UNESCO Biosphere Reserve (Fig. 4).

The *marcita* meadows is an ancient practice based on a thin layer of underground and surface water flowing over the meadows; this flow avoids the grass freezing in wintertime enabling the creation of a fertile and varied landscape. However, this is now endangered and is at risk of disappearing, due to over-industrialisation and to the construction of new infrastructure, such as the expansion of the highway. The establishment of the Ticino Park is defending, protecting and enhancing the quality of the agrarian

Fig. 4. The landscape of the *marcita* meadows: heritage at risk (Photography by Fabio Casale)

landscape, but also contributing to the preservation of the intangible heritage connected with this old practice. A series of active participatory tools have been established, for use in primary schools, with university students (digging workshops) and with farmers (participating in water management courses). Encounters, walking tours, a travelling exhibition, brochures and videos are used to raise public awareness and share cultural knowledge.

These initiatives have highlighted issues of resilience, tangible and intangible heritage, by connecting people, at local level, and promoting an alternate economic model.

4.4 Participatory Pilot on Small Towns Heritage

The Small Towns Heritage pilot, coordinated by Charles University Prague, carried out in collaboration with the Italian Ministry of Economic Development and Politecnico of Milan, analysed the representations and (re-)valuing of the heritage owned by villages and small towns in the Czech Republic, in Poland and in central Italy. Focusing on a variety of European regions, considerations were made about the liaisons among heritage objects, local history, natural and social landscapes, including how they are displayed by museums, through pageants and festivals, in heritage trails and urban spaces. The pilot identified major frameworks of identities and values to which this heritage is associated, highlighting how this understanding can help the development of more effective and innovative cultural policies (Fig. 5).

Fig. 5. Picture from 'Small towns in promotion of their cultural heritage' workshop, Prague, February 2018

5   Collection of Good Practices

During the first year of the project's life, an internal working group (composed by one representative from each project partner) was established to carry out the specific task of collecting good practices in social participation for cultural heritage research [5].

Carried out with the contribution of project partners, the resulting repository comprises currently 110 records of European and extra European participatory activities in the field of cultural heritage, with an emphasis on small-scale, localised interventions, but also including examples of larger collaborative projects and global or distributed online initiatives (Fig. 6).

Fig. 6. REACH good practice database

The database demonstrates successful cases of job creation and economic growth based on cultural heritage use and re-use, innovation in cultural tourism, and examples of improved public services for cultural heritage management.

The dataset of good practices is published as an Open Data collection on the open-heritage.eu website, under the Free Culture Creative Commons License 'Attribution-ShareAlike 4.0 International', as a browsable catalogue of resources that can support and stimulate other people's work.

The best practice collection represents a fundamental component of the Social Platform established by the REACH project, it will continue to grow, hopefully with the addition of new entries over the coming periods.

6   Online Services

The REACH Social Platform combines a physical dimension with online services.

In addition to the traditional website [10] that normally is 'frozen' with the conclusion of the EU funding period, two online services were designed to support the continuation of the platform in the digital sphere. They are the open-heritage.eu platform and the Digital Gallery.

A network of common interest was established among the project's partners and its associates. The network was enlarged with the participation of the key stakeholders who met in Brussels in March 2019 in the occasion of the 'Horizon for Heritage Research' Symposium, organised by the REACH project under the aegis of the European Commission to discuss the establishment of a permanent coordination structure.

The open-heritage.eu digital platform and the Digital Gallery of posters and videos represent the spaces to continue the coordination efforts and the collaboration among the participants in the REACH network, within a longer perspective.

6.1   Open-Heritage.eu Digital Platform

The dataset of the best practices and the resources produced by the REACH project as well as by its associate partners are hosted on open-heritage.eu (Fig. 7).

Fig. 7.   The Open-heritage.eu digital platform

Open-heritage.eu is an independent online digital platform. Even if naturally connected to the REACH project's website, the digital platform has the ambition to become a long term product, surviving to the project life-time and representing a valuable instrument to support a permanent coordination of the cultural heritage research.

The online platform provides in turn links to various services that are offered to the community of research to share knowledge and information. In addition to the thematic organisation of participatory experiences and good practices, the platform provides a rich repository of data and resources, comprising policy documents, publications, updated information on events and activities promoted by a multitude of projects and institutions.

The platform is conceived as a 'multi-actor platform', opened to contributions from its users (partners, associate partners and general visitors). It aims to attract the interest of the different stakeholders who play a relevant part in sustaining the scope initiated by the REACH Social Platform, to advance understanding and to contribute to unlocking the potential of participatory approaches and social innovation in culture.

6.2 Digital Gallery of Posters and Videos About Cultural Heritage Research

Fig. 8. The REACH digital gallery

The Social Platform launched in spring 2020 a call for posters and videos entitled 'Designing Participation for Cultural Heritage', as a contingency plan for the cancelation of the conference that was planned to take place in Pisa in June 2020, due to the pandemic. Originally thought as an instrument to accompany the conference, the Digital Gallery became an extraordinary opportunity of participation for researchers and cultural heritage institutions, to present projects' results, initiatives, innovation activities, with a particular focus on the adoption of participatory approaches (Fig. 8).

The Digital Gallery offers a rich exhibition of posters and videos tackling different themes that include: societal cohesion, sustainability and environmental/ecological responsibility, rapid societal change, narratives, place/place-making and identity.

The initiative was successfully accepted by the REACH community of stakeholders and in few months the collection has been populated by tens of multidisciplinary contributions showing the progresses of projects and new activities implemented by cultural heritage organizations and research centres in collaboration with civic participation.

The gallery is hosted by the website of the REACH project website and will remain accessible via the open-heritage.eu platform, in the coming years, when more submissions will contribute to gather and to share innovative ideas and results.

Thanks to its diversity and heterogeneity, the Digital Gallery is an excellent example of resilience and participation that can inspire actors of the cultural heritage community to adopt and develop more participatory practices.

7 Conclusion

The REACH project highlighted the role of participatory approaches in the preservation, (re-)use and management of cultural heritage and demonstrated how social participation and civil engagement stoke the vital and dynamic dimension of heritage fostering its resilience.

The results of pilot experiences together with the development of participatory models helped to define the features of a resilient European cultural heritage, able to innovate and to survive to social changes and cultural transformations. The COVID-19 crisis represented a concrete case where resilience of cultural heritage was experimented and participatory approaches demonstrated their value.

By analysing several institutional proposals and initiatives, the REACH project produced a selection of participatory models and concrete experiences that demonstrate a strong capacity of the European cultural field to foster positive reactions by the society and an active participation of citizen into the promotion and preservation of the European heritage. The collection of good practices produced a wide and multidisciplinary database that is accessible to the whole community of cultural heritage institutions and open to further and future contributions. The open-heritage.eu digital platform provides access to a wide and varied range of papers, data and links that document experiences and practices produced by the work of a multi-disciplinary community of researchers. The REACH Digital Gallery is a live witness of the richness and diversity of approaches taken by European researchers to valuing cultural heritage.

During its time life, REACH produced, gathered and documented participatory practices in culture and cultural heritage using both the experiences produced in the framework of its pilots and the knowledge and investigations developed by other projects and professionals who collaborated with REACH and joined its network.

All together, the results of the REACH Social Platform are offered to the cultural heritage community to continue the construction of a permanent coordination of their research. Such coordination will be able to deliver stronger impact and wider benefits to the European society, contributing to the transition towards the ambitions of the new Horizon Europe programme.

Acknowledgements. The authors wish to express their gratitude to the members of the REACH Consortium for their active engagement in the project.

Special thanks should be given to Prof. Neil Forbes, Project Coordinator, for his professional guidelines and to Tim Hammerton, Project Manager, for his constructive suggestions and valuable support in every stage of the project.

References

1. Alfarano, N., Debernardi, E., Fresa, A., Melani, F., Pardini, E.: Re-designing access to cultural heritage for a wider participation in preservation, (re-)use and management of European culture (2020)
2. Europe in a changing world - Inclusive, innovative and reflective societies Homepage in the website of the European Commission about Horizon 2020 research and innovation programme. https://ec.europa.eu/programmes/horizon2020/en/h2020-section/europe-changing-world-inclusive-innovative-and-reflective-societies. Accessed 15 Sep 2020
3. György, E., Sonkoly, G., Oláh, G., Kieft, E., Hammerton, T.: REACH D.3.1 Participatory Models (2019)
4. Heron, J., Reason, P.: A participatory inquiry paradigm. 274–294 (2017)
5. Colella, S., Crawley, M.L., Hammerton, T.: REACH D6.4 Resilience and social innovation in cultural heritage: a collection of best practices (2020)
6. UNESCO website, Preserving our heritage. https://en.unesco.org/content/preserving-our-her itage. Accessed 27 Oct 2020
7. György, E., Sonkoly, G., Oláh, G., Hammerton, T.: REACH D5.2 Minority heritage pilot results (2020)
8. Berlekamp, F., Crawley, M.L., Hammerton, T.: REACH D 5.3 Institutional heritage pilot results (2020)
9. Ticino Park territorial plan. https://ente.parcoticino.it/il-parco/la-tutela-del-paesaggio/abaco-del-territorio-del-parco/. Accessed 28 Sep 2020
10. REACH Social Platform website. https://www.reach-culture.eu/. Accessed 15 Sep 2020

Project Papers: Tools for Education

Virtual Heritage Learning Environments

Eimear Meegan[1]([⊠]), Maurice Murphy[1], Garrett Keenaghan[2], Anthony Corns[3], Robert Shaw[3], Stephen Fai[4], Simona Scandura[1], and Alain Chenaux[2]

[1] Virtual Building Lab, Dublin, Ireland
maurice.murphy@TUDublin.ie
[2] Technological University of Dublin, Dublin, Ireland
[3] Discovery Programme, Dublin, Ireland
[4] CIMS Carleton University, Ottawa, Canada

Abstract. The change and restrictions in how we react with cultural heritage because of the COVID-19 pandemic has created an urgency in advancing remote and digital access to objects and sites. This paper outlines the process for developing Virtual Learning Environments (VLEs) using digital recording and modelling of architectural heritage and archaeology. Virtual Reality (VR) software, game engine platforms and WEB platforms are outlined which can be applied to represent heritage sites in addition to emerging screen based technological learning systems. The application Historic Building Information Modelling (HBIM) and Game Engine Platforms for creating Virtual Learning Environments (VLEs) is also examined. The design-theory based on Virtual Learning Objects for cultural heritage is explored. Two case studies are explored for their potential to create Virtual Heritage Learning Environments. Finally, a design framework is proposed for developing Virtual Heritage Learning Environments.

Keywords: Virtual Heritage Learning Environments · Historic BIM · Game engine platforms · Heritage education learning

1 Virtual Learning and Digital Heritage

1.1 Introduction

The reduced access to cultural heritage sites in response to the COVID-19 crisis has created an increased demand for alternatively accessing virtual representations of historic buildings and their environments, consequently, it is necessary to enquire.

1. What are the most suitable tools and design systems?
2. What the implications are for education in conservation and valorization of cultural heritage?

Virtual Reality (VR) software, game engine platforms and WEB platforms are now commonly applied to represent heritage sites and are enhanced with the use of handheld devices and ubiquitous computing. The emerging screen based technological learning

© Springer Nature Switzerland AG 2021
M. Ioannides et al. (Eds.): EuroMed 2020, LNCS 12642, pp. 427–437, 2021.
https://doi.org/10.1007/978-3-030-73043-7_35

Fig. 1. Digital recording and surveying heritage sites in Ireland (Discovery Programme)

systems are also a contributing factor. In parallel the digital automation for surveying and recording heritage objects and environments has resulted in large and very useful data sets from GPS, laser scanning and digital photogrammetric surveys. This survey data when used for archaeology and architectural heritage is enriched with the addition of knowledge and information content attached as semantic attributes to a digital object. Digital objects then move from static to dynamic representations and can then be used for information and knowledge sharing for both education and valorization of cultural heritage (Fig. 1).

The key issues in identifying and applying virtual and digital systems and their implications for education in conservation and valorization of cultural heritage are examined in this paper. The application of virtual simulation for learning or other educational scenarios requires an awareness of how to replicate and simulate numerous and complex behaviors that exist in the real world. Software platforms create interactive 3D content for multiplatform publishing and promote knowledge-sharing communities.

1.2   Tools and Design of System - Factors and Influences

Virtual and Augmented Reality
Virtual Reality (VR) digitally recreates a real-world scenario using a range of software and hardware platforms, Augmented Reality (AR) on the other hand superimposes some of these VR experiences as digital elements in the real world. They are used interchangeably and share some of the same software and hardware technology, but the interactive experience is noticeably different. VR offers the user degrees of freedom, that is it is confined in a computer generated world view while AR provides degrees of freedom in that it uses visual and auditory senses to provide you with sensory information overlaid on the world that you are surrounded in. Virtual Reality utilizes software and hardware platforms to simulate and re-create numerous and complex behaviors that exist in the real world. Sherman and Craig (2003), describe VR as virtual worlds which are constructed in 3D space using computer graphics. This is enhanced by a virtual human presence as an immersive experience with user interaction, navigation and sensory experience with the virtual world and its objects [1]. The continuing evolution of VR computer simulation

software has generated lower cost, accessible and more intuitive tools. These tools are now used for the development of AR/VR learning environments [3, 5, 6].

Virtual Heritage - Historic Building Information Modelling
Building Information Modelling (BIM) is a virtual representation of a building, its structure, materials, and environment, providing the associated information (the "metadata") related to its design, construction and future lifecycle. Historic Building Information Modelling (HBIM) is an extension of BIM for the physical and knowledge management and conservation of architectural heritage.

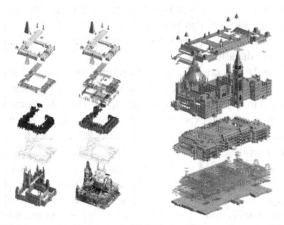

Fig. 2. Scan to HBIM Ottawa Parliament see CIMS https://cims.carleton.ca/#/projects?projectFilter=All

HBIM involves the digital recording of historical buildings using remote sensing (laser scanning, digital photogrammetry) or combinations of digital surveying and manual techniques. The acquired survey data is then processed improving the data organisation and adding intelligence using BIM software platforms. Because of the difficulties in accurately representing the variety of complex and irregular objects occurring in historic buildings existing BIM libraries of parametric objects need to be rebuilt and coded. In addition, as the building exists and is represented by a remotely sensed model, systems to map the intelligent library objects onto digital or other survey data were also developed. Cultural heritage researchers have recently begun applying Building Information Modelling (BIM) to historic buildings. The intelligent data or information contained in the model can range from geometric and spatial to material, structural, environmental, cultural and economic. Most of the research carried out in past few years was case study-based and was initiated by educational institution in different countries such as Carleton University in Canada. The methodology used by these researchers to develop HBIM involved data collection using laser scanning and modelling historic architectural elements graphically using BIM software platforms (see Fig. 2) followed by mapping 3D objects in the point cloud data, [7–13].

Virtual Heritage - Game Engine Platform

While BIM platforms have the potential to create a virtual and intelligent representation of a building, its full exploitation and use is restricted to narrow set of expert users with access to costly hardware, software and skills. The testing of open BIM approaches IFCs and the use of game engine platforms is a fundamental component for developing much wider dissemination. The nature of videogame engines is scalable and multiplatform and can potentially be viewed on a variety of systems with different performance capabilities, from tablets to sophisticated virtual reality workstations. Working with large data sets require also, intuitive tools and rapid workflow and capabilities for lighting, mapping and material editors to replicate real world 3D. A packaged 'game file' is designed to execute in a standalone fashion, requiring no additional proprietary software installed on the end-users computer system. In addition, Augmented Reality (AR) and immersive experiences using wearable technology enhance the experience whether for entertainment or education [14].

The virtual worlds are constructed in 3D graphic modelling platforms before they are exported into game engine platforms and only contain geometry and texture and are therefore limited to applications for visualisation. The enhancement of the 3D visualisation model for immersive experience with user interaction is generated within the game engine platform. Intelligent information enhanced models on the other hand facilitate the integration of data from different sources, scales and disciplines into a single cohort model. Exporting a BIM model into a game engine allows for a packaging of BIM data that can be used in a simplified and more intuitive for the user. With regards to educational applications, game engines can give public access to information, places and objects that are usually restricted, virtual models produced can allow for these to be experienced, [15–17]. Game engines can be applied to make two major contributions to architectural conservation: they can allow a low-cost method of making an HBIM model more easily accessible to actors in the building industry; and they can be used for educational purposes to facilitate dissemination of knowledge of cultural heritage, particularly in museological applications.

2   A Theoretical Design Framework Based on Heritage Learning Objects

2.1   Learning Objects and HBIM

If Historic Building Information Modelling (BIM) and Game Engine platforms are incorporated into the design for Virtual learning in building conservation, it offers a very different experience from classroom-based learning. The concept of HBIM libraries which are digital objects representing historic architectural elements which are brought together to virtually represent historic structures. In virtual learning environments these libraries become virtual Similar to object orientated programming, Learning Objects systems (LO) exist as elements or entities in digital format and can be reused as content in WEB based learning environments. Learning Objects systems (LO) exist as elements or entities in digital format and can be reused as content in WEB based learning environments.

In Fig. 3 above digital learning objects are available for WEB-based visualization of a large range heritage objects and structures from the EU 3D Icons project. The main

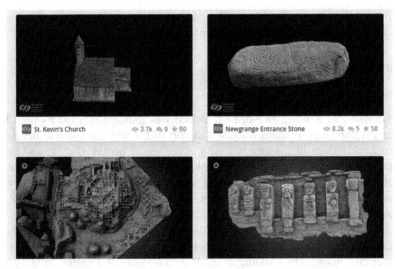

St. Kevin's Church   3.7k 9 60   Newgrange Entrance Stone   8.2k 5 58

Fig. 3. Digital heritage available at https://sketchfab.com/discoveryprogramme

computing elements are metadata standards and system specifications such as levels of scale, level of detail of data and cross platform interoperability in this case assisted with the WEB platform SketchFab. In addition to 3D geometry and texture the types of digital resource that can be reused to support learning include images or photos, live data feeds, live or pre-recorded video or audio snippets, text, animations, and web-delivered applications such as a Java applet, a blog, or a web page combining text, images and other media. Learning Objects (LO) as knowledge-based objects are self-contained and reusable and described by their meta-tags which include their history, meaning, quality and destination. LO elements are units which make up the content and the LO can be singular or a combination of elements. The IEEE Learning Object Metadata Standard (IEE) specifies the syntax and semantics of learning object metadata describing levels of detail (aggregation) and learning resource types. The aggregation detail ranges from the smallest elements (raw media data or fragments) to secondly a collection of elements for a lesson, thirdly a collection of lessons or modules for a course and finally a set of courses that lead to a qualification [19–21].

2.2 Learning Objects - Cognitive Elements

The cognitive and learning elements are equally important as texture geometry and must be acknowledged in design and delivery of Learning Objects. It is therefore a case of deciding what type/combination of digital resource is used and to what level of detail and scale to correspond with the participants' pace of learning, prior knowledge held and other criteria. The main cognitive elements for LOs are the conceptual structure of the area of learning, the student's aptitudes and the appropriate delivery and assessment systems. Learning is an active process of building rather than acquiring knowledge and instruction is a process of supporting that construction rather than communicating knowledge resulting in learners actively participating in the learning process. Learner inclusion and participation becomes a design fundamental for LO systems through the inclusion of generative learning environments [22–24].

3   Case Studies

3.1   Case Study - Armagh Observatory

The observatory at Armagh in Northern Ireland was founded in 1790 by the Church of Ireland Archbishop, Richard Robinson as part of his wider scheme to develop the fabric and institutions of the city following a prolonged period of strife and neglect. Students who are studying the module in Building Conservation in the Dublin Institute of Technology undertook the digital recording and 3D CAD modelling of the Observatory. The emphasis is on learning by doing so low-cost accessible recording and modelling tools are used by the students.

In the case of the Armagh Observatory the aim of the proposed project was to create a 3D computer based model of the observatory its instrument positions and the location of the meridian markers by building a virtual terrain model and virtual building model placed in the terrain. The final result as a full virtual model of the building and its markers can then be employed for simulating the instruments in their position in the observatory and earths meridian used to measure declination, the angle between the star and the celestial equator. The buildings, the landscape, the instruments and the night sky replications as Heritage Learning Objects are illustrated in Fig. 4 and the bottom right hand side of the Figure shows the on-site survey using GPS.

On-Site Leaning – The Missing Factor in Virtual Learning
The fact that the students carried out on-site surveys giving them a tactile real-life experience is missing from the virtual only learning experience. So, it is necessary to replicate as best and include the site experience from documentation of this experience. An example of this on-site learning allowed students to apply their theoretical knowledge from the classroom to practice by appreciating the various steps and potential errors arising when recording and processing GPS data. Data was collected in the WGS84 geodetic coordinate system using a GNSS receiver in Network Real-Time Kinematic (NRTK) mode. In NRTK mode, the GNSS receiver requires a connection through a mobile connection to a network of fixed base stations to correct in real-time for major sources of errors. Several measurements were recorded at each point of interest along the Meridian's line, In most cases, observation could only be record-ed at the base of the monuments or on positions estimated as being as close as possible to the alignment of the Meridian. Where issues related to poor mobile network connection or poor satellite geometry arose (in particular when measurements were taken too close to a building or monument), observations were subsequently removed. All data collected was then exported from the data logger and the GNSS data was converted to the Irish National Grid.

3.2   Virtual Learning Objects as a Shape Grammar for Archaeology

In Fig. 5, below a shape grammar is developed for reconstructing the Romanesque door case of a 12th century Irish church, Kilmalkeader. The grammar learning objects are based

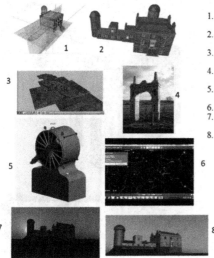

1. The modelling of the Observatory building from drawings
2. The rendered object imported into Unity Game Engine
3. The 3D landscape model exported as kmz file from Google Earth
4. The Meridian field marker for observing longitude
5. The 3D model of the mural circle telescope for observing the planets and meridian markers
6. Night sky model
7. Observatory building night sky in Unity game engine
8. Observatory building night sky in Unity game engine

Fig. 4. The pilot model virtual replication of Armagh Observatory

on the remaining elements of the door-case from laser scan and traditional surveys and interviews with archaeological experts. The grammar initially develops the primitives for the opening of the archway and columns. The Romanesque carving and the complexity of the stones making up the arch are determined from a Boolean operation production rules based on the non-terminal shape on the bottom left through to the terminal block shape with carvings. The virtual replication of the door-case and structure is mainly achieved by converting the laser scan and photogrammetric data to solid 3D models. The replication of complex geometries and shapes require authenticity and accuracy for digital reconstruction can also be an evolved process as more information comes to light.

3.3 Virtual Historic Dublin – Interaction with Heritage Learning Objects

In this case study interaction with the Heritage Los are introduced using game engine software platforms. Virtual Historic Dublin is a dynamic digital repository and portal based on modelling an Lidar scan of the historic center of Dublin City. The combination of digital recording, modelling and data management systems enable the interaction with complex, interlinked three-dimensional structures containing rich and diverse underlying data. End users can encompass architectural and engineering conservation, education and research, in addition to public engagement and cultural tourism. Two major aerial based 3D mapping surveys which were carried by the School of Engineering UCD in 2008 and 2015 and funded by Science Foundation of Ireland and European Research Council (1.8 Million Euros). The survey data includes most of Dublin City's medieval and classical historic areas.

Irish Parliament Game Engine Interpretation
As part of the Virtual Historic Dublin, the Historic BIM model of the Irish Parliament

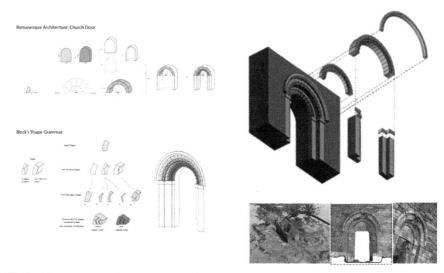

Fig. 5. Shape grammar for Romanesque door-case, exploded model of door-case and scan survey

building and complementary digital assets were imported into Unity 3D, Unreal Engine 4, and Twinmotion. HBIM model was exported from Autodesk Revit as an FBX file. Although the FBX format is standard in game design, many other file formats are usable in game engines. The imported assets retain their groups, families, and texture maps; however, materials often do not transfer over. This can be corrected by baking materials as textures or by remapping assets with new materials inside the game engines. Assets can also be reloaded if changes need to be made. Updated models maintain material adjustments, location, and script attachments. Architectural Visualization platforms and game engines have different uses for dissemination. Visualization programs provide easy to use curated tools for model showcasing and video creation while game engines facilitate purpose-built interactions. Despite the interactivity limitations of arch-vis tools, Twinmotion still serves as an effective platform for model viewing. The application's BIMmotion feature allows user to explore digital models with navigation capabilities, VR compatibility, and video attachments through a standalone executable file. With any game engine there is more freedom to build custom interactive experiences, industry standard game engines carry extensive toolboxes for terrain editing, physics simulation, animation, advanced lighting and for VR/AR, and real-time rendering. For the Timeline application, the conceptualized features were prototyped in Unity with five historic map models. The Unity game engine was chosen to develop the timeline application because of its quality rendering accessibility, asset store, and reputation. Unity also has a large community of independent game developers and plenty of online tutorials, forums, and open source scripts for basic video game features (Fig. 6).

Figure 13. Morphology evolution Irish Parliament

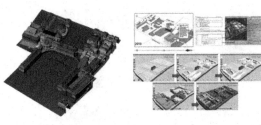

Fig. 6. Irish Parliament - Leinster House, Aerial Scan and HBIM model imported into Unity Game Engine Platform and Morphology Evolution Irish Parliament - Leinster House, Augmented Virtual Reality – Virtual Historic City

4 Conclusion

The Figure below is adapted from the work of Graff 2007 [24] and can be applied to cultural heritage for design of Virtual learning Environments (VLEs). Like most systems, technical requirements are software and hardware based but then link into the requirements of teaching from simple active linear text, general 3D models, vision maps, videos, animations, chat, forum and emails and navigation to more complex virtual reality. Technology will allow synchronous, or real-time, communication which takes place like a conversation, which is the concern of the teacher. Asynchronous, takes place outside of real-time, is the concern of both teaching and pedagogic content. The user is very concerned with ability of the system to be user friendly in ease of delivering and teaching the student. While the application of Information and Communication Technologies ICT can supply VLEs the development and adaptation of Virtual Reality with VLEs can give the impression to the learner of being there whether it is the classroom, the lab or the heritage site. This is described as Immersive learning and with novelty and innovation introduced using both Virtual Reality and Augmented Virtual Reality in game engine platforms the experience of the user can be further enhanced to create a perceived immersed learning experience (Fig. 7).

Generic Influential Factors and Causalities for Heritage Virtual Learning Environments

Like other sectors, Heritage Virtual Learning Environments are also subject to rapidly evolving software and hardware systems. The influence of technology learning systems is also related to learner digital media literacy and changing attitudes of the traditional lecturer/researcher from a mental concept of; 'what has always worked', to embracing virtual learning technology. New influences must be capable of providing the supports and services needed to enable students engage with the subject on a deep level and educator's time to learn how to harness these learning systems. Design factors for learning systems should include: (i) expanding access and convenience; noting the challenges with disparities in digital infrastructure and learner to learner engagement between groups, (ii) fostering authentic learning; noting how including activity based learning such as problem based learning and replacing on-site experience with other models will ensure learners are active contributors to their knowledge and learning.

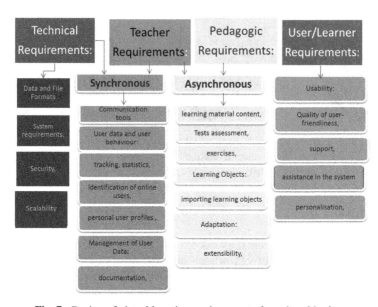

Fig. 7. Design of virtual learning environments for cultural heritage

References

1. Sherman, W., Craig, W.: Understanding Virtual Reality. Interface, Application and Design. Morgan Kaufmann Publishers, Burlington (2003)
2. Tikhomirov, V.: Smart education as the main paradigm of development of an information society (key note speech). In: Inaugural International Conference on Smart Technology-based Education and Training (STET 2014) (2014)
3. Schroth, C., Christ, O.: Brave new web: emerging design principles and technologies as enablers of a global SOA. In: Proceedings of the IEEE International Conference on Services Computing - SCC 2007, pp. 62–69 (2007). 0-7695-2925-9/07
4. Sanou, B.: The world in 2013: ICT facts and figures. International Telecommunications Union (2013)
5. Johnson, L., Adams Becker, S., Cummins, M., Estrada, V., Freeman, A., Ludgate, H.: NMC horizon report: 2013 higher education edition. The New Media Consortium, Austin, Texas (2013)
6. Adams Becker, S., Cummins, M., Davis, A., Freeman, A., Hall Giesinger, C., Ananthanarayanan, V.: NMC horizon report: 2017 higher education edition. The New Media Consortium, Austin, Texas (2017)
7. Fai, S., Sydor, M.: Building information modelling and the documentation of architectural heritage: between the 'typical' and the 'specific'. Paper presented at the Digital Heritage International Congress (Digital Heritage) (2013)
8. Garagnani, S.: Building information modeling and real world knowledge: a methodological approach to accurate semantic documentation for the built environment. Paper presented at the Digital Heritage International Congress (DigitalHeritage) (2013)
9. Graham, K., Chow, L., Fai, S.: Level of detail, information and accuracy in building information modelling of existing and heritage buildings. J. Cult. Heritage Manag. Sustain. Dev. **8**(4), 495–507 (2018). https://doi.org/10.1108/JCHMSD-09-2018-0067

10. Hichri, N., Stefani, C., Veron, P., Hamon, G., De Luca, L.: Review of the «as-built» BIM approaches. J. Appl. Geomatics (2014)
11. Murphy, M., McGovern, E., Pavia, S.: Historic building information modelling – adding intelligence to laser and image based surveys of European classical architecture. ISPRS J. Photogramm. Remote Sens. **76**, 89–102 (2013)
12. Oreni, D., Brumana, R., Della Torre, S., Banfi, F., Barazzetti, L., Previtali, M.: Survey turned into HBIM: the restoration and the work involved concerning the Basilica di Collemaggio after the earthquake (L'Aquila). ISPRS Ann. Photogramm. Remote Sens. Spatial Inf. Sci. **II-5**, 267–280 (2014)
13. Merschbrock, C., Lassen, A.K., Tollnes, T.: Integrating BIM and gaming to support building operation: the case of a new hospital (2014)
14. Yan, W., Liu, G.: BIMGame: integrating building information modelling and games to enhance sustainable design and education. In: Predicting the Future [25th eCAADe Conference Proceedings] Frankfurt am Main (Germany), pp. 211–218 (2007)
15. Boeykens, S.: Using 3D design software, BIM and game engines for architectural historical reconstruction. Paper presented to the CAAD Futures (2011)
16. Chenaux, A., Murphy, M., Keenaghan, G., Jenkins, J., McGovern, E.: Combining a virtual learning tool and onsite study visits of four conservation sites in Europe (2011)
17. Wiley, D.A.: The learning objects literature. https://opencontent.org/blog/wp-content/upl oads/2007/07/wiley-lo-review-final.pdf. Accessed 19th Mar 2017
18. Akpinar, Y.: Validation of a learning object review instrument: relationship between ratings of learning objects and actual learning outcomes. Interdiscip. J. E-Learning Learn. Objects **4** (2008). Editor: Heinz Dreher
19. Bannan-Ritland, B., Dabbagh, N., Murphy, K.: Learning object systems as constructivist learning environments: related assumptions, theories, and applications. In: Wiley, D.A. (ed.) The Instructional Use of Learning Objects (Bloomington, IN, Agency for Instructional Technology and Association for Educational Communications & Technology), pp. 61–97 (2002)
20. Buzzetto-More, N., Pinhey, K.: Guidelines and standards for the development of fully online learning objects. Interdiscip. J. Knowl. Learn. Objects **2**, 96–104 (2006)
21. Cohen, E., Nycz, M.: Learning objects e-learning: an informing science perspective. Interdiscip. J. Knowl. Learn. Objects **2**, 23–24 (2006)
22. Porter, D., Curry, J., Muirhead, B., Galan, N.: A report on learning object repositories review and recommendations for a Pan-Canadian approach to repository implementation in Canada for CANARIE Inc. (2002)
23. Convertini, V.N., Albanese, D., Marengo, A., Marengo, V., Scalera, M.: The osel taxonomy for the classification of learning objects. Interdiscip. J. E-Learning Learn. Objects **1**, 125–138 (2006)
24. Graf, S.: Adaptivity in learning management systems focusing on learning styles. Ph.D. thesis, Vienna University of Technology, December 2007

Ex Machina: An Interactive Museum Kit for Supporting Educational Processes in Industrial Heritage Museums

Athina Bosta, Dimitrios Katsakioris, Andreas Nikolarakis, Panayiotis Koutsabasis(ID), Spyros Vosinakis(ID), and Modestos Stavrakis(✉)(ID)

Department of Product and Systems Design Engineering, University of the Aegean, 84100 Syros, Greece
{dpsd16068,dpsd15043,dpsd15083,kgp,spyrosv,modestos}@aegean.gr

Abstract. The aim of our project was to create an interactive museum kit in order to prepare young elementary students for their visit the Industrial Heritage Museum of Hermoupolis, enhancing their experience and promoting a "hands-on" learning approach. This paper presents field research, design decisions and the evaluation of the Ex Machina Museum Kit. The system comprises of 4 tangible team games, 4 documentary-style videos presenting information relative to the theme of the museum's collections as well as an interactive storytelling and decision-making game. Finally, a preliminary evaluation presents the benefits that this project would provide to the elementary school students visiting the museum.

Keywords: Interactive museum kit · Industrial cultural heritage · Storytelling · Interactive game · Interaction design

1 Introduction

As part of the Interactive Systems Design course at the University of the Aegean, we were prompted to create a board game as a visit companion for a museum of our choosing at the region of the island of Syros. From a field visit to the Industrial Museum of Hermoupolis, it became evident that a number of ideas can be explored to fulfill the design brief. This museum was chosen as it houses an extensive collection of diverse industrial exhibits, too many to go over in the limited time of the tour without any previous knowledge.

We focused on primary school students, researched museum-pedagogical issues, and interviewed teachers as well as the museum employees (guide, curator, and archivist). We realized that even though the students are excited about the visit, they usually don't retain the majority of the information that they are being presented. We wanted to create a system that would stimulate the students' interest, encourage them to actively ask questions during the visit, and help them retain more information after their visit. Our research led us towards playful learning, tangible interfaces, and group activities supported by interactive technologies. With those in mind, we created an interactive system that embraces the whole visiting experience. It includes the student preparation phase

© Springer Nature Switzerland AG 2021
M. Ioannides et al. (Eds.): EuroMed 2020, LNCS 12642, pp. 438–449, 2021.
https://doi.org/10.1007/978-3-030-73043-7_36

before the visit with games and short documentary-style videos and an interactive story-telling phase to supplement the learning experience [1–3]. The interactive museum kit is meant to be sent to schools before their visit in order to support the learning processes related to the actual museum content [1, 4].

2 Methodology

We aimed to design an interactive museum kit that will prepare elementary school students for their upcoming school visit to the museum and, also, enhance their visitor-experience. During the formation of the design brief and preliminary research, some typical challenges we would have to overcome were: a) the interactive museum kit should be compatible with the current museum practices (curation and available educational programs), b) to present the learning content with the appropriate pedagogical practices, c) to be aligned with the Greek national educational curriculum and meet teachers' pedagogical preferences, and d) to provide engaging and playful activities for students.

In order to address these challenges, we followed an iterative design approach that was presented to us during the university course [5]. In Fig. 1, each studio design phase is presented. In the following paragraphs, we describe how each of them was adapted for our project.

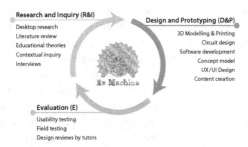

Fig. 1. The iterative design approach followed

2.1 Research and Inquiry (R&I)

This phase included desktop research as well as contextual inquiry, which acted as complementary to the findings related to on-going works and trends [6, 7]. The former referred to related projects and interactive systems achieving similar goals and/or offer similar user experience (UX), and to educational theories that will help us combine museum-teaching content with the appropriate technologies in order to accomplish specific learning objectives [2, 8]. As for the latter, there were two situations we needed to gain an understanding of them: museum approaches and teaching practices in elementary school. Therefore, we conducted semi-structured interviews with both the director of the Industrial Museum of Hermoupolis and four (4) elementary school teachers, who gladly accepted our invitation.

2.2 Design and Prototyping (D&P)

This phase covered the aspects of conceptual design and prototyping, including 3D modeling and printing, circuit design, and software development. The first step was to specify the learning content and collect information about it: the history of Hermoupolis (capital of Syros Island), its foundation, and flourishing throughout the 19th and early 20th century. Taking into consideration the museum's curation and comments from teachers, we concluded that our interactive system should embrace the whole museum visiting experience, which begins in the classroom and ends at the museum. For this reason, it took the form of a museum kit.

The presented system architecture consisted of two parts (see Fig. 2): a) classroom pre-visit activities and b) museum activities during the school visit. We designed four (4) tangible mini-game artifacts each one including playful learning activities for a group of 3–5 students, which take place in the classroom. At the museum, after the guided tour, students, forming self-selected groups, participate in an interactive storytelling game. In this game, they help the hero to establish a textile factory by collecting relevant exhibit items from different museum collections and guiding his decision.

2.3 Evaluation (E)

The Evaluation phase includes preliminary empirical testing activities about the implemented technologies and prototypes and a field study with user participation.

The first part of the evaluation was iteratively conducted throughout the design process in the classroom by tutors and other university students. Its main focus was to gather feedback about the usability of the tangible mini-games artifacts and the interactive storytelling game in order to address potential issues in time.

The following field study took place in a school class simulation room regarding the pre-visit activities, and, as for the interactive storytelling game, in the setting of the Industrial Museum of Hermoupolis, with high-fidelity prototypes and user participation. This part's objective was to evaluate the design goals, usability, and also overall user-experience (UX) of our educational interactive system.

3 Related Work

Interactive systems that influenced our work are briefly presented in this section. Emphasis is given on projects and technologies that introduce storytelling approaches, decision-making activities, or aim to enhance UX in museums (before, during, or after the visit).

"Museum in a Box (MiaB)" [9] is an educational interactive system that brings museum content to schools by providing them with hand-held tangible replicas of real exhibits in the form of 3D-prints, card-postal, documents, pictures, maps, etc. Every kit is tailor-made to meet the specific needs and content of the museums. The system uses a Raspberry Pi board along with an NFC Reader and two speakers. Users interact with NFC-embedded physical objects to hear an audio story associated with each one. The idea of 3D-printed tangible replicas, which allows students to interact safely with museum

items, as well as the concept of connecting them with a story influenced creatively our work.

"*A Gift for Athena*" [10] is an augmented reality application for the British Museum, related to the Greek exhibits and the "Gallery of the Parthenon". The game is about the celebration of Athena's birthday at the Acropolis. Users are asked to return the gift (tunic) of the goddess by completing the silhouette recognition and the exhibit collection using their mobile's camera to be able to retrieve it. As a result, the interest in the exhibits is being increased due to the playful learning and engagement. The game parts that our team examined are the characters which create a thematic context (conditions, space, time), set either short-term goals (solving each challenge) or long-term ones (offering a gift/tunic to the goddess), and challenge the player to act (interaction with the application and connection with the real environment) to achieve them. Also, the use of the exhibits as part of its storytelling and plot development, creating connections between the real (Museum) and the virtual world (application) determined the role of the exhibits in the "Ex-Machina" museum kit and the gamification of the students' museum experience.

"*Tinker Island*" [18] is a strategy mobile game about survival on an unknown island. Players have to survive through decision-making activities. The narration function is activated during exploration and describes the player's condition, who is called upon to make decisions to reach its end. Each exploration area unfolds a different plot. Player's choices can lead to the continuation of the narrative, either with a negative or a positive effect, and finally to the completion of the narrative, which will determine his status. We found it interesting to incorporate the concept of continuation alternatives in the narrative for the interactive storytelling game in the museum. In this way, different game experiences will be offered depending on players' choices.

4 Research and Inquiry

4.1 A Definition of Museum Kits

A museum kit (or Museum-in-a-box) is a portable collection of loanable items for educational purposes, which includes, for instance: museum artifacts or replicas, illustrations, and other audiovisual materials, teaching resources, educational games, etc. [3, 11]. It can be implemented before, during, and/or after the school visit to a museum. However, according to Black [3] conducting pre-visit activities helps students get familiarized with the museum content. It is a common practice among museums to provide a variety of educational kits covering a wide range of themes. Every kit should be developed carefully by articulating specific learning goals and providing methods by which these goals will be accomplished and assessed.

4.2 Educational Approach

Among the different functions museums perform, education is one of the most prominent as they provide various learning experiences to their visitors [12]. However, the settings within which learning takes place (e.g. usually self-motivated, flexible museum/learning content, no evaluation, etc.) make them non-formal learning environments [12, 13].

Taking these into account, Constructivism as a theory of education seems appropriate to be applied to museum contexts [14], and hence, our educational interactive museum kit was designed and developed from a constructivist perspective.

Constructivism maintains that learning happens in social contexts and requires the active participation of the learners in which they construct their new understanding by reflecting on their living experience and their prior knowledge [14]. Furthermore, according to Hein, active participation can be achieved by fostering a supportive learning environment that engages learners in both hands-on and minds-on activities and encourages them to interact with each other, to experiment, and discover new meanings. Probably, the most important point here is that learners' newly acquired knowledge should not be evaluated based on external reality factors (true/false conditions), but whether it is coherent and leads to reasonable actions.

5   Design and Prototyping

As the collection of exhibits in the Industrial Museum of Hermoupolis is diverse, we decided to design four (4) games, for the major sections of the museum. The museum has six (6) sections, the first is about the beginning of Hermoupolis, typography, and glassware, the second is about trade the main reason why the island's economy flourished during the 19th century, the third and fourth rooms house exhibits related to marine travel and maritime craftsmanship, the fifth room contains exhibits related to industrial cultural heritage while the sixth room houses periodical exhibits and therefore was not included. Considering the limited time for our project we chose to fully prototype three (2) mini-games.

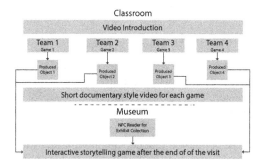

Fig. 2. "Ex Machina" system architecture

Through a set of interviews, we realized that the time teachers could dedicate to a museum kit is limited so it's not realistic to assume that all pupils would be able to play with all games. For this reason, we composed short videos (1–2 min long) meant to be seen after each group of kids finishes their game. This way each group of pupils will have general knowledge of all the topics of the museum but will be "experts" in the room whose game they played. From interviews we conducted with teachers it became even more evident that, especially in primary school, teamwork is promoted, and pupils learn better when they use "hands-on" approaches to solve problems or puzzles. Therefore, following the constructivist principles, we have integrated these concepts, as well as "learn by doing" and experimentation into the playful learning activities of tangible mini-games. Moving forward with our project we took into account that the system we designed was not to overshadow or affect the museum tour itself. For this reason, we decided to design an additional game for the end of the tour to "embrace" the whole visit from start to finish in such a way that our system coexists harmoniously with the museum and enhances the overall experience rather than undermine the museum itself. In order to make the final project more coherent, we designed a narrator who will accompany and advise the pupils throughout their interaction with the museum kit. We chose this character to be Mr. Elpidoforos Ladopoulos because, to this day, the ruins of his factory remain in the area and we have rich records of his life and work as well as of his descendants.

Finally, we considered it important to keep a souvenir in the classroom or for each student individually. So, we designed the games in such a way as to produce items that students can then keep for themselves. We also made sure that the items created during class would be used during the final game at the end of the visit, thus making the pupils realize that whatever they were creating in class has value.

5.1 Introductory Video

When the museum kit is connected to the computer, an application launches, and the character of Mr. Ladopoulos appears on the screen. He introduces himself to the pupils and puts them in the historical context in which the story takes place. Then he talks about the games that the class will play and says that the whole process will be completed in the museum. Finally, it prompts the teacher to share the games so that the pupils may start.

5.2 Mini-games

The Beginnings of Hermoupolis - Typography

After studying the exhibits of the room, we quickly decided that this game would be a letterpress composing stick that the pupils would be asked to complete. We chose one newspaper from those in the display case. We found in the public library of Hermoupolis an article from a 19th-century local newspaper which speaks for the inauguration of the new factory of Mr. Ladopoulos and we adapted it to language understood by pupils. We removed letters from the text that the pupils would be asked to put in the correct places in order to complete the article. When the article is completed correctly, the pupils should get tempera and paint the plate. Then they take the printed paper which will become the "produced object" and print the text on it. Note at this point, the increased difficulty since the plate is read from right to left, its letters, as well as what the pupils had to fill in are flipped horizontally in order to be printed correctly on the paper.

We considered it appropriate to have a check to confirm that the letters have been placed in the correct places on the plate. We made a circuit with LEDs that light up when each row is completed correctly. The system consists of a battery and 14 LEDs connected in series. The circuit is completed by placing the correct letter in the correct position. Each individual letter contains a wire in specific positions that correspond only to the specific letter. Also, for this game as well as the "Maritime Heritage Room", we have designed an instruction booklet which users should read carefully to understand the steps of the process and complete the game.

Maritime Heritage

Even though this is largely occupied by the Steam Ship "Patris" shipwreck exhibition and our original idea was to build a game similar to "Battleship", we considered that this idea has no future so much at the level of interaction as well as creativity, so we decided to design a game that would have to do with the telegraph. Pupils are asked to listen to and understand a sequence of Morse code and complete the "Produced Item" given to them. Having filled in all the words they need to send, a response message will be revealed. This system consists of an Arduino Uno, connected with 2 Buttons, 1 LED, and a Buzzer, which are contained in a 3D printed case. The "Produced Item" they are asked to complete is an order form and the message they need to send is a confirmation.

Trade

This game would be a kind of locked safe, the code of which would be given in the form of a puzzle to the pupils through production notes. They would be asked to identify numbers and keywords to calculate its combination. Inside the safe is a check which will serve as this game's "Produced item".

Industrialization

The idea Industry room's game is a 3D gear puzzle. The pupils have to put the gears that would be given to them, in the right places so that when they turn a crank, a hidden door opens a compartment containing the produced object: an "engineering diploma" (Fig. 3).

Fig. 3. Prototyped mini-games and museum kit suitcase

5.3   Application for the Video Presentation

After completing the games, the teacher asks the pupils what they did in the game they played and asks them to say a few words about their experience. Then, every team in turn takes their mini-game artifact (each game artifact has an NFC tag at its base) and places it in the special place on the museum kit.

The museum kit has an Arduino Uno with an NFC scanner integrated and is connected with the class computer. The relevant software, which we developed with Unity and C#, is also installed there. When the NFC reader recognizes the embedded NFC tag, it triggers the video playback of the 1–2 min long documentary-style videos that refers to the contents of the corresponding room of the museum. Their content emerged from our close collaboration with the director of the Industrial Museum of Hermoupolis as well as bibliographic research. The videos were composed by the members of the group, exclusively for the purposes of the museum kit. After the presentation of the fourth video, Mr. Ladopoulos appears and in a short video invites the pupils to the Industrial Museum of Hermoupolis to help him with a problem he faces and reminds them not to forget to bring with them the items they made.

5.4   Game in the Museum

The idea for the game at the end of the visit is a story that pupils shape through choices they make as they play. We wanted to give pupils the opportunity to explore the museum at their own pace and make interesting choices through discussion. In this game we have implemented some constructivist practices mentioned by Ebitz [15]: construction of knowledge through narrative by the main animated character of the story, co-construction of meaning through conversation between students during the selection procedure of museum exhibits for the interactive story game, and story completion based on the choices made by students as performance (Fig. 4).

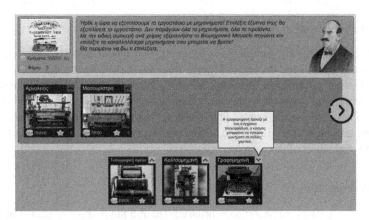

Fig. 4. Screenshot from the interactive storytelling game

The museum kit is connected to a computer, a touch screen, and a projector. Pupils operate a device that allows them to scan cards from exhibits they see to add to their "collection" letting them choose them to move the story forward. Their choices affect the plot and the final story produced at the end of the game. Throughout the story, pupils are asked to collect exhibits with NFC Reader, scan the items they produced in the classroom and, at one stage, discuss with each other and vote from a list of options.

6 Evaluation

6.1 Purpose

A formative usability test was conducted in order to observe and record useful comments, views, and problems of the potential users and university students specialized in product and system design engineering, for the prototype of the museum kit, to highlight ways to improve it [16, 17]. The participation of design students contributed to the holistic supervision of the museum kit, as they could distinguish the parameters that compose the project both at the prototype and conceptual level.

6.2 Target

The main objectives were to observe if the participants would complete the challenges as the design team expected and if they would find interesting and educational the presented information. Specifically, the observation was about the time and the way of the mini-games' completion and the participants' steps comprehension in the game: "The establishment of a textile factory".

Also, an important goal was to carry out the evaluation as close to the real conditions as possible. The evaluation was consisted of two phases: the first took place in a classroom as a simulation of a school classroom in the Department of Product and System Design Engineering because of the equipment granted, and the second, at the Industrial Museum of Hermoupolis.

6.3 User Identification

The participants were five people (n = 5), two (2) of whom were 12 years old pupils of the primary school and the three (3) were students of the Department of Product and Systems Design Engineering between the ages of 22 and 24. Of all the participants, only one child had visited the museum again and remembered that it was related to Hermoupolis' factories that existed in the past, without details or any information about the historical context of the time. The remaining participants would make their first visit during the evaluation of the system.

6.4 Implementation

The evaluation took place on 1st of February 2020 and the first phase started in a room of the Department of Product and Systems Design Engineering and lasted about an hour. There, pupils and university students were divided into 2 different groups: the first one could deal with the mini-game of Typography and the second with that of Maritime heritage. After solving the mini-game, each group presented to the class the challenge they were called to complete, and videos associated with these mini-games were shown. These documentary-style videos presented information about the historical context of Hermoupolis, and a member of the design team, linked the information provided with the content of the Museum, avoiding the disclosure of the exhibits and information of the tour, emphasizing more the social, political, and economic conditions of the past.

The second phase started in the Industrial Museum of Hermoupolis and lasted about an hour and a half. Participants were given a short tour from the museum director and formed one group, (limited participants), which played the game: "The establishment of a textile factory". During playtime, the team had to collect the exhibits they considered most suitable for each selection round by using the designed NFC reader device, return to the museum equipment area and decide on its final selections, which influenced the narrative and end of the game. The group also had to place the produced objects (check, engineer's diploma, newspaper, order form) on the museum kit at specific phases of the narrative. The design team did not intervene during the evaluation, it formulated short questions after the completion of a user task, asked participants to complete a questionnaire, and conducted semi-structured interviews at the end of each phase.

6.5 Evaluation Results

After each phase, questionnaires were given to teams, which are the Typography (2 people), the Maritime (3 people), and Museum activity (5 people) team. The first phase's questionnaire was the same for both teams, but because user experience comes from interacting with a different mini-game, two different tables were created (Fig. 5).

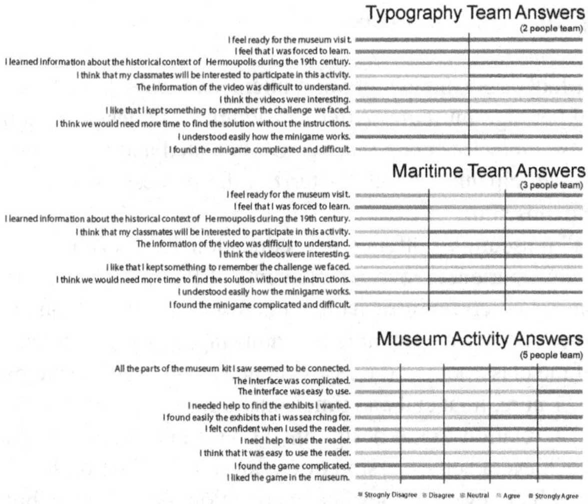

Fig. 5. Results from Typography, Maritime Mini-Games, and Museum interactive Storytelling (each section on colored bars represents a participant response)

Also, the completion task time of each phase and the total time of each one were recorded. It was observed that time durations are close to the initial assumptions of the design team (classroom-2 teaching hours and museum-1 h). Additionally, a difference in difficulty between the two mini-games was noticed. Although the Typography team completed its task approximately 4 min faster, it's important to mention that the Maritime team consisted of adult design experts. Thus, it is understood that the telegraph is a little

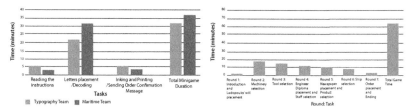

Fig. 6. Task analysis

more difficult than the letterpress composing stick and needs some modifications that will facilitate its interaction with users (Fig. 6).

Finally, a spontaneous discussion between teams was observed, immediately after the completion of the first phase. Pupils and design students exchanged their experiences explaining the process of solving mini-games and information about produced objects. During the second phase, the team constantly exchanged opinions on the collection and selection of exhibits, was carefully reading the museum labels for more information, and trying to balance the money with the options (expenses/reputation) offered by the scanned exhibits in the game.

7 Summary and Conclusions

The design team looked for interesting and interactive ways to engage an educational visit to a cultural heritage museum. After researching and designing a museum kit for the Industrial Museum of Hermoupolis, the team created and tested the prototype with the assistance of participants who characterized the process as more attractive than a simple visit to the museum.

"Ex Machina" museum kit offers a new educational approach to the Hermoupolis' Industrial Museum experience, reviving elements of the historical context that's referring to. Mini-game interactions attracted the interest of the evaluation participants, who described the process at least enjoyable and amusing. A strong project limitation was the simulation of the classroom in the assessment as well as the participation of limited pupils in it. Furthermore, financial and time constraints contributed to the discrepancies in the prototype, in relation to the design intentions, and as a result, changes must be done in order to achieve a better version of the museum kit. Also, the museum kit uses museum exhibits, which reveal the aesthetic perception, skills, and technical progress of the past and brings visitors in contact with various aspects of the daily life, equipment, and people who lived in earlier periods. In this way, museum visit becomes more experiential, visitors understand the value of the cultural heritage and express their respect for it. The interactive activities of the museum kit can be the connection with the past and the remarkable achievements of previous historical periods, through engagement with the exhibits hosted in the museum, forming a pleasant experience, and enhancing an active cultural participation.

References

1. Anderson, D., Lucas, K.B.: The effectiveness of orienting students to the physical features of a science museum prior to visitation. Res. Sci. Educ. **27**, 485–495 (1997). https://doi.org/10.1007/BF02461476
2. Andre, L., Durksen, T., Volman, M.L.: Museums as avenues of learning for children: a decade of research. Learn. Environ. Res. **20**, 47–76 (2017)
3. Black, G.: The Engaging Museum: Developing Museums for Visitor Involvement. Psychology Press, Hove (2005)
4. Diamond, J., Horn, M., Uttal, D.H.: Practical Evaluation Guide: Tools for Museums and Other Informal Educational Settings. Rowman & Littlefield, Lanham (2016)
5. Koutsabasis, P., Vosinakis, S., Stavrakis, M., Kyriakoulakos, P.: Teaching HCI with a studio approach: lessons learnt. Presented at the Proceedings of 22nd Pan-Hellenic Conference on Informatics Conference (PCI 2018), Athens, Greece (2018)
6. Holtzblatt, K., Wendell, J.B., Wood, S.: Rapid Contextual Design: A How-to Guide to Key Techniques for User-Centered Design. Morgan Kaufmann, Burlington (2004)
7. Preece, J., Sharp, H., Rogers, Y.: Interaction Design: Beyond Human-Computer Interaction, 4th edn. Wiley, Chichester (2015)
8. Antoniou, A.: A methodology for the development of museum educational applications: visitor inspired museum adaptive learning technologies (2009)
9. Espiritu, A.: A Museum in a Box. https://museuminabox.org/boxes/. Accessed 14 Sep 2020
10. A Gift for Athena I MW2015: Museums and the Web (2015). https://mw2015.museumsandtheweb.com/bow/a-gift-for-athena/. Accessed 14 Sep 2020
11. Marcus, A.S., Stoddard, J.D., Woodward, W.W.: Teaching History with Museums: Strategies for K-12 Social Studies. Taylor & Francis, Milton Park (2017)
12. Hooper-Greenhill, E.: Museums and Their Visitors. Routledge, London (2013)
13. Eshach, H.: Bridging in-school and out-of-school learning: formal, non-formal, and informal education. J. Sci. Educ. Technol. **16**, 171–190 (2007). https://doi.org/10.1007/s10956-006-9027-1
14. Hein, G.E.: Museum education. In: A Companion to Museum Studies, pp. 340–352. Wiley (2006)
15. Ebitz, D.: Sufficient foundation: theory in the practice of art museum education. Vis. Arts Res. **34**, 14–24 (2008)
16. Rubin, J., Chisnell, D., Spool, J.: Handbook of Usability Testing: How to Plan, Design, and Conduct Effective Tests. Wiley, Indianapolis (2008)
17. Lazar, J.: Research Methods in Human-Computer Interaction. Wiley, Chichester West Sussex (2010)
18. Tinker Island - Survival Story Adventure. https://play.google.com/store/apps/details?id=com.kongregate.mobile.tinkerisland.google&hl=en_US. Accessed 26 Oct 2020

Creative Industries and Immersive Technologies for Training, Understanding and Communication in Cultural Heritage

Eleftherios Anastasovitis[1,2,3] and Manos Roumeliotis[1]

[1] University of Macedonia, 156 Egnatia Street, 54636 Thessaloniki, Greece
info@pyrseia.gr, manos@uom.gr
[2] Centre for Research and Technology Hellas, 6th km Charilaou-Thermi Road, 57001 Thermi, Thessaloniki, Greece
[3] Pyrseia Informatics, 37 Ippokratous Street, 55134 Thessaloniki, Greece

Abstract. Creative industries, such as cinematography and videogames, have invaded everyday life, offering fun and entertainment. The progress of immersive technologies provides breathtaking experiences to the users of creative digital productions. Through virtual reality the player can interact with the elements of the virtual world in a physical way. The conversion of games into serious ones, transformed them as innovative educational tools, for training in every scientific field. Cultural Heritage is an inexhaustible source of inspiration that feeds the creative industries with ideas, scenarios, and stories Moreover, the needs for the training of Cultural Heritage professionals and scientists, offer very interesting scenarios that can be implemented by the combination of serious games and virtual reality, under the prism of Lifelong Learning. In this paper, the significant effect of three-dimensional animation, full-immersive serious games, and virtual reality for better understanding, communication, and training in Cultural Heritage is being presented. Three use cases that creative industry and immersive technologies apply on tangible and intangible Cultural Heritage, highlight the importance of multidisciplinary collaborations. In this context, the transformation of historical references into a meaningful three-dimensional video animation production and the design of a full-immersive serious game in VR is the first example. The emblematic Antikythera Mechanism, consists the second use case that led our research team in the creation of the innovative Virtual Museum of the ancient technological achievement. Finally, the design and the execution of Lifelong educational programmes for training in CH through creative industries and immersive technologies is the third use case.

Keywords: Cultural Heritage · Virtual reality · Serious games · Animation · Creative industries · Immersion · Training · Lifelong Learning · Educational programme

1 Introduction

The creative industries are directly related to Culture as they are a subset of Cultural Heritage (CH) and they should not be considered foreign to CH. Cinematography and

© Springer Nature Switzerland AG 2021
M. Ioannides et al. (Eds.): EuroMed 2020, LNCS 12642, pp. 450–461, 2021.
https://doi.org/10.1007/978-3-030-73043-7_37

videogames are consisted by various specialties and experts with different scientific or professional background. The adoption of technologies, full-immersive (e.g. Virtual Reality, VR), or low immersive (e.g. Augmented Reality, AR, and Mixed Reality, MR), in creative industries offers breathtaking experiences to users [1]. However, their technical nature raises issues of technophobia, which can easily be overcome through training.

The concept idea and the design of a scenario are the cornerstones for the success in creative industries. The more interesting the concept of a production is, the more acceptance it gains. Through movies and three-dimensional (3D) video animation productions, the recreation and representation of meaningful stories is being achieved. Furthermore, the introduction of virtual reality in cinematography, offers the new experimental type of VR cinema, where the spectator is equipped with the full-immersive Head Mounted Display and lives the movie in completely breathtaking way. Cinematography can be used for better communication and understanding of various types of information, meanings, methodologies, and procedures, as supplementary material for educational purposes. In this direction, 3D and full-immersive serious games in virtual reality simulate difficult, stressful, dangerous and high-risk situations for the training of professionals or personnel of an organization, such as in Industry, in Health, in Army, and so on. In a simplest version, these applications can be used for better understanding and communication of concepts and information [2].

Cultural Heritage is an inexhaustible tank for the creative industries and immersive technologies that provide concept ideas and game scenarios that stimulate the interest of the users. Tangible and intangible Cultural Heritage consists of artifacts, archives, archaeological sites, shipwrecks, buildings from different periods, stories, history, myths, as well as paintings, music, contemporary arts and more. In this context, creative industries and cutting-edge immersive technologies can be applied for the development of various types of digital applications for physical or remote visitors of CH organizations [3]. Moreover, serious games and immersive technologies can also be applied for the training of the personnel and the professionals of an CH institute, as innovative educational tool. The simulation of a virtual disaster in a museum, can safely train the user in stressful and difficult situations. Furthermore, a simulation of the excavation in an underwater archaeological site, such as a shipwreck, through full-immersive VR system, can train a professional in dangerous and unprecedented conditions.

In this paper, the impact of creative industries and immersive technologies such as 3D graphics, serious games, and virtual reality, in training, better understanding, and communication for tangible and intangible Cultural Heritage is being presented. The overview of the presentation follows the next structure. In section two, Herodotus, the father of History, triggers a multidisciplinary research that the results feed the creation of a 3D video animation production and the design of a serious game in VR. In section three, the Antikythera Mechanism, the emblematic and innovative ancient device, gathers the interest of different sciences and leads Cultural Informatics in the design and the development of next generation Virtual Museum, the experiential VM. In section four, immersive technologies and creative industries are transformed into educational means for training in Cultural Heritage, under the prism of Lifelong Learning. An extended discussion is provided in section five, while last section the conclusions are being highlighted.

2   A Scriptwriter from the Past

In this section, historical references trigger multidisciplinary researches that feed the creative industries with concept ideas and scenarios for the implementation of a) a 3D video animation production, and b) a full-immersive serious game in VR. Both different types of productions target the representation, better understanding, and communication of Cultural Heritage to the general public.

2.1   Storytelling and Multidisciplinary Research

Herodotus provides important information about the events that preceded and followed the siege of the ancient city of Potidaea during the winter between 480 to 479 B.C. (History, VIII, 126–129). The historical storytelling was proved by recent extensive geological and seismic researches in the North Aegean basin and the Thermaikos Gulf that was the first historical reference to the phenomenon of tsunami (sea-wave of gravity), which was a savior for ancient Potidaea. Herodotus' description is very detailed about the phenomenon of low tide, which preceded the violent flood that led to the destruction of much of the Persian forces and their retreat to Thessaly. In fact, Herodotus attributes the phenomenon to the wrath of Poseidon, due to the desecration of the temple and its statue, which were located on the suburbs of the ancient city, by the Persians. Although there are no traces of the exact location of the temple, it's remains are found today in the Byzantine wall of Potidaea (see Fig. 1).

Fig. 1.   The a) western part of the b) Byzantine wall of Potidaea.

Herodotus' description aroused the interest of seismologists, who investigated the faults of the wider area for the existence of a sufficient point, which could activate the mechanism of genesis of a tsunami. The seismological researches located the specific rift in the basin of the North Aegean, a few kilometers northwest of Skopelos Island [4]. The specific fault is capable of causing earthquakes from 6.5 to 7.5 Richter, with violent vertical displacement of the fault by 2 to 3 m, as well as possible underwater landslide, in the North Aegean Trench, at a depth of 1,000–1,100 m.

For their part, the geologists conducted research in the wider area of Thermaikos Gulf, drilling in coastal swamps and lagoons, i.e. places where such violent geological phenomena are stored, as there are deposited materials and organisms from the sea (shells and coals). Geologists, proved the presence of violent phenomena, while the dating of the recent layers coincides with the period described by Herodotus [5]. However, the periodicity of the phenomenon is equally important, every 2,500 years, as a corresponding violent event was detected at a greater depth of drilling.

2.2 Tsunami in Ancient Potidaea: A 3D Representation

A research was conducted to gather data and information related to the tsunami described by Herodotus and proven by geological and seismological researches [6]. Unluckily, archeological evidence to seal the event were not found. The results of this Master dissertation [6] led to write the script for the design and development of a 3D video animation production, which compose different research fields, for a better understanding of historical events, with scientific documentation (see Fig. 2).

Fig. 2. A 3D representation of the Temple of Poseidon in ancient Potidaea.

The 3D video animation *Tsunami in ancient Potidaea* represents the historical events that took place in 480 to 479 BC. And compares them with the results of the geological and seismological researches, which relate to the same historic event [7]. The representation was implemented with the exclusive use of 3D graphics and the simultaneous support of the sound.

2.3 Phlegra-VR: A Full-Immersive Serious Game

The *Phlegra-VR* is based on the 3D video animation *Tsunami in ancient Potidaea* and is its transfer to the world of videogames, using the impressive and innovative technologies of virtual reality. Through *Phlegra-VR* the user, as a protagonist (first person), will participate in the execution of missions, according to the synthesis of interesting scenarios, starting from the dissemination of the result of the Battleship of Salamis.

The individual stories (levels) of *Phlegra-VR* will be scalable, in terms of the difficulty of their completion, while in the same context will move the usability of the system, so that even the most novice users in virtual reality systems, will be trained in good practices by the beginning of the game, enhancing their experience (see Table 1). As the videogame is based on historical data and scientific research, it deserves to be treated as a serious game, without reducing the crucial characteristic of the entertainment.

Table 1. Level description of *Phlegra-VR* videogame.

Level	Title	Mission
1	The talking walls	Transition to the past during the exploration of the Byzantines wall of Potidaea
2	The early bird	To expel successfully the Persians from the Kassandra peninsula right after the Naval Battle of Salamis
3	Under pressure	Strengthen the defense of the city, repel the attacks of the Persians and reveal plans of betrayal
4	The broken trident	Support the defense of the city, repelling the final attack, aiming to force the Persians to retreat, right after the earthquake and the historical tsunami

3   Observing the Celestial Dome via an Ancient Device

In this section, the impact of cutting-edge immersive technologies through the creative industry of serious games leads to a) the digital reconstruction of the fragments of the emblematic Antikythera Mechanism, and b) the evolution of Virtual Museums to their next generation that embed full-immersive Cultural experiences.

The Antikythera Mechanism concentrated the interest of different sciences. Astrophysics consider it as the absolute astronomical device of the ancient era [8]. Engineering treats the Antikythera Mechanism as an unreal human invention, possibly the most extraordinary device for the ancient technology [9]. Computer Science is still trying to resolve the enigmas that have been survived in the fragile and corroded fragments of the first-ever analogue computer [10]. All hopes for the recovery of additional information for the Mechanism are pinned on the ongoing underwater archaeological excavations carried out in the site of the ancient shipwreck, in the sea of the Aegean.

3.1   Virtual Museum for the Antikythera Mechanism

Through the research on the datasets of the Antikythera Mechanism Research Project [11], the authors succeeded to 3D reconstruct the fragments of the Antikythera Mechanism. Using the full-immersive technologies of VR [12], in the context of a game engine [13], designed and developed a Virtual Museum (VM) that hosts this unique exhibition. The user can hold and examine the reconstructed fragments with the virtual hands (see Fig. 3). Moreover, the observation of the inner structure of each fragment, is now possible. Through an extensive evaluation by end-users the whole research was crowned with success, regarding the usability, the usefulness, the high degree of photorealism, and the immersion in the virtual cosmos [14].

Fig. 3. The *Virtual Museum for the Antikythera Mechanism* is tested by end-users.

3.2 Mechaneus-VR

One of the crucial results of the aforementioned evaluation, was the motivation and desire of the evaluators to be able to accomplish additional game scenarios in the context of the Virtual Museum. This observation led the research team to consider the combination of game industry in the context of a VM. In other words, the Virtual Museums are being transformed from narrative into experiential. In *Mechaneus-VR*, the user can act in the era of the Antikythera Mechanism, and through defined game scenarios will be able to gain all the knowledge about the structure and its functionalities [15].

4 Recursive Training Through Immersive Technologies

In this section, the training in immersive technologies and creative industries through the use of immersive technologies is being presented. The design of the innovative Lifelong Learning educational programme in the context of Master dissertation in Adult Education [16] is the core of first subsection. The design, the execution, and some interesting results from two Lifelong Learning programmes that the research team was responsible for, in *University of Macedonia*.

4.1 Design of an Innovative Educational Programme

The possibility of using new forms of knowledge representation in a Lifelong educational programme was the subject of designing the *Researching the virtual Antikythera Mechanism* [17]. Specifically, the possibility of designing an educational program, based on the principles of Lifelong Learning [17], was explored, which incorporated new types of knowledge representation, such as 3D graphics and game engines. These new tools that come from creative industries, were both learning objects and supervisory tools. The purpose of this study was to determine their positive impact on a heterogeneous educational team, which would engage in research around the Antikythera Mechanism, studying the digital data that would be freely available to the public. The design of the innovative training programme included the part of the accounting evaluation for the future improvement of the Lifelong educational programme *Researching the virtual Antikythera Mechanism.*

The cardinal objective of the training programme is the more efficient communication of the Cultural Heritage with the public. The purpose of the proposed research is to design a detailed self-funded educational programme, which will be aimed at a group of adults, and concerns the understanding of the functions of the Antikythera Mechanism, using the 3D graphics and game engines, both as cognitive objects, as well as supervisory means, to enhance learning outcomes. The design of the programme proposes group-centered and collaborative learning, under the constant encouragement of the instructor within a flexible educational structure, for the more efficient integration of innovative forms of knowledge representation in the study of open digital data of the Antikythera Mechanism.

The specific objectives of the research are: a) the design of an educational programme for the multidisciplinary study of the Antikythera Mechanism by adult learners, who come from different scientific fields; b) a description of the forms and techniques with which the Antikythera Mechanism can communicate effectively with the training team of the programme; c) the correlation of the use of 3D graphics and virtual reality environments, and d) the possibility of integrating them into a collaborative Lifelong educational programme. The hypotheses posed by the Lifelong training programme *Researching the virtual Antikythera Mechanism* are depicted on the following Table 2:

Table 2. The hypotheses of the design of the Lifelong educational programme *Researching the virtual Antikythera Mechanism.*

Hypothesis	Statement
H1	The use of 3D graphics can enhance collaborative learning in a Lifelong training programme
H2	The integration of 3D graphics and virtual gaming machine environments as supervisory tools can have a positive effect on teamwork in a Lifelong educational programme
H3	The integration of 3D graphics and game engine environments as supervisory tools has a positive effect on the cooperation of heterogeneous groups of learners in a Lifelong training programme
H4	The study of the Antikythera Mechanism can be carried out effectively by integrating 3D graphic and game engine into a Lifelong educational programme, for trainees from different scientific backgrounds

4.2   The Case of VRGamesLab

In 2018, the research team designed to separate Lifelong educational programmes, namely a) the *3DLab: "3D graphics and animation in the entertainment industry"*, and B) the *VRGamesLab-i: "3D serious games for Culture and Education using Virtual Reality"*; for training in creative industries and immersive technologies. The *3DLab* was focused on the training of participants in the technologies and techniques of design and development of successful digital producers, with the use of 3D graphics and the art of 3D animation, for their application in the representation of events through 3D animation of independent narratives.

In 2019, the aforementioned training programmes were merged into the *VRGamesLab-II*. The scope of *VRGamesLab-I* and *II* is the training of participants in the technologies and techniques of design and development of successful games for serious purpose for Culture and Education, with the use of 3D graphics in full-immersive VR environments. The identities of the proposed educational programmes are being depicted in Table 3.

Table 3. The identity of the lifelong educational programmes.

Programme	Duration	Type	Evaluation
3DLab	250 h in 4 months	**Mixed**: 75 h with physical presence, 175 h via asynchronous distant learning	1 × teamwork project. Each team was consisted by 3 members. min. Threshold: 5/10
VRGamesLab-I	250 h in 4 months	**Mixed**: 75 h with physical presence, 175 h via asynchronous distant learning	1 × teamwork project. Each team was consisted by 3 members. min. Threshold: 5/10
VRGamesLab-II	450 h in 8 months	**Mixed**: 40 h with physical presence or synchronous distance learning, 410 h via asynchronous distant learning	4 × personal project min. Threshold in average: 5/10

Both editions of *VRGamesLab* were executed once. The trainees were 7 and 19 respectively. Their background was from Education, Culture, Engineering, Informatics, and Fine Arts. The mass majority ($N = 24$) succeeded to complete the training programmes. Only two trainees withdraw their participation for personal reasons in the middle of *VRGamesLab-II*. In total, 20 digital productions were completed successfully, fulfilling the threshold. The structure of the Lifelong educational programme (see Table 4), in combination with the requirements of each of the four personal projects, minimized the level of technophobia and converted the *VRGamesLab-II* into an entertaining educational experience.

Table 4. The structure and used technologies during the *VRGamesLab-II* Lifelong training programme.

Section	Subject	Technologies
1	Introduction in 3D graphics and Virtual Reality	Oculus
2	Designing the virtual environment in game engines	{Unity, Unreal [18]}
3	3D modeling for virtual cosmos	{Blender [19], Cinema4D [20], Maya, 3DSMax}, {GIMP, Inkscape, Photoshop, Illustrator}
4	User interface in game engines	{Unity, Unreal}, {GIMP [21], Inkscape [22], Photoshop, Illustrator}
5	User experience in game engines	{Unity, Unreal}
6	Lights, shadows, and shaders	{Blender, Cinema4D, Maya, 3DSMax}, {Unity, Unreal}
7	Animation in game engines	{Blender, Cinema4D, Maya, 3DSMax}, {Unity, Unreal}
8	Simulation in game engines	{Unity, Unreal}
9	Virtual Reality and game engines	Oculus, {Unity, Unreal}
10	Production and distribution of 3D serious game in Virtual Reality	Oculus, {Unity, Unreal}, {Premiere, OpenShot [23]}, Audacity [24]

5 Discussion

5.1 Overcoming Technophobia

Immersive technologies and more specifically virtual or mixed reality equipment embodies all recent technological achievements. On the contrary, the majority of CH professionals and curators come from a theoretical base that usually causes a phobia to new media. The implementation of sophisticated applications such as serious games that combine the educational and entertaining aspects significantly reduces the technophobia. Through well designed gamification and the maximization of the feeling of presence and immersion in the virtual world, the player focuses on the completion of the mission acting in physical way even if the trainee is equipped with cutting edge VR devices.

The dynamic of creative industries has a significant influence in the implementation of breathtaking educational experiences in the CH sector. Professionals in cultural organizations need to actively participate during the pre-production and the main phase of the production for an experiential training application. Lifelong educational programmes aim to knowledge transfer of designing and development immersive and educational virtual experiences for training in CH. New knowledge about a) game scenario, b) 3D modeling, c) texturing and materials, d) animation, e) storytelling, f) development in game engine, and g) implementation for VR devices, reduces the technophobia.

The basic funding for museums and archaeological sites is the income by the tickets from the visitors. In addition, the extroversion of Cultural Heritage organizations involves them in research and innovative multidisciplinary projects, both in national and international contexts. The mutual understanding of the restrictions and special needs of each scientific sector is more than welcome. The technical partners need to respect the rules that exist in the management of cultural assets and information. On the other hand, a spherical knowledge by CH professionals, about the uses and the challenges of the technological achievements, not only restrict the technophobia, but increases the level of communication during the preparation and the implementation of any co-funded project.

5.2 Evaluation

Every serious game application is based on predefined scenarios that the user needs to execute successfully. By completing a mission, the player feels happy for the achievement. In case the goals are not met by the player there are always multiple chances to retry. In addition, the progress of the fulfillment of the objectives is depicted on a graphical score bar or on the level of experience. In this context, the user of an immersive serious game always feels and knows the level of completion of any educational task. Immersive technologies that are used as training tools enhances the self-evaluation of the trainee in a playful environment, free from any stress and anxious situations that a controlled and supervised context provides. The user acts more as a player of the serious game than a trainee in an evaluation system.

The results of an execution of a serious game can be published on a table with high-scores or with the top level of experience that the user achieved. These results provide a useful feedback to educators for the level of readiness of the trainee, to execute the simulated scenarios in real conditions. Game engines offers statistics and analytics from the behavior of the user during the application. These game analytics reflects the interactions of the trainee and various types of information, such as the time that the player spent for a procedure, the selected route to avoid obstacles, or the sequence of activities to complete a mission. By monitoring the behavior of trainees in a safe and fully controlled virtual environment, human resources department of a CH organization can easier predict potential dangers and strengthen the weaknesses of their staff.

5.3 Safety and Health Issues

The major advantage of using immersive technologies for the training of CH professionals is the safe and controlled educational environment that is being provided. Through convinced virtual reality cosmos, a diver archaeologist can execute the pre-defined serious game scenario that simulates all safety protocols during an underwater excavation. In the same context the trainee can take crucial decisions during a simulated disaster in a CH organization, such a fire destruction in a monument, a flood in a museum, or an earthquake in an archaeological site, trying to apply a dis-aster recovery plan. Moreover, designed game scenarios with full immersive virtual reality equipment aim in better preparation of conservators during the manipulation of rare, valuable, and fragile artifacts.

The nature of immersive technologies provides various solutions during an urgent and crucial period of a pandemic. Cultural Heritage organizations can apply a distribution and an exploitation plan of their digital solutions for their remote visitors. From the security of their homes, users can access the creative digital content of a museum or an archaeological site, using their personal equipment and keeping all the health protocols far from crowding. In same manner, immersive serious games can be used remotely for training purposes in Cultural Heritage, during public health restrictions. The creative industries ensure the effective communication of the CH organizations in a pandemic period, whether they are visitors or their personnel.

6 Conclusions

In this contribution we presented the impact of creative industries and immersive technologies in Cultural Heritage, through indicative use cases that our research team works on. More specifically, through a 3D video animation we represented a historical reference of a catastrophic phenomenon that seismologists and geologists consider it as the first ever description of a tsunami. The extension of this research leads to the design of a VR serious game for the revival of the history.

Full-immersive technologies in combination with serious games designed and developed the next generation of the virtual museums, the experiential one. The user can better understand in an innovative way the Cultural Heritage, acting in the era of the Antikythera Mechanism. The storytelling and the completion of predefined missions provides a compact knowledge of the ancient technological multidisciplinary achievement.

Lifelong Learning shows remarkable progress in its digital transformation. With fairly quick reflexes Adult Education tries to adopt in its innovative practices the use of the creative industries and immersive technologies. The sector of Cultural Heritage provides the field for experimental applications, using serious games and virtual reality as educational tools for the training of CH professionals and personnel. Moreover, creative industries promote the multidisciplinary collaboration between Cultural Heritage and various sciences, in every discrete phase of producing any digital application.

References

1. Anastasovitis, E., Nikolopoulos, S., Kompatsiaris, I.: Experiencing the impossible through virtual and augmented reality. In: Proceedings They are Not Silent After All... Human Remains in Archaeological Museums: Ethics and Displays, Hellenic Ministry of Culture and Sports, Athens, 31 October–01 November 2019 (2020). submitted for publication
2. Bellotti, F., Kapralos, B., Lee, K., Moreno-Ger, P., Berta, R.: Assessment in and of serious games: an overview. In: Advances in Human-Computer Interaction, vol. 2013 (2013). Article no. 136864, 11 pages. https://doi.org/10.1155/2013/136864
3. Economou, M., Pujol, L.: Educational tool or expensive toy? Evaluating VR evaluation and its relevance for virtual heritage. In: New Media and Cultural Heritage, pp. 242–260 (2008)
4. Papanikolaou, I.D., Papanikolaou, D.I.: Seismic hazard scenarios from the longest geologically constrained active fault of the Aegean. Quatern. Int. **171**, 31–44 (2007)
5. Reicherter, K., et al.: Holocene tsunamigenic sediments and tsunami modelling in the Thermaikos Gulf area (Northern Greece). Zeitschrift für Geomorphologie Supplementary Issues **54**(3), 99–125 (2010)

6. Anastasovitis, E.: Tsunami in ancient Potidaea: a 3D representation. Master dissertation, University of the Aegean (2014)
7. Pyrseia Informatics: Tsunami in ancient Potidaea. https://pyrseia.gr/Ereuna_Tsunami.html. Accessed 15 Sep 2020
8. Seiradakis, J.H., Edmunds, M.G.: Our current knowledge of the Antikythera mechanism. Nat. Astron. **2**(1), 35–42 (2018)
9. Efstathiou, K., Basiakoulis, A., Efstathiou, M., Anastasiou, M., Seiradakis, J.H.: Determination of the gears geometrical parameters necessary for the construction of an operational model of the Antikythera Mechanism. Mech. Mach. Theory **52**, 219–231 (2012)
10. Roumeliotis, M.: Calculating the torque on the shafts of the Antikythera Mechanism to determine the location of the driving gear. Mech. Mach. Theory **122**, 148–159 (2018)
11. Freeth, T., et al.: Decoding the ancient Greek astronomical calculator known as the Antikythera Mechanism. Nature **444**(7119), 587–591 (2006)
12. Oculus. https://www.oculus.com/. Accessed 15 Sep 2020
13. Unity. https://unity.com/. Accessed 15 Sep 2020
14. Anastasovitis, E., Roumeliotis, M.: Virtual museum for the Antikythera Mechanism: designing an immersive cultural exhibition. In: 2018 IEEE International Symposium on Mixed and Augmented Reality Adjunct (ISMAR-Adjunct), Munich, pp. 310–313. IEEE (2018). https://doi.org/10.1109/ISMAR-Adjunct.2018.00092
15. Anastasovitis, E., Roumeliotis, M.: Designing an edutainment serious game for the Antikythera Mechanism in virtual reality. In: Helin, K., Perret, J., Kuts, V. (eds.) The Application Track, Posters and Demos of EuroVR: Proceedings of the 16th Annual EuroVR Conference - 2019 VTT Technical Research Centre of Finland, VTT Technology, Tallinn, no. 357, pp. 94–97. IEEE (2019). https://doi.org/10.32040/2242-122X.2019.T357
16. Anastasovitis, E.: Designing an educational program for adult trainees, by using three-dimensional graphics and interaction in virtual environment of a game-engine: the case of the Antikythera Mechanism. Master dissertation, Hellenic Open University (2017)
17. Rogers, A., Horrocks, N.: Teaching Adults. McGraw-Hill Education, New York (2010)
18. Unreal. https://www.unrealengine.com/en-US/. Accessed 28 Oct 2020
19. Blender. https://www.blender.org/. Accessed 28 Oct 2020
20. Cinema4D by Maxon. https://www.maxon.net/en/. Accessed 28 Oct 2020
21. GIMP. https://www.gimp.org/. Accessed 28 Oct 2020
22. Inkscape. https://inkscape.org/. Accessed 28 Oct 2020
23. OpenShot. https://www.openshot.org/. Accessed 28 Oct 2020
24. Audacity. https://www.audacityteam.org/. Accessed 28 Oct 2020

Short Papers: DATA Acquisition and Processing

Short Papers: Digital Data Acquisition Technologies in CH / 2D and 3D Data Capture Methodologies and Data Processing

Application of Digital Fabrication Technologies in Reproducing of a Wooden Component in Heritage Buildings

Anna Norina[✉] and Shixing Liu[ORCID]

School of Design, Shanghai Jiao Tong University,
800 Dongchuan Road, Shanghai 200240, China
liushixing@sjtu.edu.cn

Abstract. This current study is aimed to demonstrate the application of innovative digital surveying and digital fabrication technologies to physically replicate elements of the wooden heritage structure. During practical part was created and the attested framework included preliminary on-site surveying with pictures processed through Photogrammetry pipeline to document the current state of the prototype element with the 3D model. Then, the virtual model is integrated into an algorithmic modeling program to generate coded milling paths. The result is a ½ scale prototype, crafted by robotic arm technologies from wood stock.

Keywords: Digital heritage · Robotic manufacturing

1 Introduction

The motivation to preserve wooden architecture has been increased extensively in recent years align with overall environmental awareness and interest to the previous experience of construction with renewable materials.

By observing earlier studies regarding the conservation and restoration of architecture worldwide, it can be depicted that researches are focused on different approaches to assess and document old wooden buildings including traditional, manual measuring and analysis of archive materials. Nevertheless, some works implement new investigating methods for heritage objects analysis with digital technologies.

Considering that many wooden constructions were destroyed due to material age and weakness, as well as a restorative intervention towards them was not properly documented, technologies of digital surveying appear to be the most perspective approach. Technologies, such as digital photogrammetry, 3D laser scanning to get an object's 3D points cloud model is one of the most precise ways of recording [1]. Results of examination when merged to 2D and 3D documentation databases can be open to new updates [2].

Moreover, wood, which is historically used for rendering of an original architectural object, unlike drawing was previously neglected in architectural research. Some recent studies reconsider physical modeling, from wood material specifically, as an effective

© Springer Nature Switzerland AG 2021
M. Ioannides et al. (Eds.): EuroMed 2020, LNCS 12642, pp. 465–473, 2021.
https://doi.org/10.1007/978-3-030-73043-7_38

tool in design and documentation [3–5]. Integrated with 3D digital technologies, physical shaping has the potential to create precise replicas of old forms without actual intervention into cultural heritage [6]. Digitally crafted representations of wooden heritage prototype can exhibit the inheritance of manual craftsmanship in the context of present building state.

This current study's aim is to demonstrate the application of innovative digital surveying and digital fabrication technologies to physically replicate elements of the wooden heritage structure. During practical part was created and the attested framework included preliminary on-site surveying with pictures processed through Photogrammetry pipeline to document the current state of the prototype element with the 3D model. Then, the virtual model is integrated into an algorithmic modeling program to generate coded milling paths. The result is a ½ scale prototype, crafted by robotic arm technologies from wood stock.

2 Framework

2.1 Technology Background

Robotic Arm Technologies. Recent advancements of digital fabrication technologies are involved to embody architectural forms and enrich its variety, complexity through combining human design with machine labor [7]. Robotic arms, automated and programmable, are widely recognized in the automobile industry and industrial areas that require high accuracy. A variety of tools (cutting, milling etc.) allows robotic arms digitally to manufacture shapes by using tools in 6 axes direction. Nevertheless, automated arms are employed for precise assembling [8].

Some researchers consider the greatest potential of easily shapeable and lasting material of wood to integrate computational modeling into scalable physical representation [9]. For purposes of preservation and restoration, robotic systems are a supplement for accurate fabrication of scaled prototype geometry as well as elements for restorative intervention. The study offers to employ robotic systems (KUKA) supplied by a milling tool to craft the wooden heritage element ½ scale replica.

2.2 Research Methods, Methodological Route

Object of Study. The object of the study is the church of the All-Merciful God, Kostroma, Russia (1712) (see Fig. 1a). The building is a good example of the "Klet" type temple, typical for the Kostroma region in the 18th century. It represents the longitudinal composition of connected opened volumes ("Klets") on the same axis. The of the church consists of a single-domed quadrangle of the temple, a pentahedral apse, a refectory, a porch with a bell tower, and a porch towering above it. The construction exhibits the art and experience of manual skilled carpentry represented in a variety of joints and carvings [10]. The selected prototype element is the carved pillar of the western porch. It is one of the most specific for this building to be further surveyed and replicated with means of robotic systems (see Fig. 1b).

Fig. 1. a) Church of All-Merciful God. Kostroma, Russia; b) the pillar, prototype element.

Methodological Route. The objective of the experimental part of the study is to create and attest an algorithm to survey prototype's geometry and integrate 3D data into programmed code to recreate the shape in ½ scale with means of the robotic arm (KUKA). Methodologically, the technological pipeline of different programmable processes that led to the result: Prototype data acquisition – Prototype 3D modeling – Programming – Digital fabrication (see Fig. 2).

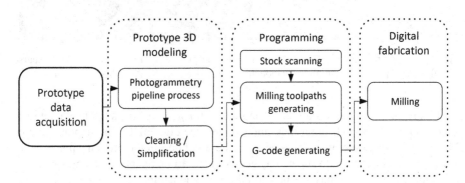

Fig. 2. Methodological route of the research.

The decision to involve Digital Photogrammetry technologies to portray the prototype's virtual model is based on availability. The method is widely used in heritage objects' digital model reconstruction, documenting, and implementing virtual reality. Latest software generation, including commercial and Open-Source based, as COLMAP ©, Autodesk ReCap ©, Meshroom Alice Vision © process the multiple imageries unstructured data through Photogrammetry Pipeline algorithms to extract the object 3D model. The procedure divided into multiple stages to allow to control of the outcome of every step. The final quality is highly dependent on the characteristic of input data (images). Control measuring is essential to scale the generated model and testify its reliability.

Prototype Data Acquisition. During the on-site inspection, the prototype element was surveyed with 150 pictures from different angles to be compiled into the 3D model by photogrammetry software Alice Vision Meshroom © on the following phase. Control measurements have been executed on site to geometrically scale a virtual model and validate the accuracy of 3D data.

Prototype 3D Modeling. Selection of 27 pictures is distributed into Alice Vision Meshroom © to generate a 3D model through the photogrammetry pipeline. Meshroom Alice Vision © model generating process includes 3 stages divided into 8 steps: images matching (Feature Extraction, Image Matching, Features Matching), sparse modeling (Structure-from-Motion, Depth Maps Estimation) and dense modeling (Meshing, Texturing) (see Fig. 3a–d) [11].

Fig. 3. Photogrammetry pipeline results. a) Prototype picture; b) images matching; c) sparse modelling (3D points cloud); d) dense modelling (texturized mesh). Alice Vision Meshroom ©.

Firstly, images passed Feature Extraction and Image Matching steps to extract relevant details patches and similarities among them (see Fig. 3b). On the step of Features Matching, 90 photometric matches between the set of descriptors from the paired input images were obtained and validated by geometric filtering. Sparse modeling's aim is to find the geometric relationships behind all observations through locating of 3d scene points and calibrating of all cameras. On the next step, Depth Maps Estimation, SfM algorithm extracts the depth value of each 2D pixel for all 27 cameras. Thus, the cloud of 356 655 points with 3D dimensional coordinates is formed (see Fig. 3c). On the Meshing step, all depth maps are fused to generate 3D Delaunay mesh consisted of 712 344 faces. On the concluding step, Texturing, UV maps were created based on middling pixels color values. The texture file was distributed to the disk along with the generated prototype mesh (see Fig. 3d) [11].

The resulted raw mesh consisted of 2 separate 3D meshes included noise and artifacts of undesired details. In order to be acceptable for the programming stage, the model needed to pass necessary cleaning from repeated faces and errors and merged into holistic geometry. Thanks to MCNell Rhinoceros ©/Grasshopper 3D © algorithmic

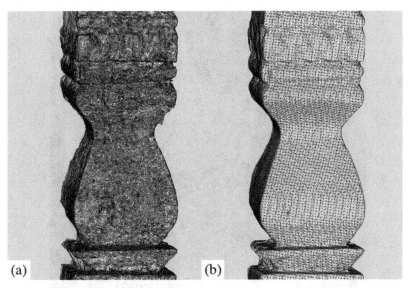

Fig. 4. a) Scanned fragment raw mesh data. b) Simplified and cleaned mesh. MC Neel Rhinoceros ©/Grasshopper 3D ©.

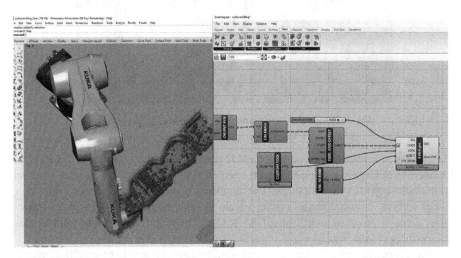

Fig. 5. Programming of trajectories and simulation of milling process. KUKA|prc ©.

design software the mesh was restructured into quadratic mesh to organize consistent structure (see Fig. 4). The texture of the surface is neglected on the following stages of programming and digital fabrication. Final mesh was geometrically scaled and validated by examining with control measurements.

Programming. The aim of this stage is to create G-code contained milling trajectories for the robotic arm tooled by spindle to get prototype shape from a wooden plank.

Fig. 6. Milling of ½ scale prototype element. KUKA|prc ©.

The plank geometry, scanned with Sense 2 © portable scanner, is imported to MC Neel Rhinoceros ©/Grasshopper 3D © to be compared with the prototype to recognize an optimal strategy to extract the shape. The number of bounding curves, divided prototype model surface, is encoded and converted into robotic arm spindle movement trajectories through programming tools of KUKA|prc © plugin for MC Neel Rhinoceros ©/Grasshopper (see Fig. 5).

The density of pathways (trajectories) is calibrated accordingly to spindle diameter. Robotic arm's movements were simulated virtually with the component of KUKA|prc © to find the possible collisions to be fixed before testing G-code on the material. Created G-code, is exported into the robotic arm directory to apply and testify during the fabricating stage to mill the prototype geometry from wood stock.

Digital Fabrication. Following testing of the milling process on stock wood with robotic arm tooled by spindle had displayed that the default encoded speed of arm movement along the wooden surface caused seizing into the material. It was stipulated to make reverse steps and adjust the speed written in code. After several consequent tests, the arm's speed was adjusted speed to 25% of default as optimal.

Another constraint has been imposed by the impact of spindle tool on fixed wooden plank shear movement depending on position relative to the table. The minimum shear appeared when stock wood is fixed in a horizontal position comparing to a vertical one. Consequently, the code was rewritten appropriately with milling trajectories for 4 sides of the element. Final G-code, digitally simulated and tested, was distributed into KUKA arm directory for detail milling accordingly to the generated pathways (see Fig. 6).

3   Future Steps

Based on the experience of creating the algorithm to reproduce one element of a wooden heritage structure, the framework to replicate the entire building needs to be optimized. The constructive elements information to be organized in a database contained information about their position and relation to the whole building hierarchy. Subsequently, every element can be extracted and reproduced.

With regards to the comprehensive data management of complex architectural objects, BIM (Building Information Model) technologies are on the edge of scientific interest. BIM modeling, mostly designed for new building processes, recently applied to the irregular geometry of heritage objects [12, 13].This method named HBIM (Heritage Building Information Model) is considered to be part of further development of the Church of Merciful God replication framework (see Fig. 7).

Fig. 7. Future development of wooden heritage building replication framework. Principal scheme.

The necessary preliminary step in order to start working with BIM modeling is portraying the whole building geometry. The recent development of digital sensing technologies offers effective methods (laser scanning) to record and archive artifacts without cause of irreparable damage. On the current stage, the entire building has been surveyed with 3D terrestrial laser scanner RIEGL 400 ©. The result, georeferenced 3D points cloud, to be processed through a 3D modeling program to generate NURBS surfaces.

The following stage is extracting and mapping building elements into data families in BIM modeling program. The main challenge of the planned study is finding an algorithm to process surveying material to depict wooden building joining structure. Such a macro zoom is credential to preserve the authenticity and constructive fidelity of prototype objects in the created replica.

Moreover, robotic systems' involvement for the fabrication of all elements and assembling into a heritage building replica model is considered to be one of the forthcoming steps of further research discourse.

3.1 Conclusion

The main contribution of this study is the design of a framework including novel technologies to heritage structures surveying and representation: photogrammetric technologies, digital fabrication with the assistance of automotive arm systems, algorithmic design. Thus, the study examined the methodology to document through physical model one element of a wooden heritage building, Church of the All-Merciful God, without violation of prototype integrity.

The model, produced with digital fabrication technologies presents a state of prototype element geometry. The created framework is attested to be part of replicating of the whole construction. On the other hand, this approach can be potentially integrated into the future restoration of wooden heritage buildings.

References

1. Porzilli, S., Bertocci, S.: 3D digital systems for the documentation and representation of the wooden heritage between Finland and Russia: survey methods and procedures for detailed analysis. In: Bianconi, F., Filippucci, M. (eds.) Digital Wood Design. LNCE, vol. 24, pp. 565–593. Springer, Cham (2019). https://doi.org/10.1007/978-3-030-03676-8_22
2. Gottardi, C., Balletti, C., Florian, S., Guerra, F.: Digital technologies for cultural heritage: 3D representation of complex wooden structures. In: Bianconi, F., Filippucci, M. (eds.) Digital Wood Design. LNCE, vol. 24, pp. 511–532. Springer, Cham (2019). https://doi.org/10.1007/978-3-030-03676-8_19
3. Yuan, P.F., Chai, H.: Reinterpretation of traditional wood structures with digital design and fabrication technologies. In: Bianconi, F., Filippucci, M. (eds.) Digital Wood Design. LNCE, vol. 24, pp. 265–282. Springer, Cham (2019). https://doi.org/10.1007/978-3-030-03676-8_9
4. Franco Taboada, J.A.: Wood as an essential material in architectural and civil engineering models from the renaissance to the architectural avant-garde. In: Bianconi, F., Filippucci, M. (eds.) Digital Wood Design. LNCE, vol. 24, pp. 285–320. Springer, Cham (2019). https://doi.org/10.1007/978-3-030-03676-8_10
5. Bianchini, C., Ippolito, A., Senatore, L.J.: The wooden models of the Vatican Basilica by Antonio da Sangallo and Michelangelo: survey, modelling and interpretation. In: Bianconi, F., Filippucci, M. (eds.) Digital Wood Design. LNCE, vol. 24, pp. 321–342. Springer, Cham (2019). https://doi.org/10.1007/978-3-030-03676-8_11
6. Valenti, G.M., Conti, C., Romor, J.: Representing with wood: Carlo Lucangeli and the model of the Flavian Amphitheatre. In: Bianconi, F., Filippucci, M. (eds.) Digital Wood Design. LNCE, vol. 24, pp. 343–373. Springer, Cham (2019). https://doi.org/10.1007/978-3-030-03676-8_12
7. Santorso, K., Ambrosz, B., Krobath, R., Brell-Cokçan, S., Braumann, J., Sampl, G.: Robotic Woodcraft. Towards the Craftsmanship of the Future. University of Applied Arts Vienna (2017)
8. KUKA AG © official webpage. https://www.kuka.com/. Accessed 12 Aug 2020
9. Menges, A., Schwinn, T., Krieg, O. (eds.): Advancing Wood Architecture – A Computational Approach. Routledge, Oxford (2016). https://doi.org/10.4324/9781315678825
10. Historical and Cultural monuments of Kostroma. Online Encyclopedia. https://enckostr.ru/showObject.do?object=1804537436. Accessed 12 Aug 2020
11. Alice Vision © official webpage. https://alicevision.org/#photogrammetry/. Accessed 12 Aug 2020

12. Brumana, R., Oreni, D., Barazzetti, L., Cuca, B., Previtali, M., Banfi, F.: Survey and scan to BIM model for the knowledge of built heritage and the management of conservation activities. In: Daniotti, B., Gianinetto, M., Della Torre, S. (eds.) Digital Transformation of the Design, Construction and Management Processes of the Built Environment. RD, pp. 391–400. Springer, Cham (2020). https://doi.org/10.1007/978-3-030-33570-0_35

13. López, F., Lerones, P., Llamas, J., Gómez-García-Bermejo, J., Zalama, E.: A Review of heritage building information modeling (H-BIM). Multimodal Technol. Interact. **2**(2), 21 (2018). https://doi.org/10.3390/mti2020021

ESTIA: Disaster Management Platform for Cultural Heritage Sites

Adam Doulgerakis[1]([✉]), Anastasios Kanellos[1], Stelios C. A. Thomopoulos[1],
George Alexios Ioannakis[2], Fotios Arnaoutoglou[2], Petros Pistofidis[2],
Anestis Koutsoudis[2], Theodora Pappou[3], Byron Protopsaltis[3], and Stelios Gkouskos[4]

[1] Integrated Systems Laboratory, Institute of Informatics and Telecommunications, National Center for Scientific Research Demokritos, 15310 Athens, Greece
{adoulgerakis,tassos.knl,scat}@iit.demokritos.gr
[2] Clepsydra Digitisation Lab, Athena Research and Innovation Centre, ILSP Xanthi's Division, 67100 Xanthi, Greece
{gioannak,fotarny,pistofid,akoutsou}@athenarc.gr
[3] SOFiSTiK Hellas S.A., 10433 Athens, Greece
dora@sofistik.gr, byron@fides-dvp.de
[4] Terracom S.A., 45221 Ioannina, Greece
sgous@terracom.gr

Abstract. ESTIA is a research and innovation project that aspires to develop a comprehensive platform allowing the forecast, detection and management of incidents that are related with the risk of structural fires within Cultural Heritage (CH) settlements and sites. ESTIA aims to (a) enhance the management and preservation of CH, (b) limit the risks of fire incidents within traditional settlements and CH sites, (c) provide competent authorities with tools for training, coordination and support for an efficient response to fire incidents, (d) effectively protect and guide inhabitants and visitors, (e) suppress structural damages in historic buildings, historic settlements and CH sites and assets, (f) support and promote cultural events and tourism in harmony with the particular requirements of CH preservation. By incorporating advanced procedures for the semi-automatic digitization of the CH built environment as well as an advanced system that simulates the development of the complex phenomena of fire propagation and human crowd behaviour, the platform is an effective tool that on one hand, assists competent authorities in assessing the fire related risks and on the other, serves as a training tool and offers fire management capabilities for first responders and civil protection officers.

Keywords: Tangible cultural heritage · Historic settlements · Historic buildings · Structural fire · Fire incident prediction · Fire incident risk assessment · Crowd simulation · Fire propagation simulation · 3D modelling · Visual analysis · Geometry analysis · Ontological segmentation · Annotation · Photogrammetry

1 Introduction

The protection of tangible Cultural Heritage (CH) assets from catastrophic fire events is of paramount importance, especially considering the challenges posed by recurrent dire

© Springer Nature Switzerland AG 2021
M. Ioannides et al. (Eds.): EuroMed 2020, LNCS 12642, pp. 474–481, 2021.
https://doi.org/10.1007/978-3-030-73043-7_39

climatic conditions. Only recently, a series of unfortunate events (i.e. Mycenae 2020, Nantes Cathedral 2020, Notre Dame Cathedral 2019, Ancient Olympia 2007) confirmed the imperative need for innovative and effective strategies to be implemented towards the protection of CH against fire incidents. Tangible CH includes buildings and settlements that are classified as historic or traditional, often featuring significant morphological, architectural, and structural characteristics. In Europe, there are numerous occasions of historic towns and settlements with a dense and unplanned development of the urban fabric, as well as traditional building construction methods based on flammable and vulnerable materials posing an increased risk of structural fire incidents. Additionally, the densely constructed urban areas and unplanned settlement development increase the risk of extensive fire spread, while impeding the intervention of first responders and the safe evacuation of inhabitants and visitors. A structural fire incident within densely constructed and populated areas may result in human casualties, substantial financial losses as well as irreversible material and structural damages in CH assets. Notably, even in cases of small-scale incidents, the restoration of damages and the preservation of the structural integrity are usually high-cost and time-consuming tasks that must also conform to regulations and directives of CH management authorities.

2   Literature Review

Currently, a number of international initiatives and organisations promote the establishment and the adoption of policies aiming to address challenges in CH preservation and resilience from natural or manmade hazards [1, 2], while notable progress has been made through research in this field [3, 4]. In the case of fire risk assessment, several methodologies exist for the evaluation of CH buildings, while some attempts have been made to evaluate complete CH urban areas [5]. In several cases, statistical methods are applied (e.g. the Gretener method, F.R.A.M.E., F.R.I.M, A.R.I.C.A) to derive fire risk indicators that can identify particular vulnerabilities. However, in such cases, the geometry of the built environment is not considered, as they rely on 2D representations, while also adopting certain simplifications in the behaviour of developing fire. More recently, there has been progress in the field of performance-based CH fire risk assessment using numerical simulations. Fire scenarios in historic buildings have been simulated using more accurate Computational Fluid Dynamics (CFD) models such as the NIST Fire Dynamics Simulator (FDS) [6], while in some cases this has been coupled with human occupant behaviour simulation software, such as STEPS [7] and EVAC [8]. Regarding CH urban areas, the Pyrosim fire simulation software has been used to analyse a fire incident to evaluate risk factors and mitigation planning in a historic residential area [9]. An analysis of evacuation times is performed, but it is determined statistically and does not involve simulation of individual inhabitants. However, in all the aforementioned approaches, the built environment to be analysed is represented in simplified 3D models (for individual buildings) or 2D GIS maps (for urban areas). In most cases, these input data are collected through in situ inspection and manual documentation of related observed information (e.g. building height, building materials), leading to considerable human resource requirements as well as higher risks of introducing errors and lower fidelity of the analysed environment. Furthermore, the impact of the fire to the health of human inhabitants does not appear to be considered in the simulation-based approaches, while real-time operation of simulations for training purposes is not supported. Even the evacuation simulations that use CFD techniques for training purposes, are either based on pre-calculated fields (T2eC and FVTVE) or are over-simplified (Walkthrough-CFAST) [10]. Pre-calculated fields provide zero-fidelity to crowd reaction for changing scenario conditions during incident evolution, cannot support high-fidelity scenarios and thus cannot fulfil training requirements.

3   The ESTIA Research Project

ESTIA is a research and innovation project that aspires to develop a comprehensive platform allowing the forecast, detection and management of incidents that are related with the risk of structural fires within CH settlements and sites. ESTIA, aims to (a) enhance the management and preservation of CH, (b) limit the risks of fire incidents within traditional settlements and CH sites, (c) provide the competent authorities with training, coordination and support for an efficient response to fire incidents, (d) effectively protect and guide inhabitants and visitors, (e) suppress the structural damages in historic buildings, historic settlements and CH sites and assets, (f) support and promote cultural events and tourism in harmony with the requirements of CH preservation.

3.1   The ESTIA Platform Development

ESTIA brings forward an advanced ICT platform, composed of autonomous connected subsystems and components, that is highly configurable to address the needs of a wide range of relevant stakeholders and allow customised deployments according to each case's particular requirements. ESTIA incorporates an advanced system that simulates the development of the complex phenomena of fire propagation and human crowd behaviour, assisting competent authorities in assessing the fire-related risks and offering training to first responders and field officers. Additionally, the platform offers an effective fire incident management system that includes fire-detection capabilities and a specialised Decision Support System, enhancing authorities during the management of a developing fire incident. For the achievement of the project objectives, it was necessary to develop computational algorithms and to establish procedures stemming from discrete research fields (e.g. visual and geometrical analysis, 3D reconstruction, computational fluid mechanics, autonomous agent systems, data fusion).

3.2   Cultural Heritage Built Environment Digitisation

Nowadays, 3D digitisation is considered common practise within both research and industry applications and the increased number of 3D digitised data available in combination with a wide range of rising opportunities have led many researchers to work towards their interpretation. The segmentation of digital representations of urban areas based on semantics is considered today an active research domain. In [11, 12], researchers propose the exploitation of aerial imagery, LIDAR data and machine learning approaches, for the segmentation of land use/cover through classification, focusing also in urban areas

Fig. 1. Upper Left: Multispectral imaging capturing UAV. Upper Right: Built environment 3D reconstruction and material-based mesh segmentation. Bottom: 3D digital reconstruction based on multi-image photogrammetry.

(buildings, trees, streets etc.). In another case, satellite imagery and lidar data were used to identify building damages through the extraction of areas with vegetation, bare land (pavement and soil) and shadows [13]. Within the framework of the ESTIA research project, the 3D digitisation of the old town of Xanthi, was performed using both RGB and near infrared imagery (see Fig. 1). The near infrared imagery was collected with an in-house built multispectral camera, that was mounted on a commercial drone (DJI Inspire 2). The multispectral camera relies on single-board computer clustering, that is coupled with infrared camera modules. A novel segmentation process was established that allowed (i) the creation of a 3D model of old town of Xanthi that is accompanied by a multilayer texture map from near infrared and RGB imagery and (ii) the segmentation of the 3D model by exploiting near infrared and RGB information on its texture. Six types of materials (i.e. metal surfaces, building walls, cobbled-roads granite kilns, ceramic roof-tiles, high and low vegetation) were identified that also exhibit morphological characteristics and context related to fire propagation and crowd behaviour simulators. The proposed 3D mesh segmentation is based on the following three supervised learning methods: Logistic Regression (LR), Support Vector Machines (SVM) and Artificial Neural Networks (ANN). The LR model was used to identify if the six classes are separable using a linear decision boundary, whereas SVMs and ANN were applied due to their power to discriminate in non-linearly separable datasets. The machine learning approaches were implemented in TensorFlow and Keras API while their performance evaluation was based on a benchmark dataset (training and validation datasets) derived from the 3D model of the old town of Xanthi.

3.3 Simulation-Based Fire Risk Assessment

The ESTIA platform incorporates modelling and simulation tools offering an advanced and versatile simulation-based fire risk assessment tool. By introducing semi-automated methods for the detailed digitisation of the built environment, the ESTIA risk assessment approach can be widely employed for the assessment of fire risks in both indoors and outdoors environments, involving individual buildings as well as complex settlements. ESTIA integrates computational models for the simulation of fire incident development, the emergent human crowd behaviour based on feedback from the fire incident, and the damages caused on the built environment. ESTIA allows the generation and simulation of fire incident scenarios for the assessment of the risk factor associated with fire incidents under various circumstances. The simulation results can be reviewed within a dedicated interactive and intuitive data visualisation environment, indicating potential vulnerabilities, and graded localized risks of high granularity to the user. The data-rich result interpretability can thus improve risk assessment and is expected to allow the establishment of efficient intervention plans and the optimisation of fire prevention and mitigation measures.

ESTIA incorporates advanced CFD algorithms for the simulation of complex phenomena such as fire propagation and the diffusion of its volatile by-products within the built environment (see Fig. 2 Right), while considering weather conditions, building materials' properties and fire-fighting interventions. Concerning the physical models for the simulation of fire and hazardous gas spread in buildings, simplified algebraic or statistical models, simplified zonal models, and general purpose CFD have been previously used with very long computing time, far beyond real time simulation [14]. General-purpose CFD methods have been adapted for fire and gas simulation in enclosed domains such as NIST Fire Dynamics Simulator (FDS). In the framework of the PYRONES research project, a simplified yet accurate CFD approach has been developed to be applicable for interactive use and physical training purposes [15]. The new algorithm is based on the Fast Fluid Dynamics technique, FFD [16] and is parallelized for use on GPUs. It uses many parts of the original CFD code as they are [17], especially the unstructured numerical mesh, to exchange data between the two simulations and ease the calibration procedure of the FFD simulations according to the CFD ones. In that case, the combined simulations focused on indoor spaces with no interaction with the surrounding environment. For fire simulation in outdoor environments, general purpose CFD software are widely used in the literature with excessive requirements for experienced users and in-depth knowledge of pre-processing and modelling CFD simulations. In the framework of the ESTIA research project that also focuses on outdoor environments and as the execution of multiple scenarios in reasonable time is sought, an FFD code is being extended for real-time simulation of fire and toxic gas spread in the urban environment. To this end, the atmospheric boundary layer is incorporated as an inflow boundary condition along with wind rose and atmosphere stability data obtained from local weather data. Various turbulence models are examined for the simulation of environmental flows with extended regions of separated and recirculating flow. The entrapment of toxic gases in street canyons of the dense traditional architecture is investigated.

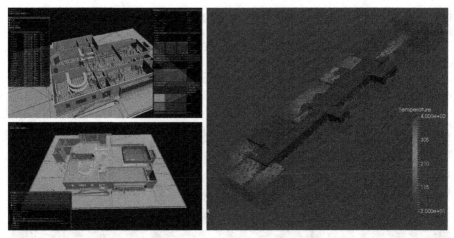

Fig. 2. Left: Human crowd behaviour simulation engine. Right: CFD based structural fire propagation simulation engine. [15]

ESTIA also implements advanced multi-agent systems algorithms for the simulation of the complex behaviour of the human crowd (see Fig. 2 Left) as an emergent phenomenon based on the simulation of the individual agents' behaviour and movement, while considering the impact of the fire incident to the human organism. The development of the ESTIA Crowd Simulation Engine, builds upon a crowd simulation model using a cognitive model based on emotional and sociological parameters to influence the strategic decisions of agents. [15, 18]; An advanced, state of the art crowd simulation model has been developed, employing both individual agent cognition architectures as well as overall imposed aggregate dynamics, that can display medium to large-scale crowds in real time and that can be utilized in any bounded area (i.e. building interiors and exteriors, stadiums, or open-air festivals). The resulting simulation solution can scale seamlessly between small and large-scale crowds while displaying a behavioural multiformity indicative of a virtual environment with realistic psychological, emotional, and cultural diversity. The coupled CFD/FFD and Crowd simulations can be optimised for accuracy or for interactive real-time execution of fire event scenarios in the scale of a settlement by incorporating climate data, urban geometries, materials, and applying models for external aerodynamics in urban spaces. The development of real-time techniques for predicting physical and complex phenomena ensures that ESTIA can also be used as a training tool where trainees will be able to interact with the ESTIA simulation engine by managing simulated resources within a 3D virtual environment (Fig. 3).

3.4 Incident Management and Decision Support

ESTIA includes an Incident Management Component that can receive and visualise alerts and data from multiple sources (i.e. GSM and IP alert and fire detection systems, Image-based fire detection systems, the ESTIA Mobile App for civil protection), enabling effective real-time incident detection, monitoring and crisis management (see

Fig. 3 Right). A Decision Support System, analyses and compares pre-executed simulation scenarios results with real-time data and informs the user for the possible development and outcome of ongoing fire-incidents. The incident management component is connected to the ESTIA Mobile App for civil protection, through which civilians will be able to report on fire incidents and the authorities will be able to broadcast evacuation instructions and alert messages.

Fig. 3. Left: Visualisation for training and fire risk assessment. Right: Incident management

Acknowledgment. This research has been co-financed by the European Union and Greek national funds through the Operational Program Competitiveness, Entrepreneurship and Innovation, under the call RESEARCH CREATE INNOVATE (project code: T1EDK-03582). We thank Xanthi's Fire dpt., the Civil Protection dpt. of Thrace's decentralised administration, and the service of modern monuments and technical works of East Macedonia and Thrace.

References

1. Bonazza, A., et al.: Safeguarding Cultural Heritage from Natural and Man-Made Disasters - A comparative analysis of risk management in the EU. Corporate Author(s): Directorate-General for Education, Youth, Sport and Culture (European Commission) (2018). 207 pp.
2. COMMISSION STAFF WORKING DOCUMENT Action Plan on the Sendai Framework for Disaster Risk Reduction 2015–2030 A disaster risk-informed approach for all EU policies, SWD (2016) 205final/2
3. ARCH Saving Cultural Heritage. https://savingculturalheritage.eu/. Accessed 16 Oct 2020
4. ProteCHt2save. https://www.interreg-central.eu/Content.Node/ProteCHt2save.html. Accessed 16 Oct 2020
5. Granda, S., Ferreira, T.M.: assessing vulnerability and fire risk in old urban areas: application to the historical centre of Guimarães. Fire Technol. **55**(1), 105–127 (2018). https://doi.org/10.1007/s10694-018-0778-z
6. Giraldo, M., Rodríguez-Trujillo, V., Burgos, C.: Numerical-simulation research on fire behavior of a historic industrial building. In: Jasieńko, J. (ed.) 8th International Conference on Structural Analysis of Historical Constructions Proceedings, Wrocław Poland (2012)

7. Caliendo, C., Ciambelli, P., Del Regno, R., Meo, M.G., Russo, P.: Modelling and numerical simulation of pedestrian flow evacuation from a multi-storey historical building in the event of fire applying safety engineering tools. J. Cult. Heritage **41**, 88–199 (2020)

8. Arborea, A., Cucurachi, G., Mossa, G.: Performance-based fire protection of historic buildings in the Italian perspective: a simulative approach. In: Proceedings of the XVII Summer School "Francesco Turco", Venice (Italy) (2012)

9. Tanachawengsakul, T., Mishima, N., Fuchikami, T.: A simulation study on fire evacuation routes in primary stage for a historic canal residential area. Procedia - Soc. Behav. Sci. **216**, 492–502 (2016)

10. Kuligowski, E.D., Peacock, R.D., Hoskins, B.L.: A Review of Building Evacuation Models, 2nd edn. NIST (2010)

11. Gibril, M.A., et al.: Mapping heterogeneous urban landscapes from the fusion of digital surface model and unmanned aerial vehicle-based images using adaptive multiscale image segmentation and classification. Remote Sens. **12**, 1081 (2020)

12. Farah, I., Boulila, W., Ettabaa, K., Ahmed, M.B.: Multiapproach system based on fusion of multispectral images for land-cover classification. IEEE Trans. Geosci. Remote Sens. **46**, 4153–4161 (2009)

13. Wang, X., Li, P.: Extraction of urban building damage using spectral, height and corner information from vhr satellite images and airborne lidar data. ISPRS J. Photogramm. Remote Sens. **159**, 322–336 (2020)

14. Zanzi, C., Gómez, P., López, J., Hernández, J.: Analysis of heat and smoke propagation and oscillatory flow through ceiling vents in a large-scale compartment fire. Appl. Sci. **9**, 3305 (2019)

15. Kanellos, T., et al.: PYRONES: pyro-modeling and evacuation simulation system. In: Proceedings of the SPIE 9842, Signal Processing, Sensor/Information Fusion, and Target Recognition XXV, 984216 (2016)

16. Jin, M., Zuo, W., Chen, Q.: Improvements of fast fluid dynamics for simulating air flow in buildings. Numer. Heat Transfer Part B Fundam. **62**(6), 419–438 (2012)

17. Stokos, K.G., Vrahliotis, S.I., Pappou, T., Tsangaris, S.: A comparative numerical study of turbulence models for the simulation of fire incidents: application in ventilated tunnel fires. Cogent Eng. **2**, 1000509 (2015)

18. Kountouriotis, V.I., Paterakis, M., Thomopoulos, S.C.A.: iCrowd: agent-based behavior modeling and crowd simulator. In: Proceedings of the Signal Processing, Sensor/Information Fusion, and Target Recognition XXV, vol. 9842, p. 98420Q. International Society for Optics and Photonics Publisher (2016)

Digital Traceological and Mechanoscopic Methods in the Study of the Stone Surface of Historical Objects

Michal Cihla and Jaroslav Valach[✉]

Institute of Theoretical and Applied Mechanics of the Czech Academy of Sciences, Prosecká 76, 190 00 Prague 9, Czech Republic
{cihla,valach}@itam.cas.cz

Abstract. The paper deals with the use of photogrammetry based on the structure from motion method to create digital models of surfaces necessary for the study of traces of stonemasons on the surface of stone elements of architectural monuments using traceology and mechanoscopy. The result of the project dedicated to these tool traces will be a knowledge system that will link information about traces with tools, materials, and buildings. This knowledge tool will enable both new ways of asking questions about the development of Prague and better protection of cultural heritage by suggesting suitable restoration intervention technologies.

Keywords: Traceology · 3D digital models · Building cultural heritage · Surface topography

1 Introduction

The authenticity of architectural monuments is conditioned not only by the preservation of the original materials during conservation and restoration interventions but also by the preservation of the craftsmanship used in the creation of the monument. Traces of the work of stonemasons are therefore an integral part of the expression of the monument and deserve full attention. In addition to the aesthetic effect, these traces help to reveal the working practices of medieval masters and the development of the craft over time. Trace documentation also allows deducing the shape of the tool and how to work with it. The above reasons explain the importance of studying and preserving traces of tools on the surfaces of historic buildings.

In this paper, we would like to discuss the objectives and methods of a new project funded by the Ministry of Culture of the Czech Republic entitled "Building stone surface topography and its application in the field of stone features restoration". The presented project was launched this year and will last until 2023. It maps the stone-work of the representative subset of historical buildings in the Prague monument reserve, creates a knowledge system that will enable a new way of performing research in the field of architectural heritage. The findings will be linked to the existing geographic information system (GIS) of the National Heritage Institute (NPÚ) [1], in which they will act as a separate GIS "layer". The research will also guide the sensitive procedures of the restoration

M. Ioannides et al. (Eds.): EuroMed 2020, LNCS 12642, pp. 482–488, 2021.
https://doi.org/10.1007/978-3-030-73043-7_40

of stone elements. The project will make it possible to monitor the development of stone crafts and the relationship between the type of material and the chosen process, between the function of the object and its appearance. But also the transformation of preferred tools over time, or record the gradual opening and depletion of stone quarries in Prague and its surroundings. The collected data will make it possible to reveal the significance that the builders attached to the material if they chose a source of stone other than the nearest one for the construction. These and other cross-disciplinary questions - from history, archeology, petrology, and 3D digital models - are the project's contribution to "digital humanities", allowing new types of questions to be asked that independent and separated from each other - work in the archive and work in the field - could not answer.

The organization of the paper is as follows, at first it introduces the problems associated with inappropriate procedures in the restoration of monuments, then the main part is devoted to explaining the method for studying traces and possibilities of current methods of recording 3D shape for its development, and finally, the conclusion shows the expected results.

2   Motivation - Sensitive Restoration Protecting Tool Marks

The methods used to record tool traces will be used to assess the properties of restoration procedures - for example, for surface cleaning, the loss of material will be assessed, the texture of the surface as an indicator of the sensitivity of intervention. For this purpose, a set of typical building materials was selected, which after processing following the original procedures will undergo artificial aging and accelerated soiling, to be subsequently cleaned by various technologies - water blasting, sandblasting, chemical cleaning, and laser cleaning. After the evaluation, a methodology of suitable restoration procedures will be summarized in "field guidelines".

Fig. 1. Pedestal sculpture with surface detail before and after restoration. The cleaned surface shows material loss and abrasion.

The importance of choosing a sensitive method of restoration of monuments, in this case cleaning of soiled surfaces, is shown in Fig. 1. The figure compares the sculpture's pedestal before and after the intervention, with the condition after cleaning showing signs of abrasion.

The issue of insensitive restoration is not new. Already during the renovations in the 19th century, mistakes were made when the surfaces were modified with contemporary tools and the original appearance and traces were lost forever. During the inspection of the monument, it is therefore important to observe traces of individual instruments, which are atypical at the time. It can indicate a complete replacement of the stone element or just a repair of the original stone. Assumptions about the stone surface can be decided by observing the originality of the joints. To understand the clues, we need to understand the individual tools, their morphology and how to work with them [2–4]. But it is necessary to record the traces using traceology in the first place.

3   Digital Traceology

Traceology is the science of identifying and examining traces. This field has developed mainly as a specialized branch of criminology studying traces of the crime. In our case, attention is paid to the investigation of historical traces, where we speak by the analogy of historical traceology, ie mostly of traces of craft activity in historical contexts [5]. The result of these analyzes is an effort to uncover the way a craftsman works. The traceology of the stone deals with traces in the material and the subsequent reconstruction of the instrument and the process itself, but it also investigates the edge of the instrument itself. The use of traceology is not limited to construction surveys. In archeology and related fields, traceology is a popular experimental method for the reconstruction of instruments and their use [6–8].

The ambition of the project is to get to know the historical development of the stonework craftsmanship. To achieve this goal, a representative set of architectural monuments in Prague was selected. The record of each object is supplemented by thorough photo documentation. These photographs are then cataloged and used to identify both the method of craftsmanship and the working tool. As a method of documentation, we also use the so-called relief photograph, which is typical for its side lighting and thus the emphasis on the examined traces. The work pattern recorded in this way is only two-dimensional (hereinafter only 2D), but with a very clear raster of traces. Currently, with the availability of 3D technology, we started recording the surface as a spatial digital model, which helps us in the future study of traces that can be performed on the digital model, without the need to return to the place. We use the method of so-called mechanoscopy for the trace analysis itself.

3.1   Mechanoscopy

Mechanoscopy uses traces to determine the shape of the instrument that produced them. The result of this analysis is an attempt to reveal the workflow of a historical craftsman for a given stone surface appearance. Mechanoscopy works with a 3D model of the examined object. We have two methods that are currently used to obtain digital models. On the one hand, there is a laser profilometer and on the other hand photogrammetric scanning, used more often. The basis of photogrammetry is spatial analytical geometry in the selected coordinate system of images. The quality of the photogrammetric model depends on the quality of the data - a set of surface photographs and reconstruction software. The laser profilometer uses the triangulation method to create a model surface; its disadvantage is the limited area of the studied surface and low productivity. Therefore, a photogrammetric approach, implemented in the structure from motion method, is currently significantly more suitable for mechanoscopy [9].

3.2 Equipment

The basis for photogrammetric documentation is a high-quality, high-resolution digital SLR, a fixed-focus lens and a set of lights that provide a choice of both directional and diffuse illumination of the surface, the lights can be lit continuously or as a flash.

A 3D model of the surface with its topography is created from sets of photographs using Agisoft Photoscan Professional. Sections and surface profiles are studied using the Global Mapper application. The output of the program is shown in Fig. 2.

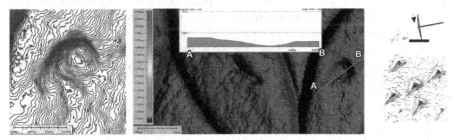

Fig. 2. Topography of a double-pick trace expressed in contour lines, using a 3D surface with an example of a depth profile and using a hand line art drawing.

3.3 Copies of Tools and Experimental Workshop

The mechanoscopy procedure optimally involves first deriving the shape of the tool from the marks on the surface and then manufacturing and using the reconstructed tool to verify that working with the derived tool results in the same marks. Each working procedure with a given tool has its characteristics, which are reflected in the trace on the respective surface. Creating a catalog of historical traces after machining is then the result of understanding the ways of working with stone tools in a historical context. Weight and shape matching is important in making copies of tools. The difference between the contemporary and original composition of the tool material is not important.

3.4 Trace Identification

Our goal is to identify correctly the traces indicating stone production activity [2, 3]. It is necessary to distinguish between tool traces, which can be either static or dynamic. By static, we mean traces arising from the perpendicular contact of the functional part of the tool with the material, while dynamic ones are created by the active movement of the given tool. By raster of traces, we mean the arrangement of traces on the surface. The grip of the tool as well as the stonemason's position at work or the position of the processed stone block affects the raster. The rasters are thus recognizable spike, parallel, fan-shaped, cross-shaped, or diagonal. A trace may overlap with another trace. Another type of trace is a secondary trace, i.e. so-called unwanted trace. They are caused either by wear and tear of the object or by an unplanned impact of a foreign object. According to the identified traces, it is, therefore, possible to position the tool in question in relation to the stone and to hold the tool with a stone-mason, and then to design the tool used and the procedure for working with it.

4   Results - An Example of the Relationship Between Surface Traces and Workflow

The connection between surface traces and workflow deduction is illustrated in Fig. 3. It shows the appearance of the stone surface, the appearance of the tool and the work of the stonemason with the tool. Similarly, most elements of a representative set of Prague's architectural monuments will be documented in the catalog.

Despite the passion for modern information technology, we would like to emphasize the importance of hand line-art drawing documentation, which abstracts from the secondary details of photography and serves as an ideographic shortcut for similar details and contexts.

By close observation of stone surface traces, one can infer the following work procedure: If it was necessary, the stonemason first removed the largest irregularities of a roughly broken block of stone with a double-pick, which he then cut into a regular block. In addition to pointed shaft tools, the so-called bossing hammer was used for the initial treatment of the face, which work with the sharp edge of the hammer striking surface. The hammer was used mainly in the creation of bossed masonry [10]. The actual normal formation of the block began by creating a straight smooth path at one long edge of the stone block. The stonemason cut it out with regular blows of a wooden mallet on a narrow chisel. In the same plane, which the stonemason checked with a ruler, a perimeter path was cut at the edge on the shorter side of the stone block and gradually on both remaining sides. The perimeter path defined the plane of one of the block faces on all four edges. The other surfaces of the block were prepared in the same way, while the stonemason was checked rectangularity. To complete the basic preparation of the inner part of the stone block, a double-pick was usually used. Only to finalize all sides of the block into a uniform surface with a characteristic pattern of traces after machining, the stonemason used a smooth or jagged ax or a smooth wide or narrower jagged chisel. Sculptures and more demanding architectural elements or parts were also processed with these tools, but sometimes they were still cut and polished.

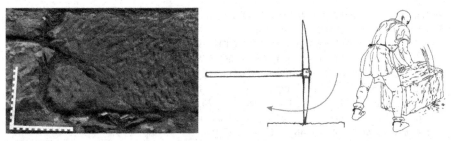

Fig. 3. Example of recording traces after the work of a stonemason. Reconstruction of work movement (middle part) and attitudes of the stonemason at work (right).

5 Conclusions

The knowledge system of tools' traces will be continuously expanding by new data acquisition during construction surveys and will become a self-contained source of knowledge and research. The accumulated knowledge would enable the search for new contexts and patterns in the development of stonemason crafts and construction methods of a long historical period and an extensive construction area of Prague.

The organization of the database is based on the findings of previous research, which concerned the creation of a knowledge system of buildings' damage based on the semantic web called MONDIS [11].

The records are designed to include photo documentation, a 3D model of the surface in which selected profiles can be studied, but also a drawing interpretation of typical trace markings to serve as a key to determining the tools used, similar to the key in botany to determine plants.

Information about the building will be drawn directly from the National Heritage Institute's catalog of architectural monuments. Similarly, information about the source of the stone will be linked to a database of historic quarries around Prague. In this way, the consistency of the information in the database is maintained.

The trace database will serve not only to document individual objects and their elements, but also as a tool for field explorers to identify the tools used to create a particular surface appearance.

Acknowledgement. The presented work is carried out within project "Building stone surface topography and its application in the field of stone features restoration" is supported by the program of applied research and development of national and cultural identity (NAKI) of the Ministry of Culture of the Czech Republic – grant No. DG20P02OVV021.

References

1. Protectes Heritage Catalogue. https://pamatkovykatalog.cz/uskp, Accessed 14 Sept 2020
2. Cihla, M., Panáček, M.: Úvod do problematiky středověkých technologických postupů opracování stavebního kamene, in: Forum Urbes Medii Aevi Vi, Brno (2011)
3. Havlíček, L.: Mechanoskopie, stopy a znaky řemeslných nástrojů, Praha (1940)

4. Bečka, J.: Tribologie, 23–25, Praha (1997)
5. Bláha, J.: Traces of construction techniques and processes. In: Hoffsummer, P., Eeckhout, J. (ed.) Matériaux de l'architecture et Toits de l'Europe/Materials of Architectural Heritage and Historical Roofs of Europe, Les Dossiers de L'IPW, 6, Namur, pp. 140–150 (2008)
6. Molloy, B., Wiśniewski, M., Lynam, F., O'neill, B., O'Sullivan, A., Peatfield, A.: Tracing edges: a consideration of the applications of 3D modelling for metalwork wear analysis on Bronze Age bladed artefacts. J. Archaeol. Sci. **76**, 79–87 (2016)
7. Adams, J.L.: Ground stone use-wear analysis: a review of terminology and experimental methods. J. Archaeol. Sci. **48**(1), 129–138 (2014)
8. Girya, E., Fedorova, D., Stepanova, K., Malyutina, A., Kolpakov, E., Kulkov, A.: Technical means and research perspectives in archeological traceology. Stratum Plus **1**, 131–143 (2019)
9. Aicardi, I., Chiabrando, F., Lingua, A.M., Noardo, F.: Recent trends in cultural heritage 3D survey: the photogrammetric computer vision approach. J. Cult. Herit. **32**, 257–266 (2018)
10. Bessac, J.C.: L'outillage traditionnel du tailleur de pierre, Paris (1993)
11. Cacciotti, R., Blaško, M., Valach, J.: A diagnostic ontological model for damages to historical constructions. J. Cult. Herit. **16**(1), 40–48 (2015)

Finite Element Analysis of Ancient Thousand Pillar Temple in Southern India

Soma Shekhar Reddy⊙, Sai Arjun Chevitipalli⊙,
Venkata Dilip Kumar Pasupuleti$^{(\boxtimes)}$ ⊙, and Prafulla Kalapatapu⊙

Ecole Centrale College of Engineering, Mahindra University, Hyderabad, India
{venkata.pasupuleti,
prafulla.kalapatapu}@mahindrauniversity.edu.in

Abstract. Ancient structures are a path to understand the cultural heritage and traditions that existed long ago. They become an important link in transferring knowledge from the past to present and future generations. Southern Indian has thousands of temples out of which a few are known for their uniqueness in construction and stability. In this research, a thousand pillar temple built during the 12th century AD in Hanamakonda, Telangana State has been considered. It is the finest example of Kakatiya's architecture, being completely built with stone spreading across the planar dimensions of 34 m × 34 m and a height of 9.5 m. Its foundation is believed to be laid in the sand at a depth of 6 m. A complete three-dimensional finite element numerical model is developed considering all the complex geometries, different types of columns, and *mandapas* to form the integrated temple model. Stresses in Individual structural elements are calculated to understand the role of complex geometry. Global stresses are computed to understand the load flow and stability of the structure for the gravity analysis.

Keywords: Numerical modelling · Ancient structure · Thousand pillar temple · Gravity analysis · Stone structure

1 Introduction

The beginning of Indian civilization dates back to the era of 3000 BC and is largely known as the Indus valley civilization. It is one of the oldest and largest urban civilizations in the world. It mainly consisted of two major cities named Mohenjo-Daro and Harappa [1, 2]. Beginning from the first town planning and evolution of materials in construction, India has seen many architectural marvels in the form of temples, palaces, forts, walls, and gates. Most of these structures are a few hundred to thousands of years old, which might need remedial measures to preserve them. The materials used are deteriorating and structural distress are observed due to natural and man-made disasters [3].

Shweta, (2008) has carried research on building science of Indian temple architecture, where the author has largely discussed construction material, the evolution of architectural styles of both Nagara (Northern style) and Dravidian (Southern styles) with distinct features. The author has also mentioned the different number of pillar temples

© Springer Nature Switzerland AG 2021
M. Ioannides et al. (Eds.): EuroMed 2020, LNCS 12642, pp. 489–498, 2021.
https://doi.org/10.1007/978-3-030-73043-7_41

built in Southern India with a comparison to Northern India [4]. Kakatiyas said to have ruled for more than 300 years during which they have built several stone temples with beautiful architecture spread across Hanumakonda, Warangal, Pillalmarri, and Palampet on various occasions. Some of the prominent examples of Kakatiyan architecture are Thousand pillar temple, Ramappa Temple, Warangal Fort, Kakatiya Kala Thoranam, and Ghanpur temple [5]. Even though the Kakatiyan architecture is an evolution from Chalukyan architecture, the style, technology, decoration show the skill and influence of the Kakatiyan sculptor. The Ramappa Temple, Thousand pillar temple, and Warangal Fort have common features showing the interchange of cultural values and unique attestation of the Kakatiyan tradition.

Understanding the historical structures can help us learn more about the old techniques used during construction and path to preserve them. With the evolution of computing technology, it has been an easy task for the development of numerical models to predict the structural behavior for existing and future loads. Ronald et al., (2018) have modelled and analyzed *gopuram* (multi-tiered entrance gateway) and the *mandapam* (pillared multi-purpose hall) for seismic loads with variation in tiers and pillars. Different analyses; namely linear, non-linear, static, and dynamic analysis were carried out for the *gopuram*. Most of the numerical models considered simplified geometry and analyzed for the structural stability for various loads due to man-made or natural disasters [6]. Sharma et al. (2019) also carried out a very similar study of South Indian temples' *gopuram* for gravity and lateral forces through finite element models. The *gopuram* has been modelled as the multi-leaf masonry structure, which is an ancient technique to resist the lateral forces. Their study was the reason behind structural distress and the collapse of *Vijayagopuram* at Srikalahasti, Andhra Pradesh in India in May 2010 [7, 8].

In this paper, an attempt is made to develop a three-dimensional model of the most complicated structure: the *"Thousand Pillar Temple"* of the Kakatiyan Era, constructed during 1175–1324 CE with a special focus on the geometrical detailing. There were very few studies that addressed the major reasons for the fine structural carvings of columns and beams. Firstly, for the religious-cultural belief and secondly, the geometry itself might play a vital role in transferring the loads throughout its life. Gravity analysis is carried to understand the load transfer and structural stability. One of the major reasons for not considering lateral loads is due to the belief that the temple is built on a foundation called the "sandbox technique" which is known to resist the lateral loads developed due to floods or earthquakes [9]. Preliminary work was discussed in the research by Kondem et al. (2018). The author demonstrated the thousand pillar temple as an example of the beam-column framework and developed a three-dimensional model, but only analyzed for a single *mandapam* [10]. Whereas our current study considers the complete modelling of the temple.

2   About Thousand Pillar Temple

The geometry of the Thousand Pillar temple from the aerial view is star-shaped and triple shrined hence called *Trikutalaya*. It was built at the end of the Chalukyan dynasty and early Kakatiyan dynasty. The temple is sculptured with one thousand pillars and this site is recognized as a world heritage site by UNESCO (5889) [11]. An ancient technique, "Sandbox" is considered for the foundation, which became extinct in the current construction world. Sandbox technique uses traditional material like Jaggery, Gallnut, Terminalia Chebula, and powdered granite. These were all mixed with the sand and filled in deep pits, which were covered by rock beams. This foundation technique largely helps in resisting the lateral loads. Figure 1 shows the different external and internal views of the temple captured during our research team visit.

Fig. 1. External and internal views of the thousand pillar temple

3 Numerical Modelling

Earlier, one of the biggest challenges of heritage or historical structures was getting the precise dimensions for numerical modelling. Due to various constraints, it was not always possible to get all the dimensions of the structures but thanks to the current technology, we can accurately measure all the dimensions of external and internal parts of the structure. The authors have visited the temple and column dimensions have been measured manually from the site in three dimensions (x, y, z) and all other dimensions have been interpolated from the images.

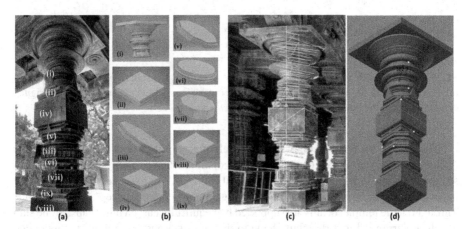

Fig. 2. (a) Column with numerical Geometrical segregation (b) Individual component modelling (c) Scaling for image processing (d) Concatenation of all the individual components

Figure 2(a) shows a original column with segregation marking of different geometrical components with roman numbers, and the respective components have been modelled carefully as seen in Fig. 2(b) so that all the geometrical aspects are considered for the numerical analysis. All the dimensions for different parts have been interpolated from the images using photogrammetry techniques as given in Fig. 2(c). Once all the sections of the column are developed, they are combined to form one single column as shown in Fig. 2(d). A similar methodology has been carried carefully for all other components of the temple for precise modelling. Figure 3 shows the other three types of pillars, beam modelling, beam-pillar joint, and multiple *mandapams*.

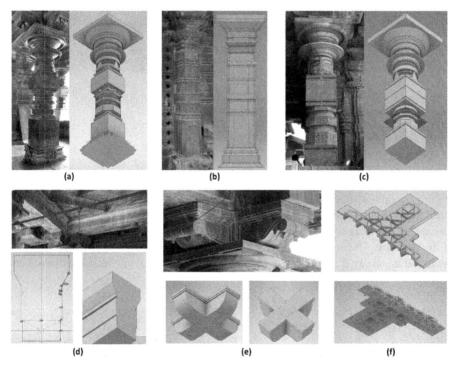

Fig. 3. Columns with developed three-dimensional models (a) Column type-2 (b) Column type-3 (c) Column type-4 (d) Original beam with beam dimensions and extruded model (e) Original column cap with the developed model (f) Multiple *mandapas*

The wall of the temple comprises of closely placed pillars with fine carvings and a thickness of 1.45 m. Pillars of the temple are distinguished by their geometrical cross-section into four types and not by the surficial carvings Whereas beams are considered to be similar as there has not been much change in the geometry except in their lengths. Throughout the temple, beams are supported by beautifully carved pillar caps. Stone slab panels are arranged in a rhombus shape to the close sky view forming' a *mandapam*. Figure 4 demonstrates all the aforementioned aspects with the detailing of the wall, *Garbha Gruha*, Sanctum, and two external views.

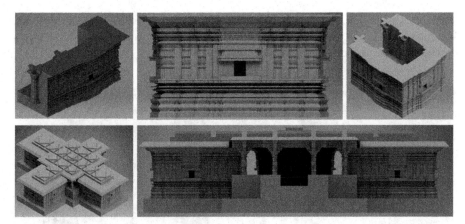

Fig. 4. Merging of pillars to make a wall, sectional views of Sanctum, complete three-dimensional model with a perspective view and side view

4   Analysis and Results

Granite stone material is considered for the study and its behavior is assumed to be isotropic. Physical properties of the stone are taken as follows: Youngs Modulus (E) is 55000 MPa, Poisson's Ratio (υ) is 0.25, Shear Modulus (G) is 27000 MPa, and Density (ρ) is 2700 kg/m^3. The analysis is carried for individual components, specifically for different pillars types and for the global structure to understand its behavior. As the structure is mammoth and made of stone, gravity analysis is largely predominant. The whole structure is assumed to be monolithic and modelled as a monolithic structure. In reality, the whole temple was constructed using granite and sandstone. For this analysis, polished granite properties have been considered as given above. The meshing of the structure is based on the fine carvings of the columns and other detailed components. Analysis of elements and the temple has taken a huge amount of time and space in

Table 1. Column types with model, meshing, max stresses, and displacements

S.No	Figure no	Column type	Height (m)	Meshing (Nodes, Elements)	Max. Von-misses stress (MPa)	Max. disp. (mm)
1	5	C-1	3.369	N-83065, E-49910	0.5412	0.005214
2	6	C-2	3.369	N-89071, E-57123	0.3322	0.003607
3	7	C-3	2.287	N-78272, E-47972	0.5620	0.002955
4	8	C-4	2.287	N-95214, E-49910	0.7302	0.002946

terms of computation. Fig-5 shows four images regarding the CAD model, Meshing, Von-misses stress and displacement modelled in Autodesk Inventor and Table 1 shows the column type, its height, mesh details, and max stresses.

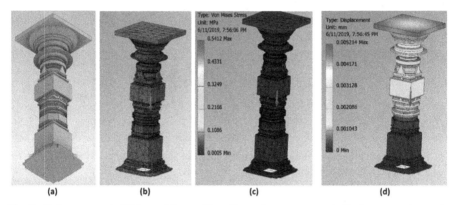

Fig. 5. Column type-1 CAD model, meshing, Von-misses stress and displacement due to its self-weight

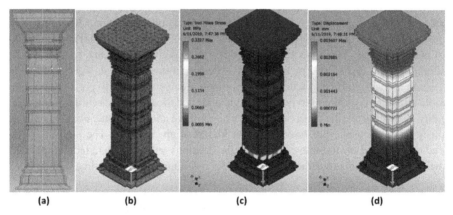

Fig. 6. Column type-2 CAD model, meshing, Von-misses stress and displacement due to its self-weight

Table 1 shows the comparative analysis obtained between different columns across the Fig. 5, 6, 7 and 8. It is observed that even though the columns are of similar height and base dimensions, they are found to undergo different stress distribution due to their self-weight which is clear from the table. Also, the absolute variation of stress is observed to be 0.21 MPa and 0.168 MPa for the column's height 3.369 m and 2.287 m respectively. This indicates that all the numerical models developed with an assumption of similar column modelling will not fetch a realistic behavior or response. Similarly, if the obtained displacements are compared, they are very small to be perceived by the naked eye but in a comparison between the columns the absolute difference is very high and this will affect

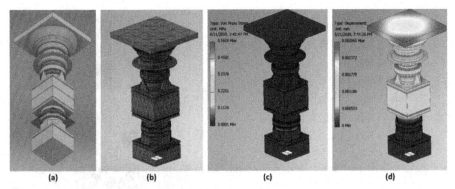

Fig. 7. Column type-3 CAD model, meshing, Von-misses stress and displacement due to its self-weight

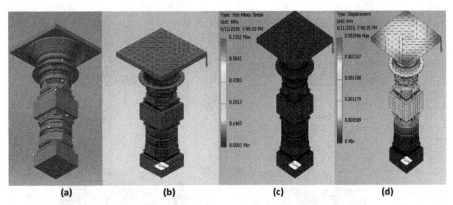

Fig. 8. Column type-4 CAD model, meshing, Von misses stress and displacement due to its self-weight

the overall behavior of the temple if the finer geometrical details are not considered. The degree of difference in both the stresses and displacement will be much higher for the complete modelling analysis compared between similar columns and different columns with fine geometrical consideration and the differences can be much higher for smaller differential settlements or lateral loads applied due to seismic movements or floods.

Analysis of columns has been easier compared to the complete thousand pillar temple model. Figure 9(a) shows the plan of the real temple, Fig. 9(b) shows two images of fine meshing of the wall and the meshing of the complete temple model which consisted of 1,12,92,666 nodes and 77,03,990 elements. Computation time for the linear static gravity analysis of the complete model has almost taken 80 h on a workstation. The same figure also shows the meshing ranges from coarse to fine depending on the geometrical modelling. For example, a simple plane box stone has a coarse meshing but all the columns are of fine meshing, so the wall which is made by the multiple columns is of fine meshing increasing finite elements and nodes. The dynamic or non-linear analysis would take weeks to months, which might be taken in future work. Four results for the

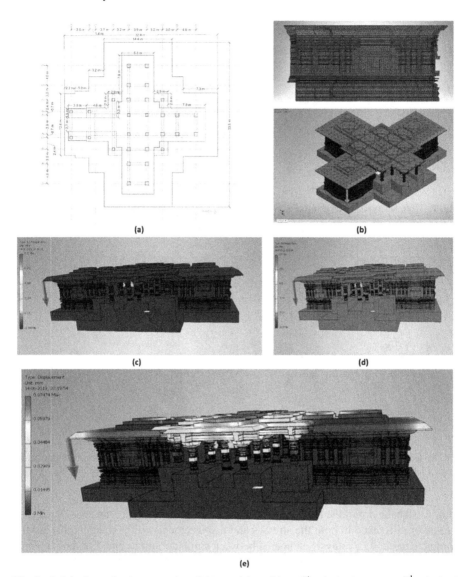

(a)

(b)

(c)

(d)

(e)

Fig. 9. Original temple plan, complete CAD model meshing, 1st Principal stresses, 3rd Principal Stresses and displacement due to its self-weight

temple have been presented, principal stresses in different directions, von-mises stresses, and displacement contour. Figure 9(c) shows the first principal stress with a maximum value of 8.15 MPa, but the figure shows largely the structure has similar stress distribution and of the value 1.75 MPa, the maximum value is observed at the sudden change in the geometry and is restricted to very few locations. Similar stress behavior is observed for the 3rd Principal stresses as seen in Fig. 9(d). Figure 9(e) shows the displacement at different locations in the temple. It can be observed that large displacements are observed exactly at the open and raised *mandapam*. That is the only location where the columns are spaced far away and the remaining temple *mandapams* are all placed on a wall made with columns, which is the major reason for negligible displacements.

5 Conclusions

Modelling historical structures is as challenging as the analysis itself, due to a lack of information on many fronts' dimensions, materials used, internal locking mechanisms, foundation type, and arrangements of slab elements. Most importantly, historical structures are difficult to construct even in the modern era. Considering all the limitations and data interpretation techniques, an attempt is made to model one of the most ancient structures of India which has not been modelled before and remains a mystery in many dimensions. This study has been moderately successful in modelling the complete structure with almost fine structural details that play a vital role in the gravity analysis. It is understood that as models get larger, computational costs are higher. Currently based on the material properties, boundary conditions, and elemental cross-section maximum displacement is found at the entrance of the temple and the edges. To predict more of its behavior, further studies have to be carried out for various combinations of loads.

Another major conclusion from the study is that columns cannot be assumed similar or uniformly modelled in the numerical modelling. The fine geometrical considerations of the columns will increase the understanding of the structural response, structural stability, and load transfer for both gravity and lateral loads.

6 Future Studies

Further extension of the work will be carried out by considering various other loads especially flood and earthquake loads because the structure has experienced both the loads during its lifetime. There could be occurrences of minor earthquakes in that area in the future for which it has to be analyzed. Apart from that, contact analysis between different elements may enhance our understanding of the structure and a more accurate behavior can be predicted.

References

1. Fairservis, W.A.: The script of the Indus Valley civilization. Sci. Am. **248**(3), 58–67 (1983)
2. Nisha, Y.: Reconstructing the history of harappan civilization. Social Evol. Hist. **10**(2), 87–120 (2011)
3. Menon, A.: Heritage conservation in India: challenges and new paradigms. In: Proceedings of the SAHC2014—9th International Conference on Structural Analysis of Historical Constructions, Mexico City, Mexico, pp. 14–17 (2014).
4. Vardia, S.: Building science of Indian temple architecture (Doctoral dissertation) (2008)
5. Ronald, J.A., Menon, A., Prasad, A.M., Menon, D., Magenes, G.: Modelling and analysis of South Indian temple structures under earthquake loading. Sādhanā **43**(5), 1–20 (2018). https://doi.org/10.1007/s12046-018-0831-0

6. Sharma, S., Menon, A., Haridasan, H., Samson, S.: Structural behaviour of gopurams in south indian temples. In: Aguilar, R., Torrealva, D., Moreira, S., Pando, M.A., Ramos, L.F. (eds.) Structural Analysis of Historical Constructions. RB, vol. 18, pp. 929–937. Springer, Cham (2019). https://doi.org/10.1007/978-3-319-99441-3_100

7. Cakir, F., Kocyigit, F.: Architectural and structural analysis of historical structures. GRAĐEV-INAR **68**(7), 571–580 (2016). https://doi.org/10.14256/JCE.1182.2014

8. Eaton, R.M.: A social history of the deccan: 1300–1761. Cambridge University Press, Cambridge (2005). ISBN 978-0-52125-484-7

9. Daka, T., Udatha, L., Pasupuleti, V., Kalapatapu, P., Rajaram, B.: Ancient sandbox technique: an experimental study using piezoelectric sensors. In: Ioannides, M., et al. (eds.) EuroMed 2018. LNCS, vol. 11197, pp. 173–184. Springer, Cham (2018). https://doi.org/10.1007/978-3-030-01765-1_20

10. Kondam, N., Poddar, B., Pasupuleti, V., Singh, P.: Three dimensional modeling and analysis of ancient indian structures. In: Ioannides, M., et al. (eds.) EuroMed 2018. LNCS, vol. 11197, pp. 11–20. Springer, Cham (2018). https://doi.org/10.1007/978-3-030-01765-1_2

11. UNESCO Home page. https://whc.unesco.org/en/tentativelists/5889/, Accessed 14 Sept 2020

Numerical Modeling and Modal Analysis of Puranapul an Ancient Arch Bridge

Abhinav Kolla[(✉)] [iD], Ravi Naga Sai Kurapati [iD], Sree Satya Venkat Meka [iD],
Venkata Sai Madhu Dinesh Vitakula [iD], and Venkata Dilip Kumar Pasupuleti [iD]

Ecole Centrale College of Engineering, Mahindra University, Hyderabad, India
{abhinav170113,ravinagasai170116,sreesatyavenkat170136,
venkatasaimadhudinesh170138}@mechyd.ac.in,
venkata.pasupuleti@mahindrauniversity.edu.in

Abstract. Masonry arch bridges are known to be the nation's valuable infrastructure systems for decades especially, in a country like India. Most of the masonry arch bridges prevailing since ancient times are still serviceable which, profoundly indicates their robustness in design and construction methodology. Abandoning such important bridges will influence the transportation practices and economy of the nation. Inadequate proficiency or knowledge of masonry structures and its testing procedures has been the most common reason to abandon them. The absence of proper maintenance and monitoring of the health of heritage structures can lead to deterioration at a much faster pace. In this study, an ancient heritage masonry arch structure 'PuranaPul' bridge which was built based on the keystone concept and inaugurated in the year 1578 across the river Musi in Hyderabad was considered for investigation of its health through visual inspection and non-destructive testing (NDT). And the same bridge is numerically modeled using commercially available software ANSYS in three dimensions for assessing the basic mode shapes of the structure.

Keywords: Masonry arch bridge · Heritage structure · Visual inspection · Finite element model · Modal analysis · Health assessment

1 Introduction

Masonry arch bridges are one of the robust and prevalent types of structures constructed for transportation practices until the early years of the twentieth century. They are many masonry arch bridges around the world which hold a history of thousands of years of service [1]. These bridges are heritage structures, which symbolize the cultural heritage of many nations across the world. Due to their age, it's natural that they have undergone continuous deterioration from the environmental exposure and external natural or man-made loads [2]. So, it is important for us to safeguard these structures and to preserve them for the future generations. A thorough understanding and precise knowledge of structural behavior of these bridges is extremely mandatory to maintain its structural integrity and also, such studies assist in coming up with some cost-efficient retrofitting

© Springer Nature Switzerland AG 2021
M. Ioannides et al. (Eds.): EuroMed 2020, LNCS 12642, pp. 499–510, 2021.
https://doi.org/10.1007/978-3-030-73043-7_42

methods. Due to the heritage behind these Structures it always brings in awareness in many researchers to seek fascinating experimental and theoretical understanding of these structures [3]. Hyderabad is known to be founded by Muhammed-Quli Qutb Shah, the fifth sultan of the Golconda kingdom in the year 1591 and is one of the largest cities in India located in southern central region of the country along the river Musi [4]. Hyderabad is known for its heritage and most of the structures are almost 400 years old and most of the monuments located in Hyderabad are built with masonry and lime as binding material largely. In this study, we have considered one of the first Masonry arch bridge constructed on the musi river connecting old Golconda to the Karwan area. This bridge is popularly called Puranapul or 'Old Bridge' or 'Bridge of love'. This bridge is constructed in the year 1578 fourteen years before the foundation of Hyderabad city i.e. 1591. The bridge is built of sandstone and contain 22 arches, it is 185 m long, 10.9 m broad and 12.8 m above the bed of the river musi [5] as shown in the Fig. 1.

Fig. 1. Puranapul Masonry Arch Bridge (a) Side view (b) Path way used by street vendors (c) extreme arches (d) location of measurements taken for one complete arch (e) Railing wall on either side of passageway

The Puranapul arch bridge in its lifetime has been restored two times due to heavy floods in the year 1820 and 1908 [6]. Figure 1(b) shows the bridge is currently used by the vegetable vendors and not used for commercial vehicle passage from last ten years as it has not been assessed for structural stability and integrity. Figure 1(c) and Fig. 1(d) shows the locations which are accessible for structural health assessment to be carried.

This study had also been focused on the sizes of stones used for construction and properties of binding material to understand its deterioration. But this research papers limits itself to the fundamental analysis of the structures based on the materials properties obtained from the site for the sandstone. And Fig. 2 shows the schematic representation of the complete bridge consisting all the 22 arches with varying ground level at the ends. It also shows the dimensions in detail, each arch opening is 5.9 m and its height is 10 m from the bottom earth level. Arch thickness is 0.7 m and pier thickness is 2.95 m. All the dimensions have been measured manually using the measuring tools such as measuring tapes and laser distance measurer during the visual inspection of the bridge. The dimensions of the arch bridge are measured precisely in-order to make sure that they are close enough to the actual dimensions of the bridge. The errors in the dimensions that occurred during the visual inspection phase are very negligible which thereby depicts that the measurements considered are accurate.

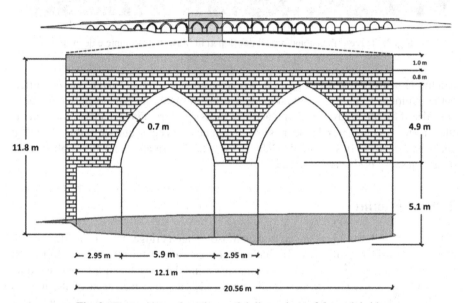

Fig. 2. Front view and componential dimensions of the arch bridge

In-order to have a proper visualization of the bridge, a three dimensional model with precise detailing has been developed using Autodesk Maya and rendered using Arnold as seen in the Fig. 3. There have been multiple trails for importing the same model in to FEM software but we faced difficulties in importing multiple layers. So, in this paper structural health of a masonry arch bridge which is 442 years old is assessed with a keen visual inspection and numerical analysis of the same is carried in order to access its current condition. The study has also attempted to know the current load carrying capacity by its frequency. The visual inspection phase mostly comprised of examining the materials used for construction, any structural damages to the structure, and taking accurate measurements of the entire bridge to build the numerical model, all in turn to give us better understanding of the structure.

For generating three-dimensional model for analysis, a finite element-based software ANSYS is used. This software was picked because of its simplicity in the complex modeling, incorporation of material properties, application of loading and boundary

Fig. 3. Three-dimensional model developed in Maya with complete detailing

conditions. This Software can generate a precise numerical model and test under different conditions of the load to investigate its structural integrity. The loading conditions considered for this study are gravity and live loads apart from modal analysis to find the fundamental frequency and other possible frequencies. In consequence of this numerical analysis, principal stresses, mode shapes, and total deformations for the applied loads on the masonry bridge are assessed.

2   Background

A Lot of research work is being carried on Masonry arch bridges from many decades all around the world, but still it is still a challenge to create a realistic model [7]. Toth et al. [8] had detailed a good review on the past numerical models developed for understanding the behavior of masonry arches. Author have also detailed that most of the models which were developed using FEM for 2D or 3D masonry structures are continuum based but masonry is fundamentally a discrete system. Few researchers have developed two dimensional models with plain strain assumption and binding materials as the spring to understand the failure mechanism [9–11]. Other group of researchers have concentrated on the material properties for more suitable behavior of masonry arch bridges [12–14]. Similarly, few other researchers have developed numerical models with consideration of contact analysis between the stones for more specific deformation and sliding behavior [15]. Even though lot of studies have been carried based on dimensional (1D, 2D, 3D), material properties (young's modulus, linear, non-linear), contact behavior (normal, shear), continuum or discrete and loading conditions, still linear continuum models play vital role in understanding the behavior of the masonry arch bridges, especially if the bridge does not have any structural damage. So, the current study had largely been concentrated on the continuum modelling and incorporation of material model for understanding its behavior.

3   Numerical Modeling

The bridge is 185 m long, 10.9 m broad and 12.8 m above the bed of the river and has 22 arches. The thickness of the spandrel walls and arch is 10.7 m as shown in Fig. 2. This bridge was constructed using sandstone as the primary material for arches, spandrel walls, and abutments. Special site investigation for the substructure has not been carried. It is observed the structural stone joints are filled with lime mortar and we also observed that there is no structural damage or seepage of water from top of the passage into bridge, which indicates that the structure is still in a good condition. Analysis of this masonry arch bridge is carried using commercially available finite element-based software in a macro modeling approach due to its minimalistic computational effort. Three-dimensional approach modeling is preferred for the better understanding in ANSYS workspace by creating a finite element by providing properties mentioned in Table 1 i.e., density, young's modulus, and poisons ratio of the material used in the construction of the bridge. As the study is conducted on an ancient masonry arch bridge comprised of the same type of material across arches, spandrel wall, and abutments, the material properties of the bridge are assumed from appropriate literature [7].

Table 1. Physical and mechanical parameters of the masonry arch bridge

Parameter	Units	Value
Compressive strength	MPa	66.9
Tensile strength	MPa	3.7
Youngs modulus	GPa	1.13
Poisons ratio	n/a	0.279
Unit weight	kN/m^3	27.5

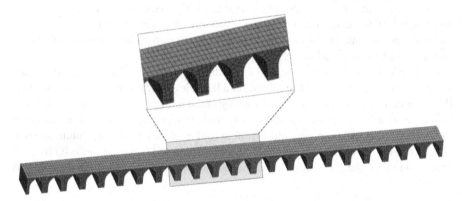

Fig. 4. Finite element model of the bridge with meshing

Three dimensional finite element model developed for the complete bridge is shown in Fig. 4 with stone masonry properties. The model is tested for three types of meshes coarse (1.2 m), medium (0.6 m) and fine (0.3 m) but the results obtained were in the similar line. Current model has 31,103 nodes and 5,376 elements in total. As the bridge is symmetric in nature, an individual arch numerical model is also developed and analysis has been carried for modal and gravity analysis.

4 Numerical Analysis and Results

Majorly numerical analysis is carried for three cases one gravity analysis to understand the scale of deformations for the self-load and live load apart from seeing the maximum permissible stress and strains. Second, modal analysis is carried to know the longitudinal and transverse mode shapes with their respective frequencies. Lastly dynamic analysis is carried to understand the seismic response with the foundations of the bridge being fixed. As this bridge consists of 22 uniform arches located equidistantly along its entire span to perform the numerical analysis on such kind of huge structures there is a need for high computational power, hence due to lack of high computational power, the analysis is done in a macro modeling approach as stated in a relatable literature [16] with a descent meshing size to obtain satisfactory results.

4.1 Gravity Analysis

To understand the deformations in detail, a single span of the total bridge is considered including the dead weight material which was used for laying the road on top of the bridge and deformations, stresses, strains are shown in Fig. 5(a–c) respectively. The maximum deformations are found to be 5.01 mm and observed at the mid of the span, maximum strains are found to be 0.00183 and maximum stresses are found to be at the corners in the range of 2.06e6 Pa.

On the application of the earth's standard gravitational force uniformly over the deck of the bridge along the negative y-direction, the following results were obtained, the total deformation of the bridge tends to be maximum at the centers of all the arches with a value of 0.14018 mm deformation in the negative y-direction and minimum at the two end surfaces and foundations of the bridge with zero deformation as shown in the Fig. 6 and it is similar that of individual span.

Figure 7 shows the equivalent strain distribution all over the bridge and maximum strain is observed to be 0.03716 and at the foundation level and reentrant corners, whereas the minimum strain is observed exactly on top of the piers projected to the passage way surface as seen in the figure. Whereas Fig. 8 shows the equivalent stress distribution over the bridge and behavior is very much similar to that of strain. The maximum stress is observed to be 4.17e5 Pa at the corners of the foundation and minimum stress is observed exactly on top of the piers projected to the passage way surface as seen in the enlarged figure.

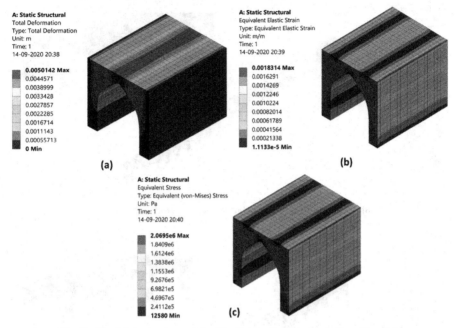

A: Static Structural
Total Deformation
Type: Total Deformation
Unit: m
Time: 1
14-09-2020 20:38

0.0050142 Max
0.0044571
0.0038999
0.0033428
0.0027857
0.0022285
0.0016714
0.0011143
0.00055713
0 Min

(a)

A: Static Structural
Equivalent Elastic Strain
Type: Equivalent Elastic Strain
Unit: m/m
Time: 1
14-09-2020 20:39

0.0018314 Max
0.0016291
0.0014269
0.0012246
0.0010224
0.00082014
0.00061789
0.00041564
0.00021338
1.1133e-5 Min

(b)

A: Static Structural
Equivalent Stress
Type: Equivalent (von-Mises) Stress
Unit: Pa
Time: 1
14-09-2020 20:40

2.0695e6 Max
1.8409e6
1.6124e6
1.3838e6
1.1553e6
9.2676e5
6.9821e5
4.6967e5
2.4112e5
12580 Min

(c)

Fig. 5. Total deformations of the Single span bridge due to its self-weight

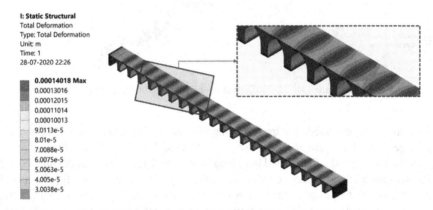

I: Static Structural
Total Deformation
Type: Total Deformation
Unit: m
Time: 1
28-07-2020 22:26

0.00014018 Max
0.00013016
0.00012015
0.00011014
0.00010013
9.0113e-5
8.01e-5
7.0088e-5
6.0075e-5
5.0063e-5
4.005e-5
3.0038e-5

Fig. 6. Total deformations of the bridge due to its self-weight

4.2 Modal Analysis

Modal analysis is carried out to understand the behavior and characteristics of the masonry arch bridge, which are vital when structure is subjected to dynamic loads [17]. Figure 9 and Fig. 10 shows first six mode shapes and respective frequencies obtained from modal analysis for single span and complete bridge (Tables 2 and 3).

Boundary conditions are similar to that of gravity analysis, bottom and end abutments are fixed. Figure 10(a) shows the first fundamental frequency 513.29 Hz in longitudinal mode and Fig. 10 (c) shows the first transverse mode of frequency 637,7 Hz. Total six

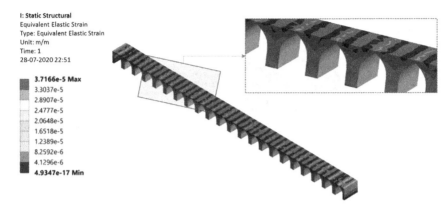

Fig. 7. Equivalent elastic strain distribution over the bridge due to its self-weight

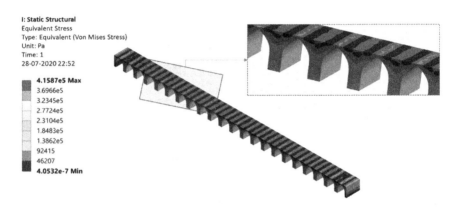

Fig. 8. Equivalent stress distribution over the bridge due to its self-weight

modes have been presented with first three longitudinal and first three transversal modes. The range of frequency are observed to be 513.29 Hz to 721.47 Hz for the first ten mode shapes and they are equally divided in to longitudinal and transversal modes shapes due to the symmetry of the structure. Modal analysis has also been carried for the model with only bottom fixed and obtained frequencies range from 483.13 Hz to 656.92 Hz. When the same is done for single arch masonry structure the frequencies of the first ten mode shapes ranged from 318.06 Hz to 1933.3 Hz.

4.3 Dynamic Analysis

The bridge is analyzed for seismic behavior to known the maximum deformation. As the Purnapul stone masonry bridge is located in the earthquake Zone-II according to IS 1893:2002, which has the zonation factor of 0.10 i.e. maximum horizontal acceleration that can be experienced by the structure in this zone is ten percent of acceleration due to gravity. To simulate the dynamic loading conditions for understanding the seismic behavior, the bridge is subjected to lateral accelerations that, were recorded on 21st Jan

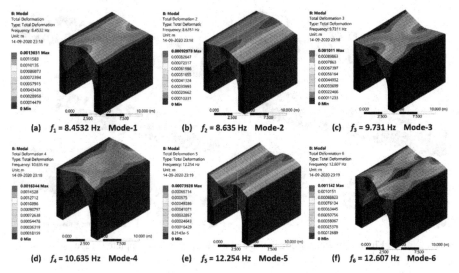

Fig. 9. Natural frequencies and mode shapes for single span of the bridge

Table 2. Natural frequencies and mode shapes values for single span of the bridge

Mode shape	Frequency (Hz)
Mode – 1	8.4532
Mode – 2	8.635
Mode – 3	9.731
Mode – 4	10.635
Mode – 5	12.254
Mode – 6	12.607

2001 in Bhuj, India. Which is one of the major earthquakes of magnitude 7.7 M_w and PGA of 0.6 g y[18] damaged short structures compared to the taller structures. The ground acceleration is applied to the model in the both the directions to the know the maximum possible deformation of the bridge. Figure 11 shows the maximum deformations for the dynamic analysis carried out and the maximum deformations are found to be very minimal 1.4×10^{-6} m and 6.14×10^{-8} m in x and z directions respectively. There are two major reasons for the negligible deformations, first one would be due to the continuum modeling and second is due to its lesser height. So the structure is quite adequate for lateral loads also, but more precise modeling and detailed material properties can predict more probable behavior.

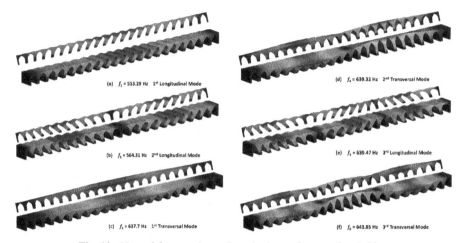

Fig. 10. Natural frequencies and mode shapes for complete bridge

Table 3. Natural frequencies and mode shapes values for complete bridge

Mode shape	Frequency (Hz)
Mode – 1	513.29
Mode – 2	564.31
Mode – 3	637.7
Mode – 4	639.32
Mode – 5	639.47
Mode – 6	643.85

Fig. 11. Maximum deformations of the bridge for the Bhuj Earthquake ground motion in both the directions.

5   Conclusions

A 442-year-old Purna pul stone masonry bridge with 22 arches was first visually inspected and based on observations, structural analysis has been carried using finite element method for static, dynamic loads and to investigate the response of the structure, as it was abandoned from past ten years. Currently it is used by street vendors effecting the structural stability and functionality. To the authors knowledge structural load carrying capacity or any other related tests have not been carried to qualitatively assess the structural stability. So, an attempt is made to understand the minimal nature of the structure and its stability. And based on the numerical analysis carried for static and dynamic, current configuration of the stone arch bridge is adequate to take its self-weight and live loads coming from the vehicular traffic. As expected maximum deformations are observed to be at the mid of the arch and principal stresses show that they are very much in the permissible limit. Stone piers are also found to be stronger based on the numerical analysis. Numerical modeling and analysis are always considered to be very effective tool in assessing the structural health of the current heritage structures for prospective conservation and preservation. Quality of the numerical analysis is always higher and nearer to the insitu behavior if nondestructive testing results are incorporated in the numerical model. The future of the work will be extended to incorporation of the material properties in the numerical model and compared with the vibrational studies.

References

1. Sarhosis, V., De Santis, S., de Felice, G.: A review of experimental investigations and assessment methods for masonry arch bridges. Struct. Infrastruct. Eng. 12(11), 1439–1464 (2016)
2. Mai, K.Q., Lee, S.M., Lee, K.: Assessment of historic stone arch bridge characterization: experiments and numerical model. Proc. Inst. Civil Eng.-Struct. Build. 172(7), 480–489 (2019)
3. Sevim, B., Bayraktar, A., Altunişik, A.C., Atamtürktür, S., Birinci, F.: Assessment of nonlinear seismic performance of a restored historical arch bridge using ambient vibrations. Nonlinear Dyn. 63(4), 755–770 (2011)
4. MIT Libraries Homepage. https://dome.mit.edu/handle/1721.3/45288
5. Appendices: Conservation of Historical Building and Areas in Hyderabad City. 1st edn. Hyderabad Urban Development Authority, Hyderabad (1984)
6. MIT Libraries Homepage. https://dome.mit.edu/handle/1721.3/20097
7. Banerji, P., Chikermane, S.: Condition assessment of a heritage arch bridge using a novel model up-dation technique. J. Civil Struct. Health Monit. 2(1), 1–16 (2012)
8. Tóth, A.R., Orbán, Z., Bagi, K.: Discrete element analysis of a stone masonry arch. Mech. Res. Commun. 36(4), 469–480 (2009)
9. Ford, T.E., Augarde, C.E., Tuxford, S.S.: Modelling masonry arch bridges using commercial finite element software. In: The 9th International Conference on Civil and Structural Engineering Computing, Netherlands, pp. 161–203 (2003)
10. Cavicchi, A., Gambarotta, L.: Two-dimensional finite element upper bound limit analysis of masonry bridges. Comput. Struct. 84(31–32), 2316–2328 (2006)
11. Gilbert, M.: Limit analysis applied to masonry arch bridges: state-of-the-art and recent developments. In: 5th International Arch bridges Conference, pp. 13–28 (2007)
12. Jiang, K., Esaki, T.: Quantitative evaluation of stability changes in historical stone bridges in Kagoshima, Japan, by weathering. Eng. Geol. 63(12), 83–91 (2002)
13. Audenaert, A., Fanning, P., Sobczak, L., Peremans, H.: 2-D analysis of arch bridges using an elasto-plastic material model. Eng. Struct. 30(3), 845–855 (2008)

14. Crisfield, M.A.: Numerical methods for the non-linear analysis of bridges. Comput. Struct. **30**(3), 637–644 (1988)
15. Kamiński, T.: Three-dimensional modelling of mason-ry arch bridges based on predetermined planes of weakness. In: 5th International Conference on Arch Bridges. Madeira, Portugal, pp. 341–348 (2007)
16. Caddemi, S., et al.: 3D discrete macro-modelling ap-proach for masonry arch bridges. In: IABSE Symposium 2019 Guimarães, Towards a Resilient Built Environment - Risk and Asset Management, Guimarães, Portugal, 27–29 March 2019 (2019)
17. Bayraktar, A., Türker, T., Altunişik, A.C.: Experimental frequencies and damping ratios for historical masonry arch bridges. Constr. Build. Mater. **75**, 234–241 (2015)
18. Iyengar, R.N., Kanth, S.R.: Strong ground motion estimation during the Kutch, India earthquake. Pure Appl. Geophys. **163**(1), 153–173 (2006)

Photogrammetric Survey for the Architectural Restoration of Ecclesiastical Cultural Heritage Monuments: The Case Study of the Church of the Holy Cross in Tochni

Zoe Georgiou[1], Maria Philokyprou[1], and Kyriacos Themistocleous[2,3]($\boxtimes$)

[1] Department of Architecture, University of Cyprus, Nicosia, Cyprus
[2] Department of Civil Engineering and Geomatics, Cyprus University of Technology, Limassol, Cyprus
k.themistocleous@cut.ac.cy
[3] Eratosthenes Centre of Excellence, Limassol, Cyprus

Abstract. This paper investigates the methodology of the digital documentation of an ecclesiastical monument in Tochni, Cyprus. The study very briefly describes the architectural history of the monument, as well as the changes that resulted in its current ruined condition. A photogrammetric survey of the monument was conducted to obtain its architectural elements, and subsequently conduct a restoration proposal. The aim of the survey is to investigate the use of photogrammetry using UAVs to examine historical monuments, in order to have a better understanding of the structure and elements that are difficult to measure and study in detail through traditional documentation.

Keywords: Digital media · Photogrammetry · Digital capture · Monuments · UAV · Ecclesiastical monument

1 Introduction

There is a plethora of historic monuments in Cyprus that have not been documented. There is also a dire need for the conservation and restoration of specific cultural heritage structures. The documentation process can be carried out using both traditional and digital means. Ecclesiastical monuments – that very often incorporate different historical periods – are considered significant cultural heritage sites in Cyprus. Although there is a predominance of Byzantine churches in Cyprus, it should be noted that there are also a large number of Gothic churches. The case study, which is the Church of the Holy Cross in Tochni, Cyprus, can be considered a Gothic church [1]. Many elements of the building – such as the pointed arches, ornamental ribbed vaults, variety of types and sizes of stones in the masonry, rich decorative features and wall heights – are very difficult and time consuming to be accurately surveyed by traditional means. In addition, the ruinous condition of the church makes the detailed survey and preparation of a comprehensive restoration proposal even more difficult.

© Springer Nature Switzerland AG 2021
M. Ioannides et al. (Eds.): EuroMed 2020, LNCS 12642, pp. 511–522, 2021.
https://doi.org/10.1007/978-3-030-73043-7_43

Nowadays, the process of documenting buildings has been enriched with the use of digital techniques that have made possible the accurate documentation of sites that are difficult to capture by traditional means. Digital media, such as photogrammetry and Unmanned Aerial Vehicles (UAVs) have made the documentation process easier and less time consuming than traditional media. Indeed, digital techniques using UAV and photogrammetry can document and provide data on cultural heritage sites and can help towards the understanding of their changes over time [2]. Photogrammetry using UAV images provides continuous covering of the object in a high-resolution context, producing a highly dense and textured 3D point cloud model [3, 4].

Photogrammetry makes precise measurements from images to determine the relative locations of points in space, and can be done as aerial, terrestrial and satellite. Also, photogrammetry software can utilise images to create 3D models and renderings. Recent developments in photogrammetry technology provide a simple and cost-effective method of generating relatively accurate 3D models from 2D images [5–7].

The equipment and instruments used for photogrammetry have evolved to a great extent. Aerial images taken from UAVs are the primary data for the process of photogrammetry. The photogrammetric software used in this study is Agisoft Metashape. Photos can be taken from any position, providing that the object to be reconstructed is visible on at least two photos. Both image alignment and 3D model reconstruction are fully automated by using Ground Control Points (GCPs). The final result is in the form of a point cloud and a surface model.

2   Case Study

The church of the Holy Cross is a medieval church from the 14th century [1, 8, 9], situated in the village of Tochni in the South-East of Cyprus. The church was designed following the main principles of the Gothic Style [1]. The site is located at the centre of the traditional village of Tochni; a settlement that is characterised by steep narrow streets, surrounded by small scale vernacular dwellings (Fig. 1). The church is located on a small slope, east of the newer church of Saints Constantine and Helen, erected over an ancient bridge. The Church of the Holy Cross is now in ruins.

The village of Tochni is historically connected with the arrival of Agia Eleni on the island, bringing with her the 'Holy Cross' [1, 8]. Some testimonies state that the church was rebuilt on the site of an earlier church that is said to have been found by Agia Eleni on her return from the Holy Land. The Gothic church is connected to another Byzantine church on its south. The church under study is considered by some scholars [1, 8, 9] to have been built after the discovery of the Holy Cross by a shepherd named George. Enlart assumes that the Lords of the island insisted on sharing the church of the Holy Cross with the Greeks and attached a Latin Chapel to it. According to the same author [1], it was the Egyptian Mamelukes who were responsible for setting fire to the monument in 1426.

The ecclesiastical complex has been declared an ancient monument by the Department of Antiquities since 1930. An excavation and cleaning of the area was carried out by the Department in 1935. Since then, no effort has been made to restore or support the monument. The church complex has been in ruins for several years.

Fig. 1. Aerial image of the village centre, showing the Church of the Holy Cross

2.1 Architecture of the Church (Typology)

Today the Gothic church is in a ruinous condition. Only its northern, eastern and western walls are preserved, as well as a small part of its roofing vaults. The south Byzantine church, attached to the south is in worse condition, as only the lower part of its walls are still visible today. This second adjoining attached church is believed to have functioned together with the Gothic church [10]. According to some scholars [10], the complex can be considered as a two-aisled church, with two semi-circular apses of sanctuary. In the south apse of sanctuary, there is evidence of Byzantine murals on the walls.

From the ruins of the complex, it is evident that there were two entrances to the west (one leading to the Gothic church and one to the Byzantine), as well as a secondary door in the southern part of the Byzantine church. In the Gothic church there is no entrance in the northern wall. Between the two churches, there are traces of columns and pilasters that probably separated the two structures. At the junction of the two churches it seems that the stones do not cross, a fact that proves that the two churches were not built at the same period. It seems that the northern Gothic church was added later with the arrival of the Latins on the island. The addition of new structures in the form of aisles affixed to Byzantine churches so they could be used as Latin chapels, are marked from the time of the Frankish occupation on the island. Meanwhile, in the countryside chapels instead of churches began to be attached to Byzantine type churches [10]. Today, in the southern part of the Gothic church under study, there is a window that in the past seems to have served as a door that probably connected the two sanctuaries of the ecclesiastical complex. This also justifies the view that the two churches operated together, at least at some period of the past.

Recent excavations by the Department of Antiquities revealed the original floor of the complex that is still visible today. The difference in the floor paving between the two churches is evident; a fact that also proves that the two churches were built in a different chronological period (Fig. 2).

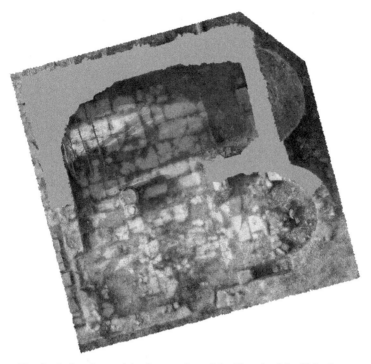

Fig. 2. Ortho-photo of the floor paving of the Church of the Holy Cross

2.2 Morphological Gothic Elements of the Church

The Gothic church in this study incorporates a number of Gothic elements, especially in its superstructure. From the missing roof of the church, only some pointed elaborated ribs, parts of the vaults and the spring of a probable cruciform are still visible today. The cruciform, as well as the pointed arches and ribbed vaults, are elements found in Latin and Catholic churches. Although cruciform vaults with ribs appeared in Byzantine churches in Greece, the dating and the effects/additions they have undergone over time are not certain. Through a study of old photographs and drawings of which a part of the roof of the Gothic church is preserved (Fig. 3), it appears that the roof structure incorporated a pointed semi-dome that covered the east apse of the sanctuary and a higher pointed barrel vault covering the eastern part of the church next to the apse. However, the exact form of the vaults that cover the central part of the church remains unknown. The morphological study and identification of the abovementioned elements of the church, and especially the form of the roofing, is anticipated to be achieved with the completion of its digital imprint.

Fig. 3. **Left:** Photo of the Church of The Holy Cross (Department of Antiquities-1937) **Right:** Drawing of the Church of The Holy Cross (Camille Enlart-1987)

3 Methodology

In the documentation of historical structures, there is always a challenge when complex irregular elements exist and require a full 3D virtual reconstruction with high resolution, geometric and radiometric accuracy. In recent years, different methods have been used for surveying cultural heritage monuments, including laser scanning and photogrammetry. UAVs provide a much better imaging geometry, and are beneficial for documenting areas not visible from the ground level, with reduction of occlusions. UAV aerial imagery in combination with photogrammetry are emerging technologies which provide an innovative approach to the 3D documentation of cultural heritage [11]. UAV applications for cultural heritage are mainly focused on documentation, observation, monitoring, mapping, 3D modelling and 3D reconstruction [12], as well as digital maps, digital orthophotos, digital elevation models (DEM) and digital surface models (DSM) [13].

In order to document the Church of the Holy Cross, the following methodology was used, as featured in Fig. 4. A survey of the area was conducted using a UAV which was geo-referenced with GCPs. The images acquired by the UAV were subsequently imported into photogrammetry software in order to create a 3D model. The remainder of the methodology includes importing the 3D model into Building Information Modelling (BIM) software, which will be used to create restoration drawings. By using BIM, cultural heritage experts will be able to understand the geometry and the construction methods of the church, and create construction drawings to restore the cultural heritage site as accurately as possible [14].

In this study, the first two parts of the methodology are used. Future research will focus on the third and fourth parts of the methodology.

Fig. 4. Methodology

3.1 Survey with UAVs and GCPs

In several places, the study area around the monument was inaccessible due to the presence of stones that fell from the structure, as well as the intense vegetation around the ecclesiastical complex. In order to acquire the images necessary for the aerial survey, a DJI Mavic 2 Pro UAV, complete with a Hasselblad 20MP camera and 1-inch sensor was used for documenting the church complex. The height of the UAV camera was placed at an average of 10 m. To define the reference system of the model and accurately orient the structure, 13 well-distributed GCPs were placed on natural features around the site, to improve the accuracy of the photogrammetric survey (Fig. 5). In order to establish the best accuracy, the 13 GCPs were geo-referenced using the CYPOS permanent station network with the LTM CGRS93/Cyprus Local Transverse Mercator projection coordinate system and the Cyprus Geodetic Reference System 1993 Datum.

As the study area was not flat, the GCPs were placed at different elevations around the church at the top and bottom of the fencing wall at the east elevation. The UAV took images at several different heights and angles of the monument. The images were then processed with the GCPs in order to find the exact coordinates for each point. To get optimum results using photogrammetry the camera on the UAV was calibrated and adjusted for optimal exposure, aperture, shutter speed and sensor sensitivity, in order to produce clean, sharp images by reducing image blurring, image noise, retain sharpness and appropriate depth of field.

Fig. 5. Placement of ground control points

The image sequence captured from the UAV consisted of 1,110 images which were oriented in different directions (Fig. 6). The first step in the programme's procedure is Structure for Motion (SfM) photogrammetry which was used to provide an accurate documentation of the church [15]. SfM software is a valuable tool for generating good quality meshes from images in a semi-automatic way, because each image is geo-tagged with the coordinates at each camera location. At this stage the software analyses the datasets including the camera locations, detecting geometrical patterns in order to reconstruct the virtual positions of the cameras used to align the images [16].

The workflow for SfM photogrammetric processing requires that at least two overlapping images are available (a stereo pair), in order to produce a digital surface model (DSM). The DSM derived from two overlapping images creates a relief displacement and corrects image geometric distortions. The final resulting ortho-image is free from any geometric distortions and can be treated as a floor plan and/or elevation.

Fig. 6. Images from UAV used for photogrammetry

3.2   3D Models with Photogrammetric Texture Mapping

The proper methodology for modelling cultural heritage sites and monuments is still debated amongst the cultural heritage community, especially regarding the accuracy of the documentation and the difficulty of retracing the correct shape of the structure [17]. Historical buildings are irregular and characterised by heterogeneous and complex shapes, structural damages, and deformations to the architectural elements. Point clouds and mesh surfaces represent complex objects that cannot be described by simple geometric rules and are difficult to project onto a 2D drawing. 3D parametric modelling speeds up the modelling phase by allowing for an easy semantic enrichment and by creating an 'intelligent' model that can adapt to a specific geometry and structure.

In historic building documentation, the texture of the surface and any decay or damage to the materials is important information which will enrich the 3D model and show the thematic information of the materials. Mapping textures is needed for any restoration or conservation interventions that affect the façade of a building. The main outputs of photogrammetric surveys – which are created by stitching and processing hundreds or thousands of images – are 3D points clouds, 3D surfaces, ortho-photos and Digital Elevation Models [15].

The advantage of using photogrammetry is the creation of a 3D digital model that possesses laser scan quality geometry with photorealistic texture mapping. The photogrammetry software that was used in this study was Agisoft Metashape. Agisoft refines the camera position for thousands of images and aligns the images. Based on the estimated camera positions, the programme calculates depth information for each camera, to be combined into a single dense point cloud model. After the dense point cloud has been reconstructed, it is possible to generate a polygonal mesh model based on the dense cloud data. The completed alignment of the cloud data is then used to develop a surface mesh model, which allows for draping of the imagery by creating and building a texture from the original images and overlaying the imagery onto the model mesh [5, 18]. The finished model can be exported in various formats for display, or imported into other 3D analysis software.

4   Results

During the study, a Mavic 2 Pro UAV, complete with a Hasselblad 20MP camera and 1-in. sensor was used to acquire aerial images of the church. The images were processed with SfM within Agisoft Metashape photogrammetry software. Photogrammetry uses a Multi-Viewpoint Stereo (MVS) algorithm in order to build a dense point cloud in virtual space. The size of the dense cloud can reach into millions or billions of points, and by using the dense cloud's 3D point positions, it creates the geometrical mesh for each surface. A texture map is calculated from the colour information from each pixel of the original images and the 3D geometry. The result is a textured 3D model that can be measured with a precision.

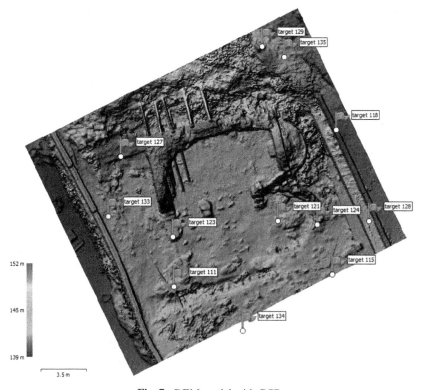

Fig. 7. DEM model with GCPs

From the dense cloud 3D points, a DEM model was generated by using an automatic elevation extraction mechanism from each point (Fig. 7). A precise, high resolution orthophoto was produced by using the DEM model and the orthogonal projection of the images, creating an accurate plan of the site. The orthophoto (Fig. 8) features detailed textures on the floor and walls, as well as evidence of the differences between the Gothic and Byzantine elements of the ecclesiastical complex.

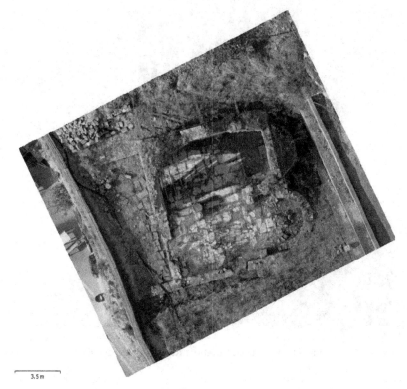

3.5 m

Fig. 8. Orthophoto

A 3D model of the Church of the Holy Cross provided the ability to examine the building from all angles (Fig. 9). The resulting 3D model showing the real representation of the church elements, shapes, and textures was needed in order to examine the architecture and extract the geometry for the correct interpretation of the original geometric structure.

The front elevation (Fig. 10, left) and side elevation (Fig. 10, Right) shows the damage of the church's exterior walls.

Fig. 9. 3D model of the Church of the Holy Cross

Fig. 10. Left, front elevation, **Right,** side elevation

5 Conclusions

When the documentation is used for restoration purposes, an accurate, detailed 3D model is needed in order to produce reliable construction drawings. However, traditional methods of documentation require expensive and time-consuming methodologies. The integration of different modelling techniques such as photogrammetry can provide feasible solutions. Building elements such as walls, vaults, semi-domes and floors are created using a modelling workflow in order to adhere to surveyed data geometry and point clouds to reach the highest level of accuracy. Such techniques and solutions use photogrammetry in combination with parametric modelling into the BIM environment. Further research can focus on exporting the 3D model into BIM and afterwards conducting restoration drawings. This will prove invaluable for the conservation and restoration of cultural heritage monuments, especially for structures with complicated plans and elevations, or different historic phases.

Acknowledgements. The aforementioned project is part of the Master's Thesis of Zoe Georgiou (Interdepartmental Master on Conservation and Restoration of Historic Buildings and Sites) at the University of Cyprus. Using the process of photogrammetry within the documentation helped shed a light on the diverse elements of the monument, and will lead to a proposal for the support and restoration of the monument in the next phase.

Using UAVs and photogrammetry for documentation is part of the activities of the ERATOS-THENES: Excellence Research Centre for Earth Surveillance and Space-Based Monitoring of the Environment's 'EXCELSIOR' project, which has received funding from the European Union's Horizon 2020 Research and Innovation programme, under Grant Agreement No 857510, as well as from the Government of the Republic of Cyprus, through the Directorate General for the European Programmes, Coordination and Development (www.excelsior2020.eu).

References

1. Enlart, C.: Gothic art and the renaissance in Cyprus. In: Trigraph Limited, pp. 337–340 (1987)
2. Rodríguez-Gonzálvez, P., et al.: 4D reconstruction and visualization of cultural heritage: analyzing our legacy through time. In: ISPRS Proceedings - International Archives of the Photogrammetry, Remote Sensing and Spatial Information Sciences, vol. XLII-2/W3, pp. 609–616 (2017). https://doi.org/10.5194/isprs-archives-XLII-2-W3-609-2017
3. Hirschmuller, H.: Stereo Processing by Semiglobal Matching and Mutual Information. IEEE Proc. Trans. Pattern Anal. Mach. Intell. 30(2), 328–341 (2008)
4. Wenzel, K., Abdel-Wahab, M., Cefalu, A., Fritsch, D.: High-resolution surface reconstruction from imagery for close range cultural heritage applications. In: International Archives Photogramm. Remote Sensing Spatial Information Science, Proceedings, vol. XXXIX-B5, pp. 133–138 (2012). https://doi.org/10.5194/isprsarchives-XXXIX-B5-133-2012
5. Themistocleous, K., Agapiou, A., King, H., King, N., Hadjimitsis, D. G.: More than a flight: the extensive contributions of UAV flights to archaeological research – the case study of curium site in Cyprus. In: Ioannides, M., Magnenat-Thalmann, N., Fink, E., Žarnić, R., Yen, A.Y., Quak, E. (eds.) EuroMed 2014. LNCS, vol. 8740, pp. 396–409. Springer, Cham (2014). https://doi.org/10.1007/978-3-319-13695-0_38
6. Themistocleous, K., Danezis, C.: Monitoring cultural heritage sites affected by geo-hazards using in situ and SAR data: the choirokoitia case study. In: Hadjimitsis, D.G., et al (eds.) Remote Sensing for Archaeology and Cultural Landscapes. SRS, pp. 285–308. Springer, Cham (2020). https://doi.org/10.1007/978-3-030-10979-0_16. Print ISBN: 978-3-030-10978-3, Electronic ISBN: 978-3-030-10979-0
7. Themistocleous, K., Ioannides, M., Agapiou, A., Hadjimitsis, D.G.: The methodology of documenting cultural heritage sites using photogrammetry, UAV and 3D printing techniques: the case study of Asinou church in Cyprus. In: Proceedings of the Third International Conference on Remote Sensing and Geoinformation of Environment Proceedings, 16–19 March 2015 (2015)
8. Jeffery, G.: A Description of the Historic Monuments of Cyprus, Nicosia (1918)
9. Gunnis, R.: Historic Cyprus, Nicosia (1936)
10. Chrysochou, N.: Η Αρχιτεκτονική της ορθοδόξου μονής της Παναγίας του Σίντη στην Πάφο. Συμβολή στη Μελέτη της θρησκευτικής αρχιτεκτονικής της Ενετοκρατίας στην Κύπρο, Λευκωσία (2003)
11. Caprioli, M., Mancini, F., Mazzone, F., Scarano, M., Trizzino, R.: Proceedings of the UAV surveys for representing and document the cultural heritage. In: Proceedings of the XIII International Forum, Aversa Capri, 11–13 June 2015 (2015)
12. Remondino, F., Barazzetti, L., Nex, F., Scaioni, M., Sarazzi, D.: UAV photogrammetry for mapping and 3D modeling-current status and future perspectives. In: Proceedings of the International Archives of the Photogrammetry, Remote Sensing and Spatial Information Sciences Proceedings, Conference on Unmanned Aerial Vehicle in Geomatics, UAV-g 2011, Zurich, Switzerland, vol. XXXVIII-1/C22 (2011).

13. Patias, P., Kaimaris, D., Georgiadis, Ch., Stamnas, A., Antoniadis, D., Papadimitrakis, D.: 3D mapping of cultural heritage: special problems and best practices in extreme case-studies. In: Proceedings of the ISPRS Annals of the Photogrammetry, Remote Sensing and Spatial Information Sciences Proceedings, 2013 XXIV International Cıpa Symposium, Strasbourg, France, 2–6 September 2013, vol. II-5/W1 (2013)

14. Themistocleous, K., Mettas, C., Evagorou, E., Hadjimitsis, D.G.: The use of UAVs and photogrammetry for the documentation of cultural heritage monuments: the case study of the churches in Cyprus. In: Proceedings of the SPIE 11156, Earth Resources and Environmental Remote Sensing/GIS Applications Proceedings X, 3 October 2019, vol. 111560I, (2019). https://doi.org/10.1117/12.2533056

15. Themistocleous, K., Evagorou, E., Mettas, C., Hadjimitsis, D.: The documentation of ecclesiastical cultural heritage sites in Cyprus. In: Proceedings of the SPIE 11534, Earth Resources and Environmental Remote Sensing/GIS Applications Proceedings XI, 22 September 2020, vol. 115340Y (2020). https://doi.org/10.1117/12.2574015. (2020).

16. Themistocleous, K.: The use of UAVs for cultural heritage and archaeology. In: Hadjimitsis, D.G., et al. (eds.) Remote Sensing for Archaeology and Cultural Landscapes. SRS, pp. 241–269. Springer, Cham (2020). https://doi.org/10.1007/978-3-030-10979-0_14. ISBN: 978-3-030-10978-3

17. Barazzetti, L., Banfi, F., Brumana, R., Oreni, D., Previtali, M., Roncoroni, F.: HBIM and augmented information: towards a wider user community of image and range-based reconstructions. In: Proceedings of the ISPRS - International Archives of the Photogrammetry, Remote Sensing and Spatial Information Sciences Proceedings, vol. XL-5/W7, pp. 35–42 (2015). https://doi.org/10.5194/isprsarchives-XL-5-W7-35-(2015)

18. Meszaros, J.: Aerial surveying UAV based on open-source hardware and software. In: Proceedings of the International Archives of the Photogrammetry, Remote Sensing and Spatial Information Sciences Proceedings, vol. XXXVIII-1/C22 (2011)

Short Paper: 2D and 3D GIS in Cultural Heritage

Mapping Cultural Heritage: CLIO MAP, Montenegro

Olga Pelcer-Vujačić[1]([✉]) [iD], Marko Krevs[2] [iD], and Zerina Ćatović[1] [iD]

[1] Historical Institute, University of Montenegro, Bulevar revolucije 5,
81000 Podgorica, Montenegro
[2] Department of Geography, Faculty of Arts, University of Ljubljana, Ljubljana, Slovenia
marko.krevs@ff.uni-lj.si

Abstract. The paper highlights the need for the digitization of cultural heritage to propose the first national mobile geoinformatics application. Unusually varied cultural heritage in the country that strongly relies on tourism income urges the need to build a new, exportable, interactive tool. In that sense, this article demonstrates the process flow in the online cultural map creation and its further development and sustainability. Being the first on market, loaded with data provided by experts from several fields also brings challenges, which this paper elaborates. Hence, a case-study of the ArcGIS Online services usage in the Montenegrin cultural landscape provides a great overview of the issues in drafting a national register of cultural heritage: from technical obstacles, policies of selection until the interpretation of the data and preservation.

Keywords: Montenegro · GIS · Cultural heritage · Mobile app

1 Introduction

Montenegro has been a crossroads of civilizations whose traces are still visible today, creating a particularly rich and varied cultural heritage, from prehistoric to modern times, leaving researchers with almost unlimited space for their pursuits. Therefore, a need for comprehensive, accurate and, easily available online mobile services is high, especially in the area of Montenegrin cultural heritage, both in scientific and touristic purposes.

Having in mind the unacceptable void in this domain, a two-year ongoing project Montenegro on the political and cultural map of Europe – CLIO MAP started in Spring 2019. The main goals of the CLIO MAP project are to enrich the knowledge base on historical, social, and cultural processes, resulting in the present Montenegrin cultural landscape, determine its characteristics and current incarnations, as well to develop the new, digital tool (commercial mobile application) for their further valorization in commercial purposes and preservation. Similar heritage-oriented databases worldwide showed great importance in cases of natural disasters and human activities, but also preservation memories of local communities and their stories that are usually not a part of public discourses [7, 9, 18].

© Springer Nature Switzerland AG 2021
M. Ioannides et al. (Eds.): EuroMed 2020, LNCS 12642, pp. 525–532, 2021.
https://doi.org/10.1007/978-3-030-73043-7_44

The planned activities cover the continuum from deciphering historical contexts creating certain segments of heritage, its elements, characteristics, monuments, and artifacts. They consist of desk (archival, librarian, and other collections) and field (location survey, drawing plans, taking the photo and video material, interviews) researches. It is envisaged to have c.ca 500 monuments and artifacts of cultural-historical heritage on the territory of Montenegro covered and relevant data processed. They are selected according to the chronological, thematic, problem, and territorial dimension. Moreover, we will cover both tangible and intangible cultural heritage in addition to the sometimes neglected field of creative industries. Data collected will be presented on the project website www.cliomap.me. It will be of great help both as an educational tool for the local population not familiar with their own historical and cultural treasure, as well as for the ever-growing number of foreign visitors (Fig. 1).

Fig. 1. Screenshot of CLIO MAP website

The principal research institution in this project is the Historical Institute, University of Montenegro with Montenegrin and foreign partners from the Sapienza University, University of Warsaw, University of Ljubljana and Institute for Strategic Thinking from Ankara, Turkey. The project team comprises of scholars and experts from many different fields of human sciences – historiography, linguistics, history of art, GIS, photography, architecture, law, and political sciences. Their expertise will come together into a joint, problem-oriented story, finding a recognizable place of Montenegro within the complex domain of European and Mediterranean historical and cultural identity.

The creation of the multi-layered GIS database, containing wider contents of cultural heritage entries, will become a national hub for this category, online available and accessible, with the support of national stakeholders such as the Ministry of tourism and sustainable development, National tourist organization, and local agencies. Planned both for Android and iOS, it will cover all the major types of operative systems that contemporary smartphone and tablet devices use, so it will be readily available to the widest group of users possible. It will be both in Montenegrin and English language, with an open possibility to be translated in other world languages.

2   Evolving Geoinformatics Foundations of Montenegrin Cultural Heritage Database

Establishing a database within the CLIO MAP project was a necessary task to support the idea of making information on cultural heritage usable in an example of an online or mobile application for touristic use, a kind of "virtual geo-museum of cultural heritage". GIS applications have so far been only occasionally used in Montenegrin historical research, mostly by the same team [15]. Furthermore, drafting a Montenegrin cultural heritage database represent the foundations of a national register of cultural heritage.

Web GIS consists of an online map, linked to one or several online geographic databases. It may be mainly designed to present data in a map form, but usually includes several other functionalities for their users, like changing the map visualizations, filtering and reclassifying data, contribute new data, analyse data, provide services like navigation, export data, and maps, to list some of the usual. Another major characteristic of Web GIS is the ease of is access and use: only internet access and devices already known to users are needed. A modern Web GIS is usually "the front-end of a much larger GIS" [10], that may "blend data from multiple governmental, industry, non-profit, or community data sources, including data gathered by citizen scientists" [10].

For this project, we have closely followed a Slovenian example [17], based on ArcGIS Online services. Establishing a digital register of immovable cultural heritage in Slovenia started in 1991, followed by its several co-ordinations with legislative changes, organization of reporting to the register, redesigning of the database, in 2009 also upgraded by a register of intangible cultural heritage. Despite similar visual and functional impression, CLIO Map Web GIS developed in almost inverse order. The three Web GIS applications within the project have been developed before the digitalization of the register even started. Consequently, some of the decisions, like how to organize, classify, visualize the cultural heritage goods in the database, even which contents and attributes to be included, have been discussed and re-designed iteratively during the project. This process did not bring the final solutions for the national register of cultural heritage yet, but had several important effects:

- speeded up the learning of the stakeholders in the project, by active participation, especially by using the Web GIS tools;
- raised several relevant questions, related to the content, and to the technological solutions, that will need to be addressed in the national register;
- provides usable and convincing visualizations of the cultural goods, based on a stable cloud solution tested in numerous similar projects all around the world;
- raises awareness of the existing ICT solutions and possibilities to support scientific, educational, and public services related to the cultural heritage;
- stimulates ideas of possible future uses of both: similar technological solutions and the established database within other projects.

The creation of the database was mostly carried out by a geoinformation expert, using ArcGIS Desktop and ArcGIS Online in the following major phases:

- designing the content of the database: a cataloguing card, listing the descriptions, resources, photo documents, external links, basic categories, spatial, temporal definitions and authoring regarding the cultural heritage sites; designing the geodatabase following the design of the content from the previous step and publishing it online;
- developing a simple-to-use online GIS application dedicated solely to enter point-objects of the cultural heritage goods and their attributes;
- developing a more complex online GIS application that allows entering point-objects and polygon objects, editing of the content and spatial position of the objects, query the database, export data in table or map form;
- developing a dashboard-type of an online GIS application, dedicated to present the collected data in different forms, including the linked multimedia
- entering data to the database; performing a quality assessment of the data;

The geoinformation environment used to support the activities within the project CLIO Map is ArcGIS Online (https://www.arcgis.com). This cloud-based platform provides some of the best adjustable solutions for collaborative mapping, map and database editing, and online presentation, which were needed in our project. The same platform has been adopted in many projects that needed similar functionalities [12, 17]. Among the functionalities within the project we are working on basic data collection, including (collaborative) mapping; editing capabilities for content-related and geographic information; map-based presentation of the database, including capabilities of detailed inspection of individual items in the database, their selection, classification; maps, tables, photos, and other online information. All the information is in visual form (text, maps, photos). The future national database might include also audio materials (like recordings of speech in dialects, storytelling) or multimedia (like video, interactive video). The application will be continued to be updated and upgraded with new entries and data after the project expiration, bearing in mind its sustainability and prolonged relevance. The data collected in the database will offer in-depth analysis, which will also result in the identification of infrastructural gaps and opportunities for further development, including system development, data aggregation, and online learning (Fig. 2).

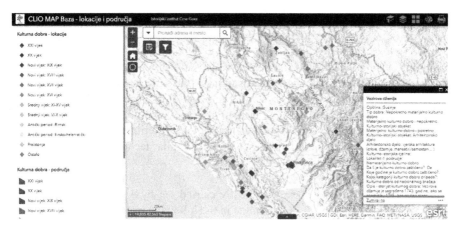

Fig. 2. Screenshot of CLIO MAP database on ArcGIS Online

3   Mobile Application

In this particular moment, there is no mobile application covering the Montenegrin cultural and historical attractions, possible for valorisation within the tourism offer. The requirement for integration all different aspects within a single application, using textual, visual, and audio means, has raised many different issues about the planning and production of cultural content for mobile usage, together with usability aspects regarding the design and distribution of a mobile app. The application is developed by the commercial partner, Identity & Promotion, and its lead consultant, Ilija Perić.

The concept is that mobile features such as geolocation and real-time interaction can be used to provide personalized up-to-date and interactive cultural heritage content, in real-time (Fig. 3).

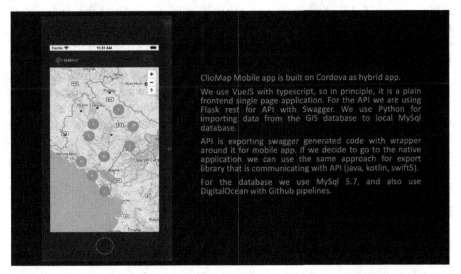

Fig. 3. Screenshot of the app with development explanation

The presentation of cultural heritage rests mostly on appealing visuals. Images could encounter the problem when used on mobile devices, due to the limited size and quality of the screen. This means that users will not be able to enjoy details (for example of a painting or monument). If it is required to display details, it can be useful to enlarge it as a separate image. High-contrast images are better and it is preferable to focus on a few elements rather than use an image full of different details. Interactive maps are one of the most successful features of smartphones, being very useful for showing location-based information [3]. In the case of the CLIO Map project, our main target is tourists visiting the country, so we will provide them with an offline map that was based on the free wiki world map OpenStreetMap (https://www.openstreetmap.org), a leading open-source map. We will also add links to the standard Google Map for users with suitable data plans or connected to a WiFi network.

The updating process should be carefully planned, since every time the content is changed, users have to download the whole app from the app store again, an operation that can be annoying or forgotten. It is therefore advisable to create an automatic updating system that regularly checks and downloads content updates from the web without forcing the user to download and reinstall the whole app.

This application, which keeps the potential for constant upgrading and continued relevance, will be maintaining its sustainability for a prolonged period since the market for cultural tourism in the country is expected to grow.

4   Possible Outcomes

The web is rapidly adapting to provide an increased sense of community, including in cultural and museum spheres [2]. Social networking and collaborative features could be integrated within an app, providing users with the possibility of collaborative feedback and interaction [5, 13]. An increasing number of interactive cultural apps is expected, allowing user-generated content as well as professionally written content. On our website, our young researchers started a blog as part of the popularization of history as a discipline among a wider audience.

In very close relation to our project, and even more to its potential further developments, are discussions on using digital cultural heritage resources for tourism recommendations by cultural institutions [14], studying the usability of geoinformatic mobile application about cultural heritage [3, 4], using geocaching in cultural heritage tourism [6] using location-aware mobile devices for searching and browsing a large number of general and cultural heritage information repositories [1], as well as using mobile augmented reality in teaching about cultural heritage [16].

5   Challenges

The free narrative formats of historic and cultural heritage research are in opposition to an online setting that relies on structured data for access and use. Any kind of heritage GIS system always integrates inclusive and very detailed documentation data on physical characteristics of heritage properties and settings through textual reports, drawings, and photographs. Most of these systems have a common problem, they only use GIS for recording properties' position without additional data integration through the geo-referencing approach. We believe we should study and analyze the reality in multi-dimensional and integrated approaches, fostering at the same time the "socialization" of spatial information. There is a feeling that there are no data standards for conservation information yet.

Another challenge is the interoperability of the cultural heritage data – between different institutions or disciplines as well as between national information systems. Even within EU directive INSPIRE, implemented to establish interoperable data exchange framework, Data Specification on Protected Sites was primarily designed for the natural protected sites. Fernandez Freire [8] proposed to adequately extend the missing characteristics necessary for the cultural heritage spatial data infrastructure. Also, the Korean Cultural Heritage Data Model is challenged by the integration of one heterogeneous heritage dataset among various heritage institutions [11].

Memory institutions may have a public commitment to preserve, but one cannot talk about digital culture preservation without talking about value. What is important to some current or prospective users is not necessarily important to others. For this reason, one of the main issues is the importance of collaboration between all the interested sides, both in the creation and the evaluation of digital map, in order to avert possible dominance of one category or specific identity narrative about the past. As mentioned, in this intention we rely heavily on local areas and small communities whose voice is not usually represented.

Acknowledgments. This research was supported by the Ministry of Science of Montenegro financing the project *Montenegro on the political and cultural map of Europe – CLIO MAP*. We are thankful to our colleagues who helped in collecting the data and provided expertise that greatly assisted the research. All photos and graphic material are made by team members. All the data in this paper are published with the consent of the Project Coordinator, dr Radoslav Raspopović.

References

1. van Aart, C., Wielinga, B., van Hage, W.R.: Mobile Cultural heritage guide: location-aware semantic search. In: Cimiano, P., Pinto, H.S. (eds.) EKAW 2010. LNCS (LNAI), vol. 6317, pp. 257–271. Springer, Heidelberg (2010). https://doi.org/10.1007/978-3-642-16438-5_18

2. Beler, A., Borda, A., Bowen, J.P., Filippini-Fantoni, S.: The building of online communities: an approach for learning organizations, with a particular focus on the museum sector. In: Hemsley, J., Cappellini, V., Stanke, G. (eds.) EVA 2004 London Conference Proceedings, pp. 2.1–2.15. EVA International, UK (2004). https://arxiv.org/abs/cs.CY/0409055

3. Boiano, S., Bowen, J.P., Gaia, G.: Usability, design and content issues of mobile apps for cultural heritage promotion: The Malta culture guide experience (2012). arXiv preprint arXiv: 1207.3422, https://doi.org/10.14236/ewic/EVA2012.12

4. Bollini, L., De Palma, R., Nota, R., Pietra, R.: User experience & usability for mobile geo-referenced apps. a case study applied to cultural heritage field. In: Murgante, B., et al. (eds.) ICCSA 2014. LNCS, vol. 8580, pp. 652–662. Springer, Cham (2014). https://doi.org/10.1007/978-3-319-09129-7_47

5. Borda, A., Bowen, J.P.: Virtual collaboration and community. In: Information Resources Management Association, Virtual Communities: Concepts, Methodologies, Tools and Applications, pp. 2600–2611. IGI Global, Hershey (2011). https://doi.org/10.4018/978-1-60960-100-3.ch809

6. Corrieu, H.D.: The use of geocaching in cultural heritage tourism. Master thesis. Erasmus Mundus Joint Master Programme, Universities of Ljubljana, Southern Denmark and Girona (2017). https://www.cek.ef.uni-lj.si/magister/corrieu2942-B.pdf

7. Costanzo, A., et al.: A smartphone application for supporting the data collection and analysis of the cultural heritage damaged during natural disasters. In: Proceedings 2018–2 (ECSA-4 2017), p. 121. MDPI, Basel (2018). https://doi.org/10.3390/ecsa-4-04930

8. Fernandez Freire, C., et al.: A cultural heritage application schema: achieving interoperability of cultural heritage data in inspire. Int. J. Spatial Data Infrastruct. Res. **8**, 74–97 (2013). https://doi.org/10.2902/1725-0463.2013.08.art4

9. Isakhan, B.: Creating the Iraq cultural property destruction database: calculating a heritage destruction index. Int. J. Heritage Stud. **21**(1), 1–21 (2015). https://doi.org/10.1080/13527258.2013.868818

10. Kerski, J., Baker, T.: Infusing educational practice with web GIS. In: de Miguel González, Rafael, Donert, Karl, Koutsopoulos, Kostis (eds.) Geospatial Technologies in Geography Education. KCG, pp. 3–19. Springer, Cham (2019). https://doi.org/10.1007/978-3-030-177 83-6_1

11. Kim, S., Ahn, J., Suh, J., Kim, H., Kim, J.: Towards a semantic data infrastructure for heterogeneous cultural heritage data - challenges of Korean cultural heritage data model (KCHDM). In: Digital Heritage International Conference, pp. 275–282. IEEE, Granada (2015). https://doi.org/10.1109/DigitalHeritage.2015.7419508

12. Krevs, M., et al.: Portal "Uporabna geografija" (Portal "Applied Geography"). https://uporabna.geografija.si/

13. Liu, A., Bowen, J.: Creating online collaborative environments for museums: a case study of a museum wiki. Int. J. Web Based Commun. 7(4), 407 (2011). https://doi.org/10.1504/IJWBC.2011.042988

14. Natale, M.T., Piccininno, M.: Digital cultural heritage and tourism recommendations for cultural institutions. Uncommon Cult. 6(2), 52–64 (2015). https://journals.uic.edu/ojs/index.php/UC/article/view/6204

15. Pelcer–Vujačić, O., Kovačević, S.: A GIS database of montenegrin katuns (Kuči Mountain and Durmitor). In: Ioannides, M., et al. (eds.) EuroMed 2016. LNCS, vol. 10059, pp. 72–80. Springer, Cham (2016). https://doi.org/10.1007/978-3-319-48974-2_9

16. Petrucco, C., Agostini, D.: Teaching cultural heritage using mobile augmented reality. J. e-Learn. Knowl. Soc. 12(3) (2016). https://www.learntechlib.org/p/173477/

17. Register of Cultural Heritage of Slovenia. Open data portal. https://gisportal.gov.si/rkd

18. Rizvić, S., Sadžak, A., Buza, E., Chalmers, A.: Virtual reconstruction and digitalization of cultural heritage sites in Bosnia and Herzegovina. Pregled Nacionalnog centra za digitalizaciju 12, 82–90 (2008)

Short Papers: Remote Sensing
for Archaeology and Cultural Heritage
Management and Monitoring

Geoinformation Technologies for Conservation of Cultural Heritage

Stefan Stamenov[✉] and Vanya Stamenova

Space Research and Technology Institute – Bulgarian Academy of Sciences, Sofia, Bulgaria

Abstract. Cultural heritage today is endangered by many factors, some natural and most of them anthropogenic. The natural factors include vegetation, growing trees, some disasters, as earthquakes, atmospheric processes, etc. Among the anthropogenic factors there is also related to vegetation – agriculture and the cultivated crops, and related to construction activities and mining. Due to these factors the cultural heritage needs careful preservation and conservation activities and measures. The monitoring is probably the best way to provide a constant or frequent observation of the status and condition of the cultural sites. The provided method for monitoring is based on combination of satellite imagery and aerial photos, GIS mapping and integration of all the data into a geodatabase. The case study in this paper is the first capital of Bulgaria, Pliska, one of the most important archaeological reserves in Bulgaria.

Keywords: Monitoring · GIS · Remote sensing · Archaeology · Cultural heritage

1 Introduction and Rationale

Today, as never before, cultural heritage is at risk. Negative processes are resulting primarily from the impact of the modern anthropogenic environment. Archaeological sites are destroyed mainly by massive constructions in urban areas, by mechanized cultivation of agricultural land and by active treasure hunting activity. A large number of archeological sites are also at risk as a result of the implementation of large-scale infrastructure projects (construction of roads, pipelines, railways, hydro facilities). All these problems of preserving the historical heritage place forward the need to develop innovative methods based on geoinformation technologies, which will ensure faster, more accurate and larger collection and storage of information about archaeological sites. The documentation of the current state of the archaeological monuments is essential and the information obtained from it allows to define measures for the conservation of the archaeological site. In recent decades, with the development of technologies, various non-destructive methods have become increasingly used in archaeological research. Their role is growing mainly because they have a non-destructive impact on the site. Non-destructive methods allow us to collect and analyze basic information about the site without interfering with the cultural layer. In archeology, the application of geoinformation technologies solves critical tasks related to the documentation, processing and storage of spatial data for the archaeological site.

M. Ioannides et al. (Eds.): EuroMed 2020, LNCS 12642, pp. 535–542, 2021.
https://doi.org/10.1007/978-3-030-73043-7_45

The preservation of cultural heritage is a priority at national, European and global level, which is enshrined in the Convention concerning the protection of the world cultural and natural heritage, adopted by UNESCO in Paris in 1972 [1], European Convention on the Protection of the Archaeological Heritage, adopted in 1992 in Valletta [2] and Cultural Heritage Act of Republic of Bulgaria [3]. One of the main priorities in European archaeological science, is the digital documentation and storage of information about archaeological sites, as the documentation of archaeological sites is considered as part of their conservation and follow-up activities related to their physical preservation and conservation.

The current paper aims to develop a method for monitoring the current state of archaeological sites, discovered and studied in the past, and those which are only located but not studies yet, based on the use of geoinformation technologies – remote sensing and GIS technologies for the Outer Town of Pliska, the first Bulgarian capital.

2   Study Area and Current State of Research

The Bulgarian Medieval capital Pliska is located in the Northeastern part of Bulgaria, near Shoumen town (Fig. 1). It consists of an Outer town, covering an area of 21,9 km^2 and surrounded by a large earthen rampart and ditch, and an Inner town (Fig. 2). Medieval Pliska is one of the most important archaeological reserves in Bulgaria.

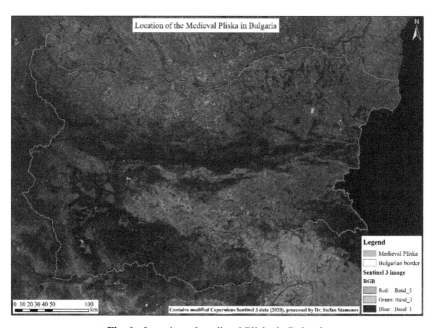

Fig. 1. Location of medieval Pliska in Bulgaria

Due to the huge spatial extent of the Outer City (21.9 km^2) the accumulation of data from its archaeological mapping is a continuous process that began more than 115 years

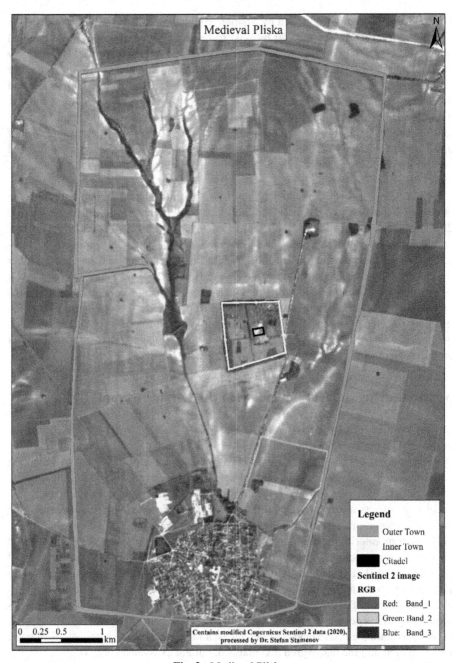

Fig. 2. Medieval Pliska

ago with the first purposeful survey presented in the archaeological map of K. Shkorpil [4] and going through several stages till nowadays. The archaeological mapping of the

Outer city of Pliska was continued by Stamen Mihailov's team in the 1940s and 1950s. They have used the map compiled by Shkorpil and additional discovered and studied objects were added on it [5]. The archaeological survey and mapping of the Outer City continued in the 1980s by Petrova. Her research was the first attempt to map the outer city of Pliska using aerial photographs and their visual deciphering [6]. A complete and detailed map of the Outer City of Pliska was made by Yanko Dimitrov in the 1990s [7, 8 and 9]. The map was made on the basis of the data published until then, as well as terrain surveys and drilling observations conducted by the author. In the framework of a Bulgarian-German research project in 1997−2001 a geophysical survey was carried out, for the purposes of which GIS methods and aerial photographs from the 1980s were used [10].

The first terrain archaeological survey using geoinformation technologies and the building of the first geo-database for the Outer City were carried out in the period 2010−2012, as a part of a research project of NAIM - BAS by a team of SRTI-BAS including the authors of this paper. The geodatabase contains remote sensing data, large-scale topographic maps and archaeological information [11, 12]. It has been further developed and completed within the Ph.D. thesis of Dr. Stefan Stamenov as a result of which the first spatial model for the Outer City of Pliska has been created [13–15 and 16]. The created spatial model provides an opportunity to continue the work on mapping the Outer City of Pliska and to develop methodological approaches based on geoinformation technologies for the purposes of monitoring and preserving the study of archaeological sites on the territory of the Outer town of Pliska.

3   Monitoring the Current State of the Outer Town of Pliska

One of the priorities of the archeological surveys in the Outer Town of Pliska is the purposeful mapping of the monuments, which will contribute to the continuation of the systematic study of the Outer City and to better preservation, research and socialization of the archaeological sites. For sites of high scientific value occupying a large area, where research continues over 100 years, the application of a monitoring system is important because it collects information about the current state of archaeological sites over time and this information serves to plan measures for their management and protection. The GIS-based monitoring of the archeological sites in the Outer town of Pliska is based on the already developed spatial model of the Outer town of Pliska and the created geodatabase [13]. The geodatabase should be further supplemented and updated with information on the archaeological sites that will be monitored, retrieved from the available publications. The essence of the proposed monitoring includes three main parts - monitoring the vegetation cover; monitoring agricultural activities like cultivating soil, plowing, planting, etc. and land cover changes; and monitoring the archaeological sites, both explored and the discovered and mapped, but not excavated (Fig. 3).

The monitoring of the natural vegetation includes recognizing the different types of vegetation – trees, shrubs, herbaceous and observing their changes, especially in the areas where archaeological sites are discovered and explored. These observations are performed using high resolution satellite images. The visual interpretation and vegetation indexes as NDVI and SAVI are used for fast analysis of the vegetation cover for the

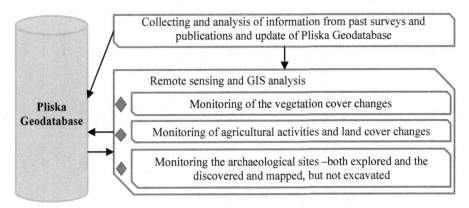

Fig. 3. GIS-based monitoring of the archaeological sites in the outer town of Pliska

whole territory of Pliska. The self-growing shrubs and trees around the archaeological sites make the sites difficult to access and also destroy them.

The regular monitoring on yearly basis of the agricultural activities is important for the conservation and preservation of the archaeological sites and cultural heritage of the Outer town of Pliska, because most of its territory is used for agriculture as seen from the map of the land cover (Fig. 4).

The Outer town of Pliska is an archaeological reserve, where only certain agricultural activities are allowed. The plowing of the fields should be done no more than 30 cm in depth in order to protect the undiscovered and unexplored archaeological sites on the territory of Medieval Pliska. Another restriction related with the agricultural activities is that the planting of orchards and perennials is prohibited. This requires the changes of the land cover types also to be monitored, especially the changes in the agricultural lands, as well as the new construction activities, including changes on the territory of the modern town of Pliska, located in the southern part of the Outer town. The information about which fields are sown and which are plowed is extremely important also for the planning and conducting of terrain archeological surveys of new sites.

Besides monitoring the entire area of the Outer city, the individual archaeological sites should be monitored as well. The already explored sites and the sites under exploration should be documented regularly after conductance of archaeological surveys and excavations using UAVs or satellite data. Some of the discovered and explored sites are overgrown with shrubs and trees, which not only make it difficult to access them, but also the root system of the trees can damage and destroy the archaeological remains.

The archaeological sites which are only discovered and mapped on the field, but not explored yet are threatened by the agricultural land cultivation. The risk is that the archaeological remains beneath the surface can be destroyed during the plowing. Some of the discovered in the past archaeological sites are left as unplowed areas in the fields and farmers do not have to cultivate them. The monitoring of these sites is very important, because sometimes these recommendations are not strictly followed, and during the process of visual interpretation of aerial photos from 2006 and 2010 and satellite image

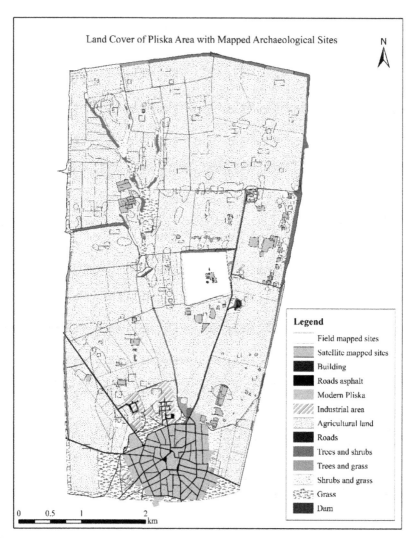

Fig. 4. Land cover of Pliska with all mapped archaeological sites by Shkorpil, Mihailov, Petrova, Dimitrov and Stamenov (4, 5, 6, 9, and 13)

from 2009 we found that some sites have been plowed, and the information for them can be lost. Examples of such archaeological sites are shown on Fig. 5 and Fig. 6.

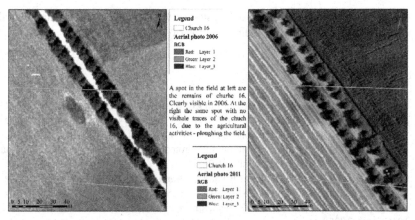

Fig. 5. Archaeological site (church 16 according to the nomenclature of Pliska archaeological sites) destroyed by plowing the agricultural field

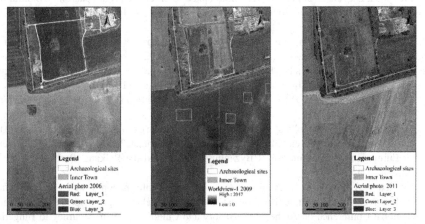

Fig. 6. Destroyed archaeological site as a result of agricultural land cultivation, located southern of the Inner town of Pliska

4   Conclusions

The monuments of the Bulgarian Early Medieval capital Pliska are an important part of our cultural heritage and are extremely important for the national identity and as a part of the European archaeological science, they provide important information about the development of the main centers in Early Medieval Europe. The importance of the terrain archaeological survey and mapping of the archeological sites in the Outer Town of Pliska is indisputable, because the lack of specific information about its settlement structure in the written sources. The remote sensing methods and GIS technologies provides for better documentation of the archaeological sites and thus contribute to the conservation and preservation of the cultural heritage. The development of a GIS-based methods for monitoring the archaeological sites serves for regular documentation of the archaeological sites and tracking their condition over time.

References

1. Convention concerning the protection of the world cultural and natural heritage. UNESCO. Adopted by the Council of Ministers of Bulgaria on February 4, 1974 and in force since 17 September 1975, promulgated in State Gazette (SG), Issue 44 of 27 May 2005
2. ETS No.143 European Convention on the Protection of the Archaeological Heritage (Revised), CoE 1992. Accessed 7 July 2012
3. Cultural Heritage Act of Republic of Bulgaria, promulgated in State Gazette (SG), Issue 19 of 13.03.2009, amended issue 16/26.02.2016, issue 52/8.07.2016
4. Шкорпил, К.: Материалы для болгарских древностей. АбобаПлиска. ИРАИК т. 10, София (1905)
5. Михайлов Ст.: Археологически материали от Плиска/1948 – 1951г./. Известия на Археологическия институт XX, 49 – 191 (1955)
6. Петрова, П.: Към въпроса за историко-археологическата топография на Външния град на Плиска по данни на аерометода. В: Плиска–Преслав, том 5, pp. 44–76, Шумен (1992)
7. Димитров, Я.: Нови данни за археологическата карта на Плиска В: Приноси към българската археология, т. 1, pp. 58–67, София (1992)
8. Димитров, Я.: Плиска. Материали за картата на средновековната българска държава. В: Плиска-Преслав, т. 7, pp. 247–263, Шумен (1995)
9. Рашев, Р., Димитров, Я.: Плиска - 100 години археологически разкопки. Шумен (1999)
10. Henning, J.: The metropolis of Pliska or, how large does an early medieval settlement have to be in order to be called a city? In: Henning J. (ed.) Post-Roman Towns, Trade and Settlement in Europe and Byzantium vol. 2 Byzantium, Pliska, and the Balkans, Berlin-New York, pp. 209–241 (2007)
11. Stamenov, S., Aladjov, A.: Application of geographic information systems for surveying archaeological site Pliska. In: Bulgaria in the World Cultural Heritage – Papers from the Third National Conference on Archeology, History and Cultural Tourism - Journey to Bulgaria, pp. 675–692, "Konstantin Preslavski" University of Shoumen, Shoumen (2014)
12. Aladjov, A., et al.: Archaeological map of Pliska NIAM-BAS. Sofia (2013)
13. Stamenov, S.: Spatial model and chronological analysis of the medieval town of Pliska based on aerospace and ground-based data. Prof. Marin Drinov Publishing House of Bulgarian Academy of Sciences, Sofia (2019)
14. Stamenov, S.: Computer-aided visual interpretation of WorldView-1 satellite image of the Medieval Town of Pliska. In: Proceedings of the Sixth Scientific Conference with International Participation Space Ecology Safety – SES 2010, Sofia, pp. 284 – 288 (2011)
15. Stamenov, S.: Modern land cover and land use of the outer town of the medieval Bulgarian capital Pliska using satellite images with high spatial resolution. In: Proceedings of the 7th Scientific Conference Space Ecology Safety – SES 2011, Sofia, pp. 236 – 240 (2012)
16. Stamenov, S., Naydenova, V., Aladjov, A.: GIS-based concept for conservation of the archaeological site of Pliska. In: Naydenova, V., Stamenov, S. (eds.) Proceedings of the First European SCGIS conference "Best practices: Application of GIS technologies for conservation of natural and cultural heritage sites", pp. 63–71, SRTI-BAS, Sofia (2012)

The Application of Digital Integration Strategy for Cultural Heritage Conservation – the Case Study of Qionglin Settlement in Kinmen County

Alex Yen[✉], Wun-Bin Yang, Hui-Chun Chang, and Chao-Shiang Li

China University of Technology, No. 56, Sec. 3, Hsing-Lung Rd, 116 Taipei, Taiwan
alexyen@cute.edu.tw

Abstract. Integrated preservation is an important trend in the maintenance of cultural heritage, and borrowing value is the benchmark. Preserving the tangible and intangible value, counseling public participation and digital technology activation are all important tasks. In the process, mature digital tools are used for dating and assist to strengthen preservation work is an important key internationally at this stage.

This research takes the reconstruction of the historical site program- Reconstruction of Qionglin's Millennium Settlement History as an example to explore how to plan and individually introduce and integrate strategies for digital technology in each project.

The results of the study found that the introduction of digital technology into the sub-projects accelerate efficiency but also the effectiveness of the program. At the same time, the results of the program can be integrated through pre-planning and placed on the geographic information system (GIS) platform, fully interactive and efficiently.

Keywords: Cultural heritage · Digital integration strategy · Qionglin settlement

1 Introduction

More than 80 years have passed since the 1931 "Athens Charter" was issued. Many international charters and conventions have been proposed internationally, mainly focusing on the preservation, restoration, and maintenance of cultural heritage, supplemented by records for preservation and research. The "Quebec Declaration" adopted by the 16th General Assembly of ICOMOS in 2008 noted:

Considering that modern digital technologies (digital databases, websites) can be used efficiently and effectively at a low cost to develop multimedia inventories that integrate tangible and intangible elements of heritage, we strongly recommend their widespread use in order to better preserve, disseminate and promote heritage places and their spirit. These technologies facilitate the diversity and constant renewal of the documentation on the spirit of place.

© Springer Nature Switzerland AG 2021
M. Ioannides et al. (Eds.): EuroMed 2020, LNCS 12642, pp. 543–553, 2021.
https://doi.org/10.1007/978-3-030-73043-7_46

In the same year, "ICOMOS Charter on the Interpretation and Presentation of Cultural Heritage Sites" also stated that "International cooperation and sharing of experience are essential to developing and maintaining standards in interpretation methods and technologies."

The digital technology of cultural heritage in practices, including the investigation and research of cultural heritage conservation, restoration design, operation management, disaster prevention monitoring and social education, as well as other stages of integration work, the public participation, digital learning, and value-added applications. The innovative management system should be integrated to further establish a cognitive business model based on a digital platform. This study takes the Regeneration of Historic Site Program in Qionglin settlement of Kinmen as an example. It enables tangible and intangible cultural heritage to obtain effective understanding, interpretation and added value, as well as sustainable inheritance, forming a complete cultural heritage preservation system.

2   The Process of Digital Technology Assisting the Preservation of Cultural Heritage in Taiwan

The early digital preservation in Taiwan was mainly used for historical materials, paintings and images in museums, and for the extensive preservation of flat objects; while cultural relics and antiquities were mostly preserved in physical objects, with little further involvement. In recent years, regarding the technology of digital preservation of cultural heritage, due to the trend of the International Charter for the Conservation of Cultural heritage and the widespread use of related technologies, Taiwan has gradually developed digital solutions for the preservation of cultural heritage. Through the use of different types of digital technologies, hope the complete preservation of tangible and intangible cultural heritage has opened a milestone in the digital preservation of cultural heritage.

In the past decade, the process of digitization has accumulated a considerable amount of digitization projects, but for such a wide range of collection projects, there is still a problem of integrated resources for cultural heritage projects. Cultural heritage is important knowledge inherited by predecessors, and are also important competitive assets and business opportunities in various countries. How to effectively apply them? The above international trends can see the blueprint for the preservation of cultural heritage in the future. In addition to the assistance of digital technology, it must also incorporate knowledge and research from different disciplines to achieve the integrity preservation of cultural heritage. Thus, the concept of "digital integration" technology is an important topic at present; only a good knowledge management policy can achieve the continuation and renewal of cultural heritage use. The digital application of cultural heritage refers to how to effectively apply the data after production and management to practice. The technology of digitizing cultural heritage has gradually moved from individual technologies to the concept of "integration" of data (Fig. 1).

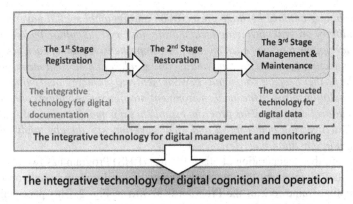

Fig. 1. Conceptual diagram of the integrative technology for digital cognition and operation.

3   Regeneration of Historic Sites Program: Reconstruction of Qionglin's Millennium Settlement History

3.1   The Launch of the Regeneration of Historic Sites Program

Taiwan's cultural heritage has been preserving since the promulgation of the Cultural Heritage Preservation Act in 1982. After nearly 40 years of hard work and accumulated experience, the Cultural Heritage Bureau was established in 2012, and Taiwan's cultural heritage preservation has also become more mature. Under the influence of international trends, the cognition of cultural heritage has tended to be diversified, and the interpretation and presentation of value are not limited to architecture and history. It requires the integration of multiple disciplines and departments and effectively presents the cultural heritage. The value of culture must be transformed from a single architecture to the concept of "sites" by effectively presenting the meaning and value of cultural heritage to the country, place, and people.

In order to further implement the Cultural Heritage Preservation Act, the Ministry of Culture launched the Regeneration of Historic Sites Program which selects 39 sites across Taiwan to benefit from the investment of 6.4 billion NT dollars since 2016. The Program aims to revitalize cultural heritage resources at a community level and also to regenerate the regional cultural landscape through public investment. It is promoted as a cultural citizen movement by including continuing community engagement and conversations to raise the awareness of cultural heritage conservation. In addition, the Program takes historical memory and the cultural context into account by considering the pluralistic imagination and uses of the heritage space. This leads to the reconnection of the contemporary community with heritage places through their involvement with cultural governance (MOC 2018). Based on the core concept of cultivating cultural development and increasing cultural engagement,

The program transcended conventional single-point, single-building, and case-by-case cultural heritage preservation methods and proposed the regeneration of historic sites as the central tenet for a public infrastructure investment project.

By combining cultural heritage preservation and regional spatial governance, this interdisciplinary program involving local culture, history, and culture technology combines the development plan of each ministry or comprehensive plan of each government, thereby connecting locals to the land and recalling relevant historical memories.

With the further deepens community development and promotes local culture residing in people's relationship with the local environment, strengthening culture connotations to boost the cultural economy. This program establishes a comprehensive cultural preservation policy involving both central and local governments, thereby applying culture preservation into civilian lifestyles.

At present, the Regeneration of Historic Sites (RHS) Program has twenty-two "onsite" projects to implement the integrative policy of local-culture-based conservation. The conceptual framework of the Program is shown in Fig. 2. This paper takes 'Representing the Glory of Thousand-year Settlement in Qionglin'- one of the RHS projects as the study case.

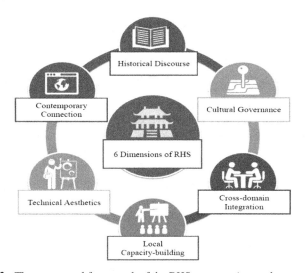

Fig. 2. The conceptual framework of the RHS program (www.rhs-moc.tw/).

3.2   Reconstruction of Qionglin's Millennium Settlement History

Qionglin settlement was listed as heritage in 2012; the local communities work together with the public sectors and scholars by proposing the "Qonglin Settlement Preservation and Redevelopment Plan" in 2013–2014. Based on the previous conservation works and the collective consensus, the "Reconstruction of Qionglin's Millennium Settlement History" program was preceded with 43 sub-projects from 2017 to 2021.

Background. Qionglin is a settlement with traditional clan culture at its core. It is situated within the Kinmen National Park. Qionglin is a highlight among the 150 traditional settlements of Kinmen because it conserves more than 400 traditional buildings while also supporting a wealth of intangible cultural heritage values. The settlement reflects the continued conservation of the living culture of Southern Fujian culture including festivals and important folk traditions. The number of Qionglin's ancestral temples and the beauty of architecture are also crowned in the whole county (Fig. 3–5). The Qionglin ancestor's cautious pursuit of the ancestors is the example of "Living Minnan Culture". In 2012, Qionglin Settlement was designated as the historic settlement according to Taiwan's Cultural Heritage Preservation Act.

Fig. 3. The view of Qionglin settlement.

Fig. 4. Location of Kinmen on the map of Taiwan.

Qionglin is a singly-surnamed Tsai village, beginning from the time that the Tsai Clan moved from Guang Zhou to Fujian, as far back as the Five Dynasties (907–960 A.D.). The residents all share the same family name–Tsai. It is apparent that the core for shaping the existence of Qionglin Settlement, including its historical development, the spatial composition, and the prosperity of Tsai families, lies in its clan-based traditions (CPRC 2017). Kinmen's clan-based culture adheres to Chinese traditional values handed down from ancient times and has been further nurtured by Southern Fujian traditions. Although like most of the island of Kinmen, it has been impacted by the diaspora cultures brought back by the returning emigrants and by a strong military presence, the village

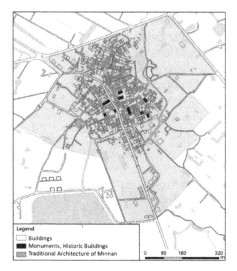

Fig. 5. The monuments and historic buildings in Qionglin settlement.

stands as an example of credible Living Heritage manifested by the architectural designs of the ancestral shrines, ancestor worship and other religious rituals, the organization and maintenance of lineages – each of which, in turn, is profoundly connected with the formation of the settlement texture and the life of its people. A farming-schooling-based tradition is advocated by the clan-based culture in the Qionglin settlement.

Objectives. In 2013–2014, combined with the participation of the public, a consensus was formed to complete the "Qionglin Settlement Preservation and Redevelopment Plan". In July 2016, the Kinmen County Government, in line with the cultural policy of the Central Government's "Reconstruction of Historical Sites Project", the Kinmen County Bureau of Culture proposed the "Qionglin Chua's Millennium Settlement Reproduction" project. The plan is divided into 4 years and the total funding is approximately US$ 6.93 million, the main goals are:

Strengthen the investigation, research, and planning of cross-domain integration of cultural heritage in Qionglin settlement.

Implement the participation of residents in Qionglin settlement and promote multiculturalism.

Establish the integrity of the basic information and digital files of cultural heritage in the Qionglin settlement.

Preserve intangible cultural heritage and folklore activity guidance and training.

Develop the digital preservation of cultural heritage, and promote the establishment and navigation of historical space scientific and technological resources.

Sharing the experience of rebuilding the historical site, and driving the preservation and activation of the Kinmen settlement.

The execution conception of Qionglin's RHS Program (Fig. 6) is based on the diversification of cultural heritage values, the places conservation, the application of digital technology, and the connection between the tangible/intangible cultural heritage and the grassroots. It aims to establish a cultural heritage conservation ecosystem by streaming cultural contents into the creative economy.

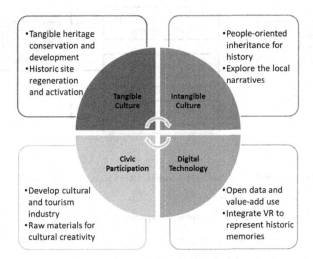

Fig. 6. The execution conception of Qionglin's RHS program.

The Program's Framework. The development of 'Reconstruction of Qionglin's Millennium Settlement History' integrates the previous heritage conservation initiatives as the foundation. The framework of the program is shown in Fig. 7. The sharing of experience is also part of the main tasks in the RHS Project. Besides taking Qionglin as the main object, it aims to extend the influence to other settlements in Kinmen.

4   Execution Strategy

4.1   UNESCO World Heritage 5Cs Strategic Objectives

By highlighting the value of Kinmen culture, this program will be based on the concept of world heritage described in "Operational Guidelines for the Implementation of the World Heritage Convention (2015)", and will discuss and discuss Kinmen's core value in depth. In 2007, the 5Cs strategy for the implementation of World Heritage Convention (WHC 2018) was promoted by the World Heritage Committee, based on the Budapest Declaration (2002's 4Cs strategy) by including the 'fifth C' for 'Communities' (See Fig. 8). This means that the integration of various government sectors and the community are recognized as an extremely important aspect of heritage conservation work. Heritage and Democracy was the main theme of 2017 ICOMOS General Assembly, emphasizing issues relevant to the communities impacted by World Heritage listings.

The execution strategy of this case is the implementation of concepts such as "bottom-up integration, cultural-based spatial governance", and integrates the concept of 5Cs strategy into this case. The content is explained as follows:

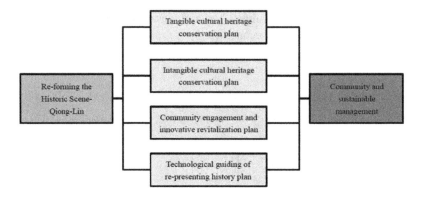

– Scene: Qionglin settlement, 8 national monuments, 400 traditional buildings, battlefield
   governance.

– History: 1600-year traditional settlement and living Southern Fujian culture

– Re-presenting: Ancestor worship in Qionglin, seasonal events and festivals, folk life

Fig. 7. The reconstruction of Qionglin's Millennium settlement history program's framework.

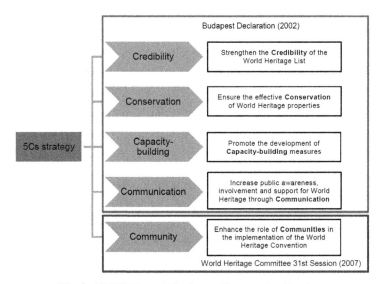

Fig. 8. UNESCO world heritage 5Cs strategic objectives.

Credibility. Complete basic research materials to support the development of related industries, cultural creation, tourism, talent training, and marketing.

Conservation. In addition to the protection of cultural heritage in the settlement, other software and hardware construction are also important tasks. Related work includes the restoration and landscape renovation of traditional buildings, dilapidated houses, street houses and modern buildings in Qionglin settlement.

Capacity Building. It includes the preservation of cultural heritage is combined with school education and the curriculum is introduced; Integrated marketing and promotion of local cultural industry; and Training of local interpreters.

Communication. Actively communicate with Qionglin local NGOs and invite them to serve as consultants in this case. In addition to communication with the private sectors, the integration and coordination of the public sectors are also ongoing.

Community. It includes Qionglin settlement annual calendar and activity calendar; Local creation and identification support, encouraging communities from all walks of life to participate in the preservation, activation and value-added use of cultural heritage; as well as cultural heritage education and inheritance, schools are encouraged to handle cultural resources and environmental education activities and teaching plan design, inherit teaching, take root down, and continue to improve and popularize culture and art.

4.2   The Preliminary Project-in-Progress: Digital Interpretation and Presentation of Cultural Heritage Based on Knowledge Ontology

This case uses the ontology to establish the interpretation data of the life cycle of cultural heritage, including tangible and intangible cultural heritage data and based on the CIDOC CRM (CIDOC Conceptual Reference Model) as the foundation of the ontology, importing the contents of the current national cultural heritage database in Taiwan and establish a knowledge ontology model. The presentation platform uses the Arches presentation platform based on international interpretation data standards and combines advanced geographic information system functions to improve traditional database search and organization problems and enhance the relevance of data context. It is positive for the promotion of Taiwan's cultural heritage in line with international standards the meaning.

This Qionglin program team participates the Arches- an open-source software platform developed jointly by the Getty Conservation Institute and World Monuments Fund for cultural heritage data management. The Arches Platform is a comprehensive solution for data management, data discovery and visualization, and project/task management. The digital resources of Qionglin settlement are available on the platform since January 2020 (Fig. 9), in which shows the information of cultural heritage based on the concept of Cultural Heritage Lifecycle in different types, including the data of basic designated registrations, surveys, management-and-maintenances.

Digital technology for the conservation of cultural heritage has moved towards more diverse and different types of technologies, including data interception technology, data management, communication media and knowledge promotion, etc. In order to enhance the demand and presentation of cultural heritage value interpretation, the application of integrated digital technology and data content is the important key, and the integration results will promote the future development and value-added application of Qionglin settlement. Figure 10 shows the digital integration system for Kinmen Qionglin.

Fig. 9. Kinmen Qionglin on the Arches platform (kinmen.cute.edu.tw/).

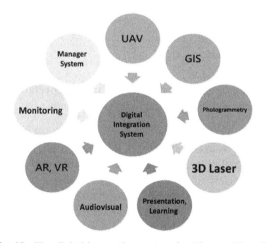

Fig. 10. The digital integration system for Kinmen Qionglin.

5   Conclusion

With the coming of the 21st century, a variety of well-developed new technologies offer a great addition to more traditional conservation and restoration techniques. At the same time, the development of Digital Technology not only provides faster and more accurate information to the record of cultural heritage (Documentation) but also advances the use of data; value-added applications (AR, VR, MR); and virtual classrooms taking access to best heritage conservation practice to an unprecedented level. The benefit of Digital Cultural Heritage (DCH) is now an essential issue that cannot be neglected.

It is an inevitable trend to use digital technology to assist in the preservation of cultural heritage. With the development of society and technological advancement, an integrated preservation structure is an inevitable trend. In the case of Kinmen Qionglin, the implementation mechanism of settlement preservation and redevelopment was established based on the concept of World Heritage 5Cs, and the corresponding digital technology was also introduced. The results of the implementation found:

Digital technology is getting mature and universal. However, in the process of implementation, how to grasp the essence of cultural heritage and properly interpret and present them is an important key to success and effectiveness.

3D GIS can provide a platform for the integration and presentation of various digital data.

The format and standard of the data are still important issues in the integration of various digital results, especially when the data needs to be opened and exchanged. This work that is set by the country and shared with the world cannot be avoided.

At present, the work of reconstructing the historical site in Qionglin is still under implementation and is expected to be completed in August 2021.

Due to the gradual expansion of the scope and direction of development of cultural heritage, the required management and monitoring data are also multiplying. An integrated management platform should be used to achieve proper management. With the development of digital preservation concepts and technology, based on the concept of cultural heritage preservation and management, it is possible to achieve a common exchange of archive formats in the future. In terms of education, the application of digital integration strategy in cultural heritage should be widely promoted, and relevant materials should be provided to increase the awareness of cultural heritage conservation, such as public inquiry, action navigation, action management, management and maintenance application, disaster prevention and monitoring, 3D GIS dynamic information and other diversified enhancements. Digital value-added platforms will make a broader contribution to the preservation, activation and reuse of cultural heritage in the future.

Acknowledgement. Thanks for the supports from Ministry of Science and Technology, the Interdisciplinary Research Project, MOST-108-2625-M-163 -001, and the Bureau of Cultural Heritage, Ministry of Culture, the College of Cultural Heritage Project, 109-Re-12 to this study.

References

World Heritage Committee. Operational guidelines for the implementation of the World Heritage Convention. UNESCO World Heritage Centre (2008)

ICOMOS. The ICOMOS Charter for the Interpretation and Presentation of Cultural Heritage Sites (2008)

ICOMOS. Québec Declaration on the Preservation of the Spirit of Place (2008)

ICOMOS. The Athens Charter for the restoration of historic monuments (1931)

WHC, World Heritage Centre. The 'fifth C' for 'Communities', (2018). https://whc.unesco.org/en/decisions/5197/. Accessed 2 July 2018

MOC, Ministry of Culture. The Information Counselling Platform for Regeneration of Historic Sites Program, (2018). http://www.rhs-moc.tw/index.php?inter=about&id=1. Accessed 2 Oct 2020

Land Movements Estimation in Amathus Archaeological Site in Limassol District with In- SAR DIn-SAR Methodologies

Despina Makri[✉], Athos Agapiou, Diofantos Hadjimitsis, and Christiana Papoutsa

Cyprus University of Technology, Archbishop Kyprianos Street 30, 3036 Limassol, Cyprus
dn.makri@edu.cut.ac.cy

Abstract. Amathus archaeological site is one of the most important monuments (memorials), which remains for up to 2300 years. Last decades, archaeological sites, face anthropogenic and natural disturbances. One of those is the land movements that come from landslides or earthquakes. Improved remote-sensing techniques and new data more contemporary can assist in archaeology because it provides extensive area coverage and access in difficult-to-reach archaeological sites. In the present study, we investigate the use of Synthetic Aperture Radar Interferometry (InSAR) in land movement estimation near archaeological sites. We applied the D-InSAR (Differential Synthetic Aperture Radar Interferometry) methodology in Sentinel-1 data. These data are free and available from Copernicus Open Access Hub. The methodological framework was implemented in SNAP software (Sentinel Applications Platform), which is free and available from the European Space Agency. The analysis had three main steps: a) to prepare the data and check the suitability, b) the production of the interferogram, and c) the production of displacement map in meter units. The results have shown that in the area of interest, the hazard of land movement is low.

The abstract should summarize the contents of the paper in short terms, i.e. 150–250 words.

Keywords: Archaeological site · Amathus · Land movement estimation

1 Introduction

The archaeological sites are alive parts of our cultural heritage. Land movement estimation close to cultural heritage sites is crucial for the protection and conservation of the monuments. The technique which is the most widespread (common) in land movement estimation is the InSAR- Interferometric Synthetic Aperture Radar [1–7]. These studies have shown the significance and the ability of the technique in emergencies and the success in the monitoring of hazardous areas. On the contrary, Mantovani et al. 2019 find suitable the method for the majority of dynamic phenomena, although the application in active landslides is still tricky. The Interferometric Synthetic Aperture Radar can be implemented with two primary techniques the Differential SAR Interferometry (DInSAR) and the Persistent Scatterer Interferometry (PSI). DInSAR is an affordable

© Springer Nature Switzerland AG 2021
M. Ioannides et al. (Eds.): EuroMed 2020, LNCS 12642, pp. 554–561, 2021.
https://doi.org/10.1007/978-3-030-73043-7_47

method that provides quantitive data (measurements) of ground deformation in the case of subsidence [8]. The method uses SAR images to produce displacement maps. The Differential SAR Interferometry is described in various studies which concern ground deformation [1, 8–10]. PSI is the technique that uses groups of DInSAR image stacks for the purpose of the estimation of ground deformation [11]. This technique uses data time series and allows the investigation of spatio-temporal variability of terrain deformation [4, 11, 12]. The comparison of two methods DInSAR and PSI accomplished in the study of Fárová et al. (2019). In the validation, with in situ measurements, the PSI technique corresponded better.

Last six years, technological advancements contribute to Earth observation with new and more accurate instruments. Sentinel-1 satellite scan the Earth in wide-area coverage, every six days, providing with different types of high-resolution data. Sentinel-1 imagery is a useful tool for different types of deformation, for example, caused by earthquakes [2, 3, 6] or by mining [8]. The data can be used for landslides detection [5] or to monitor Highway stability [10]. The majority of the studies stated in the suitability of the data. The open-access policy, under the Copernicus program, in conjunction with the wide-area coverage with different resolution for four modes, make Sentinel-1 data helpful in the research community.

In the present study, we demonstrate preliminary results produced by the DInSAR technique for the estimation of land movement and the risk assessment near archaeological sites. The analysis was carried out in the framework of a European funded project: RESEARCH — H2020-MSCA-RISE-2018.

2 Data-Methodology

The archaeological site of Amathus is an ancient city which is dated back to 300 BC. In this city, the kingdom was built. Amathus is located in the Limassol district on the southern coast of Cyprus (34° 42' 45" N, 33° 08' 30" E). Amathus is a large ground surface that covers about 0,4 km^2 and has eight significant monuments such as the Acropolis, Agora and baths, the palace, the temple of Aphrodite, the port, the Walls, the Necropolis, and the Basilicas. The remains of the town can be found till today, in Limassol, close to Agios Tychonas.

For the land movement estimation in Amathus archaeological site, Sentinel-1A SAR (Synthetic Aperture Radar) observations were used. Satellite Sentinel-1A was launched in the spring of 2014 with Copernicus Programme from European Space Agency (ESA). The high temporal resolution (every twelve days for Sentinel-1A or every six days for Sentinel-1B) and the difference in spatial resolution, accordingly the imaging mode (e.g., IW, EW, SM, WV), make the data useful for many applications. In the present study, the data used had a spatial resolution of 5 × 20 m and coverage 250 km and provided free from Copernicus Open Access Hub (website last visit: 09/2020: https://scihub.cop ernicus.eu/dhus/#/home). We used a pair of Sentinel-1A images and implemented the interferometric analysis.

- S1A_IW_SLC__1SDV_20200307T035122_20200307T035148_031564 _03A2F8_3D60

- S1A_IW_SLC__1SDV_20200705T035127_20200705T035154_033314
  _03DC1C_EBDA (Fig. 1) and (Fig. 2), Table 1.

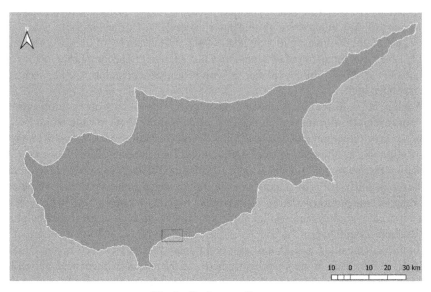

Fig. 1. Study area- Cyprus

The data processing chain is applied in the Sentinel Application Platform (SNAP) software (version 7.0.0 since 09/2020) that is freely available from ESA's website (http://step.esa.int/main/download/snap-download/). After downloading data, we check the suitability of the image pair creating a stack. In this stack is measured the coherence between the two images. The coherence has values between 0 and 1. The higher the rate, the more accurate the interferometric analysis will be. The coherence is a measure that changes as a consequence of the different land cover types. For example, urban and constructing areas are more coherent in comparison with vegetated areas that can change the coherence. In reality, the changes in coherence values are changes in the phase noise. [1, 2].

The methodological framework continues with the production of the interferogram. In this step, a Digital Elevation Model (DEM) subtracts the topographic phase. Next, the Multilook reduces the speckle noise, and the Goldstein filter enhances the output. With the use of the SNAPHU operator, we accomplish the phase unwrapping. Next, the unwrapped phase converts to displacement, and finally, the results are geometrically corrected, and the relative displacement converts to measurable displacement.

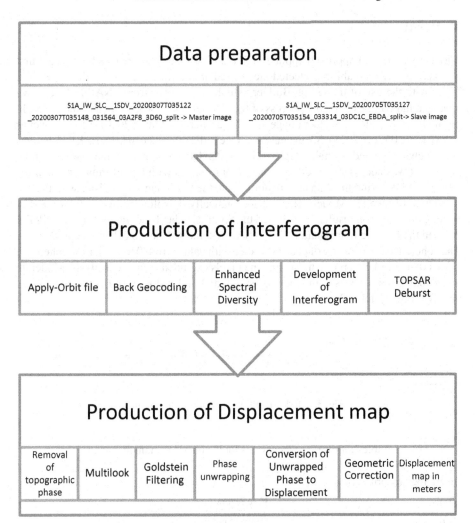

Fig. 2. Data processing chain for land movement estimation

Table 1. Sentinel-1 characteristics

	Characteristics	
Sentinel-1A	**Mode**	Interferometric wide swath
	Polarization	VV + VH (dual)
	Level	L1
	Product type	SLC

3   Results

The methodological approach applied in SNAP software. The imported data were first checked for their suitability, selected the desired area of interest, and finally were split. Then, with the use of the Graph Builder, which is provided from SNAP Software, we created a model to execute the process of the Interferogram formation automatically. In the analysis, we select the older image as a master (here 07 March 2020) and the newer as a slave (here 05 July 2020). So, the master image is the reference map to track the changes in the new image and is finally depicted in the displacement map. In the first step of the process, it was necessary to add metadata in our images with the information about the satellite Orbit during the data acquisition. Then, the two images coregister with the use of a Digital Elevation Model, which is automatically downloaded by the software. For better Coregistration results, we selected the Shuttle Radar Topography Mission (SRTM 3 s) and the Bicubic Interpolation. The InSAR technique leads to coherence production. The coherence is a measure of phase variance with values from 0 to 1 [2]. Low coherence values 0−0.3 indicate phase noise, and the pixels excluded from the analysis. Moderate values 0.3–0.6 are pixels with land movement, and high values 0.6–1 is the no changes area [2] (Fig. 3) Table 2.

Fig. 3. Model-1- production of interferogram

Table 2. Processing parameters for the intereferogram formation

Interferogram formation	
Tools	Parameters
Orbit state	Sentinel precise
Digital elevation model (DEM)	Shuttle radar topography mission (SRTM 3 s)
DEM resampling method	Bicubic interpolation
Polarization	VV (Vertical- Vertical)

After the interferogram formation, we created a second model for the next methodological steps. First, we exclude from the analysis the influence of the elevation, with the use of a DEM (SRTM 3 s). In this step, a topographic phase band is derived. The Multilook reduces the phase noise, and the Goldstein phase filtering enhances the signal-to-noise ratio. As a result, the quality of the produced interferogram (Fig. 4).

Fig. 4. Model-2- data preparation for the production of the displacement map

Till now, the interferogram is in the wrapped phase within the scale of 2π. The interferometric phase transforms to topographic height with the unwrapping operation, with the SNAPHU software. After this process, we convert the unwrapped phase to relative displacement (the pixels have a metric value). Finally, the image is geometrically corrected with WGS 84, and the low coherence pixels are excluded from the produced displacement map.

The data processing chain we followed led in the production of a displacement map. The vertical displacement values ranged from -90 mm$-$ 130 mm. In the analysis, we excluded the pixels with low and moderate coherence> 0.6. We did not take into consideration the vegetated areas because of their seasonal changes. The displacement map refers to the unchanged areas such as urban areas.

In the present study, the displacement in the Amathus archaeological site is 0 mm. No displacement detected in any of the monuments such as the Acropolis, Agora and baths, the palace, the temple of Aphrodite, the port, the Walls, the Necropolis, and the Basilicas. However, near the archaeological site, there are constructed areas (urban, ndustrial areas, or leisure facilities) that seem to be affected by the deformation (Fig. 5).

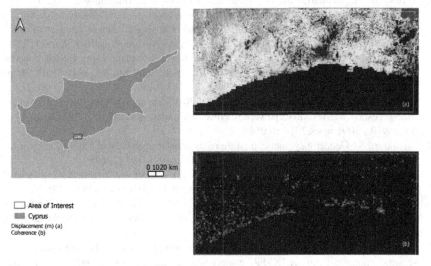

Fig. 5. Displacement map

4   Conclusion

This work concentrated on the land movement estimation, and the potential hazard may have on cultural heritage sites, such as Amathus archaeological site, Limassol. We present the preliminary results of our analysis. In the methodology we followed, we deduced that the area is not affected by land movements. However, urban and industrial areas near the site have a considerable impact. We used open-source software SNAP/SNAPHU, which are provided from the European Space Agency (ESA) (http://step.esa.int/main/download/snap-download/).

One of the essential tools for the protection and conservation of archaeological sites is monitoring. From 2014, that launched Sentinel-1, we have big availability in SAR images, free of charge, providing wide-area coverage for four modes and a medium spatial resolution. In this way, Sentinel-1 data seem to be a powerful tool in the field of archaeology.

The D-InSAR technique is a cost-effective technique that very quickly, we can have significant results for the area of interest. This technique can be used complementary in monitoring and the decision making for the stakeholders. Limitations of the Sentinel-1 still exist, as the vegetated areas cannot be recorded effectively.

Acknowledgments. This work is supported by the Research Executive Agency (REA) under the powers delegated by the European Commission under Grant Agreement number: 823987 — RESEARCH — H2020-MSCA-RISE-2018.

References

1. Tzouvaras, M., Kouhartsiouk, D., Agapiou, A., Danezis, C., Hadjimitsis, D.G.: The use of Sentinel-1 synthetic aperture radar (SAR) images and open-source software for cultural heritage: an example from paphos area in Cyprus for mapping landscape changes after a 5.6 magnitude earthquake. Remote Sens. **11**, 1–13 (2019). https://doi.org/10.3390/rs11151766
2. Goorabi, A.: Detection of landslide induced by large earthquake using InSAR coherence techniques – Northwest Zagros, Iran. Egypt. J. Remote Sens. Sp. Sci. 0–10 (2019). https://doi.org/10.1016/j.ejrs.2019.04.002
3. Dias, P., Catalao, J., Marques, F.O.: Sentinel-1 InSAR data applied to surface deformation in Macaronesia (Canaries and Cape Verde). Procedia Comput. Sci. **138**, 382–387 (2018). https://doi.org/10.1016/j.procs.2018.10.054
4. Montazeri, S.: Geodetic synthetic aperture radar interferometry. DLR Dtsch. Zent. fur Luft- und Raumfahrt e.V. - Forschungsberichte. 2019-January, 1–197 (2019)
5. Mantovani, M., et al.: New perspectives in landslide displacement detection using sentinel-1 datasets. Remote Sens. **11**(18), 2135 (2019). https://doi.org/10.3390/rs11182135
6. Dai, K., et al.: Monitoring activity at the Daguangbao mega-landslide (China) using Sentinel-1 TOPS time series interferometry. Remote Sens. Environ. **186**, 501–513 (2016). https://doi.org/10.1016/j.rse.2016.09.009
7. Casagli, N., et al.: Landslide mapping and monitoring by using radar and optical remote sensing: examples from the EC-FP7 project SAFER. Remote Sens. Appl. Soc. Environ. **4**, 92–108 (2016). https://doi.org/10.1016/j.rsase.2016.07.001
8. Pawluszek-Filipiak, K., Borkowski, A.: Integration of DInSAR and SBAS techniques to determine mining-related deformations using Sentinel-1 data: the case study of rydultowy mine in Poland. Remote Sens. **12**(2), 242 (2020). https://doi.org/10.3390/rs12020242
9. Calò, F., et al.: Enhanced landslide investigations through advanced DInSAR techniques: the Ivancich case study, Assisi. Italy. Remote Sens. Environ. **142**, 69–82 (2014). https://doi.org/10.1016/j.rse.2013.11.003

10. Fárová, K., Jelének, J., Kopačková-Strnadová, V., Kycl, P.: Klárov 3, 118 21 Prague 1, Czech Republic; jan.jelenek@geology.cz. Czech Geol. Surv. 1–23 (2019). https://doi.org/10.3390/rs11222670
11. Devanthéry, N., Crosetto, M., Cuevas-González, M., Monserrat, O., Barra, A., Crippa, B.: Deformation monitoring using persistent scatterer interferometry and sentinel-1 SAR data. Procedia Comput. Sci. **100**, 1121–1126 (2016). https://doi.org/10.1016/j.procs.2016.09.263
12. Crosetto, M., Monserrat, O., Cuevas-González, M., Devanthéry, N., Crippa, B.: Persistent scatterer interferometry: a review. ISPRS J. Photogramm. Remote Sens. **115**, 78–89 (2016). https://doi.org/10.1016/j.isprsjprs.2015.10.011
13. http://step.esa.int/main/download/snap-download/. Accessed 15 Sep 2020

Short Paper: On-Site and Remotely Sensed Data Collection

A Survey on Current Heritage Structural Health Monitoring Practices Around the Globe

Laxmi Manisha Gandham⬡, Jaswanth Reddy Kota⬡, Prafulla Kalapatapu⬡, and Venkata Dilip Kumar Pasupuleti(✉)⬡

Ecole Centrale College of Engineering, Mahindra University, Hyderabad, India
{laxmimanisha170117,jaswanthreddy170114}@mechyd.ac.in,
{prafulla.kalapatapu,
venkata.pasupuleti}@mahindrauniversity.edu.in

Abstract. Heritage structures have a significant role in the nation's history. They may be acknowledged for several reasons – age, structural magnificence, religious reasons, historical events or persons they hosted, construction challenges they had in era they were built, and so on. Preserving heritage structures is prestigious and challenging task. Furthermore, an accurate knowledge of the behavior of a structure is becoming more important as new construction and conservation techniques are introduced. Historical Structures have been exposed to environmental conditions for very long time leading to the different degrees of malfunctioning at elemental or global level. In order to assess the health of the structure, this paper presents the review on various methodologies adopted by different countries around the world in assessing and monitoring of Heritage structures. Special focus on latest technologies like Artificial intelligence and sensors are discussed to address these challenges. A number of meaningful features have been monitored through extracting from SHM data.

Keywords: Heritage structure · Structural health monitoring · Artificial intelligence · Heritage structure preservation

1 Introduction

The preservation of the heritage structures is a thought of concern from governing authorities to a common person, largely due to fear of loosing identity, details of history and cultural significance. The major challenge is to conserve and restore these historical structures as they represent important event in the history of any city or a nation [1]. During the 2nd Congress of Architects and Specialits of Historic Buildings, at venice in 1964 provided for the creation of the International Council of Monuments and Sites (ICOMOS) for the protection of historical buildings [2]. In 1972, United Nations Educational, Scientific and Cultural Oragnization (UNESCO) has started World Heritage Convention for listing, protection and conservation of reneowed heritage sites and monuments all over the world [3]. In the year 1975, European Charter of the Architectural Heritage mentioned that apart from historical buildings, even natural and artificial minor

© Springer Nature Switzerland AG 2021
M. Ioannides et al. (Eds.): EuroMed 2020, LNCS 12642, pp. 565–576, 2021.
https://doi.org/10.1007/978-3-030-73043-7_48

buildings in ancient towns are also to be considered in Heritage [4]. Following to that, all the nations rich in heritage and historical sites have started their own conserva- tion and preservation of heritage organizations at both city and national level [5]. Even though there are many preservation organizations, Heritage structures are still at the large risk due to lack of appreciation, architectural significance, constructional values and improper structural health assessment apart from rapid growth of urbanization. In the past few decades, there were many heritage structures which have lost their structural stability and integrity leading to the partial damage. To name the few the Civic Tower of Pavia, Italy [6]; the bell tower of St.Magdalena in Goch, Germany (Gantert Engineering Studio 1993); Cathedral of Noto, Italy [7]; the bell tower of the St. Willibrordus Church in Meldert, Belgium [8]; "Maagdentoren" in Zichem, Belgium [9]; Church of Kerksken, Belgium [10]; Chowmahalla Palace partial collapsed after heavy downpour in India [11]. Largely it is living historical structures which built a bridge of knowledge between the past and future generations [12]. So, it becomes very important to conserve, preserve, protect and if needed restoration to be carried of the heritage structures.

World Heritage Convention (WHC) of UNESCO has divided the world into five geographic zones namely Africa, Arab states, Asia and the Pacific, Europe and North America, and Latin America and the carribbean and listed 1121 properties by Jun 2020 as seen in the Fig. 1 all over the globe as the heritage sites. Further, it is taking all the necessary actions to preserve and protect with the help of nations government [13].

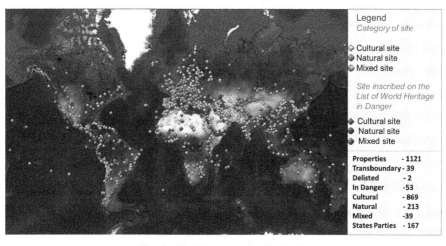

Fig. 1. World heritage list [Ref. 13]

This study also follows the same order in detailing various methodologies adopted in various geographic locations for heritage structural health assessment and monitoring.

2 Background of Structural Health Assessment and Monitoring

To understand and access the phenominal change in geometry, material, boundary con- ditions and loading compared to its original state is known to be Structural Health

Assessment (SHA) and if the same is continued to observe day by day changes is called Structural Health Monitoring (SHM). Largely these changes are termed to be deterioration or damage assessment. Extensive research on SHA and SHM is being undertaken form past three decades, but only in last one decade there were approximately 17000 research papers published in various national and international journals [14]. Out of which less than one percent have been published on SHM of heritage structures, where as there has been much research carried on Nondestructive Techniques (NDT) for the assessment and preservation of heritage structures. Most commonly used NDT tests are multispectral images, geophysics data (ground-penetrating radar [GPR]), flat-jack tests, infrared thermographic images, laser scanning data and ultrasound [15–17]. Choosing the most appropiate method requires careful decision that always takes into account of structural significance and parallely considering its physical condition. SHA is carried in three steps, first on-site visual inspection which requires prior experience and expertise, works only in accessible regions of structure, has interruption and down time, labour intensive, second, carrying out NDT tests and sample extraction for laboratory analysis and finally detailed analysis which is time consuming [18]. Considering the limitations of NDT, rise in digital technology has led to quantify heritage detrioration and detrioration live monitoring [19]. Figure 2 shows the complete structural health monitoring process in detail without much focus on the instrumentaion, largely detailing the methodologies used. Methodology choosen is directly related to structure type and parameters measured [20].

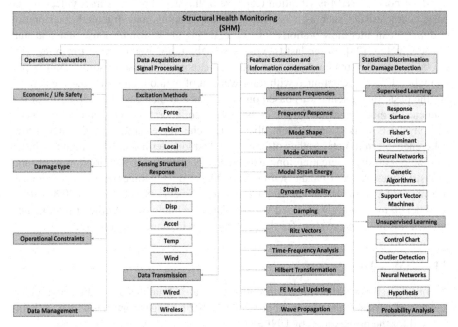

Fig. 2. Structural health monitoring process [modified from Sohn et al. 2003]

In SHM, three major aspects of sensor sub-system are variable, sensor and location of sensors. Variable largely deals with loads, environmental conditions, global or local responses. Global response deals with acceleration and deformation whereas local response includes strain, displacements, crack and fatigue at the elemental level [21]. Health monitoring system of heritage structures has started in the early 1970's, one of the early structures which was monitored was Hangzhou Tiger Hill tower, which is also called leaning tower of China to observe its tilt, settlement, ground subsidence and displacement in the year 1978 [22]. Structural health monitoring of historical structures and monuments with temporary or permanent may lead to optimal economic resources for repair or rehabilitation activities especially after natural or man-made disasters [23].

3   SHM of Heritage Structures Around the World

As mentioned above for systematic consideration of case studies around the world which are being health monitored, this study has chosen region wise which were classified based on the geographical locations by World Heritage Convention (WHC) of UNESCO are Africa, Arab states, Asia and the Pacific, Europe and North America, and Latin America and the Caribbean. Lot of research work has been carried by various organizations and research based academic institutes on prototype and actual scale structural health monitoring. But there is significant difference in use of SHM in various geographical locations and same has been discussed in detail.

Back bone of SHM is vibration response of the structure as it directly depends on basic characteristics such as mass, stiffness and damping, and structural deterioration or damage can alter the vibration response assuming the known response of actual state of the structure [24]. In the last two decades' vibration-based concept for monitoring the heritage structures has improved and seen exponential raise in studies and implementation [25–27]. Continued with improvement of methodologies to find the damage but the basic fundamental was based on vibrations and then calculated in terms of frequencies or modal analysis. In the early 1990's, collaboration between civil engineers and physicists worked on different fiber optic technologies and decided to adopt low-coherence interferometry as they offer an excellent long-term stability, a high resolution and the possibility of creating long-gauge sensors suitable for the monitoring of large civil structures. And in 1993 the SOFO "Surveillance des Ouvrages par Fibers Optiques", was named for Structural monitoring with Optical Fibers [28, 29]. In early 2000's structural health monitoring was added with the latest technology of Artificial Intelligence, but still it is in the naïve stage for the application to heritage structures [30].

3.1   SHM in Africa

According to the world heritage convention there are 34 nations under the geographical location of Africa. And there are approximately 102 heritage properties which are being focused for the preservation by UNESCO.

Rock-hewn Churches of Lalibela (Ethiopia): Rock-hewn churches of Lalibela situated in the northern-central part of Ethiopia known to be carved 800 years ago on a living volcanic rock. Due to the continuous weathering and human activities the churches have resulted in structural damages. The first restoration is of damaged churches is said to be taken during 1920 and now they are continuously monitored [31]. Rüther and Palumbo have presented structural health assessment and conservation by laser scanners, photogrammetry, GPS and total stations, which will help in creating the three-dimensional digital model which will become the base for continuous assessment [32]. Authors have not found any heritage structure in Africa under the lense of structural health monitoring. But there are many active initiatives all around the African continent of the conservation and preservation of heritage structures and their culture [33].

3.2 SHM in Arab States

According to the world heritage convention there are 19 nations under the geographical location of Arab States. And there are approximately 86 heritage properties which are being focused for the preservation by UNESCO.

The minaret of Ajloun's mosque, Ajloun, Jordan: Hamdaoui et al., presented a work on Structural Health Monitoring of the minaret of Ajloun's mosque, Ajloun, Jordon which is seven and half century old using ambient vibrations largely from wind forces. Figure 3a shows the complete dimensions of the historical monument and Fig. 3b shows the original structure from the site, Fig. 3c shows the locations of accelerometer sensors deployed to record the vibrations and Fig. 3d shows the first 12 modes obtained from the analytical solution. Dynamic characteristics obtained from the SHM and material properties obtained from the extraction samples are incorporated in the analytical solution and compared experimentally and analytically, which were in the good agreement [34, 35]. Similarly, El-Attar and Osman, 2004 have studied Al-Sultaniya minaret located in Egypt and constructed in the year 1340 both experimentally and analytically [36].

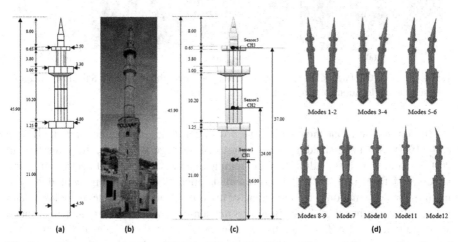

Fig. 3. a. Dimensions of Ajloun Mosque Minaret b. Ajlourn Mosque Minaret c. Location of sensors d. modes obtained from analytical analysis [34]

3.3   SHM in Asia and Pacific

According to the world heritage convention there are 36 nations under the geographical location of Asia and Pacific. And there are approximately 284 heritage properties which are being focused for the preservation by UNESCO. There has been lot of research carried on SHM of heritage structures in this region. This research work as restricted to different SHM Techniques used.

Seok-Ga Pagoda, Kyung-Ju, Korea: Seok-Ga Pagoda constructed in 8th century in the court of the Bulkook (Bulguksa) temple, Kyung-Ju, Korea. The three-story pagoda represents the finest style of Korean Buddhist pagodas that evolved from China's multistoried pavilion-type wooden pagodas. Deterioration of material, environmental exposure and non-uniform settlements made stones to move and tilt. Absence of mortar between the stones is leading to free movement of stones putting the entire structure at risk. Long base sensors and inclinometers were installed to calculate the differential settlement as seen in the Fig. 4 [37].

Fig. 4. a. Seok-Ga Pagoda b. Openings created between the stones c. Schematic diagram representing the locations of sensors d. Installed sensors [37].

In continuation that most of the nations under Asia and Pacific started SHM in early 1990's for understanding the responses of heritage structures. To name few, in 2007 sensors were installed in BaoGuo Temple to assess the material deterioration and structural deformations [38]. Shi has presented optical fiber monitoring methodology to monitor the deformation and temperature of the wall of DongHua Gate of the Forbidden City [39]. Wang has used Fiber Brag Grating sensors for the Tibetan ancient wooden structure to assess the deformations and joint behavior [40]. Toshikazu et al.. used the CCD imaging system as a structural health monitoring of Jojakkoji Temple in Kyoto, Japan to observe the response for natural disasters like earthquakes and typhoons [41]. Dhapekar and Saha have presented implementation of SHM using Rapid Visual Survey (RVS) for Bhand Dev temple, India [42]. Salvatore and Eleonora have carried SHM using digital portable tromometre for dynamic vibrations on Radha Krishna temple (Teku) and Pancha Deval complex (Pashupati) which were damaged due to 2015 Gorkha earthquake [43]. Annamdas et al., have briefly detailed the SHM applications and developments specially form the view of Asia [44].

3.4 SHM in Europe and North America

According to the world heritage convention there are 61 nations under the geographical location of Europe and North America. And there are approximately 626 heritage properties which are being focused for the preservation by UNESCO. There has been lot of research carried on SHM of heritage structures in this region too. Infact most of the structural health monitoring of heritage structures is largely taken up in Europe compared to the whole world. Apart from that regular international conferences and workshops related to SHM of heritage structures are conducted.

Villa Reale Monza, Italy: The instrumentation of the Villa Reale in Monza was one of the first applications of permanent remote monitoring using 'Surveillance des Ouvrages par Fibres Optiques' SOFO sensors. It also showed that the advantages of long-gauge sensors were also relevant to the monitoring of timber and masonry structures [45].

The Roman Arena of Verona: Very recently it was equipped with a health monitoring system to get the vibration characteristics of the monument using accelerometers and control the surveyed crack pattern through displacement transducers [46]. Figure 5a shows the aerial view of the Arena, Fig. 5b shows the Arena's wing; Fig. 5c shows the structural strengthening scheme and Fig. 5d shows the location of the static sensors deployed at the site.

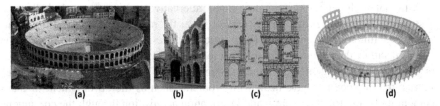

Fig. 5. a. Aerial view of the Arena; b. Detailed picture of the Arena's Wing; c. scheme of the strengthening; d. Location of static sensors [46].

As mentioned above there are many structures in Europe which are currently instrumented with live monitoring system. Casarin et al., presented the use of non - contact monitoring system for evaluating the crack openings in fresco surface for SaladeiBattuti – Conegliano Cathedral [47]. Anastasi et al., presented SHM using wireless sensors of the church of St. Teresa in the Kalsa district in Palermo, Italy. The main objective of the study was to observe structural deformations and stresses due to consolidation process which is taken up, the church was damaged due to earthquake occurred in the year 2002 [48]. Duvnjak et al., used the method of residual strain measurement on Peristyle of Diocletian's Palace in Split. This method involves attaching single strain gauge to the surface, drilling a hole in the vicinity of the gauge and then measuring the residual strains [49]. Ferraioli et al., has presented a research on health monitoring of Santa Maria a Vico bell tower using ambient vibration measurements and incorporation in the numerical model [50]. The Morris Island Lighthouse is instrumented with a discrete SHM system that consists of crack meters and temperature sensors. The system was implemented in 2007 prior to the start of a foundation stabilization to monitor any adverse effects due to intervention works [51].

4   Artificial Intelligence in SHM

Largely research related to Heritage Structures should address the following questions.

1. What is the life time of a cultural heritage structure?
2. What do we have to protect the monuments from?
3. How can we preserve and/or improve the level of safety of monuments?
4. What should we do to extend the life time of cultural heritage structures?

And the two important factors should be accounted for: to know the history of the construction and its architectural and structural characteristics and managing the maintenance of the structure. For the second aspect, the usual maintenance procedures are the classic maintenance on request, which implies a retrofitting intervention only if a damage is already occurred, and the recurring preventive maintenance, which is aimed to prevent any damage [52]. The limitation of the first approach is that the damage is already occurred and the maintenance works, if still possible, require the interruption of the use of the building with obvious negative economic effects. The disadvantage of the second approach is the difficulty in the definition of the optimum maintenance period.

Artificial Intelligence (AI) provides suitable alternative solutions for such challenges. AI strategies have been progressively received over the most recent decade for demonstrating real time issues concerning basic structural assessment and monitoring. This is a direct result of their huge ability to catch relations among input and output data that are nonlinear or complicated to figure mathematically. The first uses of AI techniques in structural engineering have dealt with problems such as the development of management tools for structural safety and information acquisition through the continuous monitoring, which is to be preferred, whenever possible. In general, AI methods have been utilized for SHM and damage identification and detection, performance assessment, structural sustainability, reliability [53, 54]. The second focus is on how AI is applied to conservation of heritage buildings. This can progress by investigating and developing a new automated tool for preventive conservation of heritage structures in urban centers based on models of AI. Indeed, AI transforms a problem with high dimensionality to a lower dimensional representation.

Using AI in the heritage structural assessment and monitoring, our survey around the globe understands the various case studies demonstrated by few authors. Ebrahim Nazarian et al. [55] describes development of a machine learning (ML)-based platform for condition assessment of building structures in the aftermath of extreme events. Evaluation of the proposed method was accomplished by using it for the characterization of damage in a turn-of-the-century, six-story building with timber frames and masonry walls. Tawfik et al. [56] the study has mainly concerned with the crack damage and do not considers the other pathologies that can affect a surface structure such as Alkali-silica reaction (ASR), efflorescence, carbonation of concrete, and scaling. Author proposed the method of pre-trained learning Deep Convolutional Neural Networks (DCNN) model with Transfer learning for the detection of seven classes of old building damage in Medina of Fez and Meknes in Morocco. Rachel Martini et al. [57] has proposed a methodology based on non-destructive tests used to characterize historical masonry and later to obtain information regarding the mechanical parameters of these elements. A mechanical characterization tool was developed applying the Artificial Neural Networks (ANN), which can be used for historic granite walls. From all the trained ANNs, based on the errors attributed to the estimated elastic modulus, networks with acceptable errors were selected. Andres Jose Prieto et al. [58] demonstrated the functional service life of built heritage. A fuzzy inference system and a multiple linear regression models were proposed and a multiple linear regression analysis is applied in order to rank the variables in terms of influence in the serviceability estimation of heritage buildings. The experiment is carried on a sample of 100 parish churches, located in Seville, Spain.

The final goal in our study is the reduction of the damage and so of the maintenance works and costs, and the increase of the safety check level by understanding the background concepts of AI and finding the necessity of AI through the various case studies of SHM system for monitoring civil engineering structures. The study clearly presents the potential of intelligent software applications like AI in the field of SHA and SHM. Therefore, AI enables exploiting the interaction from all these formulated problems, which in turn leads to robust solutions using various methods within.

5   Conclusions

The paper reports the application of structural health monitoring techniques and methodologies for the structural safety and reliability assessment of historic buildings and monuments. Advanced SHM data processing for uncertainty quantification and reduction in static and dynamic monitoring parameters have been demonstrated. The main aim is to determine, with a high level of confidence, the structural behavior of historic buildings. A special consideration was given for SHM platforms. A benchmark report was carried out aiming to understand and illustrate the current state-of-the-art in the field of SHA and SHM for heritage structures. Case studies described in the literature presents the review on various methodologies adopted by different countries around the world in assessing and monitoring of Heritage structures. Special focus on latest technologies like Artificial intelligence and sensors are discussed to address these challenges. The survey made in the paper on the assessment and monitoring of heritage structures and the inclusion of latest technologies will become baseline of understanding and scope for the researchers in this field to develop new strategies for conservation and preservation of Heritage structures.

References

1. da Silva Gonçalves, L.M., Rodrigues, H., Gaspar, F. (Eds.).: ondestructive techniques for the assessment and preservation of historic structures. CRC Press (2017)
2. Thirty years of ICOMOS = Trentième anniversaire de l'ICOMOS. Other. ICOMOS, Paris, 145p. ICOMOS Scientific Journal (1993–1999), 5. [Book] (1995)
3. "The World Heritage Convention – Brief History/ Section "Linking the protection of cultural and natural heritage"". UNESCO World Heritage Centre. Archived from the original on 26 May 2020. Accessed 17 July 2019
4. Zhang, S.: International Charter for the Protection of Urban Cultural Heritage and Selection of Domestic Laws and Regulations. Tongji University Press (2007)
5. https://en.wikipedia.org/wiki/Cultural_heritage. Accessed 28 July 2020
6. Binda, L., Gatti, G., Mangano, G., Poggi, C., Landriani, G.S.: Collapse of the civic tower of Pavia: a survey of the materials and structure. Masonry Int. 6(1), 11–20 (1992)
7. Binda, L., Baronio, G., Gavarini, C., De Benedictis, R., Tringali, S.: Investigation on materials and structures for the reconstruction of the partially collapsed Cathedral of Noto (Sicily). WIT Trans. Built Environ. 42 (1970)
8. Ignoul, S., Van Gemert, D.: Bell Tower of Church of St (No. D00466). Willibrordus. Internal Report, report (2006)
9. Ignoul, S., Van Gemert, D.: Maagdentoren at Zichem. D00394, Triconsult NV, internal report, in Dutch (2007)
10. Verstrynge, E., Schueremans, L., Van Gemert, D., Hendriks, M.A.N.: Modelling and analysis of time-dependent behaviour of historical masonry under high stress levels. Eng. Struct. 33(1), 210–217 (2011)
11. https://indianexpress.com/article/cities/hyderabad/hyderabad-rains-chowmahalla-palace-crash-6480150/
12. Embaby, M.E.: Heritage conservation and architectural education: an educational methodology for design studios. HBRC J. 10(3), 339–350 (2014)
13. https://whc.unesco.org/en/list/&order=region. Accessed 30 July 2020
14. Cawley, P.: Structural health monitoring: closing the gap between research and industrial deployment. Struct. Health Monit. 17(5), 1225–1244 (2018)
15. Wehr, A., Lohr, U.: Airborne laser scanning—an introduction and overview. ISPRS J. Photogrammetry Remote Sens. 54(2–3), 68–82 (1999)
16. Lillesand, T., Kiefer, R.W., Chipman, J.: Remote Sensing and Image Interpretation. John Wiley & Sons, Hoboken (2015)
17. Li, Z., Chen, J., Baltsavias, E. (Eds.) Advances in Photogrammetry, Remote Sensing and Spatial Information Sciences: 2008 ISPRS congress book, vol. 7. CRC Press (2008)
18. Valença, J., Gonçalves, L.M.S., Júlio, E.N.B.S.: Damage assessment on concrete surfaces using multi-spectral image analysis. Constr. Build. Mater. 40, 971–981 (2013)
19. Zheng, Y.: Digital technology in the protection of cultural heritage Bao fan temple mural digital mapping survey. Int. Arch. Photogrammetry Remote Sens. Spat. Inf. Sci. 40 (2015)
20. Sohn, H., et al.: A Review of Structural Health Monitoring Literature: 1996–2001, pp. 1–7. Los Alamos National Laboratory, USA (2003)
21. Li, H., Ou, J.: The state of the art in structural health monitoring of cable-stayed bridges. J. Civ. Struct. Health Monit. 6(1), 43–67 (2016)
22. Chen, R.: Suzhou Yunyan Temple Tower Maintenance and Reinforcement Project Report. Cultural Relics Press, 2008 (2008)
23. Comanducci, G., Cavalagli, N., Ubertini, F.: Vibration-based SHM for cultural heritage preservation: the case of the S. Pietro bell-tower in Perugia. In: MATEC Web of Conferences, vol. 24, p. 05002. EDP Sciences (2015)

24. Prabhu, S.A.: Structural health monitoring of historic masonry monuments (Doctoral dissertation, Clemson University) (2011)
25. Armstrong, D.M., Sibbald, A., Fairfield, C.A., Forde, M.C.: Modal analysis for masonry arch bridge spandrell wall separation identification. NDT E Int. **28**(6), 377–386 (1995)
26. Ellis, B.: Non-destructive dynamic testing of stone pinnacles on the palace of Westminster. Proc. Inst. Civ. Eng. Struct. Build. **128**(3), 300–307 (1998)
27. Gentile, C., Saisi, A.: Ambient vibration testing of historic masonry towers for structural identification and damage assessment. Constr. Build. Mater. **21**(6), 1311–1321 (2007)
28. Glisic, B., Inaudi, D.: Fibre Optic Methods for Structural Health Monitoring. John Wiley & Sons, Hoboken (2008)
29. Inaudi, D., Elamari, A., Pflug, L., Gisin, N., Breguet, J., Vurpillot, S.: Low-coherence deformation sensors for the monitoring of civil-engineering structures. Sens. Actuators Phys. **44**(2), 125–130 (1994)
30. Smarsly, K., Lehner, K., Hartmann, D.: Structural health monitoring based on artificial intelligence techniques. Comput. Civ. Eng. 111–118 (2007)
31. Delmonaco, G., Margottini, C., Spizzichino, D.: Analysis of rock weathering and conservation strategies for rock-hewn churches of Lalibela (Ethiopia). Protect. Hist. Build. PROHITECH **9**, 137–142 (2009)
32. Rüther, H., Palumbo, G.: 3D laser scanning for site monitoring and conservation in Lalibela world heritage site, Ethiopia. Int. J. Heritage Digit. era **1**(2), 217–231 (2012)
33. Thorn, A.: The Preservation of Great Zimbabwe: Your Monument, Our Shrine (2008)
34. Bani-Hani, K.A., Zibdeh, H.S., Hamdaoui, K.: Health monitoring of a historical monument in Jordan based on ambient vibration test. Smart Struct. Syst. **4**(2), 195–208 (2008)
35. Hamdaoui, K.: Historical monument health monitoring based on ambient vibrations. Master Thesis, Department of Civil Engineering, Jordan University of Science and Technology, Irbid, Jordan (2006)
36. El-Attar, A., Osman, A.: Seismic response of two historical Islamic Minarets. In: Proceedings of the Third European Conference on Structural Control (3ECSC), Vienna, Austria (2004)
37. Glisic, B., Inaudi, D., Posenato, D., Figini, A., Casanova, N.: Monitoring of heritage structures and historical monuments using long-gage fiber optic interferometric sensors–an overview. In: The 3rd International Conference on Structural Health Monitoring of Intelligent Infrastructure, Vancouver, pp. 13–16, November (2007)
38. Wu, M.P.: Discussion on the problem of building heritage monitoring under the concept of preventive protection. Ancient Archit. Technol. **2012**(02), 26–29 (2012)
39. Shi, Y.L.: A study on distributed optical fiber monitoring for platform of Donghua gate in the forbidden city, p. 2016. Nanjing University, Beijing (2016)
40. Wang, J., Yang, N., Yang, Q.S.: Structural health monitoring system for heritage buildings. J. Beijing Jiaotong Univ. **34**(1), 100–104 (2010)
41. Toshikazu, H., Chikahiro, M., Yasushi, N., et al.: Seismic and wind performance of five-storied Pagoda of timber heritage structure. Adv. Mater. Res. 133–134:79–95 (2010)
42. Dhapekar, N., Saha, P.: Structural health monitoring of historical monuments by rapid visual screening: case study of Bhand Deval Temple, Arang, Chhatisgarh. India. Res. Dev. (IJCSEIERD) **3**(3), 131–140 (2013)
43. Salvatore, R., Eleonora, S.: Damage assessment of Nepal heritage through ambient vibration analysis and visual inspection. Struct. Control Health Monit. **27**(5), (2020)
44. Annamdas, V.G.M., Bhalla, S., Soh, C.K.: Applications of structural health monitoring technology in Asia. Struct. Health Monit. **16**(3), 324–346 (2017)
45. Del Grosso, A., Torre, A., Rosa, M., Lattuada, B.: Application of SHM techniques in the restoration of historical buildings: the royal Villa of Monza. In: 2nd European Conference on Health Monitoring, Munich, Germany, July 2004

46. Lorenzoni, F., Casarin, F., Caldon, M., Islami, K., Modena, C.: Uncertainty quantification in structural health monitoring: applications on cultural heritage buildings. Mech. Syst. Sign. Process. **66**, 268–281 (2016)
47. Casarin, F., da Porto, F., Modena, C., Girardello, P., Kleidi, I.: Optical Structural Health Monitoring of the Frescoes in the Conegliano Cathedral, Italy
48. Anastasi, G., Re, G.L., Ortolani, M.: WSNs for structural health monitoring of historical buildings. In: 2009 2nd Conference on Human System Interactions, pp. 574–579. IEEE, May 2009
49. Duvnjak, I., Damjanović, D., Krolo, J.: Structural health monitoring of cultural heritage structures: applications on peristyle of Diocletian's palace in split. In: 8th European workshop on structural health monitoring, EWSHM, vol. 4, pp. 2661–2669, January 2016
50. Ferraioli, M., Miccoli, L., Abruzzese, D.: Seismic risk assessment of the Santa Maria a Vico bell tower. ambient vibration measurements and numerical model tuning. In: 3rd International Conference on Protection of Historical Constructions PROHITECH 2017, pp. 1–13. IST Press (2017)
51. Blyth, A., Napolitano, R., Glisic, B.: Documentation, structural health monitoring and numerical modelling for damage assessment of the Morris Island Lighthouse. Philos. Trans. R. Soc. **377**(2155), 20190002 (2019)
52. Laory, I., Trinh, T.N., Smith, I.F., Brownjohn, J.M.: Methodologies for predicting natural frequency variation of a suspension bridge. Eng. Struct. **80**, 211–221 (2014)
53. Bandara, R.P., Chan, T.H., Thambiratnam, D.P.: Frequency response function based damage identification using principal component analysis and pattern recognition technique. Eng. Struct. **66**, 116–128 (2014)
54. Bandara, R.P., Chan, T.H., Thambiratnam, D.P.: Structural damage detection method using frequency response functions. Struct. Health Monit. **13**(4), 418–429 (2014)
55. Nazarian, E., Taylor, T., Weifeng, T., Ansari, F.: Machine-learning-based approach for post event assessment of damage in a turn-of-the-century building structure. J. Civ. Struct. Health Monit. **8**(2), 237–251 (2018)
56. Masrour, T., El Hassani, I., Bouchama, M.S.: Deep convolutional neural networks with transfer learning for old buildings pathologies automatic detection. In: Ezziyyani, M. (ed.) AI2SD 2019. AISC, vol. 1104, pp. 204–216. Springer, Cham (2020). https://doi.org/10.1007/978-3-030-36671-1_18
57. Martini, R., Carvalho, J., Arête, A., Varum, H.: Non-destructive method of the assessment of stone masonry by artificial neural networks. Open Constr. Build. Technol. J. **14**(1) (2020)
58. Prieto, A.J., Silva, A., de Brito, J., Macías-Bernal, J.M., Alejandre, F.J.: Multiple linear regression and fuzzy logic models applied to the functional service life prediction of cultural heritage. J. Cult. Heritage **27**, 20–35 (2017)

Short Papers: Modelling and Knowledge Managemen

Short Papers: Interactive Environments and Applications

Interacting with Cultural Heritage Through Shape Representation Techniques in 3D Modeling Environments

Begüm Moralıoğlu[1]([envelope]) [iD] and Begüm Aktaş[2] [iD]

[1] Architectural Design Computing Graduate Program, Istanbul Technical University, Institute of Informatics, Istanbul, Turkey
[2] Department of Architecture, Altınbas University, Istanbul, Turkey

Abstract. Three-dimensional (3D) representation of cultural heritage in a digital environment is coming into prominence for documentation of geometric and semantic details and the interpretation of shape representation from academic studies to commercial practices. To interpret cultural and historical shapes, the use of the computational medium is expanding with developing technologies. Advanced 3D design and development applications appear every day with distinct functions. However, not every technology provides designers a convenient medium to create, explore, and think naturally. In that sense, digital design mediums and tools become important to enhance the interactivity level with cultural heritage for designers through different interfaces. Particularly, the utilities of design interfaces are essential for preserving reconstructing ruined cultural heritage in the digital design mediums. In this study, we investigate the designers' creative design process in the context of shape representation methods within the possibilities of two different 3D design interfaces as a computer and virtual reality (VR) interfaces. At first, we conducted a shape exploration exercise to generate the 3D model pieces of the Dark Church in Cappadocia. And then, we used the generated 3D model pieces in a shape representation exercise to observe the seeing, imagining, and acting abilities of designers in computer and VR environments.

Keywords: Cultural heritage · Shape representation · 3D design interfaces

1 Introduction

Design is an inherent human ability that consists of a series of critical decisions in an iterative and highly complex process responsive to many factors [1]. The ultimate objective of the design process is to produce visual representations of the designed entity with enough completion and coherence to allow its construction or the simulation, physically or mentally [2]. At the core of the whole design process lies transforming the ideas and thoughts to the visual representations in the designers' minds. However, the ability to transfer thoughts efficiently requires knowledge and practice. The level of knowledge underlines visual-spatial [3] or visual-mental [4] cognitive ability for identification, generation, and integration processes of 2D shape recognition, 3D modeling, or

M. Ioannides et al. (Eds.): EuroMed 2020, LNCS 12642, pp. 579–587, 2021.
https://doi.org/10.1007/978-3-030-73043-7_49

transitions between 2D to 3D shape representation mediums and tools. Changes between each medium and tools are difficult for designers, especially if there is little information about the design context. It can be hard to interact with a ruined building and interpret the architectural elements efficiently in cultural heritage projects. Today's shape representation mediums and tools are mostly based on 2D representation techniques, although the shapes we perceive and interact with are in 3D. A combination of 2D and 3D with VR technology is providing to be the next frontier for research, teaching, and dissemination [14]. The shape representation exploration of cultural heritage through visual-spatial interfaces is the primary motivation of this study as the designers think and create in 3D design mediums.

The main goal of the study is to observe the creative design process of designers in different 3D design environments to understand the effects of design interfaces on them while they are seeing, perceiving, and discovering the shapes and sub-shape relations of cultural heritage. In the end, the capacity and ability to transform knowledge into the representational outcomes will be defined by emphasizing the actions of the designers in two different 3D design mediums as VR and computer environments. Because, on computer screens, the senses are mostly limited to visual and audible experience. Interaction is bound to devices such as the mouse and keyboard. However, with readily available virtual reality hardware and software, it is possible to change the quality and quantity of interaction with the virtual environment [14]. Within the development of interactive technologies, utilization of the VR technologies in the cultural heritage is widely used for research, tourism, teaching, protection, and documentation, and so on. Thereby, VR is playing an active role in sustainable and transparent management, protection, and research of cultural heritage. Gaitatzes et al. [15] analyzed the interactive virtual environments developed at an institution of informal education and discusses the issues involved in developing immersive interactive virtual archaeology projects for the broad public. In addition to them, Loizides et al. [16] used VR to evaluate results of experiments that are useful in shaping their future actions in this area that involve user-centered design and presentation of virtual environments displaying Cypriot Cultural Heritage and Art in public spaces. That study had a relatively similar approach to compare the technological developments of VR from using keyboard controls for navigation to current devices and how this improvement affected user experience.

In the first part of the study, architectural information is collected on the dilapidated Dark Church to understand and interpret the form of the facade. Since most of the facade is missing today, it was necessary to find any instructions on the facade's original state. After that, ten masters and Ph.D. students worked on the facade to break into pieces like a puzzle as a shape exploration exercise. Next, the abstract model pieces of the facade are created related to the data provided from the shape exploration exercise. The model pieces are then placed in a file as a Rhinoceros document and as a VR scene in Microsoft Maquette software. Since most people are still not familiar with VR technology in the year 2020, it is assumed that the experiments should involve not only designers but also a wide variety of people with a shared interest in interacting with 3D design environments. Thus, the next phase of the study is planned as a set of comparative experiments, including a pilot study with architectural design students and visitors of the Sónar+ D Istanbul 2020 event. In this final phase, participants are asked to bring the model pieces together like a 3D puzzle in the computer and VR environment as the shape representation exercise. This study aims to contribute to developing 3D modeling and visualization tools in cultural heritage studies in the context of interacting and interpreting shape relations and representations in 3D interfaces.

2   Shape Representation in Heritage

The developing 3D mapping technologies like photogrammetry and laser scanning have made 3D digitization of cultural heritage possible to capture the existing geometries and appearances of the objects [8]. The information they obtained to encourage designers to interpret their architecture and create digital representations accordingly. In the case of destroyed or ruined heritage, digital interpretations and representations can help preserve data and tell history to the next generations [9]. In this study, a ruined architectural heritage site is selected to contribute the future studies on discovering the missing parts of the structure.

The knowledge and preservation of cultural heritage are based on an in-depth, layered, and interdisciplinary understanding of the sites, especially when the monuments are on edge between natural and artificial as well as between archaeology and landscape, like rupestrian (cave) architecture often is [10]. Both the constructive method and direct relationships between the interior and exterior of a settlement make rupestrian architecture unique and unfamiliar for visitors and researchers. The Dark Church is one of the churches with rupestrian architecture in Göreme National Park and surrounded by many other cave churches and monastery units (see Fig. 1).

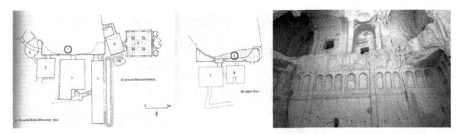

Fig. 1. The plan of the Dark Church complex with the south wall of the courtyard [12].

The Dark Church is identified as one of the 11th century Byzantine churches in Cappadocia [11]. The rooms of the church are constructed as subtraction of inside the rock as two-floor plans. Cross planned church is built as four columns and nine bays. With the exceptions of the north, south, and west arms, which are barrel-vaulted, the bays are covered with domes [11]. On the south side of the courtyard, there is an open-fronted vestibule with a flat ceiling (see Fig. 1).

The facade of the Dark Church is constructed as a rock-cut facade; however, some parts of the facade open their windows to the outside courtyard. The parts surrounding the courtyard have been lost for years, and there is no record of the last time they were complete. Wallace [11] stated that the facade of the vestibule is articulated with two pilasters. In the upper level of the wall, there is a frieze of blind keyhole-shaped niches arranged in groups of two to four, separated by pilasters. The wall of the vestibule is divided into three sections by pilasters [12]. These are the complete knowledge that is acquired for this study on the facade. There is no source for the original shape of the ruined parts to the best of our knowledge.

3 Methodology of the Study

In design, particularly in architectural design, seeing, talking, writing, drawing, and modeling methods, as well as verbal or nonverbal representation, are widespread among the designers and architects. According to Schön [13], a designer sees, moves, and sees again. Designers explore possibilities through understanding and observing by seeing as a visual thinking approach. In this sense, seeing is one of the reasons that design is a spontaneous and non-linear process. Vlavianos states that seeing and perceiving operations enable designers to create unique ideas every time instead of fixing them on the same perspectives [14]. In all this "seeing," the designer not only visually registers information but also constructs its meaning; s/he identifies patterns and gives them meanings beyond themselves [13].

This study utilizes the shape representation method by emphasizing interaction with seeing, imagining, and acting phases to generate or manipulate the given shape through the visual-spatial model (see Fig. 2). In the context of this study, we conducted a set of experiments to evaluate the efficiencies and effects of 3D modeling inter-faces on a computer, and in a VR environment for cultural heritage.

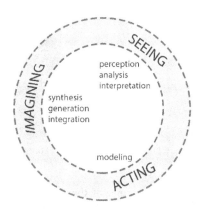

Fig. 2. Shape representation methodology of the study.

The state-of-art shape representation method adapts the visual-spatial model to 3D design interfaces to understand the creative design process by interacting with cultural heritage in different design mediums [Adapted from 15]. Seeing includes perception, analysis, and interpretation phases of the process. Imagining encapsulates synthesis, generating, and integrating phases. Acting contains verbal and non-verbal methods like sketching, drawing, and 3D modeling in different mediums. Synthesis enables participants to summarize the entire outcome of the seeing phases for generation and integration of the given representation of cultural heritage. Therefore, the participants are expected to manipulate the knowledge and internalized data to generate and integrate them into the creative design process to complete missing parts of the cultural heritage site in the acting phase.

Although these three design activities seem to be following actions, they are all intertwined in the design process. Each time participants see a shape, the shape is processed and evaluated, and each new evaluation generates a different solution as in reflection in action [13]. The 3D puzzle approach supports the visual-spatial model by allowing participants to perceive the shapes each time through their contours. Even though the model pieces are also equipped with regional information, participants need to detect and match the contours to put together the pieces. Therefore, 3D physical puzzles are typically used to help the engagement of the audience in the interpretation of archaeological artefacts in a museum exhibition. A puzzle can be seen as a game but also as a complex activity that archaeologists undertake to reassemble fragments [16]. In addition, a hybrid human-computer strategy to solve the extremely complex 3D puzzle problems for archeological environments [17] are also studied recently.

According to the psychophysical experiments, people can pick up the edges despite crowded scenery [18]. Therefore, the 3D puzzle elements in different 3D design mediums perform as a novel method to detect edges, perceive shapes, and understand sub-shape relations. Since each design medium has unique features to represent the shape information, the shape perception is different in each environment. The impact of the 3D design mediums on the shape perception of cultural heritage is essential for this study to evaluate the impact of 3D design interfaces on the creative design process for the conversation and promotion of the cultural heritage in digital environments like virtual museums, or even heritage games.

4   Shape Exploration & Representation Exercises

In this study, to state and evaluate the efficacy of 3D design interfaces to interact with cultural heritage through shape representation techniques, experiments are conducted in two parts as shape exploration and representation exercises. In the first part of the experiments, ten master's and Ph.D. students examined the Dark Church facade through the images and made sketches to show the pieces they think will be relevant to understand the shape and sub-shape relations (see Fig. 3). The results coming from the shape exploration exercise are evaluated, and some similarities are found between the sketches determining the pieces for the shape representation exercises (see Fig. 4). So, the 3D model pieces of the facade are created for the computer and VR environment accordingly.

In the second part of the experiments, four architecture students brought the 3D model pieces together in the computer and VR environment, and twelve visitors of the Sónar + D Istanbul 2020 event brought the 3D pieces together only in the VR environment. In the beginning, each participant, both architecture students and visitors of the Sónar + D Istanbul 2020 event, experienced the facade for 5 min through a 360° photo by using VR goggles. Then architecture students tried to complete the church's

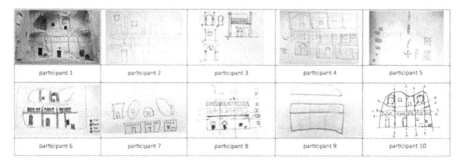

Fig. 3. Shape exploration for the facade of the Dark Church by ten masters and Ph.D. students.

Fig. 4. The result of the shape exploration exercise.

facade in 5 min through the Rhinoceros file provided for the computer environment. Following that, they had 5 min again to complete the church's facade in the Microsoft Maquette VR application. The visitors of the Sónar + D Istanbul 2020 also had 5 min to complete the facade in VR. In the end, we have different representations of the facade of the Dark Church in two different 3D modeling environments, both mostly in the VR environment, to evaluate further for the use of shape representation techniques in different design mediums for interacting cultural heritage (see Fig. 5 and Fig. 6).

The unfamiliar geometry and topology of the Dark Church enable participants for the interrelation of the entire phases of the proposed methodology, which are seeing, imagining, and acting.

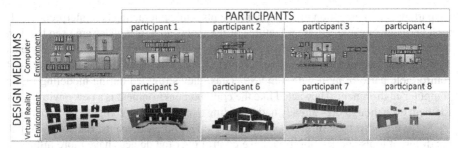

Fig. 5. The preliminary result of the shape representation exercise with architecture students.

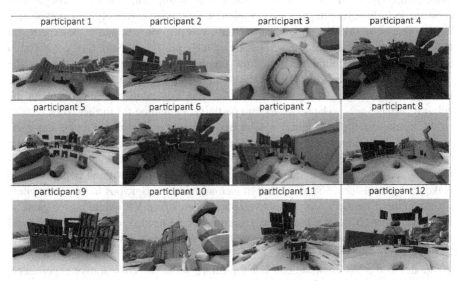

Fig. 6. The result of the shape representation exercise with Sonar İstanbul participants in the VR environment.

5   Conclusion and Further Study

This study explores the importance and effects of the 3D digital design mediums and tools on interacting cultural heritage through the creative design process in shape representation methods. Therefore, a two-phased shape exploration and representation experiment is conducted in computer and VR environments.

Within this study, it is assumed that participants may struggle in the digital design mediums that are unfamiliar to them like 3D modeling in the VR environment. Nevertheless, the preliminary results show that familiarity with the design medium does not affect interacting and interpreting cultural heritage shapes. One of the other results shows that all architecture students completed the facade as a planar surface in the computer environment. In contrast, they completed the facade as a curved surface in the VR environment (see Fig. 5). The visitors of the Sónar + D Istanbul 2020 event also completed the facade as a curved surface in the VR. That shows that tools and mediums affected the participants' perception in both environments while interacting and interpreting cultural heritage. Notably, different features of the tools and how devices are used have an influence on the preliminary results of this study. In the computer environment, students used the drag and drop command to complete the facade; nevertheless, they were not comfortable performing it with a mouse. Thus, they struggled during modeling in the computer environment. They acted like the computer environment is a new environment for them even though they already had modeling experience in a computer environment.

Since the utilization of the tools has more effect on participants, the ability to use the different tools and the ability to have control over the devices have more influence on the results than shape representations of the facade. Besides, all participants were more comfortable and have a more intuitive relationship with VR by hand-eye-body coordination. However, they did not complete the facade as creatively as it is expected. On the other hand, in the beginning, participants were pleased to be part of the experiment to have a chance to visit the site without being there physically. Still, they got bored in a short time and they found it hard to draw attention to the shape representations of the 3D objects to complete the facade Since our aim was to create a gamified VR experience to collect data for developing a user-centered approach, more information about the cultural heritage need to be added to gain participant attention for further work.

In conclusion, the preliminary results are promising to continue studying the interaction ways with ruined cultural heritage in the 3D design environment through shape representation methods. It is also recognized that digital 3D tools are proficient enough for designers to experience the cultural heritage environment without being there to make design decisions. Using 3D design technologies is auspicious to raise awareness for the cultural heritage, via interactive applications like a VR exhibition or game at a relatively low cost. Therefore, more experiments are needed to evaluate further and understand the effect of recent 3D technologies on the creative design process. However, as far as the results show that participants work efficiently and interact more with the 3D model in the VR environment. For the future work, the comparative experiments on shape representation will be continued with more participants to decode the pattern of the importance and effects of the various design mediums and tools on interacting cultural heritage within the context of shape representation methods.

Acknowledgements. We would like to thank Prof. Dr. Mine Özkar for her valuable and constructive suggestions during the planning and development of this research work. Also, the Sonar Istanbul team and the whole participant of the experiments.

References

1. Cross, N., Dorst, K., Roozenburg, N.: Research in design thinking. In: Proceedings of a Workshop Meeting held at the Faculty of Industrial Design Engineering, Delft University of Technology, the Netherlands, 29–31 May 1991: Delft University Press (1992)
2. Goldschmidt, G.: The dialectics of sketching. Creativity Res. J. **4**(2), 123–143 (1991)
3. Bilda, Z., Gero, J.S.: Does sketching off-load visuo-spatial working memory. Studying Designers **5**, 145–160 (2005)
4. Oxman, R.: Design by re-representation: a model of visual reasoning in design. Des. Stud. **18**(4), 329–347 (1997)

5. Varinlioglu, G., Alankus, G.: Unfolding ancient architecture through low-budget virtual reality experience. IN-PLAY, 93 (2016)
6. Gaitatzes, A., Christopoulos, D., Roussou, M.: Reviving the past: cultural heritage meets virtual reality. In: Proceedings of the 2001 conference on Virtual reality, archeology, and cultural heritage, pp. 103–110, November 2001
7. Loizides, F., El Kater, A., Terlikas, C., Lanitis, A., Michael, D.: Presenting cypriot cultural heritage in virtual reality: a user evaluation. In: Euro-Mediterranean Conference, pp. 572–579. Springer, Cham, November 2014
8. De Luca, L.: Methods, formalisms and tools for the semantic-based surveying and representation of architectural heritage. Appl. Geomatics 6(2), 115–139 (2014). https://doi.org/10.1007/s12518-011-0076-7
9. Vilbrandt, C., et al.: Cultural heritage preservation using constructive shape modeling. Computer Graphics Forum, vol. 23, pp. 25–41 (2004). https://doi.org/10.1111/j.1467-8659.2004.00003.x
10. Colonnese, F., Carpiceci, M., Inglese, C.: Conveying cappadocia. a new representation model for rock-cave architecture by contour lines and chromatic codes. Virtual Archaeol. Rev. 7(14), 13–19 (2016)
11. Wallace, S.A.: Byzantine Cappadocia: the planning and function of its ecclesiastical structures (1991)
12. Rodley, L.: Cave monasteries of Byzantine Cappadocia. Cambridge University Press. The Courtyard Monasteries, pp. 48–56 (1985)
13. Schön, D.A.: Designing as reflective conversation with the materials of a design situation. Knowl.-Based Syst. 5(1), 3–14 (1992)
14. Vlavianos, N.: Shape Grammars Reality (SGr): Computing in the Real World. Massachusetts Institute of Technology, Department of Architecture, MSc Thesis (2016)
15. Park, J., Kim, Y.S.: Visual reasoning and design processes. In: DS 42: Proceedings of ICED 2007, the 16th International Conference on Engineering Design, Paris, France, 28.−31.07.2007, pp. 333–334 (2007)
16. Echavarria, K.R., Samaroudi, M.: Digital workflow for creating 3D puzzles to engage audiences in the interpretation of archaeological artefacts. In: 16th EUROGRAPHICS Workshop on Graphics and Cultural Heritage (Workshop on Graphics and Cultural Heritage) (2018)
17. Adán, A., Salamanca, S., Merchán, P.: A hybrid human–computer approach for recovering incomplete cultural heritage pieces. Comput. Graph. 36(1), 1–15 (2012)
18. Elder, J.H.: Shape from contour: computation and representation. Ann. Rev. Vis. Sci. 4(1), 423–450 (2018). https://doi.org/10.1146/annurev-vision-091517-034110

Artwork Identification in a Museum Environment: A Quantitative Evaluation of Factors Affecting Identification Accuracy

A. Lanitis[1,2]([:envelope:]) [iD], Z. Theodosiou[2] [iD], and H. Partaourides[2] [iD]

[1] Visual Media Computing Lab, Department of Multimedia and Graphic Arts
Cyprus University of Technology Limassol, Limassol, Cyprus
andreas.lanitis@cut.ac.cy
[2] CYENS Centre of Excellence, Nicosia, Cyprus
{Z.Theodosiou,H.Partaourides}@cyens.org.cy

Abstract. The ability to identify the artworks that a museum visitor is looking at, using first-person images seamlessly captured by wearable cameras can be used as a means for invoking applications that provide information about the exhibits, and provide information about visitors' activities. As part of our efforts to optimize the artwork recognition accuracy of an artwork identification system under development, an investigation aiming to determine the effect of different conditions on the artwork recognition accuracy in a gallery/exhibition environment is presented. Through the controlled introduction of different distractors in a virtual museum environment, it is feasible to assess the effect on the recognition performance of different conditions. The results of the experiment are important for improving the robustness of artwork recognition systems, and at the same time the conclusions of this work can provide specific guidelines to curators, museum professionals and visitors, that will enable the efficient identification of artworks, using images captured with wearable cameras in a museum environment.

Keywords: Paintings recognition · Computer vision · Deep networks

1 Introduction

The study of museum/gallery visitors has been a rapidly evolving topic within the museum research community which is interested in optimising the overall visitor experience, while analysing visitors' activities, behaviours and experiences. In this paper we describe work related to the development of an in-museum application for tracking the artworks that a visitor is looking at, using first-person images seamlessly captured either by a wearable camera or a smartphone camera. To accomplish the artwork identification task, we utilize deep learning-based object identification algorithms tuned to recognize different artworks in a

© Springer Nature Switzerland AG 2021
M. Ioannides et al. (Eds.): EuroMed 2020, LNCS 12642, pp. 588–595, 2021.
https://doi.org/10.1007/978-3-030-73043-7_50

museum/gallery environment. The key issue considered in the work is the identification of artworks using object recognition methodologies [12], rather than dealing with the problem of art style identification or visual interpretation problem. Once an artwork is identified, information about the style and interpretation of the artwork can be retrieved from a database that stores such information.

As part of our efforts to produce a system that works with high accuracy in different conditions, we present an investigation aiming to determine the effect of different conditions on the artwork recognition accuracy. To assess the effect of different conditions on the recognition performance, we stage experiments in a virtual environment that allows the controlled introduction of different distractors. The results of the experiment are important for improving the robustness of artwork recognition systems, and at the same time the conclusions of this work can provide specific guidelines to curators, museum professionals and visitors, that will enable the use of this technology in a highly efficient manner. While there are other artwork recognition attempts recorded in the literature [9, 11], to the best of our knowledge, this is the first time that a virtual space is used for simulating different conditions in a controlled way, allowing in that way the derivation of conclusions related to the performance and limitations of artwork recognition using first-person images.

The ultimate aim of our work is to develop a dedicated application capable of identifying the artworks that a visitor is looking at, enabling in that way: a) the provision of additional information about the artwork to the visitor, and b) to register the artworks that the visitor is paying more attention as a means of automating the process of visitor experience evaluation studies [6]. The work described in this paper constitutes our first step in the application development process, where we aim to understand the effect on the identification accuracy due to the introduction of different sources of variation in images captured by a first person camera.

2   Literature Review

The new domain of computer vision focusing on the analysis of images resembling the point of view of a user, collected through wearable cameras or other smart devices, is known as egocentric or first-person vision [2]. Latest developments in image interpretation algorithms, mainly in the form of deep learning, along with the increased image capture abilities and computational power of mobile devices, facilitated the rabid development of novel egocentric applications.

In the case of cultural heritage, wearable camera technologies are often used for artwork interpretation in an attempt to enhance the interaction and experience of visitors of cultural heritage sites. Within this context Taverriti et al. [11] use the YOLO convolutional deep network for identifying eight different artworks within a museum area. Skoryukina et al. [10] also consider the problem of recognizing 2D artworks from images captured with mobile devices using a Bag-of-features approach and point geometry. Banerji et al. [1] investigate the use of convolutional neural networks as a means for extracting features from paintings that can support the tasks of painting, artist, and style recognition. Along these lines they perform experiments using different network architectures and layers.

Instead of focusing on artwork recognition, few researchers considered the problem of identifying the exact location of museum visitors based on images captured with wearable devices. Ragusa et al. [9] use first-person videos captured in the Monastero dei Benedettini, Italy, to identify the location of the visitor. Baseline location recognition performance was presented using a method proposed by Furnari et al. [4] who performs the localization task in three steps that include the steps of frame classification, negative rejection and temporal modelling of the recognized location in previous frames.

3   Paintings Identification Methodology

The process of paintings identification is carried out using a deep network tuned to classify paintings available in an exhibition area such as a museum or a gallery. To train a paintings identification network it is required to have at least one image for each painting. However, to be able to train a classification network, multiple images showing different instances of a painting are needed. To create the desirable training set, data augmentation techniques are adopted [8], that involve the transformation of a given image by changing the image scale, and by rotating the image. As a result of the data augmentation process for each painting we get multiple images showing different instances of a painting.

Recently, many object recognition tasks are performed with high accuracy using deep neural networks [5]. For this reason we have opted to utilize a deep neural network for performing the task of artwork recognition. The convolutional neural network "Squeeze Net" [5] was used due to the limited memory requirements that make it more appropriate for use on mobile devices. A pretrained version of the network trained on more than a million images from the ImageNet database is tuned for classifying paintings by initializing the convolutional layers with the pretrained weights and replacing the output classification layer with the appropriate layer size and fine-tuning the whole network architecture using the training set with paintings. During the classification phase, first-person images captured by visitors are normalized to the standard resolution and input to the tuned "Squeeze Net" allowing in that way the classification of the paintings shown, into the most similar class of paintings in the training set.

4   Experimental Evaluation

As part of our efforts for implementing an application that allows the efficient identification of paintings in a gallery, an experimental evaluation was conducted. The aim of the evaluation was to assess how different factors, frequently encountered in museum environments, affect the identification accuracy. As part of the preliminary investigation we have considered the identification of 10 paintings of renowned Cypriot artists. The main steps of the experimental set up are described below.

4.1   Creating a Virtual Gallery Environment

As a means of simulating accurately different in-museum conditions, we perform experiments in a virtual environment exhibiting the 10 selected paintings placed on a plain wall of a virtual 3D gallery (see Fig. 1). To simulate the views of a visitor, a virtual camera was placed looking towards the leftmost painting, at a height of 1.6 m and 1.5 m away from the wall with the paintings. The initial camera orientation allows the capture of images, as seen by a typical visitor. To simulate the movement of the visitor the camera is gradually moved to the rightmost painting and gradually returns to the starting position. A video showing the views of the virtual camera was recorded and all video frames were annotated to indicate frames where the virtual visitor focuses on a specific painting.

Fig. 1. The setup of the virtual gallery.

4.2   Introducing Distractors

During on-sight visits to museum/galleries exhibiting artworks, possible distractors that may affect the accuracy of automated artwork identification were defined. Identified distractors include changes in the gallery wall texture, changes in ambient light intensity, changes in camera position and orientation with respect to the observed paintings, speed of camera movement and the introduction of occluding structures in the form of additional visitors that inhibit the camera point of view. To assess the effect of the identified distractors, the appearance and overall setting of the virtual gallery and/or the settings of the camera movement were modified in a controlled way so that different distractors are simulated in a controlled way as shown in Fig. 2.

4.3   Classification

During the process of training the classifier the data augmentation techniques described in Sect. 3 were used for creating, a training set with 100 images (10 images per painting) used for tuning a "Squeeze Net" [5] for classifying paintings. During the performance evaluation stage, all frames in a video were classified using the "Squeeze Net" [5] trained for this purpose, and the correct identification performance was recorded. The performance evaluation indicator was the

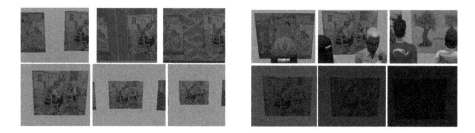

Fig. 2. Samples showing examples of different conditions simulated in the virtual environment. Row 1 (left) shows the simulation of different wall textures, row 1 (right) the introduction of virtual visitors, row 2 (left) changes in camera orientation and row 2 (right) changes in ambient lighting.

percentage of correct classification for frames where it is possible to determine the painting that the virtual visitor focuses on. Since at this stage of the experiments, the aim is to assess the effect of different conditions rather than producing the final classification system, for this set of experiments we don't consider the frames where the view is split among two paintings to an extend that it is not possible to indicated the painting on which the visitor focuses on.

4.4   Experimental Results

When the system was tested using the original settings for 99% of all frames considered (about 250 frames) the correct painting was identified. Table 1 shows how the recognition performance is affected by different simulated conditions, while Table 2 summarizes the conclusions regarding the effect of each condition on the classification accuracy.

5   Discussion

A preliminary investigation of the factors affecting the identification accuracy of paintings identification in a museum environment was presented. As part of the investigation, a deep network was trained to classify images of paintings placed in a virtual gallery. The use of a virtual gallery allows the controlled introduction of various conditions that may affect classification accuracy, enabling in that way the extraction of discrete conclusions in relation to the factors that impact the classification performance. To the best of our knowledge the results reported are unique because, unlike the ones reported by other researchers [9], they refer to the recognition of artworks in a virtual environment in the presences of simulated distractors. The results of the investigation provide a useful insight of issues that curators, museum professionals and visitors should consider to maximize the efficiency of this technology. Indicative recommendations include:

- Recommendations for gallery curators and museum professionals
  - Prefer the use of plain colors on the walls rather than textured surfaces
  - Make sure that there is strong ambient lighting in the exhibition area.
  - Limit the number of visitors allowed in a room
- Recommendations for visitors:
  - Keep a steady distance of about 1.5 m from the paintings
  - Aim to observe a painting while looking straight forward rather than looking at a painting from an angle.
  - Avoid crowded rooms

Table 1. Recognition rates for different simulated conditions

Condition	Parameters	Correct Classification Rate
Wall texture	No Texture (Baseline)	99%
	Green Stribe	95%
	Blue Stribe	94%
	Gold Fan	88%
Number of visitors	0 (Baseline)	99%
	5	92%
	10	71%
	15	83%
Distance	150 cm (Baseline)	99%
	200 cm	88%
	250 cm	78%
	300 cm	76%
Camera point of view	Forward (Baseline)	99%
	Upwards	98%
	Downwards	77%
	Left	87%
	Right	86%
Ambient light intensity	255 (Baseline)	99%
	200	96%
	150	63%
	100	27%
Camera speed	10 s	100%
	20 s (Baseline)	99%
	30 s	99%
	40 s	99%

Table 2. Conclusions regarding the effect of each condition on the artwork classification accuracy.

Condition	Comments
Wall texture	Gallery walls with textures may affect classification accuracy
Number of visitors	Increased number of visitors can cause a reduction in classification accuracy, as the point of view of the camera is occluded
Distance from paintings	As visitors move away from paintings, classification accuracy is affected. This effect may be attributed to the inability to capture details of a painting from a distance. Furthermore, as the distance between a painting and the camera increased, the proportion of the actual painting included in the point of view is reduced
Camera point of view	Changes in the camera orientation affect the classification performance, hence for optimum performance, the camera should be looking forward
Ambient light	Reduced ambient lighting has a severe effect on the classification performance
Camera speed	The speed of movement does not affect in a significant way the classification performance

While the initial results obtained prove the feasibility of this approach, there is need for further work to capitalize on the early results. Areas that need further work is the training of deep networks with enhanced training set both in terms of the number of artworks to be recognized and in terms of the variations introduced in the training set. Future work plans also involve the investigation of the effect of additional distractors both in isolation and in combination. In parallel with experiments in virtual environments, we are in the process of running experiments in a real environment in the State Gallery of Contemporary Cypriot Art, so that the results of our initial investigation will be utilized for optimizing the performance of artwork identification in a real environment.

The development of robust painting identification technology can form the basis of implementing numerous applications that aim to enhance the experience of the visitor and at the same time provide important information to curators. As far as the visitors are cornered, the identification of a painting will allow the use of mark-less augmented reality systems [3] for obtaining information about exhibits, or the activation of dedicated multimedia applications related to a painting, such as 3d visualizations [7]. At the same time useful information can be derived that includes the time spend in front of each artifact and the level of concentration of the visitor while observing an artifact. We are currently in the process of developing an application that will utilize the proposed framework to introduce the functionalities stated above.

Acknowledgements. This project has received funding from the European Union's Horizon 2020 research and innovation programme under grant agreement No 739578 complemented by the Government of the Republic of Cyprus through the Directorate General for European Programmes, Coordination and Development. We also like to thank the personnel of the State Gallery of Contemporary Cypriot Art for their support.

References

1. Banerji, S., Sinha, A.: Painting classification using a pre-trained convolutional neural network. In: Mukherjee, S. (ed.) ICVGIP 2016. LNCS, vol. 10481, pp. 168–179. Springer, Cham (2017). https://doi.org/10.1007/978-3-319-68124-5_15
2. Bolanos, M., Dimiccoli, M., Radeva, P.: Toward storytelling from visual lifelogging: an overview. IEEE Trans. Hum.-Mach. Syst. **47**(1), 77–90 (2016). https://doi.org/10.1109/THMS.2016.2616296
3. Brancati, N., Caggianese, G., Frucci, M., Gallo, L., Neroni, P.: Experiencing touchless interaction with augmented content on wearable head-mounted displays in cultural heritage applications. Pers. Ubiquit. Comput. **21**(2), 203–217 (2017). https://doi.org/10.1007/s00779-016-0987-8
4. Furnari, A., Battiato, S., Farinella, G.M.: Personal-location-based temporal segmentation of egocentric videos for lifelogging applications. J. Vis. Commun. Image Represent. **52**, 1–12 (2018). https://doi.org/10.1016/j.jvcir.2018.01.019
5. Iandola, F.N., Han, S., Moskewicz, M.W., Ashraf, K., Dally, W.J., Keutzer, K.: Squeezenet: alexnet-level accuracy with 50x fewer parameters and < 0.5 mb model size. arXiv preprint arXiv:1602.07360 (2016)
6. Loizides, F., El Kater, A., Terlikas, C., Lanitis, A., Michael, D.: Presenting Cypriot cultural heritage in virtual reality: a user evaluation. In: Ioannides, M., Magnenat-Thalmann, N., Fink, E., Žarnić, R., Yen, A.-Y., Quak, E. (eds.) EuroMed 2014. LNCS, vol. 8740, pp. 572–579. Springer, Cham (2014). https://doi.org/10.1007/978-3-319-13695-0_57
7. Panayiotou, S., Lanitis, A.: Paintings alive: a virtual reality-based approach for enhancing the user experience of art gallery visitors. In: Ioannides, M. (ed.) EuroMed 2016. LNCS, vol. 10059, pp. 240–247. Springer, Cham (2016). https://doi.org/10.1007/978-3-319-48974-2_27
8. Perez, L., Wang, J.: The effectiveness of data augmentation in image classification using deep learning. arXiv preprint arXiv:1712.04621 (2017)
9. Ragusa, F., Furnari, A., Battiato, S., Signorello, G., Farinella, G.M.: Egocentric visitors localization in cultural sites. J. Comput. Cult. Heritage (JOCCH) **12**(2), 1–19 (2019). https://doi.org/10.1145/3276772
10. Skoryukina, N.S., Nikolaev, D.P., Arlazarov, V.V.: 2d art recognition in uncontrolled conditions using one-shot learning. In: Eleventh International Conference on Machine Vision (ICMV 2018), vol. 11041, p. 110412E. International Society for Optics and Photonics (2019). https://doi.org/10.1117/12.2523017
11. Taverriti, G., Lombini, S., Seidenari, L., Bertini, M., Del Bimbo, A.: Real-time wearable computer vision system for improved museum experience. In: Proceedings of the 24th ACM international conference on Multimedia, pp. 703–704 (2016). https://doi.org/10.1145/2964284.2973813
12. Zhao, Z.Q., Zheng, P., Xu, S.t., Wu, X.: Object detection with deep learning: A review. IEEE Trans. Neural Netw. Learn. Syst. **30**(11), 3212–3232 (2019). https://doi.org/10.1109/TNNLS.2018.2876865

The Usability of Romanian Open Data in the Development of Tourist Applications

Ilie Cristian Dorobăț[(✉)] and Vlad Posea

"Politehnica" University of Bucharest, Bucharest, Romania
ilie.dorobat@stud.acs.upb.ro, vlad.posea@cs.pub.ro

Abstract. The centralization of public data and the adoption of the open data concept are directions on which governors have begun to turn their attention more and more. Unfortunately, although the efforts in this direction are increasing, the Romanian public authorities offer access mainly to semi-structured or unstructured data, which only makes their use more difficult. Only for data on museums and collections in Romania, two web portals are available, a data set in CSV format and a series of other data sets structured according to the LIDO XML Schema. In order to use these data sets, we had to consolidate them using both specific techniques for browsing and pre-processing them, and using the eCHO framework, through which the digital representation of classified cultural assets was migrated to Linked Data. Finally, the data resulting from the consolidation process was used to develop a web application through which users can more easily view this information and, based on it, create their own tourist routes directly from the application.

Keywords: Cultural heritage · Open data · Data modeling

1 Introduction

Although the centralization of public data and the adoption of *open data* [1] lead to an increase in the volume of data, they are often not published in easy pre-processing formats, are not updated or do not present a degree of detail of the resources represented as high as some public portals do. Such a case is represented by the cultural data that state institutions make public.

In the case of museums, the National Heritage Institute (INP) provides both a web platform whose interface is rudimentary and outdated to the current needs of users, and a data set in CSV format in which certain information is presented in addition to those two platforms. Also, for the representation of the collections that the museums host, INP provides both an interface similar to the one for representing museums, and a data set in XML format. Unfortunately, the use of this data for the development of a modern tourist application is burdensome and requires further pre-processing to combine data sets and increase the quality level.

This paper begins with a description of the data sources and sets used, and the techniques used for pre-processing the data sets will be presented in Sect. 3. Section 4 is intended to present the tourist platform developed based on pre-processed sets, and the

© Springer Nature Switzerland AG 2021
M. Ioannides et al. (Eds.): EuroMed 2020, LNCS 12642, pp. 596–602, 2021.
https://doi.org/10.1007/978-3-030-73043-7_51

last section is reserved to the presentation of the conclusions of the study and the further development directions.

2 Data Considerations

INP is a Romanian public institution of culture operating in the field of protection, restoration, research and promotion of cultural heritage under the subordination of the Ministry of Culture [2]. It was created following the reorganization of some public institutions subordinated to the Ministry of Culture, among which the Institute of Cultural Memory (CIMEC), whose field of activity is the digitalization of the Romanian cultural heritage. In the following, we will refer only to the INP regardless of whether the activities described were undertaken during the operation of CIMEC or after the reorganization.

The Directory of Museums and Collections in Romania[1], hereinafter referred to as GMCR[2], is a web portal launched by the INP in 1999 to promote public museums and the collections they host. Although the information on this portal is updated periodically (the last update was dated 08.31.2020), the interface remained unchanged, at the level of the years when the Internet entered the Romanian market. In addition to this portal, INP also provides a data set[3] in CSV format which, in addition to the information presented in the GMCR, also contains some additional information such as the description of the building where the museum is housed, the history of the museum, the geographical coordinates of its location, etc. (the last update of this data set was dated 05.18.2017).

Another series of data on which we focused our attention is the list of movable cultural assets classified in the National Cultural Heritage[4]. This list is a series of data sets in XML format in which are found the descriptions of no less than 36,132 cultural assets classified in the following fields: archaeology, art, decorative art, documents, ethnography, history of science and technology, history, metalinguistics, numismatics and natural sciences. For the presentation of this data, INP makes available another web portal, *clasate.cimec.ro*[5], but which unfortunately follows the same direction as GMCR, keeping an interface not suited by nature to the current needs of users.

3 Data Preparation

In order to ensure the highest possible degree of reliability, a step preceding the use of data is their pre-processing. The following will detail the steps taken to increase the level of quality of the data used.

---

[1] https://ghidulmuzeelor.cimec.ro/.

[2] GMCR is the abbreviation of the Romanian name of the web portal, *"Ghidul Muzeelor și Colecțiilor din România"*.

[3] https://data.gov.ro/dataset/ghidul-muzeelor-din-romania.

[4] https://data.gov.ro/organization/institutul-national-al-patrimoniului.

[5] https://clasate.cimec.ro/.

3.1 Directory of Museums and Collections

One of the directions of this study aims to improve the representation of information on museums and their collections. For this purpose, we consider the consolidation of the information that INP makes available on the GMCR portal with those found in the CSV data set made available on the *data.gov.ro* governmental platform, following the direction presented in Fig. 1.

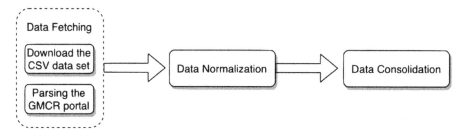

Fig. 1. Data pre-processing workflow.

The first step in the consolidation process is the actual acquisition of data. This process consists on the one hand in downloading and browsing the CSV data set, and on the other hand in programmatically browsing of the GMCR portal. For the latter, the access links to the detail pages of each museum are identified, because then we go through the detail pages one by one. At the end, we store the extracted data in two JSON sets, one for the data extracted from the CSV file, and another for the data extracted from the GMCR portal.

After collecting the raw data, a pre-processing stage follows, during which the feature names are normalized. For example, the name of the *"e-mail"* feature name extracted from the CSV file, respectively the *"E-MAIL address"* feature name extracted from the GMCR portal will be standardized according to a single format, namely: *"contact.email"*. Finally, the two standardized data sets are subject to a consolidation process following the rules below:

- if both data sets contain values for the same feature (e.g.: *"contact.email"*), only the value from the GMCR data set is retained.
- in the other cases, the identified values are kept.

Thus, keeping the set built when browsing the GMCR portal as a reference set and using the CSV set only for extracting additional information that is not found on the portal, ensures the highest possible data accuracy. This accuracy is practically due to the fact that the GMCR portal is updated more frequently than the other data set.

3.2 Movable Assets Classified in the National Cultural Heritage

For the digital representation of classified cultural assets, the Romanian authorities use a standard used by a wide range of European cultural institutions [3], the Lightweight Information Describing Objects XML Schema[6] (LIDO). However, representation through an XML schema remains trivial, given that ontology offers flexibility and a higher level of detail. Among the most important limitations that XML schemas have are:

- the represented resources cannot include semantic structures that detail their meaning.
- the concepts represented must be defined for each record (e.g.: the definition of an institution will be made for each record because there is no reference that can be reused).
- concepts from other vocabularies cannot be used to define resources, the user being strictly limited to what the schema offers.

Therefore, in order to cover the shortcomings of an XML schema, we propose to transform these data sets into semantic structures, having as reference the Europeana Data Model (EDM), a data model designed and used by Europeana[7], the largest digital library in Europe [4]. For this process, we consider the use of Enhancing the Digital Representation of Cultural Heritage Objects Framework (eCHO) [5], a framework developed to cover the need to translate data sets represented through the LIDO schema into semantic data sets, structured according to EDM.

Following the flow presented in Fig. 2, eCHO receives as input the analysed data set that it runs through, so that the LIDO features are then mapped into equivalent EDM features and classes. During the translation, the time intervals are brought to a common standard, links are created between both internal and external resources (e.g.: DBpedia), and for features that cannot be mapped, the vocabulary will be extended with new features. Finally, they will be built as extensions of the *"dc:description"* feature, a procedure that allows the extension of the vocabulary without affecting its structure.

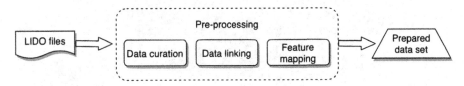

Fig. 2. LIDO to EDM workflow.

4 Data Visualization

Although data processing is a step by which their quality is validated and/or improved, the way data is exposed also plays an important role in the decision of end-users whether

---

[6] https://www.lido-schema.org/schema/v1.0/lido-v1.0-schema-listing.html.

[7] https://www.europeana.eu/en.

or not to use an application. The User Experience (UX) [6], as also defined in specialized terminology, has been designed to allow users to easily identify museums in their area of interest. More specifically, the application displays a map of the country designed through the means of Leaflet library[8], in which the counties are outlined and coloured in a different shade of blue. As can be seen in Fig. 3, the counties in which the number of museums is very small have a shade that goes to white (e.g.: Sălaj, Călărași, etc.), and the counties in which there are as many museums as possible are coloured in a shade that goes to black (e.g.: Alba, Bucharest, etc.).

Filtering of museums is as simple as possible, requiring only one click on the desired county, and the application will filter and display only the museums in the area of the selected county. When clicking outside the layers that outline the counties, the application will hide or show the markers again depending on their current status. A similar functionality to filtering is the opening of the details panel, for which users must first click on a marker displayed on the map. This action will trigger the opening of a pop-up displaying the name of the museum represented by the respective marker and a button whose role is to open a panel with more information, as in Fig. 4.

Last but not least, users have the possibility to calculate and view a tourist route composed of selected museums, the selection being made by triggering a double-click event on the desired marker. When selecting at least two markers, the route will be calculated automatically applying the formula presented in [7].

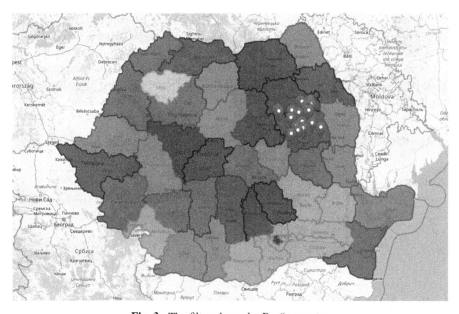

Fig. 3. The filtered map by Bacău county.

---

[8] https://leafletjs.com/.

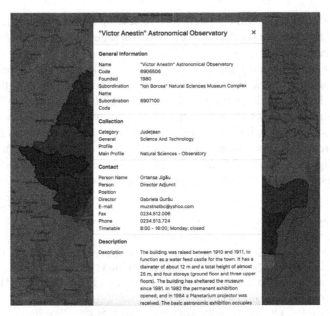

Fig. 4. The museum details pane.

5 Conclusions and Further Development

The quality of data provided by public institutions differs from case to case. If in some cases, public authorities provide data sets in machine-readable format (CSV, XML, etc.), often the representation is limited to the presentation of data on a web portal, or in hard-to-process formats such as PDF, JPEG, etc. In order for this data to be used in the production of applications, it must undergo a pre-processing step.

By analysing the data on museums and collections in Romania, we found that they are represented in several forms, depending on the represented object, as follows:

- the representation of museums is done both in CSV format and through the GMCR portal.
- the representation of classified cultural assets is done both using an XML schema and through the *clasate.cimec.ro* portal.

By applying specific procedures for aligning the two ways of representation of museums, we managed to reduce the two data sources to one that contains both the information displayed on the GMCR portal and those in the CSV file. In order to ensure the highest possible accuracy, the new data set is based on the data extracted from the GMCR portal, these being updated more frequently, the CSV data set being used only for extracting data that are not found on the portal. Also, using the eCHO framework, data on cultural assets were migrated to Linked Data, thus benefiting from an increase in the degree of data representation.

Finally, the pre-processed data were used to develop a tourist application that users can use both for a more in-depth knowledge of the museums and collections they exhibit, and for planning tourist routes.

Next, we aim to identify the most appropriate ontology for the representation of public institutions, so that we can also migrate to Linked Data the data that describe museums as institutions. Regarding the development of the UX, we aim to facilitate the design and saving of routes by extending the functionality to the possibility of changing the start/stop point and by implementing an administration panel that users can use both for editing routes and for sharing them with other users. At the same time, after the complete migration in Linked Data, we want to implement the onIQ interface [8] that will allow users to query the data warehouse using natural language.

References

1. Gurstein, M.B.: Open data: Empowering the empowered or effective data use for everyone? First Monday **16**(2–7), (2011) https://doi.org/10.5210/fm.v16i2.3316;
2. Government Decision no. 593/2011 from June 08, 2011 on the organization and functionating of the National Heritage Institute
3. de Boer, V., et al.: Amsterdam museum linked open data. Semant. Web **4**(3), 237–243 (2013). https://doi.org/10.3233/SW-2012-0074
4. Meghini, C., Bartalesi, V., Metilli, D., Benedetti, F.: Introducing Narratives in Europeana: A Case Study. Int. J. Appl. Math. Comput. Sci. **29**(1), 7–16 (2019). https://doi.org/10.2478/amcs-2019-0001
5. Dorobăț, I.C., Posea, V.: Raising the interoperability of cultural datasets: the Romanian cultural heritage case study. In: Themistocleous, M., Papadaki, M., Kamal, M.M. (eds.) EMCIS 2020. LNBIP, vol. 402, pp. 35–48. Springer, Cham (2020). https://doi.org/10.1007/978-3-030-633 96-7_3
6. Hassenzahl, M., Tractinsky, N.: User experience - a research agenda. Behav. Inf. Technol. **25**(2), 91–97 (2006). https://doi.org/10.1080/01449290500330331
7. Rinciog, O., Dorobăț, I.C., Posea, V.: Route suggestion for visiting museums using semantic data. eLearning Softw. Educ. **3**, 48–55 (2017). https://doi.org/10.12753/2066-026X-17-180
8. Dorobăț, I.C., Posea, V.: onIQ: an ontology-independent natural language interface for building SPARQL queries. In: International Conference on Intelligent Computer Communication and Processing (2020)

Short Papers: Reproduction Techniques and Rapid Prototyping in CH

Prototypes to Increase Museum Experience and Accessibility. Palazzo Mazzonis' Atrium in Turin: The Work in Progress

Francesca Ronco[✉]

Department of Architecture and Design, Politecnico Di Torino, Viale Mattioli 39, Torino, Italy
francesca.ronco@polito.it

Abstract. Today, the availability of digital scanning and computer-aided design and fabrication process open possibilities for automation that allows the reproduction of objects in different formats, facilitating the access to the cultural heritage.

Projects as Europeana, the European digital library, and "Horizon 2020 Reflective Societies 7–2014: Advanced 3D modeling for accessing and understanding European cultural assets" confirm this trend in this field.

Museums are the places where the concept of "usability" of CH has always been manifested, representing the perfect context to explore the huge potentials of modern technologies of rapid prototyping, which allow quickly reproducing an object from a 3D model, offering new opportunities of experience.

The extension of accessibility of CH to disabled people is a current topic of great importance. Physical, sensorial and cultural accessibility are to be considered essential to make the places of culture fully accessible to all visitors (MiBACT).

The research focuses on the use of digital fabrication techniques (CNC milling machine) to realize tactile architectural models to enrich the accessibility of Museo di Arte Orientale (MAO) in Turin, in a "Design for All" perspective.

The experimentation has been carried out on the vaulted system of the atrium of Palazzo Mazzonis that hosts the MAO.

Keywords: Prototyping · CNC milling machine · Tactile museum

1 Introduction

The research presented in this paper starts from an ongoing collaboration with the Museo di Arte Orientale (MAO) in Turin, located in Palazzo Mazzonis, that aims to build an accessible exposure path including tactile models of architectural spaces and of a small part of its collection.

During August 2019 was carried out a metric survey directed by Concepción López, using terrestrial laser scanning (TLS), in the frame of the international collaboration for the project "Nuevas tecnologías para el análisis y conservación del patrimonio arquitectónico", funded by the Ministry of Science, Innovation and the University of Spain.

M. Ioannides et al. (Eds.): EuroMed 2020, LNCS 12642, pp. 605–613, 2021.
https://doi.org/10.1007/978-3-030-73043-7_52

The research group, coordinated by Roberta Spallone and Marco Vitali at the Politecnico di Torino and with the participation as visiting professor of Concepción López, from Universitat Politecnica de Valencia, surveyed the atrium, the stately staircase and the first floor hall of honour of Palazzo Mazzonis.

The digital survey has been the starting point of a whole workflow that passes through two and three-dimensional virtual models and finishes with prototypes.

In the ModLab Arch and ModLab Design laboratories of the Department of Architecture and Design at Politecnico di Torino, where the author of this paper is research assistant, a series of experiments in digital fabrication are in progress, using their laser cut and CNC milling machines.

This paper is focused on the architectural model of the vaulted system of Palazzo Mazzonis atrium, in the frame of rapid prototyping as a mean to increase the accessibility in a "Design for All" perspective.

2   Digital Fabrication for Cultural Heritage

In recent years the development of 3D technologies has led to important results in the Cultural Heritage field. Project as Europeana, the European digital library, and "Horizon 2020 Reflective Societies 7–2014: Advanced 3D modeling for accessing and understanding European cultural assets" confirm this trend.

Today, the availability of digital scanning and computer-aided design and fabrication process open possibilities for automation that allow the reproduction of objects in different formats, facilitating the access to the cultural heritage [1].

The workflow starts with recording the shape of the object and finishes with its physical reproduction. Laser scanner technology allows a rapid elaboration of digital models of surfaces and complex geometries which would be very difficult to survey with traditional topographic instruments. The recent evolution of 3D terrestrial laser scanners (TLS) and related software, photogrammetric restitution techniques has brought great progress in rapid prototyping applications.

The use of digital fabrication based on metric surveying enables production of objects that replicate the true shapes. The "point cloud," obtained by photogrammetry or laser scanning, provides on one hand a record of the true state of an object in a given space–time context, and on the other hand a base for building models that can be a perfect replica of the original object or, by modifying it, its reinterpretation. The advantages of digital survey techniques are several: physical contact with sensitive objects and exhibits is not necessary; researchers and technical experts can share digital models on a global scale, and the public can enjoy museum collections in richer ways, through the experience of physical replicas [2].

The literature on digital modeling applications for CH tends to be intermingled with that on solid printing, but for some kind of models the CNC milling machine could be the best solution, as shown after.

3   Digital Fabrication for the Museums' Accessibility

Museums represent the field where the concept of "usability" of CH has always been manifested, perfect context to explore the huge potentials of modern technologies of rapid prototyping, which allow quickly reproducing an object from a 3D model, offering new opportunities of experience. The extension of accessibility of CH to disabled people is a current topic of great importance. Physical, sensorial and cultural accessibility are to be considered essential to make the places of culture fully accessible to all visitors (MiBACT). Besides, accessibility to CH is sustained by Council of Europe that adopted a new "Strategy on the Rights of Persons with disabilities 2017–2023" [3].

Contemporary technologies are an opportunity to add new "reading" tools to traditional visitor paths, transforming then in a multi-level and multi-sensory experience that includes not only the sight, but also senses of touch, smell, and hearing that contribute in the same way to our knowledge about of our surrounding reality [2].

Museums are so giving particular attention to the manipulation of objects, physical or virtual, because it creates a stronger connection than mere sight, between the individual and the object [4]. While touching the original objects would be best, this is not always feasible due to inappropriate scale, lack of tangible features or conservatory and safety concerns.

How to reproduce models that are suitable to be explored and understood during tactile experience, becomes the main issue. Computer-aided tools offer great potential for the design and production of tactile models to engage users with material culture.

3D models of statues, buildings or plans are very useful tools to involve people, particularly suitable for users with special needs, such as blind people, who rely on the sense of touch to perceive objects. The new consideration of this often-ignored public has widen the investigation field about all the experiential possibilities in the museum offer, beyond the visual one.

Today, many research and applications of digital fabrication in museum field have been realized. And over the years have been gradually combined with other technologies, creating multisensory and didactic experiences.

Digitally fabricated reliefs have been introduced to communicate bidimensional information, such as architectural facades, photos and paintings. The Tooteko app case study [5] deploys NFC technology to provide audio descriptions of a 15th century church facade in Italy.

3DPhotoworks [6], USA based company, produces coloured tactile prints that, for the "Sight Unseen" exhibition at the Canadian Museum for Human Rights have embedded touch sensors which trigger audio descriptions.

University of Vienna [4] carried out research concerning 2d and 3d artefacts conversion in tactile replicas, then enriched by audio guide, a tactile guiding system and embossed diagrams.

Other applications have used interactive 3D printed models equipped with sensors such as cameras [7], capacitive sensors and microphones [8].

The "Orasis" project deploys 3D printed exhibits, attached touch sensors, Arduino boards, and mobile app to enhance access to museums for blind users [9].

Other applications, such as the 3d puzzle activity at Brighton Museum and Art Gallery, are focused on the didactic aim of the replica and on educational and communicational aspect of the CH experience, proposing playful use of it [10].

These experiences witness that for sure one of the objectives in applied research is to create "sensorized" models [1]. Digital fabrication replicas and models have to be more and more flanked with other technologies to create remarkable added value in the museum context, confirming the need of a multidisciplinary approach to guarantee the highest possible accessibility to museums and cultural heritage in general.

4   The Case Study. Palazzo Mazzonis, Its History in Brief

Palazzo Mazzonis has been from the beginning a high-representation building for residential use, privately owned by the important noble family Solaro della Chiusa.

It is the result of the transformation of a pre-existing building (1639) and of subsequent works, wanted by Francesco Amedeo Ludovico Solaro della Chiusa and completed in 1735. This intervention has been traditionally attributed to Benedetto Alfieri, as written by Luigi Cibrario [11], even if archive documents never speak explicitly about him.

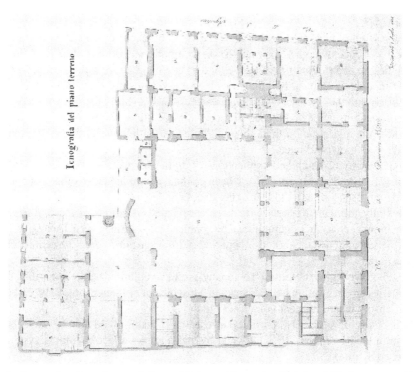

Fig. 1. Survey drawing of ground floor of Palazzo Mazzonis, 1st July 1845. Source: Archivio Storico del Comune di Torino, Tipi e dis., cart. 63, fasc. 9, dis. 1, tav III.

In the 18th century Palazzo Mazzonis assumed the current shape after various interventions. It is constituted by a central part, along via San Domenico, and other two parts embracing the central inner courtyard, linked to the road by a great colonnaded atrium. Its façade is characterized by a portal that is the only decorated part. The great atrium, adorned by an elegant stone colonnade, is connected by a sumptuous two flights staircase with stone balustrade to the hall of honor at the first floor.

Over the years it passed into the hands of several owners. In 1830, it passed to Earl Clemente Solaro della Margherita, who commissioned, in 1845 (see Fig. 1), the survey of the building (now preserved in the Historical Archive of the City), from which emerges a layout very similar to the one previous to the restoration works of 1982.

In 1870 the building was sold to a textile industrialist, Paolo Mazzonis and the ground floor was converted into the offices of the Manifattura Mazzonis S.n.c., remaining such for a century. In 1968 the company stopped its activity and the - building remained unused.

In 1980 City of Turin bought the building and in 1982 launched the restoration project, the partial renovation and functional recovery of the building as the headquarters of the judicial offices, that in 2001 were transferred to new Palace of Justice.

In 2004 it has been transformed into the Museum of Oriental Art (MAO). The final project for the construction, constitution and exhibition of the Museum was developed by the Cultural Buildings Sector with the collaboration of the architect Andrea Bruno [12, 13].

(a)   (b)

Fig. 2. Palazzo Mazzonis: a. vaulted system of the atrium near the entrance; b. vaulted system of the atrium near the courtyard. Photo by F. Ronco.

5   The Atrium from the Geometrical Analysis to the Digital Fabricated Tactile Model with CNC Milling Machine

The atrium of Palazzo Mazzonis is characterized by an area, near the entrance from the street, covered by rectangular base sailing vault intersected with a barrel vault, set on the transverse axis and corner sailing vaults (see Fig. 2a) and an area, facing the courtyard, with three aisles covered by a central sail vault and two lateral groin vaults (see Fig. 2b).

The workflow is divided in three main phases: digital acquisition (TLS), virtual reconstruction and digital fabrication. The digital acquisition carried out with terrestrial laser scanner Focus 130 × 3D model by Faro and the digital reconstruction were supported by geometric interpretations, archive drawings and on site eidotypes.

The cleaned point cloud has been imported in AutoCAD® and the detected data are discretized into a series of lines, first following rigorously the real state of the vaults and after proceeding with their geometric ideal drawing. Horizontal and vertical cutting plans are then used to obtain sections, to build the virtual interpretative model with Rhinoceros® that, in the current experimental phase, is focused exclusively on the vaulted space above the impost plane.

This model has been conceived in the perspective of tactile fruition and experience. The first step to realize a good tactile model is to start from a very simple digital model. In this sense, guidelines for tactile graphics [14] are very useful, even if they refer to the constructions of 2D models.

The voids have become solids, the spaces covered by vaults are then filled and represented in negative. The aim is to obtain a handy object, very similar to a wooden puzzle toy, that allows to perceive the intrados surface of the vaults from above.

The model will be fabricated at 1:50 scale, to be easy to handle but perceivable at the same time.

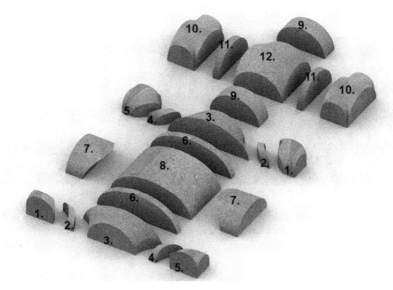

Fig. 3. Palazzo Mazzonis atrium 3d model (Rhinoceros®): different puzzle pieces, differentiated by toolpath CNC milling machine types. (1.-5.) corner sail vaults, (2.-4.) curved arc; (3.) longitudinal sail vault; (6.-9.-11.) arc; (7.-8.) barrel vault; (10.) cross vault; (12) square sail vault.

Autodesk Fusion 360 ® is the software chosen to realize this touchable model to be fabricated in Medium Density Fiberboard (MDF) with the CNC milling machine located in ModLab Design laboratory (Isel OVERHEAD® M50).

The atrium space is characterized by ten typologically different covered portions and, from the production perspective, by twelve different puzzle pieces (see Fig. 3), or twelve different milling setups (some pieces are geometrically the same but mirrored).

This correspondence between vaults and the puzzle pieces, could be useful also for didactic purpose, to help users understand difference between them and their generative shapes.

In the production phase the main task is to adapt the models or the workflow to the characteristics of the CNC milling machine and of available tool. In this case the biggest constrain is the height of the tool under the holder. The bigger piece (n. 12) at the scale of 1:50 is 4.2 cm high compared to the maximum length of 4.2 cm of the tool outside the holder. For this reason the making process will be divided into two steps: roughing and finishing.

The roughing phase will be managed with a 6mm diameter flat end mill that will follow two pocket toolpaths that cut inside the closed shape, removing all the material within the pocket to a user-specified depth. Pocket cuts have vertical sides and a flat bottom [15], giving to the object a stepped appearance.

Currently for all the pieces the toolpaths have been prepared and verified by simulation feature of Autodesk Fusion 360® software (see Fig. 4).

The finishing phase, for time reason, will be probably managed manually through a manual disk grinder located in the ModLab Design laboratory equipped with a 80 gr glass paper.

The research program foresees during next months, the fabrication of the puzzle pieces, the realization of the model of the plan to be fitted by pieces and a first round of test with visually-impaired persons.

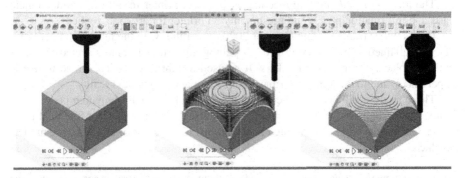

Fig. 4. Palazzo Mazzonis atrium 3d model (Autodesk Fusion 360®) the fabrication process simulation of piece n. 12 (sail vault), roughing phase: a. the stock; b. the mill toolpath; c. the obtained stepped model

6   Conclusion

Laser scanning and rapid prototyping offers great opportunities to bring back tactile experiences in our cultural heritage, extending accessibility in a "Design for All" perspective, a context where all people benefit from these improvements.

The digital fabrication techniques can be used both for models of small artworks, such as statues or paintings, and of large cultural sites, such as buildings or squares, including domes, plans and smaller details that are not directly accessible by touch.

MAO represents a great opportunity to test different digital survey and fabrication techniques, at different scales ad on different objects, for the architectural exhibition spaces and for pieces of its collection.

The current ongoing experiments are related to the architecture of Palazzo Mazzonis, started from the before mentioned digital laser scanner survey, but the program will include also the survey and the modelling of a selection of artefacts.

The final aim is to design and realize different tools to improve and expand the museum offer as tactile drawings, tactile models and information panels.

Architectural models and informative panels help any kind of user to understand the exhibition space and to be prepared for the visit, providing an overview via a guided tactile exploration. They facilitate the explanation and learning by visually impaired people who often do not have the opportunity to directly perceive certain details, such as the architectural elements [16]. Artefacts replicas are more specific and represent the second deeper step in the museum experience.

Most of literature about the generation of tactile models is focused on 3D printing method and different approaches have been designed for the production of tactile material for people with visual impairments through content [17]. The production with CNC milling machine is a challenge and at the same time open the possibility to use different materials and finishing.

The idea is to CNC milling machine or laser cut printer for all the architectonical parts and information panels and presumably 3d printer for artworks replica.

In this wider frame, during October 2020, in parallel with the fabrication activities before explained, digital survey through photogrammetry of some selected artworks will take place. Their virtual model will be used to fabricate replica, aimed to tactile experiences, and to do some experiments of virtual and augmented reality.

These models will need to be continuously tested by visually-impaired people and, thanks to the help of Dr. Franco Lepore, Disability Manager of the Municipality of Turin, test groups will be constituted to verify the effectiveness of all the tactile models produced.

Acknowledgements. This research is carried out within the framework of an agreement between the Museo d'Arte Orientale and the Politecnico di Torino. I would like to thank Dr. Marco Guglielminotti Trivel, Director of the Museum, Dr. Claudia Ramasso, museum curator and Mrs. Patrizia Bosio, from Technical and Security Office for having favored the current research and Dr. Francesco Lepore for his help in the management of the model testing phase that will take place soon.

References

1. Reichinger, A., Neumüller, M., Rist, F., Maierhofer, S., Purgathofer, W.: Computer-aided design of tactile models. In: Miesenberger, K., Karshmer, A., Penaz, P., Zagler, W. (eds.) ICCHP 2012. LNCS, vol. 7383, pp. 497–504. Springer, Heidelberg (2012). https://doi.org/10.1007/978-3-642-31534-3_73
2. Balletti, C., Ballarin, M.: An application of integrated 3D technologies for replicas in cultural heritage. ISPRS Int. J. Geo-Inf. **8**(6), 285 (2019)

3. Scianna, A., Di Filippo, G.: Rapid prototyping for the extension of the accessibility to cultural heritage for blind people. In: Gonzalez-Aguilera, D., Remondino, F., Toschi, I., Rodriguez-Gonzalvez, P., Stathopoulou, E. (eds.) CIPA International Symposium "Documenting the past for a better future", vol. XLII-2/W15, 2019, 27th, pp. 1077–1088, The International Archives of the Photogrammetry, Remote Sensing and Spatial Information Sciences, Ávila (2019)
4. Candling, F.: Art, Museums and Touch. Manchester University Press, Manchester (2010)
5. D'Agnano, F., Balletti, C., Guerra, F., Vernier, P.: Tooteko: A case study of augmented reality for an accessible cultural heritage. Digitization, 3D printing and sensors for an audio-tactile experience. ISPRS – Int. Arch. Photogramm. Remote Sens. Spatial Inf. Sci. **40**, 207–213 (2015). https://doi.org/10.5194/isprsarchives-XL-5-W4-207-2015
6. Photoworks: 3D Photo Printing Products. https://www.3dphotoworks.com/product. Accessed 19 Oct 2020
7. Reichinger, A., Fuhrmann, A., Maierhofer, S., Purgathofer, W.: Gesture-based interactive audio guide on tactile reliefs. In: ASSETS 2016, vol. 16, pp. 91–100 (2016)
8. Shi, L., Zelzer, I., Feng, C. Azenkot, S.: Tickers and talker: an accessible labeling toolkit for 3D printed models. In: CHI 2016, pp. 4896–4907 (2016)
9. Anagnostakis, G., et al.: Accessible museum collections for the visually impaired: Combining tactile exploration, audio descriptions and mobile gestures. In: Proceedings of the 18th International Conference on Human-computer Interaction with Mobile Devices and Services Adjunct, Association for Computing Machinery, New York, NY, USA, pp. 1021–1025 (2016)
10. Samaroudi, M., Echavarria, K.R., Song, R., Evans, R.: The fabricated diorama: tactile relief and context-aware technology for visually impaired audiences. In: The Eurographics Association (2017)
11. Cibrario, L.: Storia di Torino. Alessandro Fontana, Torino (1846)
12. Cornaglia, P: Guida ai Cortili di Torino. Anteprima, Torino (2003)
13. Bruno, A., Ricca, F.: Il Museo d'Arte Orientale MAO, Allemandi, Torino (2010)
14. Götzelmann, T., Pavkovic, A.: Towards automatically generated tactile detail maps by 3D printers for blind persons. In: Miesenberger, K., Fels, D., Archambault, D., Peňáz, P., Zagler, W. (eds.) ICCHP 2014. LNCS, vol. 8548, pp. 1–7. Springer, Cham (2014). https://doi.org/10.1007/978-3-319-08599-9_1
15. Rohrbacher, G., Filson, A., Kaziunas France, A.,Young, B.: Make: Design for CNC. Furniture Projects and Fabrication Technique. 1st edn. Maker Media, San Francisco (2017)
16. Rossetti, V., Furfari, F., Leporini, B., Pelagatti, S., Quarta, A.: Enabling access to cultural heritage for the visually impaired: an interactive 3d model of a cultural site. In: Shakshuki, E., Yasar, A. (eds.) Procedia Computer Science vol. 130, pp. 383–391 (2018)
17. Neumüller, M., Reichinger, A., Rist, F., Kern, C.: 3D printing for cultural heritage: preservation, accessibility, research and education. In: Ioannides, M., Quak, E. (eds.) 3D Research Challenges in Cultural Heritage. LNCS, vol. 8355, pp. 119–134. Springer, Heidelberg (2014). https://doi.org/10.1007/978-3-662-44630-0_9

BIM and Rapid Prototyping for Architectural Archive Heritage

Giulia Bertola[⊠]

Department of Architecture and Design, Politecnico di Torino, Viale Mattioli 39, Turin, Italy
giulia.bertola@polito.com

Abstract. The present work intends to show a rapid prototyping experience carried out starting from a three-dimensional model realized with the Revit 2021® software of the never realized project of the "Due ville a Capri" by the Turin architect Aldo Morbelli. The scale model was realized through the application of two digital manufacturing techniques: additive, the Fused Deposition Modeling (FDM), used for the buildings and for the external built elements made of plastic and subtractive, the Laser Beam Machining (LBM), for the slope on which the two buildings stand, realized through the superimposition of cardboard layers.

The research after a first phase of redesign of the archival documents of the project in Revit 2021® focused on the preparation of the file for the realization of the real model, defining the printing scale, the materials, the exporting the file in STL format and the necessary operations to repair the file using Autodesk's software for additive manufacturing, Netfabb®.

Keywords: Rapid prototyping · Manufacturing · BIM

1 Introduction

The present work intends to continue a study previously carried out on the archival material relating to the project of "Due ville a Capri" by Aldo Morbelli (1942) through the use of traditional techniques and tools [1] and subsequently developed through digital modeling using the BIM Revit 2021® software (see Fig. 1).

This proposal is aimed at the valorization, cataloguing, digitalization and prototyping of the Archival Heritage present in the Archives of the Central Library of Architecture "Roberto Gabetti", Politecnico di Torino, in particular the BCA Archives. Aldo Morbelli fond. Three-dimensional models and the digitization of archival records represent today a key element for a deep understanding of the architectural projects of contemporary architects. The real models built must be able to be used at different scales, for different users and for different uses and also play an important role in communication and dissemination processes [2]. Here, the author, following a brief exposition of the case study, intends to focus on the elaboration of the BIM digital model aimed at rapid prototyping, exported in STL format and corrected by Autodesk's software for additive manufacturing, Netfabb®. In the following paragraphs, an in-depth study is developed on the printing techniques most suitable for the realization of the real scale model: Fused Deposition Modeling (FDM) and Laser Beam Machining (LBM).

M. Ioannides et al. (Eds.): EuroMed 2020, LNCS 12642, pp. 614–623, 2021.
https://doi.org/10.1007/978-3-030-73043-7_53

Fig. 1. Interpretative drawings for the project of the "Due case a Capri" (Drawings by Giulia Bertola)

2 Architectural Language of Aldo Morbelli and the Project for the "Due Case a Capri"

Aldo Morbelli (1903–1963) is an Italian architect, born in Orsara Bormida in Pie-mont. In the Thirties, after graduating from the Faculty of Architecture in Rome, he founded his own professional studio in Turin. During his professional activity Aldo Morbelli deals mainly with the design of single-family houses, social housing for the INA-CASA floor, buildings for entertainment, corporate headquarters and post-war reconstruction works, also dealing with interior design and furniture design.

Aldo Morbelli's archive, preserved in the Library of Architecture "Roberto Gabetti" of the Polytechnic of Turin, contains numerous documents relating to his projects, both completed and unfinished. The figure of Morbelli, despite the fact that in the past many of his projects were recognized in internationally renowned magazines and that critics dedicated a monographic issue on L'architettura Italiana to his single-family houses, is still little studied today [3].

In the present case study, he affirms himself through a poetics that tends to a process of formal simplification, to a careful search for balance between the project and its insertion in the context, bringing out a strong reference to Mediterranean architecture. In particular, he obtains interesting poetic results through the composition of white plastered walls combined with wood and other traditional materials used for the realization of pergolas, terraces and walls.

The buildings (see Fig. 2), never realized and defined by Morbelli Casa Grande (the lower) and Casa Piccola (the higher), are located on a plot of land among the olive groves at the foot of Mount Tuoro, in the region "La Cercola". The two buildings are oriented towards the west because of the slope of the land.

The compactness of the volumes is interrupted thanks to the reference to local archi-tecture, solved through the insertion of lowered arches and the choice of white color for the floor and wall covering, without seeming vernacular. The wall masses were modelled through sinuous volutes interrupted by simple cubic volumes in which the architect went to cut out the openings.

Both buildings are enriched by large pergolas arranged along the level lines that represent an extension of the houses themselves. Even in the interior spaces there is a

Fig. 2. A. Morbelli, technical drawings of "Due case a Capri" and study sketches for the two houses in Capri (Archivi BCA. Fondo Aldo Morbelli).

clear intention to give the rooms a plastic sense: the walls and distributive elements, such as the "S" staircase of the Casa Grande adapt to the plan. The small house is on three levels, basement floor for servants and storage, ground floor with living room and kitchen, through which is accessed through a sloping wall with arched entrance, and first floor with two bedrooms. The Casa Grande is on two levels only, the lower one is intended for the living area, with the living and dining area at double height that occupies the entire front with sea view and that of the services develops towards the mountain, while the highest one is intended for the sleeping area, with four bedrooms. The architect wanted to experiment with the insertion of different types of roofing: horizontal flat, sloping flat for the small house; barrel vaulted for the big house. Until now the three-dimensional characteristics of the project were perceptible only through photographs of a real model that had been lost (see Fig. 3).

Fig. 3. A. Morbelli, the real model of "Due case a Capri" (Archivi BCA. Fondo Aldo Morbelli).

3 The BIM Model for Digital Manufacturing

For this case study, we started with the creation of a BIM digital model generated from the import of archival documents into Revit 2021®. The BIM model provides a complete representation of both geometric and semantic data [4].

By connecting these data, it is possible to reach a more complete knowledge of the project, inserting inside a single file and 3D model information about the quantities, the geometric and volumetric characteristics and the construction characteristics of the architectural artefact. Being a 3D model aimed at the realization of a full-scale object, it was necessary, before the modelling operations, to define: the printing scale, the levels of detail, the most suitable materials and rapid prototyping techniques.

3.1 Dimensional Choices and File Preparation for the Printing Phases

Depending on the scale of reproduction, real or reduced it is necessary to enrich or simplify the model depending on how it is to be made. Usually the more complex is the shape, the more complex will be the production process [2].

This case study, being referred to a project not realized, having only drawings in scale 1:100 and not being possible to have additional information about the internal structures and stratigraphies, for the BIM model and the subsequent production of the physical model, it was initially decided to keep the same scale 1:100. Later, however, it was decided to work at scale 1:200, both for the export of plans, elevations and sections and for the processing of the real model.

The choice was mainly dictated by the dimensional requirements of the printing machines. To achieve the leap in scale, the model had to be simplified using Revit 2021®'s Visibility/Graphic Overrides tools, making the elements not to be printed invisible. The model was brought to the print scale 1:200, the system families related to windows and doors and all the internal elements (partitions and stairs) except the main floors were made invisible, so that only the external envelope (roof and perimeter walls) remained (see Fig. 4).

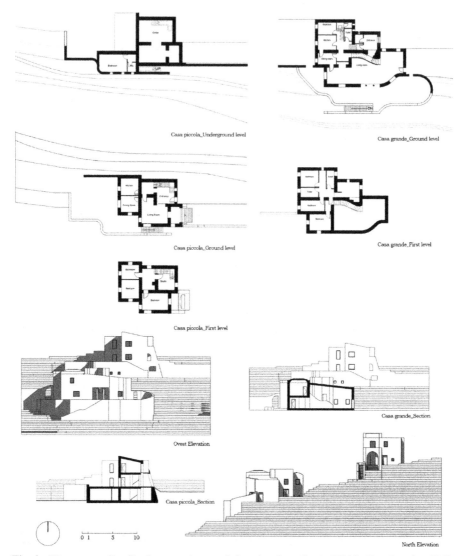

Fig. 4. "Due case a Capri", plans, sections and elevation from Revit 2021® (drawings by Giulia Bertola)

On Revit 2021®, the planes were subsequently brought to the same level so that a 2D CAD file could be exported.

As far as the terrain is concerned, the BIM model was used to make the topography of the terrain invisible and to design the terrain properly for the construction of the model. For the realization of the terracing it has been used the family category "floor" considering a thickness of the plans equal to 40 cm, in order to obtain a thickness of the real model in scale 1:200 equal to 2 mm (see Fig. 5).

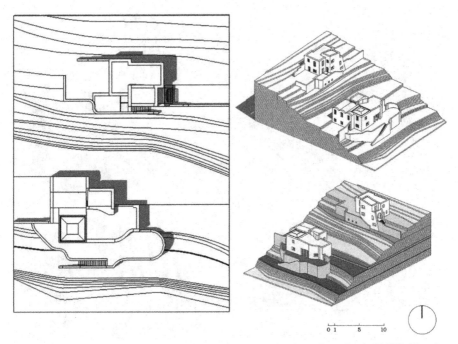

Fig. 5. "Due case a Capri", planimetric view, axonometric views from Revit 2021® (drawings by Giulia Bertola)

3.2 Exporting and Editing the File in STL Format

To proceed with the 3D printing, since an STL Exporter for Revit 2021® is not yet available, the file was exported in 1:100 scale in FBX format, imported into Rhinoceros® and then exported into STL. During the import phase in Rhinoceros®, the 3D model was scaled to scale 1:200 and the unit of measurement was changed to millimeters.

For dimensional issues related to the printing size of the machine, the models has been divided into parts: building blocks and exterior walls (see Fig. 6).

Standard Triangle Language (STL) is a format that uses small, interlinked triangles to recreate the surface of the solid model (see Fig. 7).

The level of complexity of the model determines the amount of triangles needed and their size. In turn, the amount of triangles determines the size of the file. As happened in this case, it may happen that during the conversion of the Revit file to STL, critical issues emerge and the exported file may contain some errors. These errors can be of various types: holes or blanks, inverted or intersected triangles.

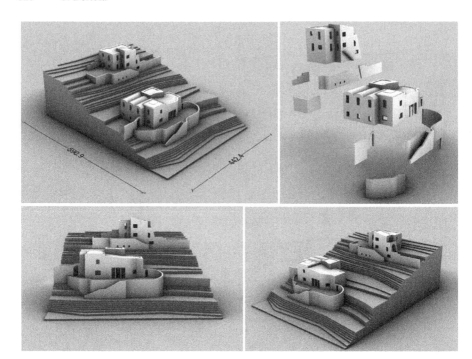

Fig. 6. "Due case a Capri", axonometric rendering view and axonometric cutaway from Rhinoceros® (drawings by Giulia Bertola)

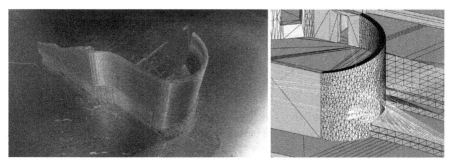

Fig. 7. "Due case a Capri", 3D printing of an external wall and axonometric view of STL file from Rhinoceros® (drawings and 3D printing by Giulia Bertola)

4   Digital Manufacturing Techniques: FDM E LBM

Digital Fabrication is a process by which solid objects can be created from digital drawings. A process capable of exploiting different manufacturing techniques, both additive, such as 3D printing and subtractive printing, laser cutting and milling.

As described above, two rapid prototyping methods were chosen for this case study: Fused Deposition Modeling (FDM) for buildings and built parts and Laser Beam Machining (LBM) for the ground [5].

4.1 Fused Deposition Modeling (FDM)

Nowadays there are several additive manufacturing processes that differ from each other depending on the different materials that can be used and how they are deposited to create the various objects. Some methods melt or soften materials to produce the layers, e.g. selective laser melting (SLM), selective laser sintering (SLS) and fused deposition modelling (FDM), while others cure liquid materials, e.g. stereolithography (SLA). The choice of a technique is usually made following some considerations made on the speed of processing, the cost, the material and the final aesthetic performance [6].

The buildings were made of plastic filament and printed using the Delta Wasp 2040 Industrial line 4.0® printer. This technique is referred to as additive manufacturing. Through a nozzle, it extrudes thermoplastic polymeric material, depositing it layer after layer on a construction surface [7].

Once the STL format was obtained, a test was made to verify the file through the software Cura, an open source slicing application for 3D printers through which an analysis of the model was carried out: thickness, stability, positioning and orientation of the model on the surface. The STL file was also automatically divided by the software into sections (slices). The software also automatically generates the support structures.

The plastic filament is conducted in a reel, pushed and melted through the extrusion nozzle. When the loose filament comes into contact with the construction plane it hardens and the rest of the material is gradually released (see Fig. 8).

Fig. 8. "Due case a Capri", 3D printing process.

4.2 Laser Beam Machining (LBM)

The soil was made of 2 mm thick cardboard using the Totrec Speedy 400® printer. Laser cutting is a process of thermal separation. The laser beam hits the surface of the material and heats it up to the point of melting or vaporizing it completely. Once the laser beam has completely penetrated the material at a certain point, the actual cutting process begins. The laser system follows the selected geometry and during this process the material is separated. From the 2D file generated by revit 2021® you can proceed with the print layout operations, defining the cutting power values using the Job Control® software.

5 Conclusion

The present work has shown the methodology of how it is possible to obtain a real model from a BIM project, having within a single file all the information necessary for an in-depth knowledge of an architectural project.

At the same time, however, numerous critical issues related to file management during the printing process have emerged.

Looking at the images related to the final model, which is still in the complete phase, it is possible to notice the difference between the correct models and not through the Netfabb® software. In the first case, the Casa Piccola has no surface defects or missing parts, in the second case, the Casa Piccola, there are many surface imperfections such as the trace of the internal floors on the perimeter walls and whole missing parts that will have to be printed separately and added (see Fig. 9).

Fig. 9. "Due case a Capri", real model (by Giulia Bertola)

For a more effective, fast and dynamic printing process, it would be necessary to add to the BIM project a 3D model made with CAD software, however, this would not allow a complete management, within a single file, of the reconstruction process of the archival project, which is the subject of this study. The future intention is to take forward the theme of prototyping from a BIM project, trying to optimize and improve the entire process as much as possible.

During the different phases of application of the BIM methodology the different heterogeneous data are collected within a single digital model. The data are then discretized to arrive at the definition of a geometric model enriched by the information of a semantic nature.

In the case of unbuilt architecture, the construction of digital models can be an opportunity to learn and clarify the aspects of architecture [8].

This cognitive process can lead to the construction of new digital representations that not only represent the virtual image of the building but become its only existential reality. We are therefore witnessing a reinterpretation of the documents and data collected during which it is necessary to take care not to generate ambiguous and confusing representations [9].

In the scenario of the digitization of archives, the 3D modeling phase allows extending the consultation of archival material, placing drawings and photographs alongside three-dimensional models that can be explored through virtual reality and augmented reality experiences, with the application of different digital interfaces, machine learning techniques, and computer supports.

The prototyping phase could, in addition to becoming an ideal context to experiment with the flexibility of the different printing techniques, give users the possibility, during the visit to the archive, to consult not only the original drawings but also plastic models that allow a better understanding of the three-dimensionality of the artifact. This could be particularly useful and significant in the case of unrealized architectures, such as those treated in this case study, and thus become the first and only physical representation of the artifact.

References

1. Spallone, R., Bertola, G.: Design drawings as cultural heritage. Intertwining between drawing and architectural language in the work of aldo morbelli. In: Agustín-Hernández, L., Vallespín Muniesa, A., Fernández-Morales, A. (eds.) EGA 2020. SSDI, vol. 6, pp. 73–85. Springer, Cham (2020). https://doi.org/10.1007/978-3-030-47983-1_7
2. Tucci, G., Bonora, V.: From real to "real". A review of geomatic and rapid prototyping techniques for solid modelling in cultural heritage field. In: International Archives of the Photogrammetry, Remote Sensing and Spatial Information Sciences, Volume XXXVIII-5/W16, 2011, ISPRS Trento 2011 Workshop, pp. 2–4. Trento, March 2011
3. Melis, A.: Architetti italiani. Aldo Morbelli L'architettura Ital. **3**, 49–72 (1942)
4. Paolini, A., Kollmannsberger, S., Rank, E.: Additive manufacturing in construction: a review on processes, application, and digital planning methods. Addit. Manufact. **30**, 100894 (2019)
5. Allahverdi, K., Djavaherpour, H., Mahdavi-Amiri, A., Samavati, F.: Landscaper: a modeling system for 3D printing scale models of landscapes. In: Eurographics Conference on Visualization (EuroVis), vol. 37, no. 3 (2018)
6. Bikas, H., Stavropoulos, P., Chryssolouris, G.: Additive manufacturing methods and modelling approaches: a critical review. Int. J. Adv. Manuf. Technol. **83**(1), 389–405 (2015). https://doi.org/10.1007/s00170-015-7576-2
7. Scopigno, R., Cignoni, P., Pietroni, N., Callieri, M., Dellepiane, M.: Digital fabrication techniques for cultural heritage: a survey. Comput. Graph. Forum **34**, 1–17 (2015)
8. Maggio, F., Scali, C.: Un disegno per isola delle femmine. Indagini digitali su gianni pirrone. In: Marsiglia, N. (ed.), La Ricostruzione Congetturale Dell'architettura. Storia, Metodi, Esperienze Applicative, pp. 222–236. Grafill (2013)
9. De Rubertis, R.: Il disegno dell'architettura, Carocci (1994)

The Vault with Intertwined Arches in Castle of Racconigi: 3D Digital Reconstruction

Fabrizio Natta(⊠)

Department of Architecture and Design, Politecnico di Torino, Viale Mattioli 39, Turin, Italy
fabrizio.natta@polito.it

Abstract. The complex approach of Guarini to each discipline (Geometry, Architecture, Philosophy, Astronomy) finds important development in his method of implementing vaulted systems.

The importance of this architectural element, which Guarini reminds as "the main part of the buildings", is reflected in the new taste of the civil architecture of the period.

The design by Guarini for the vault in the Hall of Honor in Racconigi Castle is documented in a single drawing representing the hall's cross-section. Guarini devotes particular attention to the drawing, both from the geometric and the representative point of view.

Based on this drawing we want to propose, through the most recent digital modeling and visualization methods, a three-dimensional reconstruction of this unrealized work.

The analysis method involves an in-depth examination of: Guarini's theory and his systematic approach to vaulted structures, linking Architecture and Geometry, the problems of design the artifacts, the comparison with similar shapes designed by the architect.

Through a method of representation based on geometrical principles, the aim of this paper is to give evidence – and a three-dimensional visualization – of a case study documented by an archival source, already analyzed by historians.

Keywords: Guarino guarini · Architectural drawing · Vaulted systems · 3D digital reconstruction

1 "On the Vaults, and Various Modes of Making Them"

The complex approach of Guarini to each discipline (Geometry, Architecture, Philosophy, Astronomy) finds important development in his method of implementing vaulted systems.

The importance of this architectural element, which Guarini reminds as "the main part of the buildings"[1], is reflected in the new taste of the civil architecture of the period.

---

[1] Guarini, G.: Architettura Civile. Treat. III, Cap. XXVI, «Delle Volte, e varj modi di farle» . Mairesse, Turin (1737).

© Springer Nature Switzerland AG 2021
M. Ioannides et al. (Eds.): EuroMed 2020, LNCS 12642, pp. 624–632, 2021.
https://doi.org/10.1007/978-3-030-73043-7_54

The discourse about the vaulted systems is articulated by Guarini through three texts: *Euclides adauctus* (1671), *Modo di misurare le fabriche* (1674) and *Architettura Civile* (published posthumously in 1737) [1].

In these writings are developed reasoning on the invention, construction, and calculation of surfaces and volumes of these shapes [2].

In the *Architettura Civile*, he dedicates a chapter on vaults and organized in "Observations", with continuous references to the *Euclides* in which he exposes the scientific demonstration of such contents. Guarini articulates through the observations with the numerous variables he found and those of his invention. The identification of "six round bodies"[2] (cylinder, cone, sphere, ellipsoid/oval rotation, ellipsoid/oval scalene), allow the generation of different types of vault, described and illustrated (see Fig. 1) by Guarini constituting a vocabulary on which to investigate and understand the coeval morphological and constructive issues.

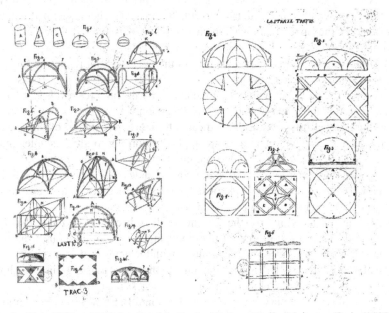

Fig. 1. Plate XIX and XX. In: Guarini, G.: Architettura Civile, Mairesse, Turin (1737).

These studies are also fundamental for understanding Guarini's method of graphic representation, which emphasizes the difficulty of "put in drawing"[3] these artifacts.

The analysis of Guarini's drawings and the recognizing of geometric rules at the basis of his design is a fundamental part of this study, which aims to find a three-dimensional visual solution to its shapes remained on paper.

---

[2] Guarini, G.: Architettura Civile. Treat. III, Cap. XXVI, Obs. I. «Delle Volte, e varj modi di farle» . Mairesse, Turin (1737).

[3] Guarini, G.: Architettura Civile. Treat. III, Cap. XXVI, «Delle Volte, e varj modi di farle» . Mairesse, Turin (1737).

The possibility of consulting Guarini's drawings, provided by the archival catalogue by Augusta Lange on the occasion of the Congress (concluded in 1670 with the publication of the proceedings) dedicated to the figure of Guarini [3], is an essential source for this type of research.

2 Guarini's Design for the Castle of Racconigi

Lange's work [4] allows us to view many drawings for Racconigi Castle by Guarini and his assistants from 1677 onwards.

The desire to transform the late medieval castle into an updated palace adapted to the popular French models of the time dates back at least to 1664, but the castle needed substantial modifications to become a new location to the Savoia-Carignano court [5].

Guarini's project is based on volumes designed in plan by his predecessors. He proposes a hall, located in the second floor level, within the walls of the inner courtyard of the old castle on which a spectacular vault with intertwined arches is set up. It is indirectly illuminated by the upper windows which natural light is filtered by an intermediate structure.

This intervention can be appreciated from the only drawing related to this project: the cross-section of the Hall of the Castle (see Fig. 2). The drawing is focused on the central part of the building, with half of the lateral rooms on three levels and not taking into consideration the underground level of the prisons.

All Guarini's efforts seem to be dedicated to the representation of this impressive vaulted structure. Watercolors colors are applied according to the principles indicated by him[4] and shading allows the understanding the spatiality of the complex structure.

As we can only refer to the section drawing to understand the spatial conformation of the hall, we have to complete its knowledge referring to other plans drawn up during the project phase by him and others architects.

Analyzing the drawings for the first noble floor it can be deduced that Guarini searched in the plan a ratio three by five, reducing the width to support the walls of the long sides of the hall in vertical continuity with the walls of the atrium [6].

The Hall is divided by half-pillars diagonal to the walls, thus dividing the short side into three bays, where large rectangular openings access the other rooms.

Through the relevant survey drawings by Giovanni Battista Borra, dated mid-fifties of the eighteenth century[5], it can be inferred that even the walls of the long side had to be divided into three larger areas.

Above the cornice it develops the vaulted structure made of intertwined arches, sails and eyes-shaped arranged around the large central opening with a total height similar to the order. The walls of the hall are raised in order to place an additional superimposed structure with the function of a light chamber – through a system of reflecting surfaces – and to mediate the presence of the sixteen large windows on the top level.

---

[4] Guarini, G.: Architettura Civile. Treat. I, Cap. VI, «Degl'Instrumenti dell'Architettur» . Mairesse, Turin (1737).

[5] Turin, Archivio di Stato di Torino, Archivio Savoia-Carignano, cat. 43, mazzo 1, fasc. 6, n. 22.

Fig. 2. Guarini, G.: Section of the hall of the Castle of Racconigi with the perforated vaulted structure. Approx. 1677. In: Turin, Archivio di Stato, Corte, Archivio Savoia-Carignano, cat. 95, mazzo 2, fasc. 121, n. 6.

2.1 Comparison with Other Guarini's Work

The solution proposed by Guarini for the Castle of Racconigi finds many references in other architectures built or only designed by him.

The system of intertwined arches is taken from its domes for churches with a central plan, mainly in the example of the church of San Lorenzo in Turin (see Fig. 3). This interweaving of arches is generated by the intersection of vertical planes on a polygonal plan with a surface of revolution. Geometry allows the system to be adopted to different solutions. In the designs for Palazzo Madama and Palazzo Carignano, instead, we find similar solutions related to the natural lighting system (see Fig. 3).

The need to have a large lighting inside the main hall leads the architect to think of a solution with a double ceiling; the first with the main vaulted structure, the second with a lightweight structure that allows to hide and filter the light from the large openings on the top level.

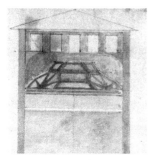
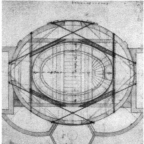
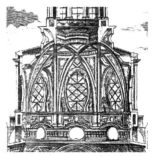

Fig. 3. Guarini, G.: Section for the vault of the hall of Palazzo Madama in Turin. Approx. 1675–1677. In: Turin, Archivio di Stato, Corte, Archivio Savoia-Carignano, cat. 43, mazzo 1, fasc. 3, n. 4; Guarini, G.: Study for the double vault of the hall of Palazzo Carignano in Turin. Approx. 1682. In: Turin, Archivio di Stato, Corte, Archivio Savoia-Carignano, cat. 95, mazzo 2, fasc. 39, n. 39); « Facies interna S. Laurentii Taurini » , detail of the cross-arched structure. In: Guarini, G.: Dissegni d'architettura civile et ecclesiastica, Eredi Giannelli, Turin (1686).

The project for Racconigi contains many of his concepts for "buildings with domes"[6], in a totally innovative way for the civil buildings of the time and where the hall represents the climax of the ceremonial path [7].

3   Geometric Approach for Shape Understanding

Guarini in the *Architettura Civile*[7] underlines the importance of the plan in his design methods [8]. The same attention is reserved in this study, so in the operations of graphic analysis and three-dimensional modeling, we wanted to investigate the construction of the plan and then make any considerations at the level of the sections.

Due to the limits in modeling of complex surfaces (expecially double curvature) of the software used, the room plan, which, as mentioned above, has a rectangular shape of ratios 3 by 5 had to be initially assumed as square. On this square plan was built the model of the vault that, finally, was modified to adapt it to the real shape of the plan.

For this reason, the construction starts from a square plan of side of about 12,6 m. (equal to 4 trabucchi[8]) in which a circumference is inscribed (see Fig. 4a). The tripartition of all sides is used to identify through diagonal lines the position of the intertwined arches (see Fig. 4b). Later the thickness of these arches (equal to about 0,50 m. or one piede liprando) has been established (see Fig. 4c). To complete the plan of the covering of the remaining fields are used ellipses tangent to the angular arches (see Fig. 4d). The remaining arcs of ellipses are radially divided (see Fig. 6e). Finally, the central opening plan is defined by circle portions (see Fig. 5f).

---

[6] Dardanello, G.: Le idee di Guarini per il palazzo con cupola di Racconigi, pp. 425–439. In: Dardanello, G., Klaiber, S., Millon, H. A. (eds.): Guarino Guarini. Allemandi. Turin (2006).

[7] Guarini, G.: Architettura Civile. Treat. II, Cap. VII. «Del modo in generale di disegnare le Piante» . Mairesse, Turin (1737).

[8] Ancient measure of length adopted in Piedmont equivalent to 3,086 meters. The trabucco could be divided into 6 *piedi liprandi* (equivalent to 0.513 m).

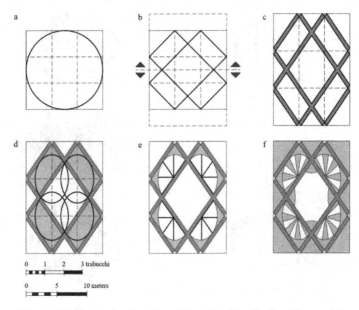

Fig. 4. Schematic plan drawing of the hall of the Castle of Racconigi.

The section of the Racconigi hall was already been object of study in its three-dimensional model since 2002[9]. The results have led to the construction of an analytical model of the arched structure and the possible overall conformation in projection in plan.

The present work focus on the geometric interpretation and choose a representation in orthogonal axonometry. The assessment of the shape tries to identified sequences and typical developments of Guarini's *modus operandi*.

Starting from a dome, the operation has been done by cutting planes of the principal shape following the diagonals identified by the tripartition of the space (see Fig. 5a); these intersections determine the internal edge of the intertwined arches (see Fig. 5b). For the creation of the arches it should be noted that these elements are not generated by cuts of the principal shape, but they are generated by conoids, what Guarini defines as *"cono che finisce in una linea"*[10] (cones that end in a line), both for the main and secondary arches of the angular sectors (see Fig. 5c).

Once the main structure of arches has been identified, perimeter lunettes with a composition of sails are placed in continuity with it (see Fig. 5d). The remaining fields use the main dome to generate empty vaulted surfaces in order to recreate four large eyeglass shapes (see Fig. 5e) for the creation of spectacular lighting effects (see Fig. 5f).

---

[9] The research has been conducted by M. Boetti and A. Raschieri edited by G. Dardanello and G. Cappelletti with the consultancy H. A. Millon. It led to the elaboration of two possible models for the restitution of the vault, starting from the hypothesis of three or five supports for the arches on the long sides.

[10] Guarini, G.: Architettura Civile. Treat. II, Cap. XXVI, Obs. IV. «Delle Volte, che nascono dal cono, che finisce in una linea» . Mairesse, Turin (1737).

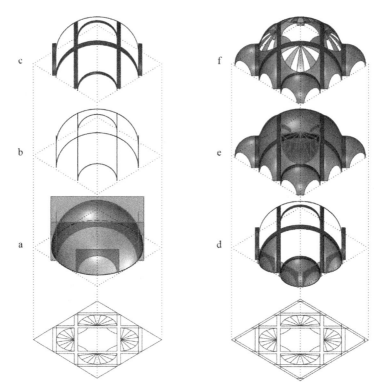

Fig. 5. Graphic analysis and digital modeling of the vault in the Castle of Racconigi.

With a geometrically composed vault in a three-dimensional space it is easy to proceed with the visualization of the object. By assigning thicknesses and including possible improvements of the three-dimensional space, it was possible to create a perspective view of the model (see Fig. 6). The creation of this visualization "without materials" aims to evaluate the how the relationship between geometry and architecture is evidenced by the particular light-effects that Guarini wanted to create.

Fig. 6. Perspective view of the digital reconstruction of the vault in the Castle of Racconigi.

4 Conclusions

The research focus on a part of Guarini's thinking about vaults, looking for a method for a deep understanding of his work, starting from the geometric components. This aspect, that characterizes each of his creations, is therefore used by Guarini not only as a compositional tool but also as a medium of expression.

The drawing analyzed is part of an extensive archive. The aim is to study the architect's theoretical and construction work in order to better understand every single part of it. The interpretation method is structured with representative techniques in adherence to Guarini's compositional thought, with the possibility of operating in a three-dimensional space to better understand the theoretical models, the design drawings and the architectures realized.

Inserted as a meeting point between representation techniques from different eras, this work tries to find a critical filter between the discipline of representation and his relationship with history of architecture, with the awareness that this theme is fertile ground for further studies and in-depth study.

References

1. Guarini, G.: Architettura Civile. Mairasse, Torino (1737)

2. Spallone, R.: "Delle volte, e vari modi di farle". Modelli digitali interpretativi delle lastre XIX e XX nell'Architettura Civile di Guarini, fra progetti e realizzazioni / "On the vaults and various modes of making them". Interpretative digital models of the XIX and XX plates in Guarini's Architettura Civile, between designs and buildings. In: Bertocci, S., Bini, M. (eds.) Le Ragioni del Disegno. Pensiero Forma e Modello nella Gestione della Complessità / The Reasons of Drawing. Thought Shape and Model in the Complexity Management, pp. 1275–1282. Gangemi, Rome (2016)
3. Viale, V. (eds) Guarino Guarini e l'internazionalità del Barocco. Proceedings of the International Conference promoted by the Accademia delle Scienze di Torino (Turin, 30 September - 5 October 1968). 2 Voll. Turin (1970)
4. Lange, A.: Disegni e documenti di guarino guarini. In: Viale, V. (eds) Guarino Guarini e l'Internazionalità del Barocco. Proceedings of the International Conference Promoted by the Accademia delle Scienze di Torino (Turin, 30 September - 5 October 1968). 2 Voll, vol. I, pp. 91–232. Turin (1970)
5. Millon, H.A.: I primi disegni per Racconigi. In: Dardanello, G., Klaiber, S., Millon, H.A. (eds.) Guarino Guarini. Allemandi, pp. 417–423. Turin (2006)
6. Dardanello, G.: Le idee di Guarini per il palazzo con cupola di Racconigi. In: Dardanello, G., Klaiber, S., Millon, H.A. (eds.) Guarino Guarini. Allemandi, pp. 425–439. Turin (2006)
7. Caterino, R.: Cupole per i saloni dei palazzi di Guarini. In: Dardanello, G., Tamborrino, R. (eds.) Guarini, Juvarra e Antonelli: segni e simboli per Torino. Silvana Editoriale, pp. 124–125. Cinisello Balsamo, Milan (2008)
8. Piccoli, E.: Disegni di Guarini per le volte di edifici civili. In: Dardanello, G., Klaiber, S., Millon, H.A. (eds.) Guarino Guarini. Allemandi, pp. 43–49. Turin (2006)

Cross Information Improvement for an H-BIM Common Data Environment

Marco L. Trani[✉], Francesca Ripamonti, and Maria Ruschi

Politecnico Di Milano, 20129 Milan, Italy
marco.trani@polimi.it

Abstract. In the construction community, the BIM approach to design, nowadays, is well-known even if still not completely spread out. Nevertheless, every design team using BIM often seems to act in its own way. In addition, the practical experience of the Con.Si.Lab. Research team, when involved in design projects, is a huge lack of information flow through different design disciplines. This issue has been evaluated as a sensible obstacle towards quality especially in H-BIM projects, where construction site problems could create loss in time and money. The research had therefore the aim to create an original standard information flow, able to structure designers' relationship starting from an information collection responsibility award given them by the BIM coordinator at the early beginning of design activities, using some dedicated synopsis tables. The team's research method had an empiric approach through many years of experience in Historical Building construction sites design and management using BIM (*i.e.* H-CoSIM, Historical Construction Site Information Modelling). The case histories collection enabled the definition of the presented information flow, based up on an ergotechnic parameters list gradually implemented and tested in many different sites. These parameters objects tables have been recently presented at the Italian Standard Body (UNI) in order to be enforced in a new release of the Italian standard UNI 11337, that provides two type of CoSIM: one at the design stage and one at the execution stage.

Keywords: BIM workflow · BIM model use · CoSIM · Construction site

1 Introduction

Nowadays, the building design process is ever more specialized in a number of different design disciplines, due to the development of new technical disciplines such as lightning engineering and energy analysis, and to the increasing interest in the so called Life Cycle Assessment. It's therefore essential to improve collaboration and sharing tools to create integrated relations between all the professionals involved in the project development. Actually, the BIM approach seems to offer a good digital solution but needs many embodied tools to achieve its best performance. Among the other, a strategic issue consists of information collecting and sharing between different design disciplines.

The European standard ISO 19650 enforced in 2019 treats the general aspects of the BIM process and the information flow of the developing phase of building project, giving

© Springer Nature Switzerland AG 2021
M. Ioannides et al. (Eds.): EuroMed 2020, LNCS 12642, pp. 633–640, 2021.
https://doi.org/10.1007/978-3-030-73043-7_55

a structured notion of Common Data Environment (CDE) as an informatics instrument to data collection and organization, comprehensive of its own usage procedure.

The standard overcome the aim of "measuring" the information content in order to avoid its excesses or defects -initially delegated to the LODs- adopting the new concept of Level Of Information Need. The key difference between the two approach lies in the concept of use, that is, the use/utility of information. For the LODs, the information request was standardized while, regarding the Level Of Information Need, the focus is on a more targeted research of the use of the necessary information in relation to the model and the design phase of interest.

The aim of the research here presented was to offer a possible solution to the problem of the complexity in managing and organizing the information workflow which leads the design teams to share a huge amount of information in a virtual environment that allows countless solutions.

The proposal defines a standard workflow that will improve a cross information approach between different disciplinary BIM models and the CDE, giving all the professionals' responsibilities in data research and sharing.

2   The State of Art

Many studies address in two main topics the complexity and the importance of interoperability and collaboration between different design disciplines involved in the building process: tools and software, in addition to networks.

While tools and software are used as measures to support collaboration in BIM-based Construction Networks (BbCNs), on the other hand network's studies have put emphasis onto the improvement of common document management tools as key facilitators of collaboration [1]. A deep analysis of process-related barriers to collaboration in BbCNs and a conceptual model was also developed [2] in order to provide a tool for project managers on BIM-enabled projects to plan their BbCNs settlement.

To improve the network efficiency in the facility management discipline of the built environment, a CDE prototype has been proposed with a web-integrated digital information with automated connectivity [3].

Historical buildings have been as well investigated setting a cloud platform aimed to unify and synchronize heritage architecture information that are connected with the BIM model and give the users all the information needed, even if not used to a BIM approach [4].

Unfortunately, research and development continue to offer solutions to improve interoperability, where professionals and software will continue to specialize creating elements outside of what has been made interoperable. Perfect interoperable integrated systems will probably never be achieved. It is therefore important to study how to design, build and operate in such a partially integrated environment [5], still having room for improvement and further studies.

Every construction element is connoted by technical data, specific for each design discipline; as a whole, those properties define the element information required by BIM, but these properties can be also of interest for different disciplines and can be modified during the design process; a useful, simple and tidy cross information method is therefore needed to go on properly in a BIM design system.

Until now a standard, linear and efficient approach to define BIM cross information has not been reached, neither to decide which professional has the right and responsibility to choose, find and share the element's data. This lack of a clear methodology leads inevitably to weigh down an already complex method, losing a lot of time in managing and organizing collaboration between disciplines. Data sets, then, have to be shared without causing excess or double information that make a BIM hard to be used. To do so, the study proposes an instrumented method able to efficiently manage the CDE and to improve and simplify the information flow in a BIM environment.

3   Construction Site Information (Default) Model

To achieve the goal above, the research investigates a standard method that, respecting current standards, is able to regulate the cross information need between all the construction disciplines helping the Standard transition from the level of information detail of an object to the level of information need, in relation to a specific model use and a project phase procedure: from definition of information requirements, through the development of the data container, to its management and its use in operation.

Starting the investigation from the design phase, was then necessary to define the information need of a tendering body assigned to the professionals involved in the proceeding via the Exchange Information Requirements (EIR). Therefore, the Level Of Information Need indicates the minimum content required during the evolution of technical and administrative procedure related to contracts.

The first discipline taken into account as a case study was Construction Site Design in an H-BIM environment since it is a very challenge area because of all the problem connected with the architectural surveys. Besides, that discipline applied to historical building can heavily affect the result of a restoration project in terms of time and money.

The Construction Site Information Model (CoSIM) at the design phase of a project consist of a "meta-design" model of the site suitable for giving an answer to productivity, sustainability, profitability as well as safety and health requirements with the aim to address and optimize the design choices of other disciplines.

Having in mind the mentioned actual standards transition, the first issue has been the definition of the Ergotechnic Model Use by creating a dedicated information framework. In order to organize all the data required, then, it has been developed an ergotechnic information breakdown structure, namely a structured parameters list, giving a predefined data sheet where to collect data connoting that model use (Fig. 1).

A complex problem to solve in order to gain uniformity and a strong information interoperability consists of identifying construction elements in an unequivocally way among the existent plenty of price lists. The "Hashtag method" (actually under a successful testing by ACCA Software and Milan Municipality) seems to be a good solution because identifies the element regardless its price structure description in the price list. Besides, referring to a specific price list in the model use allows the client to maintain control on the design budget. Note that the "appointed designer" cell refers to the BIM coordinator who has the due to decide which discipline has to fill in the shared parameters values, as explained in the next paragraph.

The information contents of the model use have been divided into Modelling Information, Alphanumeric Information and Documentation. The first information set has a general value and it supposed to be present in every model use discipline data sheet, as it is strictly related to geometric and graphic parameters that define the object as it is represented in every model. The Alphanumerical information set collects all the other data that define the object beside its modelling characteristics so that is the very level of information need of the CoSIM use, structured in operational and management data. In order not to weigh down the model, some information can be consulted in the technical/safety data sheet of the object (*i.e.* Documentation set).

OBJECT			#Name#Name#Name#Name#Name
PRICE LIST ID			Name identification
PRICE LIST ID Code			ID Code of the Price List adopted
OBJECT PRICE DEFINITION			Price structure prescription
COMPILER			Appointed designer
MODEL USE			CoSIM (Construction Site Infromation Model)
PROJECT PHASE			Design
BIM OBJECT DRAWING/IMAGE			
Modeling information	**Detail**		Rapresentation with shape and dimensions
	Dimensionality		3D
	Localization		Relative
	Look		Material colour
	Parametricity		Yes: x, y, z
Alphanumerical Information	Ergotechnic operational	Procurement	Mode of supply [...]
			Delivery carrier [...]
			Height of supply unit [m]
			Other...
		Storage	Overlapping of supply unit [...]
			Storage requirements [...]
		Handling	Handling mode [...]
			Harness mode [...]
			Length of load [m]
			Thickness of load [m]
			Other...
		Working and laying in place	Method of preparation [URL]
			Specialised labour force [...]
			Length of working element [m]
			Thickness of working element [m]
			Weight of working element [Kg]
			Other...
	Management	Disposal	Waste code [...]
		Security costs	Unit price [€/...]
Documentation	Documentation	On-call information	Techincal data sheet [URL]
			Safety datasheet (URL)

Fig.1. Level of information need – Data sheet for Ergotechnic (CoSIM) model use

4   Collecting and Sharing Cross Information for a Model Use

The level of information need of a building element is completed when all the disciplinary data sheet of the model use that refer to it (*i.e.* Architectural, Structural, ... Ergotechnic) are filled with their own information; to gain such a completeness, the BIM Coordinator has to assign to different discipline designer the due to collect and share information in a cross way. Flow chart in Fig. 2 represents (only some discipline considered) the steps necessary to reach a complete disciplinary model use. Note that a designer can be assigned to find out information not belonging to his discipline because he is appointed to by the BIM Coordinator using a "cross information" approach. Consequently, choosing a building element, designers can collect directly many other information saving time mutually with other designers. So, the BIM Coordinator has to set up the level of information need (*i.e.* for a building element, which parameters for each discipline) and apply the interdisciplinary information synopsis schedule provided by the research assigning the data giver for the information collection.

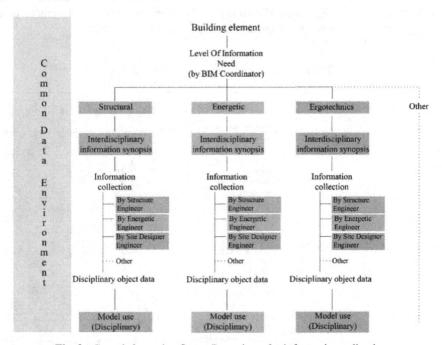

Fig. 2. Cross information flow – Data givers for information collection

5   Interdisciplinary Information Synopsis

With respect to the whole design phase, many different design discipline can be taken into account, depending on the object of the project. In order to provide the BIM Coordinator with an operational tool, it has been created an Interdisciplinary Information Synopsis Table that can automatically assign to each BIM professional designer involved his information collection due. Design areas have been divided into three categories:

• Base: including architectural, structural and plant engineering models.
• Technological: including specialist expertise such as fire engineering, acoustic, lighting and energy models.

- Ergotechnical: including CoSIM at the design phase and at the execution phase (see ERG.D. and ERG.E. in Table 1).

By checking the box of the parameters that suit the level of information need of the different models of the project, the BIM Coordinator can choose the data giver, assigning him the due to collect the requested information.

This table, which finds its application in the context of the preliminary definition of the information necessary for carrying out the contract using the BIM methodology, the table is specific for each technical element and for each Model Use.

By ticking the box in the table a disciplinary data sheet like the one in Fig. 1 is created for each designer, who receive his own data sheet with only the information he has been required highlighted, as shown in Fig. 3. The example refers to the ergotechnic information that the Structural engineer has to provide for the CoSIM.

Table 1. Interdisciplinary information synopsis.

Technical/ stratigraphic element	Model use	Information requirements	Parameters	Model								
				ARCH.	STRU.	MEP	FIRE	ACOU.	LIGH.	ENER.	ERG. D	ERG. E
X-LAM PANEL	Construction site design	Procurement	Width of supply unit [m]	☐	☐	☐	☐	☐	☐	☐	☐	☑
			Length of supply unit [m]	☐	☐	☐	☐	☐	☐	☐	☐	☑
			Thickness of supply unit [m]	☐	☐	☐	☐	☐	☐	☐	☐	☑
			Weight of supply unit [kg]	☐	☐	☐	☐	☐	☐	☐	☐	☑
			Other...	☐	☐	☐	☐	☐	☐	☐	☐	☐
		Storage	Overlapping of supply unit [...]	☐	☐	☐	☐	☐	☐	☐	☑	☐
			Storage requirements [...]	☐	☐	☐	☐	☐	☐	☐	☑	☐
			Handling mode [...]	☐	☐	☐	☐	☐	☐	☐	☑	☐
		Handling	Harness mode [...]	☐	☐	☐	☐	☐	☐	☐	☐	☑
			Height of load [m]	☐	☐	☐	☐	☐	☐	☐	☐	☐
			Width of load [m]	☐	☑	☐	☐	☐	☐	☐	☐	☐
			Length of load [m]	☐	☑	☐	☐	☐	☐	☐	☐	☐
			Thickness of load [m]	☐	☑	☐	☐	☐	☐	☐	☐	☐
			Weight of load [kg]	☐	☑	☐	☐	☐	☐	☐	☐	☐
			Other...	☐	☐	☐	☐	☐	☐	☐	☐	☐
		Working and laying in place	Method of preparation [URL]	☐	☐	☐	☐	☐	☐	☐	☐	☑
			Specialised labour force [...]	☐	☐	☐	☐	☐	☐	☐	☐	☑
			Laying mode [URL]	☐	☐	☐	☐	☐	☐	☐	☐	☑
			Height of working element [m]	☐	☐	☐	☐	☐	☐	☐	☐	☐
			Width of working element [m]	☐	☑	☐	☐	☐	☐	☐	☐	☐
			Length of working element [m]	☐	☑	☐	☐	☐	☐	☐	☐	☐
			Thickness of working element [m]	☐	☑	☐	☐	☐	☐	☐	☐	☐
			Weight of working element [Kg]	☐	☑	☐	☐	☐	☐	☐	☐	☐
			Other...	☐	☐	☐	☐	☐	☐	☐	☐	☐
	Management	Disposal	Waste code [...]	☐	☐	☐	☐	☐	☐	☐	☑	☐
		Security costs	Unit price [€/...]	☐	☐	☐	☐	☐	☐	☐	☐	☐
	Documentation	On-call information	Techincal data sheet [URL]	☐	☑	☐	☐	☐	☐	☐	☐	☐
			Safety datasheet (URL)	☐	☐	☐	☐	☐	☐	☐	☐	☐

This kind of procedures, using a draft version of the presented tools, has been tested to share information among the professional involved in the design of the restoration project of the basilica of Santa Maria di Collemaggio, L'Aquila. The church, severely damaged during the 2009 earthquake, has been the subject of an important restoration and reconstruction work BIM designed.

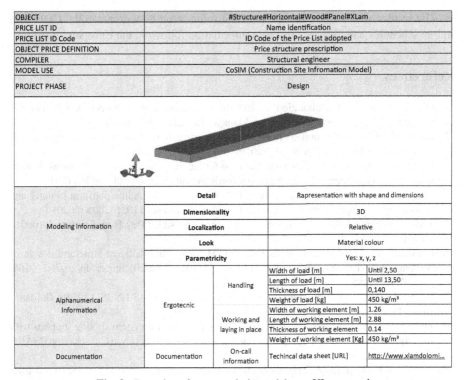

OBJECT	#Structure#Horizontal#Wood#Panel#XLam			
PRICE LIST ID	Name identification			
PRICE LIST ID Code	ID Code of the Price List adopted			
OBJECT PRICE DEFINITION	Price structure prescription			
COMPILER	Structural engineer			
MODEL USE	CoSIM (Construction Site Infromation Model)			
PROJECT PHASE	Design			

Modeling information	Detail		Rapresentation with shape and dimensions	
	Dimensionality		3D	
	Localization		Relative	
	Look		Material colour	
	Parametricity		Yes: x, y, z	
Alphanumerical Information	Ergotecnic	Handling	Width of load [m]	Until 2,50
			Length of load [m]	Until 13,50
			Thickness of load [m]	0,140
			Weight of load [kg]	450 kg/m³
		Working and laying in place	Width of working element [m]	1.26
			Length of working element [m]	2.88
			Thickness of working element	0.14
			Weight of working element [Kg]	450 kg/m³
Documentation	Documentation	On-call information	Techincal data sheet [URL]	http://www.xlamdolomi...

Fig. 3. Data sheet for ergotechnic model use: XLam panel

6 Conclusions

The site designer is the figure who collects information from other disciplines, enriching them and validating the design choices in relation to the feasibility of their realization; therefore, the study started by analysing this complex discipline, leaving space for further implementation for the other. The experience, from the point of view of Site Design, proved to be positive as the availability of clear and precise ergotechnic information has made possible to improve the phasing of the construction site design and operational planning, with positive effects also from the point of view of safety management and safety devices choices.

The exchange of information has allowed the different models of the same project to be populated defining an information set strictly related to their discipline. It is evident that the search for information from other designers, if carried out after the drafting of the project, is tiring, as is the population of models with the information necessary in the subsequent phase of their modelling. With the application of the proposed methodology this inefficiency can be improved.

An important achievement has been reached finding a way to clarify discipline roles and assignments, establishing, since the early design phase, an information and discipline hierarchy to decide which professional will have to choose the design elements and respective technical data.

The results of this study bring a possible solution on how organize the CDE with simple schedules and improve the cross information following the European standard.

References

1. Oraee, M., et al.: Collaboration in BIM-based construction networks: a bibliometric-qualitative literature review. Int. J. Proj. Manage. **35**, 1288–1301(2017)
2. Oraee, M., et al.: Collaboration in BIM-based construction networks: a conceptual model. Int. J. Project Manage. **37**, 839–854 (2019)
3. Patacasa, J., Dawooda, N., Kassemb, M.: BIM for facilities management: a framework and a common data environment using open standards. Autom. Constr. **120**, 103366 (2020)
4. Palomar, I.J., García, J.L., Valldecabres, P.T., Pellicer, E.: An online platform to unify and synchronise heritage architecture information. Autom. Constr. **110**, 103008 (2020)
5. Turk, Ž: Interoperability in construction – mission impossible? Dev. Built Environ. **4**, 100018 (2020)
6. Hamidavi, T., Abrishami, S., Reza Hosseini, M.: Towards intelligent structural design of buildings: a BIM-based solution. J. Build. Eng. **32**, 101685 (2020). https://doi.org/10.1016/j.jobe.2020.101685
7. UK BIM Framework, Information management according to BS EN ISO 19650. Guidance Part 2: Processes for Project Delivery, 4th edition (2020)
8. Zhuanga R.L., et al.: Investigating safety passage planning for system shoring supports with BIM, In: 33rd International Symposium on Automation and Robotics in Construction (ISARC 2016)
9. Schwabea, K., Königa, M., Teizerb, J.: BIM applications of rule-based checking in construction site layout planning tasks. In: ISARC, 33rd International Symposium on Automation and Robotics in Construction (ISARC 2016)
10. Singh, A.R., et al.: Optimizing site layout planning utilizing building information modelling. In: 36th International Symposium on Automation and Robotics in Construction (ISARC 2019)
11. Wu, J., Zhang, J.: New automated BIM object classification method to support BIM interoperability. In: Construction Research Congress 2018: Sustainable Design and Construction and Education, pp. 706–715 (2019)

Digital 3D Modelling for Heritage Research and Education from an Information Studies Perspective

Sander Muenster(✉) [ORCID]

Digital Humanities, Friedrich-Schiller-Universität Jena, 07743 Jena, Germany
sander.muenster@uni-jena.de

Abstract. Since more than 30 years digital 3D modelling methods have been used to support research and education about heritage and history. While an investigation on these topics is usually done from a perspective of digital humanities and cultural heritage, I investigate this topic by employing information studies methods from scientometrics, user behaviour research, and information practices. This article shows research questions and key findings from 15 completed studies that are part of an ongoing postdoc thesis work. Incorporated studies report about scholarly communities, usage practices, methodologies, technologies as well as design implications and educational strategies.

Keywords: Digital 3D modelling · Digital humanities · Practice-based education · Design implications

1 Introduction

For usual, a discourse about the use of digital 3D modelling and in particular reconstruction of cultural heritage is rather part of digital humanities and digital cultural heritage than of information studies. A main purpose of 3D models is to preserve, educate and research cultural heritage by using digital spatial modeling technologies [c.f. 1,2]. The objects of assessment can be divided into material and immaterial objects (e.g. rites or dances), differing according to the intended purpose. Another essential differentiation affecting digital modelling is between those objects which are no longer existent or which have never been realized (e.g. not implemented plans) and objects that still exist [3], which closely relates to different workflows for modelling [4]. While technological backgrounds, project opportunities and methodological considerations for the application of digital 3D modelling techniques are widely discussed in literature [e.g. 5–10], the interest guiding my postdoc thesis work is dedicated to draw a "big picture" by empirically investigating how people interact with digital 3D modelling as information, communication, and research techniques. Research questions are:

- How can digital 3D modelling techniques be learned and taught?
- What marks a scholarly culture of 3D modelling in the humanities?

© Springer Nature Switzerland AG 2021
M. Ioannides et al. (Eds.): EuroMed 2020, LNCS 12642, pp. 641–653, 2021.
https://doi.org/10.1007/978-3-030-73043-7_56

• What are technical and design implications for model creation and presentation?

Table 1. Investigational parts based on (1) area of research, (2) research interest and (3) the performed studies.

Area	Research interest	Investigation
Scholarly community	Who are main authors? What are academic structures?	[A] Social network and bibliometric analysis of publications from major conferences in the field of digital cultural heritage 1990–2015 (n = 3,917)
	What are topics?	[B] Automated topic mining of 3917 articles, manual classification of 452 articles plus 26 project reports
	Who funds projects?	[C] Qualitative content analysis of 518 projects in the field of digital cultural heritage
	What marks a scholarly culture?	[D] Three stage investigation including a questionnaire-based survey during three workshops; 15 guideline-based interviews; an online survey with 988 participants
	What are most relevant publications?	[E] Citation analysis of publication bodies from major conferences in the field of digital cultural heritage 1990–2015: n = 51,789 references out of 3,391 articles
Usage practices	What are phenomena and strategies for cooperation?	[F] 4 case studies: Data collection via expert interviews and observation. Data analysis via heuristic frameworks and grounded theory

(continued)

Table 1. (*continued*)

Area	Research interest	Investigation
	How to support cooperation in 3D modelling projects?	[G] Employment and evaluation of SCRUM as agile project management approach in an educational project seminar with 3 student teams
Methodological development	What are current challenges for 3D models?	[H] Three group discussions during workshops at national/international conferences (~60 participants); online survey with 700 participants
	What are research functions?	[I] Classification scheme developed and applied for eight projects so far
	What are recommendations for digital libraries?	[J] Recommendations for the design of digital 3D models and in particular for the field of geo-spatial approaches for humanities
Technology	How to create 3D models?	[M] Technological Pipeline development and testing for automatically creating 4D city models from historical plan and photo sources
Perception	What factors are influencing perception of 3D models?	[N] Four studies to investigate how virtually represented architecture is perceived, involving ~100 persons and using usability testing
Education	How to teach 3D modelling?	[O] Three student seminars so far to develop and test team project-based learning approaches

2 Research

Within my studies, I used a wide range of methods as well as topics derived from information studies as for instance the scientometric investigation of scientific communities, user research about perception or an empirical analysis of usage practices (c.f. Table 1). Research has been carried out since 2010 in 12 projects at local, national and EU level so far. Following, I will present some results at a glance.

2.1 A Scholarly Community

Who are Main Authors and, What are Academic Structures? Since a basic idea from sociology is that in most cases ties between individuals, like through a common authorship, will foster an exchange of ideas and information [11], we investigated co-authorship patterns with the help of a sample of publications from major conferences in the field of digital cultural heritage dating from 1990–2015. These publications were written by 4,894 people and contain nearly 14,500 links between authors of cooperative articles. A particular interest was in examining cross-nationality. As shown in Fig. 1, most were written by authors belonging to institutes in the same country (light blue). Facilitators, such as people in the top 10 in the categories of number of connections to other authors (degree), relevance as a connecting factor between author groups (between-ness centrality), or the number of publications (count), were highlighted in the graph [c.f. 12]. The giant component cluster (orange rectangle) contains 1,664 out of 2,951 authors connected to each other. This indicates that 56% of co-authors published in cooperation with just one other person. In comparison, the values for authors of the top-ranked papers in the field of chemistry are over 90% [13, 14].

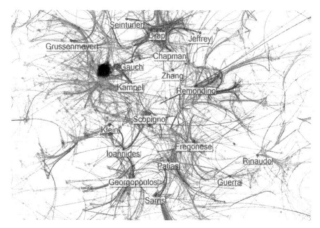

Fig. 1. Author-Co-Author Relations (n = 14,500 links, image cropped, TOP 10 in degree, count, betweenness centrality named, giant component cluster highlighted) (Color figure online)

What are Topic Areas? To investigate this topic we conducted an online survey amongst all authors of publications from major conferences in the field of digital cultural heritage [15]. Out of queried 3148 persons, 988 individuals participated and 602 completed the survey. Concerning the individual topics (cf. Fig. 2), especially data management was most frequently named, ranging from GIS and BIM to metadata schemes and data architecture. It was followed by data acquisition, photogrammetry, laser scanning and other surveying technologies. As an additional note on the survey, a large number of answers did not fit into the predefined categories and were subsumed in "Others" – in most cases specific methods or objects of research.

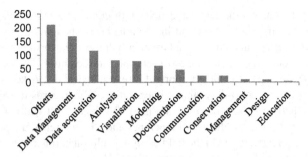

Fig. 2. Topic areas in the field of 3D modelling in humanities (Online survey, n = 825)

Similar to those findings from questioning, a discourse in the already mentioned sample of conference publications is primarily driven by technologies, and the most common keywords refer to the technologies used. Most research is around data in terms of acquisition and management, visualization or analysis. Moreover, the observed scientific discourse closely relates to practical work in terms of projects relating to specific cultural objects, technologies or practices [16]. Both indications lead to the assumption that the observed scientific community is foremost a community of practice [c.f. 17].

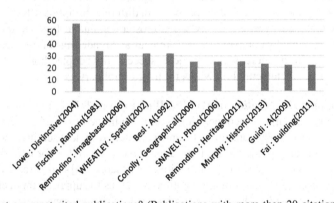

Fig. 3. What are most cited publications? (Publications with more than 20 citations from n = 51,789 references out of 3,391 articles)

What are Most Cited Publications? To investigate citations, we developed a set of C# and VBS tools to extract single references from full texts into csv and to separate authors, publication dates and title information. Within 3391 articles from our corpus 51789 references were found, amongst them 11 with more than 20 citations (Fig. 3). While most of the top cited papers describe algorithms, others like Wheatley's book on GIS for archaeology [18] provide an overview about specific fields of application.

What Marks a Scholarly Culture? Historically seen, digital heritage concentrates on tangible and intangible cultural heritage objects, and their preservation, education and research [e.g. 19]. Despite the broad variety of approaches and topics, digital cultural heritage evolved to a specific academic field with conferences, journals and various frequently contributing researchers and institutions [16]. The community is driven by researchers from European countries and especially Italy, with a background in humanities. Moreover, conference series are most relevant for a scientific discourse, and especially EU projects set pace as most important research endeavors. A key aspect of digital cultural heritage is cross-disciplinary cooperation. With regards to De Solla Price, digital cultural heritage could be seen as a mode 2 science [20] with an emphasis on cross-disciplinary teamwork, the use of machines and a joint intellectual property. Consequently, a disciplinary culture in the field of digital cultural heritage is widely common to science and engineering but less to humanities [21].

2.2   Usage Practices

What are Phenomena and Strategies for Cooperation?   To learn about these topics, we performed four case studies of 3D reconstruction projects. Data collection took place via expert interviews [c.f. 22] and observations [c.f. 23], a research paradigm combined heuristic frameworks and grounded theory research [24]. What are findings? Due to the high complexity and team-based workflows, aspects and usage practices for communication, cooperation, and quality management are of high relevance within 3D reconstruction projects. Especially if people with different disciplinary backgrounds are involved, visual media are intensively used to foster communication and quality negotiations, for example by comparing source images and renderings of the created virtual reconstruction. Furthermore, several projects successfully adopted highly standardized conventions from architectural drawings for interdisciplinary exchange.

How to Support Cooperation in 3D Modelling Projects?   Due to the finding that especially cross-disciplinary cooperation is an issue in the observed projects, we have tested Scrum as a project management framework in two student seminars so far. Since Scrum is beneficial in particular for innovation projects as well as for multidisciplinary work [25] we expected – according to cognitive load theory [26] - to decrease the time for establishing successful modes of cooperation as well as to support joint decision making. In a first course, 13 students from computing and from veterinary medicine formed three groups and produced 3D models for veterinary learning. At a glance, the use of Scrum reduced the individual load of project management for all participants but were time-consuming. In a second seminar with 80 participants from computing, geodesy, art history and education forming 10 groups we were faced with both the limitation to enroll and properly teach Scrum in such large groups and issues caused by the heterogeneous and large group sizes. Lessons learned were that interdisciplinary cooperation between the students can only take place as soon as there is absolute clarity of tasks within the individual subject area. The students of the different disciplines can only perceive each other as experts for their respective subjects if they see themselves as such. Moreover, it makes sense to specify – even for a Scrum setting - a project structure from the beginning, otherwise there is a risk that the students' self-organization will turn into arbitrariness [27].

2.3 Methodological Development

What are Current Challenges? To support a methodological development, we ran five workshops to identify prospects and demands for further development, involving around 60 researchers, as well as an online survey with 700 participants to verify findings from these workshops. Money and missing awareness were named as currently most pressuring issues (c.f. Fig. 4). Demanded are primarily the development of human resources. Further requests included sustainable and practicable approaches to access wider scientific communities, widely interoperable documentation and classification strategies, an overarching cataloguing of projects and objects as well as strategies and technologies for an exchange between different technological domains [15].

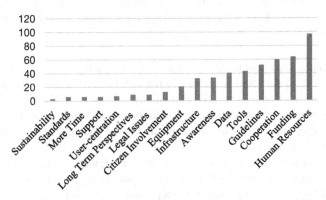

Fig. 4. What would support a further development? (Online Survey, n = 560 named items)

Table 2. Research objects of digital reconstruction

Research object	Source	Object	System
Documentation (e.g., compilation and recording of knowledge)	X		
Data quality assessment (e.g., consistency or contingency of sources)	X		
Visualization (e.g., investigation of shape or appearance)		X	
Creative process (e.g., planning or construction)		X	
Conceptualization and contextualization (e.g., typologies, functional segments, archetypical elements, provenance)	X	X	X
Numerical analysis (e.g., structural analysis, lighting)		X	
Hypothetic simulation (e.g., of hypothetic objects deriving from an architectural system)			X

What are Research Functions of Digital 3D Modelling? How do 3D technologies support research about digital heritage? Current approaches are mostly based on historical exemplification aiming to distinguish several research contexts [e.g. 28, 29]. On a more general level, the process of research and the insights to be gained are widely discussed in sociology and philosophy [i.e. 30–33]. The questions of a purpose and function of individual research, as for example the process of digital 3D modelling, require subject investigation as well. Although there are various other research approaches – such as numeric analysis methods as finite element methods (FEM) or computational fluid dynamics (CFD) – visualization is the most common way to present digital 3D reconstruction. Resulting, we developed a preliminary typology, particularly for digital 3D reconstructions. As an example of this classification, Table 2 shows types of research objectives for 3D reconstructions.

What are Recommendations for Digital Libraries? According to research about information behaviour in the humanities and particularly with regards to a scholarly use of 3D repositories [34–37], several general implications for a user centered design can be derived:

- *Cross-Domain data compilation:* Integration is a main issue in an era, where primary digitization comes of worth in relation to interoperability of existing assets. In the 3D reconstruction context several domains, such as GIS, VR, CAD, BIM, do all contribute relevant information. The postulation includes more than the models properties, and also embodies traditionally or automatically generated para- and metadata, even incomplete sets.
- *Modular middleware to replace single platforms:* Enhanced flexibility in terms of input and output along with a use of established portals and existing technical solutions can probably boost a fresh population of repositories, and consequently reach a critical user attendance, crucial in all cost/benefit considerations. A "conservative approach" focussing on existing structures favours a technical concentration on user-friendly middleware (as a broker) and stable APIs. Commercial platforms with high impact on the public may frequently outperform academic counterparts with very limited usage.
- *Persistent and multiple data access:* Data lifelines and accessibility should be extended as far as possible, whereas redundancies have to be avoided to prevent use of outdated versions. With a clearly defined authorship, responsibility and identifiers, access to a specific asset can directly reach the right partner. Existing commercial and academic platforms may provide information about projects (metadata), including links to the provider. Asset handling will largely profit from established systems like DOI.
- *Data authority of the authors:* Access to digital assets should be fully controlled by the author. Citation of digital objects, a correct reference to authorship, might be handled similar to how DOIs work in connection to publications.
- Generating additional value: Data suppliers benefit from secure archiving and structuring. It is a common place that an integration of data into a broader context substantially adds to the value. Other advantages could well be a commercial marketing of selected data. Gamification and crowdsourcing are further elements, from which research can strongly benefit.
- *Multiple ways to access information:* A digital information repository should obey the heterogeneity of purposes, disciplinary approaches and data qualities as far as

several modes to access and individual prerequisites. Furthermore, aspects of user-experience, accessibility and prominence play important roles in proposing digital platforms.

- *In-Depth-3D-Data Classification:* Since a classification of 3D content currently takes place primarily on an object scale, a segmentation and classification of parts of 3D models from point or polygon clouds data enables a more detailed knowledge integration and comparison.
- *Knowledge integration:* A major issue is to link models and knowledge bases, such as sources and information used for a 3D reconstruction. In this context, Linked Open Data became established as future-oriented technology for knowledge organization and formalization in structured data models.

2.4 Technologies

How to Create 3D Models? Especially the field of 3D retro-digitization of existing artifacts rapidly evolved during the last decades by the advent of cost-effective 3D laser scanning technologies and photogrammetry algorithms. Since the use of these techniques for creating 3D models for extant objects is highly elaborated now [38], historical images as source for photogrammetric reconstruction are difficult due to missing information to inner and exterior orientation of the camera and their very strong radiometric differences. Consequently, classical approaches like the Scale-Invariant Feature Transform (SIFT) [39], structure-from-motion or stereo matching fail or are not completely automatable [40]. Against this background, we currently test the pipeline shown in Fig. 5 which consists of four steps. Step 1 and 2 recognize similar buildings and views as well as positions and orientation of photos. Step 3 is about a vectorization of building ground plots and step 4 about a 3D model creation and visualization in a browser-based mobile virtual reality application [41]. Steps 1 and 2 of the pipeline have been tested with the current total of 1070 historical photographs of Dresden taken from the Deutsche Fotothek (www.deutschefotothek.de). A smaller subset, currently of 22 images, served as test data for the texture projection as shown in Step 4. For the VR browser application in this step, a model of the inner city of Dresden was used, containing 30 building models with LOD 2.5 and another 105 buildings automatically modeled as LOD 1.5 from historical cadaster data. To test usability, we conducted a test in which potential users were asked to use the tool to perform simulated but realistic tasks (e.g., "Please gather information on the Café Central"; "Please create a POI"; "Please examine the Old Market Square in its state in 1850"). There is much research about the interaction requirements of mobile devices [cf. 42]. Specifically, the small screen sizes and different display resolutions of these devices, as well as changes in orientation of the device from landscape to portrait mode and vice versa, are challenging for application design. Even though we are supporting both landscape and portrait mode, we found that nearly all test subjects used the interface in portrait mode. All of them were able to solve the tasks and all of them found it easy to navigate in the fourth dimension (time). Another usability issue relates to input and operation via touch with the finger [43]. It is therefore recommended to optimize all controls for finger interaction, and to increase the input area, or to visually highlight the response area. In addition, some application-specific usability challenges became apparent, specifically regarding the creation of POIs (e.g., lacking feedback after

POI creation, insufficiently labeled options, or the apparent inability to move the POI subsequent to its creation). The results of the test inform the further refinement of the user interface and user experience which is currently under development.

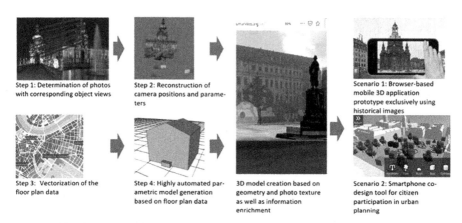

Step 1: Determination of photos with corresponding object views

Step 2: Reconstruction of camera positions and parameters

Scenario 1: Browser-based mobile 3D application prototype exclusively using historical images

Step 3: Vectorization of the floor plan data

Step 4: Highly automated parametric model generation based on floor plan data

3D model creation based on geometry and photo texture as well as information enrichment

Scenario 2: Smartphone co-design tool for citizen participation in urban planning

Fig. 5. Automated 4D modelling and mobile browser visualization pipeline

2.5 Perception

How are Virtually Represented Structures Perceived? During four studies we researched how virtually represented architecture is perceived [44]. Studies involved in total ~90 persons and used methods from usability testing. Research questions were:

- *How much detail is needed to recognize virtual architecture?*
- *How good can building properties estimated in the virtual in comparison to real world settings?*
- *How is aesthetics perceived in the virtual with regards to presentation forms?*
- *How good can mistakes be found in a visualization?*

What are findings? A current academic discourse is much about the level of detail of modelled buildings [c.f. 45]. Our findings concerning property estimation and recognisability as well as studies from other fields of visualization [46] lead to the assumption that the perception of objects is highly influenced by surroundings shown and a visual framing of a virtual object. Therefore, a suggestion for projects with a focus on estimation and recognisability may be to rather focus on a modelling of surrounding objects than on higher level of detail. There is also a long discourse about the visual representation of different degrees of hypothesis which can be roughly distinguished with regard to an enrichment of representations by explanatory elements as well as an adaptation of a representation quality [47]. However, in the context of architectural visualization a viewer effect has rarely been empirically tested. For instance, abstraction e.g. of colors has a direct influence on an assessment of perceived aesthetical qualities. Especially for visual assessment and analysis it seems to be important to mention this possible biasing. Current 3D modelling projects tend to model objects as accurate as possible. It may be questioned and is currently under investigation if subtle changes get noticed by an observer. Another finding is that geometric and radiometric errors in the digital visualizations were poorly recognized by both experts and laypersons. There were also major differences within both groups in the naming of false-positive errors. Both findings led to the hypothesis that there is no common perceptual strategy even for architectural historians - this will be tested in a next study.

2.6 Education

How to Teach 3D Modelling Competencies? Moreover, we adopted and evaluated team project-based learning approaches to support student education in digital 3D modelling. As observed in two courses so far, strategies for cooperation within student project teams for creating virtual representations evolves slowly, and mostly as reaction of upcoming problems and demands. Related competencies are highly based on implicit knowledge and experience. As consequence, a teaching of best practices prior to a project work is less effective than coaching during the project work [27].

3   Summary and Outlook

To draw the currently missing "big picture" about digital 3D modelling in the humanities, information studies can contribute methodical tools and theoretical frameworks especially to linking both, technologies and methodical ends. Within our research this ranges from the investigation of a scholarly community and related epistemic culture, via user research to implications for a design and implication of 3D models and related information systems. What are next steps in our research? Many of the already completed investigations are of qualitative nature or focus on particular aspects. Consequently, a further validation for adjacent aspects as well as a verification of findings are all-time tasks. To proceed, further investigations on the scholarly use of 3D models and historical photographs or the design of interfaces for virtual museums are under development. Since the research is intended to enhance the validation and dissemination of 3D modelling technologies in the humanities, both education and organizational development are key issues. Finally, beneficial and methodologically grounded best practice examples, an institutionalization of chairs and institutes as well as an increased awareness seem to be crucial for a further organizational establishment.

References

1. Guidi, G., et al.: 2nd International Congress on Digital Heritage 2015 (2015)
2. Georgopoulos, A.: CIPA's perspectives on cultural heritage. In: Münster, S., et al. (eds.) 5th Conference on Digital Research and Education in Architectural Heritage, DECH 2017, and First Workshop, UHDL 2017, Dresden, Germany, 30–31 March 2017, Revised Selected Papers, pp. 215–245. Springer, Cham (2018). https://doi.org/10.1007/978-3-319-76992-9_13

3. Francesco, G.D., et al.: Standards and guidelines for quality digital cultural three-dimensional content creation. In: VSMM 2008 (2008)
4. Münster, S.: Workflows and the role of images for virtual 3D reconstruction of no longer extant historic objects. ISPRS Ann. Photogram. Remote Sens. Spat. Inf. Sci. **II-5/W1**, 197–202 (2013). https://doi.org/10.5194/isprsannals-II-5-W1-197-2013
5. Arnold, D., et al.: EPOCH Research Agenda – Final Report (2008)
6. European Commission: Survey and outcomes of cultural heritage research projects supported in the context of EU environmental research programmes. From 5th to 7th Framework Programme (2011)
7. Frischer, B., Dakouri-Hild, A. (eds.): Beyond Illustration: 2D and 3D Digital Technologies as Tools for Discovery in Archaeology. University of Michigan Press, Ann Arbor (2008). https://doi.org/10.30861/9781407302928
8. Bentkowska-Kafel, A., et al.: Paradata and Transparency in Virtual Heritage (2012)
9. Bentkowska-Kafel, A.: Mapping Digital Art History (2013)
10. Kohle, H.: Digitale Bildwissenschaft (2013)
11. Granovetter, M.S.: Strength of the weak ties. Am. J. Sociol. **78**(6), 1360–1380 (1973)
12. Wasserman, S., et al.: Social Network Analysis (1994)
13. Velden, T., et al.: Patterns of collaboration in co-authorship networks in chemistry - mesoscopic analysis and interpretation. In: ISSI 2009 (2009)
14. Velden, T., et al.: A new approach to analyzing patterns of collaboration in co-authorship networks - mesoscopic analysis and interpretation. Scientometrics **85**(1), 219–242 (2010)
15. Münster, S.: A survey on topics, researchers and cultures in the field of digital heritage. ISPRS Ann. Photogram. Remote Sens. Spat. Inf. Sci. **IV-2/W2**, 157–162 (2017). https://doi.org/10.5194/isprs-annals-IV-2-W2-157-2017
16. Münster, S.: Digital cultural heritage as scholarly field – topics, researchers and Perspectives from a bibliometric point of view. J. Comput. Cult. Herit. **12**(3), 22–49 (2019)
17. Lave, J., Wenger, E.: Situated Learning: Legitimate Peripheral Participation. Cambridge University Press, Cambridge (1991)
18. Wheatley, D., et al.: Spatial Technology and Archaeology. The Archaeological Applications of GIS (2002)
19. UNESCO: Charta zur Bewahrung des Digitalen Kulturerbes, verabschiedet von der 32. UNESCO-Generalkonferenz am, Paris, 17 Oktober 2003 (2003)
20. De Solla Price, D.: Little Science - Big Science. Columbia University Press, New York (1963)
21. Münster, S., et al.: The visual side of digital humanities. A survey on topics, researchers and epistemic cultures in visual digital humanities. Digit. Scholarsh. Humanit. **35**(2), 366–389 (2020)
22. Gläser, J., Laudel, G.: Experteninterviews. In: Gläser, J., Laudel, G. (eds.) Experteninterviews und qualitative Inhaltsanalyse, pp. 111–196. VS Verlag für Sozialwissenschaften, Wiesbaden (2010). https://doi.org/10.1007/978-3-531-91538-8_4
23. Lamnek, S., Qualitative Sozialforschung. Lehrbuch (2005)
24. Bryant, A., et al.: The SAGE Handbook of Grounded Theory (2010)
25. Schwaber, K.: Agile Project Management with Scrum (2004)
26. Chandler, P., et al.: Cognitive load theory and the format of instruction. Cogn. Instr. **8**(4), 293–332 (1991)
27. Kröber, C., et al.: Educational app creation for the cathedral in freiberg. In: Spector, J.M., et al. (eds.) Competencies in Teaching, Learning and Educational Leadership in the Digital Age, pp. 303–318. Spinger, Cham (2017). https://doi.org/10.1007/978-3-319-30295-9
28. Günther, H.: Kritische Computer-Visualisierung in der kunsthistorischen Lehre. In: Frings, M. (ed.) Der Modelle Tugend, pp. 111–122. CAD und die neuen Räume der Kunstgeschichte, Weimar (2001)

29. Pfarr-Harfst, M.: Virtual scientific models. In: Ng, K., et al. (eds.): Electronic Visualisation and the Arts, EVA Conferences, London, pp. 157–163 (2013)
30. Fleck, L.: Entstehung und Entwicklung einer wissenschaftlichen Tatsache. Einführung in die Lehre vom Denkstil und Denkkollektiv (1980)
31. Peirce, C.S.: Collected Papers of Charles Sanders Peirce, vol. 1. vol besucht am 10.1.2014 (1931)
32. Latour, B., et al.: Laboratory Life. The Construction of Scientific Facts (1986)
33. Knorr-Cetina, K.: Die Fabrikation von Erkenntnis (2002)
34. Münster, S., Prechtel, N.: Beyond software. design implications for virtual libraries and platforms for cultural heritage from practical findings. In: Ioannides, M., Magnenat-Thalmann, N., Fink, E., Žarnić, R., Yen, A.-Y., Quak, E. (eds.) EuroMed 2014. LNCS, vol. 8740, pp. 131–145. Springer, Cham (2014). https://doi.org/10.1007/978-3-319-13695-0_13
35. Münster, S., Kuroczyński, P., Messemer, H.: Digital 3D reconstruction projects and activities in the German-speaking countries. In: Ioannides, M., Fink, E., Brumana, R., Patias, P., Doulamis, A., Martins, J., Wallace, M. (eds.) EuroMed 2018. LNCS, vol. 11196, pp. 599–606. Springer, Cham (2018). https://doi.org/10.1007/978-3-030-01762-0_52
36. Fernie, K., et al.: 3D content in Europeana task force (2020)
37. Rigauts, T., et al.: Web-based platforms and metadata for 3D cultural heritage models: a critical review. In: Proceedings of the 25th International Conference on Cultural Heritage and New Technologies (2020)
38. Agarwal, S., et al.: Building Rome in a day. Commun. ACM **54**(10), 105 (2011)
39. Lowe, D.G.: Distinctive image features from scale-invariant keypoints. Int. J. Comput. Vision **60**(2), 91–110 (2004)
40. Maiwald, F., Schneider, D., Henze, F., Münster, S., Niebling, F.: Feature matching of historical images based on geometry of quadrilaterals. ISPRS Ann. Photogram. Remote Sens. Spat. Inf. Sci. **XLII–2**, 643–650 (2018)
41. Münster, S., et al.: Introducing an automated pipeline for a browser-based, city-scale mobile 4D VR application based on historical images. In: Paper Presented at the ACM Multimedia - SUMAC Workshop, Seattle (2020)
42. Harrison, R., et al.: Usability of mobile applications: literature review and rationale for a new usability model. J. Interact. Sci. **1**(1), 1 (2013)
43. Nielsen, J., et al.: Mobile Usability (2013)
44. Münster, S.: Cultural heritage at a glance. Four case studies about the perception of digital architectural 3D models. In: Alonso, F. (ed.) 2018 3rd Digital Heritage International Congress (DigitalHERITAGE) held jointly with 2018 24th International Conference on Virtual Systems and Multimedia (VSMM 2018). IEEE, San Francisco (2018)
45. Kuroczyński, P., et al.: Der Modelle Tugend 2.0 – Vom digitalen 3D-Datensatz zum wissenschaftlichen Informationsmodell (2016)
46. Burri, R.V., et al.: Social studies of scientific imaging and visualization. In: Hackett, E.J., et al. (eds.) The Handbook of Science and Technology Studies, pp. 297–317. MIT Press (2008)
47. Apollonio, F.I.: Classification schemes for visualization of uncertainty in digital hypothetical reconstruction. In: Münster, S., Pfarr-Harfst, M., Kuroczyński, P., Ioannides, M. (eds.) 3D Research Challenges in Cultural Heritage II. LNCS, vol. 10025, pp. 173–197. Springer, Cham (2016). https://doi.org/10.1007/978-3-319-47647-6_9

Short Papers: Preservation and Use and Re-use

Short Papers: e-Libraries and e-Archives in Cultural Heritage

Language Independent Searching Tools for Cultural Heritage on the QueryLab Platform

Maria Teresa Artese⬥ and Isabella Gagliardi(✉) ⬥

IMATI-CNR, Via Bassini 15, 20133 Milan, Italy
{artese,gagliardi}@mi.imati.cnr.it

Abstract. The paper describes the tools for searching and visualizing local and web inventories related to intangible and tangible cultural heritage in the QueryLab platform. The pandemic outbreak has made more evident the need to offer users tools to query and enjoy interesting and educative websites by their homes. The tools presented are useful for users who are not experts in the domain of the inventories, offering predefined queries and semantic query expansion to interact with the archives. The visual suggestions, in the form of word clouds of the tags of the selected archives, help in querying the archives and retrieving the elements that come closest to the user's interests. As one of the QueryLab aims is to continue to add inventories, in the languages they are stored, visual suggestions help to overcome the language distance between the archives and the users to allow an easy and successful interaction. This paper presents QueryLab tools for searching, browsing, and displaying multimedia data, with some preliminary results.

Keywords: Intangible and tangible inventories · Innovative tools for searching and browsing · Semantic query expansion · Word cloud

1 Introduction

The pandemic outbreak of this year has made even more evident the need to allow scholars, tourists, or simply curious of the web to enjoy museums or collections of tangible and intangible cultural heritage by their homes, using tools created especially for them, whether they are inexperienced in the use of the web, subject matter or language.

Following the publication of the UNESCO's 2003 Convention for the Safeguarding of Intangible Heritage and the rules for the inclusion of endangered items in the UNESCO's list, numerous archives have been created [10]. Examples of online intangible cultural heritage archives, created after the Convention, are those in Scotland, France, Spain, concerning Europe, while South Korea, Japan, and China have defined strategies to safeguard their traditions much earlier than the UNESCO Convention. On the other hand, museums and cultural heritage collections, collectively called glams, have always had the awareness to offer their users, at different degrees of specialization, a view of their heritage.

The basic idea of QueryLab (https://arm.mi.imati.cnr.it/QueryLab) is to create a platform to integrate cultural heritage archives, whether local or remote, in a transparent

© Springer Nature Switzerland AG 2021
M. Ioannides et al. (Eds.): EuroMed 2020, LNCS 12642, pp. 657–665, 2021.
https://doi.org/10.1007/978-3-030-73043-7_57

way for users who are not aware of where the data physically resides. This paper presents QueryLab tools for searching, browsing, and displaying multimedia data, which are some of the aims of the platform.

The paper is organized as follows: after a brief section on the related works, an overview of the QueryLab platform is proposed, and the multimodal search engine is described, highlighting its characteristics. Finally, it follows conclusions, preliminary assessments, and future developments.

In this paper, all issues related to archives of (intangible) cultural heritage, their integration, tools, and models for search, navigation, and enjoyment with serious games are seen from a technological point of view, leaving to scholars and experts in the field the purely cultural part.

2   Related Works

A number of collections of cultural heritage objects are on the web with the purpose of making the contents of museums available to the users. According to the works in [8, 9], several features are appreciated by virtual visitors in their utilization of digital collections. The most valuable feature for the engagement of users is the availability of Search/Browse tools for interacting with the web. Regarding applications designed to query and browse the museums archives, innovative tools can be exploited to manage different types of data [1, 5].

While there are several sites that are the entry point for museum or tangible cultural heritage contents, the most famous of which is Europeana [6], to our best knowledge, QueryLab is the first that also deals with intangible assets. In [2, 3] the architecture of the system, with some technical details related to RESTful web services and an overview of its fruition, is described.

3   QueryLab Platform

QueryLab has been designed to be able to handle databases and inventories both local and integrated via RESTful web services (from now called web inventories). This paper will describe in detail how to search and navigate the QueryLab prototype, highlighting the differences that are encountered in the indexing, search and use of data from local databases, compared to those from databases queried through web services.

Figure 1 shows the logical schema of the QueryLab platform (this paper dives into the greenish area). The interaction/query with the remote inventories, performed using the web services provided by each of them, makes the query phase transparent to the different database locations and the addition of new inventories easy and seamless at any time. The data are queried via web services, "at their home", without any caching system or local copies that require constant updating to be always aligned to the remote inventories.

To speed up the query phase on the different local databases, an 'ICH light metadata structure' [2, 3] has been defined, starting from:

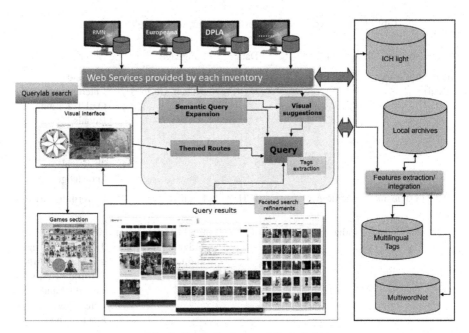

Fig. 1. Logical schema of QueryLab.

- the study and evaluation of the standard (de facto) metadata structures already in use, for example, EDM, Europeana Data Model [7],
- the structure provided by UNESCO to store information, which includes general information on cultural heritage, features, people that know and can transmit the knowledge, sustainability, data related to the inventory and references [11],
- the analysis of ICH inventories available on the web that share some common metadata, as title, UNESCO categories to which items belongs to, dates, places, …

The QueryLab platform takes into account different ways to search, browse, visualize and interact with the data coming from different sources, so as to make the user able to interact comfortably and successfully with the web site even if he is not an expert in the field, or is not familiar with the content or language in which the terms are expressed.

Different ways to interact with the databases have been designed, according to the different types of users expected, depending on their information needs and their knowledge of the topics: Experts, Communities, Tourists and Web Users.

Table 1 describes the different inventories that participate in QueryLab. It can be noticed that web inventories, in general, contain both Intangible and Tangible items, related to traditions, interviews, photos, texts, manuscripts, etc. The archives store data in different/multi languages.

Table 1. The inventories in QueryLab so far, with some characteristics

Name (source)	Country	Data	Language	Description
Intangible search (local)	Italy	ICH	Italian, English, French, German	Arts and Entertainment, Oral Traditions, Rituals, Naturalistic knowledge, Technical knowledge
ACCU Databank (local)	Pacific Area	ICH	English	Performing Arts
Sahapedia (local)	India	ICH	English (used here) and other local idioms	Knowledge Traditions, Visual and Material Arts, Performing Arts, Literature and Languages, Practices and Rituals, Histories…
Lombardy digital archive (local)	Italy	ICH, CH	Italian	Oral history, Literature, Performing Arts, Popular traditions, Work tools, Religion, Musical instruments, Family…
Museum contemporary photography (local)	Italy	CH	Italian	Architecture, Cities, Emigration, Family, Objects, Work, Landscapes, Sport…
Europeana [6] (web)	European countries	ICH; CH	Multilingual	1914–18 World War, Archaeology, Art, Fashion, Industrial Heritage, Manuscripts, Maps, Migration, Music, Natural History, Photography…

(*continued*)

Table 1. (*continued*)

Name (source)	Country	Data	Language	Description
Victoria & Albert museum (web)	UK	ICH, CH	English	Architecture, Embroidery, Costume, Paintings, Photography, Frames, Wallpaper, Jewelry, Illustration, Fashion, Manuscripts, Wedding dress, Books, Opera, Performance…
Cooper hewitt (web)	USA	CH	English	Decorative Arts, Designs, Drawings, Posters, Models, Objects, Fashion, Textiles, Wallcoverings, Prints…
Réunion des Musée Nat – RMN (web)	France	ICH, CH	French with tags in English	Photography, Paintings, Sculptures, Literature, Dances, Modern Art, Decorative Arts, Music, Drawings, Architecture…
Auckland museum (web)	New Zealand	ICH, CH	English	Natural Sciences, Human History, Archaeology, War history, Arts and Design, Manuscripts, Maps, Books, Newspapers…

(*continued*)

Table 1. (*continued*)

Name (source)	Country	Data	Language	Description
Digital public library of America – DPLA (web)	USA	ICH, CH	English	American civil war, Aviation, Baseball, Civil rights movement, Immigration, Photography, Food, Women in science…

4   Querying the Archives

QueryLab offers multimodal means of navigation and search, e.g. guided tours, keyword analysis, and serious games. In this paper, only search and browse modes will be discussed in more detail: Themed Routes, Semantic Query Expansion, and Visual Suggestions, presented in increasing order of complexity and automation.

Whatever the mode is chosen for the data search, the same query is propagated to all databases, regardless of whether they are local, or web queried. The only difference is that by querying the databases locally, it is possible to have more control over the searches made than with web-services, whose structure and the queried fields are unknown.

4.1   Themed Routes

To allow users to have a "taste" of the contents of the different inventories, QueryLab offers "predefined queries" for database searches. Starting from the semantic tags composed by 1-gram or n-grams, defined or approved by ethnographers or experts, hierarchically organized in a multilevel-level structure – WordNet style –, the basic idea is to use these tags, available in the languages of the databases both local and web queried, to allow all users to easily interact with QueryLab. Users can browse among predefined paths, exploring and retrieving semantically similar documents.

The structure defined allows easy insertion of new structured tags at any time, is seamlessly adaptable to new inventories, highlighting themes and subjects of interest to users, or topics of relevance. These tags, originally created and defined for local ICH inventories, are used with success on all the QueryLab data.

4.2   Semantic Query Expansion

Scholars or expert users may be interested in querying the archives with specific terms or keywords. Besides the simple query using terms typed in by the users, which may or may not provide some results, QueryLab offers tools to expand semantically the queries, to enlarge or shrink results, by suggesting more general or more specific terms, according to WordNet and MultiWordNet. WordNet, a large lexical database in English, where nouns, verbs, adjectives and adverbs are grouped into groups of cognitive synonyms (synsets), each of which expresses a distinct concept. MultiWordNet is a multilingual version of WordNet containing translation in different languages, as Italian, Spanish, Portuguese, etc.

By the integration of WordNet/MultiWordNet in QueryLab the semantics of terms is added [4], making it possible to:

- Seamlessly translate a term in any language of MultiWordNet;
- Structure flat list of tags into tree-shaped glossary;
- Enlarge or refine a query using the possible tree structures (associated with the different meanings of the selected term) of WordNet.

These semantic structure plug-ins can be used only on tags of the local databases. For web inventories, the visual suggestions are proposed.

4.3   Visual Suggestions

The web inventories are queried according to the RESTful protocol adopted by each inventory, generically on the descriptive data of the items. Until now, tags cannot be queried nor presented to the user in a list to be clicked. To overcome this limit and to offer all users suggestions of the possible queries, related to the one performed, the most relevant tags associated with the items are retrieved and displayed as word clouds.

These visual suggestions are part of a multi-step process to query the databases: the first step is performing a query using a simple term query, a semantic query expansion or selecting a thematic route.

The QueryLab system performs the query on all 10 databases. If the results do not satisfy the users, because a small number of items are retrieved, or none of them is significant, the visual suggestions may come to help. For local databases, the creation of visual suggestions is simple and immediate: the same tags that can be used as a possible refinement provide the material to be used. For remote databases, the data to be used are obtained via web services. Lacking a standard, each inventory required ad hoc analysis and procedures for tag extraction. By extracting the tags of the databases, the list of the tags, ordered by occurrence is then created and visualized as a word-cloud. By clicking on a tag, a new query is performed on the databases, and the process is repeated.

Figure 2 shows a word-cloud respectively for Digital Public Library of America (DPLA, USA) and Réunion des Musée Nationaux (RMN, France), after the query 'wedding' ('mariage' in French). It is important to note that RMN is a French-language database, so queries need to be translated before its use, because queries require terms in the language of the inventories.

In the case of RMN, visual suggestions are even more important, as the tags in the French language are extracted and the word cloud more useful for non-French users.

Visual suggestion, with its simplicity and its ability to extract tags in the language of the archive (and not necessarily in English), offers an extra tool to enhance the user's ability to choose and retrieve those objects that are of interest to him, even if he does not know the language of the archive perfectly.

Fig. 2. Visual suggestions for Digital Public Library of America (DPLA, USA) (left) and Réunion des Musée Nationaux (RMN, France) (right) for 'wedding' ('mariage' in French) query.

5 Preliminary Results and Conclusions

The paper describes a work in progress for the development of a platform able to search and visualize two different types of inventories, the local ones and the ones queried through web services.

The tools presented are useful for users not-expert in the domain of the inventories, offering predefined queries and semantic query expansion to interact with the archives. The visual suggestions, in the form of word clouds of the tags of the selected archives, help in identifying the tags, sorted according to the number of occurrences, and therefore extracting that elements that come closest to the user's interests. Users are provided with word clouds, a simple but expressive way to represent contents, as hints of the semantic contents of the databases and as suggestions to perform new queries.

As one of QueryLab aims is to continue to add inventories, in the languages they are stored, visual suggestions help to overcome the language distance between the archives and the users to allow an easy and successful interaction.

The work is still in progress, preliminary tests are giving positive results, but some issues have already been encountered:

- All the local databases are related only to ICH, while web inventories are mainly related to CH: no ICH web inventory has been found;
- Some web inventories are huge, with some millions of objects: a query refinement step is therefore needed to allow users to evaluate and enjoy the results. Visual suggestions could be used as a facet to refine queries and results;
- When the web inventories results are large, both tags extraction and word cloud visualization suffer: new solutions are therefore required;
- The databases are constantly growing in different languages, so new tests should be done to evaluate the results.

References

1. Artese, M.T., Ciocca, G., Gagliardi, I.: Evaluating perceptual visual attributes in social and cultural heritage web sites. J. Cult. Herit. **26**, 91–100 (2017). https://doi.org/10.1016/j.culher.2017.02.009
2. Artese, M.T., Gagliardi, I.: Sharing ICH Archives: Integration of Online Inventories and Definition of Common Metadata, vol. 8 (2019)
3. Artese, M.T., Gagliardi, I.: A platform for safeguarding cultural memory: the QueryLab prototype. Art. 18 (2019)
4. Artese, M.T., Gagliardi, I.: Multilingual specialist glossaries in a framework for intangible cultural heritage. Int. J. Herit. Digit. Era **3**(4), 657–668 (2014)
5. Ciocca, G., Colombo, A., Schettini, R., Artese, M.T., Gagliardi, I.: Intangible heritage management and multimodal navigation. In: Handbook of Research on Technologies and Cultural Heritage: Applications and Environments, pp. 85–118. IGIGlobal (2011)
6. Europeana Collections. https://www.europeana.eu, Accessed 13 Oct 2020
7. Europeana Data Model. https://pro.europeana.eu/page/edm-documentation, Accessed 12 Oct 2020
8. Lopatovska, I., Bierlein, I., Lember, H., Meyer, E.: Exploring requirements for online art collections. Proc. Am. Soc. Inf. Sci. Technol. **50**, 1–4 (2013). https://doi.org/10.1002/meet.14505001109
9. Lopatovska, I.: Museum website features, aesthetics, and visitors' impressions: a case study of four museums. Museum Manag. Curatorship. **30**, 191–207 (2015). https://doi.org/10.1080/09647775.2015.1042511
10. Sousa, F.: Map of e-inventories of intangible cultural heritage. Memoriamedia Rev. **1**(1) (2017)
11. UNESCO - Identifying and Inventoring Intangible Cultural Heritage. https://www.unesco.org/culture/ich/doc/src/01856-EN.pdf, Accessed 13 Oct 2020

Co-designing Digital Engagements with Cultural Heritage Sites in Africa: A Research Road Map for the Brandberg National Monument Area, Namibia

Martha Mosha[1](✉) 🆔 and Lorenzo Cantoni[2](✉) 🆔

[1] University of Namibia, 340 Mandume Ndemufayo Avenue, Windhoek, Namibia
mmosha@unam.na

[2] USI – Università della Svizzera italiana, UNESCO Chair in ICT to Develop and Promote Sustainable Tourism in World Heritage Sites, via Buffi 13, 6900 Lugano, Switzerland
lorenzo.cantoni@usi.ch

Abstract. This paper outlines the design of a research that would focus on the Brandberg National Monument Area, in Namibia, Southern Africa. The project seeks to find solutions by use of co-design action research with the local communities within the vicinity of the site and in the country. While an open online database is already available, with an extensive collection of archeological materials found within the site, the project will explore how to re-use and re-purpose such materials to present them not only to researchers and experts, but also to locals and to (international) tourists. In order to do so, local voices are to be fully integrated within the presentation(s), and locals' involvement will be of the utmost importance to manage communication practices as well as travelers' flows. The ultimate goal is not only to come up with different digital engagement tools, but also to end up with a digital engagement and governance framework for heritage sites, which could work in the African context.

Keywords: Co-design · Digital engagement · Cultural heritage · Digital library · Participatory design · Brandberg-Namibia

1 Introduction

"Public engagement describes the myriad of ways in which the activity and benefits of higher education and research can be shared with the public" [1]. King, Stark, and Cooke [2], explain that, "scholars have argued that the digital sphere can provide a dynamic space for two-way engagement with heritage culture, aimed at providing a complementary experience to physical visits through a range of phenomena (e.g. user-generated content, online communities, crowdsourcing projects)."

Digital engagement, at times referred to as virtual engagement is, "The use of new media in the service of cultural heritage" [3]. Digital engagement works with "substantial untapped potential to better understand the experience of end users by harnessing the

© Springer Nature Switzerland AG 2021
M. Ioannides et al. (Eds.): EuroMed 2020, LNCS 12642, pp. 666–672, 2021.
https://doi.org/10.1007/978-3-030-73043-7_58

vast amount of data that is available within heritage institutions, but which organizations frequently do not have the resources to exploit" [3]. "There is an opportunity for interaction design to take advantage of the visitors' physical experience with cultural heritage and work to integrate technology into it instead of creating a parallel and detached digital experience" [4]. One of the best ways to develop digital engagement with cultural heritage sites is by co-designing (otherwise known as participatory design), which "involve end-users and stakeholders in the ideation, design, development, deployment and analysis of the interventions" [5]. The tremendous "growth of social media, digital interaction and platforms over the last decade has brought digital culture and public participation to the fore of the field of heritage" [6].

According to the so-called ABCDE framework [7], digital technologies can help heritage tourism by improving (i) Access to high quality information about the heritage itself; (ii) Bettering the experience of people visiting the place (e.g.: through mixed reality experiences); (iii) Connecting the three main poles of the heritage experience: the heritage itself, locals and visitors; (iv) Dis-intermediating some relationships between visitors/prospects and locals; (vi) Educating main stakeholders. This research, while touching on all dimensions, will focus mainly on the access, better and connect ones.

According to the United Nations Educational, Scientific and Cultural Organisation (UNESCO) World Heritage Centre [8], the Brandberg National Monument Area, "has an exceptionally rich palaeo-archaeological heritage with a high concentration of prehistoric rock art (more than 43 000 paintings and 900 sites alone)." In addition, the Area features, "a rich biological diversity which represent 40% of the mammal and reptile species and 10% of plant species recorded from Namibia" [8].

2 Literature Review

Designing digital engagements involves "complex negotiations between stakeholders and practitioners" [9]. Watterson and Hillerdal [10] successfully worked on an, "outreach project which creatively unites science and history with traditional knowledge and contemporary engagements." The use of co-design in such projects is shared by Vagnone and Ryan [11] when they note that for one to achieve a great digital engagement experience, one should not only, "engage the communities surrounding them, but also to collaborate with visitors on the type and quality of experience they provide." To this end, "new hybrid methodologies are required in this field to enable researchers to understand technology use in actual practice" [12].

Adding digital technologies to cultural heritage sites in the end leads to, "encouraging social engagements in cultural contexts" [13]. "The design of digital into physical has to consider the complex ecology of cultural heritage with the conflicting goals of curators, visitors, and technology" [4]. In the case of technology it is noted from other studies [4, 14] that that improvements need to be made. Petrelli, Ciolfi, Van Dijk, Hornecker, Not, and Schmidt [4] highlight that, "much work is needed to create hardware and software toolkits that lower the threshold of use and allow interested parties to create digitally augmented artifacts with only minimal technical knowledge." In addition to all the above, "there is something of a discrepancy between the theory and literature on digital heritage, on the one hand, and the potential use of these tools in practice, on the other" [2].

The key lesson on designing digital engagements for heritage sites, "is the need for technical knowledge and skills paired with the high costs of interactive exhibitions that put them off" [4]. This is supported by King, Stark, and Cooke [2] who report that, "the large-scale projects often profiled in the literature are beyond the means of many institutions." However, there is research that supports that, "Researchers, creative practitioners, and heritage professionals have been progressively crafting ever more challenging digital heritage encounters for members of the public" [12].

Co-designing with the community in question is used to mitigate the extent to which outsiders influence the project as, "for outsiders to monologue a narrative on the past without making space for indigenous, or local, voices would be detrimental" [10] to the whole project. Similar sentiments as shared by Katifori, Perry, Vayanou, Antoniou, Ioannidis, McKinney, Chrysanthi, and Ioannidis [13] who questioned, "Do we have the appropriate language and tools to talk to our participants about experiences that are dynamic and unfold in time and space?" Care must be taken and Williams, and Atkin [15] notes that, "… standards, strategies and ethics of using digital media by archaeologists and heritage professionals require further investigation and critical reflection." In all, the risk factor is there as outlined by Freeman [6] that digital heritage projects have "turned out to be much more complex and nuanced: challenging established national narratives; potentially infringing on copyright; blurring notions of communities and audiences; and revealing the entanglement of corporations and algorithms in tangible and intangible forms of cultural heritage" [6].

An issue that exist is the fact that, "the open data initiative challenges the cultural heritage sector" [16]. This challenge is matched differently depending on the approach that the researchers take and can be overcome if addressed in a sensitive manner. Katifori et al. [13] summed it best by stating that, "Heritage work is increasingly understood as (at best) collaborative, co-produced, relational, and contentious."

In the end, one just has to be extra cautious when dealing with research related to such. Getting the buy-in of the community is core to digital heritage engagement projects. "If certain audience groups feel marginalized, this can lead to digital tools being deployed in inappropriate ways" [2]. Should researchers of a project not publicize the project, then the project suffers from not being used by the audience it is meant for.

2.1 The Digital Library

The core research seeks to use Harald Pager's digital collection, "the largest comprehensive rock art documentation world-wide" [17], of the Brandberg for public engagement. Harald Pager, is "known around the world for his monumental efforts to record rock paintings in KwaZulu-Natal, South Africa and in the Brandberg, Namibia" [18]. According to Petrelli, Not, Damala, van Dijk, and Lechner [19], "A wealth of digital cultural heritage content is available in on-line repositories and archives, but is used in a limited way and through rather static modes of delivery."

The digital collection is hosted by the African Archaeology Archive Cologne (AAArC), University of Cologne in Germany. Such archive was established to make the university's "archaeological collections including its important rock art documentation digitally available" [20]. It is noted that, "rock art research started in Namibia in

1963, Northeastern Africa established itself as a second focus region in the early 1980s" [21].

The AAArC has been working at digitizing their collection since 2012. The digital collection is available through Arachne – an open online central database available at https://arachne.uni-koeln.de/drupal/. Lenssen-Erz and Fäder [20] share that, "An open online archive will in the long run flatten the hierarchical order of access to the results of archaeological research and heritage archiving." The database, "combines an ongoing process of digitizing traditional documentation (stored on media which are both threatened by decay and largely unexplored) with the production of new digital object and graphic data" [21].

3   Research Issue

The Brandberg National Monument Area is a site that has been well researched with a number of collections and research papers published on the site. Harald Pager's diary has the most extensive recordings of the rock art found at the Area, and this is digitally available through the AAArC online open access database. The Diary has already been published into a book with six volumes [22–27] and still there is content that is unpublished.

Despite the digital database being made available, the public has limited access to it as they are not aware of its existence and because such a reach archive has not been designed for a direct fruition by lay-people. There needs to be some public engagement tools planned with the work available from Harald Pager's diary and hopefully others to enable easy access to information by the public.

It is with this background that the research seeks to co-design digital engagement tools around the Brandberg National Monument Area in Namibia.

4   Research Objectives

The objectives for the proposed study include to;

- Identify existing public engagement strategies used with the Brandberg National Monument Area;
- Explore the best digital engagement tools for the Brandberg National Monument Area which make use of Harald Pager's diary (and any other available research material);
- Co-design a digital engagement and governance framework for the Brandberg National Monument Area;
- Develop digital engagement tools for the Brandberg National Monument Area; and
- Evaluate and improve them based on actual usages.

5   Research Questions

The research is bound by the following questions;

- What are the existing strategies for public engagement with the Brandberg National Monument Area?
- What possible digital engagement tools would best be used for a heritage site in Africa?
- How best to co-design a digital engagement and governance framework, which work in the African context, for a heritage site?

6   Research Methodology

The proposed research would be an action design (also known as action research/science research) based on Frayling's research-through-design "foundational concept" [28]. Action-based participatory design is defined by Kensing, and Greenbaum [29] as, "a process of investigating, understanding, reflecting upon, establishing, developing, and supporting mutual learning between multiple participants in collective 'reflection-in-action.'" According to Cumbula, Sabiescu, and Cantoni [30], "Action research is mainly devoted to produce something and to sustain social change to the benefit of the stakeholders involved."

According to Hult and Lennung [31], "Action research simultaneously assists in practical problem-solving and expands scientific knowledge, as well as enhances the competencies of the respective actors, being performed collaboratively in an immediate situation using data feedback in a cyclical process aiming at an increased understanding of a given social situation, primarily applicable for the understanding of change processes in social systems and undertaken within a mutually acceptable ethical framework."

The research method, "aims to transform communities for the better, and in which positive social change is an explicit goal" [32]. Therefore, a mixed methods approach including; meeting with the community and stakeholders, workshops and focus groups, would be used as, "multiple perspectives should be incorporated throughout a research undertaking" [33].

In this case, the local communities are immediately identified to include those within the Brandberg National Monument Area and those within the National Heritage Council of Namibia. The extent to the co-design communities would be surrounding communities, government ministries, non-profit organisations, associations, and the private sector.

7   Research Ethics

For the research to be conducted, a research permit would be applied through the National Heritage Council of Namibia, "a statutory organisation of the government of Namibia established under the National Heritage Act, No 27 of 2004 …. It is the national administrative body responsible for the protection of Namibia's natural and cultural heritage" [34].

The stakeholders would be consulted prior to them being made part of the team. They would have to sign consent forms and participate in the research knowing what is expected of them. All material collected during the project would be kept safely and confidential for the duration of the project after which, they would be disposed of appropriately.

References

1. National Co-ordinating Centre for Public Engagement Homepage. https://www.publicengage ment.ac.uk/about-engagement/what-public-engagement. Accessed 31 Aug 2020
2. King, L., Stark, J.F., Cooke, P.: Experiencing the digital world: the cultural value of digital engagement with heritage. Heritage Soc. **9**(1), 76–101 (2016)
3. Kalay, Y., Kvan, T., Affleck, J.: New Heritage: New Media and Cultural Heritage. Routledge, New York (2007)
4. Petrelli, D., Ciolfi, L., van Dijk, D., Hornecker, E., Not, E., Schmidt, A.: Integrating material and digital: a new way for cultural heritage. Interactions **20**(4), 58–63 (2013). https://doi.org/ 10.1145/2486227.2486239
5. Fredericks, J., Caldwell, G.A., Tomitsch, M.: Middle-out design: collaborative community engagement in urban HCI. In: 28th Australian Conference on Computer-Human Interaction Proceedings, pp. 200–204. ACM, Australia (2016)
6. Freeman, C.G.: The implications of online connectivity for world heritage in a digital platform society. Hist. Environ. **30**(3), 84 (2018)
7. Cantoni, L.: eTourism for Heritage. Heritage and sustainable tourism: the role and challenge of information and communication technologies. In: De Ascaniis, S., Gravari-Barbas, M., Cantoni, L. (eds.) Tourism Management at UNESCO World Heritage Sites. USI – Università della Svizzera italiana Press, Lugano, Switzerland (2018)
8. UNESCO World Heritage Centre, Brandberg National Monument Area. https://whc.unesco. org/en/tentativelists/1744/. Accessed 31 Aug 2020
9. Watterson, A., Anderson, J., Baxter, K.: Designing digital engagements: approaches to creative practice and adaptable programming for archaeological visualisation. In: Electronic Visualisation and the Arts, EVA London 2020, pp. 66–72 (2020)
10. Watterson, A., Hillerdal, C.: Nunalleq, stories from the village of our ancestors: co-designing a multi-vocal educational resource based on an archaeological excavation. Archaeologies **16**(2), 198–227 (2020). https://doi.org/10.1007/s11759-020-09399-3
11. Vagnone, F.D., Ryan, D.E.: Anarchist's Guide to Historic House Museums. Routledge, New York (2016)
12. Galani, A., Kidd, J.: Evaluating digital cultural heritage 'in the wild' the case for reflexivity. J. Comput. Cult. Herit. (JOCCH) **12**(1), 1–15 (2019)
13. Katifori, A., et al.: "Let them talk!" exploring guided group interaction in digital storytelling experiences. J. Comput. Cult. Herit. (JOCCH) **13**(3), 1–30 (2020)
14. Bekele, M.K., Pierdicca, R., Frontoni, E., Malinverni, E.S., Gain, J.: A survey of augmented, virtual, and mixed reality for cultural heritage. J. Comput. Cult. Herit. (JOCCH) **11**(2), 1–36 (2018)
15. Williams, H., Atkin, A.: Virtually dead: digital public mortuary archaeology. Internet Archaeol. **40**, 1–28 (2015)
16. Stuedahl, D., Runardotter, M., Mörtberg, C.M.: Attachments to participatory digital infrastructures in the cultural heritage sector. Sci. Technol. Stud. **29**(4), 50–69 (2016)
17. Lenssen-Erz, T.: Tides of the Desert - Gezeiten der Wüste. Heinrich-Barth-Institut, Köln, Germany (2002)

18. University of the Witwatersrand, The Harald Pager Collection. https://www.wits.ac.za/roc kart/collections/the-harald-pager-collection/. Accessed 31 Aug 2020

19. Petrelli, D., Not, E., Damala, A., van Dijk, D., Lechner, M.: meSch – material encounters with digital cultural heritage. In: Ioannides, M., Magnenat-Thalmann, N., Fink, E., Žarnić, R., Yen, A.-Y., Quak, E. (eds.) Digital Heritage. Progress in Cultural Heritage: Documentation, Preservation, and Protection, pp. 536–545. Springer International Publishing, Cham (2014). https://doi.org/10.1007/978-3-319-13695-0_53

20. Lenssen-Erz, T., Fäder, E., Jesse, F., Wilmeroth, J.: Digital management of rock art: the African archaeology archive cologne (AAArC). Afr. Archaeol. Rev. **35**(2), 285–298 (2018). https://doi.org/10.1007/s10437-018-9303-5

21. Arachne Homepage. https://arachne.uni-koeln.de/drupal/. Accessed 31 Aug 2020

22. Pager, H., Breunig, P.: The Rock Paintings of the Upper Brandberg, Part I: Amis Gorge, vol. 1. Heinrich-Barth-Institut, Köln, Germany (1989)

23. Pager, H.: The Rock Paintings of the Upper Brandberg, Part II: Hungorob Gorge, vol. 4. Heinrich-Barth-Institut, Köln, Germany (1993)

24. Pager, H.: The Rock Paintings of the Upper Brandberg, Part III: Southern Gorges, vol. 7. Heinrich-Barth-Institut, Köln, Germany (1995)

25. Pager, H.: The Rock Paintings of the Upper Brandberg, Part IV: Umuab and Karoab Gorges, vol. 10. Heinrich-Barth-Institut, Köln, Germany (1998)

26. Pager, H.: The Rock Paintings of the Upper Brandberg, Part V: Naib Gorge (A) and the Northwest (Vol. 5). Heinrich-Barth-Institut, Köln, Germany (2000).

27. Pager, H.: The rock paintings of the Upper Brandberg Part VI: Naib (B). University of Cologne, Köln, Germany (2006)

28. Durrant, A.C., Vines, J., Wallace, J., Yee, J.S.: Research through design: twenty-first century makers and materialities. Massachusetts Inst. Technol. Des. Issues **33**(3), 3–10 (2017)

29. Kensing, F., Greenbaum, J.: Heritage: having a say. In: Routledge International Handbook of Participatory Design. Routledge, New York (2012)

30. Cumbula, S.D., Sabiescu, A.G., Cantoni, L.: Community design: a collaborative approach for social integration. J. Commun. Inf. **13**(1) (2017)

31. Hult, M., Lennung, S.Å.: Towards a definition of action research: a note and bibliography. J. Manage. Stud. **17**(2), 241–250 (1980)

32. McGhee, F.L.: Participatory Action Research and Archaeology. Oxford University Press, New York (2012)

33. White, B.: Mapping Your Thesis: The Comprehensive Manual of Theory and Techniques for Masters and Doctoral Research. Australian Council for Educational Research, Camberwell (2011)

34. The National Heritage Council of Namibia Homepage. https://www.nhc-nam.org/. Accessed 31 Aug 2020

Short Papers: Virtual Museum Applications (e-Museums and e-Exhibitions)

Covid-19 and Greek Museums. Digitality as a Mean of Promoting Cultural Heritage During the Coronavirus Period. New Ways of Expression

Markella-Elpida Tsichla[✉]

University of Patras, Patras, Greece
mtsichla@upatras.gr

Abstract. The coronavirus pandemic, scientifically named Covid-19, was entirely a unique phenomenon that affected the lives of billions of people around the world. The problem persists, with a happy ending not yet fully visible, even if, in due course, medical science discovers ways to reduce or eliminate this pandemic. The negative impact of the disease on people's lives has been enormous, with millions of dead people, while at the same time it affected the global economy as well as social cohesion, making life difficult for people. Culture was also a major victim of the pandemic, as the direct contacts of artists and experts with the works of art of the world cultural heritage were immediately cut off. Greece felt the negative consequences in this area, as its history and culture are linked to tourism and the promotion of its cultural heritage has suffered a major blow. Masterpieces from the past, of great his-torical importance and aesthetic value, were found in isolation as the difficulties of being approached by the international public seemed to be unsurpassed. However, "Necessity and the gods are convinced", as the ancient greeks said, so the Greek museums entered-with an unprecedented dynamism-in modern technologies and in the age of digital image, in order not to stop the "contact" of the public with the rich world of art. Therefore, at an extremely fast pace, special virtual tour programs were implemented and displayed in museums and places of culture and as it turned out, the attendance showed high numbers, as the cultural project became a "product" with the aim to be perceived by the cyber public as an intangible object with dimensions outside the "established" aesthetic pleasure. Furthermore, the result is considered to be particularly encouraging as the operation of the museums has acquired a new dynamic, a necessary condition in the functioning of the modern world.

Keywords: Pandemic · Covid-19/Corona virus · Greek museums · New Media · Digital reality · Artworks · Cultural heritage

1 Introduction

Undoubtedly, attracting visitors is the main goal of most museums around the world and for this reason they devise many ways to attract an audience that will come in

© Springer Nature Switzerland AG 2021
M. Ioannides et al. (Eds.): EuroMed 2020, LNCS 12642, pp. 675–682, 2021.
https://doi.org/10.1007/978-3-030-73043-7_59

contact with their collections. The attendance and therefore the reference to numbers of people, who show interest in works of art or cultural monuments, is not only mentioned to emphasize the need to acquire historical knowledge or aesthetic pleasure, but also for the financial independence of the museum since sustainability is also required in the cultural sector. After all, the cultural and creative industries consist exclusively of cultural products. That is why it is not accidental that in the context of the history of art and culture, relatively new sciences have been developed, such as museology, museum pedagogy, museum education and cultural economy.

However, the period of coronavirus domination in the time we are going through has completely changed the data on the reception of culture, which is without a doubt a human need that completes the human psychic personality. Adaptation to the new reality was now mandatory in order to keep people "in touch" with museums at a time when general or specific lockdowns were on the agenda around the world. In this case, the "cavalry" was called for help, which was nothing more than the invocation of technology and the implementation of specialized programs for the convenience of the public, which in this case came from all latitudes and longitudes of the earth [1].

Modern technology and new media have been the best supporters of the museums' new programs, including the Greek museums, which recently, have essentially relied on virtual reality, digitized image and interactive multimedia applications. Recognizing the potential of the internet and the importance of cyberspace in general, as been the new field of research for museums and it seems that the prospects for promoting not only collections but also the way in which culture as a "soft power" (cultural diplomacy) have been expanded thus creating a driving force for all states, regardless of their political and economic strength [2].

On the other hand, new ways of approaching and interpreting cultural heritage were discovered, with museums emerging as the most influential bodies in the public life of their countries, while art acquired new forms of expression, but also new terms for defining cultural identity [3].

The concern for culture prevailed throughout the civilized world and the use of new applications and new media for its promotion was demanded by both the state and the private sector. However, the reception of art through virtual reality - perfectly directed with the help of technology - created new relations between the object of art and the public since it is based on illusion and lack of conditions for the understanding of the human artistic creativity on one hand and for enhancing the creative nature of cultural industries on the other [1].

It is characteristic that the Greek museums and archeological sites showed an enviable adaptation to the new data, despite the initial anxiety and uncertainty about their future. Their collaboration was the top action of the Ministry of Culture, so that through the collaboration of the classic with the modern, to create a new visual world, based on new ideas and original inspirations.

2   Technology in the Service of Art and Culture. New Ideas on the Table

As it has already been said, the conditions created by the appearance of the coronavirus were unprecedented, as was the reception of culture by an audience that generally was obliged to live in conditions of complete isolation. People's lives were tested hard.

Although the museums remained closed for a long time or at best were under-operated, they remained "open" to the public with the help of digital technology and the new opportunities offered by the electronic world. The acquisition of knowledge through museum exhibits and the need for education are processes that have inherent characteristics and are inextricably linked to man. The effort to modernize museums in Greece was unprecedented so that small and large cultural institutions competed in ideas and original actions (see for example the Onassis Foundation [4]).

The group and individual exhibitions of visual artists were numerous, and some had an international tone, flooding the internet with "images" of all kinds. The Greek cultural heritage found a beloved refuge, enticing the unsuspecting Greek public to such initiatives. The theatrical works also gained a lot of popularity, being promoted with undiminished fervor by special sites, thus breaking the viewing records in similar cases (see [5]).

However, apart from the online transmission of recorded theatrical performances, the quarantine period due to covid 19 in combination with New Technologies, gave birth to new means of expression in the field of theater. It is worth mentioning the first theatrical performance in Greece, entitled "Dämmerung", which was created entirely through internet and where all the actors interpreted their role from their own environment through an online platform [6].

Regarding the museums and the promotion of the cultural heritage in the period of covid 19, remarkable efforts were made both by the state and private bodies. The world-famous Google Arts & Culture application includes Greek museums where from anywhere in the world, the digital visitor can visit their collections. Some of the museums that can be visited digitally are the Acropolis Museum, the Theocharakis Foundation, the National Gallery, the Benaki Museum, the Museum of Cycladic Art, etc. [7].

The Acropolis Museum, apart from the possibility of a digital tour in the mon-uments that offers, gives the visitor the opportunity to interact with the educational multimedia applications, "Coloring the Veil" and restoring the monuments with the "Glafka" pro-gram. The Benaki Museum has virtual tours for all its collections, the Technopolis of the Municipality of Athens has a virtual tour of the exhibition "160 years made in Greece" in combination with the Industrial Museum of Gas, while the Numismatic Museum has exhibits in a 3d representation. Also, many other institutions promote their collections and programs online, keeping in touch with the visitor even during the period of isolation (Fig. 1).

The Greek Ministry of Culture took important initiatives in order to strengthen the new artistic productions on the basis of the application of digital technology with the prospect of creating the appropriate conditions for the strengthening of the cultural institutions and their future transformation into autonomous (structural and economics) creative industries (see [8]).

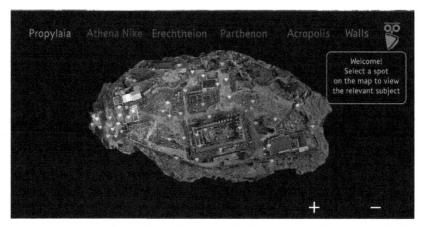

Fig. 1. Snapshot from the Virtual Tour of the Acropolis Museum (https://www.acropolisvirtualto ur.gr/)

One of the last programs with the name "All Greece one Culture", as we will see in the next chapter, deals with the connection of the ancient with the modern culture. Through this perspective new ideas were cultivated, and interesting artistic actions were created. It is not an exaggeration to claim that new values were promoted, such as, for example, the emergence of "voice" and "sound" as expressive elements, which owe their inspiration to the "confinement" of people in their homes (or hospitals) and the "silence" that followed as a necessary evil.

The examples exist to prove the reality that the world has lived (and still lives), but also to highlight Art, once again, as a "value of empathy" with universal characteristics.

Undoubtedly, the pandemic was the best occasion for Greece to integrate mu-seums and cultural sites into the world of digital technology and to create the conditions for the promotion of cultural heritage, both ancient and modern [1].

3   Greek Museums Face New Challenges During the Coronavirus Period. From the Virtual Tour to New Forms of Expression

At the first appearance of the coronavirus in Greece (second quarter of 2020) the museums after overcoming the initial shock, strengthened their technical equipment, completed the digitization of their collections at a rapid pace and offered their masterpieces to the international public "from distance", creating virtual spaces for artistic tour in order not to lose contact with the spectator audience. The result was really impressive. In particular, large museums with rich collections created special platforms with electronic exhibitions that surpassed all imagination. The success of these tests was confirmed by thousands of "visits", creating new series of friends of these museums from around the world. The largest first was presented by the New Acropolis Museum, the National Archaeological Museum, but also by the private institutions of Onassis and Niarchos in Athens. According to Hatzigiannaki [9], the culture of quarantine was manifested by the huge increase of visitation in virtual reality environments, where visitors feel the sense of "real" visit to space. Nevertheless, in the virtual visit, which is based on the theory of illusion, the visitor experiences the museum experience as a "personal experience", in the same way that the viewer identifies with the hero of a film or a literature, "It is an aesthetic experience, where the visitor, the creator, and the artwork are one, in a shared digital environment".

All this effort was based on the simple idea that museums had to maintain their role as a key pillar of the production of historical knowledge and the preservation of national identity maintaining the title of the most powerful force in creating the so-called cultural diplomacy or "soft power" (opposition to "hard power", implying the military), capable of influencing the will of factors of the international political elite.

However, the corona virus remained present thereafter (third quarter and probably in the fourth quarter of 2020), with the result that restrictions on population movements still exist and visits to cultural sites remain particularly difficult with accessibility becoming more problematic.

According to the research of the Hellenic Statistical Authority (HELSTAT) [10], the number of visitors of Greek museums in June 2020, ie the first month of their reopening from quarantine, shows a decrease of 97% compared to June 2019, while the number of visitors of archeological sites, shows a decrease of 96.4% compared to that of 2019. Regarding the entire semester of January–June 2020, which includes the months when museums and archaeological sites remained closed, museums show a decrease in traffic by 80.1% compared to the corresponding period of 2019, while the decrease in visiting at archaeological sites reaches 85.3%. However, the fact that the Louvre Museum had more online visits during the quarantine period than physical visitors throughout 2019, shows that the people's worldwide interest in museums and cultural heritage is not insignificant. Specifically, in the two months March-May of 2020, 10.5 million users visited the museum's website, while throughout 2019, physical visitors were 9.6 million [11].

Therefore, although the period we are going through, the museums are not closed like in the quarantine period, they are in a state of waiting for the period of return to everyday life. However, the universal shift in New Technologies can trigger new options, at the same time with the "natural" visit, which will make the next day, not a simple return to the previous status quo, but more creative with new solutions in terms of sustainability of museums [12, 13].

Undoubtedly the live visit to a museum is an irreplaceable phenomenon and has not changed for centuries and even now, despite the evolution of technology and the change of perceptions about the role of museums today to the extent that the potential of the digitized image and digital visiting is one of the most basic achievements of modern life - always at the level of culture. However, the direct contact of the viewer with the work of art remains a question.

For this reason, the museums in the middle of the corona virus period, have changed their plans, designing exhibitions with "real" works of art and participating artists. The initiative was taken by the Ministry of Culture with the aforementioned program and entitled "All Greece one Culture", in which there was a partnership of the services of the Archaeological Department with the administrations of museums of modern and contemporary art. Historic sites and archeological museums have opened their iconic spaces to modern artists and contemporary works of art.

Memorable are the two actions of the two largest museums of contemporary art of Greece, the National Museum of Contemporary Art of Athens (EMST) and the Metropolitan Organization of the Museum of Fine Arts of Thessaloniki (MOMus), which show the change of plans in terms of promoting the Greek cultural heritage. So, the museum of Athens carried out four artistic activities in an equal number of archeological sites in Athens: the Lyceum of Aristotle, the Archaeological Museum of Lavrio, the Roman Agora and the Temple of Olympian Zeus (Olympion). All four have an interesting rationale based on the need to divert interest from the digital world of museums and the reminder of the need for immediate and "live" expression. It is noteworthy that new ways of expression have emerged, enriching the value system of the history of art.

Specifically, in the Roman Agora, the artists Manolis Manousakis, Michail Moschoutis, Danai Stefanou, Giannis Kotsonis and Nikoleta Hatzopoulou exhibited in a group participation entitled "Deeper than Silence", which presents "sound works on the theme of silence, pause and waiting" (See [14]) (Fig. 2).

Fig. 2. Exhibition of Sound Works "Deeper than the Silence", Roman Agora (https://digitalcu lture.gov.gr)

The interesting thing about the exhibition is that instead of the illusionist perspective and virtual reality as the main way of expression in the work of art, even given digitally, the sense of hearing is skillfully used as "value" to give the atmosphere of "silence" that prevailed, during the first period of the pandemic. In addition, perhaps this work of art makes a reference to the difficulty of expression that prevails due to the mask. Thus, the sound became a carrier of a memory, but also a carrier of a performance of a situation that was experienced in a "deafening" way, the absolute silence, by almost the whole planet. Also as noted by the organizers of this "original" exhibition: "Inside the archeological site, the ancient ruins that stood empty though imposing in the silence of the days of the quarantine, will re-welcome the audience to listen to the silence and meditate on concepts such as pause and waiting. Visitors will be invited to be active listeners and to be surrendered to the frequency of sound and emotional arousal." Even in the performance of Jenny Argyriou in the temple of Olympian Zeus (entitled Phrasis) the "social distance" and the "digital alienation" are artistically commented through the interactive relationship of "speech and body with space". For the artist, the basic material of expression is the ancient speech expressed inside the ancient works, the ancient speech used to attribute the deeper meaning of the action "physically, verbally and vocally".

It is obvious that the artist and all the actors (musicians, dancers, performers, directors and others) appeal to a holistic expression in order to give the meaning of a social reality, unexpectedly unprecedented, using the maximum practices that the history of art has offered to artists over time.

The MOMus Experimental Center (Thessaloniki) took a similar view with an invitation to artists to take part in the "Open Folios" program. (see [15]). The aim is the direct and lifelong participation of artists in the contemporary art events as an attempt for a new extroverted behavior of the artists in relation to the living museum and the confirmation that the museum remains the living space of creative art of the public and of the artists themselves. The invitation was addressed to artists experimenting with new media and digital art and other related audiovisual events, that is arts that were developed more than ever due to the conditions during the coronavirus period.

In general, one has the impression that art came out of a slumber, that museums felt the need for extroversion, that is, to reopen their doors to the public and that artists realized their role as creators with consistency and responsibility to the public, who thirsts for knowledge and wants to see the new aesthetics that are formed under conditions of restriction of basic human freedoms.

4   Conclusion

The Covid-19 pandemic swept many countries on all continents, many people lost their lives and was described as one of the most negative phenomena that hit the planet after World War II. Quarantine, which was applied strictly in many rich and poor countries resulted in the deprivation of recognized human rights, such as freedom of movement and social exclusion.

Cultural institutions such as theaters, conservatories and museums around the world have implemented special programs to provide creative employment to people. Through these unprecedented conditions, the processes of digitization of the country's cultural stock has been accelerated. The leading role was played by the museums that, in addition to the digitization of their collections, made available on the internet multimedia applications, interactive programs and digital tours in order to expand the electronic public. However, the need for extroversion and the demand for the resumption of "live" activities led the museum administrations to hold events with artists in full creativity. In fact, with the partnership of the Ministry of Culture, action programs were financed, such as "All Greece one Culture", aiming at the collaboration of the contemporary art with the ancient art and the New Media. The encouraging element from the implementation of the program in addition to the occasion of the participation of many artists in this process, gave new expressive values such as the "shaping" of sounds or speech and even the creative collaboration of arts, such as the visual expression through body, movement and dance, music and space, where the specific actions are implemented with the idea of a holistic (Gesamtkunstwerk) approach to Art.

References

1. Tsichla, M.E: Virtual culture vs real culture The new reality for arts in Greece during the COVID-19 crisis. Int. J. Arts Humanit. Soc. Stud. **2**(4), 31–35 (2020)
2. Tsichla, M.E: History and art without limits. Multimedia applications in the promotion of Cultural Heritage. In: 3rd Panhellenic Conference on Digitalization of Cultural Heritage 2019. Athens: Network "PERRAIVIA" (under issue)
3. Banks, M.: The work of culture and C-19. Eur. J. Cult. Stud. **23**(4), 648–654 (2020)
4. YouTube Onassis Foundation. https://www.youtube.com/user/sgtathens. Accessed 8 Sept 2020
5. Kathimerini.gr. National Theatre: 23,500 Viewers Enjoyed Macbeth Online. (in Greek). https://www.kathimerini.gr/1072339/article/politismos/8eatro/e8niko-8eatro-23500-8eates-apolaysan-diadiktyaka-thn-makmpe8. Accessed 8 Sept 2020
6. Poulopoulou, K.: Dämmerung; The first Greek Theatrical Play Live at ZOOM. (in Greek). https://www.iefimerida.gr/politismos/neo-theatriko-thanasi-triaridi-sto-diadiktyo. Accessed 14 Oct 2020
7. Google Arts & Culture. Greece - Google Arts & Culture. https://artsandculture.google.com/entity/m035qy. Accessed 9 Sept 2020
8. Culture.gov.gr. Special Invitation to Digital Culture by the Ministry of Culture and Sports. https://www.culture.gov.gr/en/Information/SitePages/view.aspx?nID=3181. Accessed 8 Sept 2020
9. Hatziyiannaki, A.: The Quarantine Culture. The Emergency Exit During Pandemic's Social Distancing, pp. 1–10. Academia.edu (2020)
10. Hellenic Statistical Authority: Press Release Visitation of Museums and Archaeological Sites June 2020, pp. 1–5. HELSTAT, Athens (2020). (in Greek)
11. Farnworth, H: We are all in this together. Inf. Learn. Rev. Spec. Issue **2020**(2), 11–12 (2020)
12. Frankel, S.: Tips and thoughts from museums in a Covid world. Inf. Learn. Rev. Spec. Issue **2020**(2), 14–15 (2020)
13. Nos.nl. Nederlandse Omroep Stichting. https://nos.nl. Accessed 17 Oct 2020
14. Digitalculture.gov.gr. Deeper Than Silence From The National Museum. https://digitalculture.gov.gr/2020/07/deeper-than-silence/. Accessed 8 Sept 2020
15. Momus.gr. Open Folios Momus-Experimental Arts Center. https://www.momus.gr/news/open_folios. Accessed 8 Sept 2020

Reliability Analysis of an Evaluation Experiment on Cultural Websites

Katerina Kabassi[✉], Athanasios Botonis, and Christos Karydis

Department of Environment, Ionian University, 29100 Zakynthos, Greece
{kkabassi,nasbototonis,c.karydis}@ionio.gr

Abstract. This paper describes the evaluation experiment of the websites of museums' conservation labs. For this purpose an experiment has been implemented with the participation of 81 subjects and a multi-criteria decision-making model has been used for processing the results and draw conclusions about the electronic presence of the conservation labs of museums. However, the main focus of the paper is on performing a reliability analysis of the whole experiment. This analysis involved two tests, one for examining the reliability of the sample used in the evaluation experiment and another for examining the reliability of the questionnaire provided to the subjects of the evaluation.

Keywords: Reliability analysis · Intraclass correlation coefficient · Cronbach's Alpha · Evaluation experiment · Cultural websites

1 Introduction

In the last two decades, almost all museums have acknowledged the importance of online presence to meet their goals and mission. An important department of every museum is the conservation lab they have. The museums' conservation labs and the treatments which they carried out on the artifacts, many times are not obvious for the public. Nevertheless, their content may be of interest to students, researchers, archaeologists, tourists, artists for further education, and preservation guidelines purposes. As a result, in many museums, the conservation laboratories have a separate webpage.

The existence of a website does not guarantee success. Sometimes the websites are poorly developed. Therefore, many researchers have highlighted the need for evaluating websites with cultural content [1]. As a result, many studies have concentrated on evaluating museums' websites (e.g. [4, 11, 13]) or special features of those websites [7, 8]. Multi-Criteria Decision Making (MCDM) models have been used in the past for evaluating websites of environmental [9, 12], cultural [3, 5, 6, 10] or other content. However, in these experiments, the reliability of the sample and the questionnaires has not been addressed before in multi-criteria decision making evaluation experiments of cultural websites.

In this paper, we have used the same criteria and their weights as these have been described in [5] and applied a non-fuzzy model, the Weighted Product Model (WPM) [2, 17] for ranking alternatives. However, we mainly focus on testing the reliability of the

© Springer Nature Switzerland AG 2021
M. Ioannides et al. (Eds.): EuroMed 2020, LNCS 12642, pp. 683–691, 2021.
https://doi.org/10.1007/978-3-030-73043-7_60

sample used in the evaluation process and the reliability of the questionnaire provided to the subjects of the evaluation.

2 Websites of Museums' Conservation Labs

We have selected the most famous museums in Greece and abroad which include web pages for their conservation departments and we are going to evaluate and compare the twenty-nine (29) websites of the museums' conservation labs: w1-Archaeological Museum of Thessaloniki, w2-Ashmolean Museum, w3-Barberini – Corsini Gallery – Roma, w4-Benaki Museum, w5-Boston Museum of Fine Arts, w6-British Museum, w7-Brooklyn museum, w8-Byzantine & Christian Museum in Athens, w9-De Young Museum of Fine Arts, w10-Galleria Nazionale d'Arte Moderna, w11-Getty Institution, w12-Guggenheim Museum, w13-Hermitage Museum, w14-Metropolitan Museum, w15-MoMa, w16-Museo Del Prado, w17-Museum of Byzantine Culture in Thessaloniki, w18-Museum of Islamic Art – Doha, w19-National Gallery of Greece, w20-National Museum New Delhi, w21-NTNU University museum, w22-Oriental Institute Museum, w23-Rijksmuseum, w24-Smithsonian museum, w25-Tate Modern, w26-Tokyo National Museum, w27-University of Michigan Museum of Art, w28-Vatican Museum, w29-Victoria & Albert Museum,

3 Evaluation of the Websites of Museums' Conservation Labs Using Multi-criteria Decision Making

The evaluation experiment of the protected areas' websites depends on several criteria. Therefore, the use of a multi-criteria decision-making theory may prove very useful. The application of such a theory may be implemented using the following basic steps:

Step1: Defining the Criteria and Designing the Questionnaire
The criteria have been selected by Kabassi [3] and are used for designing the questionnaire:

1. **c1: Currency/Clarity/Text comprehension.**
   Question 1: How would you rate the texts of the website regarding their clarity and their currency?
2. **c2: Completeness/Richness.**
   Question 2: Do you find the content of the website adequate and complete?
3. **c3: Quality Content.**
   Question 3: How good is the quality of all content of the website (texts, images, video, etc.)?
4. **c4: Support of Research.**
   Question 4: How well does the website provide information for the support of research?
5. **c5: Consistency.**
   Question 5: How well do similar pieces of information are dealt with in similar fashions?

6. **c6: Accessibility.**
    Question 6: How easily and intuitively accessible is the website's information for any user?
7. **c7: Structure/Navigation.**
    Question 7: How good is navigation within the website and the structure of the information provided?
8. **c8: Easy to use/simplicity.**
    Question 8: How simple and easy to use is the user interface?
9. **c9: User interface-Overall presentation-Design.**
    Question 9: How attractive and engaging is the overall presentation?
10. **c10: Efficiency.**
    Question 10: How successfully and quickly are actions performed within the website?
11. **c11: Multilingualism.**
    Question 11: Is information provided in more languages?
12. **c12: Multimedia.**
    Question 12: How many different media are used to convey the information
13. **c13: Interactivity.**
    Question 13: How comprehensive and useful, nicely presented, easy to explore and use is the content of the website
14. **c14: Adaptivity.**
    Question 14: How good is the ability of the system to adapt to users' characteristics such as needs, interests, etc.

Step2: Estimation of the Weights of Criteria

The criteria are not considered equally important in the reasoning process of decision-makers. For this reason, the multi-criteria decision-making theory Analytic Hierarchy Process [14, 15] has been used for calculating weights. After making pairwise comparisons, estimations are made that result in the final set of weights of the criteria. The application of the theory, it's reasoning, and the calculations are described in more detail in Kabassi et al. [5] and are beyond the scope of this paper. As a result, the weights of the criteria as these have been calculated in Kabassi et al. [5] are: $w_{c1} = 0.34$, $w_{c2} = 0.186$, $w_{c3} = 0.325$, $w_{c4} = 0.149$, $w_{c5} = 0.172$, $w_{c6} = 0.15$, $w_{c7} = 0.214$, $w_{c8} = 0.213$, $w_{c9} = 0.164$, $w_{c10} = 0.088$, $w_{c11} = 0.242$, $w_{c12} = 0.315$, $w_{c13} = 0.196$, $w_{c14} = 0.247$.

Step3: Setting the Group of Decision-Makers

In the phase of the definition of the weights described by Kabassi et al. [5] the experts were the decision-makers. Then, the questionnaire was answered by the final group of evaluators, which consisted of 81 users (professional researchers in conservation, students at advanced undergraduate and postgraduate level, informed users and general public).

Step4: Rating Criteria for All Websites
81 potential users of the websites of museums' conservation labs were asked to interact with the 29 websites and answer a questionnaire for each website. As soon as their answers were collected, we had the values of all the 14 criteria for each one of the 29 websites.

Step5: Ranking Alternatives by Applying a Multi-criteria Decision Model
Many MADM methods estimate a crisp value for each alternative in order to form a final ranking. One such method is the Weighted Product Model (WPM). As Tofalis [16] propose WPM as more appropriate than other models in some cases. In our case, WPM seemed rather appropriate. In order to apply it, we have defined the Multi-Criteria Decision Making problem. More specifically, we had used an alternative application of WPM, which is proposed by Triantafyllou [17]. In this alternative approach of WPM, the decision-maker uses only products without the previous ratios. Therefore, for each alternative the following value is calculated:

$$P(Aw_i) = \prod_{j=1}^{n} (a_{Awj})^{w_j}, \quad \text{for K} = 1, \ldots, 29. \tag{1}$$

The term $P(Aw_i)$ denotes the total performance value of an alternative website w_i. Each one of the 81 participants had to evaluate and rate the 14 criteria for the 29 websites. For each criterion, we calculated the mean of the 81 values and a $P(Aw_i)$'s value is calculated for each website. Taking into account this value, a first categorization of the websites is presented. According to the above estimations, the $P(Aw_i)$'s values of the 29 websites are used for ranking the websites. More specifically, Table 1 presents the name of the alternative website in the first column, the museum, in which the conservation labs' website belongs, the values of $P(Aw_i)$ calculated by application of the non-fuzzy WPM, which is described in this paper, and the last column shows the ranking according to the calculations made in Kabassi et al. [6] using the fuzzy model of WPM.

The application of the WPM model to the ratings of the 81 participants of the evaluation, has revealed that the best website was considered to be the website of the conservation lab of the National Gallery of Greece. The particular website provided rich content related to the activities of the department, the different departments, the equipment, and the staff. Its content is enriched with multimedia. The user interface is well designed and generally, the website is well structured and usable. The website of the Benaki Museum in Athens was also rated high.

The comparison of WPM with fuzzy WPM that had been used in the past for ranking the same websites and is described in detail in Kabassi et al. [6] revealed that the differences are minor; the results are very similar and do not change the general picture of the electronic presence of museums' conservation labs.

Table 1. Table captions should be placed above the tables.

w_i	Conservation labs of museums	$P(Aw_i)$	Ranking non-fuzzy	Ranking fuzzy WPM[a]
w1	Archaeological Museum of Thessaloniki	42.062	11	9
w2	Ashmolean Museum	32.751	19	19
w3	Barberini – Corsini Gallery – Roma	17.272	27	27
w4	Benaki Museum	58.357	2	2
w5	Boston Museum of Fine Arts	40.167	12	13
w6	British Museum	35.282	16	16
w7	Brooklyn museum	29.365	20	20
w8	Byzantine & Christian Museum in Athens	54.079	3	4
w9	De Young Museum of Fine Arts	38.681	14	12
w10	Galleria Nazionale d'Arte Moderna	12.339	29	29
w11	Getty Institution	27.292	24	23
w12	Guggenheim Museum	44.452	8	10
w13	Hermitage Museum	54.047	4	3
w14	Metropolitan Museum	53.172	5	5
w15	MoMa	38.853	13	14
w16	Museo Del Prado	45.304	7	6
w17	Museum of Byzantine Culture in Thessaloniki	27.503	23	25
w18	Museum of Islamic Art - Doha	20.826	26	26
w19	National Gallery of Greece	62.834	1	1
w20	National Museum New Delhi	15.193	28	28
w21	NTNU University museum	28.233	22	22
w22	Oriental Institute Museum	28.719	21	21
w23	Rijksmuseum	33.428	18	18

(continued)

Table 1. (*continued*)

w_i	Conservation labs of museums	$P(Aw_i)$	Ranking non-fuzzy	Ranking fuzzy WPM[a]
w24	Smithsonian museum	36.849	15	15
w25	Tate Modern	33.693	17	17
w26	Tokyo National Museum	43.079	10	11
w27	University of Michigan Museum of Art	26.092	25	24
w28	Vatican Museum	46.386	6	7
w29	Victoria & Albert Museum	43.617	9	8

[a] According to the work of Kabassi et al. 2020b.

4   Reliability Testing for the Participants

Each one of the 81 participants interacted with the 29 websites and evaluated them by rating the 14 criteria for each website. The values given by each decision-maker to each criterion were further used for calculating $P(Aw_i)$ for each one of the 29 websites. One could easily apply the WPM model and calculate the 29 $P(Aw_i)$'s values of the evaluated websites. Similarly, another 80 tables have been generated for the rest of the users participating in the experiment.

As a result, we created a table having as rows the 29 websites and as columns the 81 users. Each cell cl_{ij} of this table contained the value of $P(Aw_i)$ for i website calculated using the values of the criteria of j decision-maker. This table provides the rating of the same websites by the different decision-makers participating in the experiment.

It is our goal to test the reliability of the different raters, which are the participants. For this purpose, we run a reliability test for participants by calculating the Intraclass Correlation Coefficient. More specifically, we use the Interclass Correlation Coefficient to find out how strongly the decision-makers participating in the experiment resemble each other on rating each website. As a result, the intraclass correlation for average measures was calculated to 0.980. More specifically, for 95% Confidence Interval, the lower bound was estimated to 0.969 and the upper bound to 0.989. These results were found very satisfactory and as a result, all participants were considered reliable.

5   Reliability Testing for the Questionnaire

Since the 81 participants of the experiment were considered reliable, we proceeded to testing the reliability of the questionnaire by calculating the Cronbach's Alpha. For this purpose, we used the raw values of the 14 criteria given by the 81 decision-makers that participated in the experiment. This procedure was implemented for each one of the 29 websites and calculated one value for the Cronbach's Alpha for each website. The values of Cronbach's Alpha the questionnaire's answers of users for each website are presented in Table 2.

Table 2. Cronbach's Alpha and Interclass Correlation Coefficient values for websites.

Website	Cronbach's Alpha	Interclass Correlation Coefficient 95% Confidence Interval	
		Lower bound	Upper bound
w1	0.871	0.825	0.908
w2	0.899	0.863	0.928
w3	0.858	0.808	0.900
w3	0.873	0.828	0.910
w5	0.856	0.805	0.898
w6	0.865	0.817	0.904
w7	0.824	0.762	0.876
w8	0.740	0.649	0.816
w9	0.777	0.698	0.842
w10	0.924	0.897	0.946
w11	0.831	0.771	0.880
w12	0.933	0.910	0.953
w13	0.853	0.801	0.896
w14	0.715	0.615	0.798
w15	0.779	0.702	0.844
w16	0.843	0.787	0.889
w17	0.939	0.917	0.957
w18	0.897	0.861	0.927
w19	0.897	0.861	0.927
w20	0.929	0.904	0.950
w21	0.773	0.693	0.839
w22	0.874	0.829	0.911
w23	0.885	0.845	0.919
w24	0.724	0.627	0.805
w25	0.858	0.808	0.899
w26	0.950	0.933	0.965
w27	0.893	0.855	0.923
w28	0.791	0.717	0.853
w29	0.810	0.743	0.865

Cronbach's Alpha of the questionnaire for the different websites ranges from 0.715–0.929. Furthermore, the Intraclass Correlation Coefficient, with 95% Confidence Interval has been calculated and the lower and higher bounds in each test are presented in Table 2. The results of the reliability analysis that involved reliability testing of the application of the questionnaire to each different website proved and confirmed the reliability of the questionnaire, irrelevant of the website one would like to evaluate. Therefore, the specific criteria and questions are reliable to be used for the evaluation of any website of cultural content.

6 Conclusions

In the past, we have used a fuzzy multi-criteria decision-making model for evaluating the websites of the museums' conservation labs [5, 6]. In this paper, we use a non-fuzzy multi-criteria decision-making model for the evaluation of websites of museums' conservation labs and make a reliability analysis of the whole evaluation experiment. The main focus of the paper is on performing a reliability analysis that involved reliability testing of the participants and reliability testing of the questionnaire. In the first test, the reliability of the participants was evaluated by calculating the Intraclass Correlation Coefficient, in order to see whether their answers were consistent. More specifically, we used the Intraclass Correlation Coefficient to find out how strongly the decision-makers participating in the experiment resemble each other. The high values of the Intraclass Correlation Coefficient in the reliability test revealed that all users had paid much attention to completing the questionnaire as their answers were consistent.

Finally, reliability tests were also performed for the questions of the questionnaire. The results of the reliability analysis that involved reliability testing of the application of the questionnaire to each different website confirmed the reliability of the questionnaire, irrelevant of the website one would like to evaluate. The results of Cronbach's Alpha in each test revealed that the specific criteria and questions are reliable irrelevant to the website that it was evaluated. Therefore, the specific questionnaire could be used for the evaluation of any website of cultural content.

References

1. Cunliffe, D., Kritou, E., Tudhope, D.: Usability evaluation for museum web sites. Mus. Manage. Curatorship **19**(3), 229–252 (2001). https://doi.org/10.1080/09647770100201903
2. Fishburn, P.C.: Letter to the editor—additive utilities with incomplete product sets: application to priorities and assignments. Oper. Res. **15**(3), 537–542 (1967)
3. Kabassi, K.: Evaluating websites of museums: state of the art. J. Cult. Herit. **24**, 184–196 (2017)
4. Kabassi, K.: Evaluating museum websites using a combination of decision-making theories. J. Herit. Tour. **14**(5–6), 544–560 (2019)
5. Kabassi, K, Botonis, A., Karydis, C.: Evaluating websites of specialised cultural content using fuzzy multi-criteria decision making theories. Informatica **44**(1), 45–54 (2020)
6. Kabassi, K, Karydis, C., Botonis, A.: AHP, Fuzzy SAW and Fuzzy WPM for the evaluation of cultural websites. Multimodal Technol. Interact. **4**, 5 (2020). https://doi.org/10.3390/mti 4010005
7. Kabassi, K, Amelio, A, Komianos, V., Oikonomou, K.: Evaluating museum virtual tours: the case study of Italy. Information **10**(11), 351 (2019). https://doi.org/10.3390/info10110351
8. Kabassi, K., Maravelakis, E., Konstantaras, A.: Heuristics and fuzzy multi-criteria decision making for evaluating museum virtual tours. Int. J. Inclusive Mus. **11**(3), 1–21 (2018)

9. Kabassi, K., Martinis, A.: Evaluating the electronic presence of protected areas managing boards in Greece using a combination of different methods and theories. J. Ecotour. **19**, 50–72 (2020). https://doi.org/10.1080/14724049.2019.1649413

10. Kabassi, K., Martinis, A.: Multi-criteria decision making in the evaluation of the thematic museums' websites. In: Katsoni, V., Velander, K. (eds.) Innovative Approaches to Tourism and Leisure. SPBE, pp. 219–221. Springer, Cham (2018). https://doi.org/10.1007/978-3-319-67603-6_16

11. Lopatovska, I.: Museum website features, aesthetics, and visitors' impressions: a case study of four museums. Mus. Manage. Curatorship **30**(3), 191–207 (2015)

12. Martinis, A., Papadatou, A., Kabassi, K.: An analysis of the electronic presence of national parks in Greece. In: Katsoni, V., Segarra-Oña, M. (eds.) Smart Tourism as a Driver for Culture and Sustainability. SPBE, pp. 433–449. Springer, Cham (2019). https://doi.org/10.1007/978-3-030-03910-3_30

13. Pallud, J., Straub, D.W.: Effective website design for experience-influenced environments: the case of high culture museums. Inf. Manage. **51**, 359 (2014)

14. Saaty, T.: The Analytic Hierarchy Process. McGraw-Hill, New York (1980)

15. Saaty, T.L.: Hu G: Ranking by eigenvector versus other methods in the analytic hierarchy process. Appl. Math. Lett. **11**(4), 21–125 (1998)

16. Tofallis, C.: Add or multiply? A tutorial on ranking and choosing with multiple criteria. INFORMS Trans. Educ. **14**(3), 109–119 (2014)

17. Triantaphyllou, E.: Multi-criteria Decision Making: A Comparative Study. Springer, Dordrecht (2000). https://doi.org/10.1007/978-1-4757-3157-6

Short Papers: Visualisation Techniques (Desktop, Virtual and Augmented Reality)

Augmented Reality Cultural Route at the Xeros River Valley, Larnaca, Cyprus

Eleftherios Ioannou[1,3]($\boxtimes$)(iD), Andreas Lanitis[2,3](iD), Athanasios K. Vionis[4](iD),
Giorgos Papantoniou[4,5](iD), and Niki Savvides[4]

[1] Department of Computer Science, The University of Sheffield, Sheffield, UK
eioannou1@sheffield.ac.uk
[2] Visual Media Computing Lab, Department of Multimedia and Graphic Arts
Cyprus University of Technology Limassol, Limassol, Cyprus
andreas.lanitis@cut.ac.cy
[3] CYENS Centre of Excellence, Nicosia, Cyprus
[4] Archaeological Research Unit, Department of History
and Archaeology, University of Cyprus, Nicosia, Cyprus
vionis@ucy.ac.cy
[5] Trinity College Dublin, The University of Dublin, Dublin, Ireland
papantg@tcd.ie

Abstract. Landscape studies have evolved into a significant branch of historical archaeological research, by placing emphasis on the ecological, economic, political and cultural values of pre-modern settled and sacred landscapes. The aim of our work is to support the systematic exploration of landscape archaeology in the Xeros River valley in Cyprus, through time, from prehistory to today, through the design and development of an Augmented Reality (AR) application. The AR application supports the exploration of pre-modern monuments and archaeological sites in the Xeros River valley, serving as a guided tour for visitors of the area. By employing image recognition and utilizing a location-based practice, the application provides the users with an immersive and educational experience. Initial reactions by experts in landscape studies indicate the potential of the application in enabling the narration and visualization of the historicity of the landscape and the fate of religious and other monuments of the past 1500 years.

Keywords: Augmented reality · Landscape studies · Xeros valley

1 Introduction

The aim of our work is to support the systematic exploration of landscape archaeology, the formation and evolution of settled and sacred places in the Xeros River valley in Cyprus through time, from prehistory to today. As part of a systematic study in this area [6], a range of informed methods and interdisciplinary approaches to Cypriot landscapes and society, including archaeological surface

M. Ioannides et al. (Eds.): EuroMed 2020, LNCS 12642, pp. 695–702, 2021.
https://doi.org/10.1007/978-3-030-73043-7_61

survey, geophysical prospection, geoarchaeology, digital Humanities and Anthropology, are employed in order to explore relevant research questions.

The Xeros River valley is located at a major junction of the Nicosia-Limassol-Larnaca motorways. The study of the archaeological material from several sites in the Xeros valley confirms continuous human habitation and land use in the area from prehistory to the present. Abandoned Turkish-Cypriot settlements, Christian and Muslim religious monuments in Kophinou and Alaminos, the Turkish-Cypriot (T/C) cemetery of Kophinou, the medieval tower and the Ottoman watermill of Alaminos, stone bridges of the British colonial period, abandoned beehives and other exceptional examples of traditional culture on the island comprise landmarks of this collective memory in the landscape of the valley today. At the same time, the presence and coexistence of these monuments in the Xeros valley in the 21st century reflect timeless and current phenomena: prosperity and symbiosis, displacement, immigration and human suffering, creation of national and religious identities, destruction of sacred sites, and abandonment (Fig. 1).

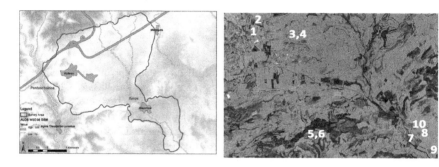

Fig. 1. The Xeros valley area (left) and the cultural route of the AR Application (right)

In this paper we focus our attention on the design and implementation of an Augmented Reality (AR) application that supports the exploration of pre-modern monuments and archaeological sites in the Xeros River valley, serving as a guided tour for visitors of the area. By employing image recognition and utilizing a location-based practice, the application provides an immersive and educational experience. The development of the contents of the application was based on historical research and on interviews and oral history accounts of community members from the villages of the Xeros river valley. The interpretive text of the application was written having in mind its possible users: international tourists, domestic tourists (Greek-Cypriots and Turkish-Cypriots) and locals. The purpose of the mobile tour application is to narrate the historicity of the landscape and the fate of religious and other monuments of the past 1500 years. The suggested route involves the following landmarks: (1) the T/C quarter of Kophinou, (2) the T/C cemetery of Kophinou, (3) the church of Panagia Kophinou and (4) the Byzantine village of Kophinou, (5) the church of Panagia Astathkiotissa and (6) the Medieval rural settlement of Astathkion, (7) the church of Agios Mamas in Alaminos, (8) the tower of Alaminos, (9) the watermill of Alaminos, (10) the T/C quarter of Alaminos (mosque and school).

Through this guided tour, visitors and current inhabitants of the Xeros valley have the opportunity to get in touch with the historical memory of the region and gain, in an indirect and novel way, an experiential contact with the monuments (religious and secular) and their surroundings. The operation of the application utilizes target images placed at the Points of Interest (POI) along the cultural route. The application encourages visitors to visit those POIs and scan the target images using their smartphones. Once a target is recognised, the users are able to see historical information about the corresponding monument while in particular cases (Panagia Kophinou and Astathkiotissa), they can observe a recreation of part of the settlement through their smartphone's camera feed. A score is maintained while the user visits each monument. The objective is to motivate the users to complete the route by visiting all the monuments/landmarks and experiencing an enhanced AR exhibition while getting information about the historical and archaeological context of each site.

2   Literature Review

While a Virtual Reality system relies entirely on computer-generated factors, AR does not allow the user to lose the sense of presence in the real world while supplementing some part of reality with virtual content [5]. AR has been used extensively to support the visualisation of cultural heritage sites and exhibits, aiming to bridge the gap between digital recreation, educational information and scientific research. The *Archeoguide* project uses specialised hardware and complicated system architecture to allow the viewers to experience the ancient Greek architecture and ancient Olympic sports events on site [8]. Zoellner *et al.* [9] proposed an AR application in which the original Reichstag building in Berlin is reconstructed while information in the form of photographs from different times are overlaid on the real scene. This application also includes an indoor, museum application focused around a satellite image of Berlin on which a 3D model of the Berlin Wall and the urban development are displayed. The *Roman Reborn* project also superimposes 3D models of Roman monuments on a large floor map in a museum installation [10]. *Dead Men's Eyes* is another AR project where a smartphone and an Arduino microcontroller are used to bring to life sights, sounds and smells at the exact place that they happened. In an outdoor AR experience, Sheffield's medieval castle is virtually restored in the Castlegate area in Sheffield city centre, where it used to stand. A large virtual object (castle) is overlaid on the mobile phone's camera view while a range of sensor data is used to tackle a variety of practical challenges that arise when employing an AR application outdoors [4].

Limitations such as constrained space in the case of large artefacts, storage of artefacts in distant sites and damaged/missing parts of archaeological arte- facts can be overcome with the use of AR. Gherardini *et al.* [2] achieved the enhancement of the fruition of artefacts and significantly advanced their visu- alisation by suggesting an AR application accessible from a mobile device and capable to be used in both inside and outside museum environments. This app-roach included the photogrammetric reconstruction of two Roman funerary lion sculptures located in Modena, Italy and their integration into an AR application.

The greatest challenge in making AR work outdoors lies in the registration problem [1]: aligning correctly the virtual with the real. Outdoor environments pose difficulties in determining the user's position and orientation while insufficient display contrast due to uncontrolled lighting conditions that hardens the registration and affects the user's experience.

3   Design of the AR Application

3.1   Aims, Specifications, Requirements

Many AR systems have been developed to support the visitors' experiences in archaeological sites and have managed to enhance user engagement. The focus of the vast majority of these applications has been the reconstruction and the process of superimposing 3D models on their corresponding real-world structures [7]. In this paper, we propose an AR application that utilises location awareness for the engagement of the users in a treasure hunt-like experience and for the registration of virtual objects in the real-world environment.

The application superimposes 3D information spheres on specific target images which are located in particular geographical locations along the path. The information spheres act as information 'hotspots' and once they are found, scanned and tapped on, they display additional information in the form of text, images, 360 viewers and 3D virtual models placed in the surrounding areas of particular locations. The application does not only allow the users to passively observe the monuments with superimposed information, but it also encourages explorations in the area by keeping a score of the targets the user has found.

Figure 2 gives an overview of the system operation. The application is devel-oped using Unity game engine and AR Foundation. The image recognition facil-ity that AR Foundation incorporates allows the recognition of target images which are placed at specific locations near the monuments. The device's sensors are also used for the support of the visitors' exploration and the registration of the virtual 3D models in the real-world environment.

3.2   Asset Collection

Except from text information that is included at each point of interest, the appli-cation is enriched with 360 panoramas images and 3D models that are placed at the surrounding landscape. 3D models used include a reconstruction of an early Byzantine basilica - built in the late 6th or early 7th century AD and on the ruins of which, the standing domed church of Panagia Kophinou was constructed later - and a 3D model of an early medieval longhouse which was created to match the typical medieval and post-medieval house-type in Cyprus and elsewhere (see Fig. 3). The 3D model of the longhouse was used for creating visualisations of settlements at nearby fields, where surface archaeological evidence suggests the location of habitation sites.

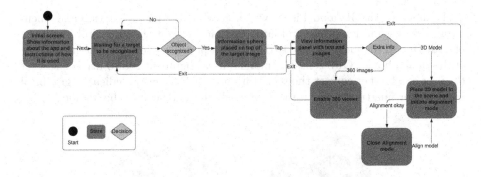

Fig. 2. State diagram - General flow of the system

3.3 Gamification

The adaptation and usage of the game technology outside of the game industry is known as gamification. Digital and serious games are attracting more and more academic attention and the value of gamification focused on heritage sites and applications is significantly increased due to the new possibilities that it encapsulates regarding user engagement and interaction with cultural heritage information. The proposed AR application is designed to embed the element of gamification by incorporating a treasure hunt game, which involves collecting virtual points by visiting particular monuments and sites and scanning specific target images that are placed there.

3.4 Placing the Virtual Model in the AR Scene

In the case of the Kophinou and Astathkiotissa churches, the user is able to visualise the medieval settlements that used to exist in the surrounding fields. Based on directions from archaeologists, multiple 3D models of the medieval longhouse were combined to create a settlement, and this was placed in the surrounding area in AR and with the use of the device's geographical location. The placement of the virtual settlements was a challenging task because the virtual models needed to be placed without the use of a marker/target image. Instead, the placement was achieved by accessing the device's location and transforming the GPS coordinates into the Unity world space. To convert between cartesian coordinate systems, scaling and rotation transforms are required. For the conversion of latitude, the difference between the required position of the 3D model and the user's location is multiplied by a constant (111,132). For longitude, assuming that the earth is roughly spherical, the arc length of a degree of longitude changes with the latitude, approaching zero at the poles [3]. The equation below captures this:

$$111319.9 * Math.Cos(latitude * (\pi/180)) \qquad (1)$$

In this way, the 3D model is spawned based on the user's location and calculating the offset in longitude and latitude that we want the virtual object to be placed. Due to the fact that the earth is not a perfect sphere and the inaccuracy of the smartphone's GPS sensor, a manual user alignment is also utilised so that the user can further correct the registration error by using a dedicated graphical interface for fine tuning the rotation, translation and scaling the 3D model.

Fig. 3. Example of a medieval longhouse and the resulting 3D model created in Blender

3.5   System Operation and Evaluation

Fig. 4 shows typical screenshots from the system operation. A video of the results is given at https://tinyurl.com/yyrgd6mj. Limitations of the system are tightly related to the difficulties of making AR work outdoors such as uncontrolled environment conditions, insufficient lighting contrast, difficulties in determining the user's position and orientation and occlusion detection. As part of future work these limitation will be addressed.

Nevertheless, it is important to note that this is the first time in Cyprus that archaeological data for the existence of lost settlements, in combination with evidence for the use of sacred monuments from the early Byzantine period to today, is translated into an AR cultural route. It is also the first time that an archaeological surface-survey project employs AR to offer back to local societies and foreign visitors a user-friendly tool for the exploration of the region's past and historical significance, in three languages, i.e. Greek, English and Turkish. The initial idea and the ultimate aim of collecting and interpreting archaeological data, followed by the creation of the AR cultural route, is to explore and acknowledge the historicity and 'centrality' of the Xeros valley through the ages. The AR route will eventually encourage locals and visitors to explore this neglected rural landscape, by appreciating the 'negativity' of the valley's collective memory, imprinted in its abandoned sites and buildings.

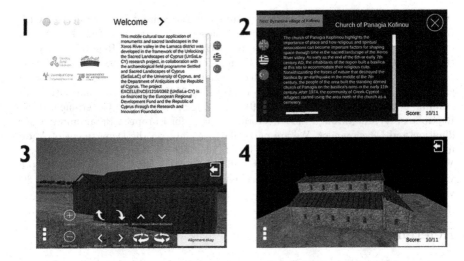

Fig. 4. The overall system in action. (1): The initial screen of the application. This welcomes the user and displays information about the application, the project and the route, (2): The panel with text and images that is displayed once a user finds and scans a target image. (3): Placement and alignment of the 3D model of the medieval settlement at the surroundings of Panagia Kophinou. (4): Viewing the reconstruction of the early Byzantine basilica

4   Conclusions

This paper presented an AR application in which the users are immersed in a treasure hunt-like game while participating in an innovative experience in terms of the act of visiting an archaeological site/monument. A location-based approach in combination with a manual user alignment allowed an adequate registration of the virtual model in the real-world environment. AR software opens up new possibilities for the enhancement of archaeological sites. We have presented an approach in which local communities and visitors have the opportunity to experience an interesting cultural route through time and through the preserved monuments and the discovered archaeological sites in the area, from the early Byzantine period to date.

As part of the future work further communication strategies will be considered following the completion of a research component of the "Unlocking Sacred Landscapes" project on the experience of the monuments by local and national visitors, as these will provide the basis for a more personal dialogue between the monuments, the audiences and the local communities. In addition we plan to stage a comprehensive user survey with multiple participants in order to evaluate the functionality, user experience and educational impact of the application. We also plan to enhance the realism of the 3D model that is placed in the surroundings by performing adaptive color normalization and by estimating the position of the sun and creating virtual shadows.

Acknowledgements. This paper was produced in the context of the Project EXCEL-LENCE/1216/0362 (Unlocking the Sacred Landscapes of Cyprus – UnSaLa-CY), co-financed by the European Regional Development Fund and the Republic of Cyprus through the Research and Innovation Foundation. We also acknowledge support by the Research Centre on Interactive Media Smart Systems and Emerging Technologies (RISE) through the European Union's Horizon 2020 research and innovation programme under grant agreement No 739578 complemented by the Government of the Republic of Cyprus through the Directorate General for European Programmes, Coordination and Development. We are particularly grateful to the Department of Antiquities for the collaboration and permissions to conduct our field research. Silversky3D VRT Ltd assisted us greatly in the materialisation of this AR application via the provision of technical equipment and expertise related to the 3D reconstructions and 360 viewers.

References

1. Azuma, R.T., et al.: The challenge of making augmented reality work outdoors. In: Mixed Reality: Merging Real Virtual worlds, pp. 379–390. Springer (1999)
2. Gherardini, F., Santachiara, M., Leali, F.: Enhancing heritage fruition through 3d virtual models and augmented reality: an application to roman artefacts. Virtual Archaeol. Rev. **10**(21), 67 (2019). https://doi.org/10.4995/var.2019.11918
3. Hockley, B.: Geolocated AR in unity arfoundation (2018). https://blog.anarks2. com/Geolocated-AR-In-Unity-ARFoundation/
4. Leach, M., et al.: Recreating sheffield's medieval castle *In Situ* using outdoor augmented reality. In: Bourdot, P., Cobb, S., Interrante, V., kato, H., Stricker, D. (eds.) EuroVR 2018. LNCS, vol. 11162, pp. 213–229. Springer, Cham (2018). https://doi. org/10.1007/978-3-030-01790-3_13
5. Ma, J., Choi, J.S.: The virtuality and reality of augmented reality. J. Multimedia **2** (02 2007). https://doi.org/10.4304/jmm.2.1.32-37
6. Papantoniou, G., Vionis, A.K.: The river as an economic asset: Settlement and society in the xeros valley in cyprus. Land **7**(4), 157 (2018). https://doi.org/10. 3390/land7040157
7. Shakouri, F., Tian, F.: Avebury portal – a location-based augmented reality treasure hunt for archaeological sites. In: El Rhalibi, A., Pan, Z., Jin, H., Ding, D., Navarro-Newball, A.A., Wang, Y. (eds.) Edutainment 2018. LNCS, vol. 11462, pp. 39–49. Springer, Cham (2019). https://doi.org/10.1007/978-3-030-23712-7_7
8. Vlahakis, V., et al.: Archeoguide: an augmented reality guide for archaeological sites. IEEE Comput. Graphics Appl. **22**(5), 52–60 (2002). https://doi.org/10.1109/ MCG.2002.1028726
9. Zoellner, M., Keil, J., Drevensek, T., Wuest, H.: Cultural heritage layers: Integrating historic media in augmented reality. In: 2009 15th International Conference on Virtual Systems and Multimedia, pp. 193–196. IEEE (2009). https://doi.org/10. 1109/VSMM.2009.35
10. Zoellner, M., Keil, J., Wuest, H., Pletinckx, D.: An augmented reality presentation system for remote cultural heritage sites. In: Proceedings of the 10th International Symposium on Virtual Reality, Archaeology and Cultural Heritage VAST, pp. 112–116. Citeseer (2009)

Digitizing the Neolithic Hypogeum

Jonathan Barbara$^{(\boxtimes)}$ ⓘ, Jeremy Grech, Joseph Camilleri, Silvio McGurk,
and Charles Theuma

Saint Martin's Institute of Higher Education, Hamrun, Malta
{jbarbara,jgrech,jcamilleri,smcgurk,ctheuma}@stmartins.edu

Abstract. The Hypogeum of Hal-Saflieni is a 6000-year-old Neolithic burial place whose microclimate is threatened by the presence of thousands of visitors all year round. Beyond digital preservation and accessibility, this project aims to provide a highly accessible experience to the virtual tourist or academic. This short paper reports on progress in faithful illumination and acoustics together with navigation aids supported by a real motion platform towards a mixed reality immersive experience. Lightweight variations such as a 360° VR film and a 360° still-based gaze-driven navigation mobile app further make such precious cultural heritage available to the wider public and serve as a basis for future enhancements towards a more immersive virtual cultural heritage experience.

Keywords: Virtual reality · Digital heritage · User experience · 360 storytelling · Gaze-driven navigation · Experimental archaeology · Serious games

1 Introduction

The underground complex of the Hypogeum of Hal Saflieni is a 6000-year-old heritage site in danger. The only prehistoric burial site accessible to the general public, its unique red ochre paintings on the ceiling and walls suffered greatly over the past century as thousands of visitors affected the highly volatile microclimate. In fact, the complex had to be closed to the public for a decade until the situation could be managed, and a controlled amount of visitors could then be allowed inside [1]. Water seeping in from various places formed puddles throughout the complex and thus wooden walkways were installed to elevate visitors and protect the passageways. These walkways are cordoned to keep hands and feet away from the paintings, walls, and cubicles scattered around the complex. As 2020 marks the 40th year since the site's inscription in the UNESCO World Heritage List, the agency curating the site, Heritage Malta, is seeking to provide more accessibility to the Hypogeum while preserving it for future generations. This short paper presents the use of virtual reality (VR) technology to address these targets while paving the way for experimental archaeology.

1.1 The Site and Its Contents

Presented as an underground prehistoric burial site, the Hypogeum of Hal Saflieni in the island of Malta features interconnected chambers across three levels, excavated during

© Springer Nature Switzerland AG 2021
M. Ioannides et al. (Eds.): EuroMed 2020, LNCS 12642, pp. 703–710, 2021.
https://doi.org/10.1007/978-3-030-73043-7_62

different periods over 2500 years. Amongst them are impressive architectural features that reflect elements found in contemporary megalithic temples above ground elsewhere on the island such as trilithons, temple facades, and ring-shaped roofs made from over-hanging stone. Most notable is the echoic chamber in the Middle level, which resonates sounds at frequencies between 40 Hz and 72 Hz [2, 3]. Having been unknowingly built over in recent centuries, it is thought that the upper level was originally above ground, with an entrance much like that of other nearby Neolithic temples as evidenced by the remains of a trilithon, whilst geographical studies suggest that the orientation of the innermost chamber, with a façade like a temple, was illuminated by sunlight every winter solstice [4]. Artefacts found in the complex during its discovery inform us on both its original excavation techniques as well as its function thereafter. Stone and bone tools sharpened to a point match holes in the wall to suggest drilling while a geological study to trace the origins of the water puddles discovered fault-lines running through the complex along which rainwater was seeping in [5]. These faults are thought to have provided smooth vertical surfaces to serve as walls for the excavated underground passageways. On the other hand, clay pottery vessels and limestone figures offer traces of the cult followed by its people, particularly the burial practice for which this complex is thought to be the main purpose [6].

As happens in many historical sites open to the public, especially in confined spaces such as the Hypogeum, the artefacts are not presented in their original context, but safely exhibited in a museum proximal to the site. This not only diminishes the understanding of the object but also removes meaning from the historical space. Curators go to great lengths to replicate relevant parts of the space within the museum through photos, models, and films but artefact de-contextualisation impacts negatively on its appreciation. Meanwhile, audio guides with narrated descriptions attempt to explain what the visitor is expected to be looking at. These are a non-intrusive solution that does not endanger the site but are limited in expressive power and relevance to actual experience.

1.2 Digital Heritage: A Fresh Outlook

The use of technology in cultural heritage over the past two decades [7] has mostly focused on digital preservation, with fidelity and realism being two major criteria, and accessibility, both to geographically distant and physically inaccessible sites. Recently, however, in a special issue on VR for Culture and Heritage, a call to focus on the provision of VR heritage experiences was made [8], demanding to go beyond preservation and accessibility. The experiential aspect of this desired direction in VR implies the need for immersion beyond the sensory perception of sight and audio, and this paper reports on an attempt to address this need in collaboration with Heritage Malta, the agency under whose custody lies the site of the Hal Saflieni Hypogeum.

2 Digitizing the Neolithic Hypogeum

Heritage Malta provided a laser scan of the site, which was used to construct the 3D environment within the Unity game development engine. Due to the primitive nature of the Neolithic site, the walls are far from flat and thus heavily tessellated and processing heavy. An effort was made to plug in the holes in the 3D model due to occlusion in concave niches and areas so as to make sure there are no gaps in the walls or floors. The orientation of the facets was not uniform: some faced towards and others away from the inside of the model. This was fixed by making the 3D model dual sided. Textures, being actual images of the complex, were augmented with bump maps and height maps, derived from said images. This processed 3D model then served as a base for further additional features listed hereunder:

2.1 Navigation

The claustrophobic nature of the complex, due to its narrow passages, was diminished by the scaling up of the model leading to a perceived miniaturization of the visitor who can navigate around the space using a drone-like craft rather than walking on two feet. This helps explain the ability to look around while moving forward and backward at a uniform speed rather than the sine-wave motion of human gait. To assist in navigation, a map of the complex with the relevant proximal area highlighted can be brought up by pressing the corresponding button on the VR controller (see Fig. 1).

Fig. 1. Context-sensitive map in VR experience (left) and Sunlight on the upper level (right) (Color figure online)

2.2 Sunlight

Whilst the complex is currently situated under a two-storey building, it is believed that the upper level was above ground. Thus, use of a software asset that provides sunlight at a given location based on time of day was made to model the illumination of the site with its present geographic location (see Fig. 1), which orientation was aligned based on GPS coordinates from official land surveys of the site. For the correct implementation of lighting, however, volume needed to be added to the model to prevent light bleed, and light barriers were created to block light from seeping in.

2.3 Audio

Whilst the first prototypes used a drone sound to mimic the visitor's avatar, this was felt to be too noisy and alien to the sanctity of the place. It felt like it was imposing the visitor's presence onto the environment rather than helping them being immersed in the complex. The sound also lacked any echoes and thus did not feel diegetic.

Therefore, in order to increase immersion, two actions were taken: the acquisition of audio profiles from the site and the selection of a number of audio clips representing action sound effects and environmental soundscapes. The former involved the capture of binaural recordings on site with source sounds inside the echoic chamber and two recordings taken: one inside and one outside the chamber (see Fig. 2). Source sounds were male basso voice chants and 16 Hz–20 kHz sweeps. For audio clips, action sound effects were chosen to represent the paintbrush strokes to accompany the red ochre paintings, the rock strikes and breaks for the building techniques, and water droplets for the large cistern situated in the upper level. For environmental sound effects, on-site recording of male basso chanting was used for the echoic chamber while an aura sonification was used around structures such as the trilithon. Due to the Hypogeum's use as a shelter during World War II bombings on the island, a recording of such an experience was used for the main chamber. Impulse responses derived from the on-site binaural recordings were used to contextualise these sounds.

2.4 Information Panels

Taking advantage of the virtual nature of the represented space while keeping the aesthetics of museum exhibits, information panels were placed at strategic locations to provide visual, filmic, and textual descriptions of the space. These panels are indicated by a minimalistic yellow floating information icon which transforms into the information panel once within reading distance (see Fig. 1). This panel orients itself towards the user allowing full visibility from any angle of approach and rotates out of the way as the virtual visitor runs through it. A voice-over narration, contextualised to the space using the abovementioned impulse responses, also starts reading out the text to the visitor, allowing one to look around while still receiving the information aurally. No reverberations reflecting the site's acoustics were added in order to place the narrator outside the virtual space, since they are not represented visually in it.

2.5 Motion Platform

To further assist in the immersion of the visitor, the drone-like experience was complemented with a real life motion platform, consisting of a bucket seat supported by three vertical pistons controlled via microcontroller interfacing with the VR machine. Such a setup allows for real movement along four degrees of freedom reflecting the visitor's movement inside the VR experience. This also had the positive effect of reducing nausea as the body's visual perception of motion was accompanied by a physical sensation of motion (see Fig. 2). Zero incidents in over 300 sessions over a weekend attended by the general public provide empirical evidence for this claim.

Fig. 2. Binaural recording in progress (left) and Motion platform at PlayCon 2019 (right)

3 Applications

The applications of this virtual experience are three-fold.

Firstly, as mentioned above, access to the Hypogeum site is limited if its preservation is to be maintained. Providing virtual representations that faithfully mimic the site provides a visitor experience that is as close to the original as possible without causing undue stress on its microclimate and state of preservation. Moreover, with the ability to virtually re-introduce the artefacts together with their descriptions, images, annotated drawings and videos provides a single access point to the site's history.

Secondly, by using digital technology popular with the younger generations, cultural heritage is being opened up to knowledge-thirsty minds willing to engage with their past. Building upon this Virtual Reality experience, meaningful interaction can be provided that leads to an informative and engaging experience.

Thirdly, by providing the most faithful possible representation of the site to the historians, this project allows for a better understanding of the tangible heritage available and also sheds light on the intangible culture that inhabited the complex thousands of years ago. The field of Experimental Archaeology requires a space within which to explore what-if scenarios and this is the strength of such a virtual representation.

4 Expanding Accessibility

The complex nature of the site's 3D model requires powerful computing and graphical processing units to handle the dynamic textured rendering for each eye, with numbers in the region of 28 million triangles and 606 million vertices. The initial attempt of making this accessible to the general public was by having it hosted at the National Museum of Archaeology in Valletta, Malta and this was indeed exhibited and launched by the Maltese Minister of Tourism, Dr. Jose Herrera. To assist the interpretation of the project itself, six screens were put up showing the stages of development from laser scan, through prototypes, to the final product on display.

However, due to the growing fears of the CoViD-19 pandemic, the museum was closed to the public the next day and with it the access to the VR experience. Due to its size, the experience could not be run on handheld devices unless a drastically reduced low polygon version was made which would reduce the fidelity of the experience and vary greatly depending on the mobile device's own level of technology.

Thus it was decided to develop two lightweight versions of the VR experience that could be propagated to the masses with a sufficient level of experience that would not belittle the levels achieved in the above detailed project.

4.1 360° Virtual Reality Film

The first version was a digital 360° recording within the VR experience which was then provided to the general public via online video sharing platforms[1] (see Fig. 3).

Viewers are taken through a pre-scripted path through the experience while having the possibility of looking around using their finger on a mobile's touch screen or mouse on a desktop PC or, if loaded onto a VR headset such as Google Cardboard, the viewer can look around using their own head. This had the added advantage that multiple visitors could experience it simultaneously on their own devices and they did not have to be physically at the museum, nor in Valletta, nor even in Malta.

The 10-min video is a linear journey throughout the site, in which a team-developed script narrates the Hypogeum's reawakening, spoken from the site's perspective, surprised at its own revival but feeling awkward at its lack of functionality.

The short film's production and direction was carried out from within the VR experience itself, picking the correct camera placement and synchronising the narration with its movement allowed the determination of the utterances and pauses as necessary.

Music that incorporated believable sounds given the Neolithic period provided a palette from which the producer could select background music that reflected the narrative emotions while a voice actor whose timbre reflected the character of an underground hollow space was employed.

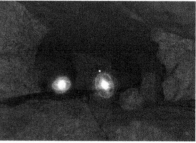

Fig. 3. The 360° VR YouTube film (left) and lightweight VR mobile app (right)

4.2 Lightweight Virtual Reality Gaze-Driven Navigation Mobile App

Another approach towards making the VR experience accessible on handheld devices involves the provision of guided virtual tours in which visitors are transported between the strategic points in the complex by simply gazing at markers positioned around them.

---

[1] https://www.youtube.com/watch?v=TQpvMWG9fws

Instead of rendering the complex environment in real-time, 360° stills taken within the virtual site representation are loaded allowing the visitors to look around until they gaze onto a marker (floating orbs) which will load the corresponding 360° still (see Fig. 3). This reduced requirement model allows the experience to be downloaded as a mobile app wherein the Google VR API has been used to maintain interaction familiarity. In order to further broaden its accessibility, care has been taken to make the teleportation mechanic as smooth as possible, using fade out to black and fade in to reduce the risk of one feeling the effects of virtual sickness. As the visitor makes their way through the complex, they are accompanied by a narrative voiceover that describes the chamber being visited.

5   Limitations and Future Work

Whilst the above work is not in its infancy, there is much work planned for the future, and here we list some of them:

- The sunlight calculations are being used for direct illumination only. Future work would reconfigure the system in order to use real-time ray tracing functionality to demonstrate how sunlight reflections would have illuminated the lower levels.
- The aural experience is based on two recordings: one inside and one outside the echoic chamber. While the phase-offset of the audio clip is adjusted to seamlessly transition from the outside acoustics to the inside acoustics, the acoustic change is very noticeable and some crossfading is needed in order to enhance the experience.
- Whilst the properties of the chamber share many commonalities with the other chambers in the complex, the variety of room sizes and orientations deserve specific recordings for more faithful contextualization but this conflicts with the aim to protect the site's inner climate.
- The placement of 3D models of artefacts originally found within the complex in the virtual representation would help inform the visitor on the use and possible rites held within such spaces, changing space to place.
- The provision of agency in the lightweight variation affords simple game mechanics such as labyrinth and maze navigation but also treasure hunts for both special site locations as well as well-placed 3D artefacts.
- The provision of agency in the original implementation, borne on strong computing power, could lead to the creation of games for engagement with the younger generations and interactive narratives allowing the virtual visitor to re-enact intangible heritage within a virtual representation of the space.

6   Conclusion

The Hal Saflieni Hypogeum suffers from problems of accessibility and preservation: two counteracting forces that cause problems to the curator. From a laser scan commissioned by Heritage Malta for its conservation, a Virtual Reality model was developed that provides accessibility to a faithful representation of the site while eliminating the contamination brought by visitors. The virtual representation has been augmented by sunlight and acoustics modelling to help provide a faithful representation that may support Experimental Archaeology and intangible heritage representation.

To this end, the main aims of this project were to.

1. mitigate damage to the environment of the site,
2. overcome accessibility issues for mobile disabilities,
3. disseminate information cheaply to large global populations who otherwise would not have had access to the physical experience,
4. assist in the interpretation of the site by a wider spectrum of scholars,
5. offer opportunities to fund the site's very expensive conservation through more restricted and exclusive physical viewing and
6. offer more up to date education assets for the 21st century classroom.

Furthermore, the representation itself has been reproduced in lighter forms in order to be made accessible on any smart device, such forms being the 360° VR film and the lightweight 360° still-driven navigation VR experience. The dissemination on public social media and content sharing platforms such as Facebook and YouTube are being studied to identify gender differentiation, if any, as well as age, race, and culture and how such models can be used in all educational levels across the world.

Acknowledgements. The authors thank Heritage Malta for provision of information on, and special access to, the Hypogeum site in Hal Saflieni, Paola, Malta.

References

1. Bonnici, A.: A Study of the Microclimate within the Hal Saflieni Hypogeum Complex. Unpublished B. Educ (Hons) dissertation, University of Malta (1989)
2. Debertolis, P., Coimbra, F., Eneix, L.: Archaeoacoustic analysis of the Hal Saflieni Hypogeum in Malta. J. Anthropol. Archaeol. **3**(1), 59–79 (2015).https://doi.org/10.15640/jaa.v3n1a4
3. Till, R.: An Archaeoacoustic Study of the Hal Saflieni Hypogeum on Malta. Antiquity **91**(355), 74–89 (2017). https://doi.org/10.15184/aqy.2016.258
4. Magli, G.: Mysteries and Discoveries of Archaeoastronomy: from Giza to Easter Island. Springer(2009) https://doi.org/10.1007/978-0-387-76566-2
5. Ercoli, A.: Geological and Structural Study of Hal Saflieni Hypogeum in Relation to Water Infiltration Problems (1992)
6. Zammit, T.: The Neolithic Hypogeum at Hal-Saflieni at Casal Paula-Malta: A Short Description of the Monument with Plan and Illustrations. Empire Press, Brooklyn (1935)
7. Refsland, S.T., Ojika, T., Addison, A.C., Stone, R.: Virtual Heritage: Breathing New Life into Our Ancient Past. IEEE Multimedia **7**(2), 20–21 (2000). https://doi.org/10.1109/MMUL.2000.848420
8. Ch'ng, E., Yiyu, C., Thwaites, H.: Special Issue on VR for culture and heritage: the experience of cultural heritage with virtual reality: guest Editors' Introduction. Presence: Teleoperators Virtual Environ. **26**(03), iii–vi (2018). https://doi.org/10.1162/pres_e_00302

Short Paper: Storytelling and Authoring Tools

The Potential of Implementing Interactive Storytelling Experience for Museums

Saif Alatrash[1(✉)], Sylvester Arnab[1(✉)], and Kaja Antlej[2(✉)]

[1] Coventry University, Priory Street, Coventry CV1 5FB, UK
{Alatrashs,Sylvester.arnab}@coventry.ac.uk
[2] Deakin University, 75 Pigdons Road, Waurn Ponds VIC 3216, Geelong, Australia
Kaja.antlej@deakin.edu.au

Abstract. This paper presents theoretical interpretations and discussions towards informing better contextualisation of displayed museum artefacts that can improve the overall visitors' experience in museums. The article examines existing academic literature related to interaction principles in museum environments and various models of communication to provide an understanding of the fundamental concept of interpretation when visitors are interfaced with museum objects. Towards enhancing the interaction and interpretation process, the paper posits that gamification and storytelling approaches when mapped against immersive Virtual Reality (VR) experience can improve visitors' motivation and immersion in the context of the presented museum artefacts.

Keywords: Cultural heritage · Storytelling · Gamification · Immersive technology

1 Introduction

This paper aims to propose a theoretical solution towards enhancing the interpretation process between the museum visitors and its displayed objects during the visit by investigating the influence of interactive, immersive technology on the visitor experience in a museum environment through storytelling and gamification theories. Overall, museums act as places of learning and archives of knowledge, bridging previous cultural history with present societies; they contain priceless pieces representing a certain era of heritage value and cultural identity (Puig et al. 2019). Each museum object holds a significant value as it embodies the cultural narratives and identities of the heritage bearers. The recent advancement of digital technology allows museum curators to implement interactive, immersive devices in their environments to increase the interpretation level for the visitors. The lack of contextualisation, however, could interfere with the actual meaning behind the museum collection. Therefore, this could lead to a misrepresentation of the cultural value of museum objects (Rahaman et al. 2019). The following discussion will provide further justifications and descriptions for each term.

© Springer Nature Switzerland AG 2021
M. Ioannides et al. (Eds.): EuroMed 2020, LNCS 12642, pp. 713–721, 2021.
https://doi.org/10.1007/978-3-030-73043-7_63

2   Visitor Interaction Principles in Museum Environments

Despite the importance of implementing Virtual Reality (VR) technology in museums to increase the amount of interpretation between the visitors and objects, there is a significant issue related to the amount of accessibility provided by museum professionals to its visitors. Exposing fragments such as artefacts could be risky due to the fragile nature (Kyriakou and Hermon 2019). A recent study by Kyriakou and Hermon (2019) involved in heritage interpretation and visitor interaction showed that interacting with museum objects through digital devices such as hand gestures isn't necessarily considered natural. The authors categorise the interaction process as the following: natural-based and gesture interaction. Natural interaction refers to tangible real-life experience without the need for human gesture or hand pose recognition, while gesture-based interactions demand a fixed pose feed from the user in order to proceed with the interaction process (Kyriakou and Hermon 2019). The nature of the interaction is necessary to determine the right equipment for interpretation. According to Lukas et al. (2015), an exhibition cannot communicate without understanding the interests of the target audience. The diversity of interests of museum visitors demands a specific classification to understand their needs. Lukas et al. (2015) categorised museum visits under the following criteria:

- *Museological characteristics*: concern with the motivation of the visits, the potential of exploring the exhibits, and the outcome of the visits.
- *Socio-demographic characteristics*: concern with the visitors' gender and age, educational background, the location of residency.
- *Range characteristics*: concern with the number of the visitors' attendance based on either group or individual visits.
- *Psychological or physiological characteristics*: concern with the nature of the visitors' behaviours and personalities such as intelligence, imagination, and memories.

The interaction process in museums mostly concentrated on the individuals rather than the multi-users such as social interaction. The recent advancement of immersive technologies offers museums opportunities to explore new methods of interaction that could drive social engagement further. Recent studies indicate the implementation of Augmented Reality (AR) technology could enhance the museum visitors' quality of experience (Geronikolakis et al. 2018). This type of technological integration has been widely used in museums, meaning visitors can be more active and involved in the experience (Bozzelli et al. 2019). A pop-up exhibition called The Lanchester Interactive Archive project based in Coventry University library, dedicated for telling the stories of Frederick Lanchester inventions through immersive technology such as augmented and virtual reality (Spanu 2020).

3   Theory of Communication in Museums

The museum sector is still holding the same principles as a place of knowledge and collection. Nevertheless, common practice revolves around the way museums communicate and interpret their content of knowledge to their visitors (Weng et al. 2020). This raises a question on how museum professionals could present and communicate the precious collection of knowledge to visitors. According to Weng et al. (2020), there are two different types of digital interpretation: the first is interpersonal, and the second is non-personal interpretation. Inter-personal interpretation involves two ways of communication as face to face interaction, usually between visitors and tour guides. While non-personal is a one-way interaction communication method that involves visitors with physical materials like museum signs. The relation between interpretation is connected with designing the actual setting to reach an appropriate level of understanding. To this extent, in a museum environment, the audience experience should approach meaning-making in order to make the outcome of the visit informative. In contrast, previous studies have shown that the interpretation could be delivered in a provocative or informative way. This creates an essential key factor for museum communication as it allows the process of interaction perceivable and understandable (Veverka 2018). According to Petersons and Khalimzoda (2016), communication models can be divided into three types:

- Linear model,
- Transactional model, and
- Interactional model.

Shannon and Weaver's communication model (1964), considered as the base of all recent transmission approaches in modern history, follows a linear direction of communication (Fig. 1). This model is concerned with sending and receiving information between two channels. The concept evolved from the necessity to improve the mass structure of interpretation to approach effective communication results between the sender and the receiver (Shannon and Weaver 1964).

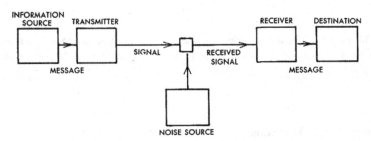

Fig. 1. Shannon and Weaver's model of communication concept (Shannon 1971, Fig. 1, p. 7).

A recent study by Petersons and Khalimzoda (2016) provides a development of a multicultural communication model, the authors unified their concepts based on different models for communication in a multicultural environment to enhance the correspondence of the communication between participants. However, the model relies on the sender's cultural background and knowledge. Therefore, acknowledging the feedback and noise limitation of the previously reviewed models, we proposed a new framework based on Shannon and Weaver's original concept, featuring the addition of two new channels between the sender and the receiver for feedback purposes. The first channel collects all the receiver's output data and returns it back to the sender again. This channel is referred to as the feedback channel. The second embedded channel is called the experience enhancement channel, which supplements the experience with a further interpretation process that can then be tested again on the museum visitors. This framework is a part of ongoing research that will be applied and tested on museum participants. The following illustration demonstrates the new communication framework (see Fig. 2).

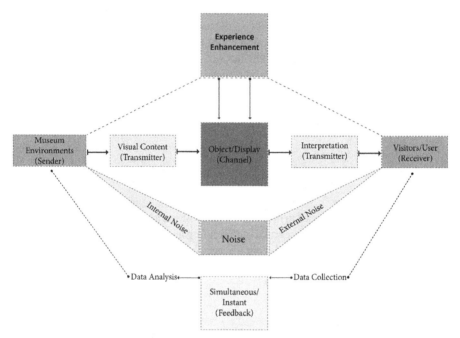

Fig. 2. This model will be tested during the research experiment to determine the framework's effectiveness on museum visitors and its objects, based on Petersons and Khalimzoda model of communication.

3.1 Storytelling in Museums

Museum collection provides the main content of a story, which can help structure a meaningful and engaging experience for the end-users (Katifori et al. 2018). Storytelling in cultural heritage refers to the process of interpretation of cultural heritage content to provide the users with the fundamental elements of storytelling, such as character, settings, plots, and the theme of the narrative. In order to approach storytelling in a heritage environment, a particular requirement and guidelines must be achieved to provide the right interpretation that connects the visitors and museum objects. A recent study by Vrettakis et al. (2019) suggests that the concept of storytelling development started as a result of postmodern heritage communication, as a tool to present collection through classification, and approaching visitor participation in a museum environment. Therefore, story and narrative are inseparable as narration constructs the baseline that contains the necessary elements of the story. This means the implementation of storytelling in museums stimulates the imagination and immersion of the visitors, providing a comprehensive, engaging experience. The use of illustration such as metaphor enhances the ability of imagination for the visitors, as the human brain becomes more active when observing visual stories (Psomadaki et al. 2019). Screenwriters usually write the ending before the middle act as that provides a better vision about the character's distention and where it is headed. The three-act structure can fulfill the journey by following a specific pattern (Bucher 2017). In this perspective, Economou et al. (2018) discuss in their projects EMOTIVE the use of emotional storytelling to change how visitors experience museums and heritage sites. The following figure illustrates the three-act plots Exposition, Climax, and Resolution (see Fig. 3).

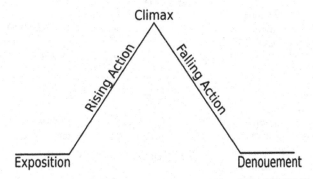

Fig. 3. Freytag's Pyramid, the Rise, and fall structure (Putria and Nurhadi 2020, Fig. 2, p. 87).

To design a digital storytelling experience in museum environments or cultural settings, an interdisciplinary approach is essential, which includes the participation of experts with specific skills to fulfill the settings' needs (Roussou et al. 2015). To design the right settings for a museum audience, the experience must contain the proper structure and contents of heritage objects. A recent study by Vrettakis et al. (2019) on digital storytelling in heritage settings shows that the actual meaning of the experience is within the content of the displayed objects. The structure of its content creates the story plot.

4 Gamification Approach in the Museum Environment

The term gamification refers to the ability to utilise game elements and design techniques in non-gaming settings and context (Deterding et al. 2011). Gamification represents a specific context of practice that allows interaction with the end-users. The concept of gamification emerged around the year of 2008 and became more comprehensive on a larger scale globally in the year of 2010 (Dopker 2014). Another definition describes it as a practice, which contains a variety of entertainment, such as a playful design, applied gaming, and games that require productivity (Deterding et al. 2011). In addition, gamification outlines two main essential concepts: first is the adaptation and prevalence of video games on the daily user basis. Secondly, game elements can provide a pleasant and engaging experience as the design of video games, in general, is based on entertainment outcome since the designed game elements can offer a certain amount of motivation for the users during the play. The utilisation of gamification concepts in heritage settings improves the way users engage with the displayed content (Dopker 2013). Hence, the use of gamification terms can supplement the interaction structure with materials and content, which can be reflected in the end-users interaction behaviour during the visits. A recent study by Sailer et al. (2017) shows a significant finding on how the implementation of gamification for educational purposes influences the learning outcome for the users from various domains. The following figure illustrates a combination of multi-dimensional elements such as learning, content, and game design in order to approach gamification in multi-domains sittings (see Fig. 3).

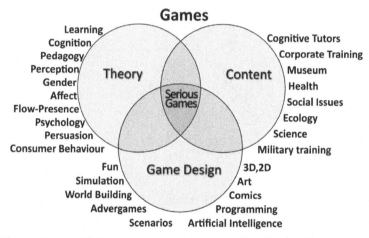

Fig. 4. The complex multi-dimensional world of gamification (Kiourt, Koutsoudis & Pavlidis 2016, Fig. 1, p. 985)

Fogg's behaviour model (2010) indicates three factors to consider that can inform how certain activities in a game can be designed, including motivation demands, the ability to perform, and the activity trigger. According to Fogg's behaviour two-dimensional scale model, the motivation level should be balanced to the amount of the activity level provided for the audience to perform. The trigger plays a fundamental key element in improving the user's motivation and ability during the experience. The following illustration provides the three main factors from Fogg's behaviour model to enhance the motivation of the end-users. It shows that the amount of motivation increases by the provided action and decreases according to the level of the ability required (see Fig. 4) (Fig. 5).

Previous gamification elements can be used as motivational factors for the visitors to increase the engagement and the learning outcomes from the experiments. To determine whether the implemented elements can be facilitated to improve the visitor's presence and reach an immersive multisensory experience. Within this framework, it has been

Fig. 5. Fogg's action model contextualise three different types to improve user motivation (Broer 2017, Fig. 2.7, p. 75)

consistently proven that gamification can provide motivational elements to the experience while storytelling as an interaction metaphor, which can be identified as the core critical elements for virtual museums (Papagiannakis et al. 2018).

5 Conclusion

This paper has provided an overview of the visitor interaction principles in museum environments. Different models of communication have been reviewed to understand the fundamental concept of interpretation between the visitors and museum object. The article shows that implementing immersive technologies in museum environments increases the interpretation between the visitors and the museum objects. Recent advancement of immersive technologies offers opportunities for museums to explore new methods of interaction that could drive social engagement further. The paper examines the value of gamification theories and approaches to improve audience's motivation and immersion during the VR experience. The key findings from the discussion are that each object holds meaning. The implementation of storytelling can represent this meaning and enhance the interpretation process during the visits as it provides better contextualisation.

Furthermore, gamification as motivational aspect enablers can motivate the visitors and enhance imagination. Utilising new forms of attraction and emotional elements as objectives and natives during the play provide the end-users with a meaningful and engaging experience. To this extent, we proposed a new communication framework as a part of ongoing research that will be applied and tested on museum participants. The framework will provide solutions for museum professionals towards enhancing the process of interpretation and contextualisation between the visitors and the museum objects, by using storytelling and gamification elements to inform the interaction aesthetics of the museum experience.

Acknowledgements. This project has been funded by the Deakin-Coventry doctoral cotutelle program. The doctoral project *Gamified Immersive Museum Experience for Engineering and Design Heritage* of Saif Alatrash is supervised by Sylvester Arnab and Kaja Antlej. We thank associated supervisors Neil Forbes, Jacqueline Cawston, and Michael Loizou at Coventry University, and Ben Horan and Meghan Kelly at Deakin University for their continuous advice and support.

References

Broer, J.: The Gamification Inventory: An Instrument for the Qualitative Evaluation of Gamification and its Application to Learning Management Systems (2017)

Bucher, J.: Storytelling for Virtual Reality: Methods and Principles for Crafting Immersive Narratives [online]. Oxford: Taylor & Francis Group (2017). https://ebookcentral.proquest.com/lib/deakin/detail.action?docID=4906521. Accessed 14 Feb. 2020

Bozzelli, G., et al.: An Integrated VR/AR Framework for User-Centric Interactive Experience of Cultural Heritage: The ArkaeVision Project'. Digital Applications in Archaeology and Cultural Heritage (2019). https://doi.org/10.1016/j.daach.2019.e00124. Accessed 10 Oct 2020.

Cawston, J.: Lanchester Interactive Archive: Case Study. in Viral Handbook. 1 edn, pp. 22–23 (2020). https://www.viraltraining.net/handbook. Accessed 20 Oct 2020

Deterding, S., Dixon, D., Khaled, R., Nacke, L. (eds.): From Game Design Elements to Gamefulness. ACM, 28 September 2011

Dopker, A., Brockmann, T., Stieglitz, S.: Use Cases for Gamification in Virtual Museums (2013). Accessed 8 Jan 2020

Economou, M, Young, H., Sosnowska, E.: Evaluating emotional engagement in digital stories for interpreting the past. The case of the Hunterian Museum's Antonine Wall EMOTIVE experiences', pp. 1–8 (2018)

Geronikolakis, E., Papagiannakis, G., Tsioumas, M.: Case study for true Augmented Reality (AR) application in industrial museum and cultural and educational center in Thessaloniki (2018). Accessed 12 Oct 2020

Katifori, A., Karvounis, M., Kourtis, V., Perry, S., Roussou, M., Ioanidis, Y. (eds.): Interactive. 'Applying Interactive Storytelling in Cultural Heritage: Opportunities, Challenges and Lessons Learned'. Held Storytelling. Springer International Publishing, Cham (2018)

Kyriakou, P., Hermon, S.: Can I Touch this? using Natural Interaction in a Museum Augmented Reality System'. Digital Appl. Archaeol. Cult. Heritage **12**, e00088 (2019). https://doi.org/10.1016/j.daach.2018.e00088. Accessed 19 Mar 2020

Najbrt, L., Kapounová, J.: Department of Information, Communication Technologies, Pedagogical Faculty, University of Ostrava, Categorisation of Museum Visitors as Part of System for Personalized Museum Tour (2015). Accessed 19 Mar 2020

Petersons, A., Khalimzoda, I.: Communication models and common basis for multicultural communication in Latvia. Society. Integration. Education. In: Proceedings of the International Scientific Conference, vol. 4, pp. 423 (2016). https://www.openaire.eu/search/publication?articleId=journrezekne::58fa7c57d7aaa7daf4ada8faf7a303a4. Accessed 11 Jan 2020

Psomadaki, O.I., Dimoulas, C.A., Kalliris, G.M., Paschalidis, G.: Digital storytelling and audience engagement in cultural heritage management: a collaborative model based on the digital city of Thessaloniki'. J. Cult. Heritage **36**, 12–22 (2019). https://doi.org/10.1016/j.culher.2018.07.016. Accessed 18 Mar 2020

Puig, A., et al.: Lessons Learned from Supplementing Archaeological Museum Exhibitions with Virtual Reality (2019)

Putria, A., Nurhadi, M.: 'Dramatic elements in Dashner's maze runner novel and film adaptation'. anaphora. J. Lang. Literary Cult. Stud. **2**, 80–88 (2020)

Papagiannakis, G, et al.: Mixed Reality, Gamified Presence, and Storytelling for Virtual Museums Lee, N. (ed.). Springer International Publishing, Cham (2018). https://doi.org/10.1007/978-3-319-08234-9_249-1.

Rahaman, H., Champion, E., Bekele, M.: From Photo to 3D to Mixed Reality: A Complete Workflow for Cultural Heritage Visualisation and Experience'. Digital Appl. Archaeol. Cult. Heritage **13**, e00102 (2019). https://doi.org/10.1016/j.daach.2019.e00102. Accessed 15 Jan 2020

Sailer, M., Hense, J.U., Mayr, S.K., Mandl, H.: How gamification motivates: an experimental study of the effects of specific game design elements on psychological need satisfaction . https://www.sciencedirect.com/science/article/pii/S074756321630855X. Accessed 9 Mar 2020

Shannon, C.E.: The Mathematical Theory of Communication. University of Illinois Press, Urbana, IL, London (1971)

Veverka, J.: Interpretive Master Planning Volume One: Strategies for the New Millennium M Useums Etc (2018). Accessed 24 Jan 2020

Vrettakis, E., Kourtis, V., Katifori, A., Karvounis, M., Lougiakis, C., Ioannidis, Y.: Narralive – creating and experiencing mobile digital storytelling in cultural heritage'. Digital Appl. Archaeol. Cult. Heritage **15**, e00114 (2019). https://doi.org/10.1016/j.daach.2019.e00114. Accessed 28 Mar 2020

Weng, L., Liang, Z., Bao, J.: The effect of tour interpretation on perceived heritage values: a comparison of tourists with and without tour guiding interpretation at a heritage destination. J. Destination Mark. Manage. **16**, 100431 (2020). https://doi.org/10.1016/j.jdmm.2020.100431. Accessed 22 Mar 2020

Short Papers: Tools for Education

The Creative School

Jennifer Siung[1]($\boxtimes$), Pier Giacomo Sola[2]($\boxtimes$), and Jo-Anne Sunderland Bowe[3]($\boxtimes$)

[1] Chester Beatty Library, Dublin, Ireland
jennys@cbl.ie
[2] Michael Culture AISBL, Brussels, Belgium
pg.sola@michael-culture.eu
[3] Heritec Ltd., Lewes, UK
jo-anne@heritec.com

Abstract. The Creative School project explores the possible mobilisation of digital cultural heritage and engagement with maker spaces models, as tools to create unusual and exciting learning opportunities. The project is developing learning modules for children and school teachers, promoting self-directed learning, critical and visual thinking skills by using cultural heritage content made available by the partner organisations. Its main outputs are: analysis of training and information needs of teachers, educators, children and also parents; development of a set of training materials focusing on the development of thinking skills through engagement with cultural heritage; development of guidelines and recommendations aimed at influencing policy makers and curriculum decision makers. The main beneficiaries of the project include primary and secondary school teachers, who, through engaging with the project will become equipped with the skills necessary to facilitate pedagogical strategies for creativity and critical thinking. Children and young people involved as participants in the Creative School project will develop the skills required to respond to the challenges offered by the Creative School curriculum.

Keywords: Digital heritage · Creativity · Critical thinking · Maker space · Schools · Teachers children

1 Introduction

The Creative School project [1] is a three-year Strategic partnership funded by the Erasmus+Programme. It builds on the outcomes of two previous Erasmus+funded projects: the Creative Museum and the Making Museum projects, that provided opportunities to generate and evaluate knowledge, clarify concepts and ideas, seek possibilities, consider alternatives and solve problems for museum professionals and audiences. Throughout the duration of the Creative School project, museum, science, arts and heritage professionals, creatives, digital practitioners and makers will be encouraged to share good practices; learn from each other; explore ways of engaging with teachers and students in schools in the development of learning resources; as well as disseminate the processes and outcomes.

M. Ioannides et al. (Eds.): EuroMed 2020, LNCS 12642, pp. 725–733, 2021.
https://doi.org/10.1007/978-3-030-73043-7_64

The Creative School project aims to use the creative and innovative methods and tools developed throughout the Creative and Making Museum projects and apply them to the development of learning modules for children and school teachers. More importantly two core ingredients the Creative School project wishes to build upon, are creativity and critical thinking skills for teachers, educators and students in schools. These skills are central in the education and development of students in schools across Europe.

According to the Organisation for Economic Co-operation and Development, in an increasingly complex world, children need to develop higher level thinking skills in order to find solutions to social, emotional and economic problems, both personally and in the context of the wider world [2]. In order to respond to the challenges of the 21st century, children need to be creative, innovative, enterprising and adaptable, with the motivation, confidence and skills to use critical and creative thinking purposefully. The Creative School responds to this need by delivering creative and critical thinking educational methodologies into schools through engagement with the cultural sector, specifically museums, galleries and science centres.

This paper presents the analysis carried out during the first year by the project partners, on training and information needs of teachers, educators and children involved in the following pilot activities of the Creative School project. As a result of this analysis, a common training plan has been defined, to organise the training materials that will be developed in the second year of the project. Thanks to teachers and educators interviewed during the course of the project as well as their contribution to the project activities; as an outcome it has been possible to define the specific training objectives.

This analysis has been prepared using desk research methods of key national and EU documents, regulations and existing practices. The purpose is to provide a broad overview and a definitive summation of the information in participating countries. With the method of desk research, partners have collected data and basic information from existing resources (national school curricula, descriptions of subjects for students, available educational materials, study/training programmes for teachers, national school strategies, and other legislation) in an effective way.

This has provided the partners with good insights into the key topics that teachers find important and are currently not sufficiently addressed, as well as key obstacles, fears, impediments, etc. in developing creative and critical thinking skills. Based on this analysis, they designed an outline of toolboxes for teachers about introducing a creative and critical thinking approach in education, focusing on selected topics and values.

The main beneficiaries of the project include primary and post-primary school teachers, who, through engaging with the project, will become equipped with the skills necessary to facilitate pedagogical strategies for creative and critical thinking. The project also explores the possible mobilisation of digital cultural heritage and engagement with maker spaces models, as tools to create unusual and exciting learning opportunities. Maker spaces are intended as community-operated workspaces, where people with common interests in technology, science, heritage and art, can meet, socialise and collaborate.

2 Creative and Critical Thinking in Europe

2.1 Definitions

There are many interpretations of creative and critical thinking skills. Pose this question to a group of museum, science centre and cultural heritage professionals and then to a group of makers the answers may vary. The terms have more recently been introduced to the school sector and they too have a number of interpretations stemming from both educational policy and practice.

As identified in the previous Creative Museum and Making Museum projects, creativity is defined as: "The ability to transcend traditional ideas, rules, patterns, and relationships to create new ideas; originality or imagination." [3, 4].

In the education sector creativity has multiple interpretations and currently is referred to in curriculum reform. One such interpretation sees it as such: "Imaginative activity fashioned so as to produce outcomes that are both original and of value." [5].

Within the museum sector, professionals, primarily those engaged with learning and audience engagement and collections management, are required to think 'creatively' on a day-to-day basis and to look outside the sector for inspiration, collaboration, partnerships and for funding. However, creativity may differ for other practitioners and this was explored and identified when working with science centres, digital, creatives and makers. Creativity is expressed through a number of ways including co-creation, ideation, hackathons or take overs of spaces and co-creating interpretations of ideas in teams as well as Maker Fairs.

According to teacher and author John Spencer [6], many schools recognise the need to prepare students for the future especially in the field of technology e.g. Artificial Intelligence, nanotechnology, 3D printing and code. However the future is difficult to predict with multiple layers of complexity and therefore it is better to prepare students for the present, develop their soft skills where machines lack in this ability to read situations using human emotions. Collaboration and empathy are key skills for students with divergent skills who need to be able to respond to an ever-changing world. Students require to be able to slow down, assess and use creative and critical thinking skills when reading the world around them. Spencer calls this Vintage Innovation; a combination of human qualities and abilities with technology and innovation. For many, the linear trajectory our parents and previous generations evolved from school to university and into the corporate work place is no longer relevant.

Now students need to utilise a multitude of skills in order to negotiate the world and classroom. Yet teachers also face challenges; how do they innovate if they lack access to the latest technology? Students and teachers require a combination of old and new learning approaches that complement each other. Spencer sees teachers as innovators with the ability to create new learning opportunities for their students. Teachers need to give students a space to innovate, experiment, express their voice and move away from a restrictive curriculum. This is reflected in the current reform of education in each of the partner countries; from didactic to innovative teaching and learning; from education policy to grassroots; from the margins to the core in collaborative programmes as reflected in the case studies presented in this analysis.

The case studies presented in this report reflect creative and critical thinking both in the classroom as well as the museum and science centre, maker spaces and beyond.

The simple definition of critical thinking is the ability to solve problems. In the 21st century classroom the 4 Cs are prevalent in the promotion and development of critical thinking skills: Critical thinking; Creativity; Collaboration; Communication.

In the education and school sectors critical thinking is often supported by other key skills such as creativity, communication and collaboration.

2.2 Covid-Culture

While writing this analysis, a global pandemic broke out at the end of 2019 and 2020. The new term "Covid Culture" emerged. How can creative and critical thinking lend itself to the Creative School project especially during prolonged times of closure of arts, cultural, science, heritage and educational organisations?

Many institutions lost visitors to their cultural sites overnight and quickly had to create new online digital content for audiences. This move from on-site to online particularly for engagement with teachers and students in school includes areas of focus for many organisations: Learning from home – online learning; Working from home; Preparation for exams; Health and wellbeing; Digital platforms; Support for the sector; Virtual school trips.

Members of the global maker community contributed to supporting the medical community at the height of the pandemic and collectively sought to design ventilators as well as face shields combining STEAM and 3D printing. Some of the members of the Creative School project were directly involved including Cap Sciences in France and Radiona in Croatia.

Lockdown of schools has had a huge impact on students' progression in learning and their academic year. Some research has been carried out such as the British Council which conducted online surveys in April and May 2020 to find out what the immediate needs and experiences of teachers of English and teacher educators were during the Covid-19 pandemic. Feedback ranged from 51–150 countries with over 9600 teachers surveyed. One report found that for most teachers remote teaching was new for the majority of them yet were confident to carry out their work online. Training was identified as a need to support this yet it was noted there is a gap in digital access for both students and teachers, e.g. poor connectivity and how to maintain prolonged engagement with students to support their learning needs as well as support parents and caregivers as they became critical in the support of students learning from home [7].

The support for teachers and students online differs greatly for each of the partner countries. What will the long-term impact of this shutdown be on students? Schools are not built to deal with extended shutdowns and yet this disruption has forced teachers and the education system to explore alternative ways of teaching. How will students make-up for lost time and regression in their learning? Can cultural, heritage, creative and scientific sectors lend to the support of teachers and students in this crisis? As society slowly reopens public spaces and schools what will learning look like in a post-pandemic world? The education sector is faced with new challenges in the management of classroom-based learning. Current discussions include a combination of learning onsite and online teaching known as blended learning. These are just a few issues raised during the course of lockdown and over time creative solutions may address some of these concerns.

2.3 Analysis of Case Studies

A number of case studies were provided by project partners to give an overview of examples across Europe including Austria, Croatia, Finland, France, Ireland, Italy, the UK.

These, as well as additional examples will be discussed, shared and give project partners insight to the current state of creative and critical thinking both in schools and the cultural, heritage, creative and scientific sectors. The project also plans to disseminate these examples as well as collate from partner country's networks across Europe and worldwide. All of this will inspire project partners to discuss and assess the current climate as well as how best to utilise good practice in their own respective organisations and networks. As these are examples, the project acknowledges this list is non-exhaustive.

Five key themes or categories were identified in the analysis of the examples submitted by partners. These are as follows:

Type 1: Museum-School Partnerships and Resources
Workshop, short project or one-off event where schools engage with the collection facilitated by a member of museum staff, educator or specialist. The museum facilitates creative and critical thinking skills in the design and facilitation of these partnerships as a means to inspire learning for both the institution and schools. These partnerships specifically link the curriculum to the museum collection as a means to reflect key skills taught in the curriculum as well as bridge the school and the museum. Resources are often developed as a key outcome of partnerships for teachers and students to access online.

Type 2: STEAM, City Councils and Maker Spaces Collaborations, Maker Fairs and Festivals
STEAM combines science, technology, engineering, arts and maths and is prevalent in the educational sector as a means of cross-curricular approaches for both teachers and students. It originates from STEM learning (science, technology, engineering and maths) incorporating the arts. STEAM promotes better problem-solving skills, increased creativity and innovation for students.

Collaboration between city council public libraries and local maker spaces and offer users access to electronics, robotics, 3-D printing, as well as metal-working, woodworking, traditional arts and craft. These are available in library spaces or converted mobile library units.

The Maker culture represents a technology-based extension of the Do-It-Yourself concept, concerned with physical objects and the creation of new devices. Typical interests include engineering-oriented pursuits such as electronics, robotics, 3-D printing, and the use of computer numerical control tools, as well as more traditional activities, such as metal-working, woodworking, traditional arts and crafts. The first Maker Faire was held in 2006 in San Francisco. See www.makerfaire.com/makerfairehistory.

Type 3: Workshops and Creative Spaces
Spaces within a heritage site, museum, science museum or creative space dedicated to creativity where audiences can participate in creative processes. These can include spaces with specialist facilities and technology such as FabLabs (Fabrication Labs), MediaLabs, Living Labs or Digital Spaces. These are often seen as places for free experimentation.

Type 4: Collaborative initiatives
Invited partners engage with the museum, heritage site or science museum over a period of time, work collaboratively with staff; co-curated exhibition, display, dedicated piece specific to learning. Often the museum and relevant organisation works with an external partner to enable this collaboration. These can be initiated by city councils, city libraries, universities, local networks for regions as well as European-funded projects e.g. Erasmus+.

3 Moving from the Theoretical to the Practical

3.1 An Analysis of the Good Practices

The organisation of case studies into different categories was the first step in understanding the different types of work that museums and cultural heritage institutions are undertaking with schools. This activity demonstrated the wide variety of different projects and programmes. The benefit of looking at the case studies in this way, allowed us to reflect on and review the different methodologies adopted. One of the challenges of undertaking an analysis like this is to make assumptions, however by presenting and organising the case studies by categories allowed us to understand some of the shared outcomes and outputs.

The second part of the analysis is to examine the commonalities that presented themselves in the case studies. These are described here as 'emerging themes' which will help inform the next stage of the project. Emerging themes are:

Challenge: allow pupils to challenge thoughts, ideas and opinions and to be challenged;

Digital: use technology where appropriate to support the pupils learning and programme outcomes.

Explore: create a space for pupils to self-develop in order to become independent learners;

Experiment: encourage experimentation.

Innovation: create opportunities for prototyping to create an understand of the creative processes;

Objects: use objects as a stimulus, to scaffold projects and mediate discussions.

Play: create opportunities to play;

Pupil-centred: ensure that pupils are active-agents in their own learning processes;

Relevance: engage with themes and ideas which interests participants;

Voice: allow space for the pupil's voice to be heard in a respectful environment.

3.2   Understanding the Needs of Teachers and Educators

Based on a synthesis of the material collected so far, these are the recommendations we can take moving forward. What do teachers need?

Clear methodologies: Teachers need to be supported in having concrete and practical methodologies to implement creative activities on critical and creative thinking;

Support for evaluation: Teachers do not know how to evaluate students on critical and creative thinking therefore there is a need to develop a methodology for evaluation;

Developing competences: Teachers need skills-set (competency framework) based on soft skills or competences students can acquire developing their own creative and critical thinking.

This analysis was produced during the pandemic at a time when schools and museums were closed; as a result, cultural institutions have been re-examining delivery of their content, predominantly to online methods. In a broad sense this is described a 'digital transformation' of engaging with audiences, which could take the form of VLE (virtual learning environments), online sessions where museum educators deliver live into the classroom via an online platform, digital resources to support collections (YouTube, online tours, downloadable materials). Whilst schools and museums have started reopen, it has become apparent that it will take some time for the pattern of school visits to return to 'normal'. Several organisations have come together to survey on a national or international scale the needs of teachers. At the time of writing, the NEMO (Network of European Museums Organisations) report on the impact of COVID-19 on museums in Europe was not available [8]. However the following reports show some interesting insights for the partnership as we move into the next phase of the project; in the UK a National Survey has been conducted by a partnership of organisations including the Arts Council and Bridge Network. The survey is a useful reflection on what has happened during lockdown in the UK but also an indicator of future opportunities and collaborations between schools and the cultural and heritage sector. In particular the respondents (mostly teachers) cited curated cultural learning resources and partnerships with cultural partners as their strongest desire going forward. In the same report, both primary and secondary teachers requested support for creativity across the curriculum. Another survey by the University of Leicester with museum educators 'Schools Visits post-lockdown' suggests that there will be an increase in activities in the future with digital components and blended learning. One of the key findings of the report says that: 'There is increased appetite for digital components in post-lockdown school visits. On average, we can expect 3 additional digital components post-lockdown than we had pre-Covid. More likely to be added are home activities, virtual tours, live lectures, online collections, bitesize talks, and social media'. As in the other national survey Teachers Resources again figure prominently. This corroborates the evidence from the partners from their own research and feedback in schools.

3.3   Recommendations for Building a Creative School

We also asked partners how the good practices and case studies could be shared in schools. In summary, the collected good practices can be effectively used classes by: introducing a new online set of educational tools for critical and creative thinking;

providing challenge and interesting ideas for engaging with heritage; creating an online database of shared knowledge; creating cross-curricular/interdisciplinary approaches to topics and themes; demonstrating good practice in design and format of resources; delivering clear learning outcomes.

Critical thinking relates to pupils (in reality to all of us) thought processes: how they take decisions, how they use their personal ideas, and how they act to solve problems. Through critical thinking students will become problem-solvers, tending to apply the same thinking processes to identify and implement the solutions to their own problems. This process works for any kind of problem - large or small. Experimenting their creativity, the students will become active learners. To reach this result they must nourish their senses, body, intellect and mind.

The Open Education Resources (OER) developed by the Creative School project should consist of a CRAFTED educational toolbox, with the following characteristics:

Cross-curricular and inter-disciplinary: Embedding creativity and critical thinking across the curriculum;

Respectful: There is a transformative learning experience when children and young people are encouraged to share their voices, opinions and personal experiences when exploring collections in an open, holistic and safe environment;

Adaptable: Each teacher should be able to work with the resource and adapt it according to the needs of the school cycle (primary, middle school or post-primary school);

Flexible: Provide flexible methods of evaluation that allow teachers to find their way around and construct their own evaluation grid. The overall objective is to determine the students' ability to follow and complete a project;

Thinking routines and strategies: Learners should be encouraged to think speculatively, to acknowledge and build on what members of their peer group are saying, and to build confidence and competence in their own ideas and evidence building.

Electronic/Digital: OER should be in digital format; simple to use and with concise instructions; no need to download applications; quick to assimilate; using images and videos, also augmented reality and virtual reality especially in the future; adopting a gameplay solution; using digital storytelling and personal stories; participatory; active involvement of the student for producing knowledge; no need for special tools.

Differentiated: Allow for teachers to interpret and adapt the resources for student's learning needs.

References

1. Creative School Homepage: https://www.creative-school.eu.
2. OECD, The Future of Education and Skills. https://www.oecd.org/education/2030/E2030%20Position%20Paper%20(05.04.2018).pdf (2018)
3. Dictionary.com Homepage, Ref: www.dictionary.reference.com.
4. Bowe, J.S., Siung, J. (ed.): Analysis of Best Practice, The Creative Museum. https://creative-museum.net/wp-content/uploads/2016/06/analysis-of-best-practices.pdf, p. 9 (2016)
5. National Advisory Committee on Education Creative and Cultural Education, All our Futures: Creativity, Culture and Education, Report to the Secretary of State for Education and Employment the Secretary of State for Culture, Media and Sport, UK, pp. 28–30 (1999)

6. John Spencer Homepage: https://www.spencerauthor.com.
7. The British Council, Teaching English, A survey of teacher and teacher educator needs during the Covid-19 pandemic, www.teachingenglish.org (2000)
8. NEMO, Report on the impact of COVID-19 on museums in Europe, https://www.ne-mo.org/news/article/nemo/nemo-report-on-the-impact-of-covid-19-on-museums-in-europe.html (2020)

The Network of the Italian University Museums for the Diffusion of the Scientific Culture

Elena Corradini[✉][iD]

University of Modena and Reggio Emilia, via Vivarelli 10, 41124 Modena, Italy
elena.corradini@unimore.it

Abstract. The first Italian University Museums Network has been constituted in 2012 for a first project, approved an financed by the Ministry of the University and Research, coordinated by Modena and Reggio Emilia, in order to monitor the most significant museums collections, to catalog their specimens with the national standard of the Central Institute for the Catalogue and Documentation for the General Catalog of the Italian Cultural Heritage and to create 80 narrative paths dedicated to environments, landscapes, stories, history of scientific instruments. All the paths have been inserted in the bilingual web portal of the Network realized for the project (https://www.retemuseiuniversitari.unimore.it) structured in order to contextualize, through both historical and territorial frameworks, significant collections and to strengthen the semantic value of the specimens identified and chosen by individual museums for their specific value within the four general themes and to create multiple contexts creating multiple contexts that explain the relationships between objects and the exhibits, not often easily understood upon their displaying.

The Network has gradually become aware of the great potential to develop educational programs and the diffusion of scientific culture: in 2015 started a second project, approved and financed by the same Ministry, dedicated to orient the students to the scientific method and culture. The museums realized 56 experiential educational paths through the individuation and the sharing of operative methods, the adoption and the use of common languages and tools, with specific attention to the information technologies, dedicated to three principal themes, biodiversity, color and time, and to seven subthemes: all are published in the second section of the Network web portal.

Keywords: University museums · Cataloguing · Scientific method

1 The Network First Project: the Cataloguing of the Collections and the Realization of the Narrative Paths for His New Web Portal

The first Network of Italian University Museums was constituted in 2012 to present at the Ministry of University and Research, within the law 6/2000 for the diffusion of the scientific culture, a project on information technologies and new realities for knowledge, networking and enhancement of the scientific cultural heritage.

© Springer Nature Switzerland AG 2021
M. Ioannides et al. (Eds.): EuroMed 2020, LNCS 12642, pp. 734–739, 2021.
https://doi.org/10.1007/978-3-030-73043-7_65

The project was approved the following year thanks to the networked cooperation of 64 University Museums, 38 collections, 9 Botanical Gardens of twelve historical Italian Universities (Bari, Cagliari, Chieti-Pescara, Ferrara, Florence, Modena and Reggio Emilia, Parma, Perugia, Rome "The Sapienza", Salento, Siena, Tuscia), with the coordination of Modena and Reggio Emilia (https://www.pomui.unimore.it/site/home.html).

The museums of the Network, with the aim of creating the first bilingual portal of the Network, have monitored their collections in order to verify their conservation as well as to identify the most significant specimens to insert them in a coherent relation, for their the symbolic value, with four thematic narrative paths: environments, landscapes, stories, history of scientific instruments.

The museums of the Network have identified 28000 specimens that have been described within specific catalog entries managed by the Central Institute for Catalogue and Documentation (ICCD) (https://www.iccd.beniculturali.it/) of the Ministry of Cultural Heritage, Activities and Tourism for the realization of the General Catalog of Italian cultural heritage.

The General Catalogue of Italian Cultural Heritage is the database that centrally collects and organizes the descriptive information on cultural heritage catalogued in Italy, the result of research activities conducted by various institutions in the territory. It allows to search information on catalogued cultural heritage in a dynamic way from SIGECweb (General Catalog Information System on the web (https://www.iccd.beniculturali.it/it/sigec-web), a web-based platform that manages the entire flow of cataloguing, from the production and diffusion of cataloguing standards, to the assignment of unique cataloguing codes, to the cataloguing of assets (archaeological, architectural and landscape, demo-ethno-anthropological, photographic, musical, naturalistic, numismatic, scientific and technological, historical and artistic), to the publication of cataloguing sheets for use on the site of the general catalog of cultural heritage (https://www.catalogo.beniculturali.it/sigecSSU_FE/Home.action?timestamp=1603277507560).

The standard are constituted by a set of rules, guidelines of method and specific terminology tools to follow for the acquisition of knowledge on the cultural heritage and for the production of their documentation. The rules for cataloguing cultural heritage include also rules for digital acquisition of the photographic images, for data transfer and also authority files cards which relate to entities (as the authors, the bibliography) in relation with the cultural heritage.

The catalogue cards are descriptive models that collect in an organized manner information on heritage, according to a cognitive path that guides the person who catalogs and at the same time controls and encodes the data acquisition according to specific criteria. The ICCD has issued different cataloguing models in relation to different specimens of the cultural heritage, organized on the basis of the various disciplines.

Every rule is made up from of the layout (the structure of the data) and the related rules of compilation, in which is indicated in detail how the individual entries must be drawn up. The observance of common rules allows, by the application of specific procedures, the interchange of information among the different players in the field of cultural heritage.

In order to catalog the 28000 selected objects/specimens, the museums of the Network have used 16 different catalog cards corresponding to the different types of demoetno-anthropological specimens (BDM layout), archaeological finds (RA); drawings (D); photographs (F); works and objects of art (OA); works and objects of contemporary art (OAC); prints (S), numismatic specimens (N), scientific and technological heritage (PST), anthropological finds (AT); six models of cards dedicated to naturalistic heritage have been added more recently, for Botany (BNB), Mineralogy (BNM), Paleontology (BNP; Petrology (BNPE), Planetology (BNPL), Zoology (BNZ) (https://www.iccd.beniculturali.it/it/standard-catalografici).

In particular, the project of the Network has allowed to experiment, through the systematic use by the various University museums, these last 6 cards dedicated to naturalistic heritage. These cards were realized on the initiative of the Conference of the Rectors of the Italian Universities (CRUI) – Museums Commission, starting from 1999, and disseminated following a "Memorandum of understanding on research, studies and training in the field of cataloguing of cultural heritage", stipulated between the CRUI-Commission Museums and the ICCD. In addition, for each of the 6 cards for the naturalistic, guidelines have been drawn up in collaboration with the ICCD to facilitate the compilation.

For the cataloguing, photographic shots of the specimens have also been made, which are essential to complete the cataloguing cards, for a correct identification of the specimens and their conservation. The photographs were fundamental for the thematic narrative paths inserted by the museums of the Network have in the web portal. To complete the cataloguing activity, a manual (currently work in progress) has been drawn up, in collaboration with the ICCD, in which the experimentation of the 6 cards for the naturalistic heritage, the AT card for the anatomical specimens, and a specific MODI card for the copies and casts are included (https://www.iccd.beniculturali.it/it/sperimentazionenormative).

All the 80 narrative paths realized, 19 dedicated to the landscapes, 18 to the environments, 25 to the stories and 9 to the history of the various Universities, 9 to the histories of scientific instrumentation, have been structured in order to contextualize, through both historical and territorial frameworks, significant collections and to strengthen the semantic value of the specimens identified and chosen by individual museums for their specific value within the four general themes. These four themes have created multiple contexts that explain the relationships between objects and the exhibits, not often easily understood upon their displaying.

The University Museums of the Network, developing a narrative approach to information, have intended to activate an effective web-based communication and dissemination strategy, able to overcome the limits that an exhibition can have, taking advantage of the fact that the same specimen can be inserted in numerous itineraries providing possible links and multidisciplinary references and becoming a starting point for multiple links to other resources of all kinds.

The contextualization of the objects/specimens within the different itineraries realized by the Museums of the Network on the four general themes and their online use through the bilingual web portal wants to be a stimulus to return to the museum, helping also to trace new visits on the territory and new ways to explore the collections. This narrative approach to information is fundamental to increase the attractiveness of museums and their collections, describing the ways in which a specimens connects to others, places, people, theories and scientific discoveries. Through this activity of digital storytelling it has been possible to expand and diversify cultural communication involving both the emotional and sensory spheres. On the bilingual web portal a similar interface has been created for each of the four sections of thematic itineraries that provides different ways to access different interactive menus on the same page.

The information management system of the bilingual web portal will represent the engine of a network of available resources online; it will aim at managing the information richness and the needs of the different subjects, giving back an integrated vision in a suitable way to spread the knowledge of cultural historical scientific and naturalistic heritage to a wide audience, as well as stimulating interest and curiosity. It means an evolution of the educational and informative role of museums in which the historical aspects are functional to a social and educational vision, in particular through a close relationship between school and local area, which proved essential especially after the pandemic, during which the museums were able to use the large amount of material available online in the portal (texts, photos, videos).

2   The Network Second Project for Method and Scientific Culture Orientation

This plural organism, the Network of Italian University Museums, has gradually become aware of the great potential to develop educational programs for the diffusion of scientific culture, which are full prerogative of what today is called the third mission of Italian Universities, after research and teaching.

In 2015, started the second project, approved and financed by the Ministry of the University and Research ((https://www.pomui.unimore.it/site/home.html). This second project of the Network (to which the Universities of Genova and Pavia and the Civic Museums of Reggio Emilia have been added), with the coordination of the University of Modena and Reggio Emilia, was finalized to the realization of experiential educational paths dedicated to the orientation to the scientific method and culture.

Starting from the historical-scientific and naturalistic heritage of the Museums of the Network, the primary objective of these paths was to promote, among the students of the IV and V High School classes, interest in scientific culture and in particular in the scientific method, retracing the historical path of the evolution of the different disciplines from the eighteenth century. The experiential educational paths realized by and within the University Museums with elementary experiments will fit, on the one side, into the school education (still generalist) and, on the other side, into the University education (highly specialist, experimental and technically advanced) in order to transmit that unifying component, common to the different disciplinary fields, that is represented by the scientific method. This meet the requirements of the experimental approach, in particular the rigorousness of method, the control and reproducibility of experiments, the distinction between results and inferences.

All the 56 experiential educational paths of non-formal education, all realized for the project whit the same method have been dedicated to three thematic areas, biodiversity and agrobiodiversity, color and time. They are published in the second section of the web portal of the Network (https://www.retemuseiuniversitari.unimore.it). In these three thematic areas, graphically represented through a conceptual map, created to summarize the process of developing the theme, 9 paths are dedicated to biodiversity and agrobiodiversity, the others 47 to the color and to the time. These are divided in seven sub-themes represented by seven conceptual maps. For the color 9 paths have been dedicated to the color in nature, 7 to the color in art and science, 4 to the color in Physics. For the time 10 pats have been dedicated to the Geology and the fossils, 6 to the measurement of the time, 9 to the human evolution, 2 to the evolution of Antarctica.

References

1. Corradini, E: POMUI. The web portal of Italian University Museums. In: Nyst, N., Stanbury, P., Weber, C. (eds.), Proceedings of the 10th Conference of the International Committee of ICOM for University Museums and Collections (UMAC), University Museums and Collections as Recorders of Cultural and Natural Communities Worldwide, Shanghai, 7–12 November 2010, Univ. Museums Collections J. **4**, 77–84 (2011)
2. https://edoc.hu-berlin.de/handle/18452/9366.
3. Corradini, E.: The new communication technologies for sharing and participatory Italian University Museums. In: Nyst, N., Stanbury, P., Weber, C., (eds.), Proceedings of the 11th Conference of the International Committee of ICOM for University Museums and Collections (UMAC), University collections and University history and identity, Lisbon, 21–25 September 2011, Univ. Museums Collections J. **5**, 133–146 (2012). https://edoc.hu-berlin.de/handle/18452/9383.
4. Corradini, E., Campanella, L.: The multimedia technologies and the new realities for knowledge networking and valorisation of scientific cultural heritage. The role of the Italian University Museums network. In: Marchegiani L., (ed.), Proceedings of the International Conference on Sustainable Cultural Heritage Management, Aracne, Roma, pp. 283–297 (2016)
5. Corradini, E.: La catalogazione e nuove tecnologie informatiche per l'accessibilità al patrimonio naturalistico. In: Mazzotta, S., Malerba, G. (eds.), Memorie del XX Congresso ANMS – Associazione Nazionale Musei Scientifici, I musei delle scienze e la biodiversità, Ferrara 17–19 Novembre 2010. Museologia Scientifica Memorie **9**, 33–39 (2013). https://www.anms.it/riviste/dettaglio_rivista/18/10.
6. Corradini, E., Campanella L.: A national project for the Italian University Museums network. In: Nyst, N., Stanbury, P., Weber, C.P. (eds.), Proceedings of the 13th Conference of the International Committee of ICOM for University Museums and Collections (UMAC), Evaluating change The University Museum, Rio de Janeiro, 10–17 August 2013, Univ. Museums Collections J. **7**, 20–29 (2014). https://umac.icom.museum/wp-content/uploads/2017/08/UMACJ-7.pdf.
7. Corradini, E., Campanella, L.,: Digital technologies for the first network of the Italian University Museums, Annual Conference CIDOC - Comité International pour la Documentation, Access and Understanding , Networking in the Digital Era, Dresden, 6–11 September 2014, Conference Paper, pp. 42–49 (2014). https://network.icom.museum/cidoc/archive/past-conferences/2014-dresden/
8. Corradini, E.: Educational itineraries of the Italian University Museums network for the lifelong guidance to the scientific culture and method. In: Garcìa Fernandez, I. (ed.) Proceedings Congreso Internacional Museos Universitarios, Tradicion y futuro, Madrid, December 3–5, 2014, pp. 489–494. Università Complutense, Madrid (2015)

9. Corradini, E.: The common and interdisciplinary itineraries of the Italian University museum network: a challenge for sharing scientific education. In: Haggag, M., Gesché-Koning, N. (eds.), Proceedings of the 13th ICOM-UMAC & 45th annual ICOM-CECA Conference, Squaring the Circle? Research, Museum, Public: a Common Engagement towards Effective Communication, Alexandria, 9–14 October 2014, Alexandria (2014), pp. 105–111 (2015). https://umac.icom.museum/wp-content/uploads/2017/08/UMAC-CECA_Alexandria.pdf.

10. Corradini, E., Campanella, L.: The Italian University Museums network for the guidance of the scientific culture. In: Monaco, G. (ed), Proceedings of the 46th annual ICOM-CECA Conference, Museum Education and Accessibility: Bridging the Gaps, 17–21 September 2015, Washington, D.C., pp. 91–97 (2016)

11. Corradini, E.: La rete dei Musei Universitari: diffusione e contestualizzazione del patrimonio culturale degli atenei, orientamento al metodo e alla cultura scientifica. In: Magnani, L., Stagno, L. (eds.), Atti del Convegno, Valorizzare il patrimonio culturale delle Università. Focus su arte e architetture, Genova 20–21 Novembre 2014, Università di Genova, Genova, pp. 131–142 (2016)

12. Corradini, E.: Percorsi formativi della Rete dei Musei Universitari Italiani per l'orientamento permanente al metodo e alla cultura scientifica. In: Borzatti De Loewenstern, A., Roselli, A., Falchetti, E., (eds), Memorie del XXIV Congresso dell'Associazione Nazionale Musei Scientifici, "Contact zone": i ruoli dei musei scientifici nella società contemporanea, Livorno 11–13 Novembre 2014, Museologia Scientifica Memorie **16**, 43–47 (2017)

13. https://www.anms.it/riviste/dettaglio_rivista/30.

14. Corradini, E.: I nuovi percorsi educativi della Rete dei Musei Universitari. In: Martellos, S., Celi, M., (eds.), Memorie del XXVI Congresso dell'Associazione Nazionale Musei Scientifici, I musei al tempo della crisi. Problemi, soluzioni, opportunità, Trieste, 16–18 Novembre 2016, Museologia Scientifica Memorie **18**, 39–44 (2019). https://www.anms.it/riviste/dettaglio_rivista/34/10.

15. Corradini, E.: Educating to the scientific method and culture in the italian university museums. Univ. J. Educ. Res. **8**(10), 4891–4896 (2020). https://doi.org/10.13189/ujer.2020.081061

ANTS: From History of Science to Future of Science

Manolis Wallace[1]([⊠]) [iD], Vassilis Poulopoulos[1] [iD], Zoi Papavramidou[1] [iD],
Ilias Tzioras[1] [iD], and John Liaperdos[2] [iD]

[1] ΓAB LAB - Knowledge and Uncertainty Research Laboratory, Department of Informatics and
Telecommunications, University of the Peloponnese, Tripoli, Greece
{wallace,vacilos,dit14158,i.tzioras}@uop.gr
[2] Department of Digital Systems, University of the Peloponnese, Tripoli, Greece
i.liaperdos@uop.gr

Abstract. ΓAB LAB (the Knowledge and Uncertainty Research Laboratory at the University of Peloponnese) is designing and implementing Argolida's Next Top Scientist (ANTS), a history of science program for minority students. ANTS draws on the biographies of celebrated scientists such as Albert Einstein and Marie Skłodowska Curie to empower students that are often found ostracized by both school and society. In a sense, the program uses the history of science as a tool to foster the future of science.

Keywords: History of science · Minority students · Empowerment

1 Introduction

The Knowledge and Uncertainty Research Laboratory of the University of Peloponnese, most commonly known as ΓAB LAB, is a research lab that specializes, among other things, in cultural informatics [1], i.e. application of technology to transform the cultural domain, and educational informatics [2], i.e. application of technology to transform the educational domain.

ΓAB LAB takes an unconventional approach in its organization, management and operation, differentiating itself from more conventional research groups, in the sense that it is tightly associated with external local and governmental entities [3]. This cooperation is bi-directional, providing the lab with real life feedback on its research results but also providing the society with an opportunity to benefit from early research results and impact the direction of research based on its current and projected needs.

A major part of the lab's connection to the society is initiative to provide educational opportunities to pupils that would otherwise not have them. This is materialized through Innovation ΓAB LAB, a nonprofit organization (NPO) belonging to the lab that provides free of charge educational programs for any pupil that may be interested. The main concept in most of these courses is to provide children with an opportunity to familiarize themselves with technology that would might be difficult for some families to either acquire or technically support, such as robotics, 3D printers and scanners, AR/VR,

M. Ioannides et al. (Eds.): EuroMed 2020, LNCS 12642, pp. 740–747, 2021.
https://doi.org/10.1007/978-3-030-73043-7_66

drones and so on. For example, we see in Fig. 1 the implementation of an educational robotics program for primary school students.

In this paper we focus on the one educational program that has a different focus. It is A.N.T.S., short for Argolida's Next Top Scientist, which aims to empower minority or otherwise marginalized students through a presentation of the history of science. Of course this is not the first time aspects of history have been used to foster skills needed in the modern world [4, 5]; but we clearly follow a different path.

The structure of the remainder of this paper is as follows: In Sect. 2 we further specify the scope of this work. Section 3 presents the outline of the educational program and reports on its earlier and current real-life implementation. In Sect. 4 we discuss the sustainability of the program and we close with our concluding remarks in Sect. 5.

2   Scope and Motivation

Achieving social equality in education is a strategic goal for ΓAB LAB and we have been working for it over the last few years. As our programs grow, we are happy to be reaching more pupils in the various locations where our programs are being offered.

Fig. 1. Innovation ΓAB LAB's educational program on educational robotics [6]

A recent analysis of the composition of our classes, though, unearthed an unexpected observation: There are certain social groups that never participate in our programs. Whilst all pupils are welcome to participate free of charge, the first year of operation has indicated that minority pupils, such as Roma children, children of immigrants and refugees and children of families that are at the most financially peril situation have not been applying for participation.

In our effort to look further into the issue, we contacted various teachers inquiring if such pupils where informed of the existence of our programs and whether there was some other prohibiting parameter. What we found out was that the pupils where actually particularly interested to participate, to some extent also jealous that they did not participate, but they considered that Innovation ΓAB LAB was "not meant for them" but for the "normal" children. It is worth noting that these are the same children that are most prone to drop out from school, before even completing primary level education, something that further limits their access to societal benefits later in life.

With that in mind, we decided to design a new educational program, aimed to empower minority students and encourage them to stay in school and pursue the most they can achieve. Thus, A.N.T.S. was born; this of course is independent from and complementary to the state's existing programs towards inclusive education.

3 The Educational Program

The educational intervention is based on the presentation of the history of science, from a societal point of view, delivering the message that everyone, regardless of origins, language, religion, ethnic group, gender etc. has the potential to excel.

3.1 Design

The educational program consists of three sections, each one serving a different goal.

The History
In the first section the educational program has the form of an intensely interactive presentation of and discussion on the history of science (see Fig. 2). We start with the presentation of an – otherwise anonymous – little girl named Maria, who has the aspiration to study but is limited by being penniless. She manages to study, while just barely managing to have enough food to survive, only to be denied the chance to use her skill and studies as a professor; she is instead told that as a woman she should rather give up her aspirations and become a housewife.

We continue following her fascinating story, with the many twists and turns that followed and the uphill battle she faced in so many occasions, and the many that she helped on the way, until the children realize – or are informed by us if they do not realize on their own – that the little Maria that we are talking about is in fact Maria Skłodowska-Curie, the greatest scientist of all times.

We later talk of a little boy that was rather odd and slow at school – only spoke at an older age, could not focus or follow rules – found it hard to finish university and was not at all appreciated by his university professors; to such an extent that he was not given even a single letter of recommendation, a fact that greatly limited his employment opportunities. He nevertheless worked on new theories on his own; but these were rejected by the scientific community of the time because he was a Jew living in Germany at the time that the superiority of the Aryan race was not to be disputed.

The story continues until the children realize – or are informed – that we are in fact following the life of the most famous scientist of all times, Albert Einstein.

Young Thomas is up next, a youngster that is thrown out of primary school in just eight weeks because his teacher assesses that he is incapable of being taught anything. His mother does not give up on him and taught him reading and writing. And then he continued reading on his own, based on his own inherent curiosity. At the age of 12 he was already almost completely deaf, which further limited his communication with others.

Fig. 2. Presenting and discussing the history of science

The attentive reader will have guessed that this is the story of Thomas Edison, America's greatest inventor of all times.

Last in this section comes that story of someone who aspired to be an inventor and was famously mocked by Albert Einstein himself for not having any potential to make a real impact on science. This is of course the story of Nicola Tesla, the undisputed greatest inventor of all times.

Throughout these stories the presentation and discussion focus on two things:

1. the environment's total belief that these individuals had little to no potential to make anything for themselves and
2. the greatness that was possible once they overcame the others' opinions and pursued their true aspirations

The narrative is of course aimed to suggest that anyone and everyone has the potential to excel, even if at some point it is considered common knowledge that they cannot; as expected, the minority pupils often find themselves identifying with the heroes of our stories, so the idea is planted that perhaps they, too, can achieve more than what seems to be considered as the ceiling of their reasonable aspirations.

The Innovation
The second section also follows the form of an intensely interactive presentation, this time discussing the notion of innovation. Through a sequence of simple examples, all based on a simple device that all the students know – the mobile phone – we discuss what is and what is not an innovation.

Very quickly the pupils learn that an innovation is.

1. Something new
2. That is used by many
3. And makes a real difference

It is of course easy to be discouraged when faced with this list. How can a minority pupil dare imagine that they can come up with an innovation, as described above, exceeding everything that has already been created by giants of science and technology such as Skłodowska-Curie, Einstein, Tesla, Edison but also Microsoft, Apple, Sony and so on.

The section closes with the group collaboratively describing a new innovation – with some careful guidance by the educators – establishing once and for all that each member of the group has the potential to be an inventor, a scientist, or anything else they put their mind to.

Fig. 3. Pupils experimenting with Augmenting and Virtual Reality

The Games

The last section of the educational program focuses on Virtual Reality and Augmented Reality. This section is not tied to the main narrative and goal of empowerment; instead, it is aimed to close the educational program with games and fun, so that pupils exit the program on a happy note, thus linking in their long term memory with positive emotions the overall experience of the educational program and the topics included in it (see Fig. 3).

3.2 Implementation

The program is primarily implemented at the laboratory's facilities in Tripoli, in the context of schools visiting the university.

This is the optimal location to implement the program, as it can be combined with a – much needed – demystification of the concept of the university, allowing pupils to consider it as something attainable.

Unfortunately, this option is not suitable, or even feasible, for everyone. Similarly, to what we have observed with our other educational programs, it is typically the most privileged schools and pupils that visit the university. Thus, we rarely have the opportunity to offer the A.N.T.S. program to its intended audience in our premises.

In this direction, it is very convenient that A.N.T.S. has been accredited by the Institute for Educational Policy, thus being included in the limited list of educational programs that can be legally implemented within school premises (see Fig. 4).

Fig. 4. Providing the program at the school location, in this example in the gym

Argolis, the geographic area where the project focuses, has six elementary schools that have "integration classes", i.e. classes for students of immigrants and other students that have limited knowledge of the Greek language and find difficulties in being integrated in the school community – both academically and socially. These types of classes are in fact the primary focus of the program. Therefore, they are our primary list of schools to visit and provide the program at location.

The program having started in early 2020, we only had the opportunity to implement it a few times due to the COVID-19 pandemic. We have now equipped ourselves with personal protection equipment, such as fabric masks for pupils and educators alike, and are awaiting to find out whether in person educational programs will be permitted by the ministry of education this year; if not we will not give up, we will merely postpone for a year.

The early feedback we have, both from the pupils at the time of the implementation as well as from their teachers when we follow up a few days later, is particularly encouraging. Still, the true test will be a few years further down the road, as a core goal of the program is to reduce the drop-out rate for minority students, a number that can be meaningfully measured only with a few years of delay.

4 Support and Outlook for the Future

We are happy to have an opportunity to provide any service to the community, and particularly to the young and least privileged, and therefore we were content to design and start the A.N.T.S program as a pro bono internal project.

Still, the program does incur some real costs, both in equipment and personnel, that would put its sustainability in question if ΓAB LAB was not supported in running it.

ARGOLIDA'S NEXT TOP SCIENTIST

Fig. 5. A.N.T.S. logo

Whilst the lab undertook the initial design and startup of the project, it is the support of the The Stavros Niarchos Foundation Public Humanities Initiative [7] that made it possible to extend it to cover a large geographic area such as Argolida. But even this funding has an expiration date.

Long term sustainability is also feasible, through the local connections that were mentioned in the first Section of this paper. An NPO named "Innovation ΓAB LAB" [6] has recently been established (its logo in Fig. 5), with the lab and local municipalities as joint members, and it has taken over the implementation of all educational programs.

The lab retains the administration of the company and the scientific supervision of the programs, whilst the municipalities take care of the funding of the activities that take place in their territory. Thus, we look to the future with hope.

5   Conclusions

In this paper we have presented project Argolida's Next Top Scientist (A.N.T.S.). The project evolves around the history of science, focusing particularly on the personal stories of renowned scientists and inventors, such as Maria Skłodowska-Curie, Albert Einstein, Thomas Edison and Nicola Tesla.

The aim of the project is to empower and motivate minority pupils in Argolida's elementary schools, with a final goal of reducing the school dropout rate for minority students, and initial results are promising.

The pandemic has put the implementation of the project on hold, but arrangements have been made to secure its long term sustainability through various collaborations with local entities such as municipalities.

Acknowledgements. In this work we are supported and partially funded by Columbia University and Stavros Niarchos Foundation via their joint initiative "The Stavros Niarchos Foundation Public Humanities Initiative".

The establishment of Innovation ΓAB LAB as a nonprofit organization (NPO) has been achieved with the support of the Municipalities of Ermionida and Messini.

Personal Protective Equipment (PPE) for the safe implementation of the program during the COVID-19 pandemic has been procured with the support of AEGEAS NPO.

References

1. Antoniou, A., Wallace, M. (eds.): Cultural Informatics 2019. In: Proceedings of the workshop on cultural informatics research and applications: state of the art and open challenges, Larnaca, Cyprus, 9 June 2019, CEUR-WS.org (2019). https://ceur-ws.org/Vol-2412/
2. Papadogiannis, I., Poulopoulos, V., Wallace, M.: A critical review of data mining for education: what has been done, what has been learnt and what remains to be seen. Int. J. Educ. Res. Rev. 5(4), 353–372 (2020)
3. Wallace, M.: Working with the society and for the society: a different way to run a cultural informatics lab. Heritage 1, 207–219 (2018)
4. Kiddey, R.R.M.: Homeless Heritage: Collaborative Social Archaeology as Therapeutic Practice (2017)
5. Ducady, G., Lefas-Tetenes, M., Sharpe, S., Rothenberg, M.A.W.: Archaeology and the common core: using objects and methodology to teach twenty-first-century skills in middle school. Adv. Archaeol. Pract. 4(4), 517–536 (2016)
6. Demetroulis, E.A., Wallace, M.: Educational robotics as a tool for the development of collaboration skills. In: Papadakis, S., Kalogiannakis, M. (eds.) Using Educational Robotics to Facilitate Student Learning, IGI Global (2020)
7. Stavros Niarchos Foundation Public Humanities Initiative Homepage. https://snfphi.columbia.edu/. Accessed 4 Oct 2020
8. Innovation ΓAB LAB Homepage. https://innovation.gav.uop.gr/. Accessed 4 Oct 2020

Scientific Investigation on Movable Cultural Heritage

Maria Luisa Vitobello van der Schoot[1,2](✉)

[1] European Jewellery Technology Network, Brussels, Belgium
info@ejtn.org
[2] Adj. Professor of History of Jewellery Technologies, Jewellery Science
and Technology Major, Milano Bicocca University, Milan, Italy

Abstract. The aim of this paper is to illustrate parts of a 45 pages scientific investigation, delivering a significative sample of the results achieved according to the authentication methodology resulting from EU funded Research Project AUTH-ENTICO – CT-044480, coordinated by EJTN GEIE. Content has been abridged according to required number of pages. Advanced scientific instrumentation allows in-depth examination of the artefact while scientific and technical scholars, with established competences on movable Cultural Heritage, interpret results.

Keywords: Authentication · Methodology · Investigation

1 Study of the Artefact

The study of this unique artefact is complex and multidisciplinary; thanks to contemporary analytical methods and instrumentation, it provides suitable evidence to endorse authenticity and pertinence to Ellenistic period.

Object typology:	Bracelet
Reference:	Private Collection
Aim of the study:	Visual, technical, scientific analyses
Object Description:	Gold armlet
Archaeological context:	Unknown

Width 16 mm. – 24 mm. - Diameter ext. 8.5 cm. – int. 7.7cm. - Weight: 47.2 gr.

M. Ioannides et al. (Eds.): EuroMed 2020, LNCS 12642, pp. 748–759, 2021.
https://doi.org/10.1007/978-3-030-73043-7_67

1.1   Materials and Technologies – An Overview

Specialized research provide evidence related to the evolution of precious metals technologies, their application to production of artefacts since its origins and geographical spread, in particular, when materials originate from different locations. Various scientific publications available are enlightening for understanding how, since over 6500 years ago, precious metals technology had advanced and was applied.

Materials

Further technical and scientific content addressing metals and precious metals in antiquity is reported, related to copper and gold [1]:

- Copper
- Copper-antimony alloys
- Copper-tin alloys
- Copper alloys with lead
- Copper-arsenic alloys
- Gold

Composition and Refining

The composition of an ancient gold object can reflect four possible practices:

1. Gold can be used "as found"

2. Gold can have silver, copper, sometimes both and occasionally other metals, alloyed with it for aesthetic, practical or even fraudulent reasons

3. Gold can be purified (refined) and employed in a pure or near-pure state

4. Gold can be refined and then alloyed down to the desired fineness by careful additions of silver, copper or other metals.

These four possibilities also represent the chronological development of gold usage. Nevertheless, as a rule of thumb, copper levels in gold were nearly always lower than silver levels – a fact true for most of the ancient world up to, and including, Roman and Byzantine times. Gold purities over 90%, and often around 95%, only became common in later times when, as suggested above, refining perhaps began to be used on a more regular basis…The recent analysis of the gold leaf on a silver plaque from the tomb of Nefertari showed it to be of high purity (99.0%) gold [2].

Technologies

Gold: Joining, Soldering, Enameling, Surface enrichment, Hammered sheet gold, Embossing, Repoussé, Round, twisted and beaded wire, Mechanical joints.

2 The Jewel

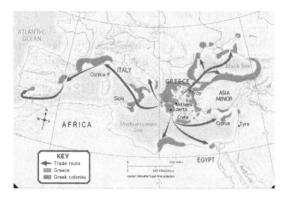

"*The Latin term for this typology of bracelet is "Armilla", "Perikarpion" when worn on the wrist, "Peribrachionion" (in ancient Greek language) when worn on the arm. Even though the armilla was frequently reproduced on Apulian vases from the Hellenistic period, such ornamental typology was absent in the funerary contest of the Tarantine and Apulian centers.*" [3]

Fig. 1. Mediterranean trade routes

From neighboring Countries, Mediterranean trade routes brought evolvement: socio-cultural and spiritual attainments reflected in the crafting skills adopted when creating precious ornaments. Metal working, in particular gold-working technology, achieved peaks of unmatched refinement, expressing the artistic and cultural growth of the various societies, such as with the Phoenician, Greek and Etruscan cultures (Fig. 1).

The Heracles Knot is the main decorative feature of this artefact: it represents a recurring theme before, during and beyond the period of reference.

The techniques used to produce the jewel are those applied and developed since thousand years, enhanced and enriched by the socio-cultural influences derived from the constant Mediterranean trade exchanges (Ref. EU funded Research Project JEWELMED -ICA3–1999-10020).

The artefact is a testimonial of gold's metallurgical evolution. From its initial steps in Varna (Black Sea, Fifth millennium B.C), the craft spread as far as Ur of the Chaldeans, to the Phoenicians, to Egypt, east to Central Asia, south to Greek Mainland and Colonies, to Sardinia, Etruria, then further West and North into Europe, reaching as far as Spain and the Hallstatt and Celtic cultures.

Such refinement can be fully appreciated when observing the Knot's floral centerpiece, its elegant and fine craftsmanship and miniature details. Twisted, plain, beaded wires were applied to sheet gold, creating edges, flowery leaves, minute petals, cells bordering the Knot, filled with colored enamels, unfortunately deteriorated, still some remains are proven by remains of silica and metal oxides on the surface.

3 Technical Overview

3.1 Technical and Morphological Description

Manufacturing Techniques

Hammered sheet gold, embossing, repoussé, round wire, twisted wire, beaded wire, mechanical joints.

The armlet consists of two main elements:

1. The shank
2. The Knot

1. The shank

Fig. 2. Microscope image of fragments from copper alloy

In order to give the body strength and stability (Pages 6, 7, X-Ray Images, Fig. 7b, c, d, Fig. 8), the sheet gold is folded around a "copper alloy core". As clearly visible in the image in Fig. 2, some fragments escaped from the shank's occasionally broken surface and were examined by XRF and SEM for characterization.

The shank is fashioned from a single sheet of hammered gold of <0.12 mm. Thickness, shaped into a ribbed hoop (Fig. 3a), enveloping a central core; the outer surface is folded into parallel corrugations, lips overlapping and covering the horizontal seam (Fig. 3b). No evidence of diffusion bonding nor soldering applied. The inner surface of the shank is smooth and burnished flat (Fig. 3c). In order to give the body strength and stability (X-Ray Images Fig. 7b, c, d), the sheet gold is folded around a "copper alloy core". Some fragments escaped from the shank occasionally broken surface and were examined by XRF and SEM for characterization, resulting in the chemical composition.

Embracing either ends of the shank's terminal parts are collar finials. (Fig. 3d). In the area overlapping the shank, a band of petal shaped cells, delicately embossed and outlined by twisted wire, (Fig. 3e) decorates both collars.

XRF analysis of fragments of reinforcing material of copper alloy escaped from the shank (Fig. 2).

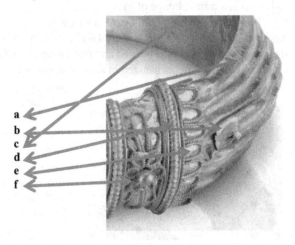

a
b
c
d
e
f

Fig. 3 Shank: details description

On the sides enfolding the Heracles Knot, the collars are bordered with plain, beaded and plain wire. Both collars are enriched by a central six petalled rosette (Fig. 3f) obtained from sheet gold; the rosette is sided by three tear drops of twisted wire, the center one more elongated than the two siding it.

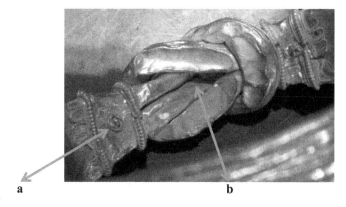

a   b

Fig. 4. a: Backside, Heracles Knot: details on curls and globules, **b**: Backside, Heracles Knot: loops intertwined, disappearing into the finials.

The rosette's center shows a pierced hole where a rivet, crowned by a large single globule resulting as well as the rosette's bud.

2. The Heracles Knot

The Heracles Knot is the armilla's most noteworthy element.

The knot is fashioned from two separate loops of sheet gold of <0.12 mm. Thickness (Fig. 5), interlocking into one another.

Fig. 5. Heracles Knot

Knot's Face

Each loop is a mirror image of the other: both embossed to a softly curved shape, lined underneath by a second plain sheet. The plain surfaced loop is slightly crinkled; the other one is enriched with decorations, its edges trimmed by braids of twisted and plain wires. The face of this loop is adorned with strands of twisted wire, organized in rhythmic, spiraling patterns. Both loops disappear, sliding into the finials, ends curved for fitting into them, as shown above (Fig. 4b).

An acanthus flower further enriches the Knot's centerpiece; its petals, of uneven size, are delicately embossed, each outlined by twisted wires. The petals are gathered to represent a corolla, embraced by a collar ring obtained from a central strand of large beaded wire, edged on both sides by twisted wire. Three oval shaped pistils emerge from the flower's heart (Fig. 6).

Fig. 6. Heracles Knot's acanthus flower

4   Scientific Methodology

When examining artefacts, non-destructive analysis of the gold alloys have always played an important role, in particular with gold work.

Elemental analysis of this artefact's surface were carried out using **XRF** (X-Ray Fluorescence) and **SEM-EDS** (Scanning Electron Microscopy - Energy Dispersive X-Ray Spectrometry). Investigation using **X-Radiography**.

OM (Optical Microscopy) and SEM (Scanning Electron Microscope) characterized the physical features of the artefact. The SEM used for this research is SEISS EVO MA15, 25 kV model, with EDS microanalysis detector, allowing to identify the compositional elements of the surface.

X-Ray Fluorescence was carried out with a portable non-vacuum instrumentation equipped with a tungsten X-Ray tube, reaching up to 35 kV and 350 μA, a silicon drift detector, Peltier cooled with its amplifier-power supply and multichannel (Amptek MCA 8000A). The resolution of the detector is 140 eV to 5.9 keV (Mn Kα). This instrumentation is able to detect chemical elements atomic number greater than 12 (Z > 12) suitable for the study of metal alloys.

OM was carried out with a Bresser stereomicroscope combined with a Canon D3000 digital camera.

The artefact complexity required application of observation techniques that would consider the whole object, such as **Digital Radiography (DR)**, as well as the use of focalized probe for investigation on each specific decorative elements.

4.1   Digital Radiography - X Ray Images

The shank is made from a single gold thin sheet (<0.1–2 mm) X-Rays easily pass through the object.

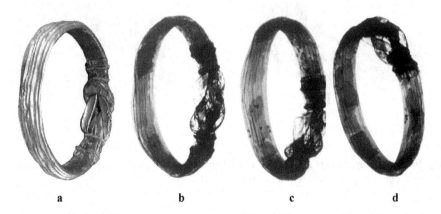

a   b   c   d

Fig. 7. a, b, c, d: Jewel's photo; X-Rays images at different angles

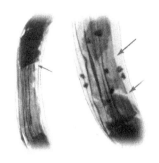

Fig. 8. X Ray image after image processing

As showed in radiographic images (Fig. 7b, c, d) the skank does not have a uniform structure, but it presents darker portion of different dimensions, due to radiopaque material. This material is not integral with the gold sheet, but is movable compared to it.

Figure 8 shows two details of Fig. 7b and 7c above. Red arrows indicate that the material inside has deliberately smooth edges while the fractures are not. This is a reinforcing sheet in copper alloy (as XRF analysis show) corroded and subsequently fragmented over time.

Figure 9a and 9b comparison between knob's visible picture and X-Ray; Fig. 9c crack detail of gold sheet, a fragment of internal material is visible; Fig. 9d digital processing of Fig. 9c. The knob's structure does not have any reinforcing material, unlike the shank. The knob is created with a gold sheet appropriately worked to produce a tubular folded on itself.

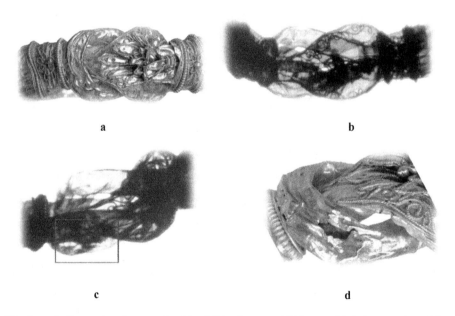

Fig. 9. a, b: Comparison between knob's visible picture and X-Ray. c: Digital processing of 9.c. d: Crack detail of gold sheet, a fragment of internal material is visible.

In Fig. 9c X-Ray shows the presence of a fragment of reinforcing sheet coming from the reinforcing material of the shank: is visible from the crack of the gold sheet too. (Fig. 9d).

4.2 XRF, X-Ray Fluorescence, SEM-EDS

Specific study areas were identified, each one of them showing elements that can be considered as diagnostic markers for the whole evaluation of the artefact. For each area highlighted, analyses and their interpretation are reported. (**A, C, E**, in the present paper).

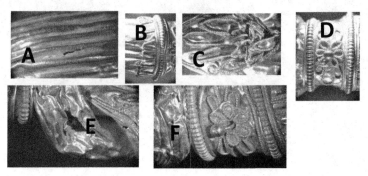

A – Study Area – XRF, X-Ray Fluorescence

The shank consists of longitudinally grooved sheet gold, showing intergranular fractures, as proved by the presence of right angles, proper of gold cubic crystallization (Fig. 10).

a . Detail of the shank   **b** . Intergranular fractures

Fig. 10. a. Detail of the shank. b. Intergranular fractures.

The measurements were taken on the artefact's outer surface: XRF detects the presence of gold (Au) as the predominant element.

Presence of nickel (Ni) is noted and could be associated with the minerals the metal was extracted from. Iron (Fe) and calcium (Ca) can be attributed to the presence of terrous material on the surface.

Concerning Copper (Cu), this could originate from the reinforced inner lamina revealed by radiography. In fact, in meas. 10 and 11, taken on the metal fracture, copper percentages increase considerably over the other two measures.

Four XRF measurements were performed on the shank, correlated spots are shown in the microscope photographs hereunder:

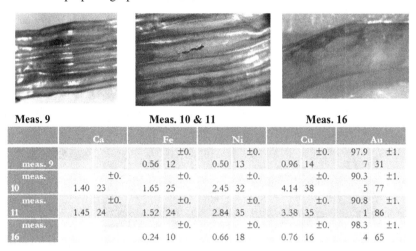

| | Meas. 9 | Meas. 10 & 11 | Meas. 16 |

	Ca	Fe	Ni	Cu	Au
meas. 9		±0. 0.56 12	±0. 0.50 13	±0. 0.96 14	97.9 ±1. 7 31
meas. 10	±0. 1.40 23	±0. 1.65 25	±0. 2.45 32	±0. 4.14 38	90.3 ±1. 5 77
meas. 11	±0. 1.45 24	±0. 1.52 24	±0. 2.84 35	±0. 3.38 35	90.8 ±1. 1 86
meas. 16		±0. 0.24 10	±0. 0.66 18	±0. 0.76 16	98.3 ±1. 4 65

A – Study Area – SEM-EDS

SEM-EDS analyses were performed on the sheet gold various micro-areas. The "back scattered" **E-Image 7** allows observation of the presence of cavities, distributed over the whole area, with presence of terrous material, as revealed by the compositional analysis, with presence of Si, Al, Mg, Ca, Fe.

With regard to sheet gold composition, the EDS **Spectrum 19** detects gold as the main element; the input for silver and copper search, as elements present in gold alloys in antique artefacts, has yielded negative results or poor concentration.

Non-constant copper presence could be attributed to the contamination of the jewel's inner support, or as a consequence of a superficial depletion intervention.

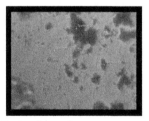

Electron Image 7

Spectrum 19

E-Images 15 and **16** below refer to magnification of the sheet gold surface, showing a modification of the structure following the natural metal kinetic crystallization. It can be observed that the crystallization processes shows either coat scratches or pre-existing lamina imperfections. (In all the analytical determinations the error can be estimated + 0.2).

Electron Image 15

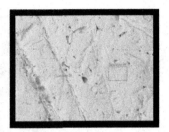

Electron Image 16

C- Study Area - XRF X-Ray Fluorescence

XRF measurements were carried out on the area in question and the results reported in Table 1 below. XRF detects copper, as X-Rays penetrate the lamina more in depth than EDS. Such results allow the hypothesis of surface depletion. Depletion can be justified by preferential copper oxidation in the gold alloy.

Table 1. XRF measurements.

	Ca	Fe	Ni	Cu	Au
meas. 1		0.37 ±0.17	1.84 ±0.37	1.12 ±0.26	96.67 ±2.33
meas. 2	0.27 ±0.17	1.56 ±0.29	0.50 ±0.22	2.70 ±0.38	94.97 ±2.23
meas. 3			0.68 ±0.20	1.26 ±0.24	98.06 ±1.98

E- Study Area – SEM EDS
SEM Investigation

As previously observed, the Heracles Knot terminals are inserted into the shank and mechanically joined by means of rivets obtained with plain round wires. A stimulating observation comes from the semi-quantitative analysis **(Spectrum 49)**, when considering the percentage content of the elements constituting the gold alloy: Au, Ag and Cu: from the bar graph, it is possible to extrapolate its value, obtaining a gold alloy having 1.5% Cu, 3.5% Ag, entirely in line with homologous alloys of the historical period of reference.

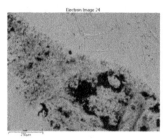
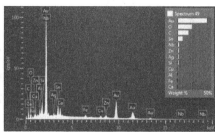

Electron Image 24   Spectrum 49

5 Discussion of Results

For the investigation, a combination of analytical techniques delivers figures based on different methodologies, which, in this particular instance, provide sufficient information for a coherent final statement. When overlapping homologous data (XRF and EDS), these prove self-consistent.

The resulting data have been discussed according to the various features that characterize the artefact, grouped according to the following themes:

- Authenticity, manufacturing techniques, conservative reconstruction

The data collected were interpreted as a function of the artistic and historical aspects related to ancient goldsmithing production and the kinetic & physic-chemical transformation of the constituting materials.

Authenticity
Coherence with similar archaeological findings. Coherence with ancient technologies. Structural changes according to recrystallization kinetics. Lack of anachronistic chemical elements, such as Cd, Cr, etc. Gold alloy composition is coherent with the period of attribution (E-Image 24, Spectrum 49, pg.10). Presence of elements characterizing ancient natural copper alloys such as As.

Manufacturing Techniques

- Coherent with the period of reference are the following techniques:

    Beaded wire
    Enamelling
    Mechanical joining pertinent (Rivet)
    Thin gold sheet
    Autogenous welding
    Pallions
    Inner copper core

- **Surface enrichment**: *To give a purer gold surface by chemical leaching. This technique, using various mixtures of alum, urine and other substances, has been employed until recent times.*

References

1. Gopher, A., Tsuk, T., Shalev, S., Gophna, R.: Earliest gold artefacts in the levant. Current Anthropol. **31**(4), 436–443 (1990). https://doi.org/10.1086/203868
2. Ogden, J., Nicholson, P.T., Shaw, I.: Section 6 Metals, Ancient Egyptian Materials & Technology, pp. 148–175 (2000)
3. Lippolis, E.: Gli ori di Taranto in Età Ellenistica. Arnoldo Mondadori Editore (1985)

Author Index

Printed in the United States
by Baker & Taylor Publisher Services